Ancient Civilizations

THE MIDDLE EAST

THE CRADLE OF CIVILIZATION REVEALED

Ancient Civilizations

THE MIDDLE EAST

THE CRADLE OF CIVILIZATION REVEALED

CHIEF CONSULTANT **Dr Stephen Bourke**

GLOBAL BOOK PUBLISHING

First published in 2008 by
Global Book Publishing
Level 8, 15 Orion Road,
Lane Cove, NSW 2066, Australia
Ph: (612) 9425 5800
Fax: (612) 9425 5804
Email: rightsmanager@globalpub.com.au

MANAGING DIRECTOR	Chryl Campbell
PUBLISHING DIRECTOR	Sarah Anderson
ART DIRECTOR	Kylie Mulquin
PROJECT MANAGER	Sophia Oravecz
CHIEF CONSULTANT	Dr Stephen Bourke
CONTRIBUTORS	Maree Browne, Professor Mark W. Chavalas, Dr Kate da Costa, Dr Peter Edwell, Dr Yosef Garfinkel, Dr Leore Grosman, Dr Lloyd Llewellyn-Jones, Dr Kevin M. McGeough, Dr Karen Radner, Dr Seth Richardson, Dr Sandra Scham, Dr Gonen Sharon, Dr Matt Waters
COMMISSIONING EDITOR	David Kidd
EDITORS	Emma Driver, Victoria Fisher, Judith Simpson, Russell Thomson
MAP EDITOR	Alan Edwards
COVER DESIGN	Alex Frampton, Kylie Mulquin
DESIGNERS	Kerry Klinner, Lena Lowe, Avril Makula, Thomson Digital
JUNIOR DESIGNER	Althea Aseoche
DESIGN CONCEPT	Alex Frampton, Stan Lamond
CARTOGRAPHER	John Frith
GRAPHICS	Althea Aseoche
PICTURE RESEARCH	Sarah Anderson, David Boehm, Emma Driver, Sophia Oravecz, Maria Stanco
INDEX	Michael Ramsden
PROOFREADER	Kevin Diletti
PRODUCTION	Ian Coles
CONTRACTS	Alan Edwards
FOREIGN RIGHTS	Kate Hill
PUBLISHING ASSISTANT	Christine Leonards

ISBN 978174048075-8

Printed in China by SNP Leefung Printers Limited
Color separation Pica Digital Pte Ltd, Singapore

PHOTOGRAPHERS
Global Book Publishing would be pleased to hear from photographers interested in supplying photographs.
Email: photolibrary@globalpub.com.au

Contributors

CHIEF CONSULTANT

Dr Stephen Bourke is a Near Eastern archaeologist, and has worked on numerous international archaeological projects since 1980, primarily in Jordan and Syria. He has written or contributed to over 70 archaeological publications during the last 25 years. Stephen currently directs the University of Sydney, Australia, excavations at Pella, Jordan, and has done so since 1992. The most recent field season occurred in 2007, with another season planned for 2009. Previously he led four seasons of renewed excavations at the Chalcolithic period type-site of Teleilat Ghassul, Jordan, between 1994–1999. His interests range from the Neolithic beginnings of urban life through to the Iron Age regional states of the late pre-Classical periods *c.* 6500–300 BCE. Current research projects include various works arising out of ongoing excavations at Pella, recently completed excavations at Chalcolithic Teleilat Ghassul, ongoing British survey and excavation work at Tell Nebi Mend in Syria, and the Homs Regional Survey. Stephen is completing a monograph on the University of Sydney work at Chalcolithic Teleilat Ghassul, and another based on his Doctoral work on British excavations at Tell Nebi Mend, ancient Qadesh on the Orontes. Connected with this earlier work, he is researching the second millennium BCE settlement history of the Homs region for the University of Durham's Homs regional survey.

CONTRIBUTORS

Maree Browne studied Classical and Near Eastern Archaeology and Prehistory at the University of Sydney. She has worked on a number of sites, principally at the University of Sydney's site at Pella, Jordan. Her main interest is in the archaeology of the ancient environment and the manipulation of this environment to benefit its inhabitants. She is currently lecturing in the Faculty of the Built Environment at the University of New South Wales, Australia.

Professor Mark W. Chavalas is Professor of History at the University of Wisconsin-La Crosse, United States, where he has taught courses on ancient Near Eastern history, archaeology, and the Akkadian language. He has had fellowships from Harvard, Yale, California-Berkeley, Brown, Cornell, Wisconsin-Madison, and the University of Arizona. He worked nine excavation seasons in Syria at Tell Ashara (Terqa), Tell Qraya, and Tell Mozan (Urkesh). His most-recent books include the co-edited *Mesopotamia and the Bible*, *Life and Culture in the Ancient Near East*, *The Ancient Near East*, and *Current Issues in the History of the Ancient Near East*.

Dr Kate da Costa is an ARC Research Fellow in the Department of Archaeology at the University of Sydney, Australia. She teaches Near Eastern and Classical Archaeology and is a director of excavation and survey projects in Jordan. Her main research interest lies in the Roman–early Islamic period in the Near East, and the interaction of foreign political powers and indigenous populations. Her current project is using archaeological methods to detect Roman provincial borders. She is also an authority on ceramic lamps from the eastern Mediterranean.

Dr Peter Edwell is a lecturer in the Department of Ancient History at Macquarie University, Australia. His current research and teaching interests focus on the lands of the eastern Mediterranean and Mesopotamia from the time of the conquests of Alexander to the late Roman period. Dr Edwell completed a PhD thesis in 2005, which focused on the expansion of Roman power in the Near East. He has traveled extensively throughout Syria and the Near East and has recently published a book about Roman control of the Middle Euphrates.

Dr Yosef Garfinkel is Yigael Yadin Professor of Biblical Archaeology at the Hebrew University of Jerusalem, Israel. He is also a curator of the museum of Yarmukian Culture at Kibbutz Sha'ar Hagolan. He specializes in the Protohistoric era of the Near East—the period of time when the world's earliest village communities were established and the beginning of agriculture took place. He has excavated numerous Neolithic and Chalcolithic sites, such as Gesher, Yiftahel, Ashkelon, Sha'ar Hagolan, and Tel Tsaf, and to date has published 12 books and over 100 articles. These contributions relate both to aspects of daily life, such as architecture, pottery and water supply, and to more spiritual aspects such as art, religion, and dance.

Dr Leore Grosman is a Researcher at the Hebrew University of Jerusalem and Weizmann Institute of Science, Israel. Her research is focused on the Near East and Levantine Corridor, in particular the origin of food production, the nature of the transition from hunting–gathering to farming modes. Beside studies of Paleolithic assemblages, she has directed, since its inception in 1995, an ongoing excavation project at Hilazon Tachtit cave (Natufian). In her 2005 PhD thesis, she introduced an additional tool for the examination of the different entities related to this time-span: computer simulation. Recently, her research focused on developing mathematical and computational tools, especially 3-D technology, for addressing archaeological issues.

Dr Lloyd Llewellyn-Jones is a lecturer in Ancient History in the School of History, Classics and Archaeology at the University of Edinburgh, United Kingdom. He is a specialist in Achaemenid Persian history and the socio-cultural history of ancient Greece and the Hellenistic world. He is the author of *Aphrodite's Tortoise: the Veiled Woman of Ancient Greece* and of numerous books and articles on Greco-Persian history. He is currently working on an edition of Ctesias' *Persica* and on a major study of the royal harem in the ancient Near East. He has made several TV documentaries on ancient Persia, including *Lost Worlds: Persepolis*.

Dr Kevin M. McGeough is Assistant Professor in Ancient Near Eastern History at the University of Lethbridge, Alberta, Canada, and is a specialist in the languages and material culture of the Bronze and Iron Age of the Near East. He received a BA in History from the University of Lethbridge, an MTS from Harvard Divinity School, and a PhD in Near Eastern Languages and Civilizations from the University of Pennsylvania. He is the author of numerous books and articles, including *Exchange Relationships at Ugarit*. Besides his interest in the past, Kevin is an avid film buff.

Dr Karen Radner is a Lecturer in Ancient Near Eastern History at University College London, United Kingdom. She specializes in the cuneiform cultures of the Middle East (third to first millennium BCE). Her primary research interests belong to Assyria, particularly the period from the ninth to the seventh century BCE. She has published on Assyria's political, social, economic, legal, and religious history extensively. Her list of published books include *Die neuassyrischen Texte aus Tall Šēḫ Ḥamad; Das mittelassyrische Tontafelarchiv von Giricano/Dunnu-ša-Uzibi,* and *Die Macht des Namens: Altorientalische Strategien zur Selbsterhaltung*.

Dr Seth Richardson has been Assistant Professor of Ancient Near Eastern History at the Oriental Institute of the University of Chicago, Illinois, United States, since 2003. He received his PhD from Columbia University in 2002, with a dissertation on the collapse of the First Dynasty of Babylon in 1595 BCE. His research interests include early second-millennium BCE Babylonian economic and administrative cuneiform texts, the intellectual history of Babylonian liver divination, and theoretical problems related to ancient Near East labor history, rebellion, and state collapse.

Dr Sandra Scham is an archaeologist, a former editor of the journal *Near Eastern Archaeology* and current Washington Correspondent for Archaeology Magazine. Sandra teaches archaeology of the ancient Near East at the Catholic University of America in Washington, D.C., United States, and has taught at the University of Maryland and Jerusalem University College in Israel. Sandra has participated in archaeological work in Israel, Jordan, and southeastern Turkey, and has a PhD in Anthropological Archaeology. Sandra is currently working with the Middle East Bureau of the United States Agency for International Development as an American Association for the Advancement of Science Fellow.

Dr Gonen Sharon is currently teaching at the Institute of Archaeology at the Hebrew University of Jerusalem, Israel. He received his PhD from the Hebrew University and wrote his doctoral dissertation on Acheulian bifacial tool technology and the significance of this technology to the study of Lower Paleolithic hominid behavior and culture. His research interests include the study of stone tool technology, the early prehistory of Africa and Eurasia, and experimental archaeology. Dr Sharon is currently excavating a Middle Paleolithic Mousterian site at Gesher Benot Ya'aqov, northern Israel.

Dr Matt Waters received his BA from the University of Notre Dame, Indiana, United States, and MA and PhD from the University of Pennsylvania. He has taught at the University of Pennsylvania and the University of Delaware and is currently Associate Professor of Classics and Ancient History at the University of Wisconsin-Eau Claire. He is an ACLS Fellow and in 2006. was awarded the Jonas C. Greenfield prize from the American Oriental Society. His research interests include Assyrian–Elamite relations and the Achaemenid Persian Empire in the mid first-millennium BCE, and cross-cultural connections between the ancient Near East and the Classical Greek world. He has published one book, co-edited another, and published articles and book reviews on ancient Near Eastern and Greek history.

CONTENTS

INTRODUCING

The Middle East

What is the Middle East?

Lying at the juncture between Asia and Africa, the Middle East is a region that has played an important role in human history. The term reflects a perception that the area is distinct, but also that the cultures within it share some common—if frequently disputed—ground.

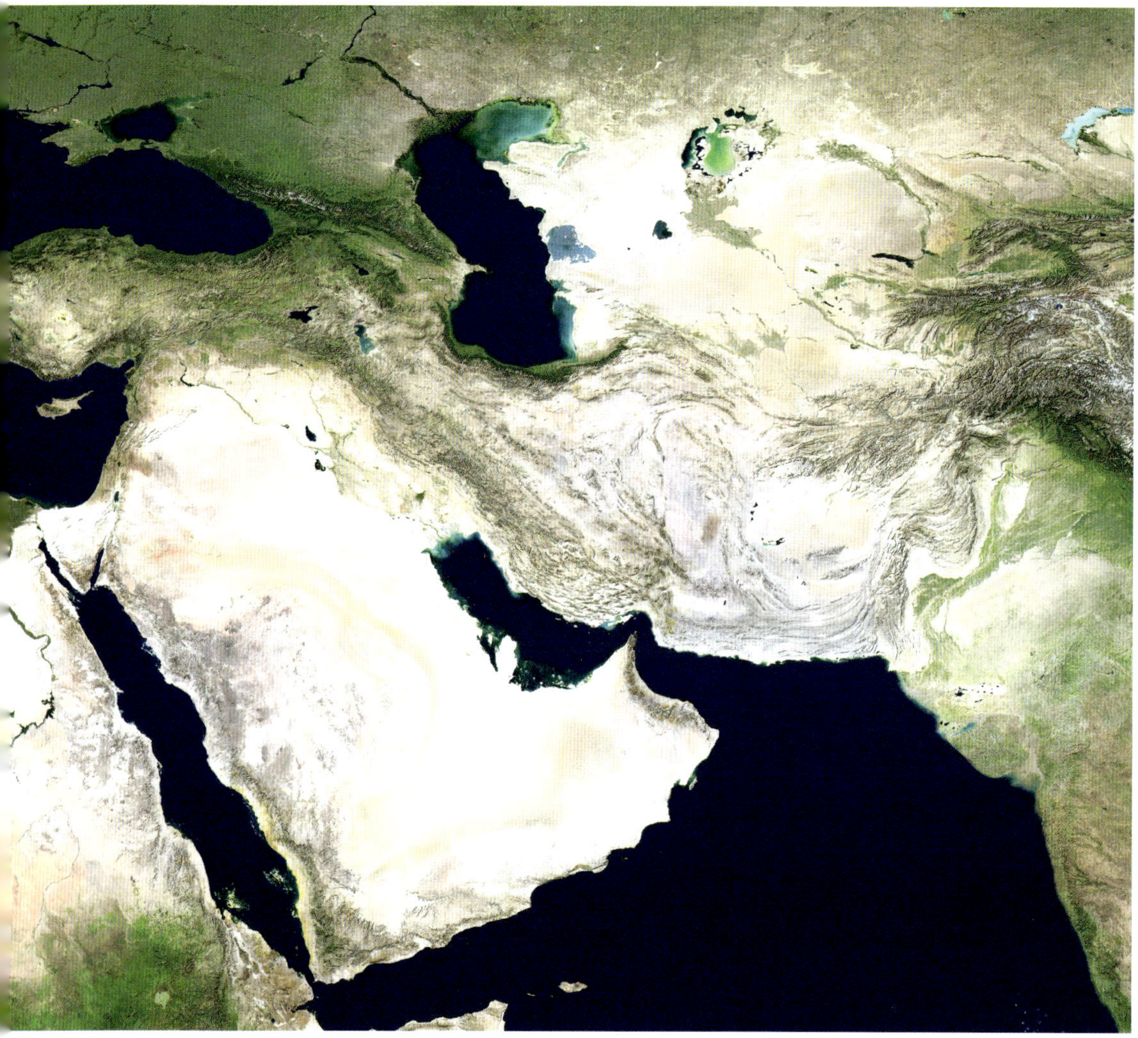

ABOVE **This satellite view of the Middle East** shows vast deserts of the Arabian Peninsula, with the Fertile Crescent above it, and the Mediterranean at far left.

The use of the term "Middle East" began relatively recently. Its first appearance in print was in a 1902 article written by the American naval strategist Alfred Thayer Mahan, who wrote of the Middle East and its strategic center, the Persian Gulf. For Mahan, the Middle East was an area between Russian and British spheres of influence, a "middle" region that was contested by the two powers. Journalists started using the term shortly afterwards, and by World War II, it had become part of general parlance.

Middle East, Near East, or Far East?

Up until World War I the term "Near East" had been more commonly used to describe this region. The term "Far East" was used to describe China, Japan, and areas on the Pacific coast of Asia. "Middle East" referred to central Asia. The Near East, then, was that part of Asia that was located closest to Europe. With the collapse of the Ottoman Empire after World War I and the rise of the Arab states, the term Middle East became more common, though archaeologists and historians still use the term Near East. Until recent years, the Middle East was thought of as part of the Orient, which encompassed all of Asia, though Westerners now generally think of the Orient as synonymous with the Far East. However, some academic programs in the United States and Britain still use the term "Orient" to refer to western Asia.

In recent years, the use of the term "Middle East" has been criticized. At the heart of much of this criticism is the perceived Eurocentrism of the term, since the designation "east" implies that there is a center of the globe, and that lies in Europe. Another criticism of the use of the term is that it obscures the actual diversity of the region: by using one vague term to encompass many polities, the true complexity of the area is not apparent.

Modern Political Divisions

Given that there are no formal boundaries that delineate the Middle East today, it is impossible to define the region solely on the basis of modern polities. Most would agree that the following countries are in the Middle East: Bahrain, Egypt, Iran, Iraq, Israel, Jordan, Kuwait, Lebanon,

LEFT **Jerusalem is an important holy city** for three of the world's major religions: Judaism, Islam, and Christianity.

Oman, Palestine, Qatar, Saudi Arabia, Syria, Turkey, the United Arab Emirates, and Yemen. All of these polities have some territory in Asia (including Egypt, which possesses the Sinai Peninsula) and by most definitions, it is this connection to Asia that makes a region Middle Eastern. In addition, several North African countries (which are predominantly Muslim) are often considered to be Middle Eastern: Libya, Algeria, Sudan, and Tunisia. Some of the former Soviet states, as well as Afghanistan and Pakistan, have also been considered part of the Middle East, although this view is less common among today's scholars and commentators.

Most of the modern political divisions of the region originate with the partitioning of the Ottoman Empire after World War I. At the Treaty of Versailles (1919), the European powers divided up the territory of the Ottoman Empire, giving France a mandate over Syria and Lebanon, and giving the United Kingdom a mandate over Iraq and what was then called Palestine. The people of Anatolia revolted against the terms of the partition of their state and formed the modern nation of Turkey. The British and French forces withdrew from the region gradually. When the British mandate over Palestine expired in 1948, the state of Israel was proclaimed, which led to warfare in the region. Disputes over Israel (and its relationship to Palestine) are still significant within the region today. The economic clout of the Middle East, particularly in the Gulf states, grew tremendously after the discovery of the massive oil reserves in the region.

Geography

For most people, the expression "Middle East" conjures up images of vast, flat deserts bereft of vegetation. In fact, although most areas are considered arid or semi-arid ecosystems, the region's geography is far from uniform. In terms of elevation, the topography of the Middle East consists of extremes. On the one hand, extensive mountain ranges are located throughout Turkey and Iran. On the other hand, the lowest point on Earth—the Dead Sea region—is in Israel and Jordan, 1,370 ft (417 m) below sea level. Israel, Jordan, Syria, and Turkey are broken up by foothills and mountain ranges, which acted as natural borders in ancient times.

One part of the Middle East is often called the Fertile Crescent, since the region that can sustain agriculture stretches in a crescent shape from Egypt to Iraq. The Arabian Peninsula, which is in the middle of this crescent, is filled with vast deserts. Until the domestication of the camel, these could not be easily traversed, and even today they provide numerous challenges to human occupation. The Syrian Desert in the north is filled with rocks and gravel and is broken up by numerous hills and valleys. The southern portion of the Arabian Peninsula is home to deserts typified by sand dunes, ever-changing in the dry winds.

BELOW **The arid sand dunes of the Arabian Desert** cover 900,000 square miles (2,300,000 square km) of the Arabian Peninsula.

Peoples and Cultures

The Middle East has long been home to diverse groups of peoples and cultures. Understanding who these people were and how they related to one another is a difficult and fascinating task.

ABOVE **A Sumerian tablet,** *c.* 2360 BCE, discussing donkeys harnessed for plowing, was discovered at Telloh, Iraq, the site of the Sumerian city Girsu.

Given that ancient notions of ethnicity and race were different from modern ones (though equally complex), scholars usually categorize ancient people according to the language that they spoke or by the polities of which they were members.

The Cultures of Mesopotamia

In antiquity, Mesopotamia (located in modern Iraq) was roughly divided into two parts: the north and the south. The earliest group to populate the region, the Sumerians (known as "the black-headed people" in ancient sources) lived in the south of Iraq. The Sumerian speakers were conquered by an Akkadian-speaking group in the last third of the third millennium BCE (the First Dynasty of Akkad). Akkadian is a Semitic language, and the Sumerian script was adopted for use with Akkadian. Both Akkadian and Sumerian were used throughout Mesopotamian history, but were eventually supplanted by Aramaic in the Iron Age (*c.* 1200–586 BCE). The people living in the north of ancient Iraq came to be known as "Assyrians," after one of their major cities (Assur). In the south, the city of Babylon rose to cultural prominence and southerners thus came to be called Babylonians.

Syro-Palestinian and Anatolian Peoples

Throughout the Bronze Age, the people most associated with the southern Levant area were the Canaanites. The Canaanites spoke a Semitic language and were organized into large city-states that dotted the region now known as Israel. They were called the Canaanites by the Egyptians, although it is unlikely they identified themselves in this grouping; they referred to themselves by their city of origin. At the end of the Late Bronze Age (*c.* 1200 BCE), these large urban centers were destroyed, and much of the civilization of the Canaanites vanished.

However, some elements of Canaanite culture did survive into the Iron Age via the Phoenicians of coastal Lebanon. The Phoenicians were skilled seafarers and eventually colonized parts of North Africa, most notably Carthage. These were the ancestors of the Carthaginians, who are best remembered for their conflict with Rome in the three Punic Wars. Throughout the rest of the Syro-Palestinian region the situation changed dramatically in the aftermath of the Late Bronze Age destructions. The Philistines, of uncertain origins, settled on the coast of modern-day Israel. The Israelites emerged in the hill country, near the Philistines. In what is now known as Jordan, the Moabites, the Ammonites, and the Edomites formed into small kingdoms.

The cultures of Anatolia were also quite diverse. The longest lived of these cultures was that of the Hittites, who spoke an Indo-European language and reached the height of their power in the Late Bronze Age. Between the Hittites

A CULTURAL HOTSPOT

Numerous cultures interacted with the Assyrians and Babylonians in ancient Mesopotamia. A group known as the Amorites moved into Mesopotamia from the Arabian deserts *c.* 2100–2000 BCE, in the Ur III period. The Amorites were originally a semi-nomadic people but after migrating to the floodplain, they mixed with the local Mesopotamian population. In the Late Bronze Age (*c.* 1550–1200 BCE), the Kassites—a people who may have come from the mountainous regions to the northeast of Syria—conquered Babylon and ruled it for an extended period of time, adopting many Babylonian traditions and customs. In the Neo-Babylonian period, numerous tribal groups vied for control of Babylon. One of these groups, the Chaldeans, was successful and the term "Chaldean" came to be used by the biblical authors and Greek writers to refer to the Babylonians.

and northern Mesopotamia was the Hurrian heartland. In the Late Bronze Age, a Hurrian kingdom, called Mitanni, was located between Mesopotamia and Anatolia, stretched across a region which now comprises southeastern Turkey, northern Syria, and northern Iraq.

The People of Ancient Iran

Iran has been inhabited for as long as Mesopotamia. However, most of our knowledge about early Iranian civilization is based on accounts from Mesopotamia. The first written language in Iran, which modern scholars call Proto-Elamite, has yet to be deciphered. While there were many earlier inhabitants of Iran, the Elamites are the first culture of Iran known by name. Elamite culture was established in Iran by 2700 BCE and lasted until 559 BCE.

Throughout the first half of the first millennium BCE, a distinct Iranian group arose in northwestern Iran—the Medes. They became an important power and helped the Babylonians defeat the Assyrians in Mesopotamia. The Medes are often credited with creating the first Iranian empire, but it was not until the Achaemenid period (559–331 BCE) that Iran was unified. This period is named for Achaemenes, the supposed founder of the dynasty, but the Achaemenids did not become a dominant power in the Middle East until the rise of Cyrus the Great in 559 BCE. This dynasty would rule Iran (and much of the east) until its defeat by Alexander the Great in 331 BCE.

The Achaemenids were enemies of the Greeks, and the wars between the two powerful states are preserved—from the Greek perspective—in the works of Classical authors such as Herodotus and Thucydides. The term "Persian" commonly refers to the Achaemenid period, which is often seen as the starting point of Persian history.

After the death of Alexander, Iran was ruled by the Seleucids, the Hellenistic successors of Alexander. The Seleucids were unable to maintain their control over Iran; their authority was then contested by the Parthians, who held power for 400 years. In CE 224 a nationalist revolt led to the rise of the Sasanian Empire.

ABOVE **Elamite culture** survived in Iran for over 2,000 years. This painted Elamite vase was made between 1000 and 800 BCE.

BELOW **On the coast of Lebanon,** archaeologists excavate the ancient Phoenician city of Sarepta (modern Sarafand).

Economy and Agriculture

The Middle East has historically been home to a diverse range of agricultural and economic activities. Despite the climatic factors, geographical realities, and political and social upheavals that severely restrict the economies of some areas, both traditional and new economic activity continues across the region.

Today, many countries in the Middle East face four major economic obstacles: they are suffering the effects of wars, sanctions, and refugee migrations; their infrastructure systems are well below international standards; their population density is high; and water is very scarce. Nonetheless, in addition to more traditional economic activities, the countries in the region have created new opportunities wherever possible. For instance, Jordan has developed a large educational and medical service sector, complemented by tourism. Lebanon is well known as a banking center. Israel's manufacturing of aviation and medical equipment, and a significant diamond-cutting trade, are well known, while Syria and especially Iraq gain export income from oil and gas.

BELOW **Olives are harvested in Abbassiyeh, Lebanon. After fruit trees, olive groves are the second most important agricultural industry in Lebanon.**

Agriculture, Herding, and Forestry

The wide range of environmental zones in the Middle East allows a variety of agricultural production, although in turn this is limited by the rainfall zone, the highly seasonal rainfall pattern, and the presence of deserts and mountainous regions unsuitable for farming. Due to better irrigation programs in the last century, horticulture—the intensive growing of tomatoes, cucumbers, salad vegetables, and herbs—has substantially increased.

Orcharding of olive, date, fruit, and nut trees has been practiced for over 6,000 years. The most important fruit tree exploited in the Middle East is the olive. It was first deliberately planted and cultivated by 4000 BCE in the western areas (i.e., modern Jordan and Israel), with other subspecies developed in Lebanon and Syria. Olive fruit can be eaten or pressed to make oil, and the wood is highly prized; there are orchards in the Middle East which may contain trees that are more than 1,000 years old. Iraq is more suited to cultivating the date palm. These trees provide food, oil, sweeteners, and building materials.

Indigenous grains in the Middle East—that is, those that existed wild and were first domesticated there—include wheat, barley, and the summer-cropped chickpea. Wild oats are also native to the Levant, but were domesticated first in Europe, then reintroduced. It is interesting to note that, despite modern agricultural practices, indigenous plants are the most common ones that are still farmed. Peas, lentils, some vetches (e.g., broad beans), and flax are also native to the Middle East and are commonly cultivated.

LEFT **A Bedouin shepherdess** herds her flock in Jordan. Despite government settlement policies, many Bedouins still live a traditional nomadic life.

Pastoralism, or the herding of sheep and goats, has been practiced since the early days of animal domestication in the region. Along the desert fringes and in the highest ranges, farming and pastoralism coexist: marginal cropping land is fertilized by sheep and goat herds, which graze on crop stubble. However, pastoralists are under pressure from many sides. Political borders make the traditional nomadic lifestyle of many Arab tribes, like the Bedouin of the Levant, nearly impossible. Modern states, which are seeking to improve the education of their citizens, have insisted that many nomadic families settle in one place so their children can attend school. As greater areas of land come under the plow or are planted out to olives, this further restricts grazing land for sheep and goat herds.

Forestry varies from country to country. Lebanon was famous in antiquity for its cedars, which were used by Egyptian pharaohs and, allegedly, in the construction of Solomon's temple in Jerusalem; the country now has a very small timber industry due to overexploitation. Jordan has most successfully pursued a forestry industry, based largely on pine timber.

Other Resources

The modern geopolitical borders of the Middle East stem in large part from the activities of European powers towards the end of the Ottoman Empire, and their carving up of territory in the aftermath of World War I. Their interest was particularly sparked by the discovery of oil in Iraq in 1908; the country has some of the largest reserves known in the world. Syria also holds oil reserves, which have been drilled since the 1960s. Most Middle Eastern countries have some oil, but much of it is so deep below the ground that it is difficult to access. There are substantial natural gas fields in Iraq, Syria, and Jordan. Iraq has reserves of other minerals, but little significant mining takes place in the region.

Building Materials

For many parts of the Middle East, mud bricks were the only building materials available until the twentieth century, and were used for around 10,000 years. Requiring only a supply of soil, some clay, and chopped straw or dung, people only needed to provide their own labor to produce them. Mud bricks have excellent thermal properties, and easily allow the construction of simple arches, and built-in furniture such as niches and benches. Regular application of lime-based renders on the outside protect to a certain extent against rain. In regions with usable stone (e.g., limestone, and basalt in the south of Syria and north of Jordan), some houses were also built of masonry.

The flat roof design was traditional, as these roofs are multipurpose: on hot nights in summer, people can sleep on the roof in whatever breeze can be found, and during the long dry months, fruits and herbs can safely be dried there. In the twentieth century, however, reinforced concrete and cement bricks began to be more widely used in building projects, replacing the traditional Middle Eastern methods.

BELOW **Manufacturing mud bricks** is still an important economic activity in parts of the Middle East. These mud bricks are drying at a factory near Neyriz, Iran.

The Importance of Water

The exploitation of water resources has been a significant problem for much of Middle Eastern history. Since much of the region is semi-arid or arid, developing strategies for water management is essential.

In many areas of the Middle East, there is only enough rainfall to support a relatively small agricultural population. However, successful water management strategies have allowed a growing human population to inhabit the Middle East for thousands of years.

Middle Eastern Rivers and Lakes

While there are many bodies of water in the region, not all of them are useful for agriculture. The Dead Sea, located in modern Israel and Jordan, is a large hypersaline sea—meaning that the salt content of the water is greater than that of an ocean. As such, the Dead Sea is useless as a source of drinking water, although its salty waters are renowned for their supposed healing effects. Its main tributary is the Jordan River, which flows through the Rift Valley, separating Israel and Jordan. The Jordan River itself is formed in northern Israel from four main tributaries. The Jordan flows through Lake Hula and the Sea of Galilee, both located in the northern part of Israel.

The term "Mesopotamia," which refers to the ancient civilization centered in Iraq, is actually a Greek word, meaning "the land between two rivers." The two rivers in question are the Tigris (on the east) and the Euphrates (on the west), which still pass through Iraq today. Both rivers flow south, from the mountains of Turkey, and join into the Shatt al-Arab Delta, which empties into the Persian Gulf. Both rivers were of central importance in ancient Mesopotamian history.

BELOW **The Dead Sea,** its shores encrusted with salt deposits, has such a high salt content that no fish or aquatic plant can survive in its waters.

LEFT **The Euphrates River,** seen here in Anbar province, Iraq, was calmer, more predictable, and more stable as a water source in ancient times than it is today.

The Seas of the Middle East

The Middle East proper is surrounded by three large bodies of water: the Mediterranean Sea, the Red Sea, and the Persian Gulf. These have played an important role in the history of the Middle East as food sources and important transportation routes, connecting polities within the Middle East to one another and to other regions of the world.

The Mediterranean Sea runs along the western edge of Israel, Lebanon, Syria, and Turkey, and along the northern edge of Egypt. Its currents are relatively stable and run counterclockwise, allowing for a stable naval transportation route between the regions of the Middle East, Europe, and North Africa.

The Red Sea separates Asia from Africa, jutting up between the Arabian Peninsula and the east coast of Africa. On the west side of the peninsula, the Suez Canal separates mainland Egypt from the Sinai Desert. On the east side, the Gulf of Aqaba coastline is largely Saudi and Egyptian, but includes coastal strips of Israel and Jordan.

The Persian Gulf is on the eastern side of the Arabian Peninsula and the western coast of Iran, and provides a southern port for Iraq and Kuwait. It is an extension of the Indian Ocean, flowing south into the Gulf of Oman and the Arabian Sea.

Water Exploitation Strategies

Two main strategies, depending on the type of water resources available, have been most common in the Middle East—collecting rainwater and diverting rivers. Along the Mediterranean coast, there is sufficient yearly rainfall to support human settlements and agriculture, but it is unpredictable. The rain may fall sporadically through the winter or come down at once over a few days. Thus, large cisterns cut into the rock play an important role in gathering and storing water.

The exploitation of rivers was also important, and was most noteworthy in ancient Iraq, which lacked sufficient rainfall for farming. The people of ancient Iraq diverted the waters of the Tigris and Euphrates directly into their fields by digging canals. Given how much silt flowed through the Tigris and Euphrates, these canals had to be constantly maintained, as attested to by numerous ancient legal records.

In modern times, dams allow more stable exploitation of water resources but bring their own unique problems, including environmental degradation and disputes over water rights. Diversions of the Jordan River and the Sea of Galilee have damaged the ecosystem of the Jordan River, and the stretch between the Sea of Galilee and the Dead Sea is now heavily polluted.

CONTROLLING THE RIVERS

Since many of the water sources in the Middle East originate in Turkey, Turkish damming projects have implications throughout the region. Both the Tigris and Euphrates have had much of their water diverted for use as a power source and for irrigation agriculture in Turkey. Syria has also dammed the Euphrates. The creation of the Tabqa Dam in 1973 formed a reservoir called Lake Assad and flooded important archaeological sites. In Iraq, which itself has numerous dams on these rivers, there is some fear that further Syrian and Turkish water management schemes may affect the main sources of water within that nation.

ABOVE **The Tabqa Dam** is located on the Euphrates River in Syria.

Archaeological Finds

The list of historical sites of world importance in the Middle East is unrivaled. From Babylon to Jerusalem, from Assyrian royal cities like Nineveh to coastal ports like Ugarit and Byblos, the region continually reveals new information about ancient societies.

Archaeological evidence in the Middle East suggests that hominid occupation began in the region 1.5 million years ago. Moving forward through history from these earliest sites, the list of discoveries in the region continues. Middle Eastern archaeological sites continue to produce evidence of the domestication of plants, sedentarization, the invention of writing, the use of ceramics and metallurgy, organized religion, the first city-states, the great empires, conquest by European forces from Alexander up to the end of the Ottoman Empire, and the development of technologically advanced cities in modern states.

In Iraq alone, of the estimated 100,000 sites which probably exist, only around 10,000 have been discovered, and only a fraction of them have been excavated. New sites are discovered daily. Some are discovered legally, but others are found by looters and never reported.

Famous Sites and Artifacts

Some Middle Eastern finds have been nothing short of spectacular. In the 1840s, Austen Henry Layard's rediscovery of Sennacherib's palace in Nineveh stunned Europe and led to many of the great nineteenth-century expeditions, although most of these were little more than object-collecting exercises funded by museums. By the late nineteenth century, more scientific work was underway. Leonard Woolley's excavations of the Royal Tombs at Ur in the 1920s and 1930s are fundamental to our understanding of ancient Sumerian culture. Similarly, the discovery of the Dead Sea Scrolls near Qumran in the West Bank in 1947 shed new light on the history of Judaism and early Christianity. The plastered skulls and stone tower of Neolithic Jericho, and the exploration of the site's Bronze Age levels by Kathleen Kenyon in the 1950s, were important not just for history but for the development of archaeology in the region.

Recent extraordinary finds have included the 15,000 tablets in the archives at Ebla (modern Tell Mardikh); the palace at Qatna (modern al-Mishrifeh) with frescoes linking Syria and the Aegean, along with untouched royal burials; 10,000-year-old plaster sculptures from 'Ain Ghazal in Jordan; and the Mitanni palace at Tell Brak in Syria. But most information comes from far more humble evidence. The slow and painstaking reconstruction of ancient life from sifted seeds dug at Neolithic sites, or the surface

BELOW **The Dead Sea Scrolls,** discovered in caves and dated from c. 335 BCE to CE 68, offered new insight into ancient Jewish religious traditions and culture.

ARCHAEOLOGICAL DATING GLOSSARY

BCE A term meaning "before the Common Era"; it is a secular form of dating that replaces the Christian form BC ("before Christ").

BP A term meaning "before the present" (i.e., before the year CE 1950); an abbreviation used in expressing dates, such as those derived from radiocarbon dating and other scientific methods.

CE A term meaning "Common Era"; a secular form of dating that replaces the Christian form AD ("Anno Domini," i.e., in the year of our Lord).

The calendar dating system familiar to us is simply one of several that have existed. The current international calendar is the Gregorian (Christian), itself a revision of the Julian (Roman) Calendar, which failed to properly calculate leap years. The Gregorian calendar uses dates beginning with the calculated birth of Jesus of Nazareth. There are many other existing calendars, including Jewish, Islamic, Hindu, Sikh, Persian, and many other highly localized systems.

LEFT **The archaeological treasures of Samarra** in Iraq have been threatened by intense military activity in the region.

collection of artifacts to establish ancient settlement patterns and changes in economic strategies, rarely makes front-page news.

Archaeological Challenges

Many of the cities and towns of the Middle East are constructed upon layers of earlier settlements. This naturally leads to conflict between the demands of archaeology, heritage management and modern development for a living city. In some cases, such as Jerusalem, the problems are magnified by the religious significance of the ancient sacred sites in the city. Important sites have also been damaged or destroyed in wars over the history of the Middle East. One recent example is the city of Samarra in Iraq, a World Heritage-listed site, which has been damaged by troops using it as a military post. Looting of sites, which supplies artifacts to the international art trade, is also a significant problem that is extremely difficult to police and contain.

Current State of Archaeology

Archaeological investigation is divided into research-based and rescue-based projects. Rescue work may involve excavation at a site recently bulldozed or targeted by looters, or it may be a planned excavation before a major infrastructure project, such as a road or dam, obscures or damages the site. Most of these excavations are carried out by personnel from local departments of antiquities, although in major building schemes, such as the Tabqa Dam on the Euphrates in Syria, foreign teams may be invited to collaborate. Both local and foreign teams undertake research work. This usually involves targeting or searching for sites to provide answers to scholarly questions. Authorities in the Middle East are particularly welcoming of foreign archaeologists, although fully collaborative projects are a more recent development.

Modern archaeology is a multidisciplinary activity. Teams include excavators who specialize in microstratigraphy, as well as colleagues from botany (pollen), zoology (animal bones), physical anthropology (human bones), geosciences (magnetic resonance studies), geology (petrography), biology (plant phytoliths), reconstruction, conservation, and cultural resource management. Surveyors, computer specialists, ceramicists, illustrators, photographers, and finds registrars record and document the material found by excavators in painstaking detail. It is estimated that all of the evidence produced from a traditional six-week archaeological dig can take a minimum of two years to process for publication.

BELOW **At a dig in Sinope,** on the north coast of Turkey, archaeologists uncover a Bronze Age layer beneath more recent structures.

The Fertile Crescent: Birthplace of Agriculture

Introduction

The roots of modern Western civilization are to be found in the ancient Near East—agriculture, urbanization, writing systems (especially the alphabet), mathematics, astronomy, law, social order, and, with the Old and New Testaments, monotheism.

This is largely due to the location of the Near East at the meeting point between Africa, Asia, and Europe, which meant it became the best informed area before the development of modern communication systems. The flow of knowledge from all over the Old World was concentrated here, so its inhabitants were the first to respond to major changes.

Stages of Human Development

About 2.5 million years ago, the earliest human activity occurred in East Africa, and *c.* 1.8 million years ago the first humans migrated from Africa into Asia and Europe through the Great Rift Valley—some of the oldest sites of human habitation have been found in the Jordan Valley of Israel. A three-stage division is useful for the understanding of human development—hunters and gatherers, early farmers, and urban societies.

Hunters and gatherers depended on nature for food, lived in seasonal nomadic sites, were organized in small communities of 20–25 people, and had an egalitarian social organization. Flint and other hard stones were used for making everyday tools. Wood was also used, but little evidence of these tools survived. Although the remains found in caves create a "cave man" image of our ancestors, there are many more open-air sites, indicating that this is not accurate.

From Farming to Urban Living

Farming communities were first established in the ancient Near East, *c.* 9800 BCE, in the area called the Levant, which lies within the modern-day boundaries of Israel, Palestine, Jordan, Lebanon, Syria, northern Iraq, and the Euphrates Valley of eastern Turkey. These early farmers cultivated fields and herded animals for food, lived in large communities of up to 1,000 in permanent villages, and had a stratified society. They invented technologies for manufacturing everyday requirements—pottery, "white ware" lime plaster vessels, figurines made from re-hydrated lime plaster, and metals. Knowledge of hydraulics enabled them to dig wells and develop maritime navigation, which led to the colonization of Mediterranean islands, such as Cyprus and Crete. The new economic and social order of the earliest urban cultures evolved into the powerful states in Mesopotamia and Egypt in the second half of the fourth millennium BCE.

The urban way of life was associated with a complex economy of farmers and specialized occupations (potters, blacksmiths, traders, artists, soldiers, and scribes). They lived in large fortified cities of a few thousand people, and had a complex, hierarchical social order. Kings and priests lived side by side with slaves in the cities. This organization of large communities under one ruler enabled large-scale construction projects. In Mesopotamia and the Nile Valley economic developments, such as the digging of irrigation canals, increased the area of land for cultivation, and population growth. Rulers and religious leaders also built extravagant monuments, like pyramids, palaces, and temples.

ABOVE **"Mesopotamia" is a Greek word** meaning "the land between two rivers"—the Tigris and the Euphrates Rivers shown here where they meet in southern Iraq.

Prehistoric Evidence

The study of hunters and gatherers and early farmers is called "prehistory." Remains at their early sites are the only evidence of how they lived. Modern research has provided considerable data about dates, climatic changes, stone-tool technology, zoology, anthropology, DNA, and much more.

Writing, invented by the first urban society (the Sumerians of Mesopotamia), was first used for economic transactions and the recording of political events—and marks the beginning of recorded history. In addition to the artifacts uncovered at sites, the ancient texts tell a great deal more about the people, including their names, songs, dreams, mythologies, and beliefs, than can ever be deduced from silent artifacts.

The Near East is a small area, but its importance to human development is unique. It was the bridge by which humans spread from Africa to Asia and Europe. In Israel, artifacts associated with burials have been found, thought to be evidence of human cognitive behavior—an awareness of an "other" reality. In this region, evidence of two different human species were found: *Homo sapiens* and Neanderthals. The Natufian culture of the Levant was the first to establish permanent villages, although their economy was still based on hunting and gathering. The first farming communities developed in the Near East and later, the first cities were established.

LEFT **The Karpass Peninsula is situated in northern Cyprus.** Cyprus was one of the first islands in the Mediterranean to be colonized in the "early farmer" phase of human development.

Out of Africa

The earliest stages of human evolution took place in East Africa, but the story of human presence in the Middle East is, from the first archaeological traces, a story of migration and occupation of new areas.

Prehistoric archaeology starts with the appearance of the first tools at the site of Gona in Ethiopia dated to 2.6 million years ago. The subsequent migration out of Africa involved hominids as well as many species of animals and plants. They can all be found in the narrow strip of fertile land between the Mediterranean in the west and the Arabian Desert in the east. This Levantine corridor was always the main highway leading from Africa to Eurasia. The African Great Rift Valley, starting in Tanzania and heading north through Kenya and Ethiopia is where most early human fossils are found. The Red Sea and the Dead Sea Rift Valleys, tributaries of the African Rift, were the most likely paths of migration.

The earliest recorded presence of hominids outside of Africa is found at Dmanisi in southern Georgia. Many perfectly preserved human fossil skulls and bones, together with stone tools assigned to the Olduwan lithic (stone tool) tradition, have been excavated from the layers embedded on top of a basalt flow dated to 1.8 million years BCE. It is apparent that the hominids who lived in Dmanisi had to cross the Levantine corridor on their way out of Africa nearly 2 million years ago.

Ancient Evidence

The earliest site in the ancient Near East, second only to Dmanisi in age, is the site of Ubeidiya in the Jordan Valley, on the margin of the Dead Sea Rift Valley 2 miles (3 km) south of the Sea of Galilee. Heavy tectonic movements, typical of this part of the world, lifted the archaeological layers upwards from below the thick cover of later sediments that accumulated in the Jordan Valley, leaving the layers tilted at a steep angle so that surfaces that used to be horizontal are now almost vertical.

BELOW **The African Great Rift Valley** is some 4,000 miles (6,000 km) in length and 35 miles (60 km) wide. This section is in Kenya.

The site is rich in stone tools and animal bones ranging from small fish and birds to elephants. Incision marks on the bones made by stone tools indicate that they were used in some way by the early humans who lived on the shore of the paleo-Lake Hula at Ubeidiya, an early member of a group of Rift Valley lakes of which the Sea of Galilee is the youngest. Whether these humans hunted the animals or were simply scavengers is an ongoing debate among scholars. Three small human teeth are the only skeletal remains of the site's inhabitants. However, the early humans who lived in Ubeidiya left behind a rich

assemblage of stone tools, which indicate that they brought with them a lithic (i.e. using stone tools) culture that can be assigned to the earliest stages of the post-Olduwan Acheulian culture of the Lower Paleolithic era.

Acheulian bifacial tools provide evidence of human migration through the Levantine corridor over the next million years. The Acheulian site of Gesher Benot Ya´aqov (GBY), 6 miles (10 km) north of the Sea of Galilee, and dated *c.* 790,000 years BCE, presents evidence of a different wave of migration out of Africa. Its layers, tilted in a similar manner to the Ubeidiya site, have exposed a rich assemblage of stone tools, which belong to a more advanced Acheulian culture. The GBY hand axes and cleavers are similar to tools found in African sites of the same age. They are made from basalt, unlike the thousands of flint hand axes found in later Acheulian sites in the Levant. The GBY tools are typical of the African Acheulian. Acheulian sites with a similar lithic tradition are known in India and the Caucasus so the site of GBY indicates that a migration wave began in Africa and reached as far east as India.

Waves of Migration

The Levantine corridor saw the arrival of the early Dmanisi hominids with their Olduwan lithic tradition *c.* 1.8 million years ago. The Ubeidiya early Acheulian peoples migrated around 1.5 million years BCE, followed by the GBY basalt cleaver makers around 0.75 million years BCE. Thousands of Acheulian hand axes have been excavated in Egypt, Jordan, Israel, Syria, and Lebanon. These flint tools may represent a final, fourth stage of the Acheulian post-GBY.

The end of the Lower Paleolithic in the Levant is dated to *c.* 300,000 years ago. By *c.* 400,000 years ago the Acheulian was replaced by the Acheulo-Yabrudian and the end of the Lower Paleolithic is marked by a new lithic tradition—the Mousterian Middle Paleolithic.

LEFT **Dmanisi in Georgia, is regarded** as "the cradle of the first Europeans." Among the artifacts shown here are a *Homo erectus* jaw, a variety of tools, and the skull of a large saber-toothed feline.

GESHER BENOT YA´AQOV (GBY)

The tools and fossil bones left by the GBY inhabitants were covered by waterlogged sediments that remained there until their recent exposure by the Jordan River. The anaerobic conditions preserved botanical and organic remains extremely rare in a site of such age. Tree logs and branches, fruit and seeds, and even bark, let us know how the Acheulian people lived. GBY has the earliest-known wooden artifact, as many as seven species of edible nuts, and the stone tools used to crack them open. One of the main contributions of the GBY lithic assemblage is a concentration of burnt flints, the remnants of ancient fireplaces and the earliest evidence of the controlled use of fire.

RIGHT **This basalt hand axe** is one of a vast number of artifacts uncovered at this site, providing a greater understanding of how early hominids lived.

Migration and Dispersal

The Middle Paleolithic of the Levant (*c.* 250,000 to 45,000 years ago) is a story of migration and dispersal. *Homo erectus* was displaced by two groups of hominids. These were our own species, *Homo sapiens sapiens* and a close relative, *Homo sapiens neanderthalensis* (Neanderthals).

In the 1970s the data from the primary sites in Europe seemed to present a clear picture: the Neanderthals, who evolved from earlier types of hominids that migrated from Africa some half a million years ago, ruled the continent for hundreds of thousands of years. They were well adapted to the cold climate of the European ice ages, and their material culture (the Mousterian) allowed them to survive for many centuries. Some 40,000 years ago Cro-Magnons appeared in Europe. Their skeletons were similar to ours and they produced a more sophisticated type of blade made from flint or obsidian cores. They also used bone tools and were the artists of the famous cave paintings and figurines of Europe.

However, in the last few decades of prehistoric research in the Levant, a very different scenario of the relationship between modern humans and Neanderthals has been uncovered.

BELOW **The western slopes of Mount Carmel** is located in northern Israel. Archaeological discoveries found here have contributed greatly to our knowledge of human development.

Neanderthals and Anatomically Modern Humans—Together?

The first prehistoric excavation in the region was undertaken by Turville-Petre in the 1920s in the Cave of Zuttiyeh in the Wadi Amud, near its outlet to the Sea of Galilee. The cap of a human skull, known as the "Galilee Man," was found, now dated to *c.* 400,000 years BP. However, the Cave of Amud, another cave in the Wadi Amud, plays a key role in our story. Here, a few Neanderthal skeletons, including that of a baby, were found. The date of the layers in which they were found is 55,000 years BP, which distinguishes them as the latest Neanderthals in the Levant. The remains of Neanderthals have also been found in other caves in the Levant. These include the Kebara Cave in Mount Carmel, in which a large and robust "classic" Neanderthal skeleton was excavated; the Cave of Tabun, in the famous Valley of the Caves in the Carmel region; and the Cave of Dederiyeh in Syria.

But here is where the story becomes complicated. Results of excavations in other cave sites in Israel indicate that they were inhabited by a different population. In the Cave of Qafzeh, located south of the city of Nazareth in the lower Galilee, a cemetery was excavated that revealed many burials of anatomically modern humans. The date obtained for this site is as early as 90,000 years BP. A similar situation is seen in the Skhul rock shelter, which is located just 330 yd (300 m) west of the Cave of Tabun. Here, a number of skeletons were excavated which displayed different combinations of modern and archaic skeletal features, all dating to between 60,000 and 100,000 years ago.

The finds from the Levant are therefore intriguing. Anatomically modern humans lived here as early as 100,000 years ago, either alongside Neanderthals yet to be discovered, or more intriguingly still, perhaps 40,000 years

LEFT **A Neanderthal burial**—some of the earliest evidence of a culture that cared for, and disposed of, the dead. Whether this is an indication of religious beliefs is a subject that is open to debate.

before late-arriving Neanderthals appeared at around 60,000 years ago. The sites from which these two types of hominids were excavated are sometimes very close together.

But this is not the end of the story. When we study the stone tools that were produced in the Middle Paleolithic sites in the Levant, we find no significant difference between the material culture or way of life of the Neanderthals and the anatomically modern humans. In all of the sites, the same Mousterian artifacts were produced by the same tool-making technology.

Same or Different?

The first anatomically modern humans were found in Ethiopia and dated to 160,000 years ago. The Levant, once again, was the main path of their migration out of Africa. This is the fifth migration wave we have been able to identify so far. But how can we interpret the finds from the Levant?

One possibility is that anatomically modern humans migrated from Africa into the Levant as early as 100,000 years BP. At *c.* 60,000 years BP they met the Neanderthals migrating south from Europe and these two populations coexisted until the appearance of the Early Upper Paleolithic industries in the Levant around 45,000 years ago. We do not know what kind of relationship these two groups had. Did they really coexist? What we do know is that they shared the same material culture, and lived in the same environment. We also know that Neanderthals had brains that were somewhat larger than ours, that they buried their dead, and took care of the old and handicapped members of their groups. But did they have the ability to talk? Archaeologists and physical anthropologists continue to debate the biological relation between modern humans and the Neanderthals. Were they a different biological species? Or were they a branch of the human evolutionary tree that came to a dead end with the appearance of anatomically modern humans? Or, as suggested from the archaeological finds of the Levantine caves, were Neanderthals and anatomically modern humans members of the same group showing skeletal differences that lie within the range of variability of the human species? Maybe the Neanderthals were not a distinct hominid species. The information we have gained from the Levant offers more questions than answers.

BELOW **The Cave of Amud in Israel** overlooks the Amud River (Wadi Amud), northwest of the Sea of Galilee, where significant Neanderthal remains have been found.

Modern Humans Emerge

The Mousterian lithic tradition of the Middle Paleolithic dominated the Levant for more than 250,000 years. And then, between 45,000 and 50,000 years ago, change came. New stone tool technologies and new ways of life can be observed from archaeological discoveries.

One of the most important of these findings comes from a small excavation of an open-air site in the deep canyon of the Zin Valley in the Negev Desert. This excavation, at Boker Tachtit, exposed an assemblage of tools produced by a technology that is definitely of Mousterian lithic origin. However, some changes had been introduced into the standard Middle Paleolithic technology resulting in end products different from any Middle Paleolithic collection of tools. The Mousterian lithic industry, based on flake tools and points, was replaced by an industry in which elongated blades were the primary form of stone tools. Thereafter, the production of blades dominated the lithic industries in most parts of the world until the end of the Stone Age. Blades with a much better edge-to-mass ratio than flakes, and the manufacture of blades from flint or obsidian cores, enabled effective and efficient production of these tools. This significant innovation in technology signaled the emergence of the Upper Paleolithic era.

Local Developments and Newcomers

The material observed at Boker Tachtit, and other Early Upper Paleolithic sites in the Levant, represents a true intermediate stage between the Middle Paleolithic Mousterian lithic tradition and the Upper Paleolithic blade industries. But who were the creators of these industries? Were they newcomers from Africa? Were they anatomically modern humans who replaced the Neanderthals in a scenario similar to the one described in Europe? It is clear that the European scenario of cultural and, possibly, biological

BELOW **The Zin Valley in the Negev Desert** is a rich source of Mousterian lithic artifacts. The Negev covers 60 percent of the land surface of Israel.

LEFT **Stone scrapers** from Ethiopia are an example of basic Mousterian lithic tools. These are dated to *c.* 160,000 BP.

replacement of Neanderthals by *Homo sapiens sapiens* cannot hold true for the Levantine emergence of the Upper Paleolithic.

The early assemblages reveal the Ahmarian tradition, which was the main lithic entity of the Levantine Upper Paleolithic. This culture is found in many sites all over the Levant and it is possible to follow a line of development from the early Ahmarian to the end of the Upper Paleolithic period. The Ahmarian lithic tradition is clearly the dominant cultural entity in the Levant for the duration of the Upper Paleolithic. However, for just a brief time, a different lithic tradition with obvious European roots entered the ancient Near East. On the coastal plain of the northern Levant, mainly in Israel and Lebanon, a few sites, mostly caves, were excavated with layers that were assigned to the "Levantine Aurignacian." In Western Europe, the Aurignacian is well known from many sites and stands as the first "true" Upper Paleolithic culture replacing the Mousterian industries. It is dated between 40,000 and 35,000 years ago. The Levantine variant comes later, falling between 32,000 and 30,000 years ago. It has a short duration and occurs in a restricted geographical area.

Immigration from Europe

The finds from the Aurignacian caves in the Levant indicate that we are looking at a lithic tradition that came into the Levant with immigrants from the north. The bearers of this distinctive European toolkit established themselves in a new region, alongside peoples still employing the older Ahmarian technology. One of the main indicators for the contact between the European and Levantine Aurignacian is a small piece of bone found in the Cave of Kebara in western Galilee. The significant part is its base, where a deep groove splits it in two to create the most typical member of the Aurignacian toolkit—the split-base bone point. This single tool indicates that the people who occupied the cave at that time were part of the Aurignacian tradition. In the prehistoric time scale, the Levantine Aurignacian period in the ancient Near East was short. Whether the newcomers from the north were pushed out by local groups or were assimilated into them to the point where they lost their lithic tradition, cannot be determined on the basis of current data.

The Upper Paleolithic in the Levant continues the story of the region as the "kings' highway" bringing cultural change and linking development between the areas of the Old World. Yet, there is one aspect in which the Levantine Upper Paleolithic is clearly inferior to the European—no cave art paintings, figurines, or engravings have ever been discovered. The reason is unknown.

The Upper Paleolithic Ahmarian culture evolved gradually into Epipalaeolithic microlith-based lithic traditions. The Paleolithic way of life was beginning to change, as larger groups of people lived longer in one place during the latter stages of the Ice Age. The world was poised for the next great cultural change—the shift from mobile hunter-gatherer bands to sedentary agricultural village societies.

BELOW **Upper Paleolithic stone and bone tools** are an indication of significant technological advances. Shown here are various blades and spearheads.

The Natufian

Since the 1930s, the Middle East, and the Levantine Corridor in particular, has provided archaeological evidence for the transition from hunter-gatherer societies to village farming. The Natufian culture (15,000–11,500 BP) is recognized as the instigator of the food-producing cultures in the Levant.

RIGHT **The Hilazon Tachtit Cave in Israel** served primarily as a place of ritual burial. It provides evidence of how ritual was integrated into domestic life.

The numerous and rapid technological changes that ushered in the Natufian period must have had a profound effect on society. The Natufian culture was first recognized in the early 1930s by Dorothy Garrod during her excavations in the cave sites of Shukbah in Samaria and El Wad in Mt. Carmel. Since then, many Natufian sites have been excavated in the Mediterranean region, the Jordan Valley, the Negev, and the Jordanian uplands.

Natufian culture is identified as a late Epipaleolithic industry, in which the most abundant form of geometric flint microlith is the small lunate. It is generally regarded as having two distinct phases based on the size and method of shaping these lunate tools—Early Natufian (*c.* 15,000–13,000 BP) and Late Natufian (*c.* 13,000–11,500 BP). The sickle-blade tool was created for harvesting various crops and is the distinguishing feature of Natufian assemblages.

Apart from the lithic component, used as the main criterion for its cultural definition, other features unique to the Natufian have been recovered from the central region of Natufian settlement, a restricted area stretching from the Mediterranean coast to the central Jordan Valley. Evidence of relatively prolific artistic activities has attracted much attention since art objects and decorative elements are rare in the material culture of the prehistoric Levant prior to the Natufian. Most importantly, a change in the spiritual outlook of the Natufians is indicated by the large organized burial grounds, a practice not previously recorded in the archaeological record.

Natufian Villages

The Natufian people reoccupied most of the caves and rock shelters that had been occupied for short periods during the Upper Paleolithic but later abandoned. Also, excavations at Eynan (Ain Mallaha) and Wadi Hammeh 27 have exposed evidence of large open-air Natufian villages. Based on distinct features of the Natufian sites and the animal remains including, also for the first time, mice, rats, and sparrows, this period suggests the emergence of sedentism—permanent, year-round settlements.

At first, communities were probably composed of hunter–gatherers whose aggregations gradually became permanent settlements, thus changing their way of life. In the latter half of the Natufian, while there are signs of a reversion to mobility, there is also a more overt expression of territorial boundaries. Towards the end of the Natufian and more definitely throughout the Pre-Pottery Neolithic A period (PPNA) that followed, there are locations that demonstrate the beginnings of settled village life and the development of agriculture.

There are indications that during the early phases of the Natufian there was a steady expansion of oak forests and steppe woodland. The area of the central Southern Levant would have been rich in food plants, including cereals, pulses, and nuts, but botanical evidence from Natufian sites is scarce. Some botanical evidence has been retrieved from a late Natufian site outside the "core area"—Abu Hureyra in Syria. A wide spectrum of potentially edible species has been identified there, including wheat, rye, lentil, bitter vetch, pistachio, hackberry, and pear. Animal remains indicate that the Natufians hunted gazelle, deer, and cattle, but there are very few remains of goats, horses, and donkeys.

ABOVE **These small flint lunates** are typical of the Natufian microlithic tools that were used for hunting and food preparation.

The Late Natufian period correlates with the well-documented climatic oscillation of the Younger Dryas. This was a signficantly drier period that lasted for about 1,000 years and marked a return to glacial conditions in northern Europe, which saw the steppe woodland belt retract.

The most prominent Natufian phenomenon, the development of permanent dwellings, is particularly evident in larger sites containing round houses. They had foundations made of undressed stone that had been collected in the immediate vicinity, and retaining walls that supported the circumference of the dwelling. These dwelling structures appear to be carefully planned, and they do not appear alone, but in small clusters.

At Hayonim Cave, for example, there are remains of six built-up round or oval structures that form two parallel series of rooms. The rooms are approximately 3 yd (2.5 m) in diameter with the perimeter wall about 1 yd (1 m) thick.

LEFT **Pioneering archaeologist Dorothy Garrod (1892–1969)** studied at Cambridge and later at Oxford. She was the first woman to be appointed professor at Cambridge.

BONE AND STONE TOOLS

The Natufian is marked by a bone industry that is far greater in quantity and contains more elaborate and varied forms and tools than any previous prehistoric culture. Objects were made of bone shafts, teeth, and horn-cores from gazelles, wolves, deer, and birds. Research indicates that bone tools were used for hide-working, and basketry. Ground-stone tools, few of which have been found in earlier periods, appear in significant numbers in Natufian sites. These include various sizes of bowls, mortars, and pestles made of limestone, basalt, and sandstone. Among them are large, fixed mortars weighing up to 220 lb (100 kg), and up to 30 inches (80 cm) deep. Recently, the ground-stone tools have been categorized into several groups relating to cooking activities: tools for pounding, mixing, milling, and grinding; serving bowls; small bowls, and plates. Natufian ground-stone tools were labor-intensive to produce, and often elaborately decorated with geometric patterns. The fact that they were carefully maintained in good condition indicates the growing importance of personal property.

ABOVE LEFT **Artifacts from Natufian sites** include bowls and mortars used for preparing and serving food.

At Eynan (Ain Mallaha), just north of the Sea of Galilee, the houses appear to be aligned along the length of a slope into which they were cut. The floors supported several installations including hearths, bins, work surfaces, and storage pits. There are also a few examples of paved floors.

In the larger centers, new regulatory mechanisms were developed to govern the ways in which nonfamily members interacted with each other.

The Growing Importance of the Dead

Natufian sites also contain evidence of a new development—cemeteries on a grand scale. During the Late Natufian period mortuary rites were developed and certain sites, such as Hilazon Tachtit Cave, functioned primarily as cemeteries for apparently more mobile populations.

From the approximately 500 burials that are known, it is difficult to discern clear-cut patterns. Bodies were usually buried in a flexed position and only occasionally in an extended position. Graves contained either a single body or several bodies of different ages and genders. Some of the bodies were decorated or wore ornamental clothing. Sometimes a stone, or stones, were placed under the head of the deceased or positioned on top of the burial to keep the body in a desired position. Many of the graves show no particular arrangement, consisting simply of a pit refilled after the burial.

There are, however, some graves that were actually constructed—the pit was partially, sometimes completely, lined with stones. More complex examples involved stone paving, such as found at Erq el-Ahmar in the Jordan Valley, or the introduction of a large, possibly ritually broken mortar into the grave pit. Sometimes stones, either lying flat or standing upright, were used to mark the graves. However, in most cases, there is nothing on the surface to indicate the location of the grave.

Toward the end of the Natufian, there is an increase in the number of secondary burials as well as a new custom of removing the skulls and burying them separately—a practice that continued into the Neolithic period.

While researchers may be divided about when plant cultivation and agriculture began, the taming, and finally, domesticating of the dog seems to have been started by the Natufian. Indeed, joint dog-man burials are found in at least two Natufian sites—Eynan (Ain Mallaha) and Hayonim Terrace.

Prolific Artistic Activities

Several stone objects bearing incised patterns were recovered from "core area" sites. These include stone slabs from Hayonim Cave, incised with a ladder-pattern motif, and carved basalt bowls from Wadi Hammeh 27, showing a meander pattern.

Both bone and stone figurines of animals and humans have been found only at the Mt. Carmel sites—Kebara, El-Wad, and Wadi Oren. Bone carvings of animals are wonderfully skilled and naturalistic, while most human figures are rendered very schematically. Large numbers of personal ornaments were recovered.

Of the thousand or so bone items recovered from the Natufian layer at Hayonim Cave, one quarter were personal ornaments—pendants and beads made of leg bones and teeth. Bone pendants, usually well-shaped oval fragments of gazelle toe and perforated at the narrow end, have been found in several Natufian sites. Most of the pendants with coloration seem to have been for burials, with only a few found in living areas. Several animal teeth, such as those of fox and hyena, that were found at Hayonim Cave and Hilazon Tachtit Cave were possibly perforated for necklaces.

Seashells, an ideal source for jewelry, are found grouped together, particularly in graves, as headdresses, necklaces, armlets, belts, or garment decorations. The dominance of dentalium shell beads, which is as high as 90 percent in the Hayonim Cave and Hayonim Terrace sites, is considered to be the cultural marker of the Natufian, indicating a major change from the assemblages of the earlier Epipaleolithic entities.

It is interesting to note that Late Natufian items unearthed at Eynan include exotic items, such as pieces of Anatolian obsidian—the first signs of the exchange network that would become well established during the Pre-Pottery Neolithic A period. The profound social and economic changes associated with the transition to agriculture (the Neolithization process) began in the Natufian, and, no doubt, entailed equally substantial ideological changes. It is not clear whether these ideological changes came before, perhaps even triggering, the economic transition, or were a response to it—a process of adjusting to living in large, permanent settlements among people who were not related by birth or marriage.

LEFT **A Natufian burial** shows the typical fetal position of burial that gives an indication of the careful treatment of the dead.

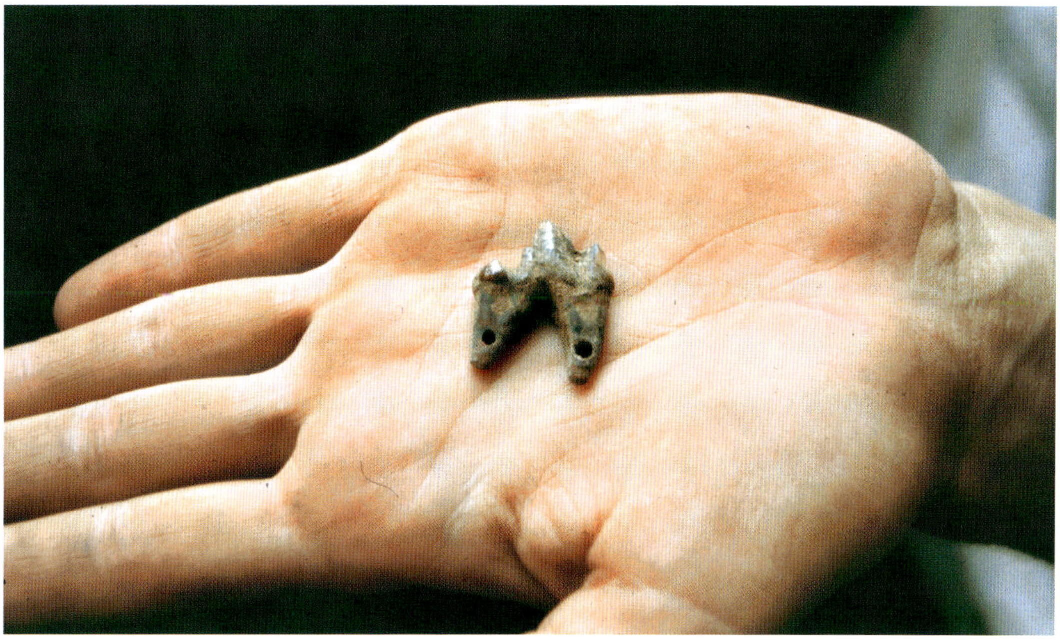

RIGHT **This canine tooth pendant** from the Hilazon Tachtit site provides evidence of the close relationship between humans and dogs.

The First Farmers

The first interest in the beginning of agriculture was shown in the 1930s by Gordon Childe who spoke of "The Agriculture Revolution." He explained that farming was in response to sudden climatic change to much drier conditions at the end of the last Ice Age.

RIGHT **Gordon Childe (1892–1958)** was an Australian who was Professor of European Prehistory in Edinburgh before becoming the Director of the Institute of Archaeology in London.

Childe suggested that the process took place in oasis environments where growing familiarity between humans and animals may have resulted in the taming of individual young animals, and gradually, full domestication. Although Childe did not work in the Middle East, his ideas were first tested there by American Robert Braidwood (1907–2003), who excavated Jarmo in Iraq in the late 1940s, which he believed was "the world's earliest village." According to his theory, the beginning of agriculture took place in the hilly area to the north of the Fertile Crescent. Other theories that attempt to explain the agricultural revolution concentrate on climatic change or the needs of a growing population. It is now evident that agriculture developed earlier in Jericho and other sites in the Levant than at Jarmo.

The First Settlements

The Neolithic period (*c.* 9800–5800 BCE) came after some 2.5 million years of hunter–gatherers. Human behavior changed from a nomadic way of life to living in permanent settlements; from dependence on wild foods to agriculture and the domestication of animals; from living in small groups to large communities; and from an egalitarian society to a stratified social order.

Kathleen Kenyon (1906–1978) excavated a sequence of four Neolithic phases at Jericho in the 1950s. These are known as Pre-Pottery Neolithic A (PPNA) and B (PPNB) followed by the Pottery Neolithic periods. This was the first time that such a detailed sequence had been recognized in the Near East and Jericho became the key site for understanding the Neolithic period. Hundreds of Neolithic sites have since been found in the Near East, creating a vivid picture of the earliest farming communities.

Pre-Pottery Neolithic A (9800–8800 BCE), the first phase of the Neolithic period, is characterized by small villages of up to 5 acres (2 ha) in size. The dwellings were round or oval structures, each containing a cooking area with a hearth and grinding stones. It appears that each building was used by a nuclear family. Artifacts for daily life were made of flint (arrowheads, sickle-blades, and axes), limestone, and basalt. Small quantities of exotic imported items were found, including Anatolian obsidian (volcanic glass), seashells, and green mineral stones. Adults were usually buried under the floors of the houses in a flexed position. Sometimes the skulls were removed and decorated with plaster, shells, and painted to resemble the living. The few art objects found are figurines of women, birds, and limestone artifacts with geometric incisions. Some scholars believe that the female figures represent a "Great Mother Goddess," who was responsible for the fertility of the land, humans, and animals.

Jericho seems to have been a regional center. Covering 6 acres (2.5 ha), it is the largest known settlement of the period, and a number of smaller sites (e.g., Netiv Hagdud and Gilgal) can be found within one or two days' walking distance. Large quantities of Anatolian obsidian and greenstone artifacts were imported to Jericho. One of the earliest monumental structures known was discovered at Jericho. It consisted of a solid stone tower approximately 28 ft (8 m) high which contained an internal staircase of 20 steps. It was used as a burial chamber. A stone wall was built next to the tower, encircling the settlement from the west. A 16-ft (5-m) wide dry moat (fosse) ran along outside the wall. Kenyon regarded these as part of a city fortification, although others think the tower functioned as an observation point, and the wall was constructed to guard against flash flooding from the adjacent Wadi Qelt. These monumental structures are unique to Jericho at this period, which suggests a much more sophisticated society than in the surrounding village communities.

ABOVE **A PPNB sickle,** with three flint blades inserted in the handle, thought to be made from animal horn, is from the Nahal Hemar Cave, Israel.

Göbekli Tepe, another regional center of this period, was discovered in the northern Levant near the modern city of Urfa. Here, Klaus Schmidt unearthed stone walls 6–9 ft (2–3 m) high, and T-shaped stone pillars 6–12 ft (2–4 m) tall. As each pillar weighs a few tons, a large group of people would have been needed to quarry and transfer them to their final location. They were decorated with engravings or high relief sculptures depicting various animals, or geometric designs. The animals are obviously male, which appears to be an important aspect of the local cult or mythology. The excellent state of preservation of the site results from the fact that the buildings were partly constructed below ground level, and were buried after use.

Established Village Communities

Pre-Pottery Neolithic B (*c.* 8800–6800 BCE) communities began to live in much larger villages as big as 34 acres (14 ha). The Neolithic way of life spread into new areas—Anatolia, Cyprus, and southeast Europe. The colonization of Cyprus indicates maritime transportation was possible. Wells from the period indicate a knowledge of water use and storage.

By this period, the typical architecture in the Levant was rectangular buildings with white plaster floors. Limestone, flint, and basalt remained the main materials used for everyday tools. The flint industry was characterized by long and elegant blades produced from a special type of core, known as "Naviform," from which arrowheads and sickle-blades were made. Exotic imported items, such as obsidian, seashells, and beads, were also found in these sites, and artifacts made from unworked copper ore have been found at Cayönü and Aşikli Hüyük in Turkey. In the Judean Desert, Ofer Bar-Yosef and David Alon discovered hundreds of items made of perishable materials in the Nahal Hemar Cave—mats, baskets, linen textiles, a complete sickle made of horn, wooden beads, and wooden tools.

BELOW **This deep trench is from Kathleen Kenyon's excavations** at Jericho in the 1950s. The great size of the prehistoric mound preserved much evidence of the earliest stages of settled life.

ABOVE **PPNA stone tower from Jericho** (*c.* 8000 BCE) may have been part of a fortification, a watchtower, or a floodwater barrier. It was finally used as a burial chamber.

Burial practices became more elaborate. Once removed, some of the skulls appear to have been disinterred, plastered, and then decorated, perhaps as part of a ceremony of worship or final burial. After long usage, groups of these skulls were buried together in pits. While there has been much conjecture about this practice, it seems that in this period we see, for the first time, the ritual use and eventual reburial of decorated human skulls.

The coming together of people in large communities created a new social order. Social stratification is evident in the variation in house sizes and the different level of access to commodities, such as burnt lime. In order to create the shared experiences that promote social order, we see the widespread use of art and cult objects. At the household level, there are small artifacts, such as human or animal figurines. Cattle figurines also start to appear in large numbers, sometimes with evidence of magic or voodoo practices, probably used to ensure success in hunting. On the community level, there are large-scale, life-size items, such as plastered skulls, masks, and statues. The first glimpses of the rich artistic expression of the period were found in Jericho. Kenyon unearthed a few concentrations of plastered human skulls which had been buried in pits. The removal of skulls had already been observed in the Pre-Pottery Neolithic A sites, but there the skulls received no special treatment. Now the skulls were plastered and sometimes seashells were inserted as eyes. When the skulls ceased to be used, they were carefully reburied in pits below house floors. This type of ancestor cult is associated with the beginning of a sedentary way of life. The skulls may have represented the community's ancestors, justifying the rights of a particular group to claim and settle down in the village and its surrounding fields.

Large statues of divine ancestors or clan gods were also found. In the southern Levant, in Jericho, and 'Ain Ghazal, where they were made of mud and plaster, they resemble the biblical and Sumerian myths of the creation of man from earth. Large stone statues of humans have been found at Nevali Çori and Göbleki Tepe, near Urfa in the northern Levant, along with stone masks dating from this period. These artifacts have openings for the eyes and mouth, as well as a means of suspension. Such artifacts indicate rituals in which community ceremonies involving elaborate public displays and group dancing formed a major component of religious activity. There are many scenes of dancing uncovered throughout the ancient Near East—a few in this period, but many more in later phases.

Developed Village Communities

The Pottery Neolithic period (*c.* 6800–5800 BCE) saw a crucial new element added to the Neolithic toolkit—pottery. This opened up new developments in household organization as pottery vessels were used for the preparation of food, cooking, storage of liquids, and stockpiling of grain in large storage jars.

Many sites of this period are small and display evidence that indicate there were numerous storage and rubbish pits, suggesting a greater accumulation of possessions. An outstanding settlement has been uncovered at Sha'ar Hagolan in the Jordan Valley. This site covers 50 acres (20 ha), and is the largest known in the southern Levant. It was a well-planned settlement with large courtyard buildings constructed along streets and a well dug down to the aquifer level. The houses ranged in size from 300–800 sq yd (250–700 sq m) and had between eight and 24 rooms built around an open courtyard.

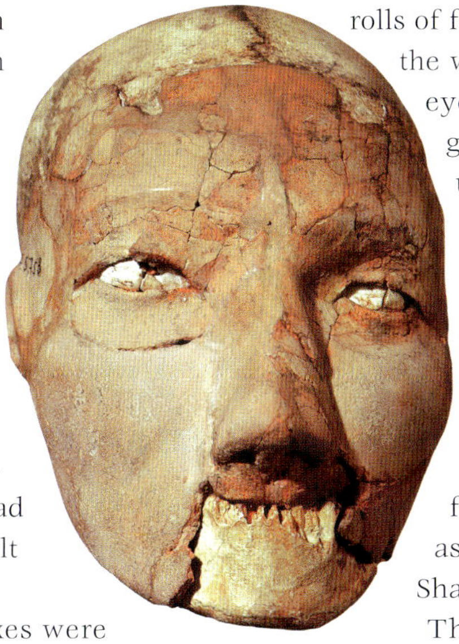

LEFT **This plastered skull from Jericho** is an example of the treatment of the dead that was widely practiced in the southern Levant during the eighth and seventh millennia BCE.

These monumental complexes were occupied by extended families, unlike the much smaller Pre-Pottery Neolithic buildings that housed smaller nuclear families. The courtyard houses are the earliest example of this architectural concept, which is still used today in the Near East and around the Mediterranean.

In Sha'ar Hagolan more than 300 art objects were found. Of special interest are baked clay figurines portraying women with wide hips and rolls of fat, seated comfortably, surveying the world through diagonal grooved eyes. The figurines are designed with great attention to detail. Some features are exaggerated, giving them a surreal appearance. Another type of figurine was made of natural limestone river pebbles. With a few incisions, and sometimes by drilling, a schematic human figure was carved onto the pebble. These two types represent mainly female figures, regarded by the exacavator as representing "the Goddess of Sha'ar Hagolan."

The overall picture is one of increasing complexity in Neolithic settlements over time. Villages became bigger and the dwellings of each family larger. New building techniques were introduced and the problem of water shortage was solved by digging wells. In an effort to support the evolving social order, elaborate community rituals were developed.

The Neolithic way of life spread into Asia, Europe, and Africa.

BELOW **This sculpture of a predator** is from a T-shaped pillar at Göbleki Tepe, near Urfa. The elaborate structure from which it comes may be one of the earliest mortuary temples ever discovered.

The Domestication of Animals

Wadi Rum Caves

This petroglyph of Bedouin camel caravans is one of many found in the 1980s in the sandstone and granite rock formations in the desert of southern Jordan. Many are believed to be over 8,000 years old.

The domestication of animals was a major breakthrough in human evolution. Agriculture enabled larger populations than could be supported by a hunter-gatherer lifestyle. Domestication of animals progressed in stages over a few millennia. At first, humans captured and kept wild animals in a protected environment. Separated from the wild population, these animals began inbreeding. Along with human selection, changes to their foraging patterns, and selective breeding via the less aggressive males, more manageable herd animals, with smaller bodies and reduced horn sizes developed. These changes can be traced through bones uncovered in archaeological sites. However, the very first stage of animal domestication leaves no direct evidence, so it is not possible to identify precisely in which archaeological period it occurred. A species chosen for domestication as a source of food lives in herds with a social hierarchy, breeds more often, and has a faster growth rate than in the wild. By *c.* 12,000 BCE, hunters and gatherers of the Natufian culture began the process of domesticating the dog. This was not done for food, but more likely for its skills in hunting, and for protection. Dog and human skeletons were found in the same burials—a clear manifestation of the famous saying that "dog is a man's best friend."

In the first stage of the Neolithic period, the domestic economy centered around growing cereals and hunting, as animals were not yet domesticated. With the advent of the Pre-Pottery Neolithic B, the herding of sheep and goats began, perhaps first in the northern

Levant, and then was introduced into the south. Animal domestication did not occur simultaneously in all areas, as hunting was still the main source of meat in some communities. In the Pottery Neolithic period, the process of domestication became more established with the introduction of two new species: cattle and pigs. During this stage, hunting wild animals decreased drastically. Most of the meat was produced from domestic animals. By the end of the Pre-Pottery Neolithic B, the arid zones of the Fertile Crescent underwent a major change. In the earlier phases they had been exploited by Neolithic hunter–gatherer communities, but now a new way of life was adopted in the desert. With herds of domesticated sheep and goats, agriculture spread into the arid areas of the Near East as full-time nomadic pastoralism. About 4500 BCE, in the Chalcolithic period, the donkey was domesticated as a beast of burden. This enabled the long-distance land transportation of goods. Domesticated horses are known in the area only from the second millennium BCE, used mainly to haul four-wheeled carts and two-wheeled chariots. Originally, the horse had been domesticated in Central Asia, but it took a long time to arrive in the Near East. The domestication of the camel took place at the end of the second millennium BCE and made crossing large desert areas possible.

Chalcolithic Pottery

These pottery figurines were discovered in a purpose-built sanctuary at the site of Gilat, a regional shrine serving the northern Negev (*c.* 4000 BCE).

There are three different aspects that indicate increased exploitation of animals in the ancient Near East. First, the number of domesticated species increased. Second, the adoption of pastoralism introduced domesticated animals into desert environments. Third, the exploitation of animals became more intensive—a process dubbed "the second revolution" by archaeologist Andrew Sherratt. This involved breeding animals for products other than meat, such as dairying, hides, hair and wool, transportation, and plowing. By analyzing animal bones found in Neolithic sites according to the proportion of males to females, and the age at which they died, it is possible to get an indication of how they were exploited.

Evidence of "Man's Best Friend"

These 12,000-year-old remains uncovered at the Eynan (Ain Mallaha) site in Israel show a human and a dog buried in the same grave.

Domestication of Animals in the Ancient Near East

Animal	Culture	Time—BCE
Dog	Natufian	12,000
Sheep and Goat	Pre-Pottery	9000
Pig	Pottery Neolithic	8000
Cattle	Pottery Neolithic	6000
Donkey	Chalcolithic	4000
Horse	Late Bronze	1500
Camel	Iron Age	1200

Permanent Settlement

The hunter-gatherer way of life ensured that population growth remained low. The move to farming and a sedentary lifestyle forever altered this situation. Living in villages allowed a larger number of children per family. The population increased dramatically and continued to double every few hundred years.

ABOVE **The Euphrates River in Kurdistan,** eastern Turkey, is typical of the type of country where agriculture and more sedentary settlements began.

RIGHT **"Mother Goddess" figures were discovered** at Sha'ar Hagolan, on the western bank of the Yarmuk River in the Jordan Valley.

This situation created a pressure that was resolved in various ways: each village became bigger, the number of villages in each region increased, and people migrated into new areas. Early farming communities spread from the Levant to nearby regions within the Near East, and then further away to Europe and Africa. The earliest village communities of the Near East evolved in the Levant—the core area of the first permanent settlements during the Natufian era *c.* 12,000 BCE. During the Pre-Pottery Neolithic A, *c.* 9800 BCE, the economic base of the early villages changed from hunting and gathering to agriculture. Plants, cereals, and legumes were first cultivated, followed later by the domestication of animals.

The Neolithic Package

Within two millennia, permanent villages were established in Asia, Europe, and Africa. The Neolithic people developed what is sometimes called "the Neolithic package": domesticated plants (wheat, barley, and peas) and animals (goats, sheep, cattle, and pigs); three typical flint tools (arrowheads, sickle-blades, and axes); water supply based on the digging of wells; various cultic characteristics ("Mother Goddess" figurines and dancing scenes); and, later, the production of pottery. These characteristics indicate to us that the Neolithic way of life was not invented in these areas independently, but was brought in from the Levant.

It was during the Pre-Pottery Neolithic B, *c.* 8800–6800 BCE, that village communities spread from the Levant into larger areas of the Near East, to Anatolia at sites like Cayönü, Aşikli, and the lower levels at Çatal Hüyük, and to the Zagros Mountains of Iraq and Iran, at sites like Jarmo and Sarab. These communities were connected to each other, as indicated by the exchange of obsidian (a volcanic glass found in the eastern Anatolian uplands, in Turkey, and Armenia). A small number of obsidian artifacts were found in many of the Neolithic sites of the Near East, from the Negev in Israel to the most eastern sites of the Fertile Crescent.

Floors of plaster made from burnt limestone were the standard floor surface for houses in the Pre-Pottery Neolithic B Levant and are known in almost every site of this period in Israel, Jordan, Lebanon, and Syria. In sites located further away, like Nevali Çori and Aşikli in Turkey, the regular dwellings were constructed without such floors but plastered floors were found in cultic buildings. Some experts believe that the idea of thick plastered floors originated in Turkey and northern Syria and when it came south it was used to pave only cultic buildings. This suggests that the Pre-Pottery Neolithic B "religion" was, therefore, an import from the north. Others think that cultic buildings were treated in this way in the south to mark them out as different from clay-floored domestic dwellings. This is seen as the beginning of the concepts of ritual purity and sacred space.

During the seventh millennium BCE Neolithic villages were established in the areas to the northern Transcaucasian region. A large horizontal exposure at Jeitun revealed the plan of a village with square houses built next to each other. Later examples, much further to the east, are indicated by the Neolithic site of Mehrgarh in western Pakistan. The early Neolithic people here herded cattle, sheep, and goats, and grew wheat and barley. From Pakistan, domestication may have spread into India, and perhaps into Southeast Asia. The domestication of plants and animals developed independently in China and may have spread from there to the islands in the southeast.

Colonizing the Mediterranean

The first colonization of the Mediterranean islands of Cyprus and Crete in the Pre-Pottery Neolithic B period indicates the existence of maritime navigation. This early date became apparent only in the 1990s, when two wells cut in rock were found in Kissonerga-Mylouthkia on the southwest coast of Cyprus. At the same time, the settlement of Shillourokambous was a flourishing village with houses, burials, and art objects. The inhabitants had brought seeds and animals that were not native to the island to Cyprus. The skeleton of a cat was found with a human burial.

The earliest-known Neolithic site in Europe was found under the famous Bronze Age palace of King Minos at Knossos in Crete, dated to *c.* 7000 BCE. Again, it indicated maritime immigration from the nearby Anatolian mainland. Not much later, agriculture spread into Europe from Anatolia. Some of the earliest European villages were found in Bulgaria, in sites such as Tell Asmak, Thessaly, the Balkans, and Romania. In these villages we find all the key elements of "the Neolithic package."

During the sixth millennium BCE, agriculture spread into Egypt. Earlier Neolithic cultures were found along the Faiyum lakeshore in Middle Egypt, and at Merimde in Lower Egypt. The everyday artifacts found at these sites include arrowheads, sickle-blades, and pottery. The first domesticated plants and animals in Egypt appear to have originated in the Levant. Agriculture spread from the Nile Valley into the desert oases to the west, and animal herding soon appeared in the arid zones in the east and south.

BELOW **This terracotta model (c. 2000 BCE) of ploughing,** found on northern Cyprus, along with other Early Bronze Age artifacts suggest cultural influences from the Anatolian mainland.

'Ain Ghazal

The most fascinating discoveries at 'Ain Ghazal are large statues of human figures found buried in pits. Twenty statues were found in one pit, about ten in a second, and just a head in a third.

A major Neolithic site, 'Ain Ghazal is located near Amman, in Jordan. It was discovered in 1974 when a new road was built between Amman and the northern part of Jordan. The site was excavated by Gary Rollefson and Zidan Kafafi in the 1980s and 1990s. Three distinct periods of occupation were noticed, one above the other, all from the Neolithic period.

This settlement started as a regular small village and after some time it expanded dramatically and reached *c.* 35 acres (14 ha), one of the largest settlements in the world at that time. It is one of the first large settlements uncovered from such an early period. More large-scale Pre-Pottery Neolithic B sites have since been found at sites such as Basta in southern Jordan.

'Ain Ghazal Houses

The typical dwelling unit consisted of one or two rectangular rooms built of mud bricks on stone foundations. The floors were made of a thick layer of white plaster, and the walls were also plastered. The production of this plaster required limestone to be burnt at about 1560°F (850°C). The excavators assumed that the intensive burning of wood for this eventually caused environmental degradation, and much of the population had to leave the site.

Some round silo-like structures were also found, along with rich assemblages of objects made of flint, limestone, and basalt. The economic base was the cultivation of various crops, which included barley, wheat, peas, lentils, and chickpeas. Meat was obtained from domesticated goats, and supplemented by hunting wild animals, such as deer, gazelle, pigs, foxes, and hares.

Community members received various kinds of burial, apparently reflecting their social status. Those with more elaborate funerals, indicated by bead necklaces, treatment with ocher, or offerings of meat, were buried in a flexed position under the floors of the houses. Sometimes the graves would be opened and the skulls removed. Some of the skulls received additional treatment, such as being painted with red pigment or plastered. In one pit, the faces from three plastered skulls were found but the skulls themselves were missing. This clearly indicates that the Neolithic plastered skulls underwent a long period of usage, which meant the removal of old plaster and the renovation of the facial features. Some people were buried in pits outside houses and others more casually disposed of in domestic refuse pits.

The most important discoveries of the period are the numerous art objects. Large quantities of zoomorphic figurines, usually representing cattle, were found—24 were buried together in one pit. Two zoomorphic figurines were found stabbed with flint items, indicating a voodoo-like ceremony, which probably took place before hunting. There were also anthropomorphic figurines representing both females and males. These small figurines would have been used by individuals or by a single family. For public ceremonies, where hundreds or even thousands of people took part, larger art and cult items would have been required. More than 40 large anthropomorphic statues have been unearthed, but it is not clear whether they represented deified ancestors or gods.

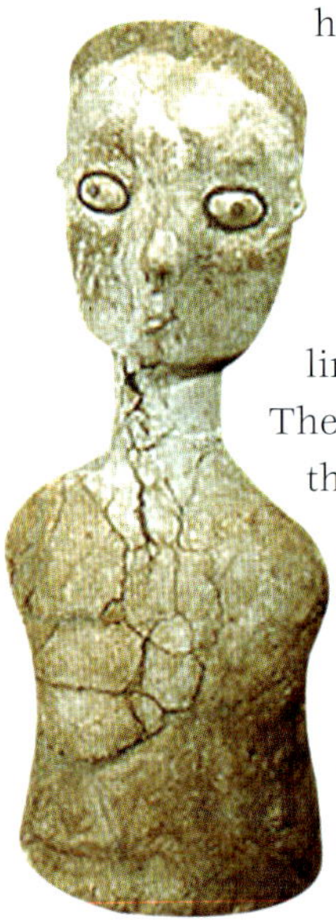

LEFT **'Ain Ghazal statues,** up to half life-size, were made of lime plaster molded over a reed skeleton, with painted features.

Pre-Pottery Neolithic C (PPNC)

This stage was recognized for the first time at 'Ain Ghazal. It bridges the gap in occupation at Jericho between the Pre-Pottery Neolithic B and the Ceramic Neolithic periods. During the PPNC,

settlements were smaller than before, architecture was simpler, and the floors were not plastered. Sometimes older structures from the Pre-Pottery Neolithic B (PPNB) were reused. The flint technology of this period was not as elaborate and furthermore the production of elongated blades had stopped. Artistic activity was minimal and large statues were no longer made. One female figurine carved from limestone is of interest as it depicts a fat female figure in a squatting position—a style that would be developed further in the female figurines of the next period.

Ceramic Neolithic

Settlements were rather small by this stage. Typical finds include pottery decorated with incised herringbone patterns, and fired-clay figurines with conical heads and stylized "coffee bean" eyes. These were made from a small lump of clay with an elongated, incised slit. The Yarmukian culture occupied the verdant regions of the Southern Levant. The largest site known in the region from this period was Sha'ar Hagolan.

Extensive artistic activity was evident at 'Ain Ghazal only during the Pre-Pottery Neolithic B, when it was a large settlement. Rich art assemblages were also discovered at the large Neolithic sites of Sha'ar Hagolan and in Çatal Hüyük. It is evident that there is a correlation between the size of a site and the amount of artistic and cultic activity. Even today large urban centers generate more such activity than small villages.

ABOVE **An 'Ain Ghazal house** showing the extensive use of lime plaster which is a feature of PPNB architecture.

THE OLDEST STATUES OF HUMANS

Three types of statues were unearthed at 'Ain Ghazal—head and torso; full bodies (including one of a woman with six fingers on each hand, and one nicknamed "Boots" as it seemed to be wearing Wellington boots); and some with two necks and heads (these could represent twins, but it is also thought that they could be married couples). A similar statue from Jericho, dated to the same period, has six toes.

RIGHT **This statue was discovered** in 1984. Study of how this particular statue was made suggests that the heads were made by one person and the torso by someone else.

Çatal Hüyük

In 1961, British archaeologist James Mellaart discovered magnificent wall paintings at Çatal Hüyük in southern Anatolia. They depicted a variety of scenes—hunting males skipping around a wild deer or bull, vultures gliding over headless human corpses, rows of handprints, and even an erupting volcano.

Other wall decorations done in raised plaster reliefs showed opposed pairs of leopards, figures with upraised arms, and numerous carefully modeled bull-skulls with attached horns, all incorporated into walls and bench decorations. These gave the site a unique position in the history of art. Çatal Hüyük is one of the most famous Neolithic sites in the ancient world. It is 40 acres (16 ha) in area, with debris to a depth of 18 yd (17 m). Its population is estimated to have been more than 5,000 people. When Mellaart excavated the site he exposed around 200 dwellings, many of them interpreted as shrines. Impressive remains were uncovered, more than from any previous Neolithic site. The thickness of the deposits, and the fact that Layer VI had been burnt, meant that wall paintings had been effectively sealed and preserved, and Çatal Hüyük became a legend. However, a peculiar history of research followed this expedition.

BELOW **This wall painting depicts a deer** being hunted and caught. A large number of similar paintings have been uncovered within the many houses in the densely populated settlement.

The Earliest City

Çatal Hüyük was composed of densely built mud-brick houses that abutted each other on all sides, creating a beehive pattern, with limited ground access to buildings. Most movement occurred across the close-set roofs, with access to individual houses via ladders. Each house had a small rectangular room, and L-shaped platforms were arranged along the walls. These platforms, probably used for sleeping, were always carefully plastered. There was a hearth in each house.

The site is characterized by rich assemblages of flint, obsidian, bone tools, beads, seals, and pottery. A unique item, found in association with a male burial, is an elongated flint dagger with a carved bone handle in the shape of a snake. Artifacts made of organic materials such as textiles, wooden plates, cups, and rectangular boxes have been preserved. Large numbers of human burials were discovered located under the raised sleeping platforms. Most are multiple burials and appear to be family burial groups. Although some houses have many more skeletons than others, some structures seem to have been more popular burial grounds, perhaps due to their sanctity.

As well as the wall decorations, many anthropomorphic and zoomorphic figurines have been found, made from clay or from a variety of stones. Of the approximately 50 anthropomorphic figurines, some are simply naked

women, while others show a woman sitting on a chair flanked by two leopards or lions. In other cases, the female is sitting directly on a leopard. Male figures are rare, although a few have been found. Engraved stone plaques are among the artifacts. One of them shows a female couple embracing—they have a common body and two heads, similar to some of the plaster statues discovered at 'Ain Ghazal. Another plaque depicts four dancing figures.

Overcoming Scandal

Mellaart's excavations at Çatal Hüyük came to an abrupt halt in 1965 when he fell into dispute with the Turkish authorities. The archaeological community had to wait a further 30 years before British archaeologists would return, bringing many new questions to be answered.

In 1993, Cambridge University archaeologist Ian Hodder renewed excavations at Çatal Hüyük. As excavation techniques had evolved greatly by then, slow and careful fieldwork became the norm, and very detailed but time-consuming analyses by the largest and most varied group of specialists ever assembled on one dig meant that initial results were slow to appear.

Five thick volumes of reports giving many new insights into the way of life of Çatal Hüyük's occupants have been published recently. They reveal that much of what was thought was known about Çatal Hüyük was incorrect. It now seems very unlikely that the cattle being consumed were domesticated, and that hunting was far more important than first acknowledged.

As Hodder's excavations have expanded, many of Mellaart's initial claims have been shown to be more reliably based than first suspected. Hodder's teams have begun to uncover unique wall decoration, including bull-skulls with attached horns, just as Mellaart found. Multiple burials have been recovered, again just as Mellaart claimed, one wearing an elaborate anklet made of animal teeth.

More fine artworks have been recovered, including a stamp seal depicting a standing bear with upraised paws. It now appears that many of the modeled and painted figures discovered by Mellaart may be of bears, rather than costumed people, as Mellaart first thought.

Recent analysis of the range of animals illustrated on Çatal Hüyük's wall paintings have shown the same restricted range of animals that were commonly fashioned in stone during the preceding PPNB period, suggesting that Çatal Hüyük's Late Neolithic inhabitants may have had much stronger links with the widespread PPNB culture of the Levant than previously thought.

As these examples suggest, there are still many surprises left to be discovered at Çatal Hüyük, one of the greatest Neolithic sites ever discovered.

LEFT **This unique double-faced vase** has incised bulls' heads on the sides. This was only discovered when it was reassembled.

BELOW **One of the terracotta sculptures found at Çatal Hüyük** is shown here. A Mother Goddess gives birth flanked by two lions, or leopards.

Late Neolithic Mesopotamia

The Late Neolithic period in Mesopotamia, part of which is also called "Early Chalcolithic," falls between two major stages in human evolution: the earlier "Neolithic Revolution" and the later "Urban Revolution."

BELOW **Tell Hassuna is the site** of the earliest-known farming community. The foundations of adobe dwellings built around open courtyards can be seen here.

Relatively little is known of this era, and we have only a fragmentary picture of the various cultural units, their geographical distribution, and chronology. The period is divided into four main stages based mainly on different ceramic traditions, reflected in vessel shape and decoration. Geographically we are dealing with northern Syria, southeastern Turkey, and Iraq. At Tell Sabi Abyad in Syria, large buildings have been found, dated to *c.* 6000 BCE. Each was divided into many small square or rectangular rooms, some of them contained stone seals and over 300 clay sealings—small, round lumps of clay, attached to a string. These were used to seal a container or a room, to show whether or not it had been opened by any unauthorized person. This clearly indicates administrative activity in the Neolithic period, as well as the evolution of a concept of personal property.

Around 6500 BCE, the Near East splintered into many small regional cultures, about which not much is known. Their economic base was agriculture: the cultivation of cereals and pulses, and the raising of livestock—goats, sheep, cattle, and pigs. Four major stages, based on the different ceramic traditions, characterized parts of northern Syria and Mesopotamia: Pre-Hassuna, Hassuna, Samarra, and Halaf.

Pre-Hassuna Cultures

The best known settlement of this period is at Umm Dabaghiyah in Syria, excavated in the 1970s

by Diana Kirkbride. She uncovered four layers of occupation, all dated to the same cultural phase. In the earliest settlements, only round pits were found. Later domestic buildings have sophisticated installations such as outdoor ovens and internal hearths and chimneys. Some walls were decorated with paintings, including images of hunting wild donkeys (onagers). Other structures have a central elongated corridor, with small chambers on both sides, each no bigger than 10 sq ft (1 sq m), too small to serve as a living space. They were probably used for storage. The pottery in the site is simple and rather crude. Some have knob-like projections around the middle of the body, which may have been used as handles, while others have decorative elements, such as human figures or animals. Similar architecture and pottery has been found at another large-scale excavation at Tell Sotto in central Iraq.

LEFT An incised vessel is one of an estimated 25,000 pottery remnants unearthed at Tell Hassuna.

Hassuna Culture

This name comes from Tell Hassuna, located near the modern city of Mosul in northern Iraq. When Lloyd Seton and Faud Safar excavated the site in the 1940s, they discovered six layers of occupation that became more substantial over time. Other sites of this culture include Yarim Tepe I, where large-scale buildings were found, suggesting they were dwellings of extended families, similar to structures from the same period uncovered at Sha'ar Hagolan in Israel.

The Hassuna culture pottery is much more advanced than that of the previous period, and includes a variety of bowls and jars, including a special type of wide, shallow basin called a "husking tray." The pottery is decorated with both red stripes and a variety of incised patterns. Human figurines of this period are depicted with stylized, "coffee bean" eyes, which were created by applying a small lump of clay with an elongated slit. This artistic convention first appeared in the Pottery Neolithic period in Jericho, spread across large areas from eastern Iran to the Balkans, and was practiced over a long period—from the ninth to the fifth millennia BCE.

Samarra Culture

This name is taken from the site of Samarra in central Iraq, excavated in 1911–1914 by Ernst Herzfeld. He published information only on the stunning Samarra culture pottery, which was then unknown, and nothing about architecture, burials, or other material culture.

At Tell esh-Sawwan, in Iraq, a large horizontal exposure of a Samarra settlement unearthed many large buildings inside an enclosure—suggesting some kind of fortification. Each building is composed of many rooms, organized in three elongated wings, and is known as a "T-shaped house." Burials were found below the floors, associated with rich grave goods, including large numbers of figurines made of clay or alabaster. Some of them have the stylized "coffee bean" eyes. The pottery is of fine quality, and was decorated with black, and, occasionally, red painted motifs. These include animals or human figures, and geometric designs arranged in intricate, symmetrical patterns with between two and six decorative bands. The necks of some jars are decorated with human figures, again with the "coffee bean" eyes. Among the outstanding items are shallow bowls decorated with four to six dancing women. Each figure is shown from the front, in a standing position, with broad hips, and bent arms and fingers. They have long flowing hair and appear to be moving in a circle. Above the women, there is a row of rather large scorpions, which are known as the symbol of Ishtar, the Goddess of Love in Mesopotamian mythology. Perhaps what we see here are the earliest roots of this tradition.

Much data on this period came from Tell Sabi Abyad, excavated by Peter Akkermans. Layer 6, which is contemporaneous with the earliest Samarran sites, had been subjected to fire. This baked and preserved the otherwise fragile clay material, and resulted in excellent preservation of the architecture and many other artifacts that would normally be dissolved over time. The architecture includes rectangular buildings divided into many rooms, some of them round. They were built close to each other, creating a

BELOW Dutch archaeologist Peter Akkermans has been leading the excavations at the Tell Sabi Abyad site in Syria since 1986.

RIGHT **This Neolithic female statuette** is believed to depict a goddess and to have been used as a tomb figure. It was found at the Tell esh-Sawwan site in Iraq.

dense settlement. The rich assemblages uncovered included stone seals and more than 300 clay sealings. Such a discovery had never been made before in any Neolithic site in the Near East. Many clay tokens were also found. These small geometric objects were used for counting, and later evolved into the earliest writing system of the Sumerians. All of these finds indicate an administration on a scale only found in urban centers. Spatial analysis of the finds provides a better understanding of the functions of the various rooms and houses. It has been suggested that these provide evidence of a relationship between two different populations—permanent farmers and pastoral nomads.

Halaf Culture

The most famous period in Mesopotamian prehistory is undoubtedly the Halaf culture, first uncovered in the early 1910s by Max von Oppenheim at Tell Halaf in the Khabur Valley of northeastern Syria. In the 1930s, the sites of Arpachiyah, Chagar Bazar, and Tell Brak were excavated by Max Mallowan, clarifying many aspects that were not known from Tell Halaf—architecture, figurines, seals, and beads. Currently, large-scale excavations are being carried out at the Halafian site of Domuztepe in eastern Turkey. Halafian sites are spread over different geographical zones—the Anatolian highlands, the base of the Zagros Mountains, and Mesopotamia. There are small changes in this culture over time, and in different geographical regions, but the main characteristics remain similar. Most of the Halafian settlements were less than 2.5 acres (1 ha) in area, indicating small communities. Many sites seem to reflect seasonal pastoral activity.

The site of Arpachiyah, excavated during the early days of Halafian research, gave the impression that they constructed no massive architecture apart from round rooms, sometimes with an elongated rectangular room abutting them. This type of building is called "tholoi," a term borrowed from Greek tomb architecture. Rounded architecture, indeed, appeared at Halafian sites, but later excavations made it clear that rectangular buildings were also constructed. Such buildings were found at Yarim Tepe II, Khirbet eah-Shenef on the Balikh, and especially at the Halafian layer of Tell Sabi Abyad. Here a building measuring 20 by 11 yds (18 by 10 m) was found.

It resembled the massive buildings that were found at this site in the earlier levels. This building had a stepped entrance and white plastered façade with niches and benches. Its ground floor had 20 rooms, too small to be lived in, which were probably used for storage.

The most significant aspect of Halafian culture is its pottery, which is among the most impressive pottery ever made in the ancient Near East. It seems that the main artistic talent of the period was invested in producing and decorating vessels in the most elaborate style. This included careful painting, sometimes with more than two colors, and a high-quality lustrous and burnished finish. This pottery tradition influences the entire Levant, as potters of the local "Wadi Rabah" culture adopted many Halafian vessel shapes.

Many stamp seals were reported from the period. They are usually around 1 in (2–3 cm) in size, and are round, square, or rectangular in shape, like buttons. On the back they have a small pierced handle for attaching string. Most seals bear geometric patterns consisting of parallel or crossed lines, checkerboard patterns, and the like. Sometimes a horned animal was depicted, but there are no complicated scenes. Many beads were also found, some of which resembled butterflies.

The Halafian produced female figurines, which present a naked figure, seated, with both hands supporting the breasts, and the pelvic area emphasized. Sometimes they were painted with red lines or dots. The heads on these figurines are rather schematic, sometimes portrayed as a simple peg.

At Domuztepe in southeastern Turkey, an extensive and complex funerary deposit was found, known as the "Death Pit." Here at least 38 individuals were recovered, together with thousands of animal bones, all highly fragmented and jumbled together. Analysis of the human bones indicates intentional killing, butchering, and cooking. This pit seems to contain leftovers of a feast in which both animal and human flesh were eaten, which might reflect cannibalism, a claim about which the excavator, Stuart Campbell, is cautious. The usual style of burial, however, was much less dramatic. Individuals were buried in flexed position, sometimes accompanied by grave goods, like pottery vessels.

LEFT **This polychrome Halaf pottery plate,** from Tell Arpachiyah near Mosul in Iraq, demonstrates a design that is typical of Halafian pottery.

THE LATE NEOLITHIC AND CHALCOLITHIC CULTURES OF MESOPOTAMIA

Culture	Major Excavated Sites	Approximate Dating
Pre-Hassuna	Umm Dabaghiyah, Yarim Tepe I (XII), Tell Sotto, Hassuna (I), Tell Bouqras	7000–6400 BCE
Hassuna	Hassuna (II–IV), Yarim Tepe I	6400–5800 BCE
Samarra	Samarra, Baghouz, Hassuna (V–VI), Tell esh-Sawwan (III–IV), Choga Mami	6000–5300 BCE
Halaf	Halaf, Arpachiyah, Chagar Bazar, Domuztepe, Tell Sabi Abyad (5)	5800–5300 BCE
Ubaid (3–4 phases)	Ubaid (XI–VIII), Eridu (XI–VI), Tepe Gawra (XIX–XIII)	5300–4000 BCE
Uruk	Uruk	4000–3200 BCE

LEFT **At Tell Sabi Abyad** excavations take place August–October each year by a team of 25 specialists and students, assisted by some 60 Syrian locals.

Mesopotamian Pottery

Neolithic Pottery Jar

The incised herringbone pattern on this jar from Sha'ar Hagolan in the Jordan Valley is typical of the Yarmukian culture of the Southern Levant in the seventh millennium BCE.

Pottery production started in the ancient Near East during the seventh millennium BCE, after a few thousand years of advanced village life. From its introduction in the Neolithic period, pottery has remained in continuous use.

Pottery vessels are useful for a wide range of purposes: storage of cosmetics or medicines in small containers; storage of liquids and grains in large containers; preparation of food; cooking directly over fire; and for serving food. Pottery has a special importance in archaeological research for a number of reasons. Once made, even if broken, it does not decay, preserving much information on ancient lifestyles. It was made in large quantities and is the most common artifact found in excavations. Different cultures usually developed specific types and styles of decoration, which can be used as a chronological marker. Pottery containers were also transferred from one region to another, indicating trade and the connections between remote areas. Finally, the mode of production reflects social organization.

The early basic vessel types, such as large wide-mouthed jars with two lug handles near the rim, appeared over vast geographical areas, and have been found in Mesopotamia, Anatolia, Greece, and as far south as Israel. Different pottery styles developed later in more confined geographical regions and chronological periods. Pottery was manufactured in a variety of open shapes, such as bowls, and basins, or closed jars. It was decorated using different techniques—painting, incising, and burnishing. Pottery kilns have been found at many Mesopotamian

Terracotta Akkadian Sculpture

This terracotta figurine believed to be a votive goddess sculpture used in cultic practices is from the third dynasty of Ur (*c.* 2190–2004 BCE).

sites. In the Halafian culture of northern Mesopotamia, the craft reached its artistic zenith with well-shaped and carefully decorated pottery, using different firing techniques. Some scholars suggest it reflects specialization and the manufacture of products for the use of elite, wealthy groups. The Halafian produced extremely elegant pottery vessels, mainly medium-sized cups, bowls, and jars, which were probably used as serving vessels at banquets. The pottery is decorated using a few colors, either in geometric designs, or depicting human figures and animals, such as cattle, birds, and snakes. A popular image was a bull's head, sometimes stylized to just the horns, which the artist manipulated into various shapes. In this period, floral motifs also appeared for the first time. Vessels were painted with flowers, trees, and branches. Human figures are quite rare, but when they do appear, nearly all are associated with dancing scenes. Sometimes these were depicted quite naturalistically, showing various dance accessories—hairstyles, masks, and dresses. In other cases, the dancing figures were portrayed in a highly stylized manner, reduced to a triangular head, two or three vertical lines for the body, and two diagonal lines for the arms. Sometimes 20 or more such figures were shown on the circumference of a vessel, creating a circle of dancing figures.

Geometric Painted Bowl from Susa, Iran
Early Susiana (*c.* 4500 BCE) pottery styles show clear influence from Mesopotamia. These designs were unknown in other parts of the ancient world.

An exceptional discovery was made at Yarim Tepe II, when two distinct pottery vessels, anthropomorphic and zoomorphic, were found buried in pits. One was in the shape of an upright naked woman with long hair. It is thought this may have been the inspiration for a whole class of so-called "violin-figurine" types, which came to dominate later cultic offerings. The other is a bulbous pot in the shape of a pig.

It seems that Halafian pottery was developed to such a high standard because it was used for prestige items. Later such items were made from gold, silver, or ivory, but in this early period such exotic raw materials were not available. Thus, elaborate pottery vessels were used as elite status symbols.

An Early Myth?

Another outstanding Halafian vessel reported from Arpachiyah is a rather small bowl with painted scenes. The outside is decorated with various geometric patterns, bulls' heads and two small human figures standing beside a large pottery vessel. On the inside, two episodes are depicted—a domestic scene showing two women weaving, and a male hunting lions. This may tell a mythological story, but it is still to be deciphered.

Painted Pottery Bowl *c.* 4500 BCE
This bowl was discovered by Max Mallowan at Tell Arpachiyah in northern Iraq. Along with many other objects, it was in a house that is thought to have belonged to a potter.

Ubaid Culture

During the Ubaid period, in the first half of the fifth millennium BCE, extensive canal networks appeared in Mesopotamia for the first time. This was a major technological development that enabled the cultivation of large fields in arid areas.

It also had far-reaching implications for the social organization. A collective effort was needed for the digging and maintenance of the canals. The increased carrying capacity of the land enabled population growth, requiring more cultivated land and larger irrigation systems.

Tell al-Ubaid in southern Iraq was excavated by Harry Reginald Hall and, later, by Leonard Woolley in the early 1920s. The Ubaid culture has five main phases in its development, with the earliest found only in southern Mesopotamia, roughly contemporary with the later Halaf cultures in the north. It is known mainly from small, deep, test pits in Eridu and Tell el-'Oueili, and represents the earliest settlement on the alluvial plain of southern Mesopotamia.

Migration or Trading?

Around 5300 BCE later Ubaid artifacts appear in ever-greater numbers in the north, west, and east, leading some scholars to speak of "an Ubaid migration" from the south into the surrounding territories. Others view this as the result of an upsurge in interregional trade. It reached as far as eastern Cilicia, the Mediterranean coast, and northern Israel to the west, and the western Iranian uplands and the southeastern shore of the Persian Gulf to the east. For the first time, southern Mesopotamia became the main cultural force in the ancient Near East, probably connected with the development of irrigation canals that dramatically increased cultivation and productivity.

Fewer people were needed for the production of food. This meant that other people could specialize in craft, trade, construction and administration.

LEFT **This Ubaid terracotta statuette of a female** is from Tell esh-Sawwan on the eastern banks of the Tigris River where five levels of occupation have been discovered.

At this stage we see large settlements surrounded by small villages. A good example of this is Tell Abada, northeast of Baghdad, where Sahah Jasim uncovered three levels of occupation. Layer II has been completely uncovered, revealing the plan of a Ubaid village with 10 large buildings. The typical house had a tripartite plan—a long, T-shaped central hall flanked by small rooms. The larger houses were probably used by extended family units. A number of sophisticated pottery kilns were excavated in the courtyards of houses.

Temples of this period were larger than domestic dwellings, and built to a standardized tripartite plan—a central wide hall with flanking side rooms. The outer walls were buttressed for added strength, and increasingly to set them apart as sacred structures. At Tepe Gawra (Layer XIII), three temples were constructed around a plaza, indicating extensive cultic activity. Parts of their walls were painted red.

Typical Ubaid pottery was hard-fired, buff-colored clay decorated with black painted horizontal bands, and wavy lines. A variety of forms, including bowls, deep goblets, pedestal bowls, and jars were made on a rotating work surface, which later developed into the potter's wheel. Other fired-clay objects included sickles, nails, spindle whorls and slingstones. While flint was imported into Mesopotamia, it is thought that the Ubaid people may have preferred to fashion these items from clay, which was cheaper and easier to replace.

Small numbers of copper artifacts, such as a ring and a chisel, were found at Tepe Gawra (Layer XVII). A large number of stamp seals were also found in Ubaid sites, including Tepe Gawra, indicating a more complex economic and social organization. The seals were decorated with geometric patterns, horned animals, snakes, vultures, and humans. Of special interest is a human figure with an animal head, usually associated with wild animals. This image later becomes the iconic "Master of the Beasts" motif, alluding to the control of wild or chaotic forces in society. Such images are common in the early levels at Susa in southwest Iran, suggesting strong Mesopotamian influence at this time.

Enigmatic Figurines

Ubaid figurines, depicting both female and male figures in standing positions, were usually found in graves. The heads are elongated, sometimes covered in bitumen. They have "coffee bean" eyes, a broad chest, slim waist, and joined legs. The heads are schematically rendered and resemble lizards, or snakes. Some female figurines hold a baby, which also has a lizard face. One male figure from Eridu holds a scepter in his hand. These slim figures are in sharp contrast to the rather fat "Mother Goddess" figurines of earlier Neolithic and Halafian times. Burials of babies in pottery vessels under the floors of houses became common, and 127 such burials were reported from Tell Abada. At Eridu a large cemetery was found, with the bodies buried extended on their backs, in contrast to earlier burials that were typically buried in a flexed position on their sides.

Ubaid social organization appears more complex than earlier Mesopotamian cultures, and may have developed into a series of competing chiefdoms. This would have taken the form of a centralized ruling authority, whether secular or priest-based remains controversial, which organized large-scale building projects (such as irrigation canals and temple complexes) by levying ever-larger agricultural taxes to pay for such construction. At the very least, there was a gradual development of social complexity and specialized agriculture, religion, craft, and industries.

ABOVE **This goblet and two bowls** from Girsu are fine examples of Ubaid pottery.

BELOW **This mud-brick courtyard building** is from Tel Tsaf, a Middle Chalcolithic site in the Jordan Valley of Israel.

Mesopotamia: The Cradle of Civilization

Introduction

Around 6,000 years ago in southern Mesopotamia the small village societies that characterized the early Neolithic period gave way to larger towns, centered on temple estates. These developed an urban life, or civilization.

Northern Mesopotamia, in the valley of the Tigris River, appears to have been settled before the south. Irrigation canals and, perhaps, the concept of the temple-centered society seem to have developed there before the Ubaid Period (5500–4000 BCE) at the confluence of the Tigris and Euphrates Rivers in the arid lowlands, and to have used the spring floods of the Euphrates to increase crop yields, borrowing the technique of irrigation from their northern neighbors. Ubaid culture, first attested at Eridu, is characterized by large village settlements and the appearance of the first public buildings in Mesopotamia. Ubaid sites also illustrate the development of smaller "satellite" settlements surrounding larger ones, and the first indications of class distinctions. A class of hereditary leaders had responsibility for the administration of the temples and their granaries, and for mediating intra-group conflict and maintaining social order.

A number of other cities came to prominence after the establishment of Eridu in the Ubaid Period. The first true urban culture to leave its mark on Mesopotamia, however, was that of the Sumerians who created their most important early center at Uruk and later at Ur. The Sumerians were first revealed to history in their earliest writing, which dates from *c.* 3500 BCE. Their language is believed to be a completely isolated one, unrelated to either Semitic or Indo-European families. The major language distinctions in the Near East are between Indo-European and Semitic languages. Indo-European is a much larger group than Semitic but, in the Near East, the number of Indo-European speakers has always been smaller. Among the ancient Near Eastern Indo-European languages are Hurrian, Luwian (Hittite), and Old Persian. The Semitic languages have been spoken historically in the Middle East, North Africa, and the Horn of Africa, as they are today. These languages included: Akkadian, Phoenician, Aramaic, Hebrew, and Canaanite among others. Sumerian is neither Semitic nor Indo-European but rather is a language isolate, that is, a language with no affinities to any other known language living or dead.

LEFT **Uruk was one of the earliest cities of Sumer.** It dates from *c.* 4000–3000 BCE. It became the first densely populated, urbanized city and a major trade center.

In addition to having the first urban culture, the Sumerians were the first people known to have used writing. The earliest use of writing was not for religious, political or literary texts but for accounting purposes. The earliest cuneiform signs resemble actual clay tokens, which were used for account keeping in pre-literate ages. These tokens were used to record the quantities of agricultural products, such as cattle and land.

Sumerian City-States

The Sumerians had many city-states, and as these grew, rivalries began to develop. Competition for resources was fierce among these cities which were located so close to each other in the south. Despite this, their agriculture was innovative. In small areas surrounding the city-states, they were able to cultivate barley, lentils, chickpeas, wheat, onions, garlic, lettuce, and mustard. The livestock they raised included goats, pigs, cattle, and sheep. In addition, they used donkeys for transport and oxen for traction.

Sumerian technology was ingenious. A system of radial canals was constructed and maintained, and they built barges (basic rafts made of thick reed bundles) capable of transporting a large volume of goods. The pottery wheel and kiln were perfected by the Sumerians. They were not, however, empire builders. In the last days of Sumerian independence, following the brief interlude represented by the Akkadian conquests, Lagash and Ur rose to prominence and became city-states of great power and influence. This is perhaps the lesson they had learned from Sargon of Akkad who created the first great regional empire *c.* 2300 BCE.

Akkad and the Ur III Renaissance

For approximately 150 years, the Akkadians controlled an area that included all of Sumer, neighboring Elam in the foothills of the Zagros Mountains, and most of Syria. The Akkadian method of government was the example that other empires were to follow. Sargon adopted several strategies to maintain control of a country: to install his daughters as high priestesses to Sin, the moon god; to install his sons as provincial governors in strategic locations; and to marry his other daughters to the rulers of conquered lands thus assuring that control of the empire rested in the hands of family wherever one might go.

After the collapse of the Akkadian Empire, a new Sumerian ruler arose at the city-state of Lagash. Gudea is known to us primarily from the multiplicity of his likenesses in stone that have been found. Later another Sumerian, Ur-Nammu, founded the Third Dynasty of Ur and inspired a Sumerian renaissance of sorts. Ur's hegemony lasted for about 100 years, until 2000 BCE when a combination of crop failures and incessant attacks from the neighboring Elamites brought the last Sumerian dynasty to an end.

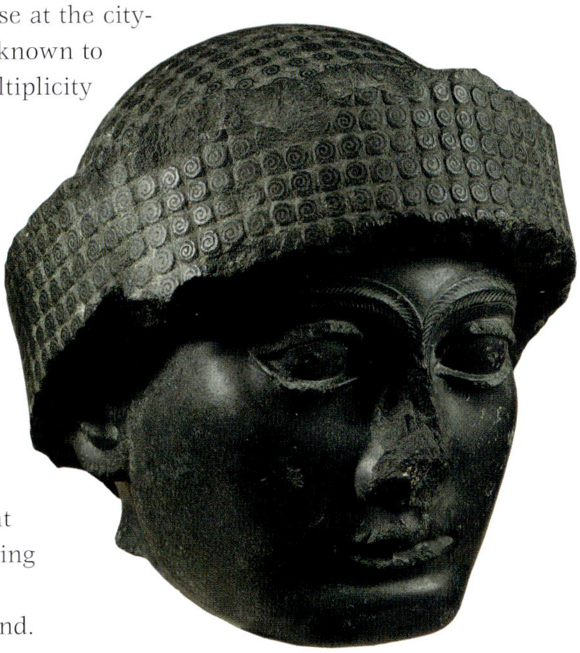

BELOW **Gudea was a much-loved ruler** of Sumer. Myriad representations of him can still be found today.

THE SUMERIAN KING LIST

Much of what we know about Sumerian political organization has been surmised from an unusual document known as the Sumerian King List. The list is an ancient text listing all kings who ruled Sumer, each local under their chief city, and including foreign rulers. This prototype document is the sole chronicle for the reigns of these earliest royals, and contains the city-state location of the kingship, along with the ruler listed by name with the length of their rule. Though kingship was believed to be handed down by the gods, it could be passed from one city to another as a result of conquest. Interestingly, the list mentions one female ruler, Kug-Bau, a tavern-keeper, who is the only ruler of the Third Dynasty of Kish.

The Sumerian Question

The nineteenth-century discovery of the Sumerian language, written on clay tablets found at sites such as Nineveh and Nimrud, gave rise to the Sumerian Question. Successive generations of scholars have not yet found an answer.

RIGHT **Hormuzd Rassam** was born in Mosul in 1826. He made several important discoveries, including the stone tablets of *The Epic of Gilgamesh*.

These questions were brought up by students of the Sumerian language, but archaeologists have complicated them with questions of their own. With the discovery of very early occupations at Uruk, it is difficult to discern when the Sumerians first built this most important early center of Sumerian civilization, if indeed they were the ones to do so.

Where Did They Come From?

Many scholars would agree with nineteenth-century Iraqi archaeologist Hormuzd Rassam that the Sumerians were in southern Mesopotamia from the outset of settlement. Others think they may have migrated into the area in the fourth millennium BCE. The consensus is that the Sumerians were skilled early farmers who were able to raise an impressive surplus of crops in an environment that was not always hospitable. Southern Mesopotamia was plagued by periodic flooding, as well as the ever-present marshlands.

Sumerian culture is generally believed to have originated in the Ubaid Period, which began around 5500 BCE. Excavations at Tell Awayli, an Ubaid site near Larsa in southern Iraq, has revealed a predecessor culture with affinities to the earlier northern Samarra culture. A late Samarran site, Choga Mami, has evidence of canal irrigation as early as 6000 BCE. Thus, Tell Awayli may indicate a kind of transition between the south and the north where the Samarrans were the first in all of Mesopotamia to practice irrigated agriculture. According to those who believe in northern origins for the Sumerians, farming peoples spread into southern Mesopotamia after they had first developed a temple-centered township society in the north.

A Combination Culture?

The scholars who believe that the Sumerians were indigenous to southern Mesopotamia have posited that they were a culture of hunters and

RIGHT **The influence of Uruk** was so significant that the archaeological culture takes its name from the site.

fishers who lived in the marshlands at the confluence of the Tigris and Euphrates Rivers, presumably the ancestors of the Marsh Arabs who have lived there into modern times. The combination of their culture with that of farmers from the north was what created Sumer. Because of Sumerian legends mentioning the site of Dilmun (Bahrain), other scholars have suggested that they came from this island situated in the Persian Gulf.

The theory that Sumer was a "combination culture" is supported by the fact that Eridu, one of the earliest Sumerian sites, is in a location where several different economic specializations might flourish. The farmers of Eridu developed a form of irrigated agriculture that could have originated in Samarra. Eridu is also close to the Arabian sea coast where fishers and hunters from the earliest periods built huts from reeds. Finally, the pastoralists (seminomadic sheep- and goat-herders living in the arid regions close to Eridu) also contributed to the formation of its distinctive way of life. There do seem to have been other cultures in Eridu during its early stages, because a few words of non-Sumerian languages seem to have entered the Sumerian vocabulary, but there is no clue as to the origins of these non-Sumerian peoples.

LEFT **Cuneiform** was the world's first writing system. It was adapted and used in various forms for more than 3,000 years.

The Sumerian Language

The Sumerian language presented difficulties to scholars from the start. To begin with, there are a great number and variety of phonetic values that can be attached to Sumerian signs. An early specialist in the language, epigrapher Joseph Halévy (1827–1917), deduced from this that Sumerian was not a true language, but rather a cryptolect, or secret code. This question was argued by Assyriologists, and Halévy's view was not completely rejected until 1897. The discussion, however, only compounded the mystery surrounding Sumerian origins. It centered on the classification of the language as either Semitic or Proto-Semitic. Today, Sumerian is considered to be a language isolate, that is, a natural language that has no demonstrable relationship with living languages.

Most scholars have concluded that the Sumerian language, in its developed form, can be found at Uruk no earlier than 3000 BCE. It is difficult to say what other languages might have been spoken then, but it is likely that in southern Mesopotamia Sumerian coexisted with a number of Semitic dialects, while in northern Mesopotamia most of the languages spoken were related to Semitic. The fact that Sumerian appears in a small and fairly isolated area adjacent to this wide range of Semitic speakers may indicate that this earliest written language was itself but a survival of an even earlier, and more widespread, continuum of similar languages.

THE DEATH OF SUMERIAN

While cuneiform writing had a long history, stretching into the first centuries CE, spoken Sumerian began to die out in the second millennium BCE. Some scholars have suggested that Sumerian was still spoken in the Old Babylonian period (*c.* 1800–1600 BCE), but increasingly rarely. As the Sumerian civilization gradually gave way to the Semitic-speaking Akkadian northerners from the twenty-third century BCE onwards, Sumerian became increasingly a language of religion and epic poetry. By the first millennium BCE only scholar priests trained for many years could hope to understand what was by then a "dead" language.

The Uruk Period

The city of Uruk so dominated the new cultural phase that followed the Ubaid that it was named for it. During the Uruk Period, Uruk achieved the status of the first great city-state in Mesopotamia.

ABOVE **These eye idols, from the third millennium** BCE, are typical of Nagar (or Tell Brak, Syria) which was developing around the same time as Uruk.

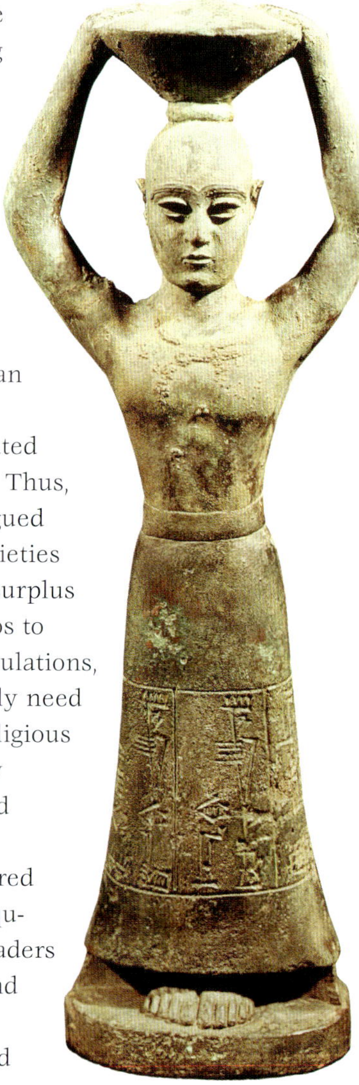

RIGHT **This bronze statuette of a porter from Uruk** (possibly carrying bricks, *c.* 3500 BCE) illustrates the craftsmanship burgeoning during the Uruk Period.

The Uruk Period is characterized by increasing social stratification, an element largely missing from the prehistoric settlements elsewhere in the Near East. Alongside the expansion of an early advanced system of regulated agricultural production, this social stratification became one of the features for early state formation in Mesopotamia at the city of Uruk.

Other than the rather formidable achievement of state-building, the Uruk Period is also known as the time in which writing first appeared. Urban centers in Mesopotamia began with the need to organize irrigation and the redistribution of surpluses to nonagricultural workers. Thus, early writing has been called "symbolic storage" in that it developed in urban environments apparently for the purpose of keeping track of goods. The earliest cities of Mesopotamia were well organized economically in comparison to the rural village societies in Anatolia and the Levant, and writing was an additional asset.

Uruk Period Government

Mesopotamia's dependence on domestic agriculture to sustain the home base, and on trade to provide the necessities for civilization not only resulted in a rapid build-up of settlements but also saw the spread of Sumerian trade colonies throughout the region, which had the effect of transforming the regional economies. The temple-city structure had less appeal abroad than the aspects of community life it fostered. The calendar of religious festivals was more than just a list of religious celebrations. It regulated the life of the people. Thus, although it can be argued that settled urban societies need an agricultural surplus and a controlling ethos to order their dense populations, they do not necessarily need the leadership of a religious authority. Less tightly regulated colonies and Sumerian-influenced city-states thus appeared in faraway places frequented by Sumerian traders and colonists. Mari and Ebla, for example, though well connected with Sumeria, did not adopt this temple-regulated style of urbanization.

The role of a central authority to collect and redistribute agricultural surpluses is a feature common to most of the cities of the ancient Near East and was probably first created in Mesopotamia during the Uruk Period. Also the specialization and standardization of industries such as metalworking, pottery, and textile-making was a major factor of urban life during this period. There was a notable increase in the number of craftsmen, and demands for their goods on the part of elite customers stimulated the already healthy trade between Mesopotamia and the rest of the Near East. In Mesopotamia the temple also exerted some control over the growth of craft industries as its demands upon artists and craftsmen were the greatest. In later times secular authorities carried out most of the administrative offices that were filled by priestly officials in the Uruk Period. The Ubaid Period had been a time in which tribal associations based on kinship were gradually transformed into a society in which authority and status was based on job status. During the Uruk Period, society abandoned the old affinities and became a true social hierarchy. The temple authorities, and its affiliated military and political leaders, were the primary stimuli for this transformation.

Archaeological Evidence

Uruk was the main settlement of this period, but the city of Nippur also grew in importance. The settlement system of Uruk was slightly different from that of Nippur. Uruk had a denser population, and Nippur became, very early in its history, a sacred city like Eridu, albeit with more of a national outlook. The improved pottery wheel, wheeled vehicles, the plow, and the pottery kiln were Uruk Period innovations that all had a marked influence on the material culture of the period. The distinctive painted pottery that spread throughout Mesopotamia during the Ubaid Period was gradually replaced by a variety of mass-produced, unpainted pottery created on a fast wheel. Bowls, especially, were turned out in great quantity and used at large community gatherings. Pottery was mass-produced at a number of centers throughout Mesopotamia. These centers were located adjacent to the densest populations and strategically positioned along trade routes. In addition to large-scale trade and exchange, it seems fairly certain that the Uruk Period saw a sharp increase in the use of slave labor. Artifacts found over a widespread area attest to the forced migrations of peoples from many different places into Sumeria.

A large proportion of resources gained through trade in timber and stone was used in temple

URUK PERIOD ARTWORKS

The nascent cities of the Uruk Period demonstrate a rapid growth of different art forms. One of these was the cylinder seal, of which we have many decorative examples from this time. The use of these seals, ostensibly to establish ownership and record agreements, became much more frequent during this period, and the seals themselves more detailed and decorative. The depictions on these seals include scenes of battle, religious celebrations, and farming and herding activities. Other sculpted stone art of the Uruk Period is largely religious in theme, illustrating scenes of worshippers, priests, and sacrificial animals. The most famous artifacts attributed to this time are probably from the transition between the Uruk and Early Dynastic Periods, but these give a good indication of the rapid growth of the arts during the Uruk phase. The carved stone Warka (Uruk) Vase depicts, in four levels, plants, sheep, men with baskets or jars, and a cultic scene, with the ruler of Uruk delivering goods to the Temple of Inanna. A famous alabaster head (the Lady of Warka), presumably of the goddess Inanna, is considered one of the earliest realistic depictions in stone of a deity. The imagery in seals and sculpture also gives us the earliest portrayals of what eventually developed into an ideology of divine kingship.

RIGHT **The Lady of Warka** disappeared from the Iraqi National Museum during the fall of Baghdad in April 2003. It was later recovered, allegedly in an orchard.

construction and maintenance. This period was the beginning of the tripartite temple plan. The earliest Uruk temples consisted of a long central hall with smaller rooms on either side and a façade with niches and buttresses. Later Uruk buildings include the famous Limestone Temple which may or may not have been entirely constructed of large limestone blocks (only the foundations have been found). The equally renowned "White Temple" of Uruk was also built at this time. The walls of this temple were covered in plaster, and niches and buttresses were also used on the outside façade.

Cities and Settlements

The size and number of settlements all over southern Mesopotamia increased dramatically during the Uruk Period. Later in the period a number of these settlements had fortifications that, no doubt, attest to the earliest beginnings of the militarization of society in the later Early Dynastic Period. With the increasing complexity of the social structure, and a growth in economic power, it is believed that secular leaders began to assert themselves in the cities—not as competition to the temple leadership but in support of it, as well as supported by it. More elite households with extended families began to build compounds within the city, close to its center. This was probably an additional factor influencing the invention and then widespread use of the seals and symbols to delineate the ownership of land and goods. This growth also helped to boost the demand for superior craftsmen and craftsmanship.

The most interesting question raised by the achievements of this largely preliterate society is what were the relations between the main cities of the alluvial plain and the outlying areas? Some scholars believe that the lack of resources in the southern alluvial plain, alongside the population growth and social stratification spurred by productive agriculture, created in this early phase a kind of preimperialism that is evidenced more fully much later in history. Other scholars have suggested that cities during this period were content to view themselves as regional centers controlling expanding hinterlands, with Uruk, by far the largest of them, operating as the chief administrative and ceremonial center. Little evidence exists to support either of these theories but, in both cases, the collapse of the "Uruk phenomenon" at the end of the period, and the fragmentation of the region into several smaller polities, argues for some kind of supra-urban organization centering round Uruk itself during the Uruk Period.

The Beginning of Writing

While the Uruk Period fostered the creation of some rather dubious achievements—social

JEMDET NASR

The Uruk ascendency over all Mesopotamia collapsed for reasons still unclear, and the following short Jemdet Nasr Period (c. 3000–2900 BCE) saw a redirection of Sumerian energies inwards. Jemdet Nasr itself is a small site south of Baghdad where excavators discovered a distinctive pottery style from the period immediately after the Uruk. The Jemdet Nasr Period is recognized as one of artistic splendor and imperial regression. The preceding Uruk Period had represented an early peak in the process of urbanization and social complexity in southern Mesopotamia. Even though the areas to the north and the east that had once been part of the Uruk Period cultural complex were developing very different cultures at the time, the Jemdet Nasr culture was known across southern Mesopotamia (i.e., the Sumerian heartland), maintaining the high standards of the Uruk Period for another century or so. In contrast to other areas, Jemdet Nasr enjoyed a time of increasing population, the expansion of irrigation systems, the growth of temple cities, increasing trade and craft specialization, and, most importantly, the increased use of writing and cylinder seals.

LEFT **This alabaster vase from Jemdet Nasr** (c. 2950 BCE) shows a procession for Inanna, with bulls and devotees. When the site was excavated in the 1920s many cuneiform texts were found.

LEFT **Uruk (seen here in aerial view)** quadrupled in size during the Uruk Period. Satellite towns sprang up around the city, heralding urbanization and social stratification.

stratification, and religious centralism, for example—it was also a time of tremendous innovation and progress. The most significant was the development of writing, begun as an administrative tool in this very specific urban context. A means to control production and exchange as well as to keep track of goods and assert ownership over assets, especially land and herds, the invention of writing, alongside the creation of cylinder seals, made it possible to communicate accurately across long distances and to be able to store detailed information for future use. It is difficult to comprehend the magnitude of this human advance, without which the knowledge of history and past civilizations would have been lost. While many other Uruk accomplishments—the temple city, the expansion of farming, herding and trade, the systemization of irrigated agriculture and the development of certain crafts—brought progress to the region, it was writing that brought it to the known world.

BELOW **Cylinder seals, such as this one from Uruk** (*c.* 2500 BCE), became invaluable for recording commercial and legal transactions as urbanization developed across the region.

From Village to City

The Ubaid culture of southern Mesopotamia was the first to develop a complex urban lifestyle. Large Ubaid villages developed some key innovations, including the pottery wheel, copper metallurgy, and irrigation technology.

Irrigation agriculture, considered the precursor to most civilizations of the ancient Near East, seems to have developed first in northern Mesopotamia. The valleys of the Tigris and Euphrates Rivers presented both an opportunity and a challenge to the people who began to settle there early in the Neolithic Period. The rivers ensured the continuous water needed to create a surplus of crops, but they also required much management and intervention to do this. If left unregulated, flash floods could wreak havoc.

Ubaid Villages

During the earliest of the Ubaid cultural phases, the city of Eridu was settled with the aid of the new irrigation technology, brought from the north, either by immigrants or perhaps more likely as an introduced idea. These flood-management techniques were well suited to the more arid south. The combination of a high water table and a relentlessly sunny climate was favorable to year-round farming—but only if the flood levels could be stringently controlled.

Large mud-brick houses and the first temples to appear in Mesopotamia signify the beginnings of complex village life. Tombs in these villages show the gradual appearance of social differentiation. Perhaps this also signals the rise of a hereditary elite who marked their status in these more elaborate burials. Public works, both practical and religious, were probably within the hands of a select few to control, and the society undoubtedly had some method of redistributing goods, as evidence of public granaries are found during this early period.

The First Temple Town

Eridu was a revelation to archaeologists. Its fabled temple proved to be a succession of 18 superimposed mud-brick structures going back to 5500 BCE or before. The temple-centered village is believed to have been yet another northern Mesopotamian development, but there is little doubt that Eridu is a phenomenon that is peculiar to southern Mesopotamia. The Eridu temple was the symbolic center of the society and went from being a social institution to a political and economic one. Mesopotamian temples controlled lands and resources, cannily managed by priestly administrators.

The religious life of the temple came to regulate the activities of the village, providing a calendar of events to dovetail with the agricultural calendar. Rituals became a significant part of everyday life, and the concept of time created in Mesopotamia was structured in accordance to a schedule of festivals.

Before Eridu became a fully fledged city-state, it had probably developed a patron god—later embodied as the Babylonian god Ea or Enki, who is associated with fresh water and knowledge.

ERIDU AND URUK IN MYTH

According to Sumerian mythology, Eridu was founded before the great flood described in *The Epic of Gilgamesh*. Enki raised the city of Eridu from the sea and made it very fertile. Eridu was also the site where the great god Anu deposited the Universal Decrees of Divine Authority for Enki to guard and later impart to the world. It was recognized as a place of impressive antiquity by the Sumerians, but Eridu was not the first village to become a true city. Much as Eridu's temple-centered society contributed to urbanization, the distinction of being the first true city belongs to a site that, according to legend, was the birthplace of the dying god Dumuzi, the consort of Inanna. This city also has another important position in Sumerian mythology–it was founded by the hero Gilgamesh, who was also its first king. This was Uruk, the progenitor of cities.

RIGHT **This clay tablet from the third millennium** BCE tells the story of Enki, the chief god of Eridu, and the origins of the world.

ABOVE **Cylinder seals and impressions from the third millennium BCE** depict the tale of Gilgamesh, the first king of Uruk and a mythical hero, and of Enkidu, his wild friend. Their exploits, encounters, and battles are recounted in an epic poem.

The association of each city with one main patron deity defines these urban centers to outsiders as sacred places, while the local gods provide protection to the citizens within. The ruler and the citizens were responsible for maintaining the cult complex for the well-being of the city, and festivals dedicated to these deities were the most important of social occasions.

The True City-State

Eridu and its temple were already almost 1,000 years old when Uruk embarked on its relatively short trajectory from large village to city. From around 4500 BCE Uruk became a center of trade because it was well positioned between the Tigris and Euphrates Rivers adjacent to many of the canals. Temple villages like Eridu dotted the banks of these waterways, taking advantage of the prosperity resulting from trade and the migration of specialized labor from other villages.

Uruk was the political and religious center of a large region. The peasants and farmers around the city were able to pay for products in market centers and, consequently, Uruk became a center of trade. By 3300 BCE, the city had two temple precincts—one for the sky god Anu, and the other for the mother goddess Inanna. It is believed that the temple area also served as the political center of the state. Uruk's products included mass-produced pottery, metal objects, carved stone seals, and decorated stone vessels. The development of a bureaucracy at Uruk made detailed record keeping ever more important. The first writing system filled this need.

RIGHT **A religious scene is depicted on the famous alabaster Warka Vase.** The vase was uncovered in the 1930s in Uruk. Here nude males carry offerings of food and drink to the goddess Inanna.

City Living

From the beginning, Sumerian towns were more than just large agricultural settlements. They developed on the basis of a model that exploited resources from the center outward rather that the hinterlands inward.

The location of the earliest towns on the river, and the creation of complex river transportation systems insured a steady flow of goods into the Sumerian settlements. This enabled the construction of elaborate temples at the center of the towns. Building work of this nature relied heavily on the economic prosperity that trade promoted, along with access to high-level engineering skills and a large and competent labor workforce.

BELOW **A stone staircase runs up the outside of a ziggurat in Ur. This was crudely reconstructed by Saddam Hussein, using bricks and cement.**

The Early Sumerian City

The temples to the local city gods were designed to be immediately visible. They were conceived of as artifical mountains, built as a series of massive brick podia, one on top of the other in a stepped arrangement, that came to be known as a ziggurat. These temples resembled hills and mountains and had ramps around the exterior to allow access—a form of sacred architecture used in Mesopotamia for several thousand years. As the temple towns became city-states, the temple elite were joined by political and military elites and, eventually, an early form of monarchy appeared, combining religious and political roles in the person of one individual. The immense food surplus that resulted from irrigated agriculture supported the elites of the city as well as its artists and craftspeople. Some of these cities had populations numbering in the tens of thousands. Administrative buildings (palaces, storerooms, workshops) were associated with the temples, and possibly dependent on them. Fields and pasturelands surrounded the cities but the Sumerians were also skilled at hunting and fishing. All these activities supported both an increased population and a variety of occupations including potters, weavers, carpenters, and

smiths. Merchants soon joined the ranks of these nonagricultural workers as the Sumerians engaged in commerce both by land and sea. By no later than the fourth millennium BCE the Sumerians had all the accoutrements of urban living—monumental public buildings, decorative arts, a variety of goods for sale, a plentiful food supply, and a skilled workforce. The only thing missing at this point was a system to make it easier to keep track of so many complex commercial transactions.

SUMERIAN CITY GODS

All Sumerian cities recognized a number of gods in common, including Anu the sky god and father of the gods, Enlil the lord of storms, and Ishtar the morning and evening star. The gods seemed hopelessly violent and unpredictable, and the life of a mortal a mere period of slavery to their whims. *The Epic of Creation* emphasizes that mortals were created to enable the gods to give up working. In addition, each city had its own god, who was considered literally to inhabit the temple and who was in theory the owner of all property within the city. Hence the priests, who interpreted the will of the god and controlled the distribution of the economic produce of the city, were venerated for their supernatural and material functions alike.

Visiting a Sumerian City

In the days before literacy, Sumer would still have presented a fairly urban face to the rest of the world. A visitor approaching an early Sumerian city would pass many farmers working in their fields with ox-drawn plows. They might then see smiths and tanners at work outside the central areas of the city. On the river would be barges ferrying a variety of goods and dominating the skyline would be the main temple or temples in the ziggurat style. The visitor entering through the city gates would begin to pass other artisans producing tools, clothing, pottery, and other items for everyday use. Near the center, close to the impressive ziggurat, merchants could be seen engaged in negotiations and utilizing an early form of record keeping involving actual clay tokens, marked to indicate a variety of products and quantities. In the precincts of the temple, the visitor would find skilled artisans producing luxury goods for priests and the city's elite.

In the space of several hundred years, the descendants of this visitor would return to the city and find temple scribes busily incising clay tablets with cuneiform signs. Cylinder seals (small stone cylinders engraved with a design) would be used to identify the client commissioning these documents. Most of the inscriptions on the tablets (which the visitor would be able to read only if they had scribal training) would relate to the administration of the temple and its lands. An inventory of the goats and sheep received that day for sacrificial use, and wage lists could also be found on these documents. The system of counting used for these inventories was based upon the unit 60—the unit of division still used today for the measurement of time and angles.

LEFT **This Sumerian clay tablet** from *c.* 2350 BCE, found at Telloh (ancient Girsu), was used to keep a tally of goats and sheep.

LEFT **Cylinder seals** were in regular use in the cities of Sumeria. The story of Idi-Ilum, a governor of Mari, is depicted here. It dates from *c.* 2000 BCE.

Religion and Politics

Urban Sumerian religion was primarily focused on the god to which the city's shrine was dedicated. Nevertheless, all Sumerian city-states revered the same deities, thus assuring that each city's temple received the respect of the residents

ABOVE **This statue of the priest-king Ebi-Il** (c. 2500 BCE) was found in the Temple of Ishtar in Mari. It is made from gypsum and lapis lazuli.

of other cities. Temples to Anu, father of the gods, and later on to the seductive Inanna/ Ishtar, the queen of heaven, could be found in Uruk. Eridu was known for its temple to Enki, god of wisdom and water, and in Lagash the war god Ninurta was venerated. The city of Ur worshipped the moon god Sin; and Nabu, the god of wisdom, favored the city of Borsippa. The city of Umma, famed for its enduring conflict with Lagash, worshipped the god Shara, a minor god associated with war.

The army, the king and the priests were in charge of the later Sumerian cities, controlling resources and waging war on a fairly unremitting schedule. These were the upper classes of society, and below them were the scribes and the temple attendants who represented a more or less simple bureaucracy, administering the city's economy and judicial system. There were elites who were not related to the monarchy, the military, or the temple. These were large landowners and successful merchants and artisans. At the lowest level of society were the small farmers, who made up the majority of the population, and slaves. This latter stratum tended to include people who had been captured in combat or during raids.

Education and the Arts

Education and art in Sumer were products of the temple society. Priests and scribes, after the invention of cuneiform writing, created a vast library of documents detailing the history of the world and its gods, and liturgical poetry. The decorative arts were also dedicated to the gods and, later, to the rulers of the cities. The elaborate mosaics, sculpture, stelae, portrait heads, and friezes symbolized the power and authority of king and deity. The kings of Ur took the creation of art to new heights, as Leonard Woolley discovered when he found the city's royal tombs in the 1920s. By the third millennium BCE, Sumerians were burying their leaders in great state, with grave goods in gold, semi-precious stones, alabaster, silver, and, most dramatically, with a retinue of soldiers, retainers and slaves, all apparently prepared to end their lives and be entombed with their master or mistress. More prosaic objects of art could be used by lesser beings. These included the artfully carved cylinder seals.

Education was primarily in writing and arithmetic. Children selected for scribal training were sent to the temple school where they laboriously copied the symbols on clay tablets until they had achieved a high level of expertise. Using clay media, they were able to smooth over mistakes, but later the best of them would be called upon to incise these symbols in stone. Thousands of the symbols had to be mastered before the student was asked to copy an entire work. Learning the standard weights and measures might have represented a much-needed break from such concentrated work.

RIGHT **This dagger with gold sheath** (c. 2500 BCE) is one of the treasures uncovered in the Royal Tombs of Ur. It shows the skill of the Sumerian craftsmen.

Relations Far and Near

The great rivers swelled, sometimes precariously, every year due to the melting of the snow in the mountains of the north. In their wake they left a rich deposit of silt across their floodplains as they approached the Persian Gulf. This was the heartland of Mesopotamian agriculture with its abundance of fish, wildlife, and date palms. A challenging environment to be sure—it was no more than a swamp in many places—but a lush one in terms of its natural resources. Though Mesopotamia yielded many riches to its early settlers, it lacked other vital materials. These still had to be imported, mainly stone, metals, and timber. Down the Tigris and Euphrates, the materials from Syria and Asia Minor came in a steady stream.

It is not clear when Sumerians began to construct boats, but a model from the middle of the fourth millennium BCE found in a grave indicates that they were common by that time. Sumerian developments were to have a flow-on affect: by the time Sumerians had begun to write, they were exchanging ideas and minor artworks with Egypt, while trading in stone and copper with the Indus Valley and Oman. They were likely to have introduced their trading partners to both the wheeled vehicle and the potter's wheel.

Social status dictated relationships within the Sumerian cities. Also, from the very earliest days of urban life, we can see that the Sumerians had developed almost a reverence for the ownership of property. Many of their documents related to property transactions between citizens, and they kept detailed inventories of their acquisitions. The scribes were employed with these transactions, when they were not required for temple business. The earliest fragmentary laws that have been found in Mesopotamia reflect this concern for property as well.

Rigid Social Structure

Civilized society came at a price for Sumerians. Most people found themselves, from birth, caught in a rigid, socially stratified system that left them with very little mobility. Part of the reason for the great inventiveness of the Sumerians was the ever more complex problems thrown up by burgeoning large-scale urban life. Such a structure demanded record keeping and organization on a scale never before required. Astronomy, the creation of the lunar calendar, the invention of increasingly complicated systems for recording the passing of time, the configuration of boundaries, and the accounting of goods and services, are all indicative of a society obsessed with control both over humans and over their natural environment.

Constant warfare, the factor that above all else contributed to the demise of the Sumerian city-state, was a later consequence of this highly structured lifestyle. Engaging in combat with one's neighbors provided an outlet for people at the lower levels of society to break away from the rigidity that characterized their lives. It had the additional benefit of annexing, albeit only temporarily, the resources of other cities. The later incarnation of the Sumerian city-state, after the demise of Akkad, may have taken some of these lessons to heart. The Third Dynasty of Ur was Sumerian in culture and language, but it was organized on the imperial model—a skill learned, no doubt, from the Akkadians.

BELOW **Hair ornaments, earrings, and necklaces** made of gold and lapis lazuli (*c.* 2500 BCE) were found in the Royal Tombs of Ur.

Cuneiform Writing

Five thousand years ago, the world's first written language appeared in Sumer. This method of transcribing languages remained in use for over 3,000 years and was used to record many languages including Akkadian, Elamite, Hittite (Luwian), Hurrian, Old Persian, and Ugaritic. Cuneiform writing began as a series of pictographs, which are symbols used to represent both concrete and abstract ideas. The symbols probably resembled the things that they stood for originally but they eventually became more abstract. The script was written primarily on clay tablets but was used for monumental inscriptions as well. Strictly speaking, cuneiform script was adapted to several different writing systems, used in logosyllabic, syllabic, and alphabetic forms.

Counting Donkeys

A tally of donkeys harnessed for ploughing is inscribed on this tablet. It is from Telloh (ancient Girsu) *c.* 2360 BCE. It is generally believed that writing developed to keep a record of harvests, herds, and land ownership, among other things.

A sharpened reed was the first instrument used to create the early cuneiform pictographs, which were laid out in vertical columns. Later, a type of pen was developed specifically to impress the symbols into clay. The characteristic wedge shapes created by this instrument were then arranged horizontally, facilitating the rapid transcription of many documents within a relatively short span of time. Cuneiform clay tablets could be recycled, sealed in clay "envelopes" or, if permanence was called for, baked in a kiln like other pottery. Tablets recovered from royal archives were those that were preserved through firing, either intentionally when they were created, or accidentally in conflagrations. Such libraries of cuneiform tablets have been found at Ugarit, Ebla, Mari, Nippur, and Nineveh.

In the fourth millennium BCE, a type of clay token began to be employed in the emerging urban centers of Mesopotamia. Examples of these have been found at Uruk, Nippur, Susa, and Ur, and seem to have been used for accounting purposes. The tokens represented specific items (for example, sheep, cattle, or wine) and were

Foundation Tablets

Foundation tablets were usually buried in the foundations of the temple to indicate who had donated to or built the temple. This foundation tablet is from the Neo-Babylonian era, *c.* 555 BCE.

Akkadian Adaptations

This clay tablet is from Tell el-Amarna in middle Egypt. It records trade and foreign relations between Egypt and the Great Powers of the day. It is in Akkadian cuneiform (*c.* 1340 BCE).

kept in cloth or leather bags. These tokens were the forerunners of the earliest cuneiform documents. The remarkable find among these early documents are the "school tablets." These indicate the development of scribal education at a very early date. Expert scribes used these tablets to teach younger students how to practice inscribing the signs accurately.

The Akkadians began to use cuneiform script in the twenty-sixth century BCE. Unlike the Sumerians, the Akkadians were Semitic-speaking, and their adaptation of cuneiform involved the creation of new equivalents for many signs in their Semitic language. By this time, the pictographic symbols had been reduced to stylised characters, but most of the later adaptations of cuneiform contained at least some semblance of the original Sumerian, making the identification of certain language classes written exclusively in cuneiform problematic. For hundreds of years thereafter Akkadian written in cuneiform was used for communications throughout the Middle East. The famous tablets found in Egypt at Tell el-Amarna, mostly from the reign of the heretic pharaoh Akhenaten in the fourteenth century BCE, were written in Akkadian.

Cuneiform writing was used by successive imperial powers in the Middle East, including the Assyrian, Neo-Babylonian, and Persian Empires. It lasted into the early Parthian period (*c.* CE 100). Following that, knowledge of cuneiform writing was essentially lost to the world until Sir Henry Rawlinson and his colleagues were able to decipher and interpret the trilingual inscription found at Behistun, Iran, in 1850.

Public and Private Use

Cuneiform was also used for public inscriptions, as a find demonstrates. A stone tablet, carved by a scribe, contains over 100 individual compartments with cuneiform pictographs. It reads "Gifts from the High and Mighty of Adab [a Sumerian city] to the High Priestess, on the occasion of her election to the temple." The development of cuneiform as a writing method for personal use is illustrated by a find (now in the Louvre in Paris) from the site of Telloh in modern Iraq, 15 miles northwest of Lagash. It is dated a century later and is a clay tablet containing a letter to the king of Lagash.

Cones of Reform

The social and economic reforms of Prince Uruinimgina are inscribed on these clay cones from Lagash (*c.* 2350 BCE). They are now in the Louvre.

Rival City-States

The city-state is one of the oldest and most widespread forms of government. Sumer is credited with the invention of the concept, although some scholars believe that it originated in northern Mesopotamia.

ABOVE **An American team excavated at the sacred city of Nippur,** *c.* 1957. Nippur was the site of the national shrine to Enlil, chief deity of Sumeria.

When the first city-states emerged, their citizens were preoccupied with maintaining canals, temples, and other public works. In the beginning, only one city, Uruk, seems to have had the honor of having a king who was considered, in title if not in fact, king of Sumer. Kingship quickly became decentralized, and it was not long before rivalries between adjacent cities began to escalate into fully fledged warfare.

Early Dynastic City-States

Throughout most of their history the people of Sumer would not recognize themselves as a unified people. The citizens of each city-state thought of themselves in terms of belonging to a particular city. Given the close association of many small, fiercely independent units, growing populations, and strictly limited agricultural resources, it is perhaps not surprising that conflicts arose over land and resources. Uruk was the first city to achieve importance as a major religious and market center. Later Nippur, famous for its national shrine to Enlil, became an important temple city, but never politically or economically influential. Instead, it found itself in the unenviable position of being a prize to be coveted by other city-states. In the third millennium BCE, any ruler who wanted to conquer another city was required to demonstrate that he was endorsed by Enlil, and controlling the city of Nippur became the primary means of demonstrating divine favor.

From cuneiform inscriptions we discover that by 2500 BCE the cities of Mesopotamia were in persistent rivalry with each other. Rulers built temples and palaces to eclipse those of other city-states and commissioned artworks and buildings to testify to and validate their own power and authority. The Old Sumerian (or Early Dynastic Period as this is called, roughly 2900 to 2300 BCE), is characterized by these competitions that eventually seem to have resulted in an increasing separation between the secular polity and its religious elites. Monumental buildings, such as palaces, attest to the diversion of resources away from religious activities.

Kish, Umma, and Lagash

Sources from the Early Dynastic Period describe a number of important rulers, the buildings they constructed, the wars they waged, and the institutions they established. Apparently Kish, like Nippur, established itself early as an important city-state. After 2500 BCE, it was common for rulers of other city-states to call themselves the king of Kish when attempting to establish sovereignty over a large area of Sumer. The cities of Lagash and Umma, which fought for many years over the fertile region between them, figure greatly in some of these texts. At some point the king of Kish attempted to draw a boundary between these cities to resolve the

RIGHT **The soldiers depicted on the Stele of the Vultures** are led by Eannatum, prince of Lagash, in his victory over their rival, the city of Umma.

dispute but his compromise was short-lived. The famous Stele of Vultures, now in the Louvre in Paris, records another, less amicable, attempt to resolve this dispute. Apparently this document commemorates the victory of the king of Lagash over the king of Umma after what appears to have been a protracted conflict.

Various scenes from this war are shown on the stele, including a heroic depiction of the victorious king in his chariot. Scholars have been able to construct some details of early warfare based upon the unusual weaponry, helmets, and lances used by the soldiers accompanying the king. The god of war, Ninurta, is to be found on the reverse side of the stele, holding the people of Umma in a large net. Apparently the king of Lagash was able to compel the king of Umma to take an oath to desist from crossing the boundary that had previously been set by the king of Kish. The enmity between Umma and Lagash continued, and there are records of the two cities having fought other enemies, which in turn engaged in continually shifting alliances with yet more cities.

A United Sumeria

It appears that the first ruler over a united Sumer was Lugalzagesi, king of Umma (reigned 2375–2350 BCE). He is said to have conquered all the other important Sumerian city-states in Mesopotamia and Syria. Every other ruler bowed to Lugalzagesi, and he had no opponent "from where the sun rises to where the sun sets," according to a royal inscription. His empire was to last only 24 years. Sargon, the ruler of Akkad, and the first Near Eastern monarch to establish a lasting empire, became the first "king of Sumer and Akkad," a title that was taken by all subsequent rulers in Mesopotamia for the next 200 years.

SUMERIAN WARFARE

The battles between cities during this time were fought mainly by foot soldiers, although some use of small chariots drawn by onagers (wild asses) is also indicated. The Sumerians were probably the first to use the chariot, but their version of the chariot was heavier and more unwieldy than later versions. It may have served as an observation platform, and to allow the king to be seen by his troops. The image of the infantry of the king of Lagash on the Stele of Vultures has the appearance of the phalanx technique later used so effectively by the Macedonian military under Alexander the Great *c.* 330 BCE.

At the beginning of city-state rule, Sumerian rulers and the military were designated by separate names. However, as warfare became more common, kings became war leaders, and new titles were invented to reflect these changed circumstances. Still later, the rulers took on the role of religious leader thereby combining in one person responsibility for directing all the important functions of the early state.

ABOVE **This scene from the Royal Standard of Ur** (c. 2600–2400 BCE) is one of the earliest-known depictions of Sumerian warfare. The Standard is a wooden box inlaid with mosaic, and was found in the 1920s.

Uruk

Uruk is the largest and most important of the early Sumerian cities. It has become synonymous with the creation of Mesopotamian civilization. According to the city's origin myth, Gilgamesh built Uruk and was its first ruler.

According to archaeologists, the city, which is today called Warka, was first settled early in the Ubaid Period (*c.* 5000 BCE). The Ubaid Period, however, was not the time of Uruk's greatest influence. It was in the following period, which is named after the city, that Uruk achieved its greatest consequence.

Early Uruk

The first great expansion of settlement at Uruk occurred in the Uruk Period, named after this "urban pulse" at Warka, which saw the site expand to over 600 hectares in size. The Uruk Period represents a transitional time during which classic Sumerian civilization crystalized. Uruk was founded on marshy but fertile land, watered by a network of Euphrates tributaries. Most of the buildings of Uruk were made of reeds and mud, but for the building of the temples, large quantities of stone were imported.

Uruk's first religious structures were in two separate precincts. The Temple to Inanna, the most important of Sumerian goddesses, was at the center of one precinct. One of the earliest buildings was the White Temple, dedicated to Inanna. Because of the rarity of stone buildings in Mesopotamia, some archaeologists believe that it was just the foundation that was of quarried limestone. In any event, this was a structure of unprecedented size in Sumer and which took a great deal of labor to construct. It contained a unique double staircase that led to the roof where the important rituals took place. Only the priests and city rulers could go there.

Later Uruk

Other buildings were gradually constructed around the White Temple, which seems to have been connected with the other, possibly later, sacred precinct of the city, that of Anu, the sky god. Anu is credited with separating heaven from earth and was also believed to be the creator of the world and humanity, the father of the gods and the creator of Inanna. The Anu temple itself is actually a series of temples dating from the Ubaid to the Uruk Period. The temple was rebuilt repeatedly over the course of 500 years. The end result, later in the history of the city, was a building that was as tall as five storeys. It was similar in plan to most late Ubaid temples, with a central room, an offering table with evidence of burning, and many interior niches.

In both the Inanna and Anu precincts, a series of large buildings was repeatedly rebuilt in ever more elaborate style, testifying to the growing wealth and prosperity of the city. The late Uruk

THE URUK MOSAIC BUILDINGS

South of the Inanna precinct, a terrace with a massive colonnade was built. This colonnade may have been designed as an impressive entrance. Staircases connect the colonnade to the courtyard of the precinct, and the columns consisted of two rows of supports, made of mud brick and bundles of reed to stabilize these bricks. The finishing of the columns was one of the most intriguing features of Uruk architecture. Many thousands of colored clay cones were laid in a bed of clay around the columns and arranged to form the earliest complex polychrome mosaic ever created. An entire temple covered with these cones, the Stone-cone or Mosaic Temple, was located between the Inanna precinct and the Anu ziggurat.

RIGHT **Colored clay cones were used in sophisticated mosaics** to decorate columns in public buildings in Uruk (*c.* 3200 BCE). They also protected the walls and columns from erosion.

LEFT **The city of Uruk** dominated the skyline of southern Mesopotamia. The temple of Anu, with its stone foundations, was one of many impressive public buildings.

Period was one of intense construction, and many temples were built on different levels. In the fourth millennium BCE, houses surrounding the precincts became larger, indicative of the growing populations managed out of these administrative buildings. Uruk was a city that clearly represents several stages on the way from agricultural settlement to large urban center.

The Symbolic Significance of Uruk

By the middle of the fourth millennium BCE Uruk was the largest settlement in Mesopotamia, rising out of the marshlands of southern Mesopotamia as a true urban center, dominated by its remarkable temples and impressive public buildings. Sculptures were erected in the city, perhaps the first public sculptures in the world. Uruk's importance in later Mesopotamian history, however, was more symbolic than actual. The kings of other city-states would often refer to Uruk in documents and attempt to compare themselves with the mythical kings of Uruk.

Up to the beginning of the Early Bronze Age (the Early Dynastic Period), Sumerian culture, as exemplified by that of Uruk, appeared in locations all over the Near East, from central Iran to the Egyptian Nile Delta. The Early Dynastic Period (2900–2300 BCE), a time of city-state domination in Mesopotamia, brought a new system of government to the region that seemed to eclipse the kind of temple-city political organization that Uruk represented. The fortifications surrounding the site suggest that it was vulnerable to the rivalries that grew up between city-states in this later Early Dynastic Period—perhaps because the city retained its religious significance. Certainly, the tradition that Uruk had been built by Gilgamesh achieved more significance in Early Dynastic times. Although he may have been a real king of the city, his role as a hero in later stories and epics is indicative of a later Sumerian view of their legendary origins than a strictly accurate portrayal of early Sumerian Uruk.

LEFT **In this stele from Uruk** (*c.* 4000 BCE), a king of Uruk hunts a lion with a bow and arrow.

The Rise of Lagash

Lagash was one of the oldest and most significant of the Sumerian city-states, and became one of the most prosperous and powerful in later Sumerian times, when it came to dominate such centers as Uruk and Ur.

ABOVE **King Eannatum, as the god Ningirsu,** is seen in this relief from the Stele of the Vultures from Girsu (*c.* 2450 BCE) leading his troops from his chariot.

The city-state of Lagash achieved particular prominence several times in the third millennium BCE, both before and after it was conquered by the Akkadians. Throughout its history, it was ruled by independent kings who managed to thwart, for the most part, the incursions of the Elamites on their eastern borderlands, and the city-state of Kish to their north. It was considerably spread out and encompassed three large centers: Lagash itself, its economic center; Girsu, its political and religious center; and Nina, a temple precinct. Its major rival was the city of Umma, its closest neighbor, with which it was engaged in a struggle for many years—a struggle Lagash eventually won. The famous Stele of Vultures, now in the Louvre Museum in Paris, details the epic clash between Umma and Lagash, and a magnificent silver vase shows a lion-headed eagle grasping a lion in both of its talons. These relics indicate that Lagash was a consistently bellicose neighbor—and one practiced in the art of war.

The Expansion of Lagash

The king of Lagash was charged with the task of protecting the city in the name of deity. The land around the city was owned partly by the king, partly by the temple, and the rest by private citizens, and it was over land that the legendary dispute between Umma and Lagash arose. King Eannatum of Lagash began the feud with Umma over the placement of a boundary between the cities. A particularly fertile property was in dispute, and the canal on it was controlled by Umma but used by Lagash. As the feud escalated, the king of Umma ordered the draining of the canal, and Eannatum then advanced on Umma and conquered it. Inscribed boundary monuments testifying to the contentious relationship between the cities have been found near Girsu (present-day Telloh).

The people of Lagash were known to be somewhat belligerent themselves and were the first Sumerians to ever engage in a revolt against their rulers. Tax increases and a restriction on their freedoms seem to have been the cause for this action. The man who became king as a result was Urukagina who is known for his reforms to combat corruption and seems to have been the creator of the first law code in Mesopotamia.

LAGASH RELIGION

The people of Lagash, like all Sumerians, were polytheists, although not all the gods were represented by temples in the city. The local favorites were Nina, a goddess of war and fertility related to Inanna/Ishtar, and Ningirsu, a Lagash version of the Sumerian war god Ninurta but who had the additional responsibility over irrigation (perhaps reflecting the consistent arguments between Lagash and its neighbors over the management of the canals). Ningirsu was the patron deity of the city, the protector of its fields, and the figure in whose name the king waged war. The symbol of the "Lord of Girsu," the lion-headed eagle, eventually became the symbol of Lagash itself.

LEFT **Ur-Nanshe, the first king of the dynasty of Lagash,** is depicted here (Girsu, *c.* 2500 BCE) carrying a basket of bricks on his head to construct a temple.

Conquest and Resurgence

Several hundred years after Urukagina's reign, the city lost its independence, along with the rest of the Sumerian city-states, when the empire of Sargon of Akkad was established. Lagash became a vassal state but, unlike some of the other conquered city-states, it successfully retained its Sumerian character. It remained a city of importance under the Akkadians, both economically and in terms of its level of artistic achievements, as archaeological finds from Girsu (modern Telloh) have attested. When the Akkadian Empire ended, partly due to the depredations of the Gutians, a rather mysterious group of people from the Zagros Mountains believed to have been nomadic pastoralists, Lagash became independent again and seems to have remained so throughout the Gutian "dark age."

The "Golden Age" of Lagash arose with the disappearance of the nomadic Gutians from the scene, and the rise of Gudea, a key figure in the city's history.

Gudea, by all accounts, was a competent ruler and an excellent general. He managed to build up the city, importing materials from far and wide, at the same time as he engaged the Elamites in battle to maintain Lagash's independence. Gudea's appearance is better known than that of most rulers in Mesopotamia, as he seems to have commissioned many likenesses of himself, judging by the number that have been found. Lagash prospered under Gudea and retained some semblance of peace. He is known for having instituted reforms aimed at reducing the debt burden of poor peasant farmers to rich urban landholders. His era is also known as a time of revival in the arts at Lagash.

Decline and Conquest

Gudea's heirs found that they were unable to compete with their illustrious ancestor in fighting for the city's supremacy on many fronts. The city held its place as the artistic capital of Mesopotamia for some time but its political capital rapidly decreased. There is little doubt that in the twenty-second century BCE it came under the control of the Third Dynasty of Ur, but there is no complete picture of what happened to the city during this period. After the collapse of the Ur III empire, Lagash eventually would have fallen under the ambit of the Old Babylonian Empire whose most famous king, Hammurabi, perhaps following the example of Urukagina and, later, Ur-Nammu of the Third Dynasty of Ur, established his own law code.

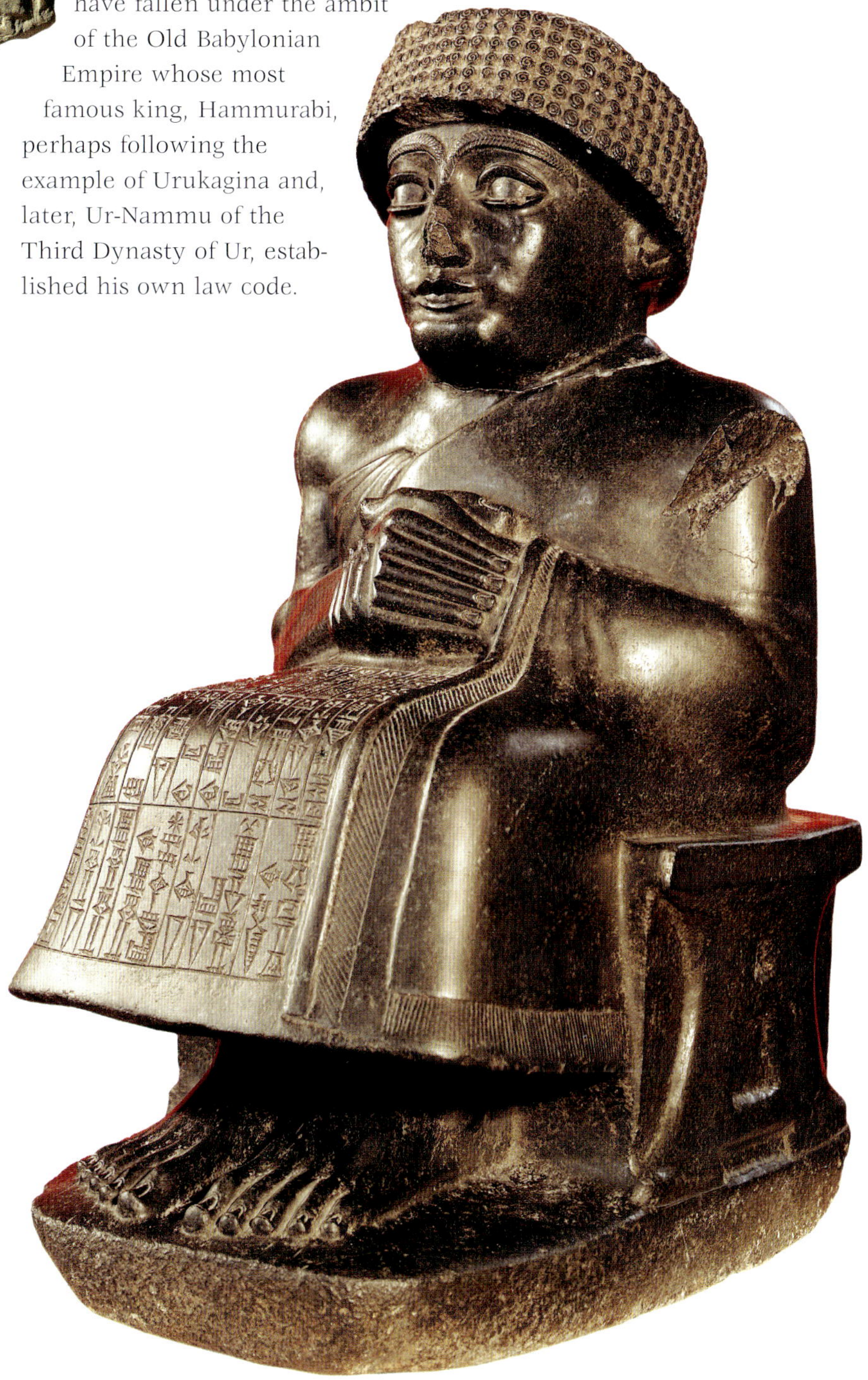

BELOW **Gudea ruled Lagash** during a time of resurgence and plenty. He was benevolent and reforming. This black diorite statue dates from *c.* 2150 BCE.

Beyond Babylon

Sargon of Akkad, the first great empire builder of his age, claimed to have built Babylon, as well as many other cities. Certainly, sources from the Akkadian period were the first to refer to the city.

RIGHT **The royal tombs at Alaca Hüyük in Turkey** (c. 2500 BCE) contained a trove of rich grave goods including gold pitchers.

In the later Uruk Period (3500–3050 BCE), before the ascendancy of Sargon, the later center of Babylon had yet to be settled. Some scholars have suggested that Babylon was the site of Sargon's capital, Akkad, but it is unlikely that this will ever be confirmed. Archaeologists have been unable so far to reach the earliest levels at this important and fascinating site as they are below the modern water table.

It has been suggested that Babylon may well have been founded as an Amorite settlement, as it is situated on the northern margins of the southern alluvial plain, in a location similar to other known Amorite foundations. It was clear from its later history that the city was a major stop on the route of Semitic peoples through Mesopotamia. The Amorites came to settle in Babylon, however, later than the Early Bronze Age. During the third millennium BCE, the Amorites probably traded with Mesopotamian cities from their homelands in the desert margins to the west of the Euphrates Valley. It was the Amorites who facilitated overland trade between Mesopotamia and the western lands of Canaan and Egypt. The name Amorite comes from the word *amurru*, the Sumerian word for "westerner." The Sumerians characterized the Amorites as a barbaric people.

Mari and Ebla

The first of the important Amorite cities was Mari. The Sumerians imported many resources and Mari was on the major trade routes to the north and west. Among the most important finds in the ancient Near East is a library of thousands of tablets found at Mari. These tablets provide invaluable information about the customs and

BELOW **The ruined city of Ebla** is about 70 miles (130 km) south of Aleppo, Syria. The site has been excavated since 1964 and is famous for the 20,000 tablets found there in 1972.

economic life of that city, as well as identifying the peoples and something of their culture. By the beginning of the third millennium BCE, Mari was becoming a center for the Near Eastern trade in tin, rare and much prized for bronze blade manufacture. Mari had an extensive irrigation system and successfully produced a surplus of food crops which added to its general prosperity.

Mari was destroyed in the twenty-third century and for some time was not rebuilt. Some scholars have suggested that Mari's principal commercial rival, the city of Ebla, had a hand in the destruction, and Ebla did benefit from Mari's decline. Although Ebla shows signs of continuous occupation from at least the Uruk/Late Chalcolithic periods of the fourth millennium BCE, its zenith came after the destruction of Mari.

Ebla, too, was the site of an impressive library of tablets which detail its economic, cultural, and political life. It was the market center for the timber and textiles that Mesopotamia imported and was a trade center for wool. Although it conducted most of its general trade with Sumer, evidence indicated that Ebla had contacts with Old Kingdom Egypt. The art and architecture of Ebla betrays a close relationship with the Mesopotamian lowlands, indicating that Sumerian culture had an impact on the art and culture of lands both near (Akkad) and far (Syria).

NonSemitic Civilizations on the Rise

While Semitic-speaking peoples began their incursions into Mesopotamia, the Hatti were establishing a major city at Alaca Hüyük in central Anatolia. The fact that their name came to be used for the Hittite kingdoms has caused some confusion. The Hatti were not Hittites or even Proto-Hittites. They were a people whose culture merged with that of the Hittites, and their language does not appear to be either Indo-European or Semitic.

Major archaeological finds at Alaca Hüyük from the Early Bronze Age were the elaborate tombs of royalty or elites. These individuals were buried with grave goods including jewelry, weapons, vessels, finials, and plaques made of gold, silver, and other metals. These artifacts are probably from a later date than those found by Leonard Woolley in the late 1920s in the Royal Tombs of Ur.

Elamites in Mesopotamia

The king of Kish, a city that seems always central to our understanding of civilizations beyond the borders of Mesopotamia, provided us with the first historical reference to the Elamites, from *c.* 2700 BCE. Sumer was later controlled by the Elamites briefly in the twenty-fifth century BCE, and some of the more powerful rulers of Sumerian city-states in turn conquered Elam for brief periods. It is only from the beginning of the Akkadian period, however, that Elam itself really enters into history. Sargon's rise was contemporary with the end of one period of Elamite rule in Sumeria. After securing Sumer, Sargon conquered Elam. He seized the Elamite capital of Susa, and set up an Akkadian provincial administration, which suppressed the use of Elamite and forced the introduction of Akkadian to the eastern courts.

ELAMITES AND PROTO-ELAMITES

While the Hattians developed a sophisticated urban civilization in central Anatolia, another enduring civilization was on the rise to the east of Sumer: the still enigmatic Elamites. The Elamites may or may not be linguistically related to the so-called Proto-Elamite culture, whose language remains undeciphered, but the largest proportion of the known Proto-Elamite texts have been excavated at Susa, a site that later was very much identified with the Elamites. Proto-Elamite was a writing system that was in use by 3050 BCE. Although Susa's Proto-Elamite culture initially showed some strong similarities to Uruk Period Sumer, from about the third millennium it began to develop its own character, combining influences from Sumer and Akkad with those from the southwestern regions of the Iranian Plateau.

ABOVE **These clay tablets detailing accounts are Proto-Elamite from Susa.** Clay tablets were frequently used for such administrative and actuarial tasks. They date from 2900 BCE.

Semitic Migrations

Though it seems clear that the Sumerians were not Semitic-speaking people, they traded with Semites to the north and south. The earliest Semitic speakers are first attested in the north of the Arabian Peninsula, and seem to have dominated north-central Mesopotamia by the fourth millennium BCE.

The first Dynasty of Kish and other northern Sumerian cities had rulers whose names appear to have been Semitic. Whether they were Akkadians or another group remains uncertain, but it is commonly assumed that the Ubaid peoples of north-central Mesopotamia, responsible for many of the critical innovations that made the Sumerian civilization possible, were east Semitic speakers. Sumerians and Semitic Akkadians, and later the Amorites, who left Arabia in the late third millennium BCE and settled in the Levant and Syria, ended up in the lower valleys of the Tigris and Euphrates Rivers. Their places of origin have never been determined, but word borrowings between Semitic languages and Sumerian have been identified. These borrowings may offer some indication of how these two groups saw each other. It is interesting to note that Sumerian words relating to writing and gardening, for example, were absorbed into the Akkadian language, while Akkadian terms relating to herding, war, and religion entered Sumerian. Later, the Sumerians worshipped some of the Semitic gods, such as the sun god and god of justice, Shamash, and Ishtar, a goddess of both love and war.

Sumero-Semitic Relations

In the beginning, the Akkadians to the north and Amorites to the west encroached upon the Sumerian city-states, but relations seem to have remained peaceful. Both Semitic cultures gained something from their contact with Sumerian inventiveness. The most obvious example is that of cuneiform writing which was adapted to many spoken languages besides Sumerian. The cuneiform writing system essentially disseminated the culture of Sumer and Akkad throughout the ancient Near East and, long after the demise of the Empire itself, the Akkadian language written in cuneiform was the standard for communication between cities throughout Mesopotamia, the Levant, Arabia, and Egypt.

By the time the Akkadians came to dominate Mesopotamia, the Sumerians seem to have been fairly well acquainted with them and with their culture. As overlords, the Akkadians determined to push that one step further and move toward linguistic assimilation. They naturally accorded greater prestige to their own language and quickly mandated that all written forms of communication adopt it. This was when cuneiform writing and Akkadian began to spread far beyond the borders of Mesopotamia. Akkadian

THE LEGENDARY LAND OF DILMUN

In addition to their myths relating to the great gods of the city-states, the Sumerians had their own version of the Garden of Eden story, set in Dilmun. Dilmun represented all things good—fertile landscapes, cool breezes, and a way of life requiring little toil. Dilmun belonged to the gods before it became a city and, according to the myth, it was a place where disease, sorrow, and death were unknown. Most scholars believe that they know the location of Dilmun. It is the island of Bahrain which from prehistoric times was a trading center connecting Mesopotamia, the Arabian coast, and the eastern lands of the Indus and Oman.

LEFT **Dilmun was the land of plenty,** where men and animals lived in harmony. This seal from Susa (third millennium BCE) depicts rams.

art achieved a similarly widespread audience and their reliefs, seals, and sculpture started to appear throughout the Near East.

Semitic Religious Philosophy

It has been suggested that the Sumerian concept that the gods were capricious, if not downright malignant, was a Semitic invention. The literature of Sumer suggests that the gods regretted the creation of humans and complained that they neglected their duties of worship. For their part, the people reflected that the gods would abandon them with little provocation, even though they dedicated their lives to serving them. The Sumerian flood myth, often compared to the one in Genesis, has one striking element. While the god of Noah destroyed mankind for its wickedness, the gods of Sumer took this drastic action because, in their opinion, humans made too much noise!

ABOVE **The moon god Sin** (left) stands on a crescent and receives a prayer. Another man prays before the symbol of Marduk, the chief of the Babylonian pantheon (*c.* 1000 BCE).

The Amorites

After the more benign Akkadians no longer ruled Mesopotamia, the Amorites, an infamous group in the Bible, began attacking Sumer. The Amorites soon came to dominate Sumer, and have been credited with founding the great city of Babylon, at which one of the legendary Amorite kings, Hammurabi, later came to power.

To the Sumerians, the Amorites were not like the Akkadians. They were described as independent nomads content to wander at will, pillaging the cities of their settled neighbors. The primary god of the Amorites was Sin, the moon god of Mesopotamia. From the second half of the third millennium BCE they had settled to the west of Sumer and were referred to in documents by the name Amurru. Their ascendancy brought many changes to the social and political organization of the region. They did not live in city-states, nor did they allot valuable resources to the temple or the monarch. Land was distributed to nonelites, and they seem to have alleviated the burden of taxes and forced labor imposed upon the common people by the Sumerian elites. Much of what we see in Amorite culture found its way into the biblical texts where descriptions of the early Israelites reflect similar cultural preferences for pastoralism, egalitarianism, and freedom from taxation.

LEFT **Ishtar/Inanna is the Sumerian goddess of fertility and warfare.** As in this terracotta relief (*c.* 2000 BCE), she is often depicted standing on the backs of lions.

Sargon of Akkad

The man who established the world's first empire is a figure around whom many fanciful tales have been woven, not least by Sargon himself. It is difficult to establish what his origins really were.

ABOVE **This diorite victory stele of Sargon of Akkad** (c. 2350 BCE) from Susa celebrates the ruler's dominance over the neighboring city-states.

THE AKKADIAN LANGUAGE

During Sargon's rule, Akkadian was adapted to the script that previously had been employed to transcribe Sumerian. The new spirit of calligraphy that is visible upon the clay tablets of this dynasty is also clearly seen on contemporary cylinder seals, with their beautifully arranged and executed scenes of mythology and festive life. Sargon's conquests introduced the Akkadian language to all corners of his empire, and it was for centuries thereafter the lingua franca or language of diplomacy in the ancient Near East. Because of this, Mesopotamian civilization has had a powerful influence on other areas in the ancient Near East, and traces of it are found in the Bible and in Greek civilization.

Many of the legends relating to Sargon seem to be reminiscent of biblical stories, which may reflect the close relationship between Mesopotamia and the Levant, even during the Early Bronze Age. One story is reminiscent of that of David's rise to power. After the king of Kish appointed Sargon to his court, the king fell into disfavor with the gods Anu and Enlil, and in a prophetic dream was told that Sargon would take his kingdom from him. He then attempted to murder Sargon and, when that failed, sent him to the king of Uruk with a message containing instructions to kill him. Sargon survived this attempt on his life as well, and later conquered Kish, Uruk, and the rest of Mesopotamia.

Kish, one of the northernmost of the early Sumerian city-states, was one of the first to be controlled by Semitic-speaking rulers. The names of rulers of the First Dynasty of Kish appear to have been Semitic but whether they were Akkadians or another group remains uncertain. This might explain the later association of Sargon with Kish, which was probably the first of the conquered city-states. From Kish, Sargon moved on to defeat Umma, which at the time was one of the largest city-states in Mesopotamia. Sargon rapidly became the most prominent ruler in the land, but the disadvantages of power soon became obvious. Some of the city-states he annexed in the wake of his conquest of Umma soon rebelled, and much effort was given over to pacifying them once and for all.

Conquest and Consolidation

Sargon expanded his rule as far as the Levant and the Taurus Mountains in Turkey. The city-states of Sumer continued to rebel and he eventually instituted changes in government that would assure his continued hegemony. He installed his daughters as high priestesses and his sons as governors. His daughter Enheduanna is particularly memorable for having composed a number of poems and prayers to the gods. Despite her seeming talent and abilities she was not successful as a priestess. The priestly classes complained that she was neglecting her duties to the moon god in favor of the goddess Inanna and she was removed from office.

Sargon's Record

Sargon's desire for trade throughout the ancient Near East brought him to Susa, the capital city of the Elamites. The only contemporary record of Sargon's reign has been found in Susa. Sargon is also mentioned in the later Sumerian King Lists as having ruled for 56 years and having built the city of Akkad. Sources indicate that his reign was troubled with rebellions and, despite his abilities, he was unable to stabilize control over such vast territories. During this historical period, when written communication was barely more than several hundred years old, such a large kingdom would have presented an insurmountable administrative challenge. There is no evidence to suggest that he was a despotic ruler, nor does it seem that the Sumerians were upset to find themselves under the authority of a Semite. Rather, the fragmented political landscape of Sumer and Elam could never be entirely reconciled to single rule as part of a regional empire.

Sargon's empire passed to his son who ruled for scarcely nine years before Naram-Sin, Sargon's grandson, came to the throne and ruled over a kingdom wracked by constant revolution for more than 30 years. The Sumerian city-states began to detach themselves early in his reign, and, soon after, he was plagued with the incursions of the Gutians from the Zagros Mountains, whom his grandfather Sargon lists among his conquered peoples. On Naram-Sin's death, the Gutians took over Sargon's kingdom and it faded from the scene. Sargon's rise from obscurity to king of the known world, for a brief time, had united all of Mesopotamia, a difficult task considering the age-old rivalries. His was the first of the great Semitic Mesopotamian empires and provided a model for the Ur III empire, and later those of Shamshi-adad and Hammurabi.

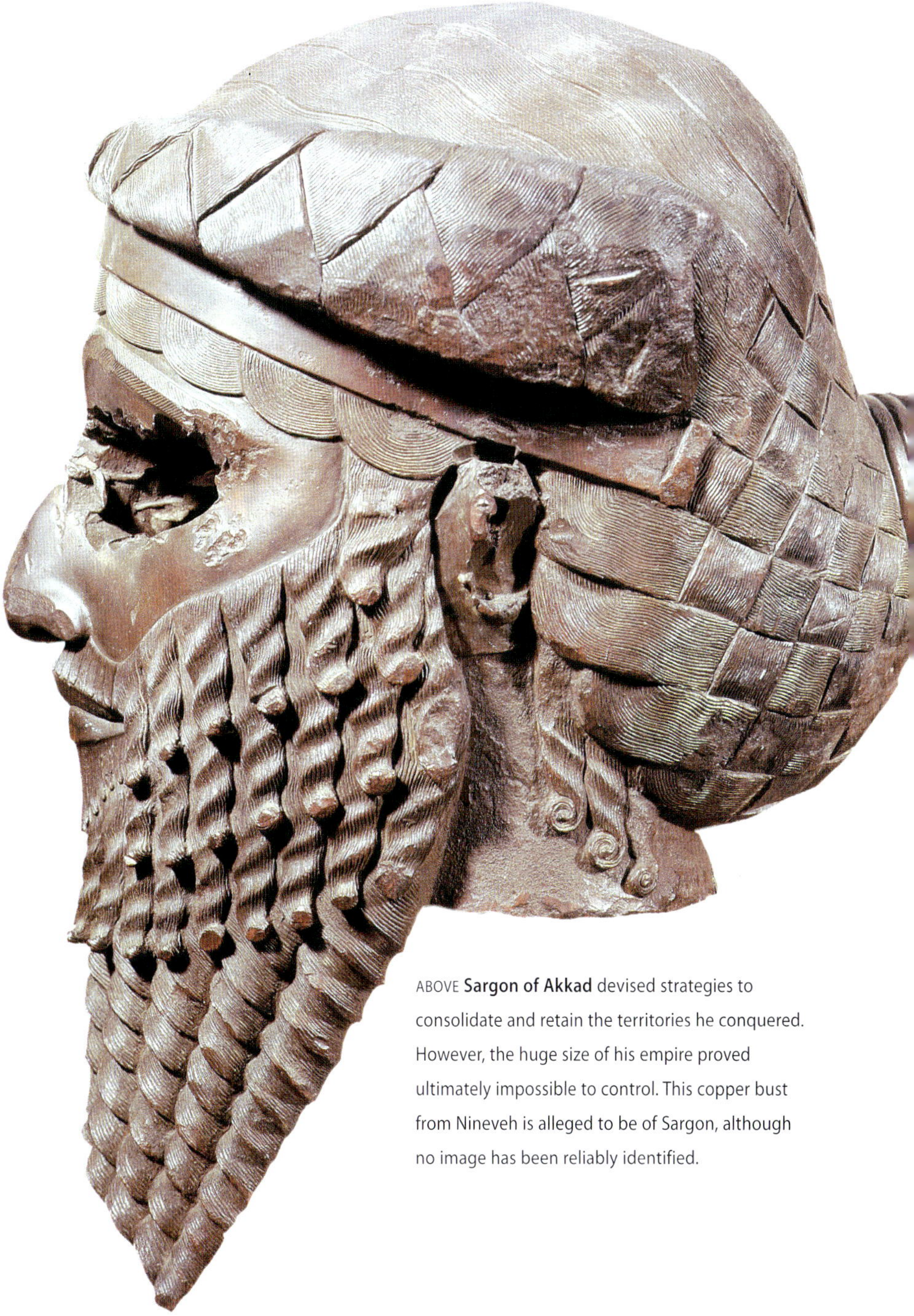

ABOVE **Sargon of Akkad** devised strategies to consolidate and retain the territories he conquered. However, the huge size of his empire proved ultimately impossible to control. This copper bust from Nineveh is alleged to be of Sargon, although no image has been reliably identified.

LEFT **Sargon stands before a tree of life** in this stone relief dating from 2300 BCE. His long reign changed the face of Mesopotamia.

The Kingdom of Akkad

As the land of Sumer suffered through its warring-states period, a powerful kingdom was forming in the city of Akkad to their north. The conquests of Sargon of Akkad (*c.* 2350 BCE) were to mark a watershed in the history of the region.

ABOVE **This statue of Manishtusu** (c. 2270 BCE) is carved in diorite. Diorite was a dense hard stone favored by the kings for its shine and for its ability to take inscriptions.

The Semitic-speaking Akkadians, led by their singularly able king Sargon, succeeded in uniting all the Sumerian city-states under his rule. From what we can gather, Akkad had grown up alongside Sumerian centers of civilization, although the precise location of the city has not been determined. Eventually, all of Mesopotamia would become known as the "land of Sumer and Akkad," a title that retained its significance in spite of the resurgence of Sumerian power during the Third Dynasty of Ur.

Cuneiform records as early as the twenty-seventh century BCE had begun to list Akkadian names and contain Akkadian words so it is difficult to determine when, in fact, the people of Akkad emerged as a distinct cultural identity. It is possible the Akkadians had taken part in the great southern Mesopotamian urban revolution of the fourth millennium. The Akkadians adopted the idea of writing from their Sumerian neighbors during the Early Dynastic Period. We find the names of Akkadian scribes in archives unearthed near Nippur not long after 2600 BCE. According to the Sumerian King List the first dynasty of Kish also seems to have included Akkadian-named rulers, suggesting early contacts in northern Sumer. The Semitic city-state of Mari, associated later with the Amorites, seems to have been one of the earliest to use the Akkadian language. Akkadian peoples had a long history in Mesopotamia before the rise of Sargon.

Aspects of Akkadian Rule

There were five kings of Akkad on the Sumerian King List: Sargon, Rimush, Manishtusu, Naram-Sin, and Shar-kali-sharri. Sargon seems to have remained on the throne for 56 years, according to this same source, while his four heirs divided the remaining 86 years among them. A few brief inscriptions record the deeds of the kings of Akkad. Copies of these by scribes in the Old Babylonian Period have also been most informative. The size of the empire beyond its southern Mesopotamian core is a matter for speculation. Certainly, at one time it included the Elamites, whose rebellions were so frequent during the reigns of the kings following Sargon. As to the other Akkadian claims of having conquered the region from the mountains of the Iranian Plateau to Syria and Lebanon, there is growing archaeological evidence.

The Akkadians revered the moon god Sin and so the office of chief priestess to this deity was one of some importance. Sargon's daughter, Enheduanna, fulfilled this role, which became hereditary, and was passed on to the daughters of subsequent Akkadian kings. Thus did Sargon seek to marry major religious institutions to the crown, while also committing his devotion and resources to the other gods of the empire. This also demonstrates the Akkadian custom, from the beginning of the Empire, of using Akkadians and relatives of the king to fill major positions.

Sargon's Successors

Having ruled for more than one-third of the period that the Akkadian Empire itself lasted, Sargon died, leaving a fairly well-established, prosperous and, unfortunately, quite contentious kingdom in the hands of his less able successors. It has been assumed by some scholars that most

of the empire was not annexed territory but tributaries. The inscriptional evidence from the reign of Sargon's son, Rimush, tells us that battles were fought with the Sumerian city-states and the Elamites continuously. How strong Sargon's control over these areas had been is difficult to discern. The records of the later kings Manishtusu, Naram-Sin, and Shar-kali-sharri also contain numerous references to battles and, except for Naram-Sin, the most able of the descendants, all died in battle—or worse; they may have been assassinated. Babylonia seemed to have been the only secure part of the empire, and the Akkadian kings were forced to stage military campaigns outside this region to protect trade rights, preserve the frontier and enforce tribute and taxation requirements. With each new campaign, Akkad became increasingly depleted of resources and was forced into ever more rapacious campaigns to bolster imperial resources.

The only king of Akkad to enjoy a strong and relatively trouble-free rule was Sargon's grandson, Naram-Sin. According to inscriptions found at widely dispersed sites, he managed to maintain control over the upper Tigris, the upper Khabur river basin, the city of Susa in Elam, and most of the important cities of southern Mesopotamia. Naram-Sin was the first "king of the four quarters of the earth," according to his own reckoning, establishing this title for future rulers of Sumer and Babylon. He was also the first king to designate himself in inscriptions as a deity assuming the title of "god of Akkad." The people of Akkad seemed to accept this designation as evidenced by documents from Nippur indicating that they swore oaths in the name of Naram-Sin.

Akkadian Script

Under the Akkadian Empire, the Akkadian language became the administrative lingua franca

ABOVE **This cylinder seal (c. 2220 BCE) of Shar-kali-sharri,** the fifth king of Akkad, shows details of buffaloes and water gods. It is now in the Louvre.

LEFT **The king Naram-Sin** is shown triumphant over the mountain people in this fragment of the Victory Stele of Naram-Sin (*c.* 2250 BCE), now in the Louvre.

of the empire, with Sumerian restricted to literary usage. Sumerian cuneiform script was not entirely suitable for the expression of Akkadian, as it was not designed to transcribe the range of sounds found in Semitic languages. Akkadian scribes, however, were able to develop a form of cuneiform that could represent Sumerian and Akkadian with equal facility. Stationed at strategic locations outside the borders of Sumer and Akkad, Akkadian soldiers spread the Akkadian language and script far beyond the borders of Mesopotamia. Elam, for example, which had an indigenous script patterned after cuneiform writing, adopted Akkadian script during the Akkadian Period and used it to write the Elamite language. Old Akkadian script was considered so aesthetically pleasing that it was used as late as the Old Babylonian era for monumental inscriptions.

BELOW **This tablet is a copy for student use** of an inscription from a statue of Naram-Sin from the Temple of Enlil in Nippur, now in the Louvre.

The Akkadian Economy

Silver from the mines of Anatolia, lapis from Afghanistan, cedar wood from Lebanon, and copper from Oman were all commodities that the Akkadians valued. They traded extensively to procure them, even to the extent of going into battle to protect trade routes. The well-excavated Akkadian site of Tell Leilan provides useful information about both trade and the domestic economy of the empire. The domestic economy was built on the agriculture of northern and southern Mesopotamia and the work of its farmers. Taxes consisted of goods in kind and labor obligations, mainly on public building projects including fortifications, temples, canals, and royal buildings. Around the twenty-sixth century BCE, the flood levels had begun to fall and, by the Akkadian Period, were much lower than previously recorded, the water table of Mesopotamia was regularly replenished from rainfall and melting snows in the mountains.

Grain storage facilities were owned and operated by the king, and rations for the nonagricultural workforce of the cities were apportioned by this central authority. Competition for agricultural resources had been a major impetus for the rivalries between Mesopotamian city-states prior to the rise of the Akkadian Empire. The Akkadians recognized this and sought to ameliorate this problem through effective organization of agricultural production. First of all, wheat fields were guarded by fortresses to protect the wheat that belonged to crown and temple. Second, with the organization, storage and rationing systems of the Akkadians, and the continuing heavy rainfall in the Mesopotamian lowlands during the Akkadian Period, they were able to avert drought and famine for over a century. Third, the Akkadian practice of recruiting farmers to work during periods of severe food shortages, under the authority of the temples, was effective in staving off famine and disaster. This scheme not only brought both useful work to men who might otherwise have become contentious over food shortages, but also such intensified cropping was to have disastrous long-term consequences for Akkadian crop production.

Portents of the End of Empire

The highly organized agricultural system of the Akkadians was plagued with more than concerns about rainfall and flood levels. The nomadic Amorites, who brought their flocks to graze on field stubble, had to be included in the system as well. Traditionally, shepherds had paid for their use of agricultural lands for pasture by providing wool, meat, and dairy products to landowners, including the temple. Under the Akkadian Empire, this system was changed to one that required taxes in the form of produce to be paid to the king. Unfortunately, when winter pasture was in short supply, the nomads would take their flocks to fields under cultivation where they would engage in conflicts with farmers. However, once the Akkadians had united northern and southern Mesopotamia and could transport wheat between the north and south, this was no longer a problem. However, it could only work as long as enough wheat was produced to supply the entire Akkadian domain.

Under the highly effective Akkadian organization of Mesopotamia's agricultural base, the empire became one of the most prosperous Mesopotamia had ever known. The balance achieved by the Akkadians in both the economic and political spheres, however, was a precarious one. Separatist tendencies in the conquered lands, along with developing tensions between farmers and herders, and even some concerns about Akkadian religious practices, which were generally tolerant, meant the empire was assaulted on political, economic, and cultural levels. Thus, while Akkad broadened Mesopotamian horizons by providing a model of a successful unified imperial control, its control was always conditional on good economic management. The power and ideology of the Akkadian Empire has always fascinated historians, particularly because the material remains of the empire—its sculpture, literature and libraries of documents—are so different from what came before and yet they serve to highlight the real achievements of the previous age. Although its short period of control seems insignificant in terms of the impressive span of Mesopotamian development, the Akkadian Empire operated as a vital transition between the chaos of warring city-states and the later regional kingdoms of Babylonia and Assyria.

CARTOGRAPHY AND ASTRONOMY

Akkad was an empire that was bound together by roads and connected through an established communications network. It also undertook the first-ever survey documenting the ownership of land. Astronomy and astrology, which became so important to the later Babylonians, developed during this period. Apparently, the standard work on the stars, used by the Babylonians, was based upon an older text that was dated to the Akkadian Period. The Akkadians also focussed on establishing a calendar. Naram-Sin established a regnal calendar, as attested by documents found in Girsu which contain statements such as "in the year in which Naram-Sin laid the foundations of the Enlil temple at Nippur and of the Inanna temple at Zabalam." The Babylonian Calendar, in which years were named in accordance with significant royal events, developed from the Akkadian Period.

ABOVE **Stone mace heads such as this one** were dedicated to the gods. This example, from Sippar (*c.* 2200 BCE), is inscribed from Shari-kali-sharri to Shamash the sun god.

LEFT **Sheep played an important role** in the Akkadian economy. This stele fragment (*c.* third millennium BCE) from Akkad is now in the Louvre.

The Akkadian Collapse

The abrupt collapse of the Akkadian Empire is a mystery. Scholars have posited various disaster-related scenarios to justify and explain the implosion and disintegration of this short-lived but powerful empire.

The Akkadian Empire extended from Mesopotamia to the Persian Gulf in the east and as far as Cilicia in Turkey in the west. During the late third millennium BCE the Empire of Akkad suddenly collapsed, after a period of only 150 years. Naram-Sin had been an able ruler, but his son came to the throne as the Gutians, a constant threat throughout the Akkadian Period, redoubled their efforts to overthrow Sargon's dynasty. Previous explanations have focussed on the lack of internal organization in the empire.

Various more specific causes have been cited, including the fractiousness of the Sumerian city-states that formed the economic, cultural, and political core of Akkad, the kingdom's wealth having been drained by constant military campaigns and the extensive resources required for the creation of a new capital city. Archaeologists have found these explanations logical but unconvincing. All the administrative problems that plagued Sargon and his descendants could have been mitigated by effective leadership. Such leadership seems to have been demonstrated not only by Sargon but by his grandson, Naram-Sin. So the reason for the sudden collapse of this powerful empire continues to interest researchers.

The Climate Hypothesis

Scholars have recently suggested that the Akkadian Empire suffered the same fate as the Egyptian Old Kingdom—namely, rapidly increasing aridity and failing rainfall throughout the ancient Near East, caused by a severe regional drought. Few details on Mesopotamian climates in this period can be gleaned from historical records, so investigators must depend on the analysis of sediments which are preserved in the ocean basins that lie close to the region.

Changes in the aridity of the region can be detected through mineralogical and geochemical analyses of a marine sediment core taken from the Gulf of Oman. This location is chosen because it lies in the path of winds that would carry dust from Mesopotamia in the event that arid conditions prevailed there. By comparing this analysis with that carried out of samples from strata dating to the Akkadian Period at key archaeological sites in the region, a direct contemporary association can be detected, strongly suggesting that a sudden shift to more arid conditions may indeed have been one of the major factors that contributed to the abrupt collapse of the Akkadian Empire.

BELOW **The ancient ziggurat at Assur** on the western bank of the Tigris was originally part of the Temple of Enlil, which may have been sacked by Naram-Sin.

LEFT **A curse upon Akkad is inscribed in cuneiform on this clay tablet.** The gods cursed Akkad when Naram-Sin destroyed the Temple of Enlil at Nippur.

The Evidence from Tell Leilan

Tell Leilan in northern Mesopotamia has provided the best comparative data to support the climate change hypothesis. This site was abandoned very soon after the city's walls were constructed, its temple rebuilt, and its grain production reorganized by the Akkadians. After this period of great activity, there is little or no trace of human activity. Soil samples taken from strata at the site reveal wind-blown sand, no trace of earthworm activity and indications of a drier, windier climate. The remains of sheep and cattle found at the site show extreme water deprivation, and it appears that thousands of people later abandoned the site to look for more fertile, rain-fed areas elsewhere.

The nomadic Gutians and the Amorites were able to move their herds closer to reliable water sources because of their age-old knowledge of pastoral routes in the region. In doing so, however, they would most likely have come into competition for scarce resources with farmers. As both settled farmers and nomads began to engage in increasing conflicts, political instability soon followed. The demise of rain-fed agriculture in the northern Tigris and Euphrates valleys was a loss to southern Mesopotamia also in terms of the agrarian subsidies that the Akkadian Empire had come to depend upon. Water levels in the Tigris–Euphrates began to drop from around 2300 BCE, reducing the land area that could be irrigated, and aggravating the already hostile relationship between herders and farmers.

The Religious Reason for the Fall

Ancient sources have blamed the fall of Akkad upon Sargon's grandson Naram-Sin and his attack on the sacred city of Nippur, where he reportedly sacked the Temple of Enlil. As a result, Akkad was cursed by the gods, and "...The great agricultural tracts produced no grain. The irrigated orchards produced neither syrup nor wine. The gathered clouds did not rain...People were flailing at themselves from hunger." In the context of recent theories concerning climate change, this explanation does not seem that far off the mark.

EARLY SEMITIC CIVILIZATIONS AND PIGS

In addition to bringing about the end of an empire, the desiccation of the ancient Near East has been suggested as the reason behind the religious proscription against eating pigs that seems to have spread throughout the Near East in the third millennium BCE. Of all the domesticated animals in the region, pigs alone require water not just for drinking but for cooling their skin, which lacks sweat glands. It was possible to find enough water during drought to sustain herds of sheep and goats, and even cattle and donkeys, but pigs would have been another matter entirely. In addition, water is the most important part of a pig's diet.

ABOVE **These young *Sus scrofa* (wild boar)** are the same breed as the animals that the Akkadians and Sumerians domesticated.

The Third Dynasty of Ur

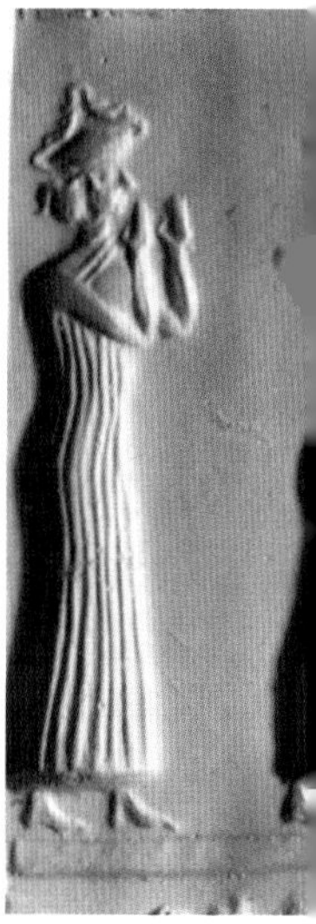

Sargon may have unified Mesopotamia, but the first (and only) Sumerian empire embodied the sophistication and urbanity of Sumerian civilization. This was the Third Dynasty of Ur, the "Sumerian Renaissance."

Coming after the domination of the Gutians, a mountain people about whom we know very little, the city states of Sumeria were looking for stability and security from foreign incursions. By all accounts, they found it in the venerable city of Uruk, where the governor raised an army to defeat the Gutians. It was a man of Ur, however, who successfully laid claim to the other cities of "Sumer and Akkad." With a combination of Sumerian wisdom and Akkadian strategic ability, Ur-Nammu came to rule as a state-builder and reformer. He also became renowned for establishing the first law code known to the world, of which only fragments have survived.

The Rise of Ur-Nammu

The dynasty created by Ur-Nammu has been debated by many scholars who question whether the Third Dynasty of Ur hegemony should be seen as an extended form of traditional Sumerian city-state rule, or a genuinely imperial administration on the Akkadian model. In any event, Ur III, as it has come to be called, came to control most of the territory formerly under Akkadian and Gutian rule, including city-states further from the center, such as Ebla, Eshnunna, and the Jeziran lands between the two city-states. Theories about how Ur-Nammu came to power are numerous. The traditional version suggests that Ur-Nammu was a military leader who supplanted the king of Uruk, who had driven the Gutians from power. According to the Sumerian King List, the king of Uruk reigned for seven years.

More recent theories begin with the proposition that the king of Uruk ruled with Ur-Nammu as his governor. Two stelae discovered in Ur include this detail in an inscription about Ur-Nammu's life. Accordingly, some scholars add to the traditional scenario the idea that Ur-Nammu led a revolt against the king of Uruk and deposed him. Still another view is that Ur-Nammu was a close relative of the king, who had asked him to rule over the city of Ur. After four years as the governor of Ur, Ur-Nammu defeated the ruler of Lagash in battle and killed the king, after which he became the "king of Sumer and Akkad."

BELOW **Ur-Nammu,** the founder of the Ur III empire, makes an offering to the seated moon god Nannar. This relief (c. 2100 BCE) is from the Stele of Ur.

Ur-Nammu Creates a Dynasty

It remains to be explained whether Ur-Nammu rose to power as a result of a hostile takeover or by the official sanction of an overlord. From the earliest Sumerian historical periods Ur and Uruk had a close relationship. Also, the defeat and denigration of rival city-state rulers was an age-old tradition. In Mesopotamia, as rulers came to control areas outside their home states, they tended to disparage defeated rivals, a practice that obscures any previous amicable relationships that might have existed between them. What does seem clear is that, by around 2100 BCE, the Third

LEFT **In this Babylonian cylinder seal impression** (*c.* 2050 BCE), a bare-headed worshipper is led by a goddess toward a seated male figure (possibly Ur-Nammu). In the inscription Ur-Nammu is described as "mighty hero, king of Ur."

Dynasty of Ur had reasserted both the authority of the south, and the culture of Sumer in Mesopotamia, as Ur-Nammu controlled the key city-states of Uruk and Lagash, as well as Ur itself. The king of Ur thus became the king of all of Sumer, and later much of Syria and Elam. The conquered territories either supported Ur with tribute or became integrated territories within the empire and supported it with taxes. Ur III can be divided into two distinct geographical and political units: one being the core of the empire under the rule of the king and the will of the state; and the other being dependencies or tributaries under independent rule but economic control by Ur. The cities of Ebla and Byblos paid tribute, as did Mari and Carchemish, either because they were controlled outright, or were threatened with conquest if they did not comply.

Shulgi—Successor to Ur-Nammu

Ur-Nammu died (perhaps in battle, as the Gutians continued to resist), and he was succeeded by Shulgi, his capable son. Shulgi continued his father's work and proceeded to make the kingdom prosperous and, in so doing, added some territory of his own to it. In fact, since Shulgi reigned for 48 years to his father's 17 years, some scholars have suggested that it was Shulgi, and not Ur-Nammu, who was responsible for the code of laws of Ur. Shulgi also completed a number of his father's building projects and reorganized the administration of the empire. During his reign the city-state rulers became provincial governors without military power, and local garrisons were installed in particularly unruly places. He had some difficulties with the land that would become

HISTORICAL RECORDS FOR UR-NAMMU

There are relatively few historical records from the Ur III Period, although there are many literary and economic documents, so the evidence for Ur-Nammu's rule is as fragmentary as his code of laws. It appears that he conquered most of the Mesopotamian city-states within a short period, after which he was able to devote most of his reign to governing. Among the important public issues to which he devoted his attention were: regulating weights and measures; forbidding the exploitation of widows and orphans; and reconstructing important temples, including the monumental ziggurat and sacred precinct at Ur. He established his dynasty by publicizing the divine sanction for his rule. His successors, Shulgi and Amar-Sin, came to be accorded, through heredity, the same divinity as their father. All three of these kings were buried side by side in the royal mausoleum at Ur.

ABOVE **This cuneiform script is a hymn to Ur-Nammu.** It lauds him as perfect, protective, charitable, fair, and guarantor of fertile lands. Ur-Nammu expanded his kingdom until he was not only king of Sumer, Akkad, and Elam, but of much of inland Syria as well.

AMORITES AND PASTORALISTS

"He is a tent-dweller. He makes no offerings, digs up truffles in the highlands, does not cultivate, eats uncooked meat and is not buried when he dies." A poem written during the Ur III period characterizes the Amorites and their pastoralist cousins. The end of the third millennium BCE seems to have been a time of population movements. Climatic changes have been cited as one of the primary reasons for the decline of the Akkadian Empire, but less than two centuries later widespread famine and drought are again being posited as one of the reasons for the decline of Ur III. It is conceivable that the canal systems, so vital to the beginning of civilization in the region, were also responsible for its decline. Salt build-up on canal-irrigated lands was a major problem for the Akkadians and remained one for the Kingdom of Ur. The nomads who plagued the Ur kings, however, were themselves in the process of settling into towns and cities and becoming farmers. This process may have been completed as early as 1800 BCE when Amorites took over the city of Babylon.

Assyria, engaging in almost annual campaigns in the north during the latter part of his reign. Before his demise, he succeeded in subduing the Hurrian, Subartian, and Assyrian populations of northern Mesopotamia. He also led numerous campaigns against the Amorites in Syria.

Ur's major antagonists, the Gutians, were still present on the outskirts of the empire and causing disruption with their constant incursions into the fertile lowlands. Shulgi's strategy to pacify anarchic Elam was to marry off his daughters to the kings of Warshe and Anshan. Later, he invaded and occupied Susa, where he installed a Sumerian governor. The Elamites rebelled, and Shulgi had to suppress a revolt in Anshan where he began instituting the practice of developing a foreign army of mercenaries to control the outlying territories. Though his queen was of Semitic origin, Shulgi viewed himself as the embodiment of all things Sumerian. His achievements included: the centralization of imperial control; the standardization of procedures and tax collection; the development of a state archive; a state army; and a national calendar. Shulgi was deified during his lifetime rather than after his death, reflecting his popularity and status among the people.

RIGHT **The name of King Shulgi** is inscribed on this diorite weight (c. 2050 BCE), now in the Louvre, France.

Shulgi's Successors

Shulgi's son Amar-Sin is known to us for his many wars against the Amorites. He was also forced to deal with the increasingly powerful Hurrians as he divided his time between building projects in the cities and war in the provinces. He may well have lost effective control over much of Syria and Elam, but was nonetheless deified during his lifetime, died of natural causes at Ur, and was succeeded by his brother after little more than a decade in power. That brother, Shu-Sin, continued Amar-Sin's battles against the Amorites, gradually being forced back into the Mesopotamian heartlands, where he constructed a wall between the two rivers to attempt to hold back the Amorite menace. He was able to annex territory in the Zagros Mountains of what is present-day Iran and to establish valuable trade relations with the Indus Valley. After only about a decade of rule, Shu-Sin died and was succeeded by a son who was to be the last of the Kings of Ur III.

Ibbi-Sin inherited ongoing troubles with Elam and the Amorites, and, in reaction, erected even more walls surrounding Ur and the city of Nippur. He was a weak king from the outset, beset by enemies on all sides, and his dwindling

LEFT **This Sumerian-language tablet,** now in the British Museum, is written in cuneiform. From the reign of Amar-Sin (*c.* 2020 BCE), it lists the barley yields of 11 specific fields.

empire began to disappear almost as soon as he gained the throne. For most of his fairly substantial reign (over 20 years by some accounts), Ibbi-Sin was confined to the city of Ur, unable to visit other territories due to the threats all around. He lost both Eshnunna and Elam in the same year. The provincial governors of most of the cities of Sumer deserted him because he offered them scant protection against the Amorites. The loyal servant he placed over the city-states of Nippur and Isin rebelled against him and detached Ur III territories in eastern Sumer, and across coastal Elam, installing his own rulers in place of Ibbi-Sin's governors. The end of his reign was marked by severe widespread famine and drought and recurring trouble from his enemies. Ibbi-Sin was finally deposed and taken as a prisoner to Elam, where he died.

The Legacy of Ur III

As is often the case with empires, it is not military success that defines the legacy of Ur III but its innovations in cultural and economic spheres. Ur III's mercantile economy was not only a means whereby the empire could obtain much-needed resources from outside its own lands, account for its trade and surpluses, and enable an established system of tribute and taxation. It was also a means of social mobility for those who wished to escape a rural life for the perhaps dubious advantages of city living. Immense numbers of texts from this period testify to its burgeoning economic growth, even during periods of protracted warfare. Ur III encouraged the mass production of other texts, such as copies of Sumerian literary works. Sumerian dominated the literary scene, while Akkadian was the official language of empire and administration. Indeed, this may have been the first period in which the great Sumerian epic poems were written down and preserved for future generations.

BELOW **Terracotta statues from Ur** (*c.* 2100–2000 BCE) represent the king (middle) flanked by two priests. These were the higher echelons of Ur III society.

Ziggurats

Ziggurat at Aqar-quf

This ziggurat was built by the Babylonian king Kurigalzu *c.* 1300 BCE. The walls of this ziggurat are 190 ft (58 m) high. The ziggurat design is popular in modern architecture round the world, especially for public buildings.

Ziggurat of Nanna

This aerial photograph shows clearly the three access ramps from ground level. Much of this structure was rebuilt (crudely) by Saddam Hussein, often using inappropriate materials.

The ziggurat is one of the earliest monumental religious structures known to humanity. It is also one of the longest lasting temple designs in Near Eastern history, dating back at least to the fourth millennium BCE and still in use in the sixth century BCE. The earliest remains of a ziggurat are at the site of Tepe Sialk in Iran. It was probably built by protoElamites who founded the city of Susa as early as the fifth millennium BCE. Later, the Sumerians, Babylonians, and Assyrians all built ziggurat temples to their gods.

The temple to Enki at Eridu offers the best example of the evolution of the ziggurat. The god Enki resided in the mythical subterranean freshwater ocean (*abzu*), the source of all the waters of the earth. Enki is the god of destiny and also the god who saved humans from the great flood in the Sumerian epics. The Temple of Enki, one of the first built by Sumerians, was an important shrine for southern Mesopotamia and accounts for the continued importance of Eridu long after it ceased to be an influential city-state. Of the 17 to 18 different structures that were built on the temple site, the earliest was quite modest in size, only about 33 sq ft (3 sq m), built in the early Ubaid Period. The building on top of this one had a niche and a platform in the middle of the room, which had traces of burning on it, probably because it functioned as an altar for burnt offerings.

The different phases of this temple proceeded during the Ubaid Period. Two of the subsequent phases are fragmentary and not well known, but the last phases of this temple in the Ubaid Period have the standard features of all later Mesopotamian temples, that is, they are simple ziggurats. These temples are in fact so different in terms of design from what went before that the excavators initially posited that they were built by a different culture. The last stages of building of the Eridu temple were in the Uruk Period and consistently follow the nascent ziggurat pattern. This indicates that this design template, which was used for all future religious buildings in Mesopotamia, had already become the standard temple design.

The succession of "steps" that characterizes the ziggurats probably reached its full manifestation near the end of the Early Dynastic Period or Early Bronze Age following the Uruk Period. By this time, the platforms might be rectangular, oval, or square in shape. The ziggurat was basically a pyramidal structure—in fact, the early Third Dynasty (*c.* 2700 BCE) pharaoh Zoser had built a seven-tier stepped pyramid at Saqqara in Lower Egypt. The building was usually made of mud brick at the core, with fired bricks on the outside. These brick façades were often glazed with different colors and arranged in designs that may have had some astrological significance. The completed form comprised two to seven tiers, with the actual shrine at the top. Access was via a series of ramps on one side of the ziggurat or a spiral ramp from the base to the summit.

Food for the Gods

The large temple dedicated to the god Nanna was built *c.* 2100 BCE by King Ur-Nammu. Sacrificial food for the gods may have been cooked on an altar at the top.

Clever, Clean Design

Special vents were built into the structure to direct the smoke from the altars away from the city. Drainage holes were also included to allow rainwater to drain away.

Sacred and Exclusive Living

Ziggurats in Mesopotamia were not meant to be places of public ritual, but rather dwellings for the gods. The succession of platforms expressed the metaphorical distance between the realm of humans and that of the gods who were believed to have a permanent home in the sky. Only priests and rulers could visit the topmost shrine and only they knew of the rooms in the base of the structure because they had the primary responsibility to care for the gods. This exclusivity conferred great authority upon the priests, and they became very influential in Mesopotamian society.

The Ur III Hegemony

After the fall of the Akkadian Empire, the kings of the Ur III dynasty developed a sophisticated form of governance. Land controlled by each city-state was split into provinces, each of which was run by a civilian governor.

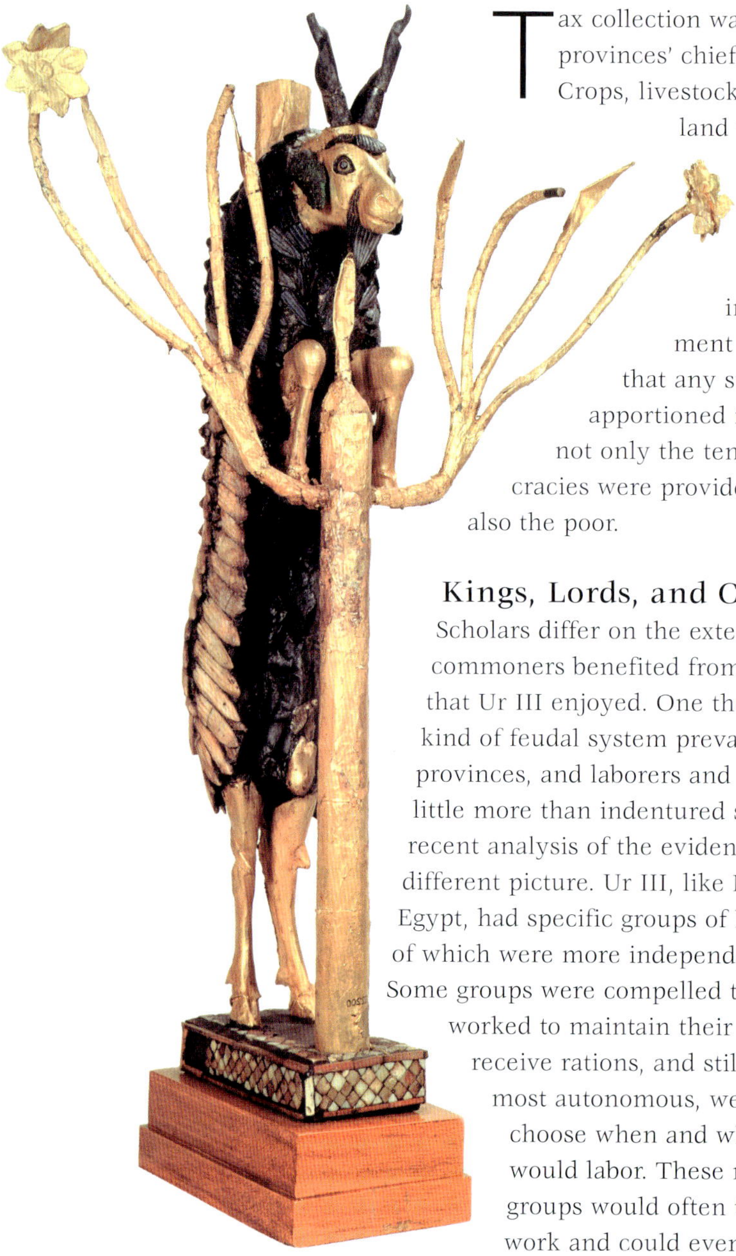

ABOVE **Sheep and goats** provided milk, wool, and meat, and were highly prized. This statue in gold, lapis, and wood is from the Royal Cemetery in Ur (*c.* 2500 BCE).

Tax collection was one of the provinces' chief responsibilities. Crops, livestock, labor, and land were all subject to taxation under Ur III. In addition, the local and imperial government would ensure that any surpluses were apportioned fairly, and that not only the temple bureaucracies were provided for, but also the poor.

Kings, Lords, and Commoners

Scholars differ on the extent to which commoners benefited from the prosperity that Ur III enjoyed. One theory was that a kind of feudal system prevailed in the provinces, and laborers and peasants were little more than indentured servants. More recent analysis of the evidence presents a different picture. Ur III, like New Kingdom Egypt, had specific groups of laborers, some of which were more independent than others. Some groups were compelled to work, others worked to maintain their property and receive rations, and still others, the most autonomous, were free to choose when and where they would labor. These more mobile groups would often travel to find work and could eventually acquire property and rise to higher positions.

Slavery was not a hereditary condition in the Near East. Most of the slaves were debtors, or had been sold by their family or were prisoners taken in conflicts. Near Eastern slaves were allowed to acquire assets and buy their freedom. Many documents attest to the fact that slaves frequently did this and negotiated their own terms with their former owners. Unsurprisingly, those laborers who were forced to work were the most reliable insofar as the provision of labor for state projects was concerned. The Ur III kings instituted many of these projects in addition to maintaining the complex and vital irrigation systems that were characteristic of all Mesopotamian civilizations. Further, they built storage facilities to support their attempt to centralize agricultural production. As the state began to control all aspects of agriculture, from sowing through harvesting to storing, the percentage of the labor force that worked on agriculture grew to be very substantial.

The Economy of Ur III

Thousands of documents have been recovered from the sites of this period, and a large proportion of these deal with economic matters.

Most of these, however, have not been analyzed according to any particular system that might give us a complete picture of the economy of Ur III. The majority are contracts relating to loans, leases of temple lands, slave purchases, and other similar subjects. Part of the problem in evaluating these and similar texts is in distinguishing between state-sanctioned contracts and privately instigated ones. The latter would include activities of individuals within the society who were independent and propertied enough to manage their own affairs. For these people both income and expenditures would be unrelated to either the temple or the palace, that is, the households of the kings and the governors.

Of the texts from Ur III that have been published, those found at Puzrish-Dagan (modern Drehem) are considered by many scholars to be invaluable for reconstructing the internal commerce. Puzrish-Dagan was a large redistribution and administrative center near Nippur that supplied the temples with sacrificial animals and was also a site for the manufacture of wool and leather. The documents recovered from this and other sites relate almost entirely to the "public" economy, which has caused many scholars to over-emphasize this sector, but they are not representative as they were found in indisputably public contexts. Texts recovered from nonpublic contexts, though few in number, cover more varied transactions.

THE WORLD'S EARLIEST BUREAUCRACY

The Third Dynasty of Ur was probably responsible for creating one of the world's first true bureaucracies. To govern the far-flung and unruly city-states of Mesopotamia, the monarchy established institutions to insure the use of official channels, the administration of people and property, and detailed accounting methods. These organizations communicated with each other through official messengers, something of an Ur III innovation. Local problems, specifically legal issues, were resolved locally whenever possible, although there was a system of appeals to higher authorities—stopping at the level of the provincial governor. There were public "civil trials," sometimes in the town square or in front of the temple, but these were rare occasions. The king and, by extension, his appointed officials were essentially the arbiters of disagreements both public and private.

ABOVE **The governor of Nippur is depicted in this cylinder seal** (*c.* 2500 BCE). Although seals often functioned as "official" documents, they also became more decorative and detailed.

Kings of Sumer and Akkad

The period of Ur III is referred to as the "Sumerian Renaissance." By this time, however, Akkadian had made such inroads into the official culture of Mesopotamia that it was used in public administration. Sumerian retained its value as the language of literature, and every educated Ur resident was required to study it, but Akkadian was the common spoken language of the empire. Consequently, the names of the members of the royal family were Akkadian, and virtually all new towns that were built during this period were given Akkadian names.

LEFT **Accounts of various agricultural activities are detailed on this tablet from Umma (Ur III Dynasty).** As more people began to move into the larger settlements and the city-state grew, commercial transactions developed. A method of recording these transactions was needed.

Decline of Ur III

Climate change, salinization, incursions, and urban restlessness have all been blamed for the end of Ur III. If these factors were all in play throughout the Ur III hegemony, why did such a troubled society endure for over 100 years?

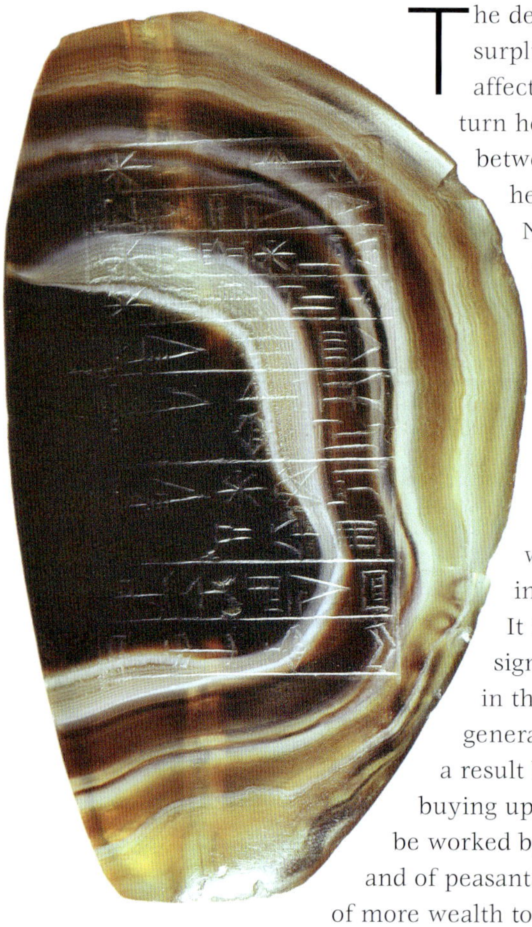

ABOVE **A dedication from Ibbi-Sin to the moon god Nanna** can be read on this polished agate from Sumer (*c.* 2000 BCE).

The declining agricultural surplus would have a profound affect on the cities, which in turn heightened competition between farmers and nomadic herders for water and land. Nomads are subject to their own political, social, and economic cycles influencing a more sedentary lifestyle during some periods, while instigating more mobility in others.

Climate change also would have an adverse impact on food production. It is unclear if this was more significant than the decline in the number of farmers in general during this period, as a result both of affluent people buying up large parcels of land to be worked by indentured laborers and of peasants attracted to the promise of more wealth to be gained through commerce in the cities. The combination of Amorites in the west and Elamites in the east created political and economic pressures on the Ur III state that lasted throughout the period. Given all of this, the real question about Ur III should not be why did it fail, but rather, how did it manage to become successful in the first place?

The Last King

Ibbi-Sin, the last of the Ur III dynasty, is scarcely credited with any administrative ability at all, but he was forced to deal simultaneously with a disintegrating urban center and a frontier population of unreconciled and warlike tribes. His empire was repeatedly attacked, and polities on its borders began to assert their independence very soon after he came to the throne. Whatever leadership abilities he might have had, they were not equal to this. He attempted to build fortifications to protect his main cities, but such walls tended to promote separatism, rather than preserving central authority. Ibbi-Sin's biggest problem, the Amorites, were not as primitive as the Sumerians supposed them to be, but the fact that they were able to cause such problems for their urban neighbors is something of a mystery. It is possible the Amorites recognized the weaknesses of Ur III and were able to exploit all the other factors affecting the decline in the fortunes of the dynasty.

Decline and Fall

We know about the last days of Ur III in more detail than many other events in Mesopotamian history because of the phenomenal record keeping of the empire. Royal correspondence, poetry, and an archive from the city of Isin tell the story of Ibbi-Sin's downfall. Ishbi-Erra, who was installed as governor of Isin by Ibbi-Sin, was a chief instigator of the king's demise. While Ibbi-Sin was away battling the Elamites, Ishbi-Erra, a man of Mari, managed to persuade him to entrust the neighboring cities of Ur to his care so that he could maintain their defenses against the

THE EVIDENCE FOR AGRICULTURAL DECLINE

The process of desertification that began during the Akkadian Empire seems to have continued during the Ur III period, and analysis of sediments from the Persian Gulf demonstrates that the rivers remained low for long periods of time. The ecological balance was so precarious that the damage of enemy raids or even mismanagement of the irrigation system would cause serious food shortages. Records tell us that during Ibbi-Sin's reign the price of grain increased exponentially. Clearly, the Amorites were responsible for some of this, at least insofar as their attacks on agricultural and irrigation systems are concerned. Their action paved the way for the more organized and powerful Elamites to invade Ur and capture its king.

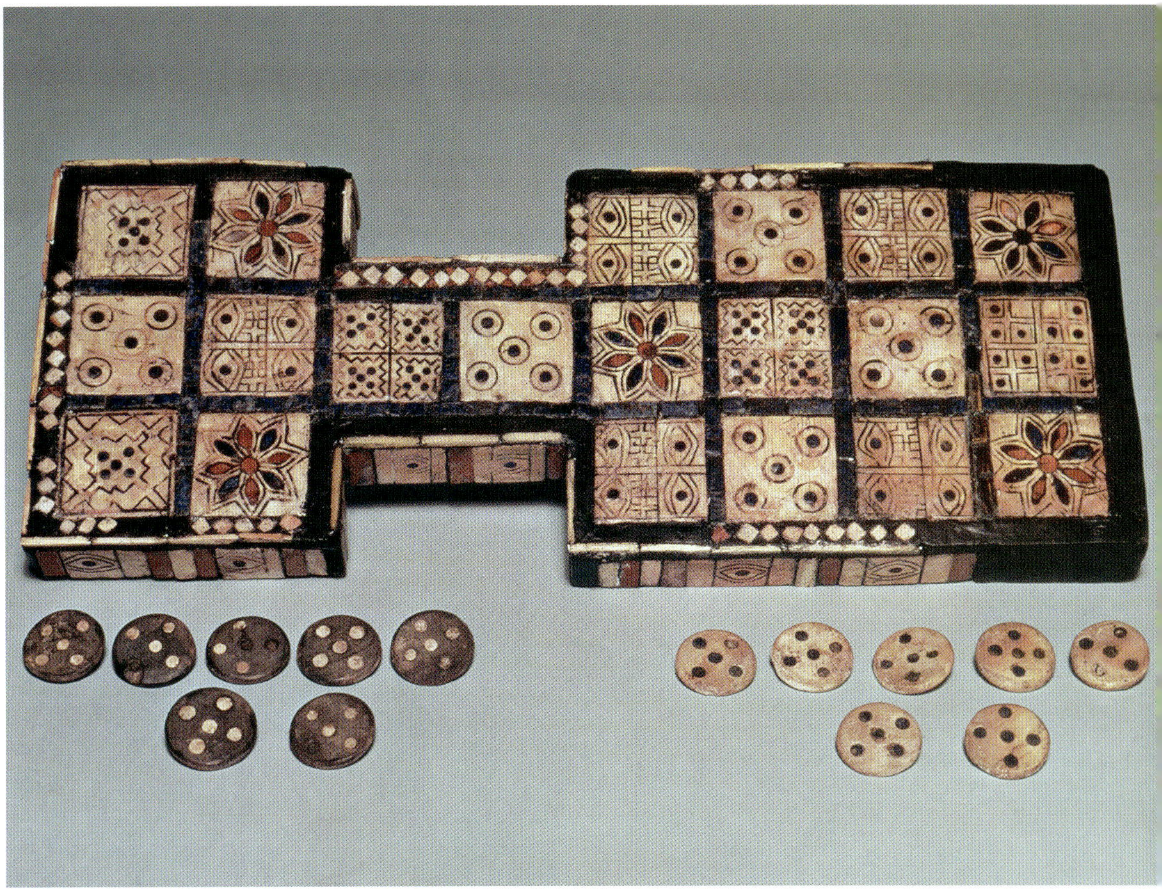

Amorites. Ibbi-Sin agreed to this, and so the cities of Isin and Nippur were given over to his command. Ishbi-Erra was apparently a smooth negotiator and a skilled communicator as his correspondence with the king clearly reveals.

After Ishbi-Erra refortified Isin, he started to assume royal privileges. He began to use his own dating methods on official documents in accordance with the date upon which he assumed his "reign." He calls himself a favorite of the god Enlil, probably to contrast his status to that of Ibbi-Sin who seems to have been perilously close to severe depression at that time. Ibbi-Sin complained constantly that Enlil hated him. Portents and omens based upon the examination of sacrificial animals confirmed this, making the king all the more despondent. Ishbi-Erra's conviction as to his "favored" status strengthened during his rule of Nippur, and in the end he proclaimed himself to be ruler over all of southern Mesopotamia, including Ur.

The End

Ibbi-Sin did not disappear from the scene, much as his former servant might have wished it. He continued to rule for 14 years after Ishbi-Erra's rebellion. The final blow was a famine that depleted the population of his city. Elegiac poetry poignantly records the end of Ur in a manner that would later be mirrored by the Book of Lamentations in the Bible. The Ur III civilization had witnesssed the apogee of Sumerian culture. The decline of Ur III is a significant dividing line between the urbanization of the Early Bronze Age and the beginning of the "age of internationalism" that developed in the Middle Bronze Age. The empire had contributed to this shift by opening up new markets all around the Mediterranean and exposing the populations of regions peripheral to Mesopotamia to Sumerian culture. It was left to the Semitic populations of Mesopotamia to take full advantage of this in the time periods to follow.

ABOVE **This games board from the Royal Tombs of Ur** (*c.* 2500 BCE), which were discovered by Leonard Woolley, is now in the British Museum.

LEFT **This Sumerian hymn (now in the Louvre, France)** is a lamentation on the ruins of Ur (*c.* 2000 BCE). The fall of Ur III provoked an outpouring of epic poetry and religious writing.

Precious Metals and Jewelry

Jewelry for the Gods
This representation of the god Ningirsu as a lion-headed eagle is made of gold and lapis lazuli (*c.* 2500 BCE). The lapis may have come from Afghanistan.

Gold and silver had to be imported into Mesopotamia, but this did not seem to have affected either the antiquity of precious metalworking there or the level of skill attained. We are still not sure where these ores came from. Sumerians became expert at this craft so quickly in the fourth millennium BCE that it has been suggested that outside influences may have inspired this innovation (the raw materials for some of the earliest artifacts have been traced to the Iranian Plateau). There are deposits of precious metals in the eastern Turkish mountains, however, and this may have been their principal source. It is also possible that the raw materials were acquired through trade with Arabia, Elam, the Oxus, Altai and Taurus Mountains, and the Indus Valley. Indus Harappa and Mohenjo-Daro used gold from the Indus River. Early gold artifacts from the Levant (Nahal Qanah) and from northern Syria (Tell Judeidah) suggest that gold found its way all over the Near East, beginning as early as the fifth millennium BCE.

The preferred jewelry designs used in Mesopotamia were natural and geometric motifs such as leaves, cones, spirals, and bunches of grapes. Sumerian and Akkadian jewelry was created from gold and silver leaf and set with many semiprecious stones (mostly agate, carnelian, jasper, lapis lazuli, and chalcedony). A number of documents have been found that relate to the trade and production of jewelry from Sumerian sites.

Later Mesopotamian jewelers and craftsmen employed metalworking techniques such as cloisonné, engraving, granulation, and filigree. The large variety and size of necklaces, bracelets, anklets, pendants, and pins found may be due to the fact that jewelry was worn by both men and women, and perhaps even children. Created both for human use and for adorning the statues of the gods, jewelry also functioned as a rare offering and, when worn, a symbol of devotion to a particular god and protection from the evil

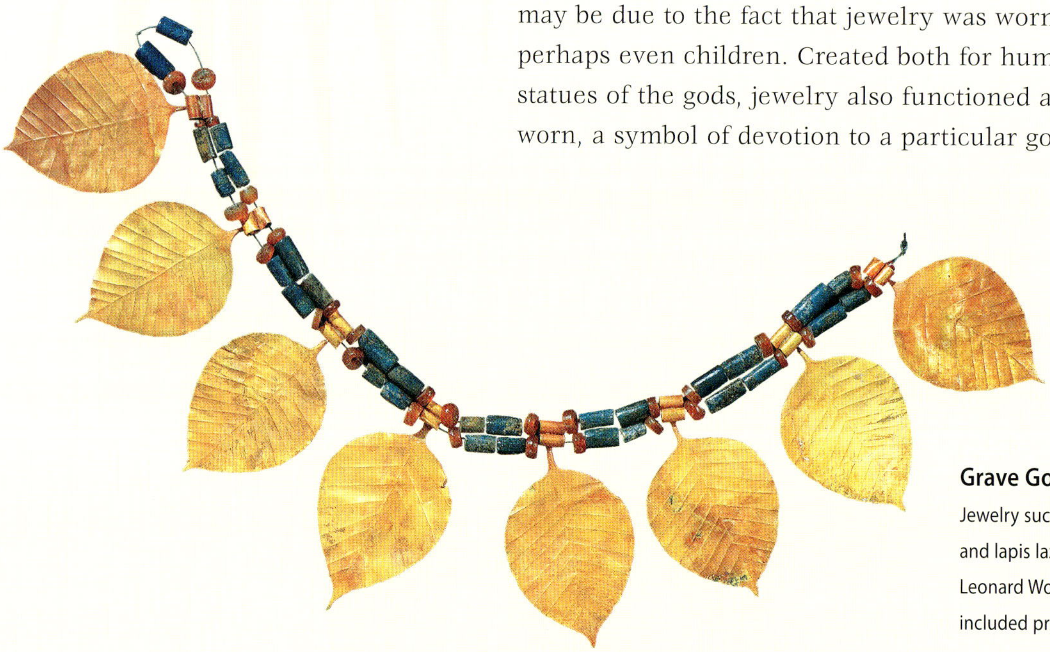

Grave Goods
Jewelry such as this necklace (*c.* 2500 BCE) made of gold and lapis lazuli was found in the Royal Tombs of Ur. Leonard Woolley excavated 16 royal tombs. Grave goods included precious metals, foodstuffs, carts, and even oxen.

A Great Honor to Die?

The women attendants buried with Queen Pu'abi were found wearing intricately made headdresses, necklaces, and other jewelry such as these (*c.* 2450 BCE).

eye. Lapis lazuli, for example, conferred the protection of the sky god, Anu, upon the wearer.

Some of the most famous jewelry in the world was recovered from Ur by Leonard Woolley who excavated the royal tombs there in the 1920s. In particular, the burial of Queen Pu'abi provides a plethora of fine examples of Sumerian craftsmanship and design. Three lapis and gold pins, three fish-shaped amulets in gold and lapis lazuli, and a gold amulet with beautifully modeled gazelle figures were found on her arms. On her head were three gold diadems, each graduated in size and held together by a gold band. The diadems each had individual designs, including interlocking rings, and poplar and willow leaves. Flowers of gold on dangling stems with blue and white decoration topped the diadem. A comb decorated with golden flowers was placed in the Queen's hair, and large gold circular earrings were placed on her ears. Her necklace had three rows of semiprecious stone beads clasped in the middle with a filigree golden flower. She wore many rings on her fingers, and her elaborately dressed retainers were decked out in pectorals, and wrist and arm bracelets. Although the royal burial must have been a stunning spectacle, it is hard to understand the apparent willing suicide of such large numbers of attendants. There is no evidence of violence, and some suggestion that a small draft of poison was given to each retainer in a shallow bowl.Whether this mass suicide was willingly undertaken to guarantee a happy afterlife, or the grim demonstration of the ruler's absolute power, we cannot tell.

A Short History of Mesopotamian Metallurgy

At first, copper metallurgy in Mesopotamia was limited to the production of small items, such as beads and hooks. By the end of the Uruk Period, however, the closed mold and lost wax methods had been introduced, making it possible to produce metal items, such as pectorals and vessels, in a range of complex forms including human, animal, and plant shapes. Sumerians became master silver- and goldsmiths by the third millennium BCE, creating works of art using different processes. The gold helmet of King Meskallam-dag (above, *c.* 2650–2550 BCE, now in the Iraq Museum) is a supreme example of the style and workmanship.

Power Struggles: Kingdoms at War

Introduction

After the collapse of the multinational Ur III dynastic polity, the Middle East at the outset of the second millennium BCE contained numerous rival states that fought for political control.

Many of the Syrian centers abandoned in the Early Bronze Age (late third millennium BCE) were reoccupied around the Middle Bronze Age (*c.* 2000–1550 BCE)—although how this came about is not clear. Rulers with Amorite names began to appear in Syria and Iraq, and dominated a number of states from Uruk and Larsa in Mesopotamia to Mari and Terqa in inland Syria, as well as Aleppo, Ebla, and Qatna in Syria.

The Rise of the Amorites

The Amorites were first mentioned in texts of the late Sargonic period (*c.* 2200 BCE). Over a century later, the Ur III kings built a wall to keep them in Syria, even though many Ur III individuals had Amorite personal names. By 2000 BCE, the Amorites had spread into much of Mesopotamia, and many cities had leaders and administrative personnel with Amorite names. They merged many of their customs with the local traditions: the Amorite chieftains of Assur identified themselves with the Assyrians, those in Babylon (a previously obscure Mesopotamian town) with the Babylonians, and so on. The Amorites in both of these cities, however, grafted their own royal genealogical traditions onto the civic "family tree" of their respective cities. For example, 17 Amorite "kings who dwelt in tents" became part of the Assyrian King List, even though they clearly were not from the city of Assur at all.

In the north, regional states began to reappear with large bureaucracies, replete with numerous textual remains at Alalakh, Mari, and Tell Leilan. The main power broker in the area appears to have been the city of Mari along the Lower Euphrates River. Thousands of cuneiform texts have been uncovered there, showing a powerful Amorite dynasty with a massive bureaucracy that ruled in the eighteenth century BCE. North along the Euphrates was Terqa, another Amorite center that ruled the Khabur River region from *c.* 1750 to 1500 BCE. Aleppo was apparently the most powerful Amorite kingdom on the coast of Syria—our evidence for this comes from archives from Alalakh and Mari.

The Emergence of New States

During the last quarter of the seventeenth century BCE, the Anatolian Hittites conquered Syro-Mesopotamia, not only sacking Babylon, but also raising havoc at Aleppo and Alalakh. This period usually marks the beginning of the Late Bronze Age (*c.* 1550–1200 BCE) in the region.

After the Hittite conquest, new polities did not manifest themselves for about a century, when an indigenous Syrian confederate empire called Mitanni was formed. In fact, Syria became the focus of large competing international polities: Egypt, the Hittites, Babylon under the Kassites, and, by 1350 BCE, Assyria. These states engaged in fierce economic and military competition, which is attested to by several sources: a cache of international correspondence from the site of Tell el-Amarna in Egypt and from the Hittite capital, Hattusa, and recently found royal letters. Though the area was ethnically diverse, Akkadian was the lingua franca of the regional polities.

There also appear to have been sophisticated bureaucracies operating in many regions across the Middle East: along the coast of Syria at Qatna and at Ugarit, a trading town where thousands of texts written in an alphabetic cuneiform script were found; and in inland Syria at Tell Munbaqa (the ancient city of Ekalte), Tell Hadidi (Azu), and Emar, a Hittite protectorate along the Middle Euphrates, where over 5,000 texts and fragments were uncovered exposing the cultural life of a satellite town.

A "Dark Age"

By 1200 BCE, the major states were in disarray. Egypt and Assyria were severely weakened, while Hatti (the Hittite kingdom) and Kassite Babylon were attacked and rapidly declined. Massive migrations into the Middle East by the so-called Sea Peoples from the Aegean in this period are supported by textual and archaeological evidence. This perhaps triggered an inland migration of West Semitic-speaking Arameans from Syria into the Tigris–Euphrates Valley, "choking off" the Assyrian and Kassite trade routes. During this so-called "Dark Age" (*c.* 1200–900 BCE), a series of small states began to coalesce in the southern Levant, later to be known from biblical texts as Judah, Israel, Ammon, Moab, and Edom. Neo-Hittite states appeared in eastern Anatolia and northern Syria, while Phoenician and Aramean states also emerged, the most famous of which was Aram-Damascus.

The Assyrian state began to regroup during the reign of Tiglath-pileser I (*c.* 1115–1077 BCE), while Babylon reclaimed its importance during the reign of Nebuchadnezzar I (*c.* 1124–1103 BCE). These "political renaissances" were short-lived, however, as both states once again lapsed into political obscurity later in the eleventh century BCE.

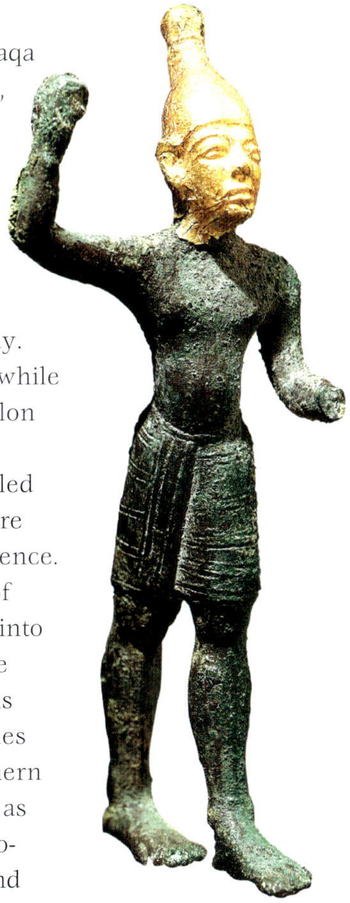

ABOVE **In the trading town of Ugarit,** as well as a rich repository of cuneiform texts, many Bronze Age artifacts have been found, such as this statuette of a god, *c.* 1400–1200 BCE.

ISIN AND THE SUMERO-AKKADIAN TRADITIONS

In this period of power struggles, a number of older sites in Syria and Mesopotamia continued in Sumero-Akkadian traditions, most notable being the southern Mesopotamian city of Isin, which consciously connected itself to the royal traditions from Sumer. It was in this city that the Sumerian King List was probably formulated, in a propagandistic attempt to legitimize its rule. The rulers of Isin continued to write in Sumerian, perhaps by then defunct as a spoken language, but rendered useful to provide continuity with the past. The law code of Lipit-Ishtar, the fifth king of the Isin dynasty (*c.* 1930 BCE), hearkened back to the Sumerian legal tradition of the third millennium BCE.

LEFT **This depiction of a soldier leading a prisoner** is from Mari, *c.* 2500–2000 BCE. Until its destruction by the Babylonians in *c.* 1760 BCE, Mari was a key independent Amorite city.

Eshnunna and Elam

Ancient Eshnunna was a significant Sumerian city in the Early Dynastic periods (*c.* 2900–2300 BCE) which gained its independence from the Ur III state *c.* 2017 BCE. When the Elamites, from Iran, captured Eshnunna (*c.* 1766 BCE), it changed the political landscape of the area dramatically.

Ancient Eshnunna—the modern site of Tell Asmar—was located along the Diyala River Valley region in present-day east-central Iraq. It came under the influence of the Ur III dynasty in the last century of the third millennium BCE, and was successful in establishing itself as an influential city-state at the outset of the second millennium BCE. About 19 kings, most presumably Amorite, are known to have reigned over Eshnunna from the city-state's independence from Ur III until its fall to the Elamites (*c.* 1766 BCE). The Mari Eponym Chronicle tells us that Ipiq-Adad II of Eshnunna was successful in conquering a number of local polities in the Diyala region by 1850 BCE, including Arrapha in northern Iraq and Rapiqum along the Euphrates River. His successor, Naram-Sin, also claimed to have conquered the city of Assur and also made advances in northern Mesopotamia from the Jebel Sinjar (a hill district of northwest Iran) all the way to the source of the Khabur River in the Taurus mountain range in Anatolia, and the Middle Euphrates Region to the city of Mari.

The Code of Eshnunna

Dadusha, the penultimate king of Eshnunna, is best known for a legal "code" containing laws concerning loans, deposits, slavery, agricultural transactions, goring oxen, marital rights, collapsing walls, and sexual offenses. It is slightly earlier than the famed Code of Hammurabi (*c.* 1770 BCE) but, like this later legal code, each of the approximately 60 extant laws are constructed with a conditional "if–then" clause, e.g., "if *x* occurs, then *y* shall be done." The laws are concerned with the three basic social groups in early second millennium BCE Mesopotamia: the *awilum* (upper class), the *mushkenum* (a difficult-to-define common class), and the *wardum* (slave class).

Editions of the Code of Eshnunna were found at Tell Harmel (ancient Shadduppum; now within the city limits of Baghdad) and Tell Haddad in the Hamrin Basin. Unfortunately, the existing copies have neither a prologue nor an epilogue, but only a brief superscription with Dadusha's name.

LEFT **The Great Goddess** statue, carved in limestone, was found at Eshnunna (modern Tell Asmar), and dated to *c.* 2800–2300 BCE.

The Capture of Eshnunna by Elam

With the help of Mari and the powerful kingdom of Babylon under Hammurabi, the Elamites from Iran captured Eshnunna *c.* 1766 BCE. Lying along the northern trade routes into Iran, Eshnunna was the first city encountered by the Iranian Elamites as they traveled down the northern trade routes from Elam. The Elamite center of Susa broke away from the Ur III state at the same time as Eshnunna; thus, when Eshnunna fell to the Elamites, it had a significant effect on the politics of the region. The Elamites moved as far as Shekna (modern Tell Leilan), but were forced to withdraw from Mesopotamia altogether when Hammurabi moved against them.

Elam

Elam was a region primarily situated in southwestern Iran. By the time the Elamites participated in the conquest of Eshnunna, they had already played a significant role in Mesopotamian politics for over 1,000 years. Most of our knowledge about them comes from Mesopotamian sources and materials from Susa, an Iranian urban center in the foothills of the Zagros Mountains that was a Mesopotamian cultural and political protectorate at various

LEFT **The Akkadian king Naram-Sin** made a treaty with Awan, an Elamite state, but other peoples were not so lucky. Here he is depicted conquering the Lullubi of the Zagros Mountains.

times. The first written documents in Iran were found here, written in an early version of Mesopotamian ideograms known as Proto-Elamite, which has not yet been deciphered.

The first written evidence of the Elamites comes from texts of the Mesopotamian Early Dynastic Period (*c.* 2500 BCE). They played a large role in the politics of the Akkadian and Ur III monarchs (*c.* 2350–2000 BCE), as these dynasts controlled Susa and often substantial parts of the Iranian plateau. The Akkadian king Naram-Sin even made a treaty (*c.* 2275 BCE) with the state of Awan, a city perhaps north of Susa. This document is the earliest known text written in Elamite, a language that is unrelated to any other known language, ancient or modern.

A century later, Puzur-Inshushinak of Awan was the first to unify the Iranian plateau and thus all of Elam, including Susa. However, the Ur III dynasts were able to control Susa and surrounding regions (i.e., Susianna, *c.* 2110–2000 BCE), and conducted marriage alliances with the Elamite kings. The Ur III state was overrun by the Elamites in *c.* 2004 BCE. Soon thereafter, the Elamites under the Sukkulmah dynasty successfully took Susa, although the bureaucratic language was primarily Akkadian, with Elamite used sparingly.

During the Isin-Larsa period in Mesopotamia (*c.* 2004–1792 BCE), the Elamites played an intimate role in the politics of the Mesopotamian region. Kudur-Mabuk, king of another Elamite state to the north of Susa, successfully placed his son, Warad-Sin, on the throne of Larsa. Warad-Sin's brother, Rim-Sin, succeeded him and became a major "power broker" within Mesopotamian politics during his reign (*c.* 1822–1763 BCE).

The End of the Sukkulmahs

The period of the Sukkulmahs ended under unknown circumstances about 1500 BCE. After this, the primary written language in Elam and Susa became Elamite (Middle Elamite period, *c.* 1500–1100 BCE), and deities with Elamite names superseded the Mesopotamian ones. The Kassite kings of Babylonia participated in dynastic marriages with the Elamite rulers of southwestern Iran. However, the Babylonian ruler Nebuchadnezzar I, king of the Second Dynasty of Isin (reigned *c.* 1124–1103 BCE), defeated the Elamites soundly, helping to end the Elamite dynasty. The Elamites continued to exist as a people, however; Elamite archers were famed members of the Persian army some 500 years later.

BELOW **This Elamite plaque of a woman weaving** found in Eshnunna is from the Isin-Larsa period, which marked a high point in Elamite culture.

Assyria and Shamshi-adad I

Shamshi-adad I was an Amorite who conquered the city of Assur in *c.* 1814 BCE. By the end of his rule 33 years later (*c.* 1781 BCE), he reigned over all of Upper Mesopotamia. His successful empire building marks him as one of the founding fathers of Mesopotamian history.

The city of Assur in northern Iraq is first noted in the last third of the third millennium BCE, during the reign of the Sargonic Akkadian kings. By *c.* 2000 BCE, it was a province of the Ur III dynasty, but with the fall of the Ur III state, the city became independent, as attested to by the thousands of mercantile documents from Kanesh, an important trading center in Anatolia (*c.* 2000–1800 BCE).

Shamshi-adad I and Assyria

According to documents found in the city of Mari, Shamshi-adad I succeeded his father Ila-kabkabum to the throne of the Amorite city of Ekallatum. (The precise location of this city is not known, but it was probably located somewhere along the left bank of the Tigris River, south of Assur.) He was forced to flee to Babylon when Naram-Sin of Eshnunna captured most of northern Iraq.

Soon thereafter he returned to Ekallatum, launching an assault on Assur, which he captured. According to the Assyrian King List, his reign began at this point, and he is credited with a reign of 33 years. Sources for his rule come from sites in the neighboring city of Mari; his capital, Shubat-Enlil (where over 1,000 texts have been found, many of which come from the period of his rule); from Shusharra (modern Shemshara in Iraq's northeast); and the aforementioned Assyrian King List. Shamshi-adad plays a significant role in the List despite his Amorite origins—his father is also mentioned. He claimed to have conquered all of northern Mesopotamia, establishing himself at a new capital, Shubat-Enlil (thought to be Tell Leilan near the eastern Khabur River in Syria).

Like the Assyrians ruling earlier during the commercial ventures to Anatolia, Shamshi-adad worked to control the northern trade routes. The Anatolian colonies, however, appear to have been disbanded during his reign. Shamshi-adad made a conscious attempt to connect himself with the earlier rulers of Akkad, claiming descent from them, and, according to a document from Nineveh, even rebuilding a temple dedicated to Manishtushu, one of the sons of Sargon of Akkad. Moreover, he also made offerings at Mari to the spirits of the departed Sargonic kings.

BELOW **Shamshi-adad I is thought to be depicted on this Babylonian stele, dated *c.* 2004–1792 BCE, which celebrates a military victory.**

Shamshi-adad I and his Rule

After capturing Assur, Shamshi-adad proceeded west to the eastern Khabur River, taking over the abandoned city of Shekhna, renaming it Shubat-Enlil, and establishing it as his seat of government. With the addition of the western territories, this new kingdom was now in the sphere of influence of the kingdom of Mari on the Euphrates. By about 1800 BCE, Shamshi-adad had successfully defeated Mari and captured the capital city. He now ruled all of Upper Mesopotamia, claiming in his inscriptions to have united the land between the Tigris and Euphrates, and closely allying himself with the king of Babylon, Hammurabi. In order to consolidate his rule, he placed his sons at strategic

Assyria after the Reign of Shamshi-adad I

Shamshi-adad's empire in northern Mesopotamia did not last long after his death (*c.* 1781 BCE), as his sons could not hold the large territorial state together. After Shamshi-adad's death, the kingdoms of Aleppo and Eshnunna combined to attack the now "two-headed" kingdom. Yasmah-adad was overthrown by Zimri-Lim of Mari, a descendant of the city-state's previous dynasts. Ishme-dagan, however, was able to continue his reign for at least another generation in a truncated kingdom centered at Ekallatum. However, when the Elamites took the city in *c.* 1765 BCE, Ishme-dagan sought refuge with Hammurabi. Though the Babylonian king helped him take back the throne, Ekallatum was reduced to a vassal city subordinate to Babylon's king. After Ishme-dagan's death he was succeeded by his son Mutu-ashkur, but his reign was brief. Mutu-ashkur was the last king known to have ruled Ekallatum, before the city disappeared from the records of Mesopotamian history.

LEFT **While excavating at Tell Leilan in Syria,** archaeologists discovered clay tablets such as this one, dated *c.* 1780s BCE, in the ruins of a temple probably built by Shamshi-adad I.

locations. Ishme-dagan I ruled from Ekallatum, while Yasmah-adad presided over the newly conquered Mari. Though both were considered kings, only Shamshi-adad took the title of "Great King," and even "King of the Universe," a title reminiscent of the Akkadian kings.

Near the end of Shamshi-adad's rule, Eshnunna raided territories in Assyria, and Shamshi-adad himself campaigned to the far west, fighting the powerful state centered in Aleppo. His troops reached as far as Lebanon, which certainly must have diverted too many troops from the center of the kingdom, and he even made a marriage alliance for Yasmah-adad with the Syrian kingdom of Qatna, although Yasmah-adad was not enthusiastic about this particular arrangement.

SHAMSHI-ADAD I AND HIS SONS

There is a significant body of correspondence discovered at Mari that provides an insight into the relationship of Shamshi-adad and his sons, especially Yasmah-adad. From these letters, it is evident that Yasmah-adad had difficulty in keeping the territories of the lower Balikh River region, especially the city of Tuttul. His father was also concerned about his fitness for rule. Moreover, Yasmah-adad expressed some irritation with his older brother, and engaged in some squabbling over territories. However, both sons continued to be loyal to their father, and did not rebel against his rule. We must also note that many of the letters at Mari are incoming correspondence to Yasmah-adad, and may not express his own opinions.

LEFT **Terracotta cooking molds** such as this one in the form of a woman (*c.* 2000 BCE) were used for baked dishes on Amorite royal tables in the time of Shamshi-adad I.

The Advent of Iron

Fragments of Iron Ore

As well as smelting iron ore, ancient Near Eastern and Egyptian societies also used various ores in jewelry, seals, and other carved objects.

Though historians and archaeologists label the Iron Age in the Near East as beginning about 1200 BCE, there is archaeological evidence of sporadic iron use in the area as early as the fifth millennium BCE. A number of specialized iron objects dating to the third millennium BCE have also been found, including an iron dagger from Eshnunna in the Diyala River area of Mesopotamia, an iron sword from an elite burial at Alaca Hüyük in north Central Anatolia, and a small fragment of iron connected to the Great Pyramid of Giza in Egypt. Textual references to iron objects have also been discovered. For example, Zimri-Lim of Mari presented an iron ring as a gift to a neighboring king (*c.* 1780 BCE). Even with the assumption that some of these items were made of meteoric iron, it is probable that some iron may have been produced as a by-product of copper smelting.

Smelting Metal

By the ninth century BCE, when this relief from Assyria was carved, smelting metal had become common in daily domestic life. Clockwise from top left, the relief shows winemaking, cooking, metal smelting, and butchering an animal.

Sporadic textual evidence from the late second millennium BCE shows that iron working was very widespread throughout the ancient Near East. A famous biblical passage in I Samuel 13:19–22 has often been interpreted to mean that in the eleventh century BCE, the Philistines—who inhabited the southern coast of Canaan—held a monopoly of the use of iron over the Hebrews, but in fact this is a misinterpretation. The passage actually states that the Hebrews had no smith in their land, and thus had to take their iron implements to the Philistines for repairs. Thus, iron working in this period may still have been a specialized activity, and not accessible to every area of the Middle East.

In any event, iron production did not supersede the working of bronze until at least 1200 BCE—although iron was considered superior to bronze, there were considerable difficulties associated with the labor involved in creating iron. However, since iron ore deposits were so plentiful, once the process for making steel was understood (i.e., allowing carbon to be absorbed into the surface of the iron), it soon became a widespread phenomenon. In fact, iron-working technology is in evidence by the eleventh century BCE in Cyprus (in a cemetery context), Har Adir in Galilee, and from Pella and the Beqa' Valley in Jordan. It is true that few, if any, iron workshops have been found before the Hellenistic period (*c.* 300 BCE), but iron smelting furnaces have been located at Tel Yin-am in Galilee, and Kamid al-Loz in Lebanon, both dated roughly to the thirteenth century BCE.

Recently, scholars working around the region of Georgia (ancient Colchis) on the eastern shore of the Black Sea have uncovered about 400 iron-working installations, tentatively dated by radiocarbon dating to 1500 BCE, a date that may require scholars to revise their views on the origins of iron production. It is well known that this area supplied the kingdoms of Urartu and Assyria with their iron in the early first millennium BCE. Certainly at the end of the second millennium BCE (*c.* 1200–1000 BCE), iron metallurgy gradually spread across the Middle East, as there are examples in Syro-Palestine, Cyprus, and Eastern Europe.

It has been argued that the simple technique of iron metallurgy made it accessible to non-elites, revolutionizing agriculture, industry, and even warfare.

Tools and Weapons

These iron axes, nails, and a knife, dated to the early second millennium BCE, were found at Mari, Syria. Although more brittle than bronze, iron tools retained their edge for longer periods than their bronze counterparts.

The Hittites and Iron Production

One of the earliest evidences of the making of iron comes from late fourteenth century BCE diplomatic correspondence from the Hittite capital of Hattusa, in north Central Anatolia. The Hittite king Hattusili III wrote to an Assyrian king—presumably Adad-nirari I, but the beginning of the letter is lost—responding to a request for iron. Hattusili claimed that his armory had none available at the time, and instead pacified the Assyrian monarch by presenting him with an iron dagger. It has often been assumed that this text implies that the Hittites began the process of smelting iron. However, there is no evidence that the Hittites originated or controlled iron production.

Iron and Gold Breastplate

This decorative breastplate, with gold lion studs, was found in the tomb of Philip of Macedon (382–336 BCE), the father of Alexander the Great.

Babylon under Hammurabi

When Hammurabi (reigned *c.* 1792–1750 BCE) came to the throne of Babylon, the city state was a small power surrounded by larger states. By the end of his reign, Hammurabi had effectively created an empire that would endure for more than 1,000 years.

Very little is known of the first few rulers of the First Dynasty of Babylon (*c.* 1894–1793 BCE) who preceded Hammurabi. In the few year names that we have (i.e., scribal statements about important annual royal events) it appears that the rulers were primarily concerned with building projects, such as temples and fortifications, and with digging canals. The rulers also were concerned with the nearby city of Sippar. There, Sabium (reigned *c.* 1844–1831 BCE) rebuilt the temple of Shamash, as well as the Marduk temple in Babylon. However, there is evidence that these monarchs also engaged in military conflicts with neighboring states. Sumu-la-el (reigned *c.* 1880–1845 BCE) claimed to have plundered Kish, an important center north of Babylon.

By the time of the final king of this dynasty, Sin-muballit (reigned *c.* 1812–1793 BCE), there were a number of significant polities in Mesopotamia, including Assyria under Shamshi-adad (reigned *c.* 1814–1781 BCE), Eshnunna along the Diyala River, as well as Isin and Larsa, states south of Babylon. Moreover, the state of Elam in modern Iran played an important role in Mesopotamian politics: Rim-Sin of Larsa (reigned *c.* 1822–1763 BCE) claimed to have defeated a coalition of powers which included Sin-muballit of Babylon.

LEFT This bronze and gold statue is thought to represent Hammurabi praying before a sacred tree, and is dated *c.* 1750 BCE. It was found in Larsa.

Like some of his predecessors, Hammurabi's name betrays an Amorite origin. The Amorites had begun to infiltrate Mesopotamia late in the third millennium BCE, and, by Hammurabi's time, reigned over a number of strategic city-states, including Assyria, Eshnunna, Uruk, and Babylon.

Hammurabi's Reign: Building an Empire

At the beginning of his reign (*c.* 1792 BCE), Hammurabi concerned himself with building activities and internal administration, including his famous legal code, rather than expanding his empire. In fact, until year 29 (*c.* 1763 BCE), only three royal year dates mention any military engagements with Babylon as a member state of a coalition of kings. Babylon appears to have been a "junior partner" with the more powerful state of Assyria, ruled by Shamshi-adad I, in the north. However, with the death of Shamshi-adad in 1781 BCE, the political landscape of Mesopotamia changed.

When the city of Mari regained its independence from Assyria, Hammurabi—perhaps in response to this—allied himself with the southern city of Larsa, which was able to conquer most of the southern region, including the states of Isin and Uruk. By *c.* 1763 BCE, however, Hammurabi was successful in defeating a coalition of kings from Elam, Assyria, and Eshnunna. A year later he defeated Larsa, thus politically uniting all of southern Mesopotamia for the first time since the Ur III dynasty over 200 years earlier. Moreover, he began to use the royal title, "king of Sumer and Akkad," and other expressions that were used by the Old Akkadian and Ur III kings from the third millennium BCE, showing a conscious attempt on his part to make a connection with the imperial past of Mesopotamia.

After the unification of southern Mesopotamia, Babylon under Hammurabi exchanged a number

of letters with the city of Mari in Syria during the reign of Zimri-Lim (reigned *c.* 1780–1760 BCE), showing that the two states were on excellent terms. Ambassadors and even troops were exchanged. However, after the end of the reign of Zimri-Lim (*c.* 1760 BCE), Mari came under the control of Babylon, and the Syrian city had its wall destroyed and was subjected to Babylonian plunder. By 1756 BCE, Hammurabi was able to conquer Eshnunna in the north, and weakened Assyria. At the time of his death in *c.* 1750 BCE, only the coastal Syrian kingdoms of Aleppo and Qatna were independent of Hammurabi's control.

Ironically, most of our information concerning Babylon during the reign of Hammurabi does not come from the city itself. Most of the material remains for the site of Babylon in the early second millennium BCE are currently under the natural water table, and thus inaccessible to the archaeologist. However, the correspondence of Zimri-Lim from Mari (mentioned above), textual sources from nearby Sippar, legal documents such as the Code of Hammurabi, and numerous scribal archives from other southern Mesopotamian centers provide valuable information about the city of Babylon and the influential reign of Hammurabi himself.

LEFT **A foundation tablet by Hammurabi** (*c.* 1760 BCE) was found in the temple of Ezida in Borsippa, just southwest of Babylon.

The Fragmentation of Mesopotamia after Hammurabi

Although all of Mesopotamia proper was under the control of a single monarch at the time of Hammurabi's death, the kingdom did not retain all of these conquered territories for long. A successor state to Mari, Khana, which was centered at the city of Terqa, declared its independence during the reign of Samsu-iluna (reigned *c.* 1749–1712 BCE), Hammurabi's successor. A little over a century later, Babylon, was a small city-state which succumbed to a Hittite invasion (*c.* 1595 BCE), thereby ending the dynasty begun by an ancestor of Hammurabi named Sumuabum, whose reign lasted *c.* 1894–1881 BCE.

Old Babylonian Life under Hammurabi's Rule

The internal workings of Hammurabi's state can be understood from the thousands of legal contracts uncovered by archaeologists, representing a diverse range of legal transactions including the liberation of slaves, the temporary hiring of workers, marriage, divorce, adoption, loans (e.g., silver, or barley), property exchange, purchases of property (e.g., houses, fields, animals, and children), property rentals (even the lease of a roof), and even lawsuits (e.g., over inheritance or property). These contracts have

RIGHT **The Code of Hammurabi** has the remains of further inscriptions at its base, indicating that the original legal text may have continued on further down the stele.

ABOVE **This sculpture of a Mesopotamian king** is possibly a depiction of Hammurabi, and was found with other artifacts looted by the Elamites in Susa, Iran.

been found at dozens of sites throughout southern Mesopotamia, revealing a bureaucratic but lively culture.

In addition, a large corpus of hundreds of letters between the king and a number of his subordinates (and between themselves) has survived. They date primarily to the last dozen years of the king's reign. In the letters, we learn that Hammurabi required Babylon to become the center of tax distribution, replacing Larsa. Moreover, a significant group of letters was sent to an official named Sin-iddinam, who was given the responsibility of governing palace affairs in a portion of the southern area of the kingdom. He was responsible for the repair and dredging of canals and dams, the regulating of water from the canals to fields, and the tax share from fields. He also needed to make sure that goods were successfully transported to Babylon from the provinces. Sin-iddinam also was required to advise the king on legal affairs, especially since Hammurabi often had to make important legal decisions. He also had to make sure that stolen property was recovered, that sufficient troops had been levied, and that any military deserters were punished.

Another official, Shamash-hazir, was originally a personal attendant to Hammurabi's son, Sumuditana, but was promoted to the position of palace steward. His duties were many, as he was responsible for overseeing the myriad estates that the king held in the south after his conquests. According to the letters, Shamash-hazir needed to make sure that the fields were adequately cared for, that they were farmed, and that renters paid their fees. He also was responsible for the state's workforce, which included specialists such as craftsmen, priests, soldiers, and manual laborers. This official was apparently an intermediary between the palace and the people, as he was often in the fields interacting with the populace and had access to a direct audience with the king himself. However, Shamash-hazir had to answer to Sin-iddinam, who held a more senior position.

Scholars have still yet to determine much about Hammurabi's personality and character. Presumably, he had a number of wives, none of whom are known by name. The letters that have survived are, as we have seen, more concerned about the daily affairs of the government and administration, and provide precious little information about his personal life.

The Code of Hammurabi and its Historical Importance

Perhaps the most famous piece of writing in the period was Hammurabi's law code, which was discovered by French archaeologists at Susa in 1901. The stele is made of diorite, and stands about 8 ft (2.4 m) high. At the top of the stele, Hammurabi stands before the seated sun god, Shamash, the god of justice. (Presumably, the

RIGHT **Hammurabi and the sun god Shamash** appear at the top of the Code of Hammurabi. The king (left) lifts his right hand to his mouth as a sign of respect.

BABYLONIAN SCRIBES

Much of the literary output during this period seems to have occurred not in Babylon itself, but south in the ancient cities of Nippur and Ur, where scribal schools flourished. Many of these schools were attached to palaces, although most appear to have been private enterprises. Numerous student practice texts, lexical lists, exams, essays of the life of a student, and copies of royal hymns have been found, providing invaluable information about the life of a student scribe and the pedagogical methods of the teachers. The school curriculum appears to have covered cuneiform writing, the Sumerian language, and the study of mathematics.

RIGHT **Clay tablets found in Babylon** (*c.* 2112–1600 BCE) attest to the range of languages in use by Babylonian scribes. These tablets include several languages, including ancient Sumerian.

stele was originally housed at Sippar in the temple dedicated to Shamash.)

Like earlier law codes found at Ur, Isin, and Eshnunna, the Code of Hammurabi is composed of three major parts: an extensive prolog, delineating the king's royal attributes and deeds; the body of 282 laws (the largest extant corpus coming from Mesopotamia); and a long epilog. Both the prolog and epilog were written in an elegant hymnic style, rivaling other pieces of Old Babylonian literature for their literary brilliance. In particular, the king claims to have become the proprietor of the holy shrines of Mesopotamian deities in the major cities of his realm (e.g., Nippur, Eridu, Sippar, Larsa, Cuthah, Borsippa, Dilbat, and even Nineveh, which was certainly outside his political jurisdiction).

The body of laws was composed in a casuistic fashion, with a conditional or hypothetical statement followed by a prescriptive statement (i.e., "if *x* occurs, then *y* shall be done"). Like the contemporary Eshnunna laws, the Code of Hammurabi dealt with a variety of criminal matters, including murder, robbery, assault, and bodily injuries, as well as a wide array of civil issues, including inheritance, adoption, marriage, real estate, and rentals. Though the actual laws appear to reflect an idealized reality rather than actual circumstances, one can learn much about the basis and principles of the culture and society of Babylon by studying their content and structure.

Old Babylonian Literature and Scribal Traditions

The literary output during Hammurabi's reign was also worthy of note. Not only have a number of legal, epistolary, and administrative texts been uncovered, but the scribes during the reign of Hammurabi saw fit to copy and preserve literary documents, such as myths and epics, from the third millennium BCE. Moreover, entirely new pieces of literature were also created in this period, which included royal hymns, as well as astronomical and mathematical documents. In fact, the period of Hammurabi's reign displays the widest array of textual forms of any period in the history of Mesopotamia.

Babylonian scribes were not only versed in Akkadian, the primary written language, but also knew Sumerian, a language which had most likely already died out as a spoken language of Mesopotamia. Hammurabi's Babylonian scribes did not merely copy the Sumerian works. For example, the scribes took a variety of different sources that had been written in Sumerian concerning Gilgamesh, the famous king of Uruk, and wove them together into an integrated epic, now known as *The Epic of Gilgamesh*, which was ultimately a new literary creation based upon older themes. In the Old Babylonian version, the hero of the epic goes through a series of tragic life events that cause him to grow experientially, thereby becoming a better king to the people of Uruk.

The Old Hittite Kingdom

Ruling from Hattusa in northern central Anatolia, the Hittites reigned over regions of Anatolia, northern Syria, and Upper Mesopotamia for 250 years (*c.* 1650–1400 BCE). In this period, called the Old Kingdom, approximately 15 Hittite kings are known to have ruled.

The term "Hittite" is derived from the name "Hatti," a term used by the Hittites (and probably pre-Hittites) for central Anatolia. The Old Kingdom of the Hittites is known because of the thousands of cuneiform texts found primarily in Hattusa, the primary capital of the Hittites during this formative period of their history.

The Origins of the Hittites

Although the precise origins of the Hittites are not known, individuals with Hittite-like names occur in Old Assyrian texts from Anatolian trade centers including Kanesh (*c.* 1920–1740 BCE). One king mentioned in the Assyrian texts was a certain Anitta (*c.* 1750 BCE) who ruled from Kushara, which was apparently southwest of Central Anatolia. Anitta, who was probably a Hittite, claimed to have destroyed the city of Hattusa, although it was rebuilt a century later. In one text, written in Hittite, he claimed to have united Central Anatolia.

The Hittite language was an Indo-European language. It shares some linguistic features with Luwian, a later language of Anatolia, and bears a resemblance to Sanskrit and Mycenaean Greek. The Hittites adopted a modified version of the cuneiform writing of Mesopotamia, perhaps learned from Assyrian merchants, or from Old Babylonian scribal traditions in inland Syria.

LEFT **This mother goddess** is from Hasanoglan, Turkey, and is dated to just before the Hittite period. Little is known about the origins or the societies of pre-Hittite peoples in Anatolia.

Hattusili I and His Heirs

The later Hittite kings did not claim descent from Anitta, however. Beginning with Hattusili I (or perhaps his father Labarna), approximately 15 kings are known to have ruled from Hattusa in the Old Kingdom. According to the bilingual (i.e. Hittite and Akkadian) Annals of Hattusili I (*c.* 1650 BCE), the Hittites expanded in Anatolia as far north as Zalpa, Arzawa to the southwest, and Ashuwa and Halpa (probably Aleppo), both south of the Taurus mountain range in northern Syria, near the Euphrates River. Furthermore, he boasted that he had eclipsed the exploits of Sargon of Akkad, who had conquered the area from the east nearly 700 years earlier.

Hattusili (reigned *c.* 1650–1625 BCE) appears to have rejected his nephew and adopted son, Labarna, as heir to the throne, and replaced him with his grandson, Mursili, as his successor. For this to happen, Hattusili required the Hittite aristocracy to take an oath of allegiance to the new heir. These internal politics of Hattusili's reign are known from another Akkadian–Hittite bilingual text, the highly propagandistic Edict (or Testament) of Hattusili I.

After his succession to the throne, Hattusili's grandson, Mursili I (reigned *c.* 1625–1595 BCE), raided as far southeast as the city of Babylon, ending the First Dynasty of Babylon, but after his death the Hittites abandoned the regions across the Euphrates River. According to a later text called the Proclamation of Telepinu, Mursili was assassinated by his brother-in-law Hantili (reigned *c.* 1595–1560 BCE), who in turn was killed by his son-in-law Zidanta I (*c.* 1560 BCE), who usurped the throne after also assassinating Hantili's son. The murderous pattern continued, as Zidanta I was killed by his own son, Ammuna, whose own sons were killed by supporters of Huzziya I, brother of Ammuna's daughter-in-law.

Huzziya I's brother-in-law, Telepinu (reigned *c.* 1525–1500 BCE), was not only successful in escaping assassination, but was able to take the throne and remove the previous monarch—this time without the need for a violent plot or assassination of his predecessor.

LEFT **An undated death mask** found in a Hittite grave represents the Hittites' belief that a person's grave acted as a portal to the underworld, or "Dark Earth."

The Proclamation of Telepinu

Our knowledge of these events in the sixteenth century BCE comes from the Proclamation of Telepinu, which contains a lengthy prolog outlining the reigns of previous Hittite kings. Considering the spate of assassinations that preceded Telepinu's reign, it is not surprising that one of the goals of his Proclamation was to establish rules of succession to the throne, which became—at least in theory—patrilinear, i.e., from father to son. Telepinu's Proclamation also attempted to ensure the stability of the monarchy itself.

However, it does not appear that the regulations of the Proclamation were put into practice. Telepinu apparently died without a direct male heir. His successor, Alluwamna, was most likely his son-in-law; he too was soon overtaken, apparently by a certain Tahurwaili, who appears to have had no genealogical ties to the crown. Three more poorly attested kings are known to have come to the throne in this period, all of whom were namesakes of previous rulers, and thus likely related to the royal family: Hantili II, Zidanta II, and Huzziya II.

The End of the Old Kingdom

It is not clear how long the period was between Telepinu's death and the reign of Muwatalli I, the last Old Kingdom monarch, but scholars estimate that about one century divides them (*c.* 1500–1400 BCE). During this period, it is probable that the Hittites maintained a strong foreign policy, as Telepinu made an alliance with Kizzuwadna, a kingdom to the southeast in the Taurus mountain highlands, made up of Luwian, Hittite, and Hurrian elements.

This period also saw the rise to prominence of the Hurrian Mitanni kingdom, centered in Syria, which defeated Aleppo and expanded to the Mediterranean coast, thus causing a number of former Hittite vassal kingdoms, including Alalakh, to switch their allegiance to the rising Mitanni state. While the Mitanni kings Paratarna and Shaustatar struggled to control the coastal region of Syro-Palestine against Thutmosis III of Egypt (reigned *c.* 1479–1425 BCE), the Hittite monarchs may have been occupied with their unstable internal dynastic affairs. In the next century, this situation would change during the 200 years of the New Hittite Kingdom (*c.* 1400–1200 BCE), when the Hittites expanded their territory to its greatest extent.

RIGHT **During the reign of Thutmosis III** (this limestone relief is from his mortuary temple at Deir el-Bahri) the Hittites remained on cordial terms with Egypt, especially as Egypt encroached further into Syrian territory.

Mitanni

The kingdom of Mitanni was a confederation of primarily Hurrian states in inland Syria and northern Iraq in the second half of the second millennium BCE. By around 1450 BCE Mitanni was the most powerful state in Upper Mesopotamia.

ABOVE **The oldest known text** in the Hurrian language is this tablet, *c.* 2150 BCE. It was found in a Hurrian temple at Urkish (modern Tell Mozan).

The history of the Mitanni state can only be partially reconstructed. The earliest king is believed to be a certain Kirta, the father of Shuttarna. The kingdom was ruled from its capital, Washukanni, which has not been located for certain. It is thought that it may have been located near the headwaters of the Khabur River in northern Syria, although scholars are not certain of the site's precise location.

Who Were the Mitanni People?

The state of Mitanni appears to have been composed mainly of Hurrians, who probably migrated from the Trans-Caucasus region in the north. The earliest attestation of the Hurrians is in the late third millennium BCE, in Sumero-Akkadian cuneiform sources from the reign of the Akkadian king, Naram-Sin. The Hurrians are described as inhabiting the northern area of Mesopotamia, especially the regions of the Khabur and Balikh River basins in Syria, as well as the Tigris River basin in northern Iraq.

By 2000 BCE, north Mesopotamia had been thoroughly "Hurrianized," with several established Hurrian states continuing to exist until the rise of the Mitanni state in *c.* 1600 BCE. From the diverse and fragmented sources available, it appears that "Mitanni" was a political term which was most often used to describe a confederation of primarily Hurrian states and vassal kingdoms. In fact, most of the vassal states had their own kings, who were likely bound to Mitanni by a treaty sworn by oath and sacrifice.

Unfortunately, no royal archives from this kingdom have been found. Knowledge about Mitanni is partially derived from royal correspondence from Egypt and Anatolia (Hittites), various sources from Assyria, and documents from Mitanni vassal states, such as Nuzi (in northern Iraq), Terqa (on the Syrian Euphrates), Alalakh (in southeastern coastal Anatolia), and Ugarit (in coastal Syria).

Mitanni Expansion

Under the reigns of Paratarna and Shaustatar, by 1500 BCE (roughly contemporary with the Eighteenth Dynasty in New Kingdom Egypt) it appears that Mitanni had expanded into most of Syria. The confederation was probably opposed by the expansion of Thutmosis III of Egypt (reigned *c.* 1479–1425 BCE). Thutmosis's annals describe victories over Mitanni in the central Syrian region of Nuhashshe. Apparently, the Mitanni continued to control the southeastern part of Anatolia (Kizzuwadna) and coastal Syria, as the kingdoms of Mukish (centered at Alalakh) and Aleppo remained under Mitanni influence. In fact, Idrimi of Alalakh claimed in his "pseudo-autobiography" that he owed his throne to the Mitanni. A later Hittite treaty indicates that Shaushtatar was successful in sacking the city of Assur in Assyria (northern Iraq) and took booty to embellish his capital city, Washukanni. It appears at this point that the area of Arrapha in Assyria (especially the town of Nuzi) was now under Mitanni influence.

HURRIAN AND KASSITE: TWO MYSTERY LANGUAGES

The Hurrian language is not perfectly understood. It has some similarities to Urartian, a language from the Lake Van region of the Trans-Caucasus that was written in the first millennium BCE. The now extinct "Hurro-Urartian" language family was apparently unrelated to other languages in the region (e.g., Indo-European and Semitic languages).

Kassite, the language of the dynasty which ruled Babylon from the sixteenth century BCE, is another poorly understood language. No Kassite texts have been attested. There are, however, two lexical texts in Akkadian and Kassite which contain about 200 basic vocabulary words (e.g., terms for colors, chariot parts, irrigation, and plants), and a handful of personal names. From them, it is apparent that Kassite is unrelated to any known language, living or dead.

Later Mitanni kings are known primarily through the Amarna letters from Tell el-Amarna in Egypt (*c.* 1370–1340 BCE), which contain evidence of the diplomatic relations between the Mitanni kings and the kings of Egypt. The warming relations between the two states were perhaps due to the rising power of Assyria, and the Hittites in Anatolia, which placed Mitanni in a precarious situation. The Mitanni king Tushratta continued a good relationship with Amenhotep III (reigned *c.* 1390–1352 BCE), as evidenced by a long letter from Tell el-Amarna. The Mitanni king even sent the ill Amenhotep III a statue of the goddess Shaushka (the Assyrians' Ishtar) of Nineveh to help cure his sickness.

ABOVE **In the royal palace of Ugarit,** archaeologists found an extensive archive of documents, some of which shed light on Ugarit's period as a Mitanni vassal state.

A State in Decline

However, the Mitanni state began to fragment, and Tushratta was defeated by the Hittite king Suppiluliuma I. The Hittites sacked the Mitanni capital, Washukanni, and installed a Hurrian vassal king, Shattiwaza. Thus, after *c.* 1350 BCE, Mitanni was no longer a major player in ancient Near Eastern politics. Moreover, the Assyrians were able to declare independence, reducing Mitanni to a small buffer state named Hanigalbat, between them and the Hittite empire. Assyrian documents record the deportation of many Mitanni citizens into this area, and the Middle Assyrian state eventually swallowed it entirely. Mitanni itself continued as a buffer state between the Hittites and Assyria for 100 more years, after which the Assyrians conquered its remaining territory. Washukanni was again sacked, this time by Assyria under Adad-nirari (*c.* 1290 BCE).

Because of their military and political power, and their central location, the Mitanni state and the Hurrians transmitted Mesopotamian culture and trade to Anatolia, Palestine, and even the Aegean. Versions of Mesopotamian epics (e.g., Gilgamesh) and other literary works have been found in both the Hurrian and Hittite languages.

BELOW **Excavations at Tell Brak** in Syria revealed a Mitanni palace and temple on the highest part of the archaeological site.

The Kassites in Babylonia

Establishing the longest lasting dynasty in the history of Mesopotamia, the Kassites ruled Babylon for over 400 years (*c.* 1570–1155 BCE). They played a key role on the Near Eastern stage, forging relationships with Assyria, Egypt, and other powerful states.

BELOW **The remains of Dur-Kurigalzu**, the capital city of the Kassite king Kurigalzu I, include a towering ziggurat. The site is approximately 19 miles (30 km) west of Baghdad.

Though the origins of the Kassites are unclear, they may have migrated from the mountains northeast of Syria (modern Kurdistan) into Mesopotamia sometime before the eighteenth century BCE, when they are first mentioned in cuneiform sources. The earliest evidence of the name Kassite comes during the reigns of Rim-Sin of Larsa (reigned *c.* 1770 BCE), and Samsu-iluna and Abieshu of Babylon (reigned *c.* 1749–1684 BCE). Royal year dates note that the monarchs had to fight Kassite troops. From these sources, we can observe that the Kassites were semi-nomadic, and were often employed as mercenaries and agricultural workers, and for public works projects. Some Kassites in this period even became integrated in Old Babylonian society, buying and selling property, and acting as officials in activities such as horse breeding and chariot building.

The Spread of the Kassites

By the early sixteenth century BCE, Kassites were living throughout Upper Mesopotamia and Syria—according to the archives at Nuzi in northern Iraq, and at Alalakh on the Orontes River. It appears that a group of Kassites controlled Khana, a small kingdom near the confluence of the Euphrates and Khabur Rivers, centered at the city of Terqa. In fact, a king with an "Akkadianized" Kassite name, Kashtiliashu of Terqa, was probably a contemporary of Abieshu of Babylon (reigned *c.* 1711–1684 BCE).

The Hittites invaded and sacked Babylon in 1595 BCE, overthrowing the First Dynasty of Babylon. For some reason they did not remain in the region, thereby leaving a power vacuum that was ultimately filled by the Kassites.

Kassites in Babylon

The long-lasting Kassite dynasty appears to have survived in Babylon for more than 400 years (*c.* 1570–1155 BCE), although the records are very sparse until the fourteenth century BCE. The later Babylonian King List designated 576 years to the Kassite dynasty, and included 36 kings. However, at least the first eight monarchs did not rule in the city of Babylon itself, and may have been ancestors of the later kings.

The first Kassite king to have ruled Babylon was either Agum-Kakrime II or Burnaburiash, in the sixteenth century BCE. At that time, the coastal portion of southern Mesopotamia was under the control of the Sealand dynasty, which first came under Kassite domination during the reign of Ulamburiash in about 1475 BCE. By the fourteenth century BCE all of southern Mesopotamia was ruled by Kassites.

Royal correspondence from Tell el-Amarna in Egypt attests to the existence of a relationship between two Kassite kings (Kadashman-Enlil I, who reigned 1374–1360 BCE, and Burnaburiash II, who reigned 1359–1333 BCE) with two Eighteenth Dynasty kings in Egypt: Amenhotep III and Akhenaten. Fourteen letters depict a relationship of equality between the monarchs, who were concerned primarily about diplomatic marriages. It is also evident that the Kassites pursued the same diplomatic policy with neighboring states including Elam, Assyria, and Hatti. In fact, the relationship with Assyria to the north was very close, as Burnaburiash married the daughter of Ashuruballit I, thereby cementing a dynastic union between the two kingdoms. However, Assyria was clearly the dominant partner in this period, as Ashuruballit invaded Babylonia and placed Kurigalzu II (reigned *c.* 1327–1303 BCE) on the throne.

Despite this, the Kassite Babylonian kingdom still continued to be an important player on the international stage. For example, a letter from Hittite king Hattusili III expressed the desire for good relations to continue with the new king of Babylon, Kadashman-Enlil II (*c.* 1263–1255 BCE). A generation later, Tukulti-ninurta I of Assyria fought a war against Kashtiliash IV of Babylon (reigned *c.* 1242–1235 BCE), defeating and then deposing the Kassite king, and placing himself on the throne of Babylon. He then handpicked a series of local dynasts to rule. Though the Kassites were able to rebel against Assyrian rule, their dynasty came to an end around 1155 BCE.

LEFT **This Kassite kudurru**, or boundary stone, depicts the goddess Bau (Gula). Kudurrus are an important source of information about economic relationships under the Kassites.

Kassite Culture

During their long rule, the Kassites were thoroughly "Babylonianized," building temples to Babylonian gods. Kassite rulers also fostered the collection and editing of many literary and religious documents (such as *The Epic of Gilgamesh* and the Babylonian Creation Epic), categorizing them and creating a literary "canon."

Much of the information concerning the internal affairs of the Kassite state comes from about 10,000 texts in administrative archives from Nippur, the sacred city of the god Enlil which, by the Kassite period, had become an important shrine for Mesopotamians. The documents imply a centralized administration, based upon a variant of the feudal model, where the king made land grants to local elites. Perhaps the most important building project enacted by the Kassite kings was the foundation for a new capital, Dur-Kurigalzu (modern Aqar-quf), built by the king Kurigalzu I (early fifteenth century BCE), north of Babylon near the confluence of the Tigris and Diyala rivers.

Although the Kassites do not appear to have produced a great number of new cultural innovations, they were responsible for the survival of the Babylonian scribal tradition, and provided southern Mesopotamia with a relatively stable rule for nearly one half of a millennium.

LEFT **This Kassite cylinder seal** from the sixteenth century BCE depicts a prayer scene, and a presentation to a god or goddess.

The New Hittite Kingdom

The New Hittite Kingdom (*c.* 1400–1190 BCE) represented the zenith of power of the Hittite state. The Hittite monarchs pacified Anatolia, subdued the Mitanni kingdom, and conquered new territories in northern Syria in the New Kingdom's 200-year rule.

The true founder of the Hittite Empire, Suppiluliuma I, did not come to power until *c.* 1344 BCE, and at least three or four kings are known to have ruled before him in the New Kingdom period.

Rulers Before Suppiluliuma I

Tudhaliya I (reigned *c.* 1400 BCE) was able to stabilize the Hittite kingdom even though the southeastern vassal state of Kizzuwadna was taken by the Syrian Mitanni kingdom. The Hittites were able to gain control of much of the territory previously controlled by the Old Kingdom rulers, and Tudhaliya I was successful in retaking Arzawa in western Anatolia.

His son, Arnuwanda I (reigned *c.* 1380 BCE) encountered difficulties with the Kaska people in the north, and Arzawa was lost, partly because of help from the kingdom of Ahhiyawa (perhaps a Mycenaean state). His successor, Tudhaliya II (reigned *c.* 1360–1345 BCE), was not able to keep the kingdom together. According to Hittite sources, rebellions occurred on every side of the kingdom, and the capital city, Hattusa, was captured and burned, although there is no archaeological evidence of the destruction.

BELOW **These figures in a Hittite relief** from Alaca Hüyük, Turkey, are thought by historians to represent acrobats (right) and a sword-swallower (left) performing in a festival.

Sometime before the monarch's death, the son of Tudhaliya II, Suppiluliuma I, participated in a doomed expedition against Mitanni. Though chronological details are not clear, it appears that the first successor to Tudhaliya was a filial namesake (Tudhaliya III) who was murdered in a coup by Suppiluliuma I (reigned *c.* 1344–1322 BCE).

The Deeds of Suppiluliuma I

Suppiluliuma I is best known through "The Deeds of Suppiluliuma," a narration, composed on at least seven tablets, which was written during the reign of his son and second successor, Mursili II. Another fragmentary text, dated from the brief earlier reign of Arnuwanda I, Suppiluliuma's first son, also describes Suppiluliuma's exploits, but "The Deeds of Suppiluliuma" is a muh more comprehensive and detailed source.

In it, it is apparent that the king removed his brother Tudhaliya III (reigned *c.* 1345–1344 BCE) from the throne. However, Suppiluliuma was successful in reestablishing Hittite power in Anatolia, making the Hittite kingdom as powerful as any state in the Near East. Furthermore, he subordinated the kingdom of Mitanni and other kingdoms in Syria (e.g., Nuhashshe, Amurru, and Ugarit) to the Hittites. These conquered kingdoms were also required to sign a long-lasting loyalty treaty with the Hittite kingdom.

Suppiluliuma and Near East Expansion

Suppiluliuma I played a significant role in the dissolution of the Mitanni kingdom. Not only did he weaken them via military involvement, he attempted to internally weaken the Syrian state by intervening in dynastic strife. A treaty written in Akkadian tells how the Mitanni prince Shattiwaza, who had fled to Hatti, was encouraged by the Hittites to move against his home country. In fact, Shattiwaza became closely tied to the Hittite state by marrying a daughter of

LEFT **The Hittite sanctuary at Yazilikaya** near Hattusa features a procession of 12 Hittite gods bearing curved sickles. A similar procession of goddesses adorns the opposite wall.

Suppiluliuma. However, the treaty makes it clear that the Hittite king was the senior partner in the relationship, and that the Mitanni prince was forced to comply with his demands.

According to historical narratives found in the Plague Prayers of Mursili II, Suppiluliuma I campaigned in Syria, taking Carchemish, and even raiding Amqa, a territory to the south controlled by Egypt (*c.* 1325 BCE). Interestingly, an unnamed Egyptian queen sent a letter to the Hittite king informing him that her husband had died (perhaps Tutankhamun), and asking for one of his sons to marry. Although he was understandably suspicious, Suppiluliuma sent his son, Zananza, to fulfil Egypt's request. However, when the prince was murdered on the trip, it caused a serious rift between the two states.

Suppiluliuma then dispatched the crown prince, Arnuwanda, to Syro-Palestine, where he was successful in his military ventures. However, according to the Plague Prayers, the prisoners and deportees brought back an epidemic to Hatti, killing many people, including Suppiluliuma himself, and his son and first successor Arnuwanda II, who reigned *c.* 1322–1321 BCE.

Mursili II

According to his annals, the next Hittite king Mursili II (reigned *c.* 1321–1295 BCE) was a youth when he came to the throne and was thus not given proper respect by other kingdoms. His eastern front was relatively secure because of a loyal brother who ruled in Carchemish, but Mursili had particular problems with the Kaska people in the northeast, claiming that they had harbored Hittite fugitives.

SUPPILULIUMA I AND NIQMADDU OF UGARIT

The treaty between Suppiluliuma I of Hatti and Niqmaddu of Ugarit, after the Syrian city's surrender to the Hittites, is a document of particular interest. The treaty opens with a historical prolog, stipulating how the king of Ugarit, Niqmaddu, was to resist starting any hostilities against the Hittites, even if he was encouraged to do so by neighboring kings. Niqmaddu was also required to pay tribute not only to the Hittite king, but to his queen, the crown prince, and even his top officials. The Ugaritic king also had to publicly abase himself before the Hittite king, witnessed by a thousand Hittite deities. Moreover, both Ugaritic and Hittite gods were to guarantee that the relationship was not to change in the future.

RIGHT **A hieroglyphic inscription of King Niqmaddu** was discovered on a fragment of a vessel in Ugarit. The treaty between Niqmaddu and Suppiluliuma covered several tablets of text, and essentially made Ugarit into a subject state of the Hittites.

According to the Plague Prayers, Mursili II spent a decade restoring order after the epidemic which swept his kingdom. He was then concerned about the supernatural reasons behind the plague, and thus discerned by oracles that the gods were angry with the Hittites because of the murder of Tudhaliya I (*c.* 1400 BCE), the Hittite invasion of Syria (which was in violation of a treaty with Egypt), and because of their neglect of certain offerings. By admitting his guilt, Mursili hoped that the gods would be appeased and have mercy upon his kingdom.

BELOW **Ramesses II** subdues his enemies (possibly the "defeated" Hittites at the Battle of Qadesh) in a heroic depiction from the Great Rock Temple, Abu Simbel, Egypt (*c.* 1275–1213 BCE).

Muwatalli II

The son of Mursili II, Muwatalli II (reigned *c.* 1295–1272 BCE), inherited the powerful Hittite kingdom. However, the Hittites had seized the Egyptian vassal kingdoms of Qadesh and Amurru. Historical narratives from Egypt reveal how the Egyptians, under the rule of Ramesses II (reigned *c.* 1279–1213 BCE), and the Hittites fought a major yet inconclusive battle near the city of Qadesh in approximately 1275 BCE. The hostile relations between the two states continued throughout the short reign of Muwatalli's son Urhi-Teshub (reigned *c.* 1272–1267 BCE), who was then deposed by one of the sons of Mursili II (and Urhi-Teshub's uncle), Hattusili III (reigned *c.* 1267–1237 BCE).

In Ramesses's twenty-first year, however, when Hattusili III had gained the throne, the two warring monarchs signed a treaty, versions of which have been found in both Hatti (in Akkadian) and Egypt, that outlined cooperation, "brotherhood," and a pact of nonaggression between the Egyptians and the Hittites. Furthermore, a diplomatic marriage was arranged between Egypt and Hatti. The territories the Hittites had taken from Egypt remained with the Hittites.

Hattusili III

Hattusili's reign is known primarily from his "Apology," a highly propagandistic autobiographical defense of his usurpation of the imperial throne from his nephew. The text also includes a description of his extremely biased perspective on the reigns of his two predecessors. In the Apology, we learn that Hattusili III was left behind to protect Hattusa when Muwatalli II moved the Hittites' imperial capital south to Tarhuntassa. In fact, he was made king of the city-state of Hakpish to the northeast. Hattusili III also participated in the Qadesh battle, after which he married Pudu-Hepa of Kizzuwadna, who became one of the most influential queens in Hittite history. Hattusili III claimed that his predecessor Urhi-Teshub treated him poorly out of jealousy. However, the future king did not act to remove his nephew until matters had become out of control, at least in his opinion. After all, Urhi-Teshub was merely the son of a concubine, according to the text of the Apology.

However, Urhi-Teshub was not killed, but exiled to Nuhashshe in Syria, where he became a "thorn in the side" of Hattusili, as he conspired with both Kassite Babylonia and Assyria to be placed back on the throne of Hatti. In exasperation, Hattusili demanded that the former king be exiled still further away. But instead, the banished Hittite monarch fled to Egypt, and thus received the hospitality of Ramesses II. Now even more frustrated, Hattusili wrote to the Kassite king, Kadashman-Enlil II, complaining that the Egyptian monarch refused to hand over the "rebel" (presumably Urhi-Teshub, although he was not explicitly named). Presumably, relations between Egypt and Hatti became strained at this point, but there is no documentation that has as yet been discovered to support this.

LEFT **This terracotta plaque,** *c.* 1300 BCE, of a seated god or goddess, was found at Emar in Syria, a vassal of the New Kingdom Hittites.

Hattusili III and International Correspondence

At any rate, there is a significant body of international correspondence between Hattusili and other powers, including Assyria, Egypt, and Babylonia, as well as vassal states. Of particular interest is correspondence with Ahhiyawa, a powerful kingdom to the west. In one fragmentary letter addressed to an unnamed king of Ahhiyawa from an unnamed Hittite king (commonly assumed to be Hattusili III), the Hittite king asked for the return of a certain Piyama-radu, whose offences were described in some detail. One can infer from the text that the Ahhiyawa were on cordial terms with the Hittites, and were also considered equals, as the king was described as "my brother."

In fact, this same Piyama-radu is again mentioned (in the past tense, though) in another letter from the Hittite king to a client king of Milawata in western Anatolia (identified currently with the Ionian city of Miletus, on the coast of the Aegean Sea). At any rate, Piyama-radu was described as the wayward king of Wilusa, which has been tentatively identified with the famous Homeric Troy (ancient Ilios). Hattusili III also received a note from Ramesses II regarding obstetric assistance for the Hittite king's sister.

The Role of Pudu-Hepa

It is also presumed that Pudu-Hepa, Hattusili's wife, wrote independently to Ramesses II, and also received correspondence from the Egyptian pharaoh. After Hattusili's death, Ramesses even afforded her the same title given to her deceased husband. About 15 letters in total that were exchanged have been recovered, although the letter heading is lost in some cases.

In fact, Pudu-Hepa issued her own royal seals, which usually was the prerogative of the monarch, and participated in the judicial affairs of the Hittite Empire. She also arranged marriages for the Hittite and Amurru royal houses, and provided a Kassite princess for Tudhaliya IV, her son (reigned *c.* 1237–1209 BCE).

Much of this activity probably occurred after the death of Hattusili III, when Pudu-Hepa was the queen mother. Hittite queen mothers were generally powerful figures, however, thus the diplomatic life and influence of Pudu-Hepa may not have been unusual in this context. Tudhaliya IV was the last significant king of this period, before the new century ushered in widespread unrest across Anatolia and the Mediterranean.

LEFT **King Tudhaliya IV** is depicted in the clasp of a god in this large relief (*c.* 1225 BCE) from the Hittite sanctuary at Yazilikaya.

Hattusa

Reconstructing the Walls

Little remains of Hattusa's once-towering city walls. Since 2005, however, a reconstruction has taken place of the mud-brick walls in one 215-ft (65-m) stretch, giving a sense of the extent of the city's original fortifications.

Hattusa, the capital of the Hittites, was located near the modern town of Bogazkoy (or Bogazkale) in northeast Central Anatolia, in Turkey. It appears to have been founded by indigenous Hattic people early in the second millennium BCE, and flourished during the period of the Assyrian merchant colonies, *c.* 1970 to 1780 BCE. The Hittite king Anitta of Kushara (located somewhere in southeast Anatolia), claimed to have destroyed and cursed it (*c.* 1750 BCE), and there is archaeological evidence of destruction about that time. The city was restored again by the Hittite king Hattusili I (*c.* 1650 BCE), and became the most influential city of the Hittites for the next 350 years.

Although relatively small when compared to other ancient Near Eastern cities, Hattusa was divided into three main zones: the upper city, the lower city, and the citadel. It was dominated by the acropolis, which was fortified in the next century with a wall 25 ft (8 m) thick, probably during the reign of Hantili II (*c.* 1475–1450 BCE). This phase of Hattusa's history was ended *c.* 1400 BCE when the city was sacked by invaders from the Kaska region in the north. Presumably, the rebuilding project began during the reign of Suppiluliuma I (reigned *c.* 1344–1322 BCE), who removed almost all of the evidence of the city's former life. Hattusa in this late Hittite Period was also ornately refurbished and expanded during the reign of Tudhaliya IV (reigned *c.* 1237–1209 BCE), the last significant Hittite New Kingdom monarch.

The city was composed of two separate sections: the royal acropolis in the southeast sector, and the lower city. To the west of the acropolis was the largest temple at Hattusa, the Temple of the Storm God, a

A Walled City

Around Hattusa's upper and lower cities were casemate walls—parallel walls with cross-walls between them, forming rooms that could be used for barracks or storage, or filled in to provide a thicker wall. Flanking towers were built at about 70-ft (20-m) intervals and included towered city gates, many of which had monumental relief sculptures, including the King's, Lion, and Sphinx Gates. All of these pointed towards the south. At the southwest entrance was the Lion Gate (pictured), named because of a pair of stone lions which guarded that area of the city. In the southeast was the King's Gate, named after a 7-ft (2-m) high sculpted male figure wearing military gear seated inside the left of the gateway. Between these two gates were two pairs of female sphinxes. The fortifications at Hattusa were over 16,000 ft (5 km) in circumference.

vast, monumental stone temple complex of over 215,000 sq ft (20,000 sq m), rivaling those temples found at Thebes in Egypt. The entire city in the late phase was enclosed by massive casemate walls which were somewhere around 25–35 ft (8–10 m) high (see feature box, below left).

Two of the city gates provided access to the lower city. Moreover, over 30 temples have been excavated in the upper city, exposing the sacral character of the area. Twenty-five of the temples were clustered together, most of which were either square or rectangular in shape. All of the temples contained archive rooms, which stored numerous documents, including a Hurrian–Hittite bilingual text, a fragment of the Akkadian version of Gilgamesh, and incantations, oracles, and temple donations. All traffic from the southern city gates went through the temple complex to get to the lower city. One scholar has argued that the layout of the city represented the Hittite view of the universe: the palace (profane area), the temple complex (sacred), and the cult district (the interface between the two).

Estimates for the size of the city range from 10,000 to 40,000 inhabitants. The myriad private houses that have been excavated most likely belonged to temple personnel, while the secular portion of the population probably lived outside the city walls. The build-up of the entire town was a supreme engineering achievement, as the Hittites had to traverse very rugged and mountainous terrain and cross massive gorges to create this powerful fortress city.

The Lower City at Hattusa

This aerial view of the excavated lower city at Hattusa shows the Great Temple, also known as the Temple of the Storm God, and its storerooms at the left of the picture.

Storing Temple Goods

Large storage jars were found in the storeroom area of the Temple of the Storm God. These vessels seem designed to hold enormous grain reserves, almost as if the city expected to be periodically crippled by major sieges.

The Mediterranean States

The political landscape of the eastern Mediterranean region during the Late Bronze Age (*c.* 1550–1200 BCE) was diverse. As well as the major polities (Egypt, Hatti, Mitanni, Assyria, and Babylonia), a host of lesser kingdoms and vassal states existed in the period.

Most of the lesser states that existed in the Late Bronze Age are imperfectly known to historians.

Ahhiyawa

Somewhere to the west of Hatti lay the kingdom of Ahhiyawa, a powerful polity mentioned often in Hittite documents of the New Kingdom period (*c.* 1400–1190 BCE), which figured prominently in Hittite affairs in western Anatolia. From the documents, it appears that Ahhiyawa was considered a diplomatic equal to the Hittite kingdom. For over a century it has been proposed that the term "Ahhiyawa" was indeed the Hittite version of "Achaia," a Homeric term for the Greeks. Although debate continues, most scholars argue that the kingdom of Ahhiyawa did indeed refer to all or part of the Mycenaean world.

Moreover, recent archaeological surveys have uncovered evidence of Mycenaean involvement in western Anatolia. In fact, Hittite records note a land called Milawata, which has been identified with Miletus, a well-known Classical Greek city on the western coast of Anatolia. Not only is Mycenaean influence found there, but the kingdom of Ahhiyawa had made Milawata subject to it by the thirteenth century BCE.

The Hittite texts describe Ahhiyawa as a kingdom that participated in the affairs of western Anatolia, either with direct military involvement or through local vassals. It does not appear that the Ahhiyawa rulers themselves controlled areas on the mainland of Anatolia, although Linear B texts from Greece make mention of workforces that were recruited from Anatolia. In fact, the relationship of the Ahhiyawa kingdom to the Hittites was often antagonistic, as both states had western Anatolia in their sphere of interest.

BELOW **Islands in the Aegean Sea** near the Anatolian coast may have been the location of the Ahhiyawa kingdom. Patmos and the Dodecanese are shown here.

Luwians

Western Anatolia was inhabited by an Indo-European group of peoples known as the Luwians, whose language was closely related to Hittite. After the fall of the Hittite New Kingdom (*c.* 1190 BCE), Luwian was the dominant language of the Neo-Hittite successor states in much of Anatolia. Though western Anatolia was called "Luwiya" in the earliest Hittite sources, the New Kingdom Hittites used the term "Arzawa lands" to denote a collection of Hittite vassal states formerly confederated in the Arzawa kingdom.

Although this region does not seem to have been politically unified during the Late Bronze Age, the Hittites mention a number of coalitions headed by the king of Arzawa, often causing tremendous havoc in the neighboring Hittite state. In fact, Amenhotep III of Egypt (reigned *c.* 1390–1352 BCE) wrote directly to the king of Arzawa, Tarhundaradu, in the attempt to enter into a marriage alliance with him (and thus establish diplomatic relations that were free from Hittite influence).

Another Luwian entity was the state named Kizzuwadna (known in the Classical period as Cilicia), an important polity in southeastern

LEFT **A clay tablet from Emar** *c.* 1300–1200 BCE, contains a contract for the sale of children. Over 1,000 cuneiform texts have been found at Emar.

Anatolia throughout most of the Hittite kingdoms. The state is first attested in the texts of Telepinu (late sixteenth century BCE), when this region declared its independence from the Hittite state. A seal impression found at Tarsus bears the name of "Isputashu, son of Pariyawatri," a ruler of Kizzuwadna who made an alliance with the Hittite king. However, because of its strategic location, it was not long before Kizzuwadna made an alliance with Mitanni, the powerful state in Syria to the east, as well as with Alalakh on the north Syrian coast during the reign of Idrimi.

The Hittite king Arnuwanda I (reigned *c.* 1380 BCE) was successful in overrunning Kizzuwadna and making it once again a vassal state of the Hittites. In fact, Tudhaliya III (reigned *c.* 1345–1344 BCE) made an extensive treaty with Sunassura of Kizzuwadna, perhaps to keep the area as a friendly buffer state to counteract the Mitanni, and to gain safe passage into Syria for military operations. Though several rebellions are recounted, Kizzuwadna remained in the sphere of the Hittites during the Hittite New Kingdom period, and even sent troop support to coastal Syria for the battle of Qadesh between Hatti and Egypt (*c.* 1275 BCE). Like Lukka to the west, a number of Neo-Hittite kingdoms came into existence in this western region after the collapse of the the Hittite New Kingdom empire in *c.* 1190 BCE.

Carchemish and Aleppo

There was a bewildering array of small kingdoms in Syro-Palestine during this period as well, a selection of which will be discussed here. Due east of Kizzuwadna on the Euphrates River was the city of Carchemish, which had apparently been autonomous for part of the Hittite Old Kingdom, although it was a vassal of Mitanni in the fifteenth century BCE. The Hittite king Suppiluliuma I established two buffer states in northern Syria in the mid-fourteenth century BCE, one at Carchemish and one at Aleppo, west of Carchemish in northern Syria, placing two of his sons on their respective thrones. Both towns continued under the direct rule of the Hittite royal house until the end of the Hittite state (*c.* 1190 BCE). Moreover, Carchemish continued as a Neo-Hittite center for five more centuries, until *c.* 700 BCE.

Both Carchemish and Aleppo are well attested in the third millennium BCE, and Aleppo, especially, was a powerful state in the early second millennium BCE, even rivaling Babylon in power. The ethnic makeup of the cities in the Late Bronze Age is not certain, but West Semitic peoples continued to inhabit the region. During this period, the monarchs at Carchemish bore Hurrian names in the early period, and Hittite ones later.

Syria and Cyprus

Further south on the bend of the Euphrates River was Emar, another town that had flourished in the third millennium BCE. It was the

RIGHT **A Neo-Hittite stele** from Tell Ahmar, just south of Carchemish on the Euphrates, shows the weather god Teschub with a lightning-bolt trident, *c.* 900–800 BCE.

main city in the small kingdom of Ashtata, which had become a Hittite protectorate. In fact, Emar was rebuilt by Mursili II in the late fourteenth century BCE and came under the direct supervision of Carchemish. Thousands of texts written in Akkadian have been recovered at Emar, many of which reveal a thriving economy which flourished without direct Hittite involvement. However, the Hittites did involve themselves directly in the juridical life of Emar.

BELOW **This bronze horned god** was found in Enkomi, Cyprus, and is dated to c. 1250 BCE.

The island of Cyprus (ancient Alasiya) was also an independent state in the early part of the Late Bronze Age. Documents from the reign of Suppiluliuma I claim that his predecessor, Tudhaliya III, conquered Alasiya in the middle of the fourteenth century BCE and imposed tribute upon them. Because of its abundance of timber and copper, the island was a strategic area for the Hittite kings. In the Amarna letters, the king of Alasiya was referred to by the pharaoh as "my brother," implying its importance in the eastern Mediterranean region.

Due west of Aleppo on the Orontes River was Alalakh, apparently the main city of the small kingdom of Mukish, best known because of a pseudo-autobiographical inscription of Idrimi, the putative founder of this Mitanni vassal in the fifteenth century BCE. Idrimi was powerful enough to make a treaty with Pilliya, king of Kizzuwadna (another tributary state of Mitanni in this period). South of Alalakh was Ugarit on the Mediterranean coast, well known because of thousands of alphabetic cuneiform texts found there, dating to *c.* 1400–1200 BCE. Though not a large state, Ugarit was a flourishing, ethnically diverse metropolis in a timber-producing region. The kings of Ugarit were caught between the two superpowers, Egypt and Hatti, and both kingdoms courted this small state. For example, Niqmaddu of Ugarit received a detailed letter from Suppiluliuma I offering support to the Ugaritic kingdom. Once he had accepted, the Hittite monarch amputated lands from the kingdom of Mukish and gave them to Ugarit.

One of the most powerful of these lesser states was Nuhashshe, east of Mukish and Ugarit, and situated between the Orontes and Euphrates Rivers. Although the name is known in the Mari and Alalakh archives earlier in the second millennium BCE, Nuhashshe did not become a coherent state (or coalition of states) until the Hittite New Kingdom. However, in one text, Suppiluliuma I claimed to have defeated the primary king of Nuhashshe, Sarrupsi, and deported the king and his family to Hattusa.

Amurru

The southern portion of Syro-Palestine was dominated by the Egyptian state. South of the Nuhashshe lands was the amorphous kingdom of Amurru, formed out of the smaller city-statelets on the borderlands between the Egyptian and Mitanni spheres of influence. The state figures prominently in the Amarna letters and in the Hittite archives. Although in the Egyptian sphere of influence, it was a constant bother to nearby vassal states. The Amarna letters make mention of two kings of Amurru, 'Abdi-Ashirta and his son Aziru, both of whom employed roving bands of peoples known collectively as the 'Apiru. In fact, three major Egyptian strongholds—Sumur, Tunip, and Ullaza—were overtaken by Amurru, as well as towns in the region of Qatna, Sidon, and Qadesh.

Probably because of the threat of Hittite involvement from the north, the Egyptian king, Akhenaten, was concerned enough to demand Aziru's presence at the Egyptian court. There are numerous Amarna letters from Rib-Adda, the king of Gubla (Byblos) on the Syrian coast, who complained bitterly to the Egyptian crown about the encroachment (and subsequent conquest) by Amurru of his territory. Since the third millennium BCE, Gubla had been a strategic trading partner with Egypt.

Other Southern Canaanite States

Further south were a number of small Canaanite principalities, all of which recognized Egyptian sovereignty. Shakmu (biblical Shechem) was the center of a vassal state apparently created by a certain Labayu, who, like the Amurru rulers, employed mercenaries from among the 'Apiru, and often terrorized neighboring territories controlled by Egypt, such as Gezer, Megiddo, and Jerusalem. However, in three Amarna letters,

WHO WERE THE LUKKA?

Other Luwian-speaking peoples known by the Hittites as the Lukka (i.e., the Lycians) inhabited southwestern Anatolia, although sources do not mention the area as an organized political state. Moreover, the Hittites do not record any treaties with the region, nor mention any kings. There were, however, many Lukka who were in the service of the Hittite state. In addition, the Lukka are mentioned in the Amarna letters from Egypt as a population that had periodically raided Alasiya (Cyprus) and even the coast of Egypt. The Lukka would become well known as the Lycians, allies of Troy in Homer's *Iliad*.

RIGHT **A Lycian necropolis** on the island of Kekova, Turkey, is dated to *c.* 600–400 BCE.

Labayu protested that he was a loyal servant of Akhenaten. Even so, with Egyptian assistance a coalition of loyal vassal states seized Labayu. Though captured, he escaped by way of bribery, but was later assassinated. One of those who complained about Labayu was Abdi-Hepa of Jerusalem, who was later branded as an outlaw, even though he asked for support against marauding 'Apiru bands.

Although the Egyptians regarded vassal rulers as Egyptian officials (they were called "mayors" in Egyptian) rather than independent kings, their administration during the early period of the New Kingdom was relatively modest. The difficulties with the Hittites that emerged for Egypt in post-Amarna times, however, subsequently prompted a more heavy-handed administration and a much heavier military presence.

BELOW **Tel Megiddo in Israel** contains Canaanite ruins that have intrigued archaeologists since their discovery nearly 80 years ago.

The Amarna Letters

The Amarna letters are the remains of an international correspondence archive found in central Upper Egypt at the site of Akhetaten (modern-day Tell el-Amarna). Since their discovery in 1887, more than 380 documents written on clay tablets have been recovered from the site.

ABOVE **This colossal statue of Akhenaten** is from the Temple of Aten at Karnak. Most of the surviving Amarna letters date from his reign (*c.* 1352–1336 BCE).

Akhetaten was the capital of Egypt for about one generation during the Eighteenth Dynasty in the mid-fourteenth century BCE. More than 380 documents were recovered in illicit excavations there, covering the years *c.* 1360–1332 BCE. This period includes the reigns of at least four Egyptian monarchs—from the thirtieth year of Amenhotep III, through the entire reigns of Akhenaten and Smenkhkare, to the first year of the reign of Tutankhamun. The letters concern the affairs and relationships between the Egyptian kings and a variety of vassal states in Syro-Palestine, as well as the peer states of Hatti, Mitanni, Assyria, and Babylonia. The major part of the archive was found in the late nineteenth century, and each letter has been assigned a sequential "EA" (i.e., el-Amarna) number.

Writing and Language in the Amarna Letters

The letters were written on clay in the cuneiform script, a writing system that was used in Western Asia (Mesopotamia, Syro-Palestine, Anatolia, and Iran), but that was not thought to have been used in Egypt before the discovery of the tablets. Most of the tablets were composed in Akkadian, the common language of international correspondence and diplomacy during the second millennium BCE. In fact, the letters from Mesopotamia to Egypt were written in the Babylonian dialect of Akkadian. However, those letters sent to Egypt from outside the Mesopotamian sphere (e.g., Syro-Palestine or Anatolia) and outgoing letters from Egypt were written in what has been called "peripheral" Akkadian, betraying some characteristics of the native languages of the writers (i.e., Egyptian, West Semitic, and Hittite). Scholars believe there was a cuneiform scribal school at Akhetaten, where Egyptian scribes learned the Akkadian language and the cuneiform script. Moreover, small selections of the letters were written in Hurrian, the primary language of the Syrian kingdom of Mitanni, and in Hittite, a language spoken in Anatolia.

Over 90 percent of the 380 extant Amarna texts are international letters or inventory lists that were part of letters. The other 30 or so texts

RIB-ADDA OF GUBLA (BYBLOS)

Rib-Adda, the ruler of Gubla (now Byblos, on the coast of Lebanon), wrote numerous letters to the Egyptian crown complaining about the rise of the Syrian state of Amurru and its leader, 'Abdi-Ashirta (later to be succeeded by his son, Aziru). The Byblian ruler wrote a series of letters outlining the threat to his "kingdom" and asking for Egyptian support, which apparently was not sent in a timely fashion (or at least in the time frame desired by Rib-Adda). Rib-Adda was eventually overthrown in a palace coup, replaced by his brother, and sent into exile in Beirut. His ultimate fate is unknown. His letters reflect the unstable political climate of the period, describing relationships with Levantine towns such as Jerusalem, Shakmu (Shechem), Lachish, and Megiddo.

RIGHT **Gubla (Byblos)**, on the Lebanese coast, was particularly vulnerable to sea attacks.

show evidence of the scribal tradition, as among the finds were Mesopotamian myths and epics, syllabaries (lists of symbols for nonalphabetic languages), lexical texts (translations of words from one language to another), and even a god list. Nearly all of the letters were found either in or near a building in Akhetaten that may have been the royal equivalent of a records office. Most of the letters were incoming ones that were received by the crown, and about 12 were either letters ready to be sent, or copies of sent letters.

Egypt and the "Great Kings"

About 40 letters are correspondence between the "great kings," i.e., those who were the pharaoh's peer. These monarchs addressed each other as "brothers," signifying equal rank. The content of the letters usually concerned the establishment or continuation of alliances, often achieved via diplomatic marriages. However, it appears that the marital arrangements were largely one-sided; Egyptian rulers were prepared to accept the daughters of peer kings as their wives, but were not interested in providing Egyptian princesses to foreign rulers. Instead of focusing primarily on so-called "affairs of state" (such as treaty negotiations and military alliances), these kings appear to have been more concerned with the mutual exchange of gifts, and argued passionately about the quantity and quality of the gifts that were transferred.

Egypt and its Vassals

The remainder of the letters shed light on Egypt's relationship to its vassals. Vassal rulers also provided gifts to the Egyptian crown. However, the relationship was considered different from that with the "brother" kings, as their goods were considered as tribute rather than presented as gifts. Moreover, they addressed the Egyptian monarchs with a variety of epithets, such as "my lord," and referred to themselves using the term "servants," even if they were kings in their own right. The rulers of the small Syro-Canaanite states subject to Egypt were often designated by the title of "mayor." It appears that the region of Syro-Canaan was divided into two or possibly three provinces, each of which was overseen by an Egyptian commissioner.

In the letters with its vassals, the Egyptians were concerned with acquiring goods and personnel, arranging supplies for troops, and ensuring obedience from the vassals. The vassals in return had a great variety of requests for the crown, depending upon their circumstances. In fact, unlike the letters in the royal correspondence, the vassals' letters refer to political events. In the northern provinces, the writers express concern over two powers that had begun to encroach upon Egyptian territories: the Hittites, who had begun to reassert their power in Syria, and a new state named Amurru, which was terrorizing other Egyptian holdings in the north.

BELOW **This Amarna letter** by Burnaburiash II, the Kassite king of Babylon (reigned *c.* 1359–1333 BCE), requests that Akhenaten send a generous gift of gold to Babylon.

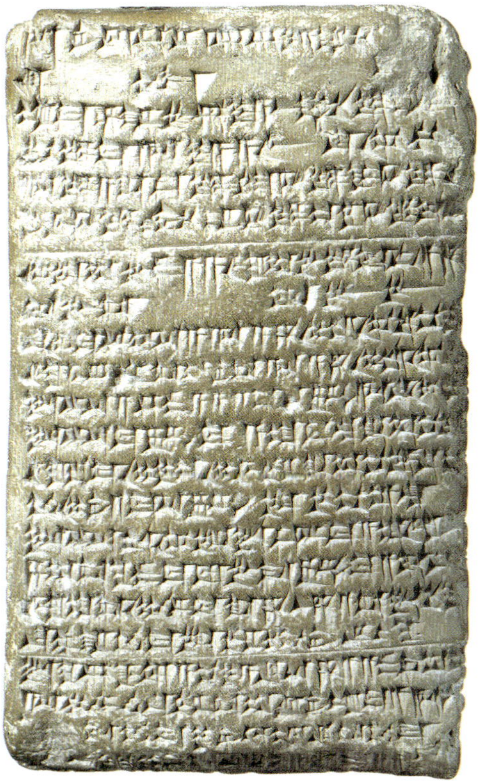

The Road to Qadesh

Because of the Hittite presence in northern Syria, Ramesses II of Egypt led a large force in his fourth year (*c.* 1275 BCE) to check their advances, culminating in a great battle near the town of Qadesh on the Orontes River.

ABOVE **The Battle of Qadesh,** from the Temple of Amon at Karnak, shows Ramesses II defeating the Hittite enemy. Egyptian depictions of the battle misrepresent Egypt's "victory" in the battle.

Qadesh (now known as Tell Nebi Mend) was a site of great strategic importance, as it lay at the crossroads of the north-south and east-west communication routes, and dominated the most convenient fords of the Orontes River south of the Lake of Homs.

Qadesh before the War

For at least two centuries before the campaign of Ramesses, Qadesh played a significant role in Egyptian international affairs in Syria. For example, Qadesh was at the head of more than 300 towns that rebelled against Thutmosis III, resulting in the coalition's defeat at Megiddo (*c.* 1457 BCE). During the reign of Amenhotep II (*c.* 1425–1400 BCE) the city continued to be hostile, and Amenhotep forced the town to acquiesce by means of a loyalty oath. By the time of Thutmosis IV (reigned *c.* 1400–1390 BCE), the Egyptians had forged an alliance with the state of Mitanni, which controlled the northern part of Syria. Qadesh, however, was at the time firmly under Egyptian control.

This situation did not remain stable for long, as northern Syria was overrun by the Hittite king, Suppiluliuma I (reigned *c.* 1344–1322 BCE), who conquered the Mitanni state and then controlled the region. During the reign of Akhenaten (reigned *c.* 1352–1336 BCE), the Egyptians twice unsuccessfully attempted to clear the Hittites from the region. This "cold war" between Egypt and Hatti continued for another generation. Understandably, Qadesh was a main point of concern between the two powerful states.

In fact, it appears that the town either changed hands or independently reversed alliances a number of times during this period. Seti I of Egypt (reigned *c.* 1290–1279 BCE) claimed to have destroyed Qadesh, which was clearly an exaggeration, as the town was back in Hittite hands soon thereafter.

Not only was Qadesh in the Hittite sphere of influence at the outset of Ramesses's reign (*c.* 1279 BCE), the neighboring kingdom of Amurru was now a Hittite satellite state, thus jeopardizing Egyptian influence in the region. Thus, the goal of the war in *c.* 1275 BCE, at least for the Egyptians, was to recover Qadesh and reassert their power.

LEFT **In this relief from Ramesses II's mortuary temple at Thebes,** the "defeated" Hittites at the Battle of Qadesh are depicted drowning in the Orontes River.

The Battle

The Hittite war had an enormous impact on the Egyptians, who recorded the event in at least two separate accounts (narrative and poetic), and created pictorial representations which included commentary. Multiple copies of both versions have been found, numbering in total about 15, and were located in various temples throughout Egypt (e.g., Abydos, Luxor, Karnak, and south at Abu Simbel). By analyzing both accounts, one can present a composite view of the battle from the Egyptian perspective.

Ramesses led four divisions of the Egyptian army towards Qadesh. While the king was with the Amun division near Qadesh, two Hittite deserters, who were in actuality spies, gave him false information as to the whereabouts of the main Hittite force. They told him the Hittites were over 100 miles (160 km) north, near Aleppo. Thus, the Egyptian king marched north past Qadesh and encamped on high ground, awaiting the main body of his army. Subsequently, the Egyptians captured two more Hittites, who, after some physical interrogation, gave the correct location of the Hittite forces—the Hittites were alarmingly close, also north of the city on the Orontes River. Unfortunately, the Egyptians were outflanked, and Ramesses soon found his division surrounded by Hittite chariot forces. Worse, the nearest supporting Egyptian division had been scattered by the surprise attack of the Hittite chariots, and the other two divisions were still some distance further to the south.

The accounts change at this point, presumably because of Egyptian ideology concerning the nature of the divine monarch, who could not possibly suffer defeat. Ramesses single-handedly broke through the Hittite forces, slaughtering many on the way. The Egyptians were soon able to regroup, "defeat" the Hittite army, and cause the Hittite monarch, Muwatalli II, to write a letter and sue for peace. One can glean from the Egyptian perspective that the Egyptians were bested in the campaign, but were most likely able to rally and fight to an inconclusive draw, thereby setting the stage for negotiations.

The Treaty

Some 15–20 years later, both powers signed a treaty, which has survived in an Egyptian version in two copies, as well as a Hittite version written in Akkadian found at Hattusa, the Hittite royal capital. The two versions are remarkably similar in nature. Both kingdoms were now responsible for maintaining a mutual nonaggression pact and a defensive alliance, extraditing fugitives, and protecting the rights of succession for each state. Furthermore, Ramesses married two different Hittite princesses over a 20-year period, and Qadesh remained, at least nominally, under Hittite control. Relations between Egypt and Hatti were relatively peaceful for the remainder of the century until the dissolution of the Hittite state (*c.* 1200 BCE). Soon thereafter, Qadesh was destroyed, probably by the Sea Peoples.

BELOW **The treaty of Qadesh** between Egypt and Hatti is one of the earliest surviving peace treaties. This fragment is dated *c.* 1255 BCE.

The Rise of Assyria

For almost 400 years after the rule of Shamshi-adad I and his sons ended, it appears that Assyria languished in subordination to Babylonian and Mitanni rule. But by the reign of Ashuruballit I (*c.* 1363–1328 BCE), the Assyrians were strong enough to throw off the Mitannian yoke and reassert themselves on the political stage.

BELOW **The ruins of Assur (modern Qalat Sharqat) are located on the Tigris River, about 68 miles (110 km) south of Mosul in Iraq.**

Knowledge about Assyria between the mid-eighteenth and mid-sixteenth centuries BCE is very limited. The only sources available are the later Assyrian King List, which provides an unbroken yet propagandistic list of rulers (*c.* 1750–1550 BCE), and isolated inscriptions which provide meager information about individuals who ruled at Assur. According to a later Babylonian Chronicle, the Assyrians made a boundary treaty with the Babylonians in this period, and it also appears that the Assyrians sent gifts to the Egyptian state. Both of these items seem to imply that Assyria was still a politically autonomous kingdom, but at some point in the sixteenth century BCE it is clear that northern Iraq was subject to the expansion of the powerful Hurrian kingdom of Mitanni in Syria.

Assyria during Mitanni Rule

The relationship of Mitanni and Assyria in this period is, however, unclear. Until nearly the end of the fifteenth century BCE, there are no extant Assyrian royal inscriptions. Thus, the rulers mentioned in the Assyrian King List may have been mayoral vassals of Mitanni, rather than kings in their own right. By the mid-fifteenth century BCE, the Mitanni king Shaustatar claimed to have plundered the city of Assur, taking silver and gold to furnish his palace at Washukanni, his capital city in inland Syria. It also appears that a handful of Assyrian officials recognized Mitanni kings as their overlords; legal texts from Assur display Hurrian-named officials. Thousands of bureaucratic texts uncovered at Nuzi, a small town in northern Iraq, also include many names of Hurrian derivation, and it is clear the Hurrian cultural influence was indeed strong. In fact, it appears from the Nuzi texts that Assyria was fragmented into a number of vassal kingdoms under Mitanni rule.

Assyrian Resurgence and Ashuruballit I

By about 1420 BCE, Assyrian royal inscriptions reappear in the archaeological record. The walls of Assur were rebuilt. A later document from Tell el-Amarna in Egypt claims that Assyrian king Ashur-nadin-ahhe II (reigned *c.* 1400–1391 BCE) exchanged gifts with the Egyptians. About this time, a Mitanni–Hittite treaty mentions an unnamed Assyrian king (perhaps Eriba-adad, reigned *c.* 1390–1364 BCE) who had declared his independence from the Hurrians. Certainly, the Assyrians had become an autonomous

political state by the beginning of the reign of Ashuruballit I (reigned *c.* 1363–1328 BCE).

Letters from Tell el-Amarna chart the rise of the newly resurgent kingdom. For example, the Kassite king of Babylon, Burnaburiash II (reigned *c.* 1359–1333 BCE) complained that the Assyrian king, who was a Kassite vassal (at least according to the king of Babylon), was treated as an equal by the Egyptian crown. In a famous letter, Ashuruballit made this explicit, showing that Assyria was a sovereign entity by attempting to form a relationship with Egypt. He sent an envoy and gifts (a chariot, two horses, and precious stones) for this purpose. However, the Assyrian king complained in a second letter that the Egyptians had not been as lavish in their gift giving, especially since the Assyrian monarch was the equal to the Mitanni king, who had received more gold from Egypt! At any rate, it is quite evident in the letters that the Assyrians were intent on being treated independently—rather than as a client state—and that Egypt responded in kind.

Another example of Assyria's importance is the fact that Ashuruballit gave his daughter in marriage to the Kassite king of Babylon, Burnaburiash. When the product of this marriage (Kara-Hardash) came to the Babylonian throne, he was eventually assassinated in a palace rebellion, so Ashuruballit avenged the death of his grandson by invading Babylon and replacing the usurper with Kurigalzu II (*c.* 1327 BCE). Ashuruballit also rebuilt major religious structures, such as the Temple of Ishtar at Assur. Clearly, by the end of his reign, Assyria had become one of the major states in the Near East.

Ashuruballit's Successors

Though there are no contemporary inscriptions from Ashuruballit detailing military campaigns, there are hints at his military ability in the records of later Assyrian kings, who claimed that he had defeated the Subarians, traditionally a Mesopotamian term for peoples in the north. Later sources also claimed that Enlil-nirari I (reigned *c.* 1327–1318 BCE), Ashuruballit's successor, defeated the Kassites in a battle in Assyria near Erbil. By the time of Arik-den-ili (reigned *c.* 1317–1306 BCE), the Assyrian kings were giving themselves the title "Mighty king, king of Assyria," once again showing Assyria's status as a major player on the political stage. However, Arik-den-ili, according to a later Assyrian chronicle, had to endure an invasion north of Nineveh from an unnamed enemy. He responded by attacking the Guti, a name for mountain peoples in the north (probably in the western Zagros Mountains).

LEFT **The walls of Assur** were made up of heavily fortified inner and outer walls and gateways. The city was extensively restored during the Middle Assyrian period.

BELOW **The reconstructed Nergal Gate** of Nineveh shows the grandeur of Assyrian architecture.

SHALMANESER AND NIMRUD

In addition to military expansion, Shalmaneser I was also concerned with building projects in the heartland of Assyria, especially in the city of Nineveh, an ancient Assyrian center (and later destined to be its last capital) where he built a palace. He also restored the great Temple of Ishtar at Assur, and founded the city of Kalah (modern Nimrud), which also became an Assyrian capital centuries later. Many economic tablets from provincial towns during this reign (e.g., Tell el-Rimah, west of Nineveh) attest to a thriving trade network, even in Anatolia—perhaps implying that the Hittite policies against Assyria were not always successful. However, even this trade network was subject to difficulties because of the ubiquitous Ahlamu people, who often blocked trade routes.

LEFT **The remains of Nimrud** include a large Middle Assyrian palace, on a hill that archaeologists call Fort Shalmaneser.

Military Expansion under Adad-nirari I

Contemporary sources abound by the time of Adad-nirari I (reigned *c.* 1305–1274 BCE), the son of Arik-den-ili, who took Assyrian military power to new heights. This Assyrian king spent a great effort against Hanigalbat (a smaller successor state to imperial Mitanni in Syria), and recorded his campaigns in a series of royal inscriptions that are, at present, the earliest extant documents detailing Assyrian military operations. In them, Adad-nirari describes geographical panoramas and records battle narratives. According to these texts, Adad-nirari's first campaign west was in retaliation for hostilities committed against the Assyrian king by Shattuara, a Hanigalbatean king. Hittite sources also describe how Shattuara was forcibly taken to Assur, where he was strongly encouraged to become a vassal of Assyria. Assyria had clearly turned the tables on the Hurrian successor state.

Despite this apparent victory, Adad-nirari saw fit to invade Syria once again, as Shattuara's son, Wasashatta, had enlisted the aid of the Hittites, but troubles in Anatolia rendered the the Hittite king unable to provide assistance to the Hanigalbatean ruler. In this second campaign, Adad-nirari claimed to have conquered the old Mitanni capital of Washukanni, and went as far west as Carchemish, which bordered the Hittites' kingdom. Thus, Hanigalbat was conquered and Wasashatta and his family group captured, effectively decapitating Hanigalbat's center of resistance against the Assyrians.

Now a powerful state, Assyria made overtures to the Hittites for "brotherhood." However, an unnamed Hittite king rejected the Assyrian monarch's request in a letter, or at least refused to acknowledge Adad-nirari as an equal. At any rate, Assyria now controlled the northern trade routes, as attested by another Hittite letter that describes the request of Hattusili III, the Hittite king, for iron and weapons from the Assyrians. Though the heading of the letter is missing, most historians date it to these monarchs, who now called each other "brother," implying an alliance of equality.

Adad-nirari I was also successful in the south with the Kassites of Babylonia. He was able to secure the Diyala River (and Zagros Mountains) as a border with the Kassites. In fact, his wars with the Kassites were celebrated in an epic, fragments of which still exist. However, the Assyrian kings began to imitate their Babylonian counterparts, as they used Standard Babylonian in their writing (rather than the Assyrian dialect of Akkadian), and the chief god of greater Babylonia, Enlil, became extremely influential. In fact, the Assyrian monarchs used "governor of the god Enlil" as one of their primary titles. Thus, the Assyrians were in many ways culturally dependent upon their southern counterparts, even during those periods in which they controlled Babylonia politically.

Shalmaneser I

The son of Adad-nirari I, Shalmaneser I (reigned *c.* 1273–1244 BCE), continued the traditions of cultural interaction with Babylon and military expansion, as attested by his annals, which were discovered at Assur. He was especially concerned with a northern people who had not previously been mentioned in documents—the Urartians, who inhabited the regions around Lake Van and the Caucasus Mountains. The Urartians are well known in Assyrian inscriptions in the early first millennium BCE as a powerful kingdom that competed with the Assyrian Empire. During the reign of Shalmaneser, however, the Urartians appear to have denoted a series of peoples, but apparently not a unified kingdom.

Shalmaneser seems to have begun the systematic deportation of conquered peoples, who were often used to shore up the workforce in the Assyrian heartland. Many Urartians in particular were used in service to the crown. In addition, Shalmaneser claims to have deported over 14,000 Hanigalbateans from Syria, who were perhaps used to work with raw materials, building projects, and on "chain gangs." It has been speculated that the native Assyrian population was not sufficient to fulfill the labor needs of this emerging state.

LEFT **The goddess Ishtar,** depicted here in a modern imagining by Evelyn Paul (1995), represented not only love and fertility but also war and hunting.

Like his predecessors, Shalmaneser had trouble with his western border with the vassal kingdom of Hanigalbat. However, this time it was not simply because of a rebellious vassal king (once again, Shattuara) but a new people named the Ahlamu, who had made their presence known. It is presumed (but not certain) that the Ahlamu people were a precursor to the Semitic-speaking Arameans known from later Assyrian sources. Caught between two regional superpowers, the king of Hanigalbat was provoked to ask the Hittites for assistance in the war with Assyria. Not only did the Hittites provide military aid, but they forbade their vassal states to trade with Assyria at all. This condition was prescribed by the Hittite king Tudhaliya IV (reigned *c.* 1237–1209 BCE) in a treaty with Shausga-muwa of Amurru (a small kingdom on the Syrian coast). Thus, the Hittites were encouraging an economic embargo on the Assyrian Empire.

ABOVE **These Urartian fortress ruins** are on a hill near Tepe Bastam in Iran. Sustained pressure by the Assyrians eventually saw the disparate Urartian kingdoms unify to confront the threat.

Although this text was probably composed a few years later than Shalmaneser I, it may represent a Hittite policy that had already been in place during his reign. However, Shalmaneser claimed to have gained control over the Hittite city of Carchemish, and even portions of Cappadocia in southeastern Anatolia. The defeat of Hanigalbat gave the Assyrians rich agricultural land and prosperous cities in their territory, and a large population for military use.

Shalmaneser I and Babylon

Shalmaneser I's relationship with Babylon is not entirely clear. However, a letter from the Hittite king Hattusili III (reigned *c.* 1267–1237 BCE) to the king of Babylon, Kadashman-Enlil II (reigned *c.* 1263–1255 BCE) implies Hattusili's concern over the interruption of diplomatic traffic between Hatti and Babylon, which was partly due to the meteoric rise of Assyria's power and their detainment of Babylonian diplomats. Relations between Babylon and Assyria would deteriorate much further, however, during the reign of Tukulti-ninurta I (reigned *c.* 1244–1208 BCE), Shalmaneser's son and successor.

Tukulti-ninurta I

Tukulti-ninurta I of Assyria (reigned *c.* 1244–1208 BCE) is one of the more interesting and enigmatic figures in ancient Near Eastern antiquity. Some have viewed the legends concerning this Assyrian king as possible inspiration for the depictions of the biblical king Nimrod and the Greek Nino (Ninus).

In a reign spanning 36 years, Tukulti-ninurta I consolidated his rule over territories inherited from his father Shalmaneser I, extended Assyrian rule into Anatolia, defeated and plundered Babylon, and founded a new capital city. Because of his brilliant victory against Kassite Babylon and its king, Kashtiliash IV (reigned *c.* 1242–1235 BCE), the Tukulti-ninurta Epic was composed, one of the most interesting historiographic and propagandistic pieces to come from cuneiform literature.

BELOW **The altar of king Tukulti-ninurta I** shows the king in prayer before two deities, each carrying wooden standards.

The Exploits of Tukulti-ninurta

Tukulti-ninurta crossed the Euphrates River in the north to attack Nairi in southeastern Anatolia, perhaps a precursor to Urartu, a powerful state that rivaled Assyria in the early first millennium BCE. He also crossed the Khabur and Balikh River basins into Syria. He even claimed to have deported 20,000 Hittite subjects into Assyria, which was surely an exaggeration. A fragmented text found in Hattusa, presumably from this Assyrian king to the Hittite Tudhaliya IV (reigned *c.* 1237–1209 BCE), describes Assyrian border raids into Anatolia, much to the Hittite king's dismay. Tukulti-ninurta, however, denied that any such event had occurred, and that his soldiers had not snatched anything from Hittite soil. Though there was some animosity, the kings described each other as "brothers," indicating their equal status.

The defeat of the Kassite king Kashtiliash IV was considered the high point of Tukulti-ninurta's reign. Kashtiliash was defeated in battle, and taken from his land in chains. Tukulti-ninurta destroyed the walls of Babylon, killed many of its inhabitants, plundered the city, and deported many Kassites and native Babylonians to Assyria. For the first time, Assyrian administrators were sent to Babylon to rule directly. In addition, he transported the statue of the god Marduk from Babylon to Assyria, where it remained for a century. He even established the Babylonian Akitu (or New Year) festival at Assur, which may have contributed to tensions with Assyrian religious personnel. Among the plunder were many Babylonian literary pieces which were wrenched from their contexts in the south and brought to Assyria. These deeds were probably considered sacrilegious, even in Assyria, as Babylon was thought to be the cultural and religious center of Mesopotamia, and they perhaps prompted the Assyrian king to justify his acts in the highly propagandistic text of the Tukulti-ninurta Epic.

Having greatly increased the size and influence of his empire, Tukulti-ninurta engaged in a series of building projects. He restored the palace of his father, Shalmaneser, in Assur, constructed yet another palace, and then founded a new capital across the Tigris from Assur, Kar-Tukulti-ninurta (i.e., fortress of Tukulti-ninurta), only about 2 miles (3 km) north of the traditional Assyrian center. The Assyrian king pointed out that this city was founded on virgin soil. It is not certain why he decided to build this new capital, although it is possible that he had experienced friction with the elite populations in Assur. However, to proceed with these building projects, he needed to exploit the forests in the eastern region of the Taurus Mountains, bringing hardship to the Assyrian vassals in the area. This may have been the catalyst for the coup that eventually led to his downfall.

ABOVE **Mythical queen Semiramis** (in foreground), imagined here by Adriaen van Nieulandt (1587–1658), was said to be the wife of Ninus, who may be based on Tukulti-ninurta I.

The Tukulti-ninurta Epic

Although in a highly fragmented form, the Tukulti-ninurta Epic is a description of Tukulti-ninurta's victory over his Kassite enemy, Kashtiliash. In a masterful way, it poetically depicts the aggression of the Kassite king (i.e., the events leading up to the battle), the actual war itself, and the Assyrian king's plunder of Babylon.

In the propagandistic Epic, the Assyrian king complains to both Shamash, the Mesopotamian sun god and god of justice, and to Kashtiliash himself, that the Kassite king had violated an ancestral treaty between the two nations, thereby justifying the coming conflict. Predictably, Kashtiliash does not act like a courageous king, but as a frightened weakling, aware of his own guilt and Tukulti-ninurta's reverence to the gods. Like other ancients (including Xerxes in Herodotean lore), the Kassite king recognizes divine portents that predict his demise.

More proof of the courageous nature of the Assyrian king is his mocking challenge to Kashtiliash, who shows his indignity by preparing an ambush, which Tukulti-ninurta is able to repel with great power, as the gods are on his side. Thus, the epic shows the "obvious" moral superiority of the Assyrian king and his gods over the morally decadent Kassite king. Even without the propagandistic ideology, it is apparent that the Assyrians were successful in achieving preeminence, in both cultural and political terms.

The End of Tukulti-ninurta

Despite Tukulti-ninurta's celebrated victory over Kashtiliash, triumph would not characterize the close of his reign. Tukulti-ninurta exercised control over Babylonia for perhaps only seven years, after which a rebellion eventually elevated Adad-shuma-usur (reigned *c.* 1226–1197 BCE), a son of Kashtiliash, to the Babylonian throne. Subsequently, a revolt also took place within Assyria. According to a later Babylonian chronicle, a palace conspiracy occurred in Kar-Tukulti-ninurta, headed by the king's son Ashurnasirpal and nobles from Assur. The Assyrian king was imprisoned and then killed. However, there must have been some confusion after his death, as another son, named Ashur-nadin-apli, succeeded him to the throne, reigning *c.* 1208–1205 BCE.

Assyria lapsed into obscurity after Tukulti-ninurta's reign. There is also a dearth of textual sources for Assyria for nearly a century until the reign of Tiglath-pileser I, who ruled Assyria *c.* 1115–1077 BCE. In fact, within one generation of the assassination of Tukulti-ninurta, Assyria briefly declined so far that it fell under the control of Babylon.

RIGHT **This statue of a monkey** was recovered from the site of Kar-Tukulti-ninurta, the king's capital city. Monkeys, although exotic animals, were often depicted in Mesopotamian art.

Tiglath-pileser I

Although Assyria had been in seeming decline for nearly a century, Tiglath-pileser I (reigned *c.* 1115–1077 BCE) was successful in reorganizing the military and once again began Assyria's military expansion into surrounding areas.

One of the key sources for the rule of Tiglath-pileser is his annals. He appears to have been the first Assyrian king to record true annals, as military events were described in chronological order, although they were not yet dated, nor were the lengths of his military campaigns recorded.

Military Campaigns

From the north came the Mushki, who were perhaps a Proto-Phrygian group that crossed the Tigris and threatened the city of Nineveh. The Assyrian king claims to have massacred them and then appears to have launched a campaign deep into Anatolia, where fragmented Neo-Hittite kingdoms existed, and reached Lake Van, where he erected rock inscriptions. He claimed to have defeated "the 60 kings of the Nairi lands," receiving many exotic animals as booty. Later, he turned due west to subdue the Phoenician states of Gubla (Byblos) and Sidon on the Syrian coast, and evidently reached the Mediterranean Sea, where he was especially interested in his success in killing a *nahiru* or "sea-horse."

In fact, this Assyrian king was quite interested in hunting activities, as he killed four wild bulls in the country of Mitanni (inland Syria), ten bull elephants in the country of Harran and in the Khabur River region, 120 lions slain on foot, and 800 more from the chariot. Even if these are gross exaggerations, they illustrate his great interest in hunting.

BELOW **Hunting was a favorite pastime** of the Assyrian monarchy, as shown in this Neo-Assyrian relief (*c.* 668–627 BCE) of a king hunting lions, from the palace of Ashurbanipal.

Tiglath-pileser I and the Arameans

In these various campaigns, Tiglath-pileser was confronted with Aramean tribes, Semitic-speaking peoples who inhabited the Euphrates River region in Syria. They were independent, semi-nomadic pastoralist tribes, loosely unified by geography rather than ethnicity. These tribes consistently evaded the Assyrian army and raided the local communities, destroying agricultural produce. Though the Assyrian king was not successful in completely subduing them, he claimed to have crossed the Euphrates 28 times to campaign against them. At any rate, it appears that he was able to keep them "at bay" on the western side of the Euphrates River.

Tiglath-pileser I in Babylon

Tiglath-pileser I also campaigned against Assyria's southern neighbor, Babylon. The Babylonian king, Nebuchadnezzar I (reigned *c.* 1124–1103 BCE), had formerly raided Assyrian territory. During the reign of Marduk-nadin-ahhe of Babylon (reigned *c.* 1099–1082 BCE), Ekallatum—which was not far from Assur—was captured. Countering, Tiglath-pileser I penetrated deep

THE "HAREM EDICTS"

Like the Middle Assyrian Laws, the Middle Assyrian Palace Decrees (or "Harem Edicts") were recovered during excavations at Assur. In their present condition, they appear to have been a composite of three centuries' worth of regulations, and thus may have been more of a reference work rather than a series of rules to follow. Nine kings from the reign of Ashuruballit I (reigned *c.* 1363–1328 BCE) to Tiglath-pileser I are referred to in more than 20 extant decrees. In sum, they were a collection of regulations concerning the behavior and actions of palace officials (primarily females and those who interacted with them). The monarchs were especially concerned with the activities in the "Inner Quarter" (or royal harem), and the preservation of its sanctity. Earlier types of decrees like this one have been found at nearby Nuzi, dating from the mid-fourteenth century BCE.

RIGHT **The city of Assur** has yielded invaluable Middle Assyrian documents. The "Harem Edicts" were first translated in the 1950s.

into Babylonia, and plundered a number of cities, including Babylon itself. He did not attempt to control the area itself and did not establish himself as king, as implied by the Synchronistic History (a text that describes the relations between the Assyrian and Babylonian kings in the late second millennium BCE). Although the later years of this Assyrian king are not recorded in the annals, a fragment of a text describes Aramean attacks and a famine in the heartland of Assyria itself. The text even suggests that the prominent city of Nineveh was captured.

Tiglath-pileser I was more than a military chieftain—he was also interested in cultural pursuits. During his reign, the Middle Assyrian Laws and Court Edicts (or Palace Decrees) were compiled, and a major library was constructed in Assur. He was also an indefatigable builder, constructing numerous monuments and temples (restoring the temple of Adad at Assur), as well as public parks and gardens.

The Middle Assyrian Laws

The Middle Assyrian Laws were apparently written and collected by Tiglath-pileser I, perhaps for his royal library or for individual scribal libraries. Most appear to be copies of originals composed at least 300 years earlier. Instead of a single systematic composition, the Middle Assyrian Laws were a series of about 15 tablets containing various legal provisions, ranging from laws concerning women (either as victims or primary participants), blasphemy, assault, sexual offenses, homicide, inheritance, veiling, witchcraft, abortion, agriculture, irrigation, pledges, deposits, theft, maritime traffic, and false accusations, to name a few. Unlike the earlier examples of Sumero-Akkadian law, such as the Code of Hammurabi, the Middle Assyrian Laws are concerned with two types of persons: free people, and male and female slaves. One tablet, labeled as "Middle Assyrian Law A," further differentiates women as wives, widows, and those of the *qadiltu* class (a type of priestess).

The death of Tiglath-pileser I, which may have been an assassination, apparently caused the Assyrians considerable dynastic confusion. Tiglath-pileser's successor was a usurper king named Saggal-apal-ekur, who reigned *c.* 1077–1074 BCE. This instability, whatever its cause, ushered in a period of disorder in Assyria that lasted for well over a century.

BELOW **These Assyrian clay cylinders** are inscribed with an account of the building projects and campaigns of Tiglath-pileser I (*c.* 1100 BCE).

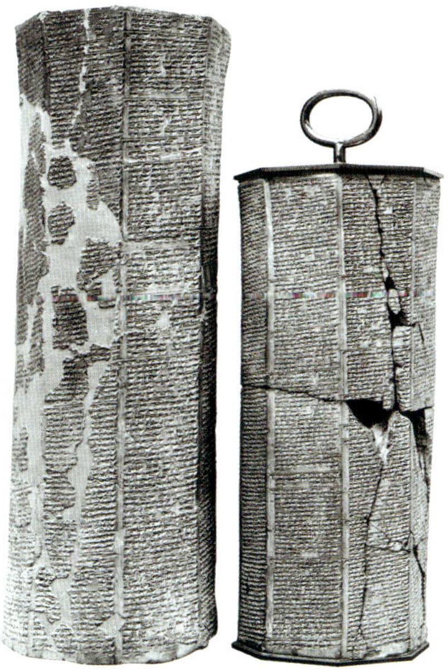

The Sea Peoples

The term "Sea Peoples" describes a variety of peoples who migrated east from the Mediterranean Sea in the later thirteenth through to the mid-twelfth centuries BCE, bringing destruction to the Aegean, Egypt, Syro-Palestine, Cyprus, and Anatolia.

ABOVE **The port of Dor in Israel**, on the Mediterranean coast, was one of the cities that succumbed to invasion by the Sea Peoples in the twelfth century BCE.

The earliest references to the Sea Peoples are scattered, and are found in inscriptions during the reign of Ramesses II (reigned *c.* 1279–1213 BCE), but they are best known from Egyptian sources of the late New Kingdom, particularly during the reigns of Merneptah (reigned *c.* 1213–1203 BCE) and Ramesses III (reigned *c.* 1184–1153 BCE). Thirteenth century BCE documents from Hattusa, the Hittite capital, and from Ugarit in Syria allude to high-level destruction that was perhaps perpetrated by the Sea Peoples. Furthermore, there is increasing archaeological evidence for destruction during this period in various coastal locales around the eastern Mediterranean, much of which has been attributed to the Sea Peoples.

Who Were the Sea Peoples?

Although the origin of the Sea Peoples is not clear, it is commonly assumed that they were mainly from the Aegean area and Anatolia. Some evidence of abandonment in this period has been found at many Mycenaean cities on the mainland of Greece, which may suggest movements of the Sea Peoples traditionally associated with Egyptian texts.

The Egyptian documents list a host of names that have been associated with the Sea Peoples: Denyen, Ekwesh, Lukka, Peleset, Sherden, Shekelesh, Teresh, Tjeker, and Weshesh. Many of these names appear similar to geographic names found in some Hittite and even Greek sources. Denyen, for example, is likely Danuna (or Danaoi), from mainland Greece, while the Ekwesh (or Akawasha) may have been the Ahhiyawa people from the Greek mainland mentioned in Hittite texts, who have been identified with the Achaeans. The Sherden (or Shardana) have been linked to the island of Sardinia, while the Shekelesh have been identified with Sicily. The Lukka were peoples mentioned in both Egyptian and Hittite sources as inhabiting southwestern Anatolia, essentially the same region that was called Lycia in Classical sources. The Teresh have been very difficult to identify, although some have connected them with the classical Tyrsenoi, ancestors of the Etruscans. The Tjeker and Weshesh have defied any firm identification. Last, the Peleset have been more convincingly identified with the biblical Philistines. In their case, we cannot be precisely certain of their original homeland, but we can determine their settlement in southeastern Palestine.

From Egyptian sources, it is apparent some groups of the Sea Peoples were known before the migrations. For example, the Lukka are mentioned as invaders in the Amarna letters in the middle of the fourteenth century BCE during the reign of Amenhotep III. Moreover, painted papyri from Tell el-Amarna show enemy soldiers that look like depictions from mainland

Greece (Mycenae). Sherden soldiers were listed in the service of Ramesses II at the battle of Qadesh (*c.* 1275 BCE).

The Mass Migrations

No one can be certain of the cause of the mass migrations of the Sea Peoples, although theories abound. Famine and sudden climate change are two possibilities. We do know that there was a wave of invasions in year five of the reign of Merneptah (*c.* 1208 BCE), and in year eight of the reign of Ramesses III (*c.* 1176 BCE). The Merneptah texts mention a group of peoples who attacked Egypt in concert with the Libyans, including the Ekwesh, Sherden, Teresh, Shekelesh, and Lukka. The Egyptians describe incorporating the survivors of these attacks into the Egyptian army. Though Ramesses III does not mention a Libyan threat, there was a coalition of Sea Peoples who invaded Egypt, and may have previously attacked Hittite Anatolia and the Syrian coast.

This invasion is depicted in great detail on the walls of the mortuary temple of Ramesses III at Medinet Habu (pictured above right), and the invaders in this instance included the peoples known as Tjeker, Shekelesh, Weshesh, Denyen, and Peleset. In this case, it is interesting to note that the invaders are depicted along with their families, and thus can be assumed to have been looking for new land in which to settle, rather than simply to raid and plunder. The texts also describe the resettlement of the Peleset in southern Palestine, as well as the Tjeker and Sherden along the coast to the north of Egypt.

Predictably, the Egyptians claimed victory over these invaders, and the Sherden people in particular are mentioned as becoming incorporated to some extent into Egyptian society during the remainder of the Ramessid era (until *c.* 1070 BCE). Furthermore, the late Ramessid literary text, the Story of Wenamun, describes the Tjeker as grasping and piratical. Many scholars have surmised that the Sea Peoples contributed to the decline and dissolution of the Egyptian New Kingdom, but there is no consensus as to the extent of that contribution.

ABOVE **Ramesses III,** at left, is shown defeating the Sea Peoples in a relief from Ramesses III's mortuary temple at Medinet Habu in Thebes, Egypt, *c.* 1150 BCE.

THE SEA PEOPLES OUTSIDE OF EGYPT

Evidence for the Sea Peoples in sources outside Egypt during this period is not clear. About 1200 BCE, 'Ammurapi, the last king of Ugarit on the coast of Syria, wrote a letter to the king of Alasiya (Cyprus), describing the enemy advance. He also asked for assistance from the ruler of Carchemish in the north, but received none. It has been assumed that the Sea Peoples are the unnamed threat in these letters, and that they were responsible for the political and social upheavals in Anatolia, causing the collapse of the Hittite state. Further west, the destruction in the twelfth century BCE of many Mycenaean centers has often been associated with these large-scale migrations. Classical tradition describes the migration of the Dorians into southern Greece in this period, but a connection with the Sea Peoples at this point is still problematic.

RIGHT **Mycenaean civilization** may have fallen victim to the chaos that engulfed the eastern Mediterranean in the twelfth century BCE; this vase (*c.* 1150 BCE) depicts Mycenaean warriors.

The Uluburun Shipwreck

The Coast Near Kas, Turkey

The area where the Uluburun shipwreck was found is dotted with rocky islands. Some historians suggest that the ship may have been blown by strong winds onto the rocks, sinking the vessel.

An ancient shipwreck off the coast of Kas in southern Turkey in the Mediterranean Sea came to light in the early 1980s. Underwater excavators labored over the shipwreck for a decade (1984–1994), with spectacular results. The ship was found in parts on a rocky slope about 165 ft (50 m) below the surface. Artifacts most likely associated with the wreck were found at least another 35 ft (10 m) below.

The ship was approximately 50 ft (15 m) long and had a badly damaged hull made of cedar wood. Portions of oars were found, as well as more than 20 anchors, some of which were over 440 lb (200 kg) in weight. Scholars have estimated that the ship might have been able to stow over 20 tons (18 metric tons) of cargo in total.

Though we cannot be absolutely certain about the ship's origin or destination, theories abound. Aspects of the ship show similarities with merchant ships from nearby regions. For example, the anchors have counterparts from Ugarit, Byblos, and Tell Abu Hawam in Syro-Palestine, as well as Kition on Cyprus. The hull has similarities to types found in ships later in Phoenicia. Thus, the ship probably originated in Cyprus or Syro-Palestine. It fits well in the Late Bronze Age (*c.* 1550–1200 BCE), and a more precise study of the dendrochronology—tree-ring analysis on the timber—places its manufacture in the fourteenth century BCE.

The cargo within the ship contained both raw materials and manufactured goods—more than 18,000 cataloged goods in all. Over 470 Cypriot copper ingots of various shapes were recovered, weighing a total of about 10 tons (9 metric tons), as well as 40 tin ingots. Approximately 175 glass ingots of greatly varied shapes and colors (e.g., cobalt blue, turquoise, and lavender) were also recovered, similar to items mentioned in letters from Tell el-Amarna in Egypt and from Ugarit on the coast of Syria. Some scholars argue that the 150 Canaanite-type jars that were found may have been used to transport incense. Other raw material items included logs of Egyptian ebony, worked tortoise carapaces, a few hippopotami teeth, elephant tusks, ostrich eggshells, and portions of sea snail shells. Manufactured goods included ceramics, metal objects, weapons, and fishing gear. Two wooden writing boards were also found, earlier by centuries than any previously attested.

Most of the objects recovered betray a Syro-Palestinian origin. However, other items appear to have originated in Greece, as Mycenaean-style seals, swords, beads, spearheads, razors, chisels, and a variety of ceramics were found. A bronze pin, spearheads, as well as a ceremonial stone macehead that were similar to styles originating in Bronze Age Romania were also found. The copper ingots have been chemically analyzed, and came from the island of Cyprus, implying that the ship was outbound from that island.

However, based upon the immense cargo and the many specialized elite items, the ship may have been bound for an elite group, perhaps even trade with royalty. Since the shipwreck was off the coast of Anatolia, it may have been going to Arzawa (in western Anatolia) or even Mycenae.

Ceramic Amphorae

Ceramic artifacts from Uluburun and other ancient shipwrecks are exhibited in the Museum of Underwater Archaeology in the city of Bodrum, Turkey.

A Hoard Fit for a King

Archaeologists uncovered thousands of manufactured goods from the Uluburun shipwreck, which included Cypriot ceramics, notably large storage jars which contained pottery and pomegranates. There were also faience drinking cups, and bronze (or copper) cauldrons and bowls. There were numerous small objects, including Canaanite-style bracelets and gold pendants, Egyptian gold objects, electrum, silver, and stone, as well as a scarab stamped with a cartouche of Queen Nefertiti of Egypt.

Other items included thousands of beads; scrap gold and silver; various small objects in ivory, tin, and bone; and numerous bronze tools (one saw, awls, drills, axes, and adzes) and weapons (spearheads, arrowheads, daggers, and swords). Fishing gear included lead net and line sinkers, netting needles, a harpoon, fishhooks, and even a bronze trident. Of special note was a miniature trumpet carved from a hippopotamus tooth (in the shape of a ram's horn). Last was a bronze female figurine with some gold plating.

The Fall of the Hittites

Exactly what events precipitated the final decline of the Hittite state in the early twelfth century BCE is much disputed by historians. Whatever the cause, the state's destruction coincided with the beginning of a "Dark Age" (*c.* 1200–900 BCE) throughout much of the Near East.

ABOVE **The Hittite sanctuary at Yazilikaya** was built in honor of Tudhaliya IV by Suppiluliuma II (reigned *c.* 1207–1190 BCE). The chamber housed a shrine to the divine Tudhaliya.

The events of the final years of the Hittite monarchy are shrouded in mystery. It appears that the deterioration of the state began during the reign of Tudhaliya IV (reigned *c.* 1237–1209 BCE). Tudhaliya engaged in correspondence with Tukulti-ninurta I of Assyria (reigned *c.* 1244–1208 BCE), and was especially concerned about Assyrian encroachment into Hittite territory. In fact, Tudhaliya forbade his own vassal state, Amurru, from having economic relations with Assyria, which may have precipitated a struggle between Assyria and the Hittites, ending in the weakening of the Hittite state. Kurunta, a cousin of Tudhaliya, captured and burned the city of Hattusa in the first decade of Tudhaliya's reign, and temporarily became king (reigned *c.* 1208–1207 BCE). Tudhaliya was able to return to power, extensively rebuild Hattusa, and engage in diplomatic relations with the Aegean power in the west, Ahhiyawa.

Suppiluliuma II: the Last of the Hittite Kings

The textual sources concerning the last days of the monarchy are very unclear and confusing. After Tudhaliya's death, his son Arnuwanda III briefly ruled (*c.* 1209–1207 BCE), but was soon succeeded by the last ruler of the New Kingdom, Suppiluliuma II, who ruled *c.* 1207–1190 BCE. There are two texts that describe the Hittite elites swearing oaths of allegiance to Suppiluliuma, one of which speaks of an internal rebellion during the reign of Arnuwanda III. We know that Suppiluliuma engaged in building projects, as he constructed a mortuary shrine in memory of his father, Tudhaliya IV, at Yazilkaya near Hattusa. He also claimed to have conquered lands in southwest Anatolia (i.e., Lycia and surrounding areas), regions that had sworn vassal allegiance to the king.

One of the few military engagements known during his reign was a naval battle off the coast of Cyprus, possibly in order to protect grain transport between Cilicia on the Anatolian coast and the port of Ugarit along the Syrian coast. The unstated enemy in this case was from Cyprus, although it is not certain whether these people were local Cypriots or foreigners (e.g., Sea Peoples) who had occupied the island. In any case, the eventual loss of grain from this area would prove to be devastating for the Hittites, who appear to have become more dependent upon foreign foodstuffs. A surviving letter from the Hittite crown to Ugarit implies defiance and rebellion on the part of this strategically located vassal state; in another letter, the Hittites urgently request Ugarit to send them a shipment of grain. Even an Egyptian text during the reign of Merneptah, dated to *c.* 1212–1204 BCE, notes that a shipment of grain was sent to Hatti for the kingdom's well-being.

ABOVE **Shipments of grain from Egypt** were essential to the Hittites, perhaps due to drought in Anatolia. This fresco is from the tomb of an Egyptian official, Wensu, in Thebes, *c.* 1500–1390 BCE.

The End of the Hittite State

Unexpectedly, the crowning blow against the Hittite state did not come from rising Assyria, which was now experiencing its own internal troubles. In fact, one can only surmise what happened. Though previous unsubstantiated theories for the collapse of the Hittite kingdom posit natural forces such as an earthquake or prolonged drought in the eastern Mediterranean region, part of the responsibility may be credited to massive migrations from the west by tribes the Egyptian sources called the "Sea Peoples." Attacks from the north from the Kaska, a nomadic people from northern Anatolia who occupied an area stretching to the shores of the Black Sea (modern Pontus), are another possibility; some evidence suggests they may have sacked Hattusa.

Whomever was responsible, there is archaeological evidence that the Hittite capital was burned and subsequently abandoned in the early twelfth century BCE. Moreover, appeals from the last king of Ugarit, 'Ammurapi, to Alasiya and Carchemish for assistance against an unnamed enemy went unheeded, except for some empty encouragement from the viceroy of the Anatolian regional capital. An Egyptian source states that Hatti, Kizzuwadna, Arzawa, Carchemish, and Cyprus were all crushed. In addition, a number of centers on the Mycenaean Greek mainland exhibit destruction layers dated to this period, and may be related to what happened further east. In any event, all of the major Anatolian states appear to have evaporated by the beginning of the twelfth century BCE. The fact that historical records from Hattusa abruptly stop during the reign of the last Hittite king may attest to this.

However, the following period is clouded in textual obscurity. Although Hattusa and Ugarit show evidence of destruction, the evidence for devastation elsewhere is not as obvious. The majority of other Hittite sites appear to have been abandoned rather than destroyed. Most Hittite scholars assume large-scale movements of people in Anatolia and elsewhere. Although nothing explicit is known until after the Dark Age (to *c.* 900 BCE), perhaps new states emerged from the collapsed Hittite kingdom (*c.* 1150 BCE).

THE NEO-HITTITE STATES

The "Neo-Hittite" states, as historians call them, were probably smaller political units in central and southeast Anatolia, and northern Syria—although almost nothing is known about them in this period. The largest of these independent polities was centered at Carchemish on the Upper Euphrates River, ruled over by a cadet branch of the Hittite royal family, descended from Kuzi-Teshub, the last imperial viceroy of Carchemish. His descendants ruled a much truncated kingdom for nearly 500 years after the collapse of Hattusa. These Neo-Hittite states survived as such until the Assyrian conquest of Syria and eastern Anatolia in the late eighth century BCE. In fact, Hittite and Luwian (an Anatolian language related to Hittite) place names and divine names persisted well into the first millennium BCE.

RIGHT **This Neo-Hittite prince** was carved between 1000 and 700 BCE, in the Neo-Hittite city of Carchemish.

A Dark Age

After the collapse of the Hittite and Kassite states, possibly assisted by the invasion of the Sea Peoples, came a period known as a "Dark Age" (*c.* 1200–900 BCE), primarily named because of a dearth of cuneiform textual resources from this period.

BELOW **This Babylonian boundary stone,** dated *c.* 1125–1104 BCE, describes an officer's military service to Nebuchadnezzar I in campaign against the Elamites.

During this Dark Age, Assyria and Egypt were politically weakened, and the disintegration of the Hittite state and the Kassite dynasty of Babylon helped to create something of a power vacuum, which brought a succession of new political players to the fore.

Babylon: The Second Dynasty of Isin

After the fall of the Kassite state in Babylonia (*c.* 1155 BCE), a local native dynasty was successful in filling the regal shoes. The founder of this new kingdom was a certain Marduk-kabit-ahheshu (reigned *c.* 1157–1140 BCE), who came from the ancient city of Isin. Thus, the dynasty has been labeled by historians as the Second Dynasty of Isin, which lasted until approximately 1026 BCE. Very little is known about the first three kings of this dynasty (also Itti-Marduk-balatu, reigned *c.* 1139–1132 BCE, and Ninurta-nadin-shumi, reigned *c.* 1131–1126 BCE). However, the fourth king of this dynasty, Nebuchadnezzar I (reigned *c.* 1124–1103 BCE), was a significant and locally celebrated monarch who left a good number of sources.

Nebuchadnezzar I

Although he left texts concerning victorious military exploits against the Assyrians, most of our evidence for the reign of Nebuchadnezzar I is derived from his campaign against the Iranian state of Elam to the southeast. By means of a series of damaging military campaigns, the Elamites had been partially responsible for the fall of the Kassite kingdom. Worse still, they had captured a number of the cultic statues, including the chief god of the city of Babylon, Marduk.

With the help of a certain Shitti-Marduk, Nebuchadnezzar I invaded southwest Iran and not only defeated the Elamite king, Hulteludish, but recaptured the statue of Marduk and returned it to its proper place in Babylon. Shitti-Marduk was granted privileges as a reward for his help. Nebuchadnezzar, however, did not capitalize on his victory in Elam, as he did not remain in the area. However, both the victory and the return of the statue were celebrated in literary texts.

Decline of Babylon

Despite these victories, Babylon under the successors of Nebuchadnezzar was politically depressed. The following three monarchs (Enlil-nadin-apli, reigned *c.* 1103–1100 BCE; Marduk-nadin-ahhe, reigned *c.* 1099–1082 BCE; Marduk-shapik-zeri, reigned *c.* 1081–1069 BCE) were clearly overshadowed by their northern royal counterpart, Tiglath-pileser I of Assyria (reigned *c.* 1115–1077 BCE), who claimed to have defeated Marduk-nadin-ahhe in battle, and burned his palaces in Babylon. Although Assyria's fortunes began to wane with the death of Tiglath-pileser, the Second Dynasty of Isin in Babylon perhaps fared even worse. The Sutu, an Aramean tribe, plundered the Temple of Shamash in Sippar in the mid-eleventh century BCE. This tragic event was probably the impetus for the great literary piece, the Erra Epic.

The fall of the Second Dynasty of Isin brought even more chaos in southern Mesopotamia. In fact, there were three separate dynasties in Babylon in the span of 47 years (*c.* 1025–978 BCE), all of which were heavily influenced by Elamites, Arameans, and even Kassites. The next king, Nabu-mukin-apli (reigned *c.* 977–942 BCE), founded the Seventh Dynasty of Babylon, which was to last over two centuries; his reign was also full of chaotic events. He suffered from constant attacks from the Arameans, who were successful in isolating Babylon from the rest of the kingdom. In addition, a number of texts describe difficulty in the collection of taxes from the provinces, most likely due to Aramean intrusions.

LEFT **Aramean peoples** spread across Mesopotamia as far as southeast Anatolia during the "Dark Age." This Aramaic carving and inscription was found in Zincirli, in southern Anatolia.

Assyrians and Arameans

Northern Mesopotamia (i.e., Assyria) fared little better than its southern counterpart after the death of its king, Tiglath-pileser I (*c.* 1077 BCE). The Arameans, who had been instrumental in weakening the kingdom of Babylon, were just as destructive in the north. The Assyrian monarch's second successor, Ashur-bel-kala (reigned *c.* 1074–1057 BCE), actually fought in concert with the Babylonians against the Aramean threat, and was successful in placing Adad-apla-iddina (reigned *c.* 1068–1047 BCE) on the throne of Babylon, thus intertwining the affairs of both states. However, dynastic intrigue plagued Assyria for the next decade. Textual sources for the Assyrian kingdom in this period are nearly nonexistent until the reign of Ashur-dan II (reigned *c.* 934–912 BCE).

During this "Dark Age," the Semitic-speaking Arameans were spread from the coast of Syria to southern Mesopotamia. Once they were firmly planted in Syria and Mesopotamia, the Aramean tribes appear to have created a number of "houses" or small kingdoms. Sources for these states are known almost solely from Assyrian and Babylonian cuneiform texts, beginning in the late tenth century BCE. There is also a small selection of Aramaic alphabetic royal inscriptions in the ninth century BCE from Syria, as well as many biblical references to Aramean kingdoms which participated in the political affairs of the united kingdom of Israel during the reigns of Saul, David, and Solomon (*c.* 1020–920 BCE).

Although Aram-Damascus was perhaps the most influential of these Aramean states, there were many others centered on the larger Syrian cities. Moreover, the Arameans infiltrated Mesopotamia so comprehensively that they became the dominant ethnic, cultural, and even linguistic force early in the first millennium BCE. The Aramaic alphabetic script soon began to compete with the more cumbersome cuneiform script native to Mesopotamia. Aramean kingdoms also competed with the Neo-Hittite kingdoms, and with the Phoenician kingdoms on the coast of Syria, which nevertheless continued to expand their trading posts around the Mediterranean.

BELOW **The oldest-known example of the Phoenician alphabet,** *c.* 1000 BCE, is carved onto the lid of this sarcophagus of King Ahiram of Byblos.

History and the Bible

The wealth of textual and archaeological information from the ancient Near East has provided many points of illumination for the Old Testament narratives of the Bible, although this is by no means a risk-free undertaking.

The period of the Patriarchs (ancestors of the tribes of Israel), the Captivity and subsequent Exodus of the Israelites from Egypt, and the period of the Judges, are all reputed to have occurred during the second millennium BCE. However, there is currently a dearth of external sources that make explicit mention of Israel, the Hebrews, or specific biblical events from this period. Therefore it is more profitable to try to ascertain how ancient Near Eastern sources illuminate cultural practices in the Old Testament.

Furthermore, literary and archaeological material may be useful in determining the historical plausibility of the biblical traditions, and comparing them with other ancient Near Eastern traditions. Of course, historical analogy does not imply historical accuracy, but can lead the scholar in the direction of the historical plausibility of the biblical record. In another vein, it is apparent that the biblical materials have likely gone through a number of editorial revisions, perhaps over a few centuries. But even if this is the case, the biblical traditions contain anecdotes, legal material, legends, and tales that exemplify contemporary cultural phenomena across the Near East.

The 'Apiru and King David

A number of Middle and Late Bronze Age sites in Syria and northern Iraq have shed some light on the Patriarchal traditions (*c*. 2000–1600 BCE). The city of Mari on the Middle Euphrates River (the reputed "homeland" of the Patriarchs) was a significant Amorite center at the outset of the second millennium BCE until *c*. 1750 BCE. The thousands of Mari texts, written in a West Semitic dialect of Akkadian, have exposed numerous comparisons with the Old Testament in the field of personal names, tribal organization (e.g., Bene-iamina, or Benjamin), rituals, prophetic texts, and other various Israelite customs. The name 'Apiru, which is possibly similar to the biblical term "Hebrew," has been found at Mari, and has also been located at the site of Alalakh in southeastern Anatolia (flourished until *c*. 1200 BCE), where the 'Apiru were viewed as an important mercenary class. It is unclear, however, how this term is related (if at all) to the biblical one.

Moreover, the pseudo-biographical inscription of Idrimi (*c*. sixteenth century BCE) found at Alalakh appears to anticipate the biographical story of David. Like David, Idrimi had to flee in the face of hostile forces, but was able to take the throne of his city with divine help, even though he was not related to the royal line.

RIGHT **Inscribed on this statue of Idrimi,** the king of Alalakh in the sixteenth century BCE, is the story of Idrimi's life which resembles that of biblical King David.

Cultural Parallels

Over 6,000 cuneiform tablets from the site of Nuzi in northern Iraq (flourished *c*. 1600–1350 BCE) have provided possible examples of cultural practices analogous to those in Patriarchal narratives—marriage contracts, deathbed blessings, pseudo-adoptions, household gods, and animal husbandry agreements. The coastal city of Ugarit (flourished *c*. 1400–1200 BCE) has perhaps provided more possible connections with Old Testament culture than any other ancient Near Eastern site. For example, numerous scholars have argued for close connections between many of the Psalms and selections of Ugaritic poetry. Many facets of Ugaritic religion that are expressed in their myths and epics (e.g., sacrifice) have remarkable similarities to the biblical sacrificial tradition. Moreover, the Ugaritic language shows such close characteristics to biblical Hebrew that many

have regarded it as simply a Canaanite dialect that was written in alphabetic cuneiform.

The relationship of Emar, a town north of Mari on the Euphrates River that flourished c. 2000–1190 BCE, to biblical studies is most acute in the religious sphere. The concept of anointing is found at Emar, as are festivals, which appear to have had various requirements that can be compared to the regulations found in Leviticus. Emar prophetic offices, loyalty oaths, inheritance texts, and even care of the dead provide other similarities to biblical Israel.

The Exodus

Although the Exodus is not mentioned in any contemporary Egyptian sources, the biblical writers of Exodus have placed the events in a plausible Egyptian context (*c.* 1400–1200 BCE). During the Egyptian Middle Kingdom period and the Second Intermediate Period, *c.* 2000–1550 BCE, there is extensive evidence for "Asiatics" (those who lived in the Palestine area) as prisoners of war, merchants, or individuals sent to Egypt as diplomatic gifts. There is also archaeological evidence for Semitic settlement in the northeast Delta area, contemporary with the rule of the Hyksos (i.e., an Asiatic dynasty).

The new Egyptian monarch mentioned in Exodus 1:8 as the "king who knew not Joseph" possibly represents a dynastic shift in Egypt, perhaps the beginning of the Eighteenth Dynasty with the accession of Ahmose I, who had expelled the Hyksos, an Asiatic dynasty (*c.* 1550 BCE). The new rulers are unlikely to have favoured Asiatics such as Joseph's people. Semitic peoples are well attested in the New Kingdom (*c.* 1550–1070 BCE), initially serving in menial roles, but gradually advancing to higher offices as the Eighteenth Dynasty unfolded. Laborers making bricks can

ABOVE **Mount Sinai in Egypt** is traditionally thought to be where Moses received the Ten Commandments, but some scholars argue the Exodus route would have been further north.

LEFT **Laborers in Egypt,** depicted here in the tomb of the vizier Rekhmire in the Valley of the Nobles, Thebes (*c.* 1425–1400 BCE), may have included many Asiatic slaves and prisoners of war.

ABOVE **A silver-plated bronze bull calf** (*c.* 1500 BCE) was found during recent excavations at Ashkelon in Israel. Its discovery illustrates one interesting element of Canaanite religion.

be seen from the tombs as early as the middle of the fifteenth century BCE, some of whom were taken as prisoners of war from Canaan, a common use of Asiatics during the reign of Thutmosis III (reigned *c.* 1479–1425 BCE) and after. Nineteenth Dynasty monarchs also campaigned in western Asia, and more frequently from the later years of Ramesses II (reigned *c.* 1279–1213 BCE), when new challenges to Egyptian rule began to emerge on their eastern borderlands. Thus, there were likely thousands of Asiatics in the Delta region, many of whom were probably assigned to building projects and to temples. Though there is no concrete evidence for the Exodus, the Merneptah Stele (*c.* 1206 BCE) is often held to mark the appearance of the people of Israel in Palestine, suggesting that the Exodus, if it occurred, had to be placed before this time.

The Golden Calf and Mesopotamian Legal Parallels

The Golden Calf, in the biblical narrative, was created by the Israelites in Moses' absence to depict Yahweh (God), but as idolatry had been forbidden, the Israelites were punished. However, the calf was probably in fact a bull calf, commonly the representation of the Canaanite storm god, Baal. It has been suggested that Aaron did not intend the calf (i.e., bull) to represent the deity, but to function as a pedestal of Yahweh, as there are numerous artistic examples where gods stand upon lions and bulls. The "breaking of the tablets" after the incident of the Golden Calf is reminiscent of Akkadian legal terminology, where the term "to break the tablet" signifies the invalidation of an agreement. In Ugaritic myth, the deity Mot was destroyed by the goddess Anath by being pulverized and scattered, in much the same way that Moses burned, pulverized, and scattered the remains of the golden calf in Exodus 32:20.

Perhaps one of the more interesting ancient Near Eastern parallels during the time of the Exodus is in the field of law. The biblical laws found in Exodus–Deuteronomy are remarkably similar to exemplars of Mesopotamian law found written in Sumerian and Akkadian as early as 2100 BCE. Both systems of law contained a similar overall structure (prolog, body of law, and epilog), similar specific structure (i.e., each law was presented in a conditional "if-then" fashion), similar content (laws concerning the goring ox, and laws relating to equal compensation for injury; i.e., "eye for an eye, tooth for tooth, life for life"). Whereas the Mesopotamian laws were generated by the king and presented to the deity (for the god's approval, presumably), the legal code of the Israelites was generated in the opposite way—it was God who created the laws and presented them to humanity.

Period of the Judges

As with previous periods, to understand the period of the Judges (*c.* 1200–1000 BCE),

THE LEGEND OF SARGON OF AKKAD

The story of Moses' birth in Exodus 2 has long been compared to the pseudo-autobiographical Legend of Sargon of Akkad (reigned *c.* 2371–2316 BCE), a powerful Mesopotamian monarch. The extant texts concerning Sargon are, however, dated to the Late Assyrian and Babylonian periods (*c.* 700–550 BCE) and it is not known whether they reflect any historical realia concerning Sargon's birth. The narrative states that Sargon was born of an entu priestess and an unknown father. For an unstated reason, Sargon was cast adrift as a baby in a reed basket on the Euphrates River. He became a foundling (a common legal concept in Mesopotamia for children who were exposed in this way and reared by others) and later became the king of Sumer and Akkad.

the historical narratives in turn must be augmented with other materials, such as documents from surrounding regions. Few inscriptions, however, have been found in Palestine during this period. Many of the inscriptions are written in a very early version of the alphabetic script on bronze arrowheads, identified by the owner's personal name and his father or master. There are also a number of very small inscriptions on potsherds that contain a few letters, seals, and some personal names.

In terms of material remains, it appears there was a gradual shift from Canaanite material culture of the Late Bronze Age (*c.* 1550–1200 BCE) to new "Israelite" settlement patterns during the Iron Age I period (*c.* 1200–1000 BCE). Scores of new sites are found in the highlands of northern and southern Canaan, and across Jordan. The largest numbers of these sites are situated in the hill country north of Jerusalem which, according to the Bible, was allocated to the tribes of Ephraim, Benjamin, and Manasseh. They are mostly smaller sites than in the previous period, unfortified, most likely inhabited by agro-pastoral communities. Many of these sites were deserted at the end of the eleventh century BCE. Some were reinhabited as towns during the Monarchy (i.e., the period of Israel under Saul, David, and Solomon, roughly 1020–920 BCE), thus showing a dramatic change in settlement patterns.

There is still evidence of Egyptian domination during the early part of the Judges period (roughly 1200–1150 BCE), as Canaanite culture persisted and a strong Egyptian presence can be seen at key sites such as Beth-Shean, Megiddo, Lachish, and Tel el-Farah. However, by the mid-twelfth century BCE, many sites experienced destruction, possibly at the hands of the Sea Peoples or even "proto-Israelites", which may be consistent with the collapse of Egyptian control in Canaan. Megiddo, Beth-Shean, and Lachish were all rebuilt shortly after their destruction, and their material remains retained both a Canaanite and a markedly Egyptianizing character. The book of Judges lists Megiddo, Gezer, and Beth-Shean as territories that were not conquered by the invaders.

In terms of architecture, the four-roomed house was common in this period, formed around a room at one end, with a courtyard divided by two rows of columns. This house type has also been found in sites in Philistia and Jordan. Few fortresses dated to this period have been found, apart from one discovered at Har Adir in the upper Galilee area. Towers are mentioned in the book of Judges at Shechem (Shakmu), Penuel, and Tebez.

LEFT **Biblical laws show many similarities** to early Mesopotamian legal texts. This tablet is a Sumerian legal text from Nippur, *c.* 2112–2095 BCE.

BELOW **Tel Gezer in Israel is the location** of the biblical site of Gezer, which formed the border between Egypt and the kingdom of Israel in the tenth century BCE.

Masters of the Known World: The Age of Empires

Introduction

The decline and eventual collapse of most ancient Near Eastern territorial states, combined with the large-scale migrations that marked the end of the Late Bronze Age, heralded a new world order, known today as the "Age of Empires."

Changes in the political geography meant the kingdom of Assyria lost many of its former holdings, but the central administration held on to its power, and Assur continued to be the center of religion and ideology. From the mid-tenth to the mid-ninth century BCE, these lost territories were regained, but Assyria's domination of the region remained under challenge. Urartu, which controlled wide parts of eastern Anatolia, contested Assyria's control over the smaller states in northern Syria and western Iran. The kingdom of Kush, with its center in modern Sudan, saw itself as heir to the pharaohs of the New Kingdom, and sought to control Egypt, and its former holdings on the Levantine coast.

The Assyrian Empire

Assyria's expansion in the second half of the eighth century BCE and the wars in Egypt, and Iran in the seventh century BCE, can be seen as reactions to these threats. As a result, Assyria became the first empire of the ancient Near East, creating an extensive road network, and relocating large parts of the population to create a uniform people. These two strategies successfully welded Mesopotamia, Syria, and the Levant together to form a cultural unit that outlasted the Assyrian Empire itself.

The Neo-Babylonian Empire

Throughout most of the early first millennium BCE, the south of Mesopotamia was politically fragmented, and a Babylonian state existed mainly in the minds of those who tried to keep the institution of the king of Babylon alive—the clergy of Marduk's temple in Babylon. Foreign leaders saw this as an opportune way to control southern Mesopotamia. The ancient cities such as Nippur, Uruk, and Ur functioned as city-states, often allied with the Aramaean kingdoms of the region—Bit-Yakin, Bit-Amukani, and Bit-Dakkuri.

The re-emergence of a unified Babylonia as a major power is the direct consequence of Assyrian intervention in the region from the mid-eighth century BCE onwards. When Assyria's power declined in the late seventh century BCE, Babylonia was able to break away from the empire, and invade the Assyrian heartland with the allied Median troops, defeating the defending armies. Babylonia inherited most of the former Assyrian countries, and the city of Babylon emerged as the supreme center of the ancient Near East. The strategies of the Assyrian Empire were continued, in particular their traditional population relocation policy.

Like Assyria, Babylonia had three main competitors—the re-united Egypt under the Saite Dynasty, Lydia in Anatolia, and the emerging Persian state in Iran. It was this Persian state that destroyed the Neo-Babylonian Empire after only seven decades. In 539 BCE Cyrus the Great, king of Persia, invaded Babylonia.

The Achaemenid Empire

With the Persian conquest, Mesopotamia's independence and its long domination of the ancient Near East came to an end. The Achaemenid Empire was larger than any of its predecessors. Cyrus conquered Media, Lydia and Babylonia, and by 525 BCE, when his son and successor, Cambyses, took Egypt, all competing states had been successfully absorbed, making Persia the first superpower—at its peak it spanned three continents, stretching from Egypt to Greece and Afghanistan. The Achaemenid rulers continued certain policies of their predecessors, most notably the royal road network, which they expanded. However, creating a uniform society was not one of the Achaemenid rulers' ideals, so the extensive resettlement policy was not resumed. The Persians regarded themselves as a distinct nation, and the king's role was to rule over subject peoples.

ABOVE **Marduk, chief Babylonian deity,** holding a bouquet, greets the scribe Ibn-Ishtar on this limestone kudurru, or deed of gift, from Uruk.

The wars between the Persian army and the Greeks during the reigns of Darius the Great (reigned 522–486 BCE), and his son, Xerxes I (reigned 486–465 BCE) still capture the imagination of many as they are often seen as symbolic of the clash between "East" and "West"—between despotism and democracy. This crude, if influential, interpretation fails to do justice to either side. In antiquity, the Achaemenids had many admirers and imitators, the most prominent being Alexander the Great (reigned 336–323 BCE), who not so much vanquished the Persian Empire, as usurped its throne while in Iran. Subsequently, both the Parthian and Sasanian rulers of Persia modeled themselves on their Achaemenid predecessors.

BELOW **This nineteenth-century CE lithograph,** by James Ferguson, gives an imagined view of the Assyrian Palace of Nimrud on the Tigris River.

Phoenicians and Neo-Hittites

The great migrations of the twelfth century BCE changed the population structure of the ancient Near East, and evidence of new groups of peoples such as the Aramaeans, the Philistines, and the Phrygians appear in the historical record.

While most of the coastal regions were affected by these changes in population, there was a remarkable continuity in the area of what we know as the Lebanese coast. This narrow strip of land between the Mediterranean Sea to the west and the Lebanon range to the east accommodated some of the most important harbor towns of the Eastern Mediterranean at this time—Tyre, Sidon, Byblos, and Arwad. The Canaanite culture of the Bronze Age continued to flourish in these city-states. They were politically independent of each other and pursued their own commercial interests, but they shared a language and formed a cultural unit.

The Greeks certainly saw them as one people and gave them the name—Phoenicians. This may ultimately be a loanword, perhaps derived from Lebanese, and it is seen as linked to the identical Greek word, which denotes both the murex snail and the color purple that was produced from that creature's glandular mucus. The production of purple dye was a closely guarded Phoenician secret, and textiles dyed with it were among the most precious and sought after among the many luxuries traded by Phoenician merchant vessels. The people of the Lebanese coast were, therefore, summarily identified as the "purple dye people."

The Cedars of Lebanon

Murex snails are not the only resource that made the Lebanese coast an excellent environment for industry and trade. Unlike today, the Lebanon range of old was covered with extensive cedar forests. Growing up to 130 ft (40 m) tall and with a very straight trunk, their timber was in demand all over the ancient Near East as a building material. Without them for roof beams, the vast halls of Mesopotamian palaces and temples could not have been built. On the Lebanese coast itself, the timber was used to build ships that could traverse the entire Mediterranean

BELOW **Phoenician warships are shown here** in this relief from the time of Sennacherib. Vessels like this were made from cedar grown in the forests of Lebanon.

Sea, and eventually sail as far as the Atlantic and Indian Oceans (via the Red Sea).

From at least the ninth century BCE onwards, the cities of the Phoenician mainland started to establish permanent settlements beyond the Lebanese coast. The first was on Cyprus, which was followed by settlements in northern Africa (most famously, Carthage), Sicily, Sardinia, and Spain. The initial impetus for this westward expansion came from Tyre, a city which, although closely allied with Assyria, was always independent. Treaties between the two states granted Tyre the privilege to access all harbors under Assyrian control, and gave it an advantage over its competitors. Not only did its trade network make Tyre rich, it also enabled the earliest cultural exchange between East and West. The most significant result of this was the spread of the Phoenician alphabet throughout the Mediterranean region.

The Heirs of the Hittites

Although the Hittite Empire collapsed in the twelfth century BCE, the Hittite language and culture survived. Several small kingdoms in northern Syria and southeastern Turkey saw themselves in a direct tradition harking back to the Great Kings of Hatti. Hence, the kings of Kummuhhu, the region that was known in classical times as Commagene, took the names of the most famous rulers of the Hittite imperial period—Suppiluliuma, Muwattali and, Hattusili. There, as well as in the other kingdoms in the region, such as Que, Arpad, and Hamath, the traditional Luwian language—the most commonly used Hittite language—and writing system continued to be used. Like cuneiform, the Luwian script uses a combination of signs representing syllables and words. It is now often described as hieroglyphic, even though it has no connection with Egypt—it is better described as pictoglyphic.

The Mesopotamian cuneiform script, the Egyptian hieroglyphs, and the Luwian pictoglyphs each use hundreds of different signs, often with multiple possible readings. The Phoenician alphabet consists of just around two dozen signs, each of which stand for exactly one sound (phoneme). The term "alphabet" derives from the names of the first two signs in the sequence: aleph "cattle" and beit "house." These names also reflect the letters' shape, each derived from a picture of an object whose name starts with the relevant sound. This is a script simple enough to be learnt quickly, without the years of training required to master the other writing systems, so literacy was no longer confined to palaces and temples where the traditional scripts continued to be used. The alphabet script, however, suited the needs of merchants and, as it could be easily used to record any language, it was adapted for many languages including Aramaean, Hebrew, Greek, Phrygian, Lydian, Etruscan, and Latin.

ABOVE **The Stele of King Mesha of Moab,** ninth century BCE, charts the successful revolt led by Mesha against Ahab of Israel, leading to the conquest of northern Moab.

A Common Identity

We should not imagine the population of these "Neo-Hittite" kingdoms as consisting exclusively of Luwians. The fact that the alphabetic script and the Aramaean language were also used in most of these states indicates a significant Aramaean influence. To consciously continue the Hittite traditions created a common identity for the people of these states and provided a unity that transcended their boundaries. This was used as a cultural defense against a common adversary, the expanding Assyrian empire.

It was ultimately in vain—in the second half of the eighth century BCE, one "Neo-Hittite" kingdom after the other was annexed by Assyria.

LEFT **This eighth-century BCE pottery vessel** is from Tyre, an important Mediterranean port that, according to Herodotus, was founded in 2750 BCE.

Israel and Judah

By the tenth century BCE Israel emerged from its tribal origins to become an important Levantine kingdom. It survived four centuries of aggression from the superstates of Assyria, Egypt, and Babylon before it collapsed in 587 BCE.

BELOW **The Victory stele of Merneptah** is inscribed with a list of defeated peoples. It was erected in 1213–1204 BCE by Merneptah in his funerary temple at Thebes.

The first time the term "Israel" occurs is on a stele of the Egyptian pharaoh Merneptah (*c.* 1210 BCE), who claims to have destroyed it. We do not know what sense of the thirteenth-century BCE term—the Egyptian writing denotes a people rather than a place—survived into the mid-tenth century BCE when dynastic "houses" of kings first formed an Israelite monarchy. The only references in the 250 intervening years are to be found in the Bible (Judges) and in archaeological remains. Those sources are not consistent and support a variety of theories about how this tribal people eventually came to build cities, temples, act on the international stage in war and peace, and write its theological history into the unique text of the Old Testament.

The biblical narrative tells of the arrival of the Israelites in Canaan after the Exodus from Egypt, their settlement of the hill country in tribes, their struggles against neighboring Canaanites and Philistines, and the efforts of judges as political leaders to codify cultic practices, and unify political rule. The historical authenticity of these events is often called into question, but it is partly corroborated by some evidence. Archaeology reveals a rapid expansion of a few hundred villages into a population of something like 100,000 people by 950 BCE.

The United Monarchy, Tenth Century BCE

The evidence derived from sources from the later Iron Age does not provide complete confirmation of the stories told in both books of Samuel and I Kings. The growing pace of warfare, particularly against the Philistines, brought more Israelite tribes into alliances to protect their lands and cult-sites. In one instance, the prophet Saul was appointed as war-leader against a Philistine advance, becoming the first acknowledged king of Israel. Yet Saul had to make military decisions in consultation with other tribal leaders, judges, and priests, such as Samuel. The stories also acknowledge the use of magic and divination alongside Yahwistic cult. A unified kingship over a territorial state called "Israel" then developed in stages under the leadership of David and Solomon (*c.* 1000–930 BCE), centered on Jerusalem as a royal city, rather than Shiloh, which was the religious capital prior to the establishment of a monarchy.

At Jerusalem, the glory of the monarchy was manifested in the wealth that poured in through trade with Egypt, Tyre, and Arabia. According to the Old Testament it was ultimately crowned by Solomon's construction of the First Temple (I Kings 6), although there is little archaeological evidence of this. The story of Israel's struggle to maintain its sovereignty is reflected in the nine biblical accounts of the pillaging of Jerusalem's Temple by various kings (mostly its own), including its destruction by Babylon in 586 BCE. The state's strength was reflected in the fortification of cities with walls and gates, the installation of governors, and a unified taxation system. This strength also translated to success on the battlefield as Israel fended off several hostile nations on its eastern border, including

Moab and Edom. Domestic tribal disunity remained an ongoing problem, however, and many areas maintained independent cult-sites (the so-called "high places"). At Solomon's death, the north and south split into the separate kingdoms of Israel and Judah.

Levantine Neighbors as Allies and Enemies, *c.* 931–800 BCE

Eight royal houses of Israel governed from three cities from *c.* 931 BCE until Assyrian domination. In those two centuries, 19 kings ruled for as little as seven days and as long as 41 years. Eight of them succeeded to the throne after the assassination of their predecessors. Judah, meantime, maintained a more stable monarchy for 345 years to 586 BCE. An unbroken line of 20 kings and one queen reigned at Jerusalem. Israel and Judah officially remained at war for about six decades, but they were just two among a dozen other states and tribal confederacies, which intermittently sparred and traded with one another. Political and cultic unity was temporary and exceptional.

After an opportunistic invasion by Egypt *c.* 925 BCE, Israel quickly mastered the arts of diplomacy. A dynastic and political alliance was cemented with Tyre by the reigns of Omri and Ahab (885–852 BCE), and control extended over Moab from the new capital, Samaria. This is reflected in a stele of Moab's King Mesha (*c.* 850 BCE), claiming to have revolted against Omri's son. Israel next became associated with powerful Damascus, supplying chariots and troops in 853 BCE for a multi-state war against expansionist Assyria. This resulted in a century-long regional stalemate, but Israeli King Jehu is famously depicted in an obelisk kneeling before the Assyrian King Shalmaneser III, post-841 BCE. The collapse of the anti-Assyrian alliance degenerated into bitter local warfare. Judah now shared Israel's hostility to Damascus, and the two states sealed a treaty with a dynastic intermarriage in 841 BCE. However, predictions of the downfall of the monarchy arose in

ABOVE **The Eastern Wall of the Temple in Jerusalem,** on the site of Solomon's First Temple which, according to the Bible, was constructed in the tenth century BCE.

LEFT **King Jehu of Israel is shown paying tribute** as he kneels before Shalmaneser III. Jehu founded the longest dynasty in Israel's history.

ABOVE **The exodus from the conquered city of Lachish,** 701 BCE, is shown here in a relief from the Palace of Sennacherib at Nineveh.

response to the theological implications of royal dependence on foreign alliances.

Judah between Assyria and Egypt

Assyria proved a divisive force, and Israel imploded. In the late 750s BCE, Menahem paid tribute to Assyria to gain its help to assassinate Shallum, the ruling Israelite king, and take the throne. Another usurper, Pekah, then turned to Damascus to support the assassination of Menahem's son in 736 BCE. Israel and Damascus now stood arrayed against Judah, and its king, Ahaz, eventually appealed to Assyria to help reinstate the balance of power. Tiglath-pileser III obliged by conquering Damascus in 732 BCE, but also helped himself to much of Israel's territory. When the Assyrians discovered that the Israelite King Hoshea was corresponding secretly with Egypt, Israel was occupied, its population deported, and the monarchy ended (721 BCE).

Judah now stood alone against an Assyrian giant, which flanked it to the west all the way down to the border with Egypt. Hezekiah, the son of Ahaz, refused to render tribute to Assyria, and corresponded with both Egypt's King Taharqa and the Babylonian rebel leader, Merodach-Baladan. The Assyrian King Sennacherib invaded Palestine in 701 BCE, destroyed the city of Lachish and sent emissaries to pressure Hezekiah to submit. The biblical and Assyrian accounts agree in some of the details about this event, yet, while II Kings recounts the destruction of Assyrian forces by the Angel of the Lord, the Assyrian annals dryly record Hezekiah's submission of tribute and his acceptance of being a vassal once again.

King and Cult: Politics under Pressure

The Old Testament interprets political and military history in terms of theological causation, rather than just history. The divine intervention of Yahweh rewarded Israel for abiding by Deuteronomic law, but, more frequently, Yahweh punished it for idolatry and other cultic lapses. It seems official Israeli religion aimed to achieve national monolatry (the worship of a single god, while recognizing the existence of others) rather than monotheism (the worship of only one, true god). Even Solomon, builder of the First Temple, is said to have built temples to other gods, and the Old Testament tells us that earlier Yahwistic cult was performed in many "high places" throughout Israel. The biblical narrative tells

RIGHT **This seventeenth-century engraving** by Matthaeus Merian the Elder is called *Josiah renews the Covenant.*

of multiple gods and cult-sites throughout the monarchy, and these outlived the Jerusalem Temple itself. Judahite kings periodically tried to centralize the cult, prohibit sacrifice, except at Jerusalem, and vilified all other cult-sites as Canaanite, and therefore foreign.

At the same time, participation in international politics demanded the acceptance, in principle, of foreign gods. Thus a second and more purist strain of religious-political thought developed through the prophetic tradition, which challenged both monarchism and idolatry. The prophetic books contain highly critical historical accounts of the many kings who tolerated idol worship, trafficked with foreign gods, or stripped the Jerusalem Temple of its treasures to fund their ambitions. The biblical history of Israel indicates that these tensions reached from Jerusalem to the battlefields of far nations.

Collapse and Legacy

After 721 BCE, Israelite refugees poured into Judah, and Jerusalem grew to an impressive size. Hezekiah's capitulation to Sennacherib, however, marked the end of this growth, and the monarchy's cult reforms collapsed. As Assyria began its slide into collapse, and Egypt and Babylon had not yet recovered from its rule, the reign of Josiah (640–609 BCE) gave Judah its last experience of independence. The rediscovery of a lost "Book of Law" in the Jerusalem Temple provided the basis for the centralizing, Deuteronomic reform, and Josiah even managed to recover some of the territory of the old Israelite state.

The recovery was not to last. Coming to the aid of the last Assyrian garrison in Syria, Necho II of Egypt was stalled briefly at Megiddo by the pro-Babylonian Josiah, who was killed in battle. A destabilized Judah struggled to fend off Egypt and Babylon in the next decades, but in 605 BCE Babylon decisively defeated Egypt at Carchemish, and won control of the region. Nebuchadnezzar II deposed first one Judahite king, Jechoniah, in 597 BCE, and then another, the rebellious Zedekiah, in 586 BCE. Jerusalem and its Temple were razed, and the king and most of the population were deported into almost 50 years of Babylonian exile. The city and Temple would eventually be rebuilt, but no independent Judean kingdom would re-emerge until long after the Babylonian, Persian, and Seleucid empires had fallen.

IS THE BIBLE HISTORY?

Readers giving credence to the Old Testament as a faithfully transmitted history of Israel see it as preserving parts of a story going back as far as the Middle Bronze Age. These views claim the existence of extensive oral and written traditions from which later texts were copied out. Readers giving "minimalist" readings, on the other hand, see a series of narratives that were often heavily edited or composed centuries after the events they described. This position holds that many of the earlier events of the Bronze and Iron Ages were folktales, or entirely fictional stories, meant to create the impression of a centuries-old Israelite history leading up to the creation of the Temple at Jerusalem, and that later events were often recast as more acceptable political apologies.

ABOVE **These images, from a Gothic, thirteenth-century CE psalter,** show the Israelites in chains before King Nebuchadnezzar (top) and before the walls of Babylon (bottom).

The Neo-Assyrian Empire

Modern scholars regard the last three centuries of Assyrian history as the Neo-Assyrian Empire. From the ninth century BCE to the end of the seventh century BCE, Assyria dominated the ancient Near East politically and economically.

ABOVE **The Gates of Balawat,** also known as The Wooden Gates of Shalmaneser III, have bands of relief in bronze, showing details of the Assyrian assault on the city of Khazazu.

In the tenth century BCE the kingdom of Assyria consisted only of what is modern northern Iraq, with the Lower Zab River as its southern border. However, within a hundred years, Tiglath-pileser I reestablished the boundaries of the state. By the reign of Shalmaneser III (858–824 BCE) they extended from the Euphrates in the west to the main ridge of the Taurus Mountains in the north. From the reign of Tiglath-pileser III (744–727 BCE) onward, Assyria's borders reached the Mediterranean Sea in the west, deep into the Zagros Mountains in the east, and far into Anatolia in the northwest. Babylonia ceased to exist as an independent state and became an Assyrian holding. At that time, Assyria's influence reached far beyond its borders: into the Iranian and Anatolian plateaus, and the Arabian desert; the Nile downstream to Egypt and Nubia (Kush); to the islands of Cyprus in the Mediterranean; and Bahrain in the Persian Gulf.

While we cannot be certain what prompted Assyria's renewed expansion in the tenth century BCE, the idea, that the holdings in the west that were then under the control of various Aramaean rulers were rightfully Assyrian lands, certainly played a crucial role. But to conquer is one thing, to stay in control is another. How did the Assyrian Empire cohere?

The City of Assur and the Provinces

Assyria was divided into administrative provinces, each under the control of a governor. By the early seventh century BCE, Assyria consisted of about 70 such provinces. The king personally appointed every governor, and they, in turn, answered directly, and only, to the king. As a rule, governorship was not hereditary. The office could not be passed on from father to son, and, to prevent dynastic ambitions, the king preferred his governors to be eunuchs, and so unable to father children. It was understood that the king was chosen by the gods and ruled by their grace. His command was law, and he could directly intervene at all levels of his empire. Despite this, the Assyrian administration was largely decentralized, and the governors were authorized to act independently on behalf of the king in their own provinces. In all routine matters, they were expected to operate at their own discretion.

The heart of the Assyrian state was the ancient cult city of Assur, no matter where the administrative capital was situated. The center of government and bureaucracy was moved from Assur to Kalah under Ashurnasirpal II in the ninth century BCE, then to Dur-Sharrukin under Sargon II in the late eighth century BCE, and finally to Nineveh under Sennacherib in the early seventh century BCE. Throughout all of these moves, the city of Assur never lost its crucial role as Assyria's ideological center because it harbored the one and only temple of the god Ashur, the focal point for the country and, to the Assyrian mind, the entire world. All who were subjects of the Assyrian king and, therefore, servants of Ashur, had to provide the temple with sacrifices. This was not only

RIGHT **The god Ashur is usually shown** in a winged disc. His left hand holds a warrior's bow, as his right hand bestows a blessing.

expected of the Assyrian provinces but also all vassal states, who also owed the king tribute.

The religious center of Assur, the various administrative capitals, and the provinces were linked by an extensive road network. Certain routes were known as "the king's roads" and used to transport the correspondence between the king and his governors, as well as for all other official business, including the movement of troops and diplomatic delegations. It is difficult to say precisely how well maintained these special roads were—modern scholars assume widely differing standards. What is clear is that the development and preservation of the network was among the top priorities of the state administration.

The King, Representative of the God Ashur

While the governors represented authority on a local level, it was the king alone who was the earthly representative of the god Ashur. The king's omnipresence and ubiquity was established and guaranteed to ensure that every subject of Assyria was, at all times, aware that the one person who was all-powerful in the state was the king, and only the king. To this end, the king maintained residences all over the empire, which he visited regularly. An entire royal household, complete with an administrative staff, supply and maintenance units, and entertainers, such as musicians and singers, lived in each of these palaces. While the inhabitants of the many Assyrian cities with royal residences may not always have known when the king was in his local palace, the grand building itself was always there, visible every day as a testament to the king's claim to power. Moreover, the king was present in the form of his statues and stelae, which took their place next to the divine images in all major temples. They were also erected at other prominent locations, such as city gates. But perhaps, most importantly, a loyalty oath tied every inhabitant of Assyria personally to the king. The oath was perceived as a spiritual essence. The oath-taking ceremony required the ritual drinking of water which prevented any breach of the agreement "from within."

The combination of a decentralized administration, and the close personal link between the people and their king, was the backbone of the Assyrian state. This was a political fixture in the ever-changing political geography of the ancient Near East from the fourteenth century BCE to the end of the seventh century BCE. Remarkably, the same clan ruled over Assyria throughout that time and, long before that, over the ancient city of Assur. The dynasty of the Assyrian kings can be traced back as far as the early second millennium BCE, making it one of the longest surviving in world history. The Assyrian king was seen on an ideological level as a creation entirely separate from, and superior to, ordinary man.

The epic Mesopotamian poem *The Epic of Gilgamesh* tells us:

> *"Ea (god of wisdom) opened his mouth to speak, saying a word to Belet-ili (goddess of creation): 'You are Belet-ili, the sister of the great gods; it was you who created man the human. Fashion now the king, man the prince! Gird the*

ABOVE **Sargon II, from the palace at Dur-Sharrukin** (Khorsabad), wrote a letter to the god, Ashur, telling of one of his campaigns. This letter has been recovered.

RIGHT **Soldiers of the Royal Guard** are shown here in a relief from Sennacherib's palace at Nineveh.

whole of his figure so pleasingly, make perfect his countenance and well-formed his body!' And Belet-ili fashioned the king, man the prince."

The idea expressed in this quote gives the royal family a special status in Assyrian society, and it helps to explain the longevity of the dynasty.

The Royal Bloodline

The office of king was reserved exclusively to the male line of this particular family. Other than that, the rules of succession were fluid, with all legitimate male members of the family—the king's sons, brothers, nephews, and even more distant relatives—having a theoretical chance to ascend to the throne. Crucially, this also included the descendents of royal consorts other than the queen (in Assyrian, "Woman of the Palace"), the only official wife of the king.

This created a rather large pool of potential successors at all times, thus ensuring that the royal bloodline was well protected against its extinction and created stability for the dynasty. This is certainly a key reason that kingship could remain so firmly in one family's control, with no other family ever gaining access to the throne, or even competing for leadership.

BELOW **Shamshi-adad** (823–811 BCE) was the younger son of Shalmaneser. His queen was Sammuramat, who is also known as Semiramis.

However, beyond belonging to this particular family, there was one more essential requirement—in order to be king, a candidate needed to be in perfect physical and mental health. Whether this condition was used to exclude certain claimants from the successions by intentional mutilation is not clear from the available sources, but this certainly remains a possibility. The practice is well known with the later Sasanian kings of Iran where unwelcome pretenders for the throne were disqualified for kingship by the removal of their ears or noses.

A large group of legitimate pretenders to the throne created the risk of internal power struggles. To avoid this prospect, the ruling king officially appointed his successor during his lifetime. We know from surviving primary sources that this choice was, and needed to be, sanctioned by the gods, yet the decision was not absolutely binding and a new crown prince could be appointed at the king's initiative.

It is not entirely clear whether this would have been a routine action that need not necessarily put the demoted candidate to shame—this would have been the case if the organization of the Assyrian state demanded the existence of a crown prince from the moment a new king was appointed—or whether this was an unusual move bound to cause resentment.

We are only aware of those instances where a change in the succession arrangements ultimately resulted in a succession war, such as the dismissal of King Sennacherib's crown prince, Arda-Mullissi, in favor of Esarhaddon. This led to Sennacherib's murder and a succession war followed in 681 BCE.

In normal circumstances, the appointed heir could use his time as crown prince to gain experience as a ruler-in-the-making and to secure his power base. Usually, he could then hope to ascend to the throne after his predecessor's natural death, and be widely accepted. Nevertheless, time and again Assyria saw controversies, and also battles for the throne; but crucially, the protagonists were all members of the royal clan.

The Assyrian Army

Assyria's expansion depended on its army. Palace decorations celebrate their vigor and discipline, but avoid showing Assyrian casualties while slain enemy soldiers are omnipresent. Modern observers are intrigued by the manned siege machines used to break through the fortifications of besieged cities, but they would be even more impressed to see the army—men, horses, and equipment—cross broad rivers with inflated sheepskins serving as flotation devices. By the ninth century BCE, it was predominantly a professional army, unlike in Middle Assyrian times when troops were mustered from among Assyrian taxpayers. Annual army service was a key component of the tax obligations attached to the tenure of land. The Neo-Assyrian army relied on contingents of professional soldiers, both of Assyrian and foreign origin. While it was the world's largest army at that time, and extremely well equipped, it did not have a significant technological advantage over the troops of the neighboring states. However, it was open to innovation, continually adopting effective strategies and methods from abroad, such as the slingshot troops that Sennacherib (reigned 704–681 BCE) added after encountering this simple but highly effective battle technique in Judah.

ABOVE **This relief from Sennacherib's palace** at Nineveh shows his troop of slingshot soldiers at the siege of Lachish, 701 BCE.

Ashurnasirpal II

Ashurnasirpal II (reigned 883–859 BCE) is best known today as the king who moved the Assyrian court away from Assur and transformed the city of Kalah (modern Nimrud) into the administrative center of Assyria and made it a spectacular monument to Assyria's renewed power.

ABOVE **This magnesite statue of Ashurnasirpal II** is from the Temple of Ishtar at Assur.

From the reign of Ashur-dan II (reigned 934–912 BCE), the Assyrian army embarked on an ambitious mission to reclaim the Assyrian territories lost during the eleventh century BCE. These were lost to a series of small Aramaean kingdoms, each named after its founder as head of its "house"—Bit-Bahiani, Bit-Agusi, and Bit-Zamani.

Recovering the Lost Territories

Within a century, Assyria annexed these states, consolidating the process during the reigns of Ashurnasirpal II and his son and successor, Shalmaneser III (reigned 858–824 BCE). Assyria now controlled all the territory east of the Euphrates, and more important bridgeheads west of the river.

Local rulers could stay in power if they accepted Assyrian supremacy, as best illustrated by the ruling family of Bit-Bahiani, whose capital was Guzana (Tell Halaf) in the northeast of modern Syria. While Shamash-nuri, and later his son, Hadad-yis'i, were recognized locally as kings, to the Assyrian king they were simply provincial governors. The life-sized statue of Hadad-yis'i, found in 1979 at Tell Fekheriyeh, bears a bilingual inscription. The Assyrian cuneiform names him as governor, and the Aramaic gives his title as king. Eventually, the local elites were replaced with Assyrian officials sent by their king to represent him. Many of these officials were eunuchs, to ensure that they would not be able to found hereditary dynasties like the Aramaean rulers whose place they had taken.

Kalah, the New Royal Residence City

Kalah was situated on the eastern bank of the Tigris, about 45 miles (70 km) to the north of Assur, the religious and ideological center of Assyria, and traditionally home to the king's main residence. Yet Ashurnasirpal relocated the entire royal court from Assur to the ancient city of Kalah after it had been completely transformed. The old settlement mound at Kalah, having grown to a substantial height during its five-millennia-long occupation, was turned into a citadel that housed only the royal palace and several temples for the most important deities of Assyria—Ninurta, Nabu, and Ishtar. There was, however, no shrine for Ashur, whose only sanctuary remained in the city of Assur. Ashurnasirpal's Kalah covered about 900 acres (360 ha)—twice the size of Assur—and it was surrounded by a fortification wall that was 5 miles (7.5 km) in length.

The most impressive building at Kalah was Ashurnasirpal's palace, known today as the Northwest Palace. With a length of 220 yd (200 m) and a width of 140 yd (130 m) it dominates its surroundings. The palace is organized around three courtyards, accommodating the state apartments, the administrative wing, and the private quarters, which also housed the royal women. Here, several underground tombs were uncovered

RIGHT **Shalmaneser III is seen here** greeting Babylonian King Marduk-zakir-shumi from the relief series on the throne of Shalmaneser III.

in 1989, one of which was the last resting place of Ashurnasirpal's queen, Mullissu-mukannishat-Ninua, the daughter of the king's cupbearer, one of the foremost officials at court. Her rich burial goods give a vivid impression of the luxury in which the king and his entourage lived. This is also clear from the decorations of the state apartments, especially the throne room in which the king held audience. Huge alabaster slabs lined the walls—featuring engraved figures and Ashurnasirpal's inscription celebrating the king's achievements.

ABOVE **Ashurnasirpal II's Palace at Kalah** has some of the finest examples of Neo-Assyrian sculpture. Winged bulls, made of alabaster, guarded the palace doorways.

Why Move the Capital?

We don't know why Ashurnasirpal moved the capital. Was Assur becoming too small for the royal court? Was its agricultural hinterland too limited to support it? Did Ashurnasirpal mean to distance himself from the old aristocratic families of Assur? Was he trying to establish the king, rather than god Ashur, as the nucleus of the state? Or was the construction of the new city an exercise in conspicuous consumption, designed to show off Assyria's wealth to the world?

Kalah was the administrative center of Assyria and the king's main residence until Sargon II (reigned 721–705 BCE) built the new city of Dur-Sharrukin, which replaced Kalah in these functions. Nevertheless, Kalah remained one of the most important Assyrian cities.

The Feast for Thousands

According to the so-called "Banquet Stele," erected in a courtyard of Ashurnasirpal's palace in Kalah, a total of 69,574 people participated in the inaugural celebrations for the new city. The local participants were joined by people from all over Assyria and 5,000 foreign dignitaries from the neighboring countries, including the Neo-Hittite kingdoms and the Phoenician cities Tyre and Sidon.

As Ashurnasirpal's guests, all these people were wined and dined for ten days in a gigantic feast whose menu is preserved on the stele: 17,000 sheep and cattle, and twice as many birds (ducks, geese, pigeons) were slaughtered, meaning that every participant's share would have been half a bird, and a very sizable portion of beef and mutton. These main courses were supplemented by venison, fish, and (less to our taste) rodents, enormous quantities of vegetables, fruit, spices, and a broad range of dairy products while 10,000 tubs of beer and 10,000 skins of wine provided relief for the thirsty.

Neo-Assyrian Sculpture

Statue of Gilgamesh

The deeds and adventures of Gilgamesh, the legendary king of Uruk (*c.* 2700 BCE), were the subject of the earliest epic poem ever written. This statue is from the palace of Sargon II.

The Assyrian kings lined their massive palaces with stone reliefs depicting their war machine in action, with themselves as heroes, and a variety of magical protective figures.

More than a dozen palaces were built between 883–612 BCE in the capital cities of Assur, Kalah, Dur-Sharrukin, and Nineveh, developing a centuries-old tradition of palace decoration. Their one-time opulence was embellished with gilding, gemstones, brightly colored paint, and exotic woods from lands as far away as India. All that remained for modern excavators to discover of this exuberance were the stone elements—thousands of stern, gray "Mosul marble" slabs carved in low relief. The Kalah palace of Ashurnasirpal II (reigned 883–859 BCE) represents the earliest phase of this sculptural tradition. Its reliefs, now scattered in museums around the world, are the most immediately familiar to modern audiences.

Ashurnasirpal's palace featured scenes of tribute-bearers in the courtyard, of the king at war in the throne room, and, in the rest of the palace, hundreds of protective genie-figures with an obstinately mysterious "Sacred Tree" motif. The gates were guarded by dozens of titanic human-headed winged bull figures *(lamassu)*, weighing upwards of 40 tons (36 metric tons). Texts reveal that other massive figures were cast in bronze, copper, and gold. Neo-Assyrian artisans continued to produce other forms of stone sculpture—including the king represented in the round, in free-standing stelae, and in cliff carvings that marked the empire's borders. Many are still visible today.

Assyrian Violence

The recovery of Assyrian reliefs, such as this relief from Nimrud which depicts soldiers in the foreground and hanged men in the background, seemed to confirm a biblical image of Assyrian cruelty. These scenes of violence were positioned in audience halls as stark reminders to vassals and allies of the very real penalties for disloyalty. Sculptures and texts depicted punishments: impalings, flayings, burnings, decapitations, the defilement of corpses. More than three million people were deported between 883–612 BCE. These abuses may be contextualized in several ways. First, more imperial subjects benefited than suffered under a *pax Assyriaca*, which effectively abolished hundreds of local wars and their horrors. Second, the most florid abuses appeared during the "high empire" (705–650 BCE) and were applied to only a few enemies to fulfill the curses of the treaties violated. Third, the practices were prominently advertised by the Assyrians themselves, to establish loyalty and desensitize their troops to violence.

By the mid-eighth century BCE, as the palaces grew larger, images of Assyria's military exploits took center stage, with refinements in perspective, detailing, and technique, producing an unparalleled mural art form. The earlier stiff, isolated figures were replaced by expansive scenes of battlefield chaos, besieged cities, and the loot from foreign nations. The reliefs took on a more documentary tone, capturing naturalism, proportion, and sense of motion, depicting swimmers crossing rivers, riders cantering through forests, and cornered lions in their death throes. Detail became a vocabulary of an all-seeing authority—the viewer sees the crab in the river, the running horse craning its neck, the trickle of women and children fleeing a city while the battle rages on.

The depictions of warfare, submission, and gruesome punishment of enemies provided the visual representations corresponding to the campaign annals—an Assyrian tradition. Frustrating to the modern scholar, the reliefs rarely correlate to the texts. The Assyrian siege of Lachish (II Kings 18), for instance, was the subject of an entire room full of reliefs in the palace of Sennacherib (reigned 704–681 BCE) in Nineveh, but some of the more sordid details of the event are not mentioned in his annals. The same annals document the simultaneous confrontation at Jerusalem in detail, but there is no representation of this in any of the reliefs. The reconstruction of reliefs in sequence has thus become a major historical art project, with the goal of "reading" the stories these kings wrote on their palace walls.

Dying Lioness Killed in a Royal Hunt

The pathos with which the lioness's suffering is illustrated is seemingly at odds with the generally accepted images of Assyrian brutality. This suggests that much violent iconography was used to shock, rather than reflect an indifference to suffering.

"Sacred Tree" Motif

A winged spirit protector, holding a purification bucket and cone, offers a libation to a sacred tree in a relief from Nimrud *c.* 875–860 BCE. The stylized tree was represented as a religious symbol for the first time during this period, and there continues to be much debate about its true meaning.

The Royal Annals

While there was a long-standing tradition of recording historical events in Assyria, these collections are preserved only as rare fragments or in very abbreviated form. Accounts of a king's most important deeds in a chronological sequence frequently survive in lengthy building inscriptions.

RIGHT **On this glazed, terra-cotta tile** from Nimrud of an Assyrian king and his attendants, it is possible to get an indication of the palace's color scheme.

BELOW **This octagonal, biconic clay prism** with cuneiform inscription is from the time of Sargon II (reigned 721–705 BCE).

These inscriptions, now known as the Royal Annals, were buried deep in the foundation courses of palaces, temples, and fortification walls, or engraved into the stone exteriors of a building. These inscriptions could either be readily visible or hidden from sight. The images on the stone reliefs adorning the walls of Assyrian palaces, and the cuneiform texts that accompany them, do not always correspond with each other. Few visitors to the Assyrian galleries in the Louvre or the British Museum would guess that the stone slabs they see also bear inscriptions on their reverse side. Both obvious, and hidden, inscriptions are also found on stone thresholds, door sockets and entrance guardian figures. It was not of primary importance that these texts were able to be read—more important was that the name of the king who had erected the building was written into its very fabric, providing an unbreakable connection between the structure and its creator.

The inscriptions hidden in the foundations served this purpose, but they also had another function—communication between past, present, and future kings. Since Tiglath-pileser I, Assyrian rulers used a special kind of clay artifact for these inscriptions. They were hollow prisms with either six or eight sides that were each inscribed in minute cuneiform script, providing space for hundreds of lines of text. Shorter inscriptions were recorded on barrel-shaped clay objects, tablets of stone, or precious metal. These were then deposited in stone boxes, and set into the foundational layers of the new building. Whenever a palace or temple was renovated, its foundation deposits were excavated, the contents studied and reburied together with those added to commemorate the present ruler. This practice was not limited to the Assyrians, but constitutes a Mesopotamian tradition that reaches as far back as the third millennium BCE. However, the prisms, which allowed very long accounts to be recorded, are characteristically Assyrian, and the detail of their royal inscriptions is without parallel elsewhere.

Sources with a Bias

Assyrian building inscriptions are among our most important sources for reconstructing the political history of the ancient Near East. They relate, from the Assyrian king's perspective, the key events of his reign. The subject matter covered was determined by convention. Events inside the boundaries of Assyria were normally ignored and the focus was firmly on interactions with the outer world, with the Assyrian king making foreign peoples "draw the yoke of god Ashur." In practical terms, this implied that the surrounding states were supposed to accept Assyrian sovereignty and pay regular tribute to the king. On an ideological level, this highlights the king's role as the representative, and agent, of his divine overlord, executing Ashur's command to "further my domain." It is therefore clear that the Royal Annals are a biased source, offering not only a subjective point of view, but also written to portray the king as his god's responsible and dedicated servant. There is no room for failure, only success, and while we stand to learn much about war between Assyria and its neighbors, we cannot expect to hear about other aspects of Assyrian foreign policy, such as trade agreements or peaceful negotiations.

The fact that the Annals are linked to building projects means that the whole of a king's reign is not documented—only the years up to the start of the construction work. Therefore, we often know very little about the later years of a king's reign. Some rulers like Shalmaneser V (reigned 726–722 BCE) died without commencing any major building projects, thus leaving no such texts.

Royal Stelae and Rock Reliefs

The inscriptions of Assyrian kings were also made on monuments that they called "the king's image," usually large monolithic stone slabs with a rounded top. These stelae were often placed in temples, or on significant natural landmarks, such as the sources of rivers, the seashore, or on mountains where they often took the form of rock reliefs. These outdoor sites were thought to provide an immediate connection with the divine world, in much the same way temples did. While monuments were set up within the Assyrian empire, many were erected outside its boundaries. The fact that "the king's image" was placed in a particular location was in itself not an indication of a permanent Assyrian claim, at least in administrative and political terms. Instead, the monument commemorates the fact that the Assyrians gained knowledge of the place, and is a lasting testament to this symbolic achievement. On the ideological level, the erection of a royal monument marks, and safeguards, that place in the "officially existing world."

"The king's image" served as a substitute for his presence. The monument always shows the king in an act of worship, while the inscription usually invokes the gods represented in the form of divine symbols. They introduce the king and his most celebrated deeds, ending with blessings for the future rulers who respect and protect the monument, and curses against those who do not.

BELOW **A larger-than-life stone relief** depicting archers is now in the Baghdad Museum.

Tiglath-pileser III

Under Tiglath-pileser III (reigned 744–727 BCE), Assyria's territories were greatly enlarged by incorporating lands to the west of the Euphrates River, and east of the Zagros Mountains' main ridge. In 729 BCE, he also seized the crown of Babylon.

RIGHT **Tiglath-pileser III is seen here on** a stone panel from his Central Palace at Nineveh. He became one of Assyria's most successful military commanders and administrators.

Unlike many personal names used today in the English-speaking world, the meaning of Assyrian names was immediately comprehensible to the people who used them. Most names are complete sentences, often prayers or blessings for the bearer of the name or those close to him. Some examples are Adad-šezibanni "O Adad (storm god), save me!", and Nabu-ra'im-ketti "Nabu (god of scribes) loves the truth."

Certain names were reserved exclusively for the Assyrian kings and commoners were not allowed to use them. To do so was a punishable offence, as shown by court records from the reign of King Ashurbanipal (reigned 668–627 BCE). Several rulers changed their birth names when ascending to the throne, and it is extremely likely that the Assyrian kings habitually used throne names. Some of these names are used repeatedly, for example, Ashur-nirari (meaning "Ashur is my help") is used by no less than five Assyrian kings.

Tiglath-pileser's Name, and other Assyrian Royal Names

The meaning of royal names is closely linked to the ideology of Assyrian kingship, and often celebrates the close relationship between the king and the gods that protect his office. Tukulti-ninurta means "My trust belongs to Ninurta (a warrior god and the son and heir of Ashur)." This is, in effect, the same name as Tiglath-pileser (correctly, Tukulti-apil-Ešarra), meaning "My trust belongs to the son of the Ešarra temple (the shrine of Ashur, Ninurta's father)." The significance of this name is obscured by the fact that we use its distorted biblical form, as is the case whenever an Assyrian king is mentioned in the Bible. This was, after all, how the memory of these rulers survived when cuneiform script was no longer in use.

Other examples of biblical versions of Assyrian royal names are: Shalmaneser for Salmanu-ašared—"Salmanu (a god closely associated with the king) is the foremost"; Sargon for Šarru-ken ("The king is true"); and Sennacherib for Sin-ahhe-eriba—"Sin (moon god) has replaced the brothers." However, this last name is not a royal name. When Sennacherib came to the throne in 704 BCE, he did not change his private name, which he shared with many other Assyrians, and which signified that his parents considered the newborn boy a replacement for his older brothers who had died as infants. Perhaps Sennacherib, who held a prominent and influential position throughout the reign of his father Sargon II (reigned 721–705 BCE), thought it unwise to "re-invent" himself as king after his father's traumatic death on the battlefield. Perhaps he preferred to send a message of continuity, and stability by maintaining the name under which he had been successful as crown prince.

Tiglath-pileser's Origins

Sennacherib's grandfather, Tiglath-pileser III, however, had adopted a new royal name when ascending to the Assyrian throne. It was a name that instantly invoked the impressive achievements of Tiglath-pileser I, the great Assyrian king of the eleventh century BCE, and this is likely to have been intentional.

As we have no archival texts from the reigns of the predecessors of Tiglath-pileser III, we do not know his private name before he took an official throne-name, or whether he had been the crown prince. In his own inscriptions, Tiglath-pileser III never mentions his father, usually invoked in this context to stress the king's legitimate claim to the throne. According to the list of Assyrian kings, he was the son of his predecessor Ashur-nirari V (reigned 754–745 BCE). Modern scholars, therefore, generally assume that, although of royal blood, he was a usurper who took the Assyrian crown by force by engineering a coup against his ineffective father.

ABOVE **Archers from Tiglath-pileser III's army** are depicted in one of the many reliefs that record Tiglath-pileser's conquests.

LEFT **An official from the court** of Tiglath-pileser III is shown praying to symbols of the gods in this limestone relief recovered from Tell Abta near Nineveh.

Assyria in the Early Eighth Century BCE

In the first half of the eighth century BCE, Assyria found itself in a precarious situation. With the rise of Urartu in eastern Anatolia, Assyrian supremacy was no longer automatically accepted by its western neighbors, the smaller kingdoms in Syria and Anatolia. The treaties binding these states to Assyria, and guaranteeing their tribute for the Assyrian treasury, were vulnerable as long as swearing allegiance to Urartu instead remained a realistic alternative. At that time, Urartu's army was certainly Assyria's equal and in 754 BCE, just when Ashur-nirari V had ascended to the Assyrian throne, Sarduri II, king of Urartu, defeated the Assyrian army in Arpad, an Assyrian vassal state in northern Syria. This glorious achievement was celebrated in Sarduri's inscriptions, and was quite clearly a disaster for Assyria. For the next few years, the troops did not leave the borders of Assyria and it was only in 749 BCE that a new expedition was mounted. This was not against Urartu, but to defend the border with Babylonia where Assyrian interests were now also endangered.

In 746 BCE a rebellion took place in Kalah, the city of the main royal residence. Tiglath-pileser III supported this revolt against Ashur-nirari V, as had the governors of Assur and Kalah. They were among the very few high officials who remained in power after a coup in 745 BCE when Tiglath-pileser III seized the throne. The insurrection

TIGLATH-PILESER'S QUEEN YABA

In 1988, the tomb of Yaba, Tiglath-pileser's queen, was discovered underneath the private wing of the Northwest Palace in Kalah; she was 30–35 years old when she died and she was buried with exquisite funerary goods. The burial was protected with a curse, threatening whoever disturbed the grave with thirst and restlessness for all eternity. It was explicitly forbidden to bury another body in Yaba's tomb, yet, later, the corpse of a second woman was laid down in her coffin. Even more bafflingly, the funerary goods identify two more queens, not just one—Banitu, the queen of Shalmaneser V (reigned 724–722 BCE), and Atalia, the queen of Sargon II (reigned 721–705 BCE). This gives rise to speculations that Yaba and Banitu were one and the same, as both names mean "The beautiful one."

RIGHT **This gold necklace is one of six** that were found in the tomb, along with solid gold anklets, a funerary crown, and other exquisite jewelry.

had clearly started in the very center of Assyria, with the backing of some of the most senior officials. Many other governors and magnates, however, were replaced, probably after they were executed when Tiglath-pileser's faction prevailed against those who remained loyal to his predecessor, Ashur-nirari V.

The Early Reign of Tiglath-pileser III

Having established himself on the Assyrian throne, Tiglath-pileser first took the army to the south and decided the situation at the Babylonian frontier in his favor. He founded two new provinces, situated along the important trade route that we know as the Silk Route. Bit-Hamban, at the headwaters of the Diyala river, and Parsua, further to the east in the Zagros Mountains, were created in 744 BCE.

The news from Assyria, indicating a dramatic shift in the ailing state's fortunes, brought the Urartian army, still under the command of the celebrated Sarduri, to the Euphrates border, and in 743 BCE Assyria and Urartu met once again in battle in Arpad. This time, the Assyrian troops were victorious and pursued the Urartian army all the way back to their capital, Turushpa.

The decade-long experiences of Assyrian vulnerability and impotence, eclipsed and threatened by Urartu, and the loss of its hold over Syria and Babylonia, more than likely caused Tiglath-pileser and his army to initiate the military campaigns in the west. This marked the beginning of Assyria's expansion to the Mediterranean coast, deep into Anatolia and the Zagros Mountains, and to the Persian Gulf. Under Tiglath-pileser, Assyria outgrew its traditional boundaries and was transformed into what today we call the Assyrian Empire.

The Conquest of Syria

After defeating the Urartian troops in Arpad, Tiglath-pileser decided to discipline this kingdom that had provided Urartu with access to Syria and to Assyria's frontier. His army waged war in Arpad for three years, and by 740 BCE had crushed all resistance. Arpad's forces had also been assisted by the troops of all its Syrian neighbors. When Arpad was ultimately defeated, the Assyrian army did not leave, as it had in previous centuries. Instead, the country was transformed into a permanent part of Assyria and two Assyrian provinces were established.

The determined resistance met in Arpad meant that the war could not end if the new Assyrian holdings were to be protected. Although the alliance against Assyria had been driven out of Arpad, it remained in existence, and was a powerful adversary. Next in line was Arpad's close ally and neighbor to the west, the influential kingdom of Hamath on the Orontes River. Hamath's troops were first defeated in 738 BCE and its northwestern territories, reaching the

Mediterranean Sea, were turned into Assyrian provinces. During this campaign, Hamath's northern neighbor on the Mediterranean coast, the Neo-Hittite kingdom of Unqi, was also conquered and incorporated into Assyria. But the state of Hamath did not collapse, and the fight for its independence continued, assisted by its allies, Damascus and Israel.

This war was won by Assyria six years later, in 732 BCE, when the troops of Hamath and Damascus were defeated, the countries invaded, and permanently annexed. At the same time, Israel was also subjugated, and the northern half of the kingdom was integrated as the Assyrian province of Megiddo.

ABOVE **This scene shows Tiglath-pileser's army** attacking a city under siege with a battering ram, supported by a phalanx of archers.

The Later Reign of Tiglath-pileser

During the reign of Tiglath-pileser III, the Assyrian forces were transformed into a professional army with specialized soldiers. These largely replaced the conscripts who provided military service during the summer months when the agricultural calendar permitted the absence of farm workers. Soldiers from the defeated kingdoms of Arpad, Unqi, Hamath, Damascus, and Israel swelled the ranks of the Assyrian army, supplemented by mercenaries from Anatolia, the Zagros Mountains, and Babylonia.

It would seem that most of the income provided by Tiglath-pileser's conquests was invested in the establishment of this professional army, and the maintenance of the new provinces. He certainly did not spend his revenue in central Assyria, where he contented himself with building only a new palace in Kalah, the so-called Central Palace. The decorated stone slabs that served as the stone paneling around the base of the palace walls provide us with Tiglath-pileser's accounts of his conquests. From the beginning of his reign, the Assyrian king had been active in Babylonia. He became the arch rival of Mukin-zeri, chief of the tribe of Bit-Amukani, who attempted to unite the politically fragmented region under his leadership, and assumed the kingship of Babylon in 731 BCE.

Tiglath-pileser saw this as a provocation and a challenge to Assyria's primacy in the region. He repeatedly led the Assyrian army against Mukin-zeri and ultimately defeated him, taking the crown of Babylon for himself in 729 BCE. For the rest of his reign, Tiglath-pileser ruled both as the king of Assyria and the king of Babylon.

LEFT **The numerous carefully inscribed slabs** like this one, showing troops of Tiglath-pileser's army attacking a Phoenician or Syrian city, provide a detailed record of how the army operated.

The Threat from Urartu

From the mid-ninth century BCE onward, Assyria had a mighty rival to the north: Urartu, to use the Assyrian name for the kingdom, which controlled what is today eastern Turkey, Armenia, and northwestern Iran.

RIGHT **This model of an Urartian city wall** (from the late eighth century BCE), comes from Toprakkale (ancient Rusahinili) in Urartu. It shows details of the city's architectural fortifications.

The name Urartu lives on as Ararat, the supposed landing place of Noah's Ark. Urartu is not a local place name, rather, from the second millennium BCE, it was the traditional Mesopotamian designation for the mountain ranges of Inner Anatolia. The people that we today label "the Urartians" called themselves and their state Biainili, which can be pronounced "Vian-ili." The name lives on today as "Van," designating both a lake in eastern Turkey and the most important settlement on its eastern shore.

The predecessor of the modern city of Van was Turushpa, capital of Urartu from the reign of Sarduri I onwards, a contemporary of the Assyrian king Shalmaneser III (reigned 858–824 BCE). In the mid-eighth century BCE, Urartu controlled the area between the three lakes of Van, Urmia (now in Iran), and Sevan (now in Armenia), and the valley of the Murat Su up to its confluence with the main branch of the Euphrates River.

The God Haldi and the City of Musasir

Sarduri I proclaimed the god Haldi as the head of the Urartian pantheon, and he and his successors erected many temples in Haldi's name. The first, and most important, sanctuary of Haldi, however, was not situated in Urartu, but in the ancient city

BELOW **Mt. Ararat in eastern Turkey,** the tallest mountain in Turkey, is traditionally thought to be where Noah's Ark came to rest after the Flood, according to the Bible.

of Musasir, capital of a small kingdom in modern Sidikan in northeastern Iraq. Musasir, as it was called by the Assyrians, was known also under the Hurrian name Ardini "The City," and it is recorded as an important settlement from the early second millennium BCE onwards. Why Sarduri chose to promote Haldi as the main deity of Urartu remains unclear, but it is perhaps significant that the former capital, Arzashkun, was situated not far from Musasir, on the other side of the Zagros Mountains. Haldi's importance in Urartu meant that Musasir held a special place throughout Urartian history. The kings were crowned in Haldi's temple at Musasir, and visited the shrine regularly as part of their cultic responsibilities. Nevertheless, Musasir retained its independence and was ruled by its own king.

Following the emergence of Biainili in the late ninth century BCE, Musasir was a buffer state between Urartu and Assyria. Both states respected Musasir's sovereignty, until Sargon II of Assyria plundered the city and temple in 714 BCE. This was celebrated in the stone reliefs from Sargon's palace in Dur-Sharrukin (Khorsabad), which show the capture of Musasir, and the looting of its temple in great detail. The depiction of Haldi's shrine, with its unique roof construction, and its façade decorated with shields, spears, and statues, is today the most famous architectural representation in Assyrian art.

Assyria and Urartu

Since the initial encounters between Assyrians and Urartians, the relationship of the two states was defined by open conflict as both competed for political and commercial control over the kingdoms of northern Syria, which provided access to the Mediterranean Sea and western Anatolia. The two rival states were separated by the soaring mountains of the Zagros and the Taurus main ridges. Urartu's influence grew steadily until it reached its pinnacle under Sarduri II (reigned 756–*c.* 730 BCE). He defeated Assyria's forces in a battle in northern Syria in 754 BCE, shattering Assyria's control of the lands west of the Euphrates, and plunging the kingdom into confusion. Only 12 years later, in 743 BCE, just after Tiglath-pileser III (reigned 744–727 BCE) had ascended the Assyrian throne, he crushed the Urartian army in northern Syria, and drove it back to Turushpa, the first time that Assyrian troops had reached that Urartian capital. This heralded Assyria's rising might and its ultimate triumph over rival powers.

URARTIAN WINE

Urartu was a wine-producing and wine-consuming nation. Several Urartian kings, most importantly Menua (reigned *c.* 810–785 BCE), had irrigation systems constructed that were to provide water for fields, fruit groves, and the very extensive vineyards that were created all over Urartian territory. According to Sargon II of Assyria (reigned 721–705 BCE), Urartian cities had wine cellars so vast that one could drink wine there as if it were water, and archaeological excavations have confirmed that Urartian fortresses contained huge stocks of wine, stored in enormous clay vessels with a holding capacity of almost 260 gal (1,000 l). Of the 70 underground storerooms of the fortress of Teishebaini (modern Karmir-Blur near the Armenian capital, Yerevan), seven were wine cellars with 360 such containers, which would have held the staggering amount of 92,000 gal (350,000 l) of wine. Today, Armenia is renowned for its wines, and, famously, Winston Churchill's favorite drink was Armenian brandy.

LEFT **The winged god Ahura-Mazda** offers libation in this stone relief from the palace of Urartu.

The Conquest of Palestine

Under Tiglath-pileser III (reigned 744–727 BCE), the kingdoms to the west of the Euphrates River were annexed, one after the other, by Assyria, a policy continued by his successors. The Mediterranean coast was to be the new western frontier.

ABOVE **Tel Megiddo in the Valley of Jezreel** in Israel was at the junction of many trade routes. It is believed to be where Armageddon—the end of the world—will occur, as prophesied in the New Testament (Revelation 16:16).

One of the states that fell victim to the Assyrian expansion to the Mediterranean Sea was the kingdom of Israel. Its conquest is well documented in the Old Testament. Assyrian royal inscriptions, with materials from the administrative archives, also provide further information.

In 732 and 722 BCE, Israel was defeated and split into two Assyrian provinces: Megiddo and Samaria. According to the Bible (II Kings 15:29) the northern part of Israel was captured by Tiglath-pileser III, who crushed the army of Pekah, king of Israel, and occupied the conquered regions. The Bible states that the Assyrian troops were summoned by Ahaz, king of Judah, Tiglath-pileser's vassal, who had asked for Assyrian help after losing the harbor of Eilat on the Red Sea to the kingdom of Edom which was allied to Damascus. In II Kings 16:7–9, we read:

> *"Ahaz sent messengers to say to Tiglath-pileser king of Assyria, 'I am your servant and vassal. Come up and save me out of the hand of the king of Aram [Damascus] and of the king of Israel, who are attacking me.' And Ahaz took silver and gold...and sent it as a gift to the king of Assyria. The king of Assyria complied..."*

Tiglath-pileser's royal inscriptions do not contain references to this invasion, which happened in 732 BCE when the kingdoms of Damascus and Hamath were conquered and added to the Assyrian state. The Israelite city of Megiddo, the center of an Assyrian province of the same name, is mentioned in several later texts, dating from the reign of Sargon II (reigned 721–705 BCE) onward.

With the north of the kingdom lost, Israel's south remained independent for another decade. It, too, was eventually occupied by Assyria in 722 BCE when Tiglath-pileser's son and successor, Shalmaneser V (reigned 726–722 BCE), conquered the capital city of Samaria, after which the newly established Assyrian province was named. The Assyrian conquest of Palestine continued.

Ashdod was defeated in 711 BCE, and this Philistine city became the center of the most southern of Assyria's provinces on the Mediterranean coast. The kingdom of Judah, however, remained independent.

The Siege of Jerusalem in 701 BCE

While relations with Assyria were mostly amicable, Judah was invaded by the Assyrian army in 701 BCE during a campaign that was meant to strengthen Assyrian supremacy in the southwest of the empire after the sudden death of Sargon II. Judah's king, Hezekiah, had allied himself with the Assyrian archenemies Merodach-Baladan II in Babylon, and Taharqa, king of Egypt and Nubia. This brought the army of Sargon's son and successor Sennacherib (reigned 704–681 BCE) to Jerusalem. The Bible (II Kings 18:31–32) reports Sennacherib's message to the people of Jerusalem, encouraging them to betray their King Hezekiah who refused to submit:

> *"Make your peace with me and come out to me! Then every one of you will eat of his own vine, and every one of you will eat of his own fig tree, and every one of you will drink the water of his own cistern, until I come and take you away to a land like your own land, a land of grain and wine, a land of bread and vineyards, a land of olive trees and honey, that you may live, and not die!"*

It is the prospect of being resettled elsewhere in the Assyrian Empire that Sennacherib is said to have used in his attempt to ensnare the people of Jerusalem. Indeed, deportation could be regarded as a privilege. People were not made to leave on their own, but together with their families, and only after they had been carefully selected. This often followed a military campaign that had, quite possibly, reduced their original home to ruins. When the sources specify who is to be relocated we find the urban elites, the craftsmen, the specialists, and scholars among them. The practice of resettling populations was a fundamental ingredient of the basic structure of Assyria and its successor states. Every population group taken away was replaced with another from elsewhere in the Assyrian Empire. This policy provided a high degree of cultural homogeneity and economic balance that characterized the ancient Near East by the mid-first millennium BCE.

ABOVE **The Western Wall** (also known as The Wailing Wall) in the old city of Jerusalem is the holiest of Jewish sites.

The Lost Tribes of Israel

Jerusalem did not submit to the Assyrian army in 701 BCE, and its people remained safe from Assyria's resettlement strategy, because Judah had renewed its treaties with the empire. In 732 and 722 BCE, however, the population of Israel had been greatly affected by this policy of forced resettlement. The phrase "the lost tribes of Israel" refers to those that were then taken away to their new homes elsewhere in the Assyrian empire. The Bible (II Kings 17:6) gives the destination only of those Israelites resettled in 722 BCE:

> *"The king of Assyria captured Samaria and deported the Israelites to Assyria. He settled them in Halah (near Mosul in northern Iraq), in Gozan on the Habor River (modern Tell Halaf in northwestern Syria), and in the towns of the Medes (in the Zagros Mountains)"*

Since antiquity there has been speculation about where the other Israelites were sent. Today, the quest continues with the help of DNA analysis.

LEFT **Shalmaneser IV attacks Hoshea of Samaria** and leads captives away behind his chariot, *c.* 725 BCE, as depicted in this illumination by French artist Jean Fouquet (1420–1481).

Sargon II

Sargon II (reigned 721–705 BCE) ascended the Assyrian throne during a countrywide rebellion. He later created a magnificent new city, known as "Sargon's Fortress" in what is now Dur-Sharrukin (Khorsabad), but just one year after it had been completed, he died on the battlefield.

ABOVE **The opulence of life at Dur-Sharrukin,** as imagined in the nineteenth-century CE, is depicted in this engraving.

ABOVE RIGHT **The cuneiform text on this clay fragment** gives details of Sargon II's ascension to the Assyrian throne in 721 BCE.

Sargon II was a son of Tiglath-pileser III (reigned 744–727 BCE), and a brother of Shalmaneser V (reigned 726–722 BCE), who he succeeded under obscure circumstances. We would expect him to be recorded in a prominent military or administrative role in the archival materials from Kalah. Although these date from Tiglath-pileser's reign, we do not know under what name he was known before he took the crown of Assyria, so he has not yet been identified. Sargon was at least 40 years old when he came to the throne, and his son Sennacherib, as crown prince, immediately assumed a responsible role in the running of the state.

It was Sargon's brother Ululayu who had been Tiglath-pileser's chosen heir. Several letters from the royal archives of Kalah in which he reports to his father, the king, document his activities before he succeeded to the throne after the natural death of Tiglath-pileser. He took the throne name Shalmaneser V. By doing so, he invoked the great deeds of namesakes such as the thirteenth-century BCE king Shalmaneser I and Shalmaneser III (reigned 858–824 BCE), who had both successfully consolidated control over the newly conquered regions that their respective predecessors had annexed to Assyria.

The new king continued his father's conquest of the west. During his short reign, regions in southeastern Turkey and Samaria, the southern half of the biblical kingdom of Israel, were established as new Assyrian provinces. Shalmaneser also ruled as king of Babylon.

Sargon Wins the Assyrian Throne

Sargon came to power in 721 BCE. His brother's fate is unknown, but there are indications that the succession was not smooth. In the one

inscription in which Sargon mentions his predecessor, he is condemned as godless and robbing the city of Assur of its traditional privileges, and he is not referred to at all in Sargon's official accounts. Sargon's throne name means "the king is legitimate," as is explained in one of his inscriptions: "My name, which the great gods assigned to me in order to uphold law and justice, to help the powerless prevail and to protect the weak."

Sargon portrays himself as the restorer of order. Did he rescue the country from a state of lawlessness under Shalmaneser V? Or was the chaos caused by a coup that he engineered? The available sources do not tell us, but it is clear that the new king met with massive opposition. We know that Sargon pardoned 6,300 "guilty Assyrians" and resettled them in Hama. This city had been the center of a rebellion under the leadership of Iau-bi'di who had gained widespread support in the west of the Assyrian empire.

The former kingdoms of Hama, Arpad, Damascus, and Israel all rose in rebellion after Sargon's rise to power. The revolt was crushed in 720 BCE and Hama was destroyed once again. The Assyrians who found themselves relocated to the ruins of this once-proud city were exiled from the empire's power center, while they had to repay the mercy of their king who spared their lives by rebuilding Hama.

The Loss of the Crown of Babylon

When central Assyria and the west rose in rebellion against the new king, Assyria's enemies in the south saw their chance. Merodach-Baladan, chief of the Bit-Yakin tribe, and the figurehead of the anti-Assyrian movement in Babylonia, announced the end of Assyrian sovereignty, and claimed the throne of Babylon for himself.

Upon hearing this, Sargon marched southwards. Merodach-Baladan reacted by joining forces with Assyria's old rival, the king of Elam. They mustered a massive army against Sargon's forces. The troops met in battle at the city of Der on the plains east of Babylon in 720 BCE. This was the same battlefield where almost two centuries later, in 539 BCE, Darius the Great defeated the army sent by the last Babylonian king, Nabonidus. Although Merodach-Baladan's troops arrived too late for active combat, the Assyrian army was pushed back by his Elamite allies, and he remained on Babylon's throne.

The Capture of Carchemish and Musasir

After a very rocky start, and the loss of the Babylonian crown, Sargon was able to consolidate his reign in Assyria. It was the conquest of Carchemish in 717 BCE that allowed Sargon to recoup the costs of the permanent, but unproductive, deployment of the army since the beginning of his reign. The massively fortified and wealthy city of Carchemish controlled an important Euphrates crossing; was positioned at a crossroads between the Mediterranean coast, Anatolia and Assyria; and profited from its role in international trade. Moreover, Carchemish was the last of the Neo-Hittite states, the Syrian heirs of the mighty Anatolian Hittite Empire of the second millennium BCE, and its king enjoyed a leading role among the Neo-Hittite kingdoms.

When Sargon attacked Carchemish, he violated the treaties with this longstanding Assyrian ally. He defended his actions by claiming that Pisiri of Carchemish had passed on information to his

LEFT **A Neo-Hittite soldier** is depicted in this stone relief from Carchemish, a city located on the border between modern-day Turkey and Syria.

enemies. Carchemish's prize was its treasury, which contained 730 lb (330 kg) of pure gold, 70 tons (63,000 kg) of silver, and huge amounts of bronze, tin, iron, and ivory. The influx of silver changed the Assyrian economy from a bronze-based to a silver-based financial system. The capture of the holy city of Musasir three years later was motivated by its wealth, rather than the treachery of its king, by which Sargon justified his actions.

The temple of Haldi, as the head of the Urartian pantheon, had received gifts and donations for over a millennium when Sargon plundered the shrine and royal palace in 714 BCE, resulting in a booty of over 1 ton (*c.* 1 metric ton) of gold and about 10 tons (*c.* 9 metric tons) of silver, and much other treasure.

BELOW **Reliefs, such as this one from Sargon II's palace** at Dur-Sharrukin, show important details of how buildings were constructed.

The Construction of "Sargon's Fortress"

After this large addition to his coffers, Sargon began the construction of Dur-Sharrukin, "Sargon's Fortress," in 713 BCE. Unlike Kalah, and Nineveh, this was an entirely new city, constructed on virgin soil in an area quite close to Kalah that Sargon had identified as the perfect site for the center of the Assyrian empire. This gigantic building project was intended to be the king's crowning achievement. In the foundation inscriptions, Sargon proudly takes credit for recognizing the potential of the sleepy village of Maganubba as the location for his new city. He bought the land from its owners, and started a massive irrigation project to provide the agricultural produce needed for the inhabitants of what was to be the largest city in Assyria—it covered *c.* 10,000 sq ft (3 sq km).

The ground plan of Dur-Sharrukin is modeled on that of Kalah but, unlike this city, which was developed from an existing settlement, Sargon's new capital was perfectly symmetrical with no concern for the surrounding landscape. The seven monumental city gates penetrate the fortification wall at regular intervals, rather than according to the needs of a pre-existing road network. The two gigantic platforms, one housing the palace and temples, the other the arsenal, were constructed from scratch.

Sargon's new palace eclipsed the buildings of all his predecessors in scale and quality. The relief scenes that adorned the palace walls depict his conquests, and also the sack of Musasir which, crucially, had funded the building works. In 706 BCE, only eight years after construction had begun, the court moved to Dur-Sharrukin.

Sargon's Triumph and Death

Sargon continued with the policy of conquest and annexation that characterized the reign of Tiglath-pileser III and Shalmaneser V, but the effort to control areas that were situated ever farther away from the Assyrian heartland began to weigh heavily. Two more provinces in the Zagros Mountains were created in 716 BCE, and were secured only after years of fighting.

The deportations from the region brought a sizable Median population to the city of Assur, which may have played a role in the fall of that city in 614 BCE. The attempt to establish the province of Tabal in Central Anatolia in 713 BCE failed after a rebellion the following year.

The annexation of Ashdod in Philistia in 711 BCE was more successful, as was the conquest and integration of the Neo-Hittite kingdoms of Gurgum in the same year, and

LEFT **A tributary is seen leading a horse** in this Assyrian relief from the Palace of Sargon II at Dur-Sharrukin, which was discovered by Paul-Emile Botta in 1843.

Kummuhhu (Commagene) in 708 BCE. The year 710 BCE saw a major triumph. Sargon finally managed to oust Merodach-Baladan from the Babylonian throne, and took the crown for himself. While his crown prince, Sennacherib, officiated in Kalah, Sargon resided in Babylon for the following three years, receiving homage and gifts from rulers from as far away as Cyprus and Bahrain. Only when the move to Dur-Sharrukin had begun did he return.

In 705 BCE, Sargon returned to Tabal in an attempt to restore the region to its former status as an Assyrian province. His army met with violent opposition and, to everyone's horror, the king died in battle, his corpse lost to the enemy.

This catastrophic event led to Dur-Sharrukin being abandoned as the royal residence. It was also thought to lie at the root of his heirs' subsequent poor fortune—Sennacherib was murdered, and Esarhaddon's reign was haunted by conspiracy and illness.

"WINGED BULLS"

The so-called "winged bull" sculptures are guardian figures, pairs of which protect the gateways of Assyrian cities, palaces and temples, including those of Dur-Sharrukin. These composite creatures have the head of a bearded man, the wings of an eagle and the body of a bull or lion, sometimes combined with fish elements such as scaly skin and fins. They can best be described as angels, acting as intermediaries between the human world and the divine, and correspond to the cherubim mentioned in the Bible. When the Assyrian royal cities were excavated from the mid-nineteenth century CE onward, winged bulls were shipped to museums in London, Paris, and Chicago, but not all reached their destination. A pair from Dur-Sharrukin, sent on their way to Paris in 1855, was lost to the Tigris. This was not the first time that boats carrying winged bulls had sunk. From Sargon's correspondence, we know of such an accident during the construction of his city, but the governor of Assur was able to recover the heavy load that his men had lost in the Tigris on the way from the quarry to Dur-Sharrukin.

RIGHT **The Winged Bull with a human face** is from the Hall of Winged Bulls in Sargon II's palace.

Nineveh

In the seventh century BCE, Nineveh was the capital of Assyria and considered to be the world's largest city. According to the Old Testament, 120,000 people lived in the city, which was so large, it took three days to cross.

Nineveh was situated on the eastern bank of the Tigris River, at its confluence with its tributary, the Khosr River, occupying a prime location on the long-distance trade network. Today, Mosul, Iraq's second largest city, covers only half of the area of the ancient Assyrian settlement. Millennia before, when Sennacherib (reigned 704–681 BCE) moved the royal court to Nineveh, and transformed the city into Assyria's political and administrative center, it had been one of northern Mesopotamia's most important towns.

Our knowledge of this earlier period is limited, as archaeological investigation has focused on the impressive architecture of the seventh century BCE. Evidence proves that Nineveh existed by the sixth millennium BCE at the latest, and was an important regional center by at least the mid-third millennium BCE.

This is suggested by the distribution of Ninevite 5 pottery which has been found across upper Mesopotamia and in northern Syria. Nineveh was the city of the goddess who was known as Inanna in Sumerian, Ishtar in the Assyrian and Babylonian language, and Shawushka in Hurrian and Hittite. The goddess was worshipped in several ancient Near Eastern cities, but Ishtar of Nineveh was considered so powerful that, in the fourteenth century BCE, Amenhotep III, Pharaoh of Egypt, asked his ally, the king of Mittani who controlled Nineveh at that time, to let her statue visit Egypt to bestow Ishtar's blessings on the ailing pharoah.

BELOW **This fragment of an enameled terracotta tile** showing two men walking is from Nineveh.

Sennacherib's New Residence City

From the creation of the Middle Assyrian kingdom in the mid-fourteenth century BCE onward, Nineveh was one of the most important cities of Assyria and was always the center of a province, but it was only under Sennacherib that Nineveh became the gargantuan city that was both praised, and condemned, in the Old Testament. The original city encompassed only the mound of Kuyunjik, and its immediate surroundings in the area north of the Khosr River.

To this Sennacherib added the territory of the formerly separate city of Nurrugum (modern Nebi Yunus), which was situated on the southern bank of the Khosr. Around this enormous area of 1,800 acres (750 ha), Sennacherib had a fortification wall of 7.5 miles (12 km) constructed. Access was through 15 gigantic gates, which were decorated with, and protected by, monumental winged bull guardians. These gates were fortresses in their own right, with an inner and an outer gate, above which were two-story rooms that housed the garrisons.

Sennacherib built his palace on Kuyunjik, and adorned it lavishly, as we know from the results of the excavations conducted in Nineveh since the mid-nineteenth century BCE. Sennacherib's building inscriptions also explain the construction of the palace in great detail.

He seems especially pleased that he used stone from a new, and conveniently located, quarry, and that the royal parks surrounding the palace contained rare plants that none of his predecessors had been able to acquire—cotton is mentioned prominently.

The Irrigation System

The new metropolis needed an enormous amount of water to irrigate the fabulous royal parks, and especially to increase the area that could be used for agriculture. Additional fields, vegetable gardens, and fruit groves were needed to provide food for Nineveh's inhabitants, whose numbers greatly increased after the expansion of the city.

In his inscriptions, Sennacherib proudly claims that he allocated a garden plot to every Ninevite.

LEFT **A protective goddess,** holding a dagger, is shown in bas-relief from the palace at Nineveh.

To provide the large amount of water necessary, the king embarked on a hydraulic engineering project to haul water directly from the springs in the mountains north of Nineveh. It was the most ambitious project undertaken during the Assyrian Empire. Aqueducts, subterranean canals, dams and reservoirs were built, all of the highest technological standard, and often lavishly decorated with reliefs and inscriptions. Over the course of fifteen years (702–688 BCE), Sennacherib's engineers constructed 90 miles (150 km) of canals.

As with every irrigation system, these waterworks needed constant maintenance and repair. When Nineveh was attacked by the Median army in 612 BCE, these elaborate engineering works were destroyed during the siege. After the fall of the empire, the impoverished citizens who remained did not have the resources to repair the aqueducts. This contributed to the rapid abandonment of the city which, without artificial irrigation, could not provide a home for its many inhabitants. Nineveh soon became a ghost town.

Sennacherib's palace was not discovered until the mid-nineteenth century CE.

BELOW **This depiction of the reconstruction of the palace at Nineveh** is a nineteenth-century CE engraving by French artist Félix Thomas.

THE PROPHET JONAH

According to the Bible, God sent Jonah, a man from the region of Nazareth, to Nineveh to prophesy the imminent doom of that godless metropolis. Jonah initially tried to escape his destiny by boarding a ship bound for Spain, as far away from Nineveh as possible. Yet, a storm arose and the sailors threw Jonah overboard. He survived, but ended up in the belly of a whale, and finally accepted his mission. He eventually reached land, and, ultimately, Nineveh, where he walked through the city proclaiming, "In forty days Nineveh shall be destroyed!" When Nineveh's inhabitants believed him and did penance, God showed mercy and spared the city—for the time being. Tradition has it that Jonah died in Nineveh, and his grave is thought to lie on the mound of Nebi Yunus ("Prophet Jonah" in Arabic).

Ashurbanipal

Ashurbanipal (reigned 668–627 BCE) is today considered the last great king of Assyria. Appointed crown prince of Assyria in 672 BCE, he succeeded, uncontested, to the throne. His reign lasted for nearly 40 years during an increasingly troubled time.

BELOW **Details of a hunting expedition** can be seen in this relief dated c. 645 BCE, one of many found at Nineveh that provides an insight into life at that time.

Ashurbanipal's father and predecessor, Esarhaddon (reigned 680–669 BCE), ruled successfully over Assyria and Babylon. The loss of his beloved wife, Ešarra-hamat, in 673 BCE may well have further undermined his already fragile health. When death seemed imminent, there were many candidates to succeed him, because he had fathered at least 18 children. At one point his son Sin-nadin-apli was mooted as the next king, but it was his younger son Ashurbanipal who eventually, in 672 BCE, ascended to the rank of crown prince of Assyria. While Esarhaddon ruled both Assyria and Babylonia, he clearly did not wish his successor to continue this practice, and so prepared the separation of the two countries by installing simultaneously another of his sons, Šamaš-šumu-ukin, as crown prince and future king of Babylon.

Both crown princes were deeply involved in important political and cultic matters, and this division of power seems to have lightened the sick king's burden. In 669 BCE, Esarhaddon set out for a campaign against Egypt, which had risen in rebellion, but he died on the way to the Nile, as far as we know, of natural causes. As he had planned, Ashurbanipal ascended to the Assyrian throne, while his brother, Šamaš-šumu-ukin, became king of Babylon.

The Struggle for Babylon

Esarhaddon had envisaged that Ashurbanipal and Šamaš-šumu-ukin would rule over their kingdoms as independent equals, linked by common interests and heritage. However, Ashurbanipal considered his brother an Assyrian vassal, and reserved a prominent role in Babylonian religious and public life for himself. Anti-Assyrian sentiment in Babylonia was fueled by the breakdown of the good relations between Assyria and the powerful Iranian kingdom of Elam, which Esarhaddon had established by signing a mutual peace treaty in 674 BCE. Elam shared a long border with Babylonia, its western neighbor, and the two states maintained close economic and political links. As tensions between Elam and Assyria grew, pro-Elamite influence in Babylonia became synonymous with anti-Assyrian plotting. The Assyrian army invaded Elam in 658 BCE, and

LEFT **This Neo-Assyrian winged lion** of glazed bricks is one of a pair from the Palace of Darius I at Susa.

sacked its ancient capital, Susa. Ashurbanipal now considered Elam his vassal state, but Assyrian control was limited, which became obvious once Šamaš-šumu-ukin, with the support of Elam and other enemies of Assyria, renounced Assyrian authority.

In 652 BCE, the king of Babylon claimed pre-eminence over Assyria, declaring Ashurbanipal to be nothing but the Babylonian governor of Nineveh. The Assyrian army was dispatched to Babylonia and, after four years of brutal war, and at great cost to the Babylonian people, finally gained control in 648 BCE. The palace of Šamaš-šumu-ukin was burnt when Babylon was taken and it is assumed he died in the fire.

Afterwards, Ashurbanipal portrayed himself as the savior and restorer of Babylon, but refrained from proclaiming himself King of Babylon. He installed someone called Kandalanu as puppet king, and Babylonia remained a separate state, clearly subservient to Assyria. Kandalanu is such an obscure character that an unlikely hypothesis, which sees Ashurbanipal and Kandalanu as one and the same person, continues to find occasional support among modern scholars.

Ashurbanipal: A Scholar, not a Soldier

With the costly wars in Babylonia and Egypt, and with Elam slipping out of Assyria's control, the reign of Ashurbanipal cannot easily be regarded as successful. However, he managed to stay on the throne for more than four decades—much longer than any of his immediate predecessors. While his grandfather, Sennacherib, had been killed by his sons, and his father's early reign had been haunted by the specter of conspiracy, Ashurbanipal's claim to the throne was apparently uncontested. Married to Queen Libbali-šarrat, Ashurbanipal ruled from 668 until at least 630 BCE, but so poorly documented are the last years of his reign, that it is difficult to establish when he was eventually succeeded by his son Ashur-et-ililani.

It is clear that, unlike previous Assyrian kings, and even his ailing father, Ashurbanipal rarely saw military action. He did not even accompany the troops on campaigns. If we recall that his great-grandfather, Sargon, had fallen in battle, this strategy, while it almost certainly prolonged his life span, was a radical departure from the behavior previously expected of an Assyrian king. While the Assyrian army was invading Elam in 658 BCE, Ashurbanipal remained in Nineveh, and prayed for success. However, when the army returned victorious, he took the leading role in the re-enactments of the battles and the triumphant processions that included the parading and public torturing of the most prominent captives.

Such performances aside, he seems to have led an isolated existence, protected and screened off from his subjects by his bodyguards, and the thick walls of his lavish new palace in Nineveh. Here he amassed what was, at the time, the biggest library in the world.

Today, Ashurbanipal is best remembered as the royal scholar on Assyria's throne.

BELOW **Ashurbanipal is depicted at a banquet** in this gypsum relief from his palace at Nineveh.

The Library of Antiquity

Ashurbanipal (reigned 668–627 BCE) aimed to transform the existing library of his royal palace in Nineveh into one that contained all human knowledge—an ambitious project, without precedent, that owes much to the king's personal interests.

RIGHT **This dictionary of synonyms** with a colophon (closing stamp), made of fired clay, is from the library of Ashurbanipal.

Ashurbanipal was highly educated and a true scholar. According to the scribes who helped him assemble the vast collection of cuneiform literature that today is known as Ashurbanipal's Library, he was learned in "the entire corpus of scribal learning, namely the craft of the gods Ea and Asalluhi (the performance of rituals), the divination series Šumma izbu (interpreting anomalous births) and Šumma alu (interpreting natural phenomena), the disciplines of exorcism, lamentation and chanting, and all other scribal learning." In his own official inscriptions, Ashurbanipal claimed:

> *I can solve complicated reciprocals and calculations that do not come out evenly. I have read cleverly written text in Sumerian and obscure Akkadian whose interpretation is difficult. I have studied inscriptions from before the Flood.*

Several of Ashurbanipal's brothers held high positions in Assyrian and Babylonian temples. His father, Esarhaddon, had also had a deep interest in the work of a scholar, and the details of cult and rituals, and had, quite possibly, been raised for such a career himself. The young Ashurbanipal may well have been destined for a priestly career before Sennacherib chose Esarhaddon to inherit the Assyrian throne, and disqualified Arda-Mullissi, the original crown prince, in 679 BCE. There can be little doubt that all Assyrian kings were literate, just like all men born into the higher echelons of society, and destined for a role in the running of the empire, but it is not at all certain that they shared Ashurbanipal's high level of erudition, and his fascination with esoteric and arcane knowledge.

Building up a Comprehensive Library

Ashurbanipal was not the founder of the Assyrian royal library—this institution can be traced back at least to the thirteenth century BCE. However, he systematically increased the holdings that he had inherited from his predecessors. To this end, he made full use of Assyria's hegemony over the known world. Whether he was motivated by a thirst for knowledge, and the wish to control this knowledge, or rather a collector's voraciousness, the library he created is today his most lasting monument. His interest in acquiring a comprehensive library made him utilize the military

WRITING BOARDS

Besides clay tablets, the cuneiform script was often recorded on writing boards. A thin layer of wax, made malleable by adding paraffin, was set into a frame of wood, or ivory. The writing was impressed into the wax with a wooden, or metal stylus. There were simple single-leaf versions, but also boards with two or more leaves, hinged together in such a way that when closed the wax surfaces were protected. Writing boards with several hinged leaves that folded up like an accordion were particularly popular for storing long compositions, such as omen collections with thousands of entries. They could be far more easily and conveniently stored than the dozens of clay tablets that would have been needed to store the same text.

RIGHT **On this fragment of a clay tablet,** (*c.* 680–669 BCE) lexical writings can be clearly seen: Sumerian pictographs are on the left, Assyrian cuneiform on the right.

successes in Babylonia and Egypt to collect, by brutal force when necessary, whatever library texts were available, and to have them brought to his growing library in Nineveh. Library acquisition records from 647 BCE list large numbers of scholarly works taken away from their original Babylonian owners in the aftermath of the war in Babylonia. So organized was Ashurbanipal's effort that he dispatched dedicated search parties to Babylonia to locate rare scholarly works.

However, not only existing library holdings were added to Ashurbanipal's collections, he also had entire libraries copied, either by the scholars in his entourage, or by local scribes. We know that he commanded the temples of Babylonia to have copies of all scholarly works in their possession made and sent to him. Captive scribes were an important resource, and contemporary reports tell how Babylonians who mastered the art of writing were used to copy texts for Ashurbanipal's library. Among them was the son of the former governor of the Babylonian city Nippur. Whenever he was not actively writing, he was kept in shackles. Whether this reflects the usual living conditions of these captive scribes, or was deemed necessary only in the case of a member of a highly influential, now disgraced family, remains tantalizingly unclear.

A Library of Clay Tablets, Writing Boards, Leather Scrolls, and Papyri

The clay tablets of Ashurbanipal's library survived the destruction of Nineveh in 612 BCE, although they were often broken into many fragments. They were recovered during the archaeological excavations conducted by British archaeologists at Nineveh in the mid-nineteenth century CE, and brought to the British Museum. Since then, ancient Near Eastern specialists have been working to catalog and decipher the rich contents of the tablets—a process still far from completion. Unfortunately, all other writing materials perished in the flames. We know that Ashurbanipal's library collections contained wax-covered writing boards and leather scrolls, as well as papyri, which were used by the Egyptian scribes and scholars active in Assyria. Around 28,000 cuneiform tablets survive from Ashurbanipal's library, but they represent only a tiny fraction of the original collection. Still, without the durable clay tablets we would have nothing at all—just as nothing remains of that other famous royal library of antiquity, the library of Alexandria.

BELOW **Scribes with hinged writing boards** and scrolls count the heads of the enemy after a battle, in this relief from the Palace of Sennacherib.

Assyria's Demise

At the end of the seventh century BCE, Assyria appeared to collapse abruptly at the very height of its power. Was it the force of the invading Babylonian and Median armies alone that caused the mighty empire to fall?

RIGHT **Ashurbanipal's troops are depicted storming a city** in this relief from the palace at Nineveh (*c.* 645 BCE).

In 674 BCE, Esarhaddon (reigned 680–669 BCE) arranged a peace treaty with Elam, Assyria's long-standing rival, and thus secured Assyria's eastern border. This gave Assyria its first chance to turn the power vacuum in Egypt to its own advantage. Egypt was politically fragmented at the time, with local dynasts ruling over small, virtually independent kingdoms in the Delta region. They reluctantly accepted the supremacy of the Nubian king, whose power base lay in what is now modern Sudan.

From the late eighth century BCE onwards, Assyrian and Nubian interests had clashed over control of the Philistine cities of Gaza and Ashdod. They were situated at a crossroad of international trade—the overland routes between Egypt and Assyria met the Mediterranean merchant ships, and the Arabian camel caravans. The Assyrian and Nubian-Egyptian armies met several times in battle, but neither achieved total control. Esarhaddon's army successfully invaded Egypt in 671 BCE after a stealthy approach through the desert, aided by Arab camel troops. The Delta rulers had to accept Assyria as their overlord, but their insurrections were supported by the Egyptian king, Taharqa, and his Nubian troops in 669 BCE, and again in 664 BCE. The Assyrians eventually forced the Nubians out of Egypt and Nekho, ruler of Sais in the Delta, and his son Psammetichus, united Egypt under Assyria's supremacy. They established the Saite dynasty, which ruled Egypt until the Persian conquest.

BELOW **In this relief, also from the palace at Nineveh,** Ashurbanipal's troops can be seen pursuing the Elamites, who are riding camels.

Assyria's ten-year military engagement in Egypt initially paid off. Egypt was at peace and Assyria's trusted vassal, and commerce blossomed. Little more than a decade later, Psammetichus, a former royal hostage at the Assyrian court, escaped from the control of his overlord, Ashurbanipal, and gained complete independence from Assyria. With relations with Elam again hostile, and the conflict in Babylonia turning into an outright war, Ashurbanipal's attention was focused elsewhere. Although Egypt's treachery was condemned in the strongest words in Ashurbanipal's royal inscriptions, no military actions followed. By the 650s BCE, the days when Assyria's army was active on all borders of the state were over.

A Shift of Power: Royal Women and Courtiers in Control

In the seventh century BCE, there is a marked concentration of power in the hands of those closest to the king. His female relatives assumed positions of great influence that contrasted sharply with the hitherto largely ceremonial role of the Assyrian royal women. This is especially pronounced in the reign of Esarhaddon when the king's mother, Naqi'a, the queen Ešarra-hammat, and the king's eldest daughter, Šerua-eṭirat, were openly involved in political decision-making, and the trend continued under Ashurbanipal.

Members of Ashurbanipal's personal entourage—his major domo, chief singer, and cook—were also given prominent positions traditionally reserved for the highest officials of the state. The fact that Ashurbanipal no longer led his army in battle distanced the governors and magnates from the king, whom they would, traditionally, have accompanied on campaign, bonding in the confines of the army camp. There were several mass executions among the members of the administrative and military elite of Assyria, fueled by Esarhaddon's and Ashurbanipal's fear of conspiracies. The capture of the city of Assur by enemy troops in 614 BCE was possible only because the ongoing process of internal disintegration had left Assyria unprotected and vulnerable.

After Ashurbanipal

Upon the death of Ashurbanipal *c.* 627 BCE, his son Ashur-et-ililani ascended to the throne after a succession war. The interests of Ashur-et-ililani, still a minor at the time, were protected by the chief eunuch, Sin-šumu-lišir, whom he described as his guardian. Sin-šumu-lišir commanded the troops on behalf of his young charge, and achieved victory, but the young king's reign ended in 624 BCE in unknown circumstances. The army commanders who had fought on his side were rewarded handsomely with land grants and tax exemptions. We don't know who Ashur-et-ililani's opponent was.

The new king, Sin-sarru-ish-kun, claimed to be Ashurbanipal's son, and there is little reason to doubt this. His name means "The moon god has installed the king," and identifies him as a man who was meant to serve the Assyrian king, not be king himself. He must have started his career as a royal official, but in what function we don't know. We can only guess what the role of Sin-šumu-lišir, a devious, gray eminence in the vein of Cardinal Richelieu, was in all this.

Babylonian Independence

Closely connected to these events in Assyria is the emergence of Nabopolassar, who proclaimed himself king of Babylon in 626 BCE, and ended Assyrian supremacy over Babylonia. A decade later his troops would march against Nineveh and Assur. An epic composition of that period celebrates Nabopolassar's rise to the throne, and portrays the Assyrian chief eunuch, Sin-šumu-lišir, clearly as a tyrant brought down by Nabopolassar. Contemporary legal texts prove that Sin-šumu-lišir had indeed assumed kingship in Babylonia in 624 BCE, but whether he had also attempted to take official control of Assyria is unclear. The much later third-century BCE account of the Hellenistic historian, Berossos, describes Nabopolassar as an Assyrian general sent by Sarakos (i.e., Sin-sarru-ish-kun) to Babylonia

BELOW **This wall casing of bronze with a gold veneer** is of King Esarhaddon and his mother, Queen Naqi'a, praying.

ABOVE **The ziggurat at Assur,** the ancient cultic capital of Assyria, where more than 16,000 cuneiform tablets have been found, is now a UN World Heritage site.

to quash a rebellion. If this information can be trusted, we might reconstruct a chain of events that sees Sin-sarru-ish-kun rise to the Assyrian throne after the demise of the boy king Ashur-et-ililani. His mentor, the chief eunuch Sin-šumu-lišir, lost his influence in Assyria, and headed south and proclaimed himself king of Babylon. The new Assyrian king sent Nabopolassar, his general, to dispose of the usurper, but once this mission was successful, Nabopolassar took the Babylonian crown for himself and ruled as king.

The Babylonian and Median Invasion of Assyria

Under Nabopolassar, Babylonia established its independence from Assyria, and Sin-sarru-ish-kun's reign as king of Assyria did not get off to a promising start, but we know little about the 14 years of his reign (623–612 BCE). In 616 BCE Nabopolassar led the Babylonian army up the Euphrates into Assyrian territory. This began the war that directly brought about the end of Assyria.

The next year, the troops of the Median king, Cyaxares, opened another front in the eastern parts of Assyria. Whether his initial involvement was due to a pact with the Babylonians, or constituted an independent opportunistic attack, is not clear, but we know that, after the Median troops had conquered Assur in 614 BCE, Nabopolassar and Cyaxares concluded a treaty there.

With Assur captured and its main temple, the shrine of the god Ashur, violated and sacked, Assyria's end had come. The state organization that it had supported disappeared within a few short years. The Assyrian empire was carved up between the Babylonians, the Medes, and also the Egyptians, who had entered the war in 616 BCE on Assyria's side. By 612 BCE the political capital, Nineveh, was under siege by Babylonian and Median troops. King Sin-sarru-ish-kun died in the battle raging around the city. Excavations of several of the city gates of Nineveh have revealed gruesome heaps of skeletons, the remains of the defenders of Nineveh whose bodies were never cleared away for burial.

The successor of Sin-sarru-ishkun, and the last ruler of Assyria, was Ashuruballit II, who ascended to the throne in 612 BCE in the temple of the moon god, Sin, at Haran. Traditionally, the Assyrian kings were crowned in the temple of Ashur at Assur, but with the city in enemy hands, this was no longer possible. While there may still

RIGHT **The remains of the city wall of Nineveh,** and the Adad Gate, are shown here after the restoration that was attempted in the 1960s.

have been hope that Ashuruballit would eventually be installed as king in the proper way, this hope was extinguished when the Assyrian troops and their Egyptian allies suffered a crushing defeat at Haran in 609 BCE and had to retreat across the Euphrates. Another battle at Haran is documented the following year, but the Assyrian forces were unable to regain control over Haran. This marks the end of Ashuruballit's efforts to keep the Assyrian state alive. His fate is unknown.

Carving up the Assyrian Empire

The Medes, it seems, had no interest in controlling any of the lands west of the Zagros Mountains, and left this to the Babylonians. But there were others who saw themselves as heirs to parts of the Assyrian empire. Egypt categorically claimed all regions west of the Euphrates formerly controlled by Assyria, while Judah's king, Josiah, aimed to incorporate the former Assyrian provinces of Megiddo and Samaria, which had previously constituted the kingdom of Israel. His ambitions were quashed in 609 BCE when the Egyptian army under Nekho II defeated his troops at Megiddo. This fateful battle gives its name to the term "Armageddon." Egypt's attempt to gain control over the regions west of the Euphrates ended when the battles at Carchemish (on the Euphrates) and Hama (on the Orontes River) in 605 BCE were decided in Babylonia's favor. Private legal texts from Dur-Katlimmu in Syria show that, by 602 BCE, Babylonian supremacy was accepted in the former Assyrian lands, and with Egypt's army defeated in 601 BCE in the battle at El 'Arish in the northern Sinai, Babylonia established itself as the unrivalled heir of the Assyrian Empire.

Assyrian Succession Wars

The Assyrian royal family's claim to the throne was uncontested. Succession conflicts arose only between competing factions within this one family, when disappointed hopefuls reacted to the installation of a rival by killing the ruler. The most notorious case is the murder of Sennacherib (reigned 704–681 BCE) who was killed by two of his sons after selecting Esarhaddon to replace the original crown prince, Arda-Mullissi. His chosen heir emerged as king only after a bloody war against his brothers and their supporters. The war between Ashurbanipal and his brother, Šamaš-šumu-ukin, for the control of Babylonia between 652 and 648 BCE was another milestone in the ongoing struggle between different factions of the royal family. The accession of Ashurbanipal's young son, Ashur-et-ililani, to the throne in *c.* 626 BCE was also preceded by a succession war. By the end of the seventh century BCE, the capacities of the state had been weakened by the conflict raging inside its boundaries, fueled by the ambitions of rival court factions.

BELOW **King Ashurbanipal is seen** riding in his chariot in this limestone relief, from the Palace of Ashurbanipal, Nineveh.

The Medes

In 614 BCE, the Median army under Cyaxares conquered the city of Assur. In the following years, the Medes joined forces with Babylonians under Nabopolassar and brought about the end of the Assyrian Empire.

ABOVE **Median dignitaries** are shown in a Persian relief in the Tripylon at Persepolis, c. 500–450 BCE. By this time, the Medes had been absorbed into the vast Persian Empire.

The Medes are well attested in the Assyrian sources from the ninth century BCE onwards, and are resolutely distinguished from the other peoples living in the Zagros mountain range. It is never clear, however, what exactly made a Mede a Mede. Was it language, religion, or something else entirely?

An Assyrian View on the Medes

From an Assyrian perspective, the various peoples of the mountain valleys of the Zagros shared many social, economic, and political characteristics. They all bred cattle and horses, and were ruled by "city lords"—hereditary political leaders of a specific region with a fortified settlement as its center. The city lords were rooted so deeply in society that even when Assyrian provinces were established in the region, they did not disappear. According to the Assyrian view, there was not one Median state, let alone an empire, but instead many small independent states with no discernible sense of solidarity among them. That these Median states all had their own commercial interests may have contributed to this perception. However, the Assyrians perceived them as a unit and distinguished them from other peoples living in the Zagros, such as the Manneans or the Singibuteans. Was language or perhaps religion the constituent element to Median identity? Assyrian sources for the Medes are unfortunately silent on this matter.

The fortresses of the Medes were situated along an overland trade route of prime importance, the later-named Great Khurasan Road, which connected Mesopotamia with central Iran. The Medians offered protection for traders traveling through, and extracted taxes from them for the service. Steady Assyrian involvement in the Zagros Mountains began in the second half of the ninth century BCE, when the formation of the Urartian state in Anatolia cut off the regions that used to supply Assyria with the horses they urgently needed for the army. Western Iran thus became the most important source of horses for the Assyrians. Horses made up most of the tribute raised from the inhabitants of the Zagros Mountains, including those dozens of small Median city-states. The contact intensified when two Assyrian provinces were founded in the region in 744 BCE, followed by another two in 716 BCE. As a consequence, Medes were found among the inhabitants of the city of Assur and also as bodyguards of the Assyrian royal family.

In the course of the seventh century BCE, it appears that Assyrian control over the Zagros provinces slipped. The Medes, as well as other more distant peoples such as the Scythians and the Cimmerians, were seen as dangerously indifferent to the political maneuvers of their Assyrian neighbors. There are no sources for the political situation in the Zagros region in the later part of the seventh century BCE, thus the events that precipitated Cyaxares becoming recognized as the "King of the Medes" by 615 BCE still remain unclear.

Herodotus about the Medes

According to the Greek historian Herodotus, writing around 420 BCE, Cyrus the Great, founder of the Persian Empire in the sixth century BCE, was the grandson of the last king of the Medes, Astyages. His account of Cyrus's birth is a lurid narrative with obvious fairytale elements—Astyages orders Cyrus to be killed, but the child survives and grows up to lead a rebellion against his grandfather. We should therefore accept the story's authenticity with extreme caution. There is no doubt, however, that Cyrus overthrew Median supremacy and gained independence for his Persian kingdom, as this is fully supported by contemporary evidence from Babylonia.

What, then, should we make of Herodotus's account of the early history of Media? He credits one Deioces with uniting the six Median tribes and thereby founding the Median state, with Ecbatana (modern Hamadan) as its capital. The Medes elected him to be their king, and Herodotus then traces Median history during the reigns of Deioces's successors Phraortes, Cyaxares, and finally Astyages. According to Herodotus, the Median state reached as far west as the Halys River (modern Kizil Irmak River), sharing a border with Lydia.

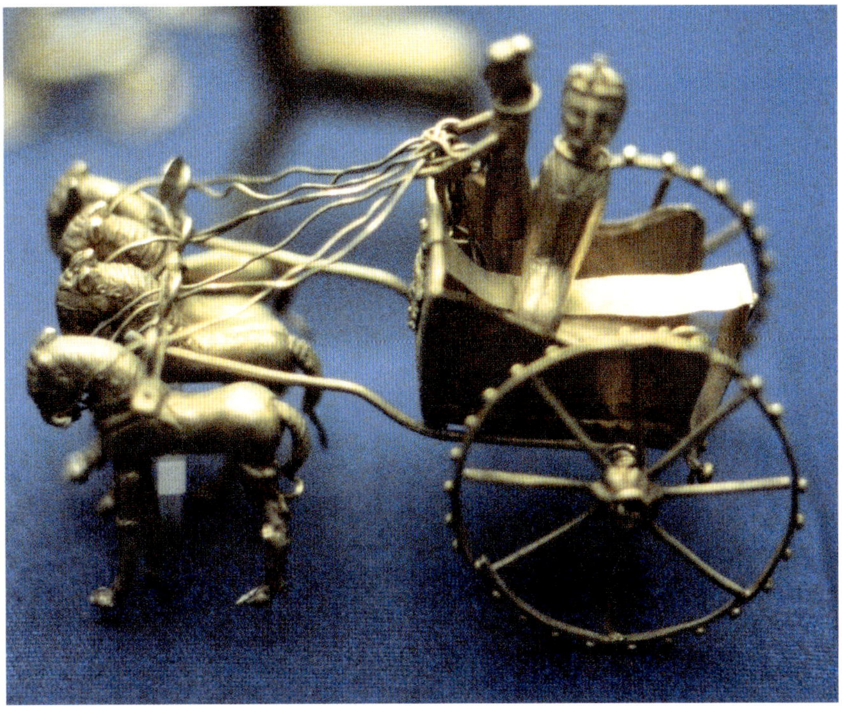

ABOVE **The figures in this chariot** are distinguished as Median by their dress. The chariot is from the Oxus Treasure (*c.* 450–350 BCE), a hoard of objects from the Achaemenid period.

World Power or Historical Phantom?

While the Babylonian sources of the late seventh and sixth centuries BCE offer independent evidence for the activities of the Median kings Cyaxares (reigned *c.* 625–585 BCE) and Astyages (reigned *c.* 585–550 BCE), the information about the Medes in the Assyrian sources of the ninth to mid-seventh centuries BCE cannot be easily reconciled with the testimony of Herodotus. Most scholars today would agree that the Assyrian texts contradict Herodotus's version of early Median history. Rather than illuminating the processes that led to the birth and evolution of the state that would lay the foundations for the Achaemenid Persian Empire, the Assyrian sources show the Medes in a very different light.

Furthermore, excavations at important Iranian sites such as Nush-i Jan and Godin Tepe would seem to support the idea that emerges so clearly from the Assyrian sources: that of small, independent Median states centered around a fortress that controlled the region and passage through it. The archaeological evidence for a vast Median state stretching the great distance from Iran to inner Anatolia, however, is conspicuously lacking in any of the relevant excavations.

Therefore, the question must be asked: is this Median Empire a historical phantom? Whatever the case, it is clear that without Herodotus's report we would not even consider its existence at all.

LEFT **The Medes were expert horse-breeders,** supplying the Assyrian war machine for over 50 years. This later Persian relief comes from Persepolis, from the palace of Darius I, *c.* 500–480 BCE.

The Chaldeans

The Chaldeans were nomadic groups who migrated into lower Mesopotamia from *c.* 1100 BCE. In later biblical and Classical accounts they became indistinguishable from the culture of urban Babylonia, and earned a lasting reputation as astrologers, mathematicians, and kings.

People called "Chaldeans" first appear in Assyrian and Babylonian records in 878 BCE, denoting sedentary tribal groups settled in the south of present-day Iraq. Although speaking a dialect of West Semitic, indicating they had emigrated from the Syrian desert lands to the west, Chaldeans were unlike the Aramean tribes also living in Babylonia, which had troubled ruling states since the eleventh century BCE. Chaldeans settled as farmers, traders, and stock-breeders in extended family units, which took the name of the elder family or house *(bitu x)*.

Chaldeans and Babylonia

Three major groups dominated some of the richest farmlands of Babylonia, arranged in villages (often fortified) along the Lower Euphrates River. From north to south, we know of 16 villages belonging to the Bit-Dakkuri group near Borsippa, 39 of the Bit-Amukani in the Uruk hinterlands, and 11 of Bit-Yakin outside of Ur and in the Gulf marshlands. More than 100 other smaller Chaldean units also used the Bit- name throughout lower Babylonia. In 703 BCE, the Assyrian king Sennacherib would report in the course of his Babylonian campaign Chaldean resistance put up by no fewer than 88 "walled cities" and 850 villages.

Although rural in location and tribal in name, Chaldeans rapidly assimilated into Babylonian culture, adopting local personal names and the pantheon of city gods. By *c.* 700 BCE, they were also living in the Babylonian cities as fully urbanized citizens—as property-owners, businesspeople, and temple elites. With their full integration into urban society, coupled with the long-term effects of Assyrian deportations of foreign peoples into the area, "Chaldeans" soon disappeared as a distinct group. This may explain the later confusion of the terms "Chaldean" and "Babylonian."

BELOW **Chaldean prisoners are led through a palm grove in this relief from the palace walls of Assyrian king Sennacherib, *c.* 700–685 BCE.**

The Political Intersect

Within one generation of their appearance in documents, Chaldeans were engaged in power politics: the Assyrian king Shalmaneser III received tribute from "Abdi-il, the Dakkurean," called "king," as early as 850 BCE. Tribal leaders called themselves only "chieftains" or "sons" of their lands, but built palaces in emulation of urban kings. Gradually they began styling themselves as "governors" and their tribal lands as "provinces."

SCIENCE OR MAGIC?

Graeco-Roman parlance also confused "Chaldeans" with Persian "Magi," reflecting a deep ambivalence as to whether Chaldean "wisdom" was science or *magic*. The term "Chaldean" gradually evoked an exoticized, superstitious Orient. Biblical literatures contributed to this image by stressing Chaldean astrology, idolatry, and divination as ludicrous and empty impieties (e.g., Daniel 2:10, Ezekiel 16:29). The fact that it was Nebuchadnezzar II, the arch-villainous Chaldean king of Babylon, who destroyed Jerusalem in 586 BCE made this layer of tarnish a mere addition to an existing reputation for cruelty (e.g., 2 Chronicles 36:17–20). One might wonder what a genuine Chaldean tribesman would have made of the late Antique notion that he had possessed the magical knowledge necessary to read omens from the stars.

The first Chaldean king of Babylon was a Yakinite chieftain named Eriba-Marduk, who wrested it from Assyrian control in the 760s BCE. His reign of temple-building and land reform was replaced by a Dakkurean one which ushered in anarchy: one governor reported that Chaldeans, Arameans, and city-dwellers "sharpened their weapons for many days...and slew one another." Calm was finally restored by a new ruler, Nabonassar (reigned *c.* 747–734 BCE), identified by the Egyptian astronomer Ptolemy as inaugurating the observation of eclipses. It is not clear if Nabonassar was Chaldean, but the later attachment of the term to Babylonian kings begins with his reign.

The next century saw Chaldean leaders seize Babylonian kingship and lead campaigns against Assyrian field armies dispatched to hunt them down. The most famous of these was the king Marduk-apla-iddina II ("Merodach-Baladan" in the biblical books of 2 Kings and Isaiah). He ruled Babylon twice; outlived four Assyrian kings; gathered military coalitions of Babylonians, Arameans, and Elamites; and reached as far as Judah to open a two-front war against Assyria. After 23 years of struggle, he was defeated by Sennacherib in 700 BCE. Despite this setback, the grit of Marduk-apla-iddina's resistance set the tone for a Chaldean-led war of national liberation that culminated in Nabopolassar's accession (626 BCE).

Chaldean Legacies

The "Neo-Babylonian" dynasty of Nabopolassar (626–539 BCE) was so insistently labeled as "Chaldean" in later ages that it now seems useless to contest the convention. It was the Greeks who chose the term to characterize a Babylonian scholarship they copied and furthered as early as Herodotus (fifth century BCE). It became expected that Greek philosophers and scientists would study "Chaldean" writings, preferably in Babylonia itself. Strabo, Diodorus Siculus, and Hipparchus were among the many who studied works of the Babylonian scholars Berossus and Diogenes the Stoic, and the astronomers Kidenas (Kidinu) and Antipater.

Greek astronomy was built from Babylonian data collections stretching back to the early second millennium BCE. Crediting Chaldean records, Claudius Ptolemy reproduced their system of solar ephemerides, Hipparchus continued work on solar and lunar eclipse prediction, and Classical calendars incorporated the length of the Babylonian solar year and synodic month. Scholars in Egypt, Syria, Athens, and Rome read translations of cuneiform works even as scholars in Uruk and Babylon continued to produce them down to the first century BCE. Yet "Chaldean" also described a hodgepodge of other literatures that fascinated Greek audiences, including romantic tales about the mythical Assyrian queen Semiramis and wisdom stories of Ahiqar.

LEFT **This inscribed brick from Babylon** (*c.* 580 BCE) includes the names of Nabopolassar and his son Nebuchadnezzar II.

BELOW **Greek astronomer Ptolemy** (depicted here in *Portrait of Ptolemy* by Joos van Ghent, *c.* CE 1475) used Chaldean records to make his own astronomical calculations over 500 years later.

The Neo-Babylonian Dynasty

Sixth-century BCE Babylon rose to become the wealthiest and largest city of its day. Under the rule of a few long-lived kings, its name came to be synonymous with opulence, high finance, and scientific knowledge.

ABOVE **A Neo-Babylonian seal** of blue-gray slipped clay shows a priest praying before the symbols of Nabu, the god of wisdom, and Marduk (possibly c. 550 BCE).

The Neo-Babylonian dynasty (flourished 626–539 BCE) held sway over an empire that was relatively peaceful and prosperous, but shorter lived and more geographically compact than the preceding Neo-Assyrian (flourished 934–612 BCE) and later Achaemenid (flourished 550–330 BCE) Empires. The cultural achievements and wealth of the era fired both the imagination and ire of later biblical and Classical writers, who sometimes referred to Babylonians as "Chaldeans," one of the most prominent tribal groups of the region.

Nabopolassar and the Origins of the Dynasty

It is not clear whether the Neo-Babylonian dynasty had tribal origins or not. When Nabopolassar (reigned 626–605 BCE), the first ruler of the dynasty, proclaimed himself king in Babylon, he did so after more than a century of Assyrian occupation. During that time, Babylonian resistance had often been led by Chaldean leaders, but later Greek sources disagree in identifying Nabopolassar either as a "king of the Sealand" (i.e., a Chaldean chieftain) or an Assyrian appointee. What is certain is that after the death of Kandalanu, the Assyrian regent, in 627 BCE, a year of anarchy and warfare followed in Babylonia, after which Nabopolassar emerged as the local victor over the divided Assyrian monarchy.

Nabopolassar next consolidated his political control over other Babylonian cities like Nippur and Uruk. He then methodically reduced the Assyrian empire by taking credit for the Median capture of Assur in 614 BCE, destroying Nineveh in 612 BCE, and crushing the last Assyrian garrison at Harran in 609 BCE. A defining victory over Egyptian forces at Carchemish in 605 BCE confirmed Babylon's hegemony. After 500 years without a stable monarchy, Babylon now controlled many of the lands only recently ruled by Assyria, including Syria, the Levant, and the Phoenician cities.

Government and the Empire at Large

Nabopolassar's crown prince Nebuchadnezzar II (reigned 605–562 BCE) ascended to the throne after despatching the Egyptian army back across the Euphrates (605 BCE).The king ruled the districts of the Babylonian heartland through a network of appointed city governors, tribal chieftains, and temple-estates. This complex arrangement was the product of a varied political landscape, which included old, wealthy temple cities and their supporting farmlands, semi-nomadic Aramean groups, and semi-independent settled villages of Chaldean tribesmen. Few records, however, allude to the structure or day-to-day operations of other parts of the empire.

In principle, Babylonians were content to continue many Assyrian policies, including rule through local power structures, mass deportations, and the installation of puppet kings and governors in key cities. Babylon, however, ruled over a very

RIGHT **This relief depicting the sun god on his throne** (ninth century BCE) was discovered by Nabopolassar in the temple of Shamash at Sippar, during his restoration of the temple.

different world. The annual warfare that Assyria had used to buttress its rule was sharply curtailed, and Babylonian royal inscriptions now focused almost exclusively on temple building. Moreover, Assyria's earlier despoiling of Elam and Urartu had opened up power vacuums that were filled by neighboring Media, Persia, and Lydia. The available sources indicate that only minor external powers, such as Cilicia, and a handful of Arabian oasis towns were ever subject to Babylonian military occupation—other than Babylon itself, which rebelled in 595 BCE.

A few examples, however, show that warfare remained an instrument of imperial rule. Judah, like many Levantine states near the Egyptian sphere of influence, rebelled repeatedly, and was subjected to military assault, mass deportations (in 597, 587, and 582 BCE), and the imposition of puppet kings, for which several books of the Old Testament remain important sources. An epic 13-year siege of Tyre which was ultimately successful—also illustrates Nebuchadnezzar's ongoing struggle to hold Syria.

The City of Babylon

The relatively few wars of aggression, however, should not distract our attention from Babylon's prominence in long-distance trade. The city directly controlled caravanserais (inns along main travel routes where merchants could rest) and ports as far-flung as present-day Medina, the Persian Gulf, and the border of Egypt. Exotic goods arrived on a regular basis from as far away as Africa, south Asia, Greece, and even the Baltic Sea. Babylon played host to merchants, mercenaries, and deportees hailing from Egypt, Caria, Judah, and Arabia. Its preeminence as a center for world trade and high finance were then reflected in Nebuchadnezzar's building initiatives, which raised Babylon to new heights of opulence.

The city occupied a staggering 3 square miles (7.7 square km), with the Euphrates running through the center of the inner fortress. In this central district were fortifications, numerous temples, one of the three royal palaces, and the Esagila temple complex of Babylon's chief deity Marduk, which included the temple-tower that was likely the model for later accounts of the "Tower of Babel." The principal approach to these magnificent structures was through the Ishtar Gate, and along the Processional Way, whose walls were lined with exquisitely glazed baked bricks representing lions, the emblems of Ishtar, and dragons, the emblems of Marduk.

The kings of the dynasty similarly renovated the temples of all the major Babylonian cities. The gods of these temples would annually "travel" to Babylon at the time of the New Year's

ABOVE **The Tower of Babel,** depicted here in an artistic imagining (*c.* sixteenth century CE), may have been based on the Esagila temple complex in Babylon, or the nearby Etemenanki ziggurat.

Festival in public ceremonial homage to Marduk. During the festival, the king would confirm his role as the appointee of Marduk by taking part in rituals emphasizing his obedience to the god.

Society and Economy

The life of the "average" Babylonian is difficult for scholars to assess. Babylon's citizens were the beneficiaries of empire, yet only urban elites were typically documented in texts. Still, indirect evidence supports the idea that a sizable class of independent rural producers persisted under the empire, and that Babylon boasted a large proletariat class of free wage-earners. Other urbanites were affiliated with institutions (temples or palaces), holding productive land or incomes in exchange for obligatory service.

Some of the more prestigious of these arrangements were permanent offices similar to modern "prebends," held by Babylonia's upper-class families who remained tightly knit by bonds of intermarriage and business. Such business ranged from the management of institutional resources such as wool and grain up to quite complex partnerships and corporations investing in land, extending credit, bankrolling import and export schemes, and buying up estates in default. The economy during this time moved away from in-kind obligations rooted in land tenure and toward payment in precious metal equivalents and commodity trading markets.

This atmosphere of privatization may have been associated with a trend toward the assertion of city-charter rights *(kidinnutu)*. Residents of Babylonian cities gained certain exemptions and privileges excusing them from royal tax payments and labor service. The source documents for this period suggest that rights of the individual generally improved, but they were primarily geared to protect business interests. For instance, the rights held by women under law were mostly restricted to protecting their dowries, which were often important aspects of business deals between families. Babylonian law also upheld the position of slaves and their children as the chattel property of slave owners.

A Center of Knowledge

The private and temple libraries of Babylonia were already famous for the literary and scientific texts they had produced and preserved. By the reign of Nebuchadnezzar, the city of Babylon was 1,500 years old; Uruk was 1,200 years older still. Over these millennia, the copying of texts as part of the training of scribes had resulted in collections of scholarship in every Babylonian city. The scribes who owned literary master works like *Gilgamesh* and *The Epic of Creation* also kept on hand manuals for archaic Sumerian spelling and translating the Code of Hammurabi. Ritual and theological tablets were shelved next to medical, mathematical, and magic or religious texts. Even the most archaic writings—sometimes more than 2,000 years old—were kept and copied even when they were poorly understood.

But Babylonian scholarship had become famous for one art above all: the astronomical sciences. This preeminence arose from a long

NABONIDUS AND ROYAL THEOLOGY

Nabonidus (and, in some garbled accounts, Nebuchadnezzar) remained famous long after his death in several legendary Greek, Persian, Hebrew, and Aramaic stories as having lapsed into madness and disease. Undoubtedly these negative traditions all stem from his attempt to impose the moon god Sin—whom his Syrian mother had worshipped—as universal and preeminent over other gods throughout the empire. The most provocative aspect of this ultimately unsuccessful program certainly would have been the challenge it presented to Marduk as the chief deity—and Babylon as the center of the empire. Yet it is difficult to determine just how divisive this experiment in royal theology truly was: the later accounts are largely politically self-interested, and both Assyrian and Babylonian kings had in fact been tinkering with various theological reformations for centuries by Nabonidus's time.

ABOVE **A tower and arch** remain at the temple of Sin in Haran, Turkey. Inscriptions at the site explain Nabonidus's divine justification for assuming the Babylonian kingship.

history of night-sky observations, and of reading omens in the movements of planets and stars. Babylonians never abandoned this intellectual connection between divination and astronomy, but there is no doubt about their accuracy or technical sophistication. Ongoing refinements by now permitted the prediction of lunar eclipses—later used by Greek astronomers—and a highly accurate calendar. Astronomical diaries routinely noted local events as well as heavenly ones, producing chronicles filled with historical events, market prices, and the level of the Euphrates.

LEFT **This cuneiform tablet from Babylon,** *c.* 500 BCE, is an astronomy text that records the ephemeris of Saturn.

This interest in time and events also extended to the Babylonian past. Aware of the depth of tradition and history beneath their feet, Nebuchadnezzar and other kings excavated the temple quarters of several cities for historical information. Their interest largely lay in reestablishing renovated temples on ancient foundations and connecting their own names with those of legendary kings. In this they succeeded, unearthing inscriptions and statues of Naram-Sin, Ur-Nammu, and Burnaburiash II (dated *c.* 2250, 2100, and 1350 BCE respectively), which they housed in a palace museum.

Turmoil at Court

After 75 years of this "Babylonian renaissance," the dynasty stumbled through six years of strife, followed by the troubled 17-year rule of its final king. Amel-Marduk (reigned 561–560 BCE, biblical "Evil-Merodach") followed his father onto the throne, but was soon assassinated by Neriglissar (reigned 559–556 BCE), a wealthy businessman who had married into the family. Neriglissar's (natural) death briefly brought his young son Labashi-Marduk to the throne in 556 BCE, but the boy was quickly murdered. Nabonidus (reigned 556–539 BCE), a court officer and co-conspirator, became king even though he was not even Babylonian; his father was an Aramean chieftain and his mother was a Syrian.

Nabonidus's coronation may have been a pretext for the enrichment and eventual succession of his son, Belshazzar. The king's military campaigns and his as-yet-unexplained nine-year stay (*c.* 553–544 BCE) in the Arabian caravan town of Tayma (Tema) left his son the undisputed regent at Babylon, although his father's theological posturings (see feature box, opposite) may have caused friction with the traditional elites of the city.

The abrupt fall of Babylon to the Persian forces of Cyrus the Great in 539 BCE thus took place within an atmosphere of court intrigues and priestly resentment, yet the collapse of the dynasty had little lasting effect on Babylonian society. The city would remain a dynamic center of high culture for several centuries to come.

BELOW **Scholars suggest this basalt stele,** *c.* 556–539 BCE, possibly from Babylon, may represent King Nabonidus himself. The figure wears the traditional dress of a Babylonian king.

Nebuchadnezzar II

Nebuchadnezzar II (reigned 605–562 BCE) transformed Babylonia from a local power into a world empire. Writers of later ages vilified him for his destruction of holy Jerusalem, and marveled at his rebuilding of a glittering new Babylon.

BELOW **Nebuchadnezzar II is a much-maligned figure** in biblical sources. This Christian depiction from the twelfth century CE shows him ordering the deaths of three Hebrew wise men.

Much of Nebuchadnezzar's kingship is celebrated (though often inaccurately) in non-Mesopotamian sources composed after his reign, and we know little of his early years. He came of age during the "nationalist" reign of his father, Nabopolassar, who had been crowned king of Babylon in 626 BCE after the death of the last great Assyrian monarch, Ashurbanipal (reigned 668–627 BCE). For ten years, Nabopolassar struggled to expel Assyrian armies from Babylonia, and what began as a local war of national liberation gradually widened into an all-out regional war with the goal of destroying Assyria entirely. Nebuchadnezzar's name ("The god Nabu-guards-the-heir") emulated a by-then ancient king, Nebuchadnezzar I. This king of Babylon reigned *c.* 1124–1103 BCE, and was famed for liberating Babylonia from a foreign Elamite threat and returning the kidnapped statue of the god Marduk to Babylon.

From Battlefield to Throne Room

Although his date of birth is not known for certain, Nebuchadnezzar II must at least have been an adult by 607 BCE, when he is known to have commanded field armies in his father's stead. (The Babylonian scholar Berossus, writing in *c.* 278 BCE, dated Nebuchadnezzar's marriage to the Median princess Amytis to 614 BCE.) In 605 BCE, still the crown prince, Nebuchadnezzar met an advancing Egyptian army which had been dispatched to support the last ragtag Assyrian garrison at Carchemish. The crown prince polished off the Assyrians and delivered a crushing blow to the Egyptians, then pursued them over 124 miles (200 km) to Hamath where, according to one of the Babylonian Chronicles, he "inflicted a defeat upon them so that not a single man returned home." The historic victory was bittersweet, however: Nabopolassar died in Babylon while his son was pacifying Syria. Nebuchadnezzar can have wasted little time reacting, since the same chronicle reports that he was crowned in Babylon 22 days later, having traveled almost 620 miles (1,000 km).

Ruling the Four Quarters

The years of Nebuchadnezzar's rule were heady ones for Babylon. Only a decade before, Assyria sat astride an empire stretching from southern Egypt to southwest Iran, while Babylon was enmeshed in a populist, regional insurgency. Suddenly, Assyria was gone, Egypt beaten back, and the young Nebuchadnezzar found himself the inheritor of much of this massive imperial realm. To keep it from falling apart into its previous constituent states, he had to act quickly to assert his power in the region.

LEFT **Little was left of Nebuchadnezzar's palace** in Babylon before the 1980s, when former Iraqi president Saddam Hussein built a new palace on its foundations.

Babylon's sphere of influence extended over Syria, Assyria, and Levantine states such as Judah, Tyre, and Sidon—but control had to be cemented with force. Unlike Assyrian royal inscriptions, Neo-Babylonian kings wrote almost exclusively about building work, so knowledge of their military campaigns is scant. Fortunately, the later Babylonian Chronicles describe the first decade of Nebuchadnezzar's rule, which appears to have been spent marching through the west to show his strength. In 604 BCE, he conquered the last independent Philistine city, Ashkelon, reducing the city "into a mound and heaps of ruins;" in 599 BCE he plundered Arab territory; the following year, he besieged Jerusalem and took it after a lengthy siege, then installed the puppet king Zedekiah (as described in 2 Kings 24:8–20 and Jeremiah 52:28–30).

Egypt, Anatolia, the Iranian plateau, and the elusive Median tribal confederacy, however, would remain beyond Nebuchadnezzar's reach. A 601 BCE invasion of Egypt ended in disaster for the Babylonians, and in 596 BCE an Elamite army was defeated only as it neared the banks of the Tigris. The next year brought danger even closer to home in the form of an attempted coup, which Nebuchadnezzar suppressed ruthlessly, according to the Chronicles: "With arms he slew many of his own army." Empire, he was learning, came at a significant price.

A City Fit for Empire

For 1,000 years, Babylon had been the royal city of Babylonia, and its chief deity Marduk celebrated through an elaborate political theology as "king of the gods." For most of the 500 years separating the two Nebuchadnezzars, however, this notion of Babylon as a seat of cosmological power was undercut by its dynastic instability and weak kings. Moreover, Assyrian sieges in 689 and 648 BCE resulted in widespread urban destruction, with only limited rebuilding afterwards.

With Nebuchadnezzar's rise to power, however, the wealth of an entire empire was suddenly channeled towards this ancient capital, and a massive building program was begun. The city of Babylon sprawled over 3 sq miles (8 sq km), which Nebuchadnezzar now enclosed within 11 miles (18 km) of newly fortified walls. At its heart lay the palace and temple district, protected by another triple-layered wall. A channel was dug out around this area so that the Euphrates flowed in to protect it as a moat. No traces of the fabled "Hanging Gardens" as mentioned by Berossus, however, can be found; some scholars suggest

BELOW **The reconstruction of the imposing Ishtar Gate** shows clearly the bull and dragon motifs—symbols of the goddess Ishtar and other deities—alternating across its surface.

RIGHT **The sacred bull,** as depicted on the Ishtar Gate, was one of the symbols of the goddess Ishtar.

this was a Greek confusion for the gardens at Nineveh built by Sennacherib, the Neo-Assyrian king (reigned 704–681 BCE).

The north entrance to this dazzling official quarter was the Ishtar Gate, a towering, regal confection of blue-glazed brick emblazoned with white dragons and lions, symbols of Marduk and Ishtar. Past the gate and two flanking palaces lay the Processional Way, which was 3,280 ft (1 km) long and led to the massive ziggurat and Esagila temple complex. Eighteen other temples and gates lay within this and the adjacent precinct, adorned with precious gemstones, gold, and exotic woods. These broad avenues were the setting for elaborate public spectacles such as the New Year's Festival (see feature box).

The End of a Dynasty

Unfortunately, our specific information becomes intermittent where the Chronicle texts break off after 594 BCE. A few obscure campaigns were documented: a partial cuneiform text describes another Egyptian campaign around 568 BCE; others suggest Nebuchadnezzar annexed Edom and Moab. An Arabic manuscript from the tenth century CE indicates a strike against Arabian tribes. Two campaigns, however, gained lasting fame. One was a 13-year siege of Tyre, the island-fortress city, finally concluded by a settlement; the feat was only ever repeated by Alexander the Great. It was the second Jerusalem campaign, however, that gained Nebuchadnezzar his lasting infamy in Western history.

Nebuchadnezzar's dynastic line after his death in 562 BCE was short-lived, although six sons and one daughter are known by name. The crown prince Amel-Marduk (biblical "Evil-Merodach") succeeded him in 561 BCE, but was assassinated by his brother-in-law Neriglissar after only two years. Neriglissar then ruled only three more years before a series of coups brought Nabonidus, an unrelated contender, to the throne as the last independent king of Babylon (reigned 555–539 BCE).

NEW YEAR'S RITES AND RITUALS

The Babylonian New Year's Festival of Nebuchadnezzar's time was when the gods of other Babylonian cities were said to journey out of their temples to visit Marduk in Babylon. It was an enactment of cosmological renewal for the land and its king, and Nebuchadnezzar would have played an important role. Preparing to meet Marduk in the Esagila temple, the king laid aside all royal regalia and recited a "negative confession" that he had not sinned or broken taboos during the year. Marduk's high priest would then administer a ringing slap across the king's face, presumably to nullify any remaining sins. Thus refreshed, the king led the remaining days of ritual and sacrifice, escorting Marduk in a grand procession through Babylon, watched by his subjects. Nebuchadnezzar's long reign would have seemed proof to the Babylonians of the festival's potency.

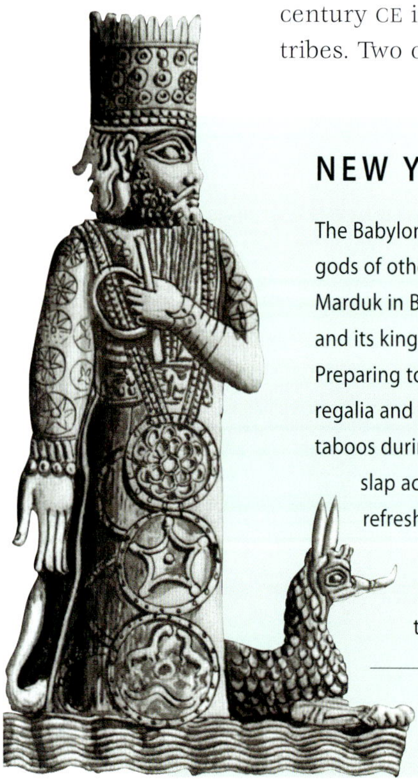

LEFT **Marduk, the chief god of the Babylonians,** is shown here with his symbol, the dragon, in a drawing made from a Kassite Babylonian relief.

Nebuchadnezzar in Near Eastern Memory

The legacy of Nebuchadnezzar was shaped by two traditions. A negative tradition formed following his second siege of Jerusalem in 587–586 BCE, when Zedekiah attempted to defect and form an allegiance with Egypt. The siege was described centuries after the fact in Josephus's *Jewish Antiquities* (written in CE 94): 18 months of privation and disease resulted in the capitulation of Jerusalem due to famine. The biblical accounts describe the flight of Zedekiah and his army, his capture and torture, and the burning of the houses of the "great men." The walls of Jerusalem were demolished, the Temple pillaged and destroyed, and the monarchy of the Israelites ended.

Though the "poor of the land" were left behind, so many were deported to Babylon that 2 Kings 25:21 concludes somberly: "So Judah was carried away out of their land." Remarkably, cuneiform texts excavated from Babylon support the authenticity of the deportation—the texts document the rations drawn and business conducted by Israelites living in exile. When the Persians permitted the exiles to return to Judah from 539 BCE, some chose to remain in Babylon where they held property and social standing, while those who returned came into conflict with those who had never left.

The divisive influence of Nebuchadnezzar's deportations was written into later Near Eastern literary traditions in different ways. The Old Testament and apocryphal writings depict Nebuchadnezzar as both rapacious conqueror and as instrument of God's judgment on a wicked, backsliding Judah. Aramaic folktales, meantime, gradually mixed in negative themes from stories about Nabonidus, confusing the two kings. Nebuchadnezzar was thus said to have been struck by madness and lived among the beasts of the wild for seven years, a story that then found its way back into the biblical book of Daniel. A wholly different line of tradition was maintained by Arab chroniclers, who struggled to reconstruct the honorable lineages of Iraq's ancient kings.

Nebuchadnezzar in European Memory

Simultaneously, a wide-eyed Orientalist fantasy grew up in Classical literature about Nebuchadnezzar as the builder of an impossibly ornate Babylon. Greek authors—Herodotus, Diodorus Siculus, and Strabo in particular—recounted in breathless terms a Babylon of gargantuan size, adorned with wonders like the Hanging Gardens (ostensibly built by Nebuchadnezzar to satisfy his Median queen Amytis, who pined for her mountainous homeland), a statue of Marduk weighing over 10 tons (9 metric tons) in solid gold, and walls encircling an area so large it took a full three days to traverse the city. Such authors often misattributed the building work to mythical figures such as "Semiramis," a figure who appeared in old Babylonian romance tales, or to anonymous "Syrian" kings.

In the centuries that followed, historians did a much better job of attributing the work to Nebuchadnezzar by name, although they repeated many of the same fables. Berossus, the famed Babylonian scholar, suggested that Nebuchadnezzar had built Babylon's walls in a mere 15 days, and in the fourth century BCE Megasthenes suggested that the king's conquests had even stretched as far as Spain. In many respects the name of Nebuchadnezzar merged with a Greek fantasy about Babylon itself. Both entered legend as archetypes of oriental despotism, seductive masks for rule by naked force, and an amoral indulgence of sensual pleasures. Both the negative tradition of the Old Testament and the half-admiring, half-horrified Classical tradition were transmitted to medieval and early modern Europe, where the memory of Nebuchadnezzar was enshrined in conflicting and often overlapping ways.

BELOW **In this illustration from the *Breviary of Isabella of Castile* (unknown Flemish artist, *c.* CE 1497), Nebuchadnezzar burns Jerusalem's books, destroying the city's sacred texts in his pillage.**

Babylon's Hanging Gardens

A Terraced Garden
While the Hanging Gardens probably did not "hang," they were possibly terraced up a hillside, as suggested in this illustration (Ferdinand Knab, *The Hanging Gardens of Babylon*, 1886).

The Hanging Gardens of Babylon are usually depicted in a highly romantic light, featuring skyscraper-high terracing, balconies spilling over with flowering plants, and a series of flowing waterfalls. These are not, however, the features that made them one of the most remarkable edifices of the ancient world. Rather, it was their extraordinary construction and planting techniques, and their sophisticated water-carrying machinery, that made them legendary to writers of the Classical era.

The Hanging Gardens are listed as one of the Seven Wonders of the Ancient World, but what—and where—was this amazing spectacle? No archaeological evidence of the gardens' existence has been found at Babylon in modern Iraq, nor is there any mention of them in the contemporary descriptions of the city. There are, however, a number of detailed descriptions of them from ancient sources of later periods, written by Diodorus Siculus (first century BCE), Strabo (first century CE), Josephus (first century CE) and others.

These various descriptions of the gardens have a number of features in common. They depict the gardens as built on a series of stepped terraces supported by stone vaults or thick walls that in turn supported a frame of beams, perhaps of palm trunks. A number of the descriptions comment on the use of stone arches supporting the beams. Overlaying these beams was reed matting that formed the base of the garden beds. Diodorus Siculus describes stone beams above which formed a series of layers, including reeds thickly impregnated with bitumen and a layer of lead to stop

Babylon or Nineveh?

An eloquent argument has been presented by Dr Stephanie Dalley of the Oriental Institute, Oxford, in favor of the gardens belonging to Sennacherib at Nineveh. This city was the site of a number of gardens during the first millennium BCE, and its gardens were depicted, in fine detail, in the wall reliefs that decorated the palaces of Nineveh. There is one wall panel, now in the British Museum (pictured), depicting a terraced garden that matches almost exactly the descriptions of the Hanging Gardens given by the ancient authors. This is the panel from the North Palace of Ashurbanipal at Nineveh depicting the garden of Ashurbanipal's grandfather, Sennacherib. It has been suggested that a water-carrying machine described by Sennacherib, which was not unlike the Archimedes screw, was used to supply water to the gardens.

moisture seepage. Above this was the soil of the garden beds. Below were cool caverns in which a person could walk.

Water flowed through the garden in a series of water channels, irrigating the beds as it flowed. The supply of water to the garden's upper terraces was critical to the survival of the plantings, and was achieved by advanced mechanical means. Strabo describes water screws alongside the stairs to the upper levels of the garden which carried the water up from the river to the gardens.

Josephus describes the gardens as an attempt to reproduce tree-covered mountains. Traditionally, gardens in Mesopotamia in the first millennium BCE would have been planted mainly with trees, and we know of a number of plants that would have been available for the gardens at that time. These trees include willows, date palms, pomegranates, olives, figs, grape vines, a variety of junipers, and various other fruit trees.

Within the various ancient sources there is confusion as to who built the garden, though tradition gives Nebuchadnezzar II (reigned 605–562 BCE) the title. This is disputed by a number of experts; some feel that the gardens described were those of Sennacherib, the Neo-Assyrian king (reigned 704–681 BCE), at Nineveh (see feature box).

Irrigating the Gardens

The Archimedes screw works by channeling water from the screw's base to its top, via turning or winding. The mechanism can be seen in this modern artwork by an unknown artist.

However, whether these gardens belonged to Nebuchadnezzar at Babylon or Sennacherib at Nineveh, they were an amazing feat of engineering and irrigation technology. Their design of elevated stone terraces went on to become a feature in the great villa gardens of the Roman Empire and thence into the Islamic and European garden tradition.

The Sack of Jerusalem

Nebuchadnezzar II's destruction of Jerusalem, its temple, and the deportation of its people to Babylon brought Judah's independent monarchy to an end. Over time, however, the exile would become a symbol of the perseverance of Jewish religion and culture.

ABOVE **This illustration, *The Siege of Jerusalem by Nebuchadnezzar*,** is from a 1470s translation of Josephus's *Jewish Antiquities* originally written in *c.* CE 94.

By the time Nebuchadnezzar II laid siege to Jerusalem in 587 BCE, the city had already endured centuries within the Egyptian and Mesopotamian spheres of influence. Only a decade before, Nebuchadnezzar had deported an Israelite royal family and thousands of prominent citizens and soldiers, but no lasting damage to the city was done. There was little to suggest that this time, in 587 BCE, A siege of the city would result in anything more than the replacement of the rebellious puppet king, Zedekiah, with a new one.

The Siege (587–586 BCE)

Israelite resistance proved uncharacteristically fierce. In the Old Testament, Jeremiah 39 and 2 Kings 25 put the length of the siege at 18 months. Zedekiah was captured with his sons, who were executed before his eyes—which were then gouged out. Although much of the population survived the ensuing destruction of the city walls and villas, one key Babylonian action elevated the event to the status of a full national calamity: Solomon's temple (the "First Temple") was stripped of its treasures and burned to the ground. For the Israelites, ritual sacrifice at the temple guaranteed their connection to Yahweh (God), and the rupture of this connection suspended the national covenant, the monarchy, and the social unity of the people.

The sack of Jerusalem became a symbol of foreign persecution, but was just as much the culmination of long-simmering internal tensions. The monarchy had been blighted by centuries of bitter partisanship and bloody coups; the practice of temple sacrifice had long been argued by the prophets as secondary to Yahweh's law; and the Babylonians cunningly exploited a long-standing gap between rich and poor classes.

The Exile (586–539 BCE)

In the aftermath of the siege, wealthy Israelites were deported to Babylon, and a governor was installed to rule over the remaining lower-caste Israelites, who were given the orchards and flocks of the deportees. It is not certain how many were taken to Babylon; Jeremiah and 2 Kings suggest that around 35,000 deportees in total were taken in 597, 586, and 582 BCE (after another uprising), which was perhaps one-sixth of the total population of Judah.

With the exiles now composing texts in foreign captivity, the Babylonian Exile entered Jewish folk mythos. "By the rivers of Babylon, there we sat down, yea, we wept, when we remembered Zion," relates the singer of Psalm 137. Yet the hardships of this "bondage" were mostly rhetorical, since the exiles were permitted to hold property, practice their religion, and engage in commerce in Babylon. Israelite genealogical, personal, and place names appear in Babylonian

cuneiform marriage documents land deeds, and banking notes around this time. This assimilation into Babylonian life was epitomized in *c*. 561 BCE by the release of King Jehoiachin, who had been originally captured in the siege of Jerusalem in 598 BCE, some 37 years earlier.

The challenges of exile were religious rather than economic or political. Idolatry, the long-detested heresy of the prophets, was the local norm of Babylonian worship. The lack of a temple forced the exiled community to turn to fasting, penitential observance, and study of the Law. This reflective mode encouraged the scribes to revisit and revise the existing Pentateuchal, historical, and prophetic writings of what would become the Hebrew Bible (Old Testament), in an effort to harmonize the literature and give the community a new focus: instead of a temple, the people would now turn to a book.

The Return (539 BCE and Beyond)

The fall of Babylon to Cyrus II (the Great) of Persia in 539 BCE ushered in a second life for Temple Judaism: the Cyrus Cylinder specified that images of captive gods could return to their temples, along with "their inhabitants." The language is vague, but is commonly taken to mean that a right-of-return was guaranteed to the exiles and other captive peoples in Babylonia. The books of Ezra and Nehemiah give substantially different estimates for the number of Jewish returnees to the former Kingdom of Judah: 2,058 and 42,360 respectively. Some propertied Jewish families remained in Babylon for centuries to come.

The first priority of the returnees was to rebuild the temple. Work proceeded haltingly, as division grew up between those who had remained in Judea and those who had been exiled in Babylon. Ezra 4 says that the Samaritan "people of the land" attempted to halt the work by writing to the Persian king, accusing the returnees of "rebuilding that rebellious and wicked city." The Persians felt secure in Judean loyalty, however, and full permission to rebuild the temple was finally given by Darius I (the Great) around 521 BCE.

This Second Temple stood as one center of the Judean community throughout its ensuing periods of foreign (Persian, Ptolemaic, Seleucid, and Roman) and native (Hasmonean) rulers. Rebuilt in 20 BCE, it was again destroyed in an uprising against Rome in CE 70. Jerusalem later suffered destruction at the hands of the Romans (CE 135), the Sasanian Persians (CE 614), and the European Crusaders (CE 1099), and enjoyed restoration under Abbasid, Mamluk, and Ottoman rulers. But these were Jerusalems no longer centered on a Jewish temple; Rabbinic and Talmudic learning exemplified the continuity of Jewish culture.

LEFT ***Joachin Taken Out of Prison*****, an engraving by F. H. van Hove** (undated), depicts the release of King Jehoiachin from captivity in Babylon, *c*. 561 BCE.

BELOW **This model of the Second Temple**, as built in 520 BCE, was based on the description of its structure by the historian Josephus in the first century CE.

The Achaemenid Empire

The Achaemenid Persian Empire, at its maximum territorial extent under Darius the Great, held sway over territory stretching from the Indus River valley to southeastern Europe, and from the Aral Sea region to northeast Africa.

RIGHT **A servant in the Achaemenid court** is depicted on a relief in the Hall of a Hundred Columns (*c.* 486–424 BCE) at Persepolis, one of the Achaemenids' capital cities.

Standing at the end of a long historical continuum in the ancient Middle East and South Central Asia, the Achaemenid Empire owed much to its forebears, but at the same time presented something new in its scope and durative power. On a modern map, the Persian Empire at its height covered territory stretching from Pakistan to Greece and from Kazakhstan to Libya and the Sudan, and it was ruled by one central authority for over 200 years—from its founding by Cyrus the Great in *c.* 550 BCE to Alexander the Great's overthrow of Darius III in 330 BCE. It was by far the largest empire in antiquity that archaeologists and historians have so far uncovered.

Sources for the Empire

The empire takes its name from Achaemenes, who, thanks to the propaganda of Darius the Great (Darius I), became the eponymous founder of the dynasty. There is no independent evidence of Achaemenes's existence beyond Darius's testimony, and Darius's rhetorical claims are to be evaluated with a large dose of skepticism. Cyrus the Great (Cyrus II) does not mention the name of Achaemenes in his genealogy, and for that main reason most modern scholars have rejected Darius's implication of a shared descent with Cyrus from Achaemenes. Thus, the term "Achaemenid Empire" may be a misnomer—especially for the early period of the Persian Empire before Darius the Great—but its use persists as it is convenient and entrenched in the literature.

BELOW **Persian royal inscriptions** were often trilingual. This plaque, in Old Persian, Babylonian, and Elamite, defines the limits of the empire of Darius I (522–486 BCE).

Until the late nineteenth century CE, knowledge of the empire's history was based almost entirely on Greek and biblical accounts, and we still rely on the Greek tradition for much of our information. The Persian Empire left an indelible impression on the early Greek historians and, through them, their successors in the Roman period and even beyond. Scholarly developments in the last century have added exponentially to that Classical base. The empire's sheer scope left records in several languages, and much more material has been lost or awaits discovery. The Achaemenids left behind royal inscriptions, which were often trilingual and inscribed in cuneiform script: Old Persian (an Indo-Iranian language), Elamite (linguistic affiliation uncertain), and Babylonian Akkadian (an Eastern Semitic language).

Many States, One King

According to ancient traditions, within roughly 50 years of the fall of Nineveh (612 BCE) and the collapse of the Assyrian Empire, three major powers dominated the ancient Middle East: the Babylonians (heirs to much of the Assyrian realm), the Lydians in western Anatolia, and the Medes in northern Iran. By the end of Cyrus the Great's reign in 530 BCE, the Persians had arisen from obscure origins to conquer each of the three great powers and additional lands besides, and during the reigns of Cambyses II and Darius the Great, the empire extended even further.

From the Assyrians and Babylonians, the Persians inherited almost 3,000 years of Mesopotamian tradition, stretching back to the earliest Sumerian and Akkadian city-states. These, in turn, fused aspects of the old Elamite civilization in Iran and their own heritage. The Persians, like their cousins the Medes, appear to have once been pastoralists, although their ultimate origins, their progression into Iran, and their settlement in the Marv Dasht plain (modern Fars province) where they founded their greatest cities are matters of ongoing debate. Since Persian is an Indo-Iranian language, many scholars track their ultimate origins in the second millennium BCE deep into Central Asia.

In addition to the new cities of Pasargadae and Persepolis, the Persians designated Babylon in Mesopotamia, Ecbatana in Media, and Susa in Elam as additional capitals. The kings made a practice of itinerant, annual alternation between the capitals. The spectacle of "the King"—the word is often capitalized in English translations

REIGNS OF THE ACHAEMENID PERSIAN KINGS

Cyrus (II) the Great, 558–530 BCE
Cambyses II, 530–522 BCE
Darius (I) the Great, 522–486 BCE
Xerxes I, 486–465 BCE
Artaxerxes I, 465–424 BCE
Xerxes II, 424–423 BCE
Darius II, 423–404 BCE
Artaxerxes II, 404–359 BCE
Artaxerxes III, 359–338 BCE
Artaxerxes IV (Arses), 338–336 BCE
Darius III, 336–330 BCE

BELOW **Tributaries from all over the empire** bring gifts for the Achaemenid king. This relief is part of a much larger series on the staircase of Darius I's palace at Persepolis (*c.* 480 BCE).

RIGHT **In this relief from the Hall of a Hundred Columns** at Persepolis (*c.* 486–424 BCE), the king is incorporated in the winged disk of the god Ahura-Mazda, indicating his divine status.

of Greek sources—in his palaces or with his retinue was unmatched. For the Greek writers who chronicled the Persian Empire, this was a foreign and awe-inspiring world, hence many Greek authors simply referred to the Persian king as "the King," with no name required—there was simply no comparable monarch.

At the same time, however, from the Greeks' frequently scornful perspective stems the persistent stereotype of the oriental despot, who maintained a tyrannical hold over his subjects (or even "slaves," as is often erroneously translated). The picture gleaned from the Persian kings' own propaganda, not surprisingly, is quite different. Carvings on the Apadana (the audience hall) of Persepolis show carefully differentiated rows of all the peoples of the empire, each portrayed in native garb and bearing gifts to the king. These are not portrayals of subjugation but of cooperation. Representations of the king upon a throne or dais, borne upward by similarly carved figures, occur at Persepolis, upon royal tombs at Naqsh-i Rustam (near Persepolis), and a statue-in-the-round of Darius the Great from Egypt.

Beliefs and Way of Life

The religious belief system (termed in modern scholarship "Mazdaism") promoted by Darius the Great evolved into the mature Zoroastrianism of the Sasanian dynasty several centuries later. Many elements of the sacred Zoroastrian books of the Avesta share a strong affinity with Indian (Hindu) traditions—a function of their shared Indo-Iranian heritage. Only the creator god, Ahura-Mazda, is consistently alluded to in Persian royal inscriptions (and portrayed, as a winged disk, on reliefs), until the reign of Artaxerxes II, when the gods Anahita and Mithra also find reference. Despite the references to Ahura-Mazda in royal inscriptions, it is difficult to discern the Achaemenid belief system, as much of what we know of it is hopelessly conflated by Greek sources. It seems clear that the Achaemenid kings did not forcibly impose this belief system upon their subjects. There is evidence for a variety of local and regional religious systems, some of which persisted and thrived in the Persian heartland alongside Mazdaean beliefs.

Much of what we know of the Achaemenid Persians' culture and lifestyle is gleaned from later tradition or external sources, especially writings of the Greeks, who were far removed on the western frontier of the empire but were perpetually aware of its omnipresent power. The historian Herodotus, writing in the mid- to late fifth century BCE, provides an important source in his description of Xerxes's invasion of Greece in 480–479 BCE. His and other accounts contain much of value, but must be treated cautiously as they are replete with Greek literary and cultural motifs. Moreover, there are no concurrent and comparable Persian narrative sources to balance the Greek perspective, so at best historians and scholars can only gain a partial understanding of events from these texts.

In the first book of his history, Herodotus discusses much of Persian customs and culture. Some of this material is bizarre and humorous, such as the assertion that the Persians deliberated on an important matter while drunk but revisited the same issue on the following day while sober; if the decision was the same after both sets of deliberations, it was adopted. Other assertions, such as Herodotus's contention that the main elements of a Persian youth's education were archery, horsemanship, and honesty coincide directly with an inscription on Darius I's tomb that clearly emphasizes his skill with the bow and horse. Darius also claimed in his inscriptions (especially at Behistun) an unyielding antagonism toward falsehood (Old Persian *drauga*), often translated as "the Lie." This attitude is consistent in Achaemenid royal inscriptions. The king, via

LEFT **Dated to the reign of Artaxerxes I** (465–424 BCE), this silver statuette shows a Persian dignitary dressed in a traveler's outfit of trousers and a cap.

his special relationship with Ahura-Mazda, cast himself as the guarantor against "the Lie."

Many later Greek and Roman writers veered further into literary motifs that emphasized the Persians' luxury and decadence at the expense of the historical accuracy of their accounts. Plato and Xenophon both provide examples of the debasement of the Persian education system to the detriment of later Achaemenid kings and the empire itself: a process that manifested itself straightaway with Cyrus the Great's sons, who were corrupted and weakened by a luxurious upbringing, with similarly deleterious effects on the empire. The Greek doctor and historian Ctesias of Cnidus (writing *c.* 400 BCE) focused on intrigue among the Persian queens and eunuchs—the infamous harem—and depicted the increasing effeminacy of the Persian kings, presenting this as a manifestation of the degradation of the empire's power. According to Ctesias, Achaemenid queens and princesses would stop at nothing to ensure their progeny's (and thus their own) exalted positions, and the fragments of Ctesias's history that we possess describe ubiquitous treachery, torture, and a complete disregard for justice and virtue.

Greek sources offer a mosaic of potential insights into the cultural and social history of the Achaemenid Empire, but it is difficult to tease out elements of reliable historical worth from such stylized accounts. Similar difficulties apply to the portrayal of Ahasverus (Xerxes I) and other Achaemenid figures who appear in books of the biblical Old Testament. One counter to the often distorted perspective of narrative Greek sources, however, is provided by the Persepolis Fortification Tablets, an archive of administrative texts found in the fortification wall at Persepolis (see feature box below). These tablets offer a window into the logistics of the administrative hierarchy, all the way up to the royal family, and the distribution of commodities all the way down to members of the lowest rungs of society. The tablets also promise insight into the agricultural, economic, and military methods and systems of the Persian Empire. The distribution of rations to workers and officials in a variety of far-flung locales and differing contexts testifies to the reach and organizational acumen of the empire's central authority. Despite over 50 years of work at the time of this writing, in many respects the analysis of the Fortification Tablets still remains in its nascent stages.

THE PERSEPOLIS FORTIFICATION TABLETS

According to the principal investigator of the Persepolis Fortification Tablets, of an estimated 20,000–25,000 tablets, about 15,000–18,000 are original documents dating from 509 to 494 BCE. A much smaller find of similar tablets from the Treasury, consisting of 114 documents dated between 492 and 458 BCE, also conveys important information to historians about the administration of the Achaemenid Empire. The majority of the tablets (roughly 70 percent) are in Elamite, with the remainder either uninscribed or in other languages such as Aramaic. The occasional Babylonian Akkadian, Greek, and even Old Persian tablets have been discovered as well. The importance of these tablets for our developing knowledge of the Achaemenid Empire cannot be overestimated.

RIGHT **This Achaemenid clay tablet in Elamite,** ***c.*** **500 BCE, is one** of 300 describing the workings of the Persian administration.

Cyrus the Great

Cyrus II, "the Great" (reigned 558–530 BCE), is without doubt one of the most important and influential figures in Persian history. Without him, Persia would not have achieved imperial status and become a world power.

ABOVE **Pasargadae, in southern Iran,** was Cyrus's capital city. The remains of the palace audience hall are shown in this photograph.

Cyrus the Great (*Kurush* in Old Persian) was the son of Cambyses I, and was born around 600 BCE in a small southwestern Iranian kingdom known as Persia (Greek *Persis*), located in the modern province of Fars.

Cyrus and the Early Persian Kings

The Persian dynasty that produced Cyrus the Great was begun *c.* 650 BCE by its first monarch, Teispes. He styled himself as "King of Anshan"—referring to an area in the southwest plateau region of the uplands north of Elam, once ruled by the powerful and culturally sophisticated Elamites—and Teispes's successors followed this naming tradition. It appears that the earliest Persian monarchs saw themselves as the rulers of Elamite lands and perhaps even regarded themselves as the natural inheritors of Elamite culture, attested to by the fact that the language, bureaucracy, and court organization of Elamite culture remained highly influential in Persia throughout the Achaemenid period.

RIGHT **Cyrus the Great** (depicted in an engraving by an unknown modern artist) was greatly admired by Alexander the Great, who eventually conquered the empire that Cyrus created.

LEFT **This gold lion** (*c.* fifth century BCE, Kanellopolous Museum, Athens) is one of many Persian artifacts that attest to the wealth of the empire founded by Cyrus.

Further knowledge about this early period of Persian history is scant. The archaeology of early Fars (*c.* 1150–650 BCE) shows a steady decline in populated settlements, but during the reigns of these first Persian kings, evidence indicates that a massive resettlement of the area took place (*c.* 650–559 BCE). This suggests some growth in the stability of the area, but little else can be gleaned with any certainty.

When Cyrus ascended to the throne of Persia in 558 BCE, there were four major empires in the Near East: Egypt, Babylonia, Lydia, and Media. Cyrus the Great was to have an impact on each of them. According to Greek historian Herodotus, the Persians were one of several Iranian tribes, each of which was a vassal state to the Medes. The powerful Median kingdom was growing so large in northern Iran that Median military aggression turned toward the wealthy area of Babylonia. In 550–549 BCE, eight years into Cyrus's reign, Babylon was saved from attack when Cyrus and a coalition of south Iranian tribes marched north to attack Astyages, the Median king. The Greek accounts given by Herodotus and Ctesias of Cnidus interpret the actions of Cyrus as a bid to break the yoke of Media, and they tie together Cyrus's defeat of Astyages with an account of Cyrus's youth and strength of character.

The Birth of Cyrus: Legend or Fact?

Legends of Cyrus the Great were no doubt common in the rich storytelling tradition of ancient Iran. Even in the Achaemenid period itself, people probably told stories of the birth, reign, and greatness of their founding imperial monarch. Herodotus reports that he knew of at least three legends about Cyrus's birth and upbringing, although he chooses to cite only one in full. In this version, Cyrus's father Cambyses I was married to a daughter of Astyages, Mandane. Following the marriage, Astyages was plagued with nightmares in which he foresaw that his future grandson would take over his throne.

When Mandane gave birth to her prophesied son, Astyages ordered the child to be slain, but Harpagus, a Median general, smuggled the infant to safety in the countryside where he was raised by a herdsman. The child Cyrus grew to maturity and developed into an outstanding youth, quickly overshadowing his friends and displaying all the qualities required of a royal leader. News of his kingly attributes reached Astyages, who invited Cyrus to court. Upon seeing the boy, the king immediately recognized his grandson and allowed him to return home to Persia to his noble parents. Cyrus then began to entertain the idea of seizing power from the Median king. He persuaded a number of Persian tribes to side with him, subsequently gaining independence from Astyages and Median rule.

In an alternative version of the story, the child Cyrus survived in the wild, reared by a wild dog. Another story suggests that Cyrus was not related to Astyages at all, and a further variation names Cyrus's parents as Atradates, a thief, and Argoste, a goatherd. These stories are part of the founding legends of Cyrus the Great, and follow a much older Near Eastern storytelling tradition of the humble birth of great leaders. King Sargon of Akkad and the biblical figure of Moses share similar founding legends with Cyrus, and all take their inspiration from different forms of popular storytelling or political propaganda.

The conflict between Astyages and Cyrus can be considered either a piece of romantic fiction or the first documented fact in Achaemenid history. Certainly the war is attested in several Greek texts and some Near Eastern sources. Contemporary inscriptions of the Babylonian king Nabonidus offer a brief account of the conflict. The Nabonidus Chronicle, written in *c.* 550–549 BCE, recalls that Astyages's army "revolted against him, captured him, and deliv[ered] him to Cyrus," whereupon Cyrus marched into the royal palace at Ecbatana, looted it, and took all the "silver, gold, goods, and valuables" back to Anshan.

Cyrus's Conquests

Following the overthrow of the Medes and the sack of Ecbatana, Cyrus turned his attention towards northern Media, including the ancient kingdom of Urartu in the area of Lake

ABOVE **The Cyrus Cylinder** was discovered at Babylon, where it had been placed soon after Cyrus conquered the city, *c.* 538–535 BCE.

Van. The chronology of this period is hazy, but it is possible that Cyrus also occupied Elam and claimed possession of Susa. Ctesias suggests that Cyrus also undertook a campaign in Bactria, but Herodotus passes off the Bactrian war as nothing more than a minor skirmish.

Better-known is the Persian campaign against the wealthy and powerful kingdom of Lydia. The Lydian king, Croesus, had brought the cities of Ionia under his rule, and his capital, Sardis, benefited from extensive trade with Mesopotamia. Only Greek sources record the fall of Lydia, but its sack meant that Cyrus was able to take other important cities along the Ionian coast, which were placed under the control of Persian governors and administrators.

By 540 BCE, Cyrus was ready to march on Babylon and moved his army into Mesopotamia, marching first on Opis and then on Sippar. He entered Babylon on October 29, 539 BCE, having already taken the Babylonian king, Nabonidus, prisoner. Apparently meeting no military resistance, Cyrus appointed his son, Cambyses II, as the city's regent, although he maintained the status quo by allowing Babylonian officials to continue in their governmental and religious offices. A Babylonian named Ugbaru was appointed as the city governor.

In the years after the conquest of Babylonia (538–530 BCE), Cyrus gained a truly international empire: Aria, Parthia, Sogdinan, and Margiana fell to him on the eastern front, while near the Jaxartes River he founded a city which the Greeks called Cyropolis. In the west, Cilicia, Syria, and Palestine came under Cyrus's rule. Although he never held Egypt, he clearly marked it out for conquest at a later stage.

In 530 BCE, Cyrus died on the battlefield in a war against the Massagetae. His legacy cannot be overemphasized: he swiftly founded a world empire of great cultural diversity. The Babylonian priests recognized him as Marduk's earthly representative, the Jews saw him as God's anointed, and the Greeks regarded him as a supreme statesman and beneficent ruler. Among modern Iranians, Cyrus is a cult figure and his tomb is still a place of veneration for millions of people.

The Cyrus Cylinder: The First Bill of Human Rights?

The Cyrus Cylinder is a barrel-shaped clay foundation offering written in Akkadian, found in excavations at Babylon in 1879 near the sanctuary of Marduk and presumably composed on Cyrus's orders. The whole document is written from a Babylonian point of view in traditional Babylonian terms, but was perhaps inspired by the inscriptions of Ashurbanipal, the Assyrian king (reigned 668–627 BCE). As an example of imperial propaganda, the cylinder attempts to legitimize Cyrus's conquest of Babylon: it emphasizes how the wickedness of Nabonidus has driven the gods out of the city, while the Babylonians themselves were forced into heavy labor to realize his vainglorious building program. Marduk looks down from heaven for a champion, and finds him in Cyrus, who is presented as the savior of the city.

Cyrus returns order to Babylon, frees the city's inhabitants from their forced labor, and allows deported peoples to return to their lands. He worships the gods piously and correctly, according to the cylinder text: "Marduk, the great lord, was well pleased with my deeds and sent friendly blessings to myself, Cyrus, the king who worships him, to Cambyses, my son...as well as to all my troops, and we all praised his great godhead." Cyrus then "signs" himself "King of the world, great king, legitimate king, king of Babylon, king of Sumer and Akkad, king of the four rims of the earth...descendant of Teispes ... of a family which always exercised kingship, whose rule [the gods]...love."

Because of its references to the restoration of deported peoples, the cylinder has been referred to as a bill of human rights; modern Iranians often take pride in the claim that Cyrus was a humanitarian. The image is enhanced by the praise of the Jews for Cyrus's deeds, for it was he who allowed the Jews to return from their Babylonian exile back to their homeland (Isaiah 45:1). As such, he is the only Gentile to receive the honor of the title "Messiah" ("Lord's

PASARGADAE: CYRUS'S PARADISE

Pasargadae (Old Persian *Pâthragâda*) in the modern Fars province was chosen by Cyrus as the site for his palace. It consisted of two small stone structures, built by Lydian stonemasons, incorporating a residential area and an Apadana (columned audience hall). The walls of the palace were decorated with painted stone reliefs inspired by earlier Assyrian models. One well-preserved male figure (pictured), a semi-divine being, borrows motifs from all over the empire: an Elamite garment, Assyrian-style wings, and an Egyptian crown. Pasargadae was planted with a formal garden, and it incorporated myriad irrigation channels in the land around the palace to ensure the gardens were well watered. The result was nothing short of a desert paradise, the modern word being derived from the Persian word for a garden—*pairidaêza* (*paradeisos* in Greek). At the edge of his garden, not far from the palace, Cyrus erected his simple tomb: a gabled building on a simple platform, inspired by Lydian funerary monuments.

RIGHT **The winged spirit relief at Pasargadae** is the best-preserved figure at the site, but in recent years it has suffered some damage. Archaeologists are considering removing the relief from the site to prevent further weathering.

Anointed"). However, the concept of "human rights" would have been alien to Cyrus and his contemporaries. While it is true that the Jews were allowed to return home, other peoples did not fare so well under Cyrus. The citizens of Opis, for instance, were massacred en masse, and, following the fall of Lydia, the population was deported to Nippur in Babylonia, where a community of Lydians is attested.

Cyrus was clearly a pragmatic ruler. This is demonstrated in his appropriation of the worship of local gods. There is no mention in the cylinder of Cyrus himself worshipping the Iranian god Ahura-Mazda. In the Akkadian text he is the tool of Marduk, just as in the Old Testament he is presented as the servant of the god of Israel.

BELOW **Cyrus the Great's tomb** (*c.* 530–515 BCE) still stands at Pasargadae.

Cambyses II and Darius I

After the death of Cyrus the Great in 530 BCE, his son Cambyses II conquered Egypt. A palace coup d'état soon plunged Persia into near chaos, but the determination, foresight, and statesmanship of Darius I ("the Great") saw the vast empire flourish.

Trained for the succession by his father, Cambyses II (reigned 530–522 BCE) had been appointed governor of Babylon, and upon Cyrus's death, he ascended peacefully to the throne. A Babylonian text, dated August 31, 530 BCE, names Cambyses as "king of Babylon, king of lands." At his accession, Cambyses appointed his younger brother, Bardiya (known in Greek texts variously as Smerdis, Tanaoxares, or Tanyoxarkes), as a governor of either Media (northern Iran) or Bactria (Afghanistan)—the Greek sources are contradictory on this point.

Cambyses II: a Mad King?

Cambyses's greatest achievement as king was the conquest of Egypt in 525 BCE, following the death of the pharaoh Ahmose (Amosis) (reigned *c.* 570–526 BCE), whose heir, Psamtek III, was defeated in battle at Pelusium. Cambyses was crowned pharaoh according to ancient rites at Memphis, with the throne name Mesuti-Re. Following the conquest of Egypt, the neighboring regions of Libya and Cyrene offered submission to the Persian forces. Cambyses marched south, down the Nile, stationing a Jewish garrison on the island of Elephantine near Aswan to protect Persian interests in the south, before advancing and conquering at least a part of Nubia.

Greek sources, Herodotus in particular, tend to portray Cambyses as a mad despot, tyrannically oppressing and murdering his subjects, committing unnatural sexual acts, and impiously debasing the religious traditions of his conquered nations. He is accused of destroying Egyptian temples and even slaughtering the sacred Apis bull, the animal incarnation of the god Ptah. Much of this vilification emanates from the accounts of Egyptian priests who were opposed to Cambyses's attempts to reduce their power and wealth. Archaeological evidence from Egypt, however, suggests that Cambyses adopted a policy of religious tolerance. Inscriptions from the Serapeum in Memphis (524 BCE) confirm that he honored the death of a sacred bull with due rites and rituals. Like Cyrus in Babylon, Cambyses co-opted the support of Egyptian nobles to maintain his sovereignty. One text celebrates the reverence shown by Cambyses to the goddess Neith: "Cambyses came...to the temple of Neith. He touched the ground before

BELOW **Cambyses II, accused of drunkenness,** shoots a young boy through the heart to prove his sobriety. This 1754 engraving (artist unknown) depicts a story by Herodotus.

LEFT **Darius I ("the Great")** sits on the throne in this relief from the audience hall (Apadana) at Persepolis, *c.* 485 BCE.

her very great majesty as every king had done, he organized a great feast." Other similar texts confirm that Cambyses II was sensitive to the religious and cultural traditions of Egypt, and that the impression of him as a mad autocrat given by Herodotus appears to be unwarranted.

Darius's Court Coup

Cambyses's death, which occurred in Egypt in the summer of 522 BCE, is shrouded in mystery: he may have died naturally or from a wound, or he may have committed suicide. According to the account by Darius in his Behistun Inscription, Cambyses had secretly killed his brother Bardiya, but a magus (Median priest) named Gaumata claimed to be Prince Bardiya and seized the throne. Cambyses, Darius maintained, killed himself. For six months the pretender Gaumata ruled Persia as Bardiya; no one was prepared to challenge him. Darius's account, which was then followed by Herodotus a century later, begins to appear particularly suspect and almost farcical when he claims that Gaumata looked identical to Bardiya, and that even his harem of wives was not able to tell the difference between the usurper and the murdered prince.

With six other Persian nobles, Darius—who was not Cambyses's heir, but the son of the governor of Parthia, Hystapses—conspired to oust Gaumata from the throne. In a palace coup of September 29, 522 BCE, the impostor was slain and Darius I, "the Great" (reigned 522–486 BCE) ascended to the Persian throne.

It is generally accepted that Darius's account of events is pure fabrication and that it actually serves to cover up the fact that Darius himself killed Cyrus's rightful successor. To legitimize his claim to the throne, Darius invented a common ancestry between Cyrus and himself—Achaemenes, the eponymous founder of their "shared" dynasty. Darius also consolidated his throne by marrying the daughters of Cyrus, Atossa and Artystone, and Parmys, the daughter of Bardiya. He allied himself to the houses of the six nobles who had aided his bid for the throne by marrying their daughters or giving his female relatives to them in marriage. He gave the six magnates his promise that they would have access to him for a personal royal audience at any time, apart from those hours he spent with his wives. By marrying into the Persian elite, Darius also ensured the expansion of the new "Achaemenid" bloodline he had established.

Not everybody accepted Darius's rule so easily, however; rebellions broke out in Babylon, Media, Armenia, Scythia, and even in Persia itself (led by a challenger claiming to be another Bardiya). Darius was ruthless in suppressing the revolts, an act that he accomplished in little more than a year. After capturing and executing the rebel leaders, he was not threatened with an uprising for the rest of his reign.

BELOW **The "Darius Vase"** (*c.* 340–320 BCE), painted by the southern Italian artist called "The Darius Painter," may represent Darius I (seated in the center).

RIGHT **Gold coins, called darics,** were introduced by Darius and produced in mints in Lydia, in the west of the Persian Empire. This one is dated *c.* 480–400 BCE.

BELOW **The tomb of Darius the Great** (*c.* 486 BCE) is cut high into the rock face at Naqsh-i Rustam, Iran.

The Administrator King

In 518 BCE, after confirming his hold on the empire, Darius was able to expand its borders as far as the Sind (and possibly the Punjab) in India; in 513 BCE he attempted to conquer the Scythians north of the Black Sea, too. In Darius's reign the empire extended from Libya to Bactria.

To aid administration of the empire, he divided it into 20 provinces called satrapies, each governed by a satrap who was usually drawn from the royal family. Each satrapy was assessed for its wealth and taxed accordingly in the form of annual tribute which had to be paid to the central administration. It was Darius who also introduced coinage into the empire. To aid communication and prompt payment of taxes, Darius constructed the Royal Road from Susa to Sardis in western Anatolia, and disseminated his royal edicts along it in multiple languages, including Old Persian, a written form of the Persian language created at his behest.

Darius was also concerned with building and engineering projects. In Egypt, he was responsible for the creation of a canal between the Nile and the Red Sea, and built temples to Egyptian gods at Hibis. On the temple walls he is depicted in full pharaonic regalia. In the Iranian heartland, the cities at Susa, Ecbatana, and Pasargadae were expanded and embellished by Darius, and he started the ambitious building program at Persepolis.

Late in his reign, Darius came into contact with the Greeks, and while he may have had ambitions to incorporate Greece into the Persian Empire—and was certainly keen to punish Athens for its interference in Persian affairs—Herodotus's account of Graeco-Persian tensions probably exaggerates the Persian response to the Greek resistance. Before he could launch a major campaign against the Greeks, Darius died in the winter of 486 BCE and was buried in a tomb at Naqsh-i Rustam, near Persepolis. It was left to his son, Xerxes I, to plan a military strike against the Greeks.

The Behistun Inscription: Reinventing the Past

High above the Royal Road near Ecbatana, carved deep into the rock face of Mount Behistun (Old Persian *Bagast na,* "place of the gods"), towers Darius the Great's monument to his kingship: his account of his accession to the Persian throne and its immediate aftermath. Almost 216 ft (66 m) below, on the mountain's slope, are the remains of Sikayuvatish, the Median fortress where Gaumata, the usurper, was assassinated by Darius and his six co-conspirators.

The inscription tells the dramatic (if distorted) story of Darius's royal accession. It is written in regular columns, using three cuneiform languages—Elamite, Babylonian,

THE FOUNDATIONS OF SUSA

A foundation inscription from Susa records how Darius enlisted workers from all over the empire to build and decorate his palace at Susa. The text was meant to advertise the vast natural resources and labor that the king had at his command.

> *The cedar timber, this was brought from a mountain named Lebanon. The Assyrian people brought it to Babylon; from Babylon the Carians and the Greeks brought it to Susa...The gold was brought from Lydia and from Bactria, which here was wrought. The precious stone[s] lapis lazuli and carnelian...[were] brought from Sogdia... Precious turquoise...was brought from Chorasmia ...The silver and the ebony were brought from Egypt. The ornamentation with which the wall was adorned, that from Greece was brought. The ivory ... was brought from Nubia and from India ... The men who wrought the wood, those were Lydians and Egyptians. The men who wrought the baked brick, those were Babylonians. The men who adorned the wall, those were Medes and Egyptians. Darius the King says: at Susa a very excellent work was ordered, a very excellent work was brought to completion.*

and Old Persian—carved into the rock face. A huge raised relief (probably once painted) dominates the surface of the stone. It shows Darius, richly bearded and wearing a crown, standing at the head of a line of rebellious kings, each one fettered to the next by a rope, their hands tied behind their backs; at the end of the line, and added at a later date, is the figure of Skunkha, the rebel from Scythia, wearing a distinctive pointed cap. Darius is depicted on a larger scale than the other figures on the relief and he places his left foot upon the belly of the prostrate figure of Gaumata, who lifts his arms in supplication. In his left hand Darius clutches a bow, a symbol of his military authority, which is echoed by the presence of two armed guards standing to his rear. The king's right hand is raised in adoration at the figure in the winged disk at the center: this is probably Ahura-Mazda, the supreme god of the Persians, who offers Darius the kingship in the form of a ring.

Throughout the inscriptions, Darius confirms his devotion to the "Wise Lord" Ahura-Mazda and attributes his success to the god: "Ahura-Mazda bestowed the kingdom upon me. Ahura-Mazda brought me aid until I had held together this kingdom. By the favor of Ahura-Mazda I hold this kingship." Darius also cites his genealogy and stresses his right to the throne by claiming a common ancestry with Cyrus the Great, both of whom, he insists, are descended from Achaemenes. But like much else in the Behistun Inscription, this is propaganda: Darius was not a member of the house of Cyrus and his ancestors, the kings of Anshan.

Darius at Susa

The Elamite city of Susa was afforded a new lease on life by Darius's building program. He selected Susa as his administrative capital and erected a large palace with an impressive Apadana, where colored glazed-brick reliefs showed bodyguards standing in strict formation. Other finds from the site include an oversized statue of Darius, which was probably made in Egypt and brought to Susa to adorn the palace.

ABOVE **The inscription at Behistun,** just visible under the stone relief, was first translated by Englishman Henry Rawlinson, who made a copy of the cliff-face inscription in 1835–1839.

Persepolis

Rising out of the sands of the Marv Dasht plain in Iran, the citadel of Persepolis is one of the great sites of antiquity, and one of the best-preserved royal palaces of the ancient Near East.

ABOVE **The archaeological site at Persepolis** includes a huge stone terrace on which its palaces stood, close to 1,450 ft (450 m) long and 1,000 ft (300 m) wide.

Darius the Great began the construction of the palace and ceremonial centre of Persepolis around 515 BCE, and it was greatly added to by Xerxes I, Artaxerxes I, and each of the successive Achaemenid monarchs. It was still in the process of being built when, in 330 BCE, Alexander of Macedon burned it to the ground—in retaliation, he claimed, for Xerxes's sack of Athens in 480 BCE.

The Palace Complex

The buildings at Persepolis were built of locally quarried stone, although the craftsmen who worked on the site were drawn from all over Persia's empire. The 20,000–25,000 cuneiform tablets (the so-called Persepolis Fortification and Treasury Tablets) attest to the presence of different peoples of the empire, all of whom received payments in foodstuffs for their labors, meticulously recorded by palace scribes.

But what was Persepolis used for? First excavated by Ernst Herzfeld and the Oriental Institute of Chicago in 1931, Persepolis was found to consist of a vast complex of military quarters, treasuries and storerooms, private living quarters, large reception rooms, vast audience halls, and rock-cut royal tombs in the nearby cliffs. Yet Persepolis was not continuously inhabited by the king and his court: the court moved between Susa, Babylon, and Ecbatana annually, coming to rest at Persepolis, it is assumed, for the festivities of Nou Rouz, the spring equinox on March 21.

It would seem that Darius planned Persepolis as a showcase of empire, for it was here that ambassadors from all over the Persian world, from Ethiopia to Elam, would congregate each year to offer tribute to the king. The sculptors working at the site recorded these scenes of imperial gift-giving in loving detail on the palace stairways: each group of tribute bearers wears "national dress" and brings gifts of precious metals, textiles, food, ceramics, and livestock to the palace. The treasury, a large many-roomed building, was begun by Darius to safeguard the gold, silver, and other costly materials presented to him as tribute.

Palace Quarters: Public and Private

The palace complex was divided into public and private spaces. Ambassadors, nobles, and courtiers would, by and large, find themselves in the outer courts of the palace, such as the Apadana (the audience hall or throne room), a vast pillared hall about 65 ft (20 m) high, in which the king held audience and received the obeisance of his court, or the Hall of a Hundred Columns, a huge indoor banqueting room built by Xerxes. Enormous courtyards were able to accommodate thousands of dignitaries and guards as they stood waiting to see the king, flanked by impressive stairways and towering entrance gates.

Courtiers and servants with close connections to the king, as well as members of the royal family, made up the inner court, and occupied living spaces at the rear of the palace complex. A series of small banqueting rooms, council chambers, and terraces have been identified at Persepolis, and it is also possible to locate the private suites of the king himself. At the far end of the private wing of palaces is a large L-shaped building that possibly served as the residential quarters of the royal harem, housing some of the wives, children, and even siblings of the monarch.

Beyond the Walls of the Palace

Despite its scale, it is clear that the whole court could not have lived on the Persepolis terrace itself. The number of servants needed to look after the needs of the immediate members of the royal family would have run into huge figures alone, while the king himself was said to have had no less than 360 royal concubines, all of whom required extensive accommodation. From the Fortification Tablets we know that in 467 BCE, some 1,348 people were employed in the royal treasury alone. So where did the majority of people at court reside?

There is archaeological evidence for a series of small palace structures surrounding the main palace platform, accommodating a few hundred people. But the greater part of the court was housed in tented accommodation scattered around Persepolis for several miles—the Persian court was, by nature, peripatetic and frequently lived out of huge tents. This would explain how so vast an infrastructure as the Persian court could leave so little trace in the archaeology of the landscape.

ABOVE **The Gate of All Nations** built by Xerxes I at Persepolis (c. 480 BCE), with its immense human-headed bulls, was the gateway through which the king received his guests.

THE LION AND THE BULL

The scene of a lion clinging onto and biting the hindquarters of a bucking bull is a common image found at Persepolis. It is located in conspicuous spaces, such as the stairways leading up to the Apadana, and is without doubt one of the most powerful and captivating images in Achaemenid art. But what does it mean? It is possible that the motif suggests that the strong bull cannot overcome the strength of the lion, the lord of beasts—in other words, that it would be futile for any country within the empire to challenge the supremacy of the Achaemenid king. On the other hand, some scholars interpret the motif as an astrological symbol, pointing to the constellation of Taurus giving way to that of Leo, thereby indicating the spring equinox and the celebration of Nou Rouz, when Persepolis was used by the king and court for the New Year festivities.

RIGHT **This lion and bull relief** appears on the staircase leading to the Tripylon, or council hall, at Persepolis.

Achaemenid Art

Achaemenid art is essentially an eclectic mix of styles and motifs drawn from different parts of the empire, but fused together to produce a distinctive and harmonious look that is distinctly recognizable as Persian. Egyptian and Assyrian motifs (such as winged disks and winged *genii*, pediment designs, and even cannons for depicting the human figure) are frequently melded together, so that Achaemenid art can be said to reflect in material form both the diversity and unity of the empire as a whole.

The art of the Achaemenid Empire serves two key purposes: it confirms the royal ideology of the unity of the empire, and it promotes the image of the monarch. In a way, all Achaemenid art is royal art since the motifs created for the glorification of the king are found time and again in almost all Persian material artifacts. These range from vast rock-cut sculptures—such as those found on the cliffs at Behistun, or in the tombs of the kings at Naqsh-i Rustam and Persepolis—to miniscule engravings found on gemstones.

Winged Lions and Gods

Imposing mythical creatures appear in glazed brick artworks at Susa, Iran, *c.* fifth century BCE. The winged disk, depicting Ahura-Mazda, hovers above them.

The king is often the central focus. He is shown as a warrior, bow or spear in hand, trampling on his enemies, or as a great mythic hero, a kind of Gilgamesh figure, who slays monstrous beasts with his sword or dagger. Alternatively, the king is depicted at a fire altar piously adoring the figure of Ahura-Mazda, the supreme god of the Persians, who takes on human form and resides in a winged disk above the altar. The king is also shown in state, wearing the lavishly decorated royal robes, progressing through his palace with attendants bearing parasols and fly-whisks; he is also shown seated on his high-backed throne as he receives courtiers in audience.

A particularly interesting motif shows the great king elevated on a throne-like platform

Lions at the Royal Table

This gold drinking rhyton from the fifth or fourth century BCE—probably from the royal table—is crafted as an exquisitely detailed winged lion, with a decoration of lotus flowers and buds under the rim.

that is raised up high by individuals from across the empire (see picture at right). Each person is identified by ethnic dress and represents a different province of the empire. In his tomb inscription at Naqsh-i Rustam, Darius the Great encourages readers to look at the accompanying reliefs to understand the vastness of the empire he held: "If now you shall think that 'How many are the countries which King Darius held?' look at the sculptures [of those] who bear the throne, then shall you know, then shall it become known to you: the spear of a Persian man has gone forth far; then shall it become known to you: a Persian man has delivered battle far indeed from Persia."

The Empire Supports the King

A detail from the tomb of Darius I (Naqsh-i Rustam, Iran) shows the motif of the empire's peoples holding up a platform, upon which stands the king.

This theme is also found in three-dimensional form in a sculpture of Darius found at Susa in 1972. Carved in Egyptian style, it shows Darius in Persian court robes standing on a rectangular pedestal, carved with kneeling individuals who raise up their hands to support the figure of the king above them. As on the tomb relief, each person is dressed in local costume and is named. In effect the statue is an empire list: an enumeration of nations subject to the king.

Ethnicity in Achaemenid Art

The Achaemenid monarchs' interest in the ethnic makeup of the empire is also apparent on the staircases leading to the Apadana at Persepolis. Here representatives of the empire are depicted in loving detail bringing tribute to the court of the king: curly-haired, dark-skinned Nubians carry elephant tusks and lead an okapi on a leash; Ionians in turbans carry silver tableware and ornamental armlets; Lydians (pictured) bear vessels; and Elamite nobles lead in a lioness and her cubs. The detailing of every delegate, every courtier and every soldier is overwhelming. Even the personality of a Bactrian camel is clear in the rendering of its face, and is a testimony to the skills of the ancient artists.

Imperial Government

In the Achaemenid Empire, although the power of the king was absolute, he ruled at the center of a complicated nexus of bureaucracy and personal relationships, and administered the empire by dividing it into smaller provinces, or satrapies.

RIGHT **Servants and officials were crucial** to the organization of the empire. This chromolithograph of Xerxes I with attendants was made from a relief at Persepolis.

For the Achaemenid kings, the empire's most important officials were the satraps, the "protectors of the kingdom," who were typically members of the Persian elite. A satrap may be considered equivalent to the governor of a province, while the term "satrapy" refers to a province. The satrap reported directly to the king.

Locating the Satrapies

Delineation of the Achaemenid satrapies is frequently attributed to Darius the Great, but it has become increasingly clear that Cyrus and Cambyses initiated the system by adopting and adapting the preexisting structures. The resulting administrative units were occasionally modified in light of political circumstances, but remained reasonably constant throughout the Achaemenid period.

It is not at all easy to reconstruct a definitive list of the empire's satrapies and to determine any fixed and firm boundaries. Specialists continue to debate the boundaries of the satraps' territories, which are not always readily discernible in the extant sources, but which typically coincide with natural phenomena such as major rivers. The presumed or claimed overlap of boundaries between satrapies often led to dissension between the satraps. Using a modern map, it is not possible to give more than approximations of where a given satrapy's territory ended.

Moreover, the various sources for Achaemenid government, and the satrapal system, are not easily reconciled. To do so requires that the lists of peoples or lands (*dahyava* in Old Persian, although the word's precise meaning is still disputed) in the royal inscriptions of Darius and Xerxes be reconciled with the different perspectives from the accounts of Herodotus and the historians of Alexander the Great's campaigns. The royal inscriptions vary in the number of *dahyava* listed, but there are usually more than 20; many are traceable to provincial territories within the preceding empires that the Achaemenids incorporated. Further, Classical sources use different words to describe the political hierarchy of the Achaemenid Empire, which leads to some confusion in identifying the precise role of the particular officials named.

The process by which these satrapies came into being is usually viewed as a replacement of previous kings or rulers by Persian satraps, who took control of those territories, with the governors (or their equivalent) of the older entities now subordinate to the satrap. Smaller administrative units within a satrapy would have retained their demarcation but varied as their circumstances changed. At the risk of oversimplification, we may view the Achaemenid king as an additional, overarching level of administration, who became the focal point.

LEFT **Satraps like Mausolus (377–353 BCE)** were key local leaders in the empire. When Mausolus died, his wife Artemisia erected him an impressive tomb, giving us the word "mausoleum."

Satraps and their Dynasties

Despite their relative independence in the day-to-day operations of their province, the satrap was ultimately responsible to the king. Satraps were not only responsible for the security of their province (and, by extension, the empire) but also for the collection and delivery of taxes and tribute to the central authority, i.e., the king. When the king had need of military forces for a major campaign, it was the satrap's responsibility to assemble the requested forces from his area.

Whenever possible, the satraps took steps to ensure that their rule became a dynastic one, as in the case of Mausolus, the satrap of Caria in southwestern Anatolia in the early to mid-fourth century BCE. Other satrap positions were devolved on a Persian elite family and became dynasties, as in the case of Artabazus in Phrygia, in northwestern Anatolia. Artabazus and his son, Pharnaces, then grandson, Pharnabazus, provide an unbroken line of satrapal rule from 479 BCE until well into the fourth century BCE.

Artabazus was a cousin to the royal family, thus a part of the extended Achaemenid clan, and this sort of connection often underlay the Persian nobility's stake in the empire. Marriage into the Achaemenid family was a high honor. The nobles' and their families' positions were thus dependent upon the empire's stability and their good graces with the king, though there were certainly occasions where the satrap, along with members of his family, spurred destabilization through revolt.

Administering the Empire

Royal secretaries and military personnel, responsible directly to the king, were critical components of satrapal administration. These individuals and their retinues helped maintain consistent and reliable communication with the king, and could also be used for strategic purposes to weed out any rebellious officials in the empire. Herodotus, for example, recounts the role of a royal messenger in the downfall of one particularly recalcitrant and murderous satrap, Oroetes. Oroetes had been appointed satrap of Sardis (Lydia) by Cyrus, but he had acted with far more independence—and far less honor—than a Persian satrap should. Moreover, he remained aloof during the crisis that preceded Darius I's accession to the throne, and did not aid the eventual victor.

To test the loyalty of Persian troops in Oroetes's satrapy, Darius sent a series of letters under the royal seal. Each letter contained a command; if the guards obeyed it, this was a signal to the messenger, Bageus, to read the next letter. When it became clear to Bageus that the satrap's guards were loyal to the king, he opened the last letter, which commanded the guards to slay Oroetes. They did so immediately. This reveals the mechanism of royal control in the satrapies, and the potential consequences of rebellious behavior.

BELOW **Military personnel** were vital to the empire; the standing army was made up mostly of Persians (Iranians) and Medes. These soldiers are from the Tripylon at Persepolis (*c.* 500–450 BCE).

The Persian Royal Road

The Persian Royal Road served as the primary conduit of communication and transport between the western part of the Persian Empire and its core. It ran from Sardis in western Anatolia to Susa in Elam.

ABOVE **In the mountains of Cappadocia, Turkey,** a family climb through the rock formations. The Persian Royal Road passed through Cappadocia, although its exact route is not known.

The Greek historian Herodotus is our main source for the Persian Royal Road. According to his calculations, it was approximately 1,500 miles (2,415 km) long, or a journey of 90 days. The route ran from Sardis, the capital of the satrapy of Lydia (in western Anatolia), through Cappadocia and Cilicia through the southeast of Anatolia, then southward through Arbela (modern Arbil), along the Tigris, east and south of Nineveh, and on toward Susa in Elam (modern Shush in Iran). An additional leg from Ephesus, one of the main Greek cities on the Ionian coast of western Anatolia, to Sardis, would add another three days in Herodotus's reckoning.

It is presumed Herodotus's calculations were based on the time an ordinary traveling company would take to complete their journey, as Persian royal messengers would have been able to travel the road much more swiftly. He describes royal staging-posts and inns along the entire route, at which messengers bearing proper authorization received rations and fresh horses (see feature box, above right).

A Network of Roads and Bridges

The Persepolis Fortification Tablets record many royal authorizations for messengers traveling the Royal Road. These documents also provide information on a number of the roads running between Susa and Persepolis. Some of these documents, supplemented by Classical sources, reveal that large work crews were involved in construction of these roads. Herodotus's account of Xerxes's invasion of Greece in 480–479 BCE also describes road-makers at work, and indicates that the army on campaign was responsible for the construction work.

The maintenance of such a far-flung network required a vast bureaucracy, and the satraps were responsible for the maintenance and safeguarding of the roads in their territories. As a comparison, Herodotus describes the difficulties Darius's army encountered during the Scythian expedition in southeastern Europe, precisely because there were no ready roads for the army to follow.

The primary roads served to facilitate rapid and efficient communication between the center and periphery, and to move military forces

ABOVE **This pontoon bridge** over the Euphrates River, built in Samawa, Iraq, in 2004, makes use of the "floating bridge" principle the Persians used to cross rivers along the Royal Road.

NEITHER SNOW, RAIN, HEAT, NOR DARKNESS...

Engraved upon the Post Office building at 8th Avenue and 33rd Street in New York is the expression "Neither snow nor rain nor heat nor gloom of night stays these couriers from the swift completion of their appointed rounds." Although widely (but erroneously) considered the United States Postal Service's official motto, the inscription is in fact a translation of a famous passage in Herodotus describing the Persian messenger system as it was established along the Royal Road:

> *There is nothing mortal that travels faster than these messengers...as many days as the whole route may be there are both horses and men divided, one horse and one man set for each day. Neither snow, nor rain, nor heat, nor night hinders them from accomplishing the course laid before them as quickly as possible. After the first one finishes his route, he delivers the instructed message to the second, the second does likewise to the third; from there in rapid succession down the line the message moves.*

quickly. Consequently, they were constructed wide enough to allow chariots or wagons—both military and cargo-carrying—to travel on them. The Royal Road crossed several rivers. Over some of these were permanent bridges; Herodotus describes one spanning the Halys River (modern Kizil Irmak River) in Anatolia, which was guarded by a fort, and likewise the Euphrates and the Tigris in Mesopotamia.

Floating pontoon bridges allowed crossing of other rivers, and many spots on the northern Tigris and the Euphrates and their tributaries were bridged in this way. Pontoon bridges provided the means for Persian armies to cross into Europe: Darius I over the Bosphorus on his campaign against the Scythians, *c.* 513 BCE, and Xerxes's bridge over the Hellespont against the Greeks in 480 BCE.

Persian Roads in Other Sources

The Greek doctor and historian Ctesias of Cnidus, writing in *c.* 400 BCE, alludes to the main routes from Mesopotamia and Persia proper to Central Asia, though the details of his writings on these have not survived. Routes across the Iranian plateau culminated in Bactria and the Indus Valley. In modern works on antiquity, the main route to Bactria across northern Iran is called the (Great) Khurasan Road, although in treatments of later periods the better-known term "Silk Road" is used. Greek writers who chronicled Alexander's military conquests and the wars between his successors refer to a number of other routes beyond the Royal Road from Sardis to Susa, including routes between Susa, Babylon, and Ecbatana (modern Hamadan).

One Aramaic document tracks travelers journeying from northern Mesopotamia to Damascus and on to Egypt, with several stops along the way listed by name. Many of these routes that traversed Greater Mesopotamia had been, like the Khurasan Road, in use for centuries and were inherited (along with the responsibility for their maintenance) by the Persian Empire. The Persian road network was vast, and formed the foundation of the communications capability that was a critical component of the empire's success.

BELOW **Sardis, at the western end** of the Royal Road, was rich in alluvial gold, and an important administrative center for the Persians in western Anatolia.

The Ionian Revolt

The Ionian city-states of Western Anatolia fell to Cyrus the Great after his conquest of the Lydian king Croesus, *c.* 545 BCE. The Ionian Revolt (499–494 BCE) marked their first attempt at independence from Persian rule.

ABOVE **This marble sculpture of an Ionian *kouros*** (male youth), dated to the sixth century BCE, is from the Aegean island of Samos, which was home to several important Ionian city-states.

Despite its difficulties of use and interpretation, our main source for the Ionian Revolt is, once again, the work of the Greek historian Herodotus. Herodotus maintained a clear and direct link between Athenian involvement in the Ionian Revolt and Xerxes's invasion of Greece almost 20 years later.

Greek Troublemakers: Aristagoras and Histiaeus

According to Herodotus, the blame for the Ionian Revolt was to be placed upon one man, Aristagoras, the tyrant of Miletus and nephew of the previous tyrant, Histiaeus. More than a decade before, Histiaeus had proven his loyalty to Darius I during the Persian campaign against the Scythians by protecting Darius's newly constructed pontoon bridge over the Bosphorus. Darius rewarded him with additional holdings, and Histiaeus consolidated his personal power in the northern Aegean to such an extent that some Persians began to view him as a potential threat. To obviate this threat, Darius made him a royal table companion, thus granting him a position of honor but allowing him to be closely monitored at court.

In 500 BCE, Histiaeus's nephew Aristagoras, now ruling Miletus, approached Artaphernes, the satrap of Sardis and the brother of Darius, with a proposal to conquer the island of Naxos in the Aegean Sea as a springboard to invading Greece itself. With Darius's approval, a Persian force was dispatched with Aristagoras, but the expedition proved a failure. Distraught at his presumed fate because of this blunder, Aristagoras feared for his position. At the same time, a trustworthy slave sent from Histiaeus arrived with a message encouraging Aristagoras to rebel. Histiaeus had tattooed the message on his slave's scalp and waited for his hair to grow back before sending him on the mission. Herodotus emphasized that this was done in order to prevent discovery by the king's many agents stationed along the Royal Road—a comment on the expansiveness of the Persian king's reach.

Creating a Coalition

Aristagoras abdicated his position as tyrant of Miletus and, with his supporters' help, expelled the other tyrants from the Ionian cities. He was able to convince many of the cities to join in his revolt against the king and, in addition, sought assistance from mainland Greeks, ultimately hoping to overthrow the entire Persian Empire. Herodotus describes Aristagoras's ill-fated attempt at securing military aid from Sparta. The Spartan king, Cleomenes, looked over Aristagoras's map of the Persian Royal Road; when he learned that it was a three-month journey from Ionia to the king's palaces, he immediately refused any assistance and ordered Aristagoras out of Sparta.

In Athens, however, Aristagoras found a more hospitable audience, as the Athenians considered the Ionians to be their kinsmen. They promised 20 ships to the Ionian cause. The Eretrians of the

RIGHT **Greek warships, of the type shown** on this Greek vase *c.* 550 BCE, were greatly outnumbered by Persian ships at the final decisive Battle of Lade.

island of Euboea (Athens's neighbors) promised five more ships. Herodotus emphasizes that those Athenian ships were the beginning of evils for both the Greeks and the "barbarians"—a term that was used generically by the Greeks for any peoples who spoke a nonGreek language. This mainland support, Herodotus argues, set the stage for the so-called Persian Wars.

Persian Victory

Aristagoras's forces were initially successful in a daring and unexpected raid against the satrapal capital of Sardis itself. During this raid the lower city was burned, including a sanctuary of the Anatolian fertility goddess Cybele. Persian forces rallied, pursued, and defeated the rebels at the city of Ephesus on the coast. It was after this that the Athenians departed, but the Ionians, along with much of the island of Cyprus and the territory of Caria (inland southwestern Anatolia), continued the revolt.

Despite some reverses, from 497 BCE onward the Persians systematically fought, defeated and reconquered rebellious cities and regions. Aristagoras was killed in battle in Thrace while seeking more resources to support the revolt. Histiaeus returned to Ionia with Darius I's permission, but was ultimately captured and brought to Artaphernes, who had discerned his part in stirring the rebellion, and put to death.

Miletus was besieged. The rebels made one final throw in a naval battle at Lade, off the coast of Miletus, in 494 BCE. Their resistance splintered, and many Ionian contingents defected as the naval battle began. The Persian forces carried the day, and effectively ended the revolt.

Not long after, Miletus itself surrendered and was reduced to slavery, and Persian forces defeated the remaining pockets of resistance throughout Ionia. The Ionians could not match Persian resources or cohesion. Many Ionian tyrants (i.e., the rulers of the city-states) owed their positions to Persia, and it was with their help—and the prospect of their resumed rule under Persian aegis—that the revolt dissipated and failed. Ionia was reduced again, as it had been under Cyrus beforehand, to subject status.

After the revolt, the satrap Artaphernes took measures to consolidate Persian control on the western borders of the empire, while Darius's eye traveled further west again, into Thrace, in southeastern Europe. His son-in-law Mardonius took an army and campaigned there in 492 BCE. The end result was that Thrace and Macedonia were brought further into the fold of the Persian Empire. This campaign laid the groundwork for the subsequent invasions of Greece proper. The Athenian (and Eretrian) support for the Ionians required a Persian response, and this was not too long delayed.

ABOVE **Miletus was one of the most powerful** of the Ionian cities on the Anatolian mainland. Today, the city's site is no longer on the coast due to the silting up of the Meander River.

Xerxes I

Despite his bad reputation in the Classical sources, Xerxes I (reigned 486–465 BCE) managed to suppress several revolts and hold the Persian Empire together. Nevertheless, squabbles at court amongst his sons led to his assassination.

RIGHT **Xerxes I stands at the entrance** to the Hall of a Hundred Columns at Persepolis. Two attendants stand behind him with a parasol and a fly-swat.

Xerxes I was the son of Darius I and Atossa, daughter of Cyrus the Great. He was appointed crown prince by Darius despite not being the eldest son of the king—the Persian monarchs did not automatically appoint the firstborn son of the king to the throne. Xerxes acknowledged this in an inscription at Persepolis: "Other sons of Darius there were, [but] this was Ahura-Mazda's desire—Darius my father made me the greatest after himself."

Why was Xerxes Chosen?

Before his accession to the throne, Darius already had a harem of wives. His eldest son, Artabazanes, was one of three children born to Darius by the (unnamed) daughter of Gobryas, and hence belonged to one of Persia's leading noble families. Had Darius promoted Artabazanes to the throne, the Gobryas bloodline would have been strengthened. But Xerxes, the son of Atossa and therefore the grandson of Cyrus the Great, represented the physical embodiment of Darius's propaganda strategy—the unification of his bloodline with the Achaemenid line of Cyrus, as noted in the Behistun Inscription. Xerxes was also born after Darius had ascended the throne, which perhaps gave him a better claim to the kingship. Herodotus, however, credits Xerxes's rise to the throne simply to the fact that "Atossa had all the power" and that she fought against rival claimants to the throne.

Sources for the Reign of Xerxes

Xerxes was crowned king in 486 BCE, and in all essentials, he continued his father's policies.

XERXES IN THE BIBLE

The Old Testament book of Esther is set in the court of Susa, and follows the exploits of the Jewish maiden, Esther, who enters the harem of King Ahasverus (Xerxes), whom she eventually marries. She uses her rank to secure the safety of the Jews from annihilation by the courtier Haman. Court intrigues form the background to the story, which is packed with incidental detail about Persian court life, palace protocol, law, and culture. It is therefore generally held that Esther was composed in the Achaemenid era, and that its author was very familiar with Persian institutions. The style of the text indicates a date of composition of approximately 400 BCE, only a few decades after the reign of Xerxes. There are no Greek words used in the text at all, a fact that clearly points to it being composed before the Hellenistic era.

LEFT **Francois Langrenee's *Esther and Ahasuerus*,** *c.* CE 1775–1780, depicts the biblical story of Esther and Ahasverus (Xerxes).

It must be noted, however, that knowledge of Xerxes's reign is almost totally confined to the western periphery of the empire, derived as it is from Greek sources. Moreover, evidence for the events of the latter years of his reign is sparse. Because of his aggressive policy toward the Greek lands, Classical sources depict Xerxes as a hubristic megalomaniac, but this is probably far from the truth.

We know very little of his family life, save that he took as his queen a noblewoman named Amastris, whose reputation suffered as much as that of her husband in the hands of the Greek historians. Her father, Otanes, was one of the nobles who had aided Darius. She bore Xerxes at least three children we know of: Artaxerxes, Darius, and Achaemenes.

A Troubled Empire

Xerxes's first task was coping with a rebellion in Egypt, which had begun just before Darius's death. After subduing it, he appointed his brother Achaemenes as satrap of Egypt. In 481 BCE Babylonia erupted in revolt. Again Xerxes drew on his close relatives for aid: the rebels were subdued by Megabyzus, Xerxes's cousin and son-in-law. Xerxes responded to the revolt by dividing the Babylonian satrapy into two: "Babylonia," embracing everything east of the Euphrates, and "Beyond the River," including everything west of the Euphrates between Palestine and Turkey.

One key aim of Xerxes was to force the mainland Greeks to acknowledge Persian power. The importance to Xerxes of bringing the Greeks under Persian control is signaled by the fact that he led the expedition to Greece himself. As Xerxes was marching his army into Greece in 480 BCE, however, a second revolt in Babylonia broke out. This renewed unrest in Babylon would explain Xerxes's hasty departure from Greece. His rapid intervention in the revolt was successful, since the province did not rebel again.

According to the later Greek historian Arrian, writing in the second century CE, Xerxes punished the city by razing the temple of Marduk to the ground and removing the god's statue from the city. Is there any truth to this tale? There are very few dated Babylonian sources from Xerxes's reign; some texts suggest a demotion in status of the city, but there is no archaeological evidence that Xerxes destroyed Babylon's temples. The city's sanctuaries and cults suffered no noticeable decline, and the New Year Festival of Marduk went ahead uninterrupted in Babylon.

Xerxes's Death

In August 465 BCE, Xerxes and his crown prince, Darius, were murdered in a court coup. The events are obscure, but the plot appears to havebeen hatched by Artaxerxes, another son of Xerxes, in a conspiracy with some powerful eunuchs. Certainly, when he was crowned the next king, Artaxerxes I (reigned 465–424 BCE) posed as the avenger of his father and brother by publicly executing the supposed assassins.

BELOW **Darius I sits on the throne, with Xerxes standing behind him,** in this relief from Persepolis. The winged disk of the god Ahura-Mazda is at the top.

War with Greece

Xerxes's invasion of Greece (480–479 BCE) marked a turning point in the history of the Western world. Greece's victory set the stage for its independent development and cultural importance, and put Athens on the path to power and prestige.

The term "Persian Wars," a label that reflects a Greek perspective, is typically applied to Xerxes's invasion, for which the Battle of Marathon (490 BCE) is often seen as the prelude. Herodotus yet again is our main source, although many Classical authors wrote about or alluded to this formative event in Greek history. There are no existing Persian sources for the period, thus we are entirely reliant upon Herodotus and his Greek and Roman successors. The perspective of the Persians must therefore be gleaned with care and skepticism from these Classical works, and extrapolated from other sources elsewhere in the empire. Herodotus wrote and presented his account later in the fifth century BCE (*c.* 420 BCE), so he had access to eyewitnesses who were several decades removed from the events.

Prelude to War

The Ionian Revolt (499–494 BCE) resulted in defeat for the Ionian states rebelling against Persian rule, but in Herodotus's telling it is an event that prefigured the critical role Athens would play in the next stages of the conflict. After describing the rebels' burning of Sardis during the early stages of the Ionian Revolt, he relays a colorful anecdote of Darius I's response. Darius discounted the Ionians, whom he considered of little importance, but asked who the Athenians were who had helped them. Upon hearing the answer Darius took his bow and shot an arrow into the sky, and prayed that he would punish the Athenians for their involvement. Darius also infamously ordered a servant to repeat to him "Remember the Athenians" three times at every meal.

In 492 BCE, Darius's son-in-law Mardonius, who was to play a key role in Xerxes's war with the Greeks, campaigned in Thrace. Although Mardonius lost his fleet in a storm off Mt. Athos, the campaign resulted in the subjection of Macedonia to Persia. In the following year, Darius's heralds canvassed Greece, seeking the submission of Greek city-states to Persian rule. Many complied, but Athens did not—and, what is more, the Athenians defied accepted convention by casting the Persian heralds into the same pit in which condemned criminals were hurled. According to tradition, the Spartans behaved similarly, throwing the Persian envoys into a well.

BELOW **The island of Samos joined the Ionian Revolt, a prelude to the "Persian Wars." The Temple of Hera visible here was one of the great regional cult centers.**

The Battle of Marathon

The Persians campaigned against Athens and Eretria (on the island of Euboea), which had also given support to the Ionian rebels. The fleet crossed the Aegean Sea in 490 BCE, and subjugated Naxos and a number of other islands, laid waste to several cities that resisted, and plundered and burned the temples in Eretria—the last act in reprisal for the burning of the sanctuaries of Sardis during the Ionian Revolt. From there, the focus turned to Athens, and

LEFT **This tomb site in Marathon, Greece,** is where the ashes of the fallen Greek soldiers were interred after the Battle of Marathon. The site is now sealed, and lies beneath a burial mound.

a landing was made at Marathon in the northeastern part of the Attic peninsula.

Herodotus's account celebrates Athenian courage and ingenuity in not only facing down the Persian forces but in choosing an opportune time to attack. With this quick action, Herodotus claims, the Persians were compelled to retreat. The Persians sailed around the peninsula with the intention of putting in at Athens's harbor, Phaleron, but a fast Athenian runner was sent to Athens to warn of the approaching Persian fleet. The port was closed, and the Persians sailed away. The "race" (and the distance) that the Athenian runner covered was the basis for the modern marathon, named after the site of their initial victory.

Xerxes's Invasion

Darius died in 486 BCE and was succeeded by Xerxes I. Once the new king had resolved his more pressing problems (i.e., revolts in Egypt and Babylonia), he prepared a full-scale invasion of Greece. Herodotus states that preparations for this momentous and cataclysmic undertaking took four years, and Xerxes himself led the massive army.

Herodotus provides statistics for the invasion force before it reached Thermopylae in Thessaly: 277,610 men on 1,207 warships, 240,000 men on 3,000 transport ships, 1,700,000 infantry, and 100,000 cavalry and charioteers, along with 300,000 men drafted from Xerxes's European holdings. This runs to a total of 2,617,610 men, and Herodotus begs off from counting the camp followers. There is no way to get to the truth of the matter, but modern estimates range from 50,000 to 200,000 for the army, and 500 to 1,000 for the navy.

The battles fought by the Greeks against Xerxes's invading army and navy have become the stuff of legend in Western history, and became so shortly after the time of the invasion. King Leonidas and the Spartans' last stand at Thermopylae, and Themistocles's trick to secure a Greek naval victory at Salamis have inspired countless retellings since. The Greek victories, including Plataea and the naval battle of Mycale, preserved Greek freedom and profoundly marked the Classical period of their history (*c*. 500–323 BCE).

As for the Persians, we discern no noticeable impact of their defeat beyond their eventual withdrawal from Europe and the end of their westward territorial designs beyond Ionia. This runs counter to the preponderant emphasis in

LEFT **A Greek vase depicts a duel** between a Persian (left) and a Greek soldier, painted sometime during the mid-fifth century BCE.

ABOVE **A Greek warship,** of the type used in the Battle of Salamis in 480 BCE, is represented on this undated fragment in the British Museum.

Greek sources on degradation and decadence in the empire from the time of Xerxes to its fall in 331 BCE—which was a full 150 years after his invasion of Greece. Such a perspective thus does not do justice to the historical reality.

The Greeks Strike Back

Sources for the next 48 years or so (*c.* 479–431 BCE) are sporadic at best, and the available material to help historians understand Persian political and military interaction with Greece is meager. However, there is significant evidence, particularly from Athens, that Persian influence left its mark on the literature, architecture, and culture of Classical Greece at its height.

Flush from their victory in 479 BCE, several Greek city-states under the leadership of Athens attempted to drive the Persians from Europe and free the Ionians. Athenian success in the Aegean and Ionia appears to have put the Persian satraps in western Anatolia on the defensive. Athenian attempts to extend their reach further, such as by supporting revolts in Egypt and Cyprus *c.* 460 BCE, resulted in failures and, ultimately, an apparent detente on the Aegean frontier.

Specialists continue to debate whether a formal treaty, which modern scholars call the "Peace of Callias", was concluded between Athens and Persia in the mid-fifth century BCE, and, if so, on what terms. It is reasonably clear, in any case, that the king and his satraps never relinquished claim to the empire's Ionian holdings, and, when advantageous to do so, they were determined to contest them.

With the outbreak of the Peloponnesian War between Athens and Sparta (431–404 BCE), the Persian Empire becomes prominent again in the extant source material: this time as a potential support to both protagonists in the war. The western satraps continued to assert Persian interests in the Ionian theater, and acted as intermediaries with Greeks who wished to deal with the king (Artaxerxes I until 424 BCE, and Darius II from 423 BCE) directly. Initial Persian inclination to support Sparta was never absolute, though the satraps seized opportunities to weaken Athenian power in the Aegean and to play one Greek side against the other.

The Revolt of Cyrus the Younger

In the final decade of the Peloponnesian War, the Persians concluded a treaty with Sparta through which the Persians provided financial and logistical support in exchange for Spartan

XERXES ON THE HELLESPONT

Xerxes's bridging of the Hellespont, by which his army crossed from Asia into Europe, became a paradigm of the hubristic and despotic behavior associated in Classical sources with the Persian kings. Herodotus's account describes this incredible feat of engineering, a pontoon bridge roughly over 3,950 ft (1.2 km) long, but its thematic approach focuses on Xerxes' stereotypically tyrannical behavior. The first bridge was destroyed in a violent storm, and Xerxes's response was not only to behead the offending engineers but also to punish the sea itself. A pair of shackles was thrown into the water, and, as his men whipped the water, Xerxes cursed: "O Bitter Water, your Master, who has done no wrong to you, visits this punishment upon you. But King Xerxes will cross you, whether you will it or not. It is right that no one of men sacrifices to you, a foul and bitter river."

LEFT ***Xerxes at the Hellespont*** by Jean Adrien Guignet (*c.* CE 1845) portrays Xerxes reaching the edge of the strait.

renunciation of any claim to Ionia. Darius II's second son, Cyrus ("the Younger"), arrived in the west with intent to ensure a Spartan victory and to end Athenian interference in Ionia. Persian money financed a navy and crews for the Spartan cause, the result being a siege and total surrender of Athens in 404 BCE. Persian dominance in Ionia was again secure, for a short while at least.

It soon became clear—at least from the perspective of the Greek sources—that the aim of Cyrus the Younger in hastening the war's end was to lay the groundwork for a Greek mercenary army that he would use in 401 BCE to overthrow his brother, the recently crowned Artaxerxes II (reigned 404–359 BCE). Cyrus's expedition and the defeated Greek army's return westward has been immortalized by Greek historian Ctesias, in his *Persica*; by the Athenian soldier Xenophon, in *Anabasis*; and in Plutarch's much later *Life of Artaxerxes*. Cyrus the Younger's revolt came to nothing when he was slain on the battlefield of Cunaxa, north of Babylon, by Artaxerxes's troops.

Trouble broke out again in Ionia for the Persians with the surprising expedition of the Spartan king Agesilaus in the mid-390s BCE. Through this campaign, the Persians discovered that mainland Greeks had not altered their intentions toward Ionia, but that now the Spartans instead of Athenians were attempting to liberate the Greek cities there. The Persians reinstituted their policy of supporting one Greek side against the other; Persian funds financed a new Athenian fleet that, this time, broke Spartan power in Ionia in 394 BCE, nine years after Athens's naval power was likewise rendered ineffectual. Continued wrangling among the mainland Greeks allowed Artaxerxes II to impose the so-called "King's Peace" upon them (387 BCE), which again ceded the Greek cities of Ionia to Persia.

A resurgent Athens, however, sporadically resumed the contest for control of Ionia. The Persians' confrontations with Greeks in Ionia and in the Aegean persisted through the fourth century BCE, until the kingdom of Macedon emerged as the primary threat both to Greece and to Persia's interests in the west. The invasion of the Macedonian king, Alexander ("the Great"), brought the Achaemenid Persian Empire to an end in 330 BCE. The empire's like was not seen again until the rise of the far-reaching Roman Empire in the first century CE, and has been seldom seen since.

ABOVE **The Alexander Sarcophagus** depicts the battle between Alexander the Great and the Persian cavalry. It was sculpted in the fourth century BCE.

The Last Achaemenids

Far from being a time of stagnation, the late Achaemenid period (404–330 BCE) saw a new spate of military activity and the reconquest of rebellious territories. Aggressive Macedonian expansion, however, did not bode well for the Achaemenid Empire.

BELOW **This Persian royal figure,** part of the gold and silver hoard called the Oxus Treasure (*c.* 450–350 BCE), may portray one of the last Achaemenid kings.

The succession in 404 BCE from Darius II to his eldest son, Arses, appears to have been relatively smooth. Arses assumed the throne name Artaxerxes II and reigned over the Achaemenid Empire for 45 years (404–359 BCE).

Artaxerxes II

Early in his reign, Artaxerxes's younger brother, Cyrus ("the Younger"), satrap of Lydia and Phrygia Minor, nursed ambitions for the throne, encouraged by his mother, Parysatis. Cyrus gathered a group of Persians and troops from his satrapy, plus a force of Greek mercenaries, including the Athenian soldier Xenophon, who has left us a valuable description of Cyrus's ill-fated revolt in his work *Anabasis*. The rebellious army met with Artaxerxes's troops at Cunaxa in Babylonia in 401 BCE and Cyrus was killed. His bid for the throne had failed to gain sufficient support among the Persian nobility, and thus Artaxerxes's power over the empire remained unshaken.

One of the first international crises Artaxerxes II faced was Egypt's attempt to break free of Persian control. Between the years of 401 and 399 BCE, the Persians were expelled from the Egyptian territory. This was a serious blow to the king, and the history of the Achaemenid Empire for the next 56 years is dominated by continuous efforts to regain control of this important province.

Meanwhile, Artaxerxes turned his attention toward ensuring that Syro-Palestine and Anatolia remained under firm Persian control, and in 387 BCE he imposed a settlement on the Greeks called the "King's Peace," whereby the Greeks were forced to recognize that the cities of Ionia would thenceforth fall under Persian control.

Artaxerxes II was the longest reigning of all the Achaemenids, and it is a pity that we know so little about him. The Greek historian-moralist, Plutarch, provides us with a largely sympathetic sketch in his *Life of Artaxerxes*: he portrays him as a generous ruler anxious to make himself accessible to his subjects, a loving and dutiful husband, and a courageous warrior prepared to share the hardships of his soldiers.

Artaxerxes III and the Reconquest of Egypt

Long reigns like that of Artaxerxes II often create problems when it comes to the question of royal succession, and in this case several mature and experienced sons were ready to jockey for position. Three of Artaxerxes II's sons, including crown prince Darius, died violent deaths, and another son, Ochus, who eventually succeeded his father as Artaxerxes III (reigned 359–338 BCE), is credited with engineering the fatalities.

The major achievement of Artaxerxes III's reign was the reconquest of Egypt in 343 BCE, after hard campaigning. By then, he had already crushed a revolt in Phoenicia, headed by the ruler of Sidon, Tennes. Artaxerxes's punishment of Sidon was swift: Tennes was executed, some of the city destroyed, and a part of its population deported, as recorded in one of the Babylonian Chronicles: "The fourteenth [year] (i.e. 345 BCE) of Umasu, who is called Artaxerxes: in the month Tishri the prisoners which the king took [from] Sidon [were brought] to Babylon and Susa. On the thirteenth day of the same month a few of these troops entered Babylon. On the sixteenth day the...women prisoners from Sidon, which the king sent to Babylon—on that day they entered the palace of the king."

With the recapture of Egypt, the reputation of Artaxerxes III for harshness and cruelty was confirmed. A seal of the king depicts him crushing his enemies and leading prisoners on a leash.

LEFT **Darius III fights from his chariot** at the Battle of Issus, as depicted in the Alexander Mosaic (House of the Faun, Pompeii, Italy, *c*. CE 75). Behind Darius, the Macedonians form a wall of pikes *(sarissas)*.

Court Coups and the Clash of Empires

Artaxerxes III and most of his family died in a veritable bloodbath (338 BCE), masterminded by a eunuch, Bagoas, who then raised the sole surviving young son of Artaxerxes, Arses, to the throne; he again took the name Artaxerxes, and reigned as Artaxerxes IV from 338 BCE. Only two years later he was murdered by Bagoas, who now supported the claims of a member of a collateral branch of the Achaemenid family, Artashata, to the kingship, a man who had a reputation for exceptional physical bravery. Once Artashata was firmly established on the throne and had adopted the throne name Darius III, he had Bagoas executed.

The reputation of Darius III (reigned 336–330 BCE) has suffered badly. Fated to be the opponent of Alexander of Macedon, whose brilliant military victories, comparable to those of Cyrus the Great in their breathtaking sweep and speed, spelled the end of the Achaemenid dynasty, Darius has gone down in history as a weak-kneed coward. In reality, he was a brave soldier who posed a serious threat to Alexander's dreams of glory. He met Alexander in battle at Issus in 333 BCE, but was forced to flee the field, leaving Alexander to capture the royal harem. Darius met Alexander in battle again at Gaugamela in 331 BCE, but once again was defeated. He fled to Ecbatana to try to raise fresh troops, pursued by Alexander, who was anxious to take him alive. He then fled to Bactria where he was killed not by Alexander, but by the satrap of Bactria, Bessus, in July 330 BCE. Alexander gave Darius an honorable funeral and, to help legitimize his claim to the Persian throne, married Darius's daughter, Stateira.

ACHAEMENID ROYAL WOMEN

Royal women played a key role in the politics of the empire and although they could not rule in their own right, they had access to power through their intimate relationships with the kings—as mothers, wives, daughters, sisters, or concubines. According to Greek sources, queen mothers of the dynasty were often active in defending the royal family from external or internal threats. However, the favor they showed to one child over another could have disastrous consequences: for example, it is clear that Darius II's wife Parysatis encouraged her much-loved younger son, Cyrus, to rebel against his elder brother, Artaxerxes II. Clearly a woman of drive and ambition, she is credited with executing and poisoning several court nobles, and even poisoned her daughter-in-law, Artaxerxes II's wife Stateira, perhaps because she saw in Stateira similar ambitions for power.

RIGHT ***The Family of Darius Pleading***, by Filippo Tagliolini (eighteenth century CE), depicts the family of Darius III after their capture by Alexander the Great.

Under Occupation: Hellenistic and Roman Conquerors

Introduction

The establishment of Greek military and political hegemony in the Middle East toward the end of the fourth century BCE, marked a revolutionary departure from previous norms, which reverberates to this day.

When Alexander III of Macedon ventured into Asia Minor in 334 BCE, no one could have predicted that his forces would march all the way to India, establishing an empire unprecedented in size. Even less conceivable were the political and cultural developments which would pave the way for the Roman Empire's domination of the eastern Mediterranean, and the emergence of Christianity and Islam. The history of the Middle East during the thousand years which marked Greek and Roman control (*c.* 330 BCE–*c.* CE 640) is fascinating and complex. It is marked by the syncretism of the relatively new cultures of Greece and Rome with the already ancient cultures of the Babylonians, Assyrians, and the coastal peoples of the Levant. Following the death of Alexander the Great in 323 BCE, a bloody series of wars were fought to carve out independent kingdoms. The victors were established as kings in three smaller empires carved out of the vast imperial legacy of Alexander. They were: the Seleucid (Asia Minor, Syria, Mesopotamia, and Iran); the Ptolemies (Egypt); and the Antigonids (Greece and Macedonia). Seleucus, one of Alexander's bodyguards, took control of the Seleucid (the largest). The Seleucid dynasty would rule as Greek (Hellenistic) kings for the following 250 years (until *c.* 65 BCE). Their empire would eventually be subsumed in the west by the Roman Empire, and in the east by the new Parthian kingdom, based loosely on the Iranian possessions of the Achaemenid Persians whom Alexander had defeated. Both Rome and Parthia had been affected by Greek culture and continued to use Greek language in the political

LEFT **The Alexander Mosaic,** (c. CE 75), from Pompeii, Italy, depicts Alexander the Great at the Battle of Issus. This encounter, fought in 333 BCE against Darius III, was the second of their three major battles for primacy in Asia.

and military administration of the former Seleucid territories in the Middle East. Increasingly, both empires were strongly influenced by the local Semite cultures of the Middle East, and in the case of Rome, this was expressed most obviously in religious terms.

Roman Power Expands

The Romans and the Parthians fought one another in the Middle East for three centuries until the Parthians were overthrown by the Sasanian Persians (CE 223) from southern Iran. Rome and Parthia fought in Armenia, Syria, and northern Mesopotamia. On three occasions in the second century CE, Roman emperors invaded the Parthian Empire (Trajan, reigned CE 114–117, Lucius Verus, reigned CE 162–165, Septimius Severus, reigned CE 194–198). As a result, Rome's power in the Middle East expanded east across modern Syria and as far as northern Mesopotamia. Armenia, Syria, and northern Mesopotamia continued to be the focus of conflict between the Romans and the Sasanians, and Roman emperors continued the tradition of regular invasions of their eastern neighbor.

Under the Sasanians, Zoroastrianism received imperial support, and by the end of the third century CE resembled a "state religion." With Emperor Constantine's adoption of Christianity in CE 312, the rulers of both empires contesting for control of the Middle East now publicly supported a monotheistic religion which they linked to the security and welfare of the state. Christianity would play an increasingly important role in the wars between the Romans and the Sasanians over the following centuries.

Byzantine and Islamic Powers in Competition

The Middle East became a more central feature of the Roman Empire as the western territories were lost in the fifth century CE. By this time, the Roman Empire effectively had two emperors: one in the west and one in the east. However, in CE 476, the last Roman emperor in the west abdicated, formally marking the political extinction of the Roman Empire in the west. The empire in the east, with its capital at Constantinople, continued to function as the Roman Empire, although modern scholars refer to this empire as Byzantium. The Byzantine Empire was centered on the Balkans, Asia Minor (Turkey) and the Middle East (Syria, Lebanon, Israel/Palestine, Jordan, and Egypt), with Christianity one of the central features of its politics and culture. The wars between Byzantium and Sasanian Persia continued until the early seventh century CE, when the Sasanian King of Kings, Croesus II, invaded Byzantine Syria, Arabia, and Egypt. These territories were conquered by Croesus II but recovered after a long ruinous war by Heraclius in CE 628. The emergence of Islam as a religion with broad appeal throughout the Arabian Peninsula was a defining event for the history of the Middle East. Within a few years, this politico-religious movement resulted in the Byzantines losing all their territories in the Middle East, and the Sasanian Persian Empire entirely disintegrated. Islam effectively became a state religion with its founder, the Prophet Mohammed, harnessing its broad appeal to unify a powerful political and military enterprise. The political and military departure of Byzantium from the Middle East was not accompanied by social oblivion. Indeed, the impact of this long period of influence of Greece and Rome on the Middle East has continued in many forms down to the present day.

ABOVE **This early fourth-century CE sarcophagus lid** is from the Archaeological Museum in Spalato, Croatia, and depicts the Emperor Constantine on his throne holding a symbol of Christianity.

The Rise of Macedonia

The reign of Alexander III ("the Great") of Macedonia (336–323 BCE) is one of the best-known periods in the study of ancient history. Alexander's sweeping military victories took his forces as far east as India, and the effects of this intrusion are still apparent.

The story of Alexander's expansion often overshadows events in the kingdom of Macedonia before Alexander set out on his eastern campaign in the spring of 334 BCE. Alexander owed much to his father Philip II, who had come to power in 359 BCE when the kingdom of Macedonia was in a very precarious position.

ABOVE **Philip II**, shown here on a silver drachma coin minted in Pella in 354 BCE, was a military strategist and innovator, diplomat, and powerbroker.

Philip II Transforms Macedonia

The Macedonian dynasty, of which Philip and Alexander became the most famous representatives, was established in the first half of the fifth century BCE by Alexander I (died 454 BCE). By the time Philip II came to power over a century later, the kingdom faced serious difficulties as the result of a military defeat at the hands of the Illyrian tribal groups, located in the mountains to the northwest of the kingdom, together with ongoing dynastic feuding. Philip's approach was to unify and expand Macedonia, emphasizing in the process his own paramount authority. Philip quickly capitalized on a military victory over the Illyrians in 358 BCE and began the process of unifying various principalities in upper Macedonia which had contributed to the kingdom's instability. He also extended Macedonia's power and influence throughout the neighboring Balkan kingdoms, including Epirus and Molossia.

As a means of tying the difficult elements of the Macedonian nobility more closely to his authority, and as a way of contracting alliances in the Balkans, Philip took several wives including Olympias of Molossia (Alexander the Great's mother) in 357 BCE. He expanded the imperial bodyguard and attracted numerous individuals as advisers and royal companions from outside Macedonia. Increasingly, Philip's most trusted advisors were not part of the dangerously divided nobility of Macedonia and drew their authority from Philip alone. Perhaps the most famous of these was the philosopher Aristotle who went to the Macedonian royal court in the capital at Pella in 342 BCE to serve as private tutor to Philip's son, Alexander. In a further attempt to make organized and sustained opposition from the Macedonian nobility more difficult, Philip established the institution of the Pages, who were the sons of nobles sent to the imperial court at Pella to be educated and form part of Philip's entourage. In short, Philip established himself as an autocrat in Macedonia and increasingly as the main power broker throughout the region of the Balkans and Greece.

Further to Philip's centralizing and strengthening of his own imperial authority, he improved the state of the imperial treasury by expanding the mining of silver and gold throughout the kingdom. The most important of these mines was at Mt Pangaeum which supplied large amounts of silver and gold from as early as

RIGHT **Olympias of Molossia**, depicted here in a marble eighteenth-century relief from the Imperial Palace in Pavlovsk, Russia, tried to preserve the throne for Alexander's son, but ultimately failed.

356 BCE. The flow of mineral resources from these mines underpinned Philip's growing autocracy and allowed him to develop the army, the most important asset of an expanding empire.

Philip's reorganization and expansion of the Macedonian army was one of the most important features of his transformation of the kingdom. He raised a considerable infantry force from the populous and fertile agricultural regions of upper Macedonia. By the time of his death in 336 BCE the army numbered approximately 30,000 men. Philip also raised a cavalry force which was very well trained and is thought to have numbered 3,000 by the end of his reign. This professional standing army was the most powerful in the whole of the Mediterranean region at this time. Under Philip, the Macedonian army was also a versatile force comprised of light-armed cavalry, allied hoplites, and the heavily armed phalanx. Together with a high level of training, this army was also equipped with experienced military engineers so that, in all, it was one of the most powerful forces yet assembled in the ancient world. Philip's army and the mineral resources financing the Macedonian treasury allowed a considerable expansion of power and influence throughout the region. Significant Balkan kingdoms, such as Molossia and Epirus, came under Macdeonian influence during his reign, and his kingdom also developed considerable power in Thrace and Thessaly. By the year 340 BCE the Macedonian kingdom had become a superpower, and this was to have ramifications for Greece to the south, and, eventually, for the vast territories east of the Bosphorus.

Philip II and the City-States of Greece

The city-states of Greece are typically considered to have reached the height of their prosperity in the legendary "Golden Age" of Greece in the sixth and fifth centuries BCE. By the time Macedonia under Philip emerged as a significant regional force in the 350s and 340s BCE, the Greek city-states no longer enjoyed such prosperity, but they still claimed to be the legitimate guardians of what it was to be truly Greek. This set them on a collision course with the expanding Macedonian kingdom, and in the latter years of Philip's reign and the early years of Alexander's reign it was to have profound consequences for Greece.

Argos, Athens, Corinth, Sparta, and Thebes were among the most important of the Greek city-states at this time, and Philip became involved in their politics. At the time of Philip's accession in Macedonia, Athens, in particular, had meddled in the affairs of the kingdom and this continued throughout Philip's reign. The situation came to a head towards the end of 340 BCE when Philip captured a fleet of ships containing grain bound for Athens, threatening the very lifeblood of the city. In 339 BCE, the city of Thebes came into conflict with Philip when he threatened one of its important allies, Locris. The threat felt by both Athens and Thebes led to their formation of an alliance that mustered an army designed to threaten Macedonia. In the late

ABOVE **This lion mosaic is from the royal palace at Pella** (*c.* 350 BCE). Pella grew in size and splendor during the reign of Philip II, and patronage of the arts flourished.

ABOVE **This relief of a Greek hoplite in battle,** from a sarcophagus (c. 300 BCE) in the Vatican Museum, shows the use of the shield and lance. Hoplites were infantrymen who fought in phalanx formation.

summer of 338 BCE, this army engaged with the formidable Macedonian phalanx at Chaeronea and was slaughtered. The Athenians lost approximately 3,000 hoplites, of whom 1,000 were killed and 2,000 taken into slavery. The Thebans also suffered heavy losses including the famous Sacred Band, an elite force established by Thebes 40 years earlier. Philip was now the most powerful figure in the whole of Greece, and Athens and Thebes were forced into alliances with the Macedonian kingdom. Indeed, all of the important cities in Greece were forced to recognize Philip's power and this culminated in the establishment of the League of Corinth in 337 BCE. The League of Corinth gave technical freedom to all cities in Greece but Philip presided over the League, with Macedonia confirmed as the supreme power.

War Between Greece and Persia

A particularly momentous decision taken by the League of Corinth at this time was to declare war on Persia. This was the immediate background to Alexander's departure on a campaign against Persia three years later. The enmity between Persia and Greece had it origins, however, in the preceding centuries. In 490 BCE and a decade later in 480–479 BCE, the Persians, led firstly by Darius I and then by Xerxes I, mounted attacks on mainland Greece. The Persians continued to threaten Greece in varying degrees for the next 150 years. A key issue in the ongoing dispute between Greece and Persia was the presence of Greek colonies on the coast of Asia Minor in territory that was under Persian rule. These trading colonies had been established from the tenth through to the sixth century BCE and their treatment by the Persians was an ongoing issue for the Greeks up to the time of Alexander. The Greek cities had long desired to avenge the Persian attacks of the early fifth century BCE, but it was only under Philip's leadership that such an attack could be considered viable due to Philip's organization and expansion of the Macedonian kingdom. A related reason for the declaration of war was Philip's desire to demonstrate that Macedonia under his rulership was an accepted member of the Greek commonwealth. One of the taunts which stung him most was that he and Macedonia were not truly Greek. The avenging of the Persian attacks on Greece 150 years earlier, and the liberation of the Greeks in Asia Minor, was designed to silence such criticism.

Philip was also exploiting a prolonged period of difficulty for the Persian royal family. The Achaemenid rulers of the Persian Empire had faced upheaval across their vast empire in the years leading up to the declaration of war by the League of Corinth, including major rebellions in Egypt and Babylon. The upheaval continued in 336 BCE when the Persian king, Artaxerxes IV, was assassinated. He was replaced by a member of the Achaemenid royal family called Artashata and took the name of Darius III. He proved to be a significant adversary who was nonetheless defeated comprehensively on three occasions by Alexander the Great. He was the last of the Achaemenid Persian kings.

THE SARISSA—A POWERFUL NEW WEAPON

Of great importance to the military advances made under Philip was the development of a powerful new weapon which would revolutionize armed conflict for centuries to come. This weapon was known as the *sarissa* and was essentially a heavy spear or pike measuring approximately 18 ft (5.5 m). The *sarissa* was used in a sophisticated formation known as the phalanx and required a high level of training and coordination to be effective. It would come to be dreaded throughout the eastern Mediterranean.

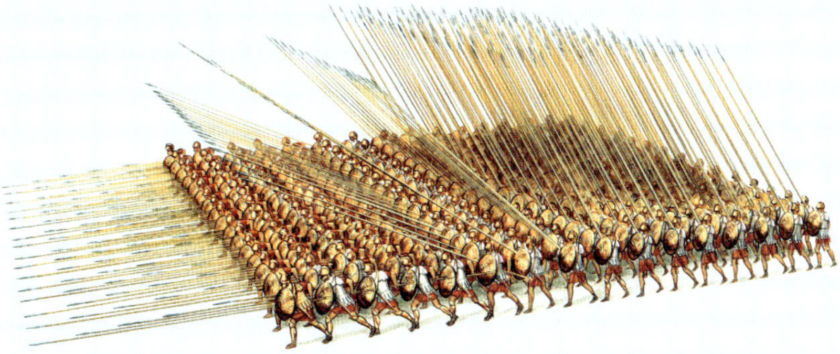

ABOVE **Regular drilling created a cohesive and surprisingly maneuvrable strike force** that was to prove invincible as long as the cavalry protecting its flanks remained strong.

Alexander III Comes to Power

The year 336 BCE was also momentous for Macedonia and Greece. In October of that year, Philip was assassinated. As a result, his 19-year-old son, Alexander, was elevated to the throne. While Philip had left Macedonia in a dominant position in Greece and the Balkans at the time of his death, the situation at the royal court was very dangerous for his young successor. The treasury was facing difficulties, making Alexander's position even more precarious. In 335 BCE, Alexander was faced with a revolt by the city of Thebes, which he ruthlessly suppressed, destroying the city in the process. With the ever-present danger of plots and intrigue within the Macedonian court, the necessity to improve the kingdom's waning financial resources, and the declaration of war against the Persians under his father in 337 BCE still in force, Alexander decided to prosecute the Persian war. In the spring of 334 BCE, he set out with a force of approximately 40,000 troops to take on the might of the Persian Empire. An advance force under Philip's general, Parmenion, had been operating in Asia Minor since 336 BCE, and once the two forces met up, the army numbered approximately 50,000 men. This force, with Alexander as its supreme commander at the age of 21, would surpass all expectations and mark the beginning of political, social, and cultural developments in the Middle East which are still being felt to this day.

RIGHT **This fourth-century CE mosaic from Byblos** depicts the birth of Alexander of Macedonia. Sources of the time claim that several omens were revealed to his father Philip II on that day. Alexander was the first of Philip's children to survive into adulthood.

The Western Conquests

Alexander's invasion of the Persian Empire began when he led an army of 40,000 men across the Hellespont. This narrow stretch of water marked the separation of Europe and Asia. Alexander appreciated the symbolism of this crossing for both his soldiers and the people he planned to conquer.

BELOW **The Hellespont, or Dardanelles,** links the Sea of Marmara with the Aegean. It is 38 miles (61 km) long by 4 miles (6 km) wide.

The advance force under Parmenion, one of Philip's most trusted generals, joined Alexander's army, swelling the numbers to 50,000 infantry and cavalry. A major battle between the Macedonian and Persian forces was inevitable as Darius III, the Persian emperor, had mustered a large army also. The strength of the Macedonian army was its infantry, while the Persian cavalry was superior to that of the Macedonians. This would be a consistent feature of wars between European and Eastern forces for centuries to come. The forces of Greeks, Romans, and medieval Europeans were stronger in infantry while Persian, Parthian, and Islamic armies excelled in cavalry and archery.

Another important feature of the wars between Alexander and Darius was the employment of Greek mercenary soldiers by the Persians in an attempt to strengthen the infantry capacity of the army. The Persian army was, therefore, a conglomerate of Greek mercenaries and Persian soldiers with varying skill levels, who were levied from all over a vast and diversified empire. This led to a number of problems for the Persians, including disagreements in the senior command, and difficulties in the heat of battle caused by different levels of training and ability among the infantry.

ALEXANDER'S DIVINE ASPIRATIONS

The crossing of the Hellespont was symbolically important for Alexander and he is said to have been the first ashore on the eastern side, hurling a spear onto the beach and claiming Asia as a spear-won land. This action consciously emulated the Greek god Heracles from whom Alexander claimed to be descended. Throughout his campaigns, Alexander consistently linked himself to the most famous Greek heroes, especially those with connections to Asia (such as Achilles and Heracles). Indeed, part of Alexander's cultivation of a heroic and perhaps divine image was the effort to outdo Heracles, some of whose exploits took place in Persia.

Alexander visited Ilium, the site of ancient Troy, which held great significance in the mythical past of Greece. Alexander sacrificed to the goddess Athena at Troy and participated naked with his Companions in a race honoring Achilles. Achilles had been one of the major figures in the Trojan War, and Alexander claimed descent from him through his links with the Molossian royal family via his mother Olympias.

RIGHT **Alexander, depicted as Achilles,** is shown in this first-century BCE glass engraving, now located in the Archaeological Museum, Naples.

The Battle at Granicus River

The Macedonian and Persian armies finally engaged at the Granicus River (near modern Koçabas, Turkey) in May–June 334 BCE. The Granicus was a small river but had very steep banks which the Persian cavalry had occupied in anticipation of the arrival of the Macedonians. Alexander's army arrived early in the evening but waited strategically until the following morning to charge across the river and take on the Persian forces. The left wing of the Macedonian army was able to absorb a concerted Persian cavalry charge before the right and center, led by Alexander himself, overwhelmed the Persians with superior infantry. The contribution of the famous and deadly *sarissa*-armed phalanx in this success was highly significant. The Macedonian victory was a crushing one, and the Greek mercenaries in Darius's army suffered heavily. Darius fled to Babylon with the remnants of his army which was in disarray after such a humiliating defeat.

Alexander Marches Down the Coast of Asia Minor

This victory opened up the rich coast of Asia Minor to the Macedonian army, with little prospect of serious opposition from the Persian garrisons stationed in its important cities. Memnon, the commander of the Greek mercenaries at the Granicus, had managed to escape, and he was given the commission by Darius to slow Alexander's advance with the remnants of his infantry. The liberation of the Greek cities of Asia Minor had been one of the reasons promoted by Alexander for his Persian campaign, and this achievement now lay before him. Taking advantage of his victory, Alexander marched towards the city of Sardis and its large Persian treasury. He then turned towards Ephesus which lay on the coast 60 miles (100 km) from Sardis. Ephesus was one of the most important cities on the coast of Asia Minor, but its Persian garrison had abandoned it in the face of Alexander's advance. In many of the cities of Asia Minor,

ABOVE **This is the view of the now-swampy location of the original Temple of Artemis at Ephesus,** burnt down by Herostratus the night that Alexander the Great was born. It was one of the Seven Wonders of the Ancient World.

factional politics had been part of their governance for some time, with factions sympathetic to Greece supporting democracy, and those supporting Persian control favoring oligarchy. This had been a particular issue at Ephesus, and when Alexander took control of the city he reinstated the previously exiled democratic leaders. In many of the cities in Asia Minor he did the same. Ephesus also had a special significance for Alexander as its famous Temple of Artemis had burned down on the night of his birth. He organized for revenue to be diverted to the temple for its ongoing reconstruction and eventual endowment.

It is easy to focus on the land-based activities of Alexander's army during this period. However, an ongoing issue for Alexander, which had not been dealt with at the battle of the Granicus, was the presence in the Aegean of a large Persian fleet. The Persian fleet caught up with Alexander when he marched to Miletus after the occupation of Ephesus. Alexander's fleet was only half the size of the Persian fleet which numbered approximately 400 ships. Fortunately for Alexander, the Macedonian fleet arrived at Miletus just before the Persians did. As a result, the Persian fleet was not able to land and could do little more than observe events from a distance. Alexander successfully captured Miletus and afterwards maintained a policy of denying the Persian fleet a landing place and not engaging with it as a way of neutralizing its power.

The next confrontation with what remained of the Persian forces in Asia Minor was at Halicarnassus. Memnon had based himself at Halicarnassus, and many of the Persian soldiers and Greek mercenaries who had evacuated the garrisons along the Asia Minor coast had fled to join him there. Memnon organized a strong defensive effort at Halicarnassus, and although Alexander succeeded in capturing much of the city, the garrison's successful withdrawal to two powerful citadels meant that the siege was ultimately unsuccessful. The siege also took a toll on Alexander's men, slowing down their progress along the coast and hinterland.

Alexander now made his way inland toward Phrygia and Cappadocia before turning south

BELOW **This scene from the Alexander Sarcophagus** shows the Macedonian cavalry dispatching Persian rivals. The defeat of the Persian army at Issus opened all of Syria and Egypt to Alexander's armies.

TYRE

Unlike most of the cities in Syria, the ancient Phoenician city of Tyre proved difficult for Alexander to capture. Tyre had been an important city for centuries, playing a leading role in the founding of trading colonies across the Mediterranean. It was also a strategic coastal base. Located on an island just off the coast of modern Lebanon, it was so well defended that a Babylonian siege lasting 13 years (585–572 BCE) was unsuccessful. After fierce fighting, Tyre refused to surrender to the Macedonians. Using, it is said, rubble from the abandoned mainland city, Alexander constructed a causeway to join the island to the mainland and finally captured Tyre. The view above looks east towards the mainland, and Alexander's mole, which joined Tyre to the mainland, can still be seen.

ABOVE **It took Alexander seven months** to breach Tyre's fortifications. The city was famous for its expensive dye, known as Tyrian purple.

toward Pamphylia and Cilicia. He was moving at a considerable pace to keep the enemy from consolidating and to engage the regrouping Persian army as soon as possible. With the Persian fleet and Memnon now more active in the northern Aegean, and even threatening Greece itself, this was a risky strategy. A number of important cities fell to Alexander during this part of the campaign, including Gordium, Ancyra, Termessus, Perga, Aspendus, and Side. At Gordium a famous event took place which has contributed to the legend of Alexander ever since. The Phrygian kings were based at Gordium, and their mythical founder had attached a wagon to a pole with a knot so intricate that no one had ever been able to untie it. It was claimed that whoever could undo the knot would become Lord of Asia. Alexander tried but failed, so he took his sword and slashed the knot in half. This was strongly symbolic of his approach to difficult problems.

The Second Confrontation at Issus

The campaigns from the Granicus to Cilicia represented 18 months of hard fighting and significant success, although some of the regions Alexander had conquered were taken so quickly that considerable resistance to Macedonian rule continued throughout the rest of Alexander's reign. Following the defeat at the Granicus, Darius III had retreated to Babylon, leaving what was left of his Greek mercenaries together with the Persian garrisons in the cities of Asia Minor to delay Alexander's advance for as long as possible. In Babylon, Darius raised a large army from across his empire and employed approximately 30,000 Greek mercenaries in preparation for the next major battle against the Macedonians. His strategy was to halt Alexander's invasion before he advanced into Syria. The two armies engaged at Issus (near modern Iskenderun, Turkey) in November 333 BCE. The battle was a rout, and the Macedonians dealt particularly harshly with the Greek mercenaries who fought for Persia. Darius was forced to flee for his life, even leaving his wife and family behind who were taken captive by Alexander. By all accounts, Alexander treated the king's family well. With Darius's army virtually destroyed, and the Persian king effectively a fugitive in his own empire, Alexander decided to continue campaigning down the Mediterranean coastline of Syria through most of 332 BCE. Unlike Asia Minor, many of the cities Alexander encountered in Syria surrendered easily and were offered friendly terms, with the exception of Tyre.

Egypt Falls to Alexander

Alexander now marched towards Egypt and met with some resistance at Gaza along the way. Towards the end of 332 BCE he arrived at Pelusium, the most significant fortification protecting Egypt, and prepared for a difficult campaign to capture the kingdom. On arrival at the fortress, however, Alexander was greeted by the Egyptians as a liberator; in fact throughout the kingdom he enjoyed a similar reception as the Persians had been deeply unpopular with the Egyptians. Alexander's army and fleet sailed up the

BELOW **Alexander** is depicted in this statue from Karnak in Pharaonic attitude and dress. The notion of king as living god appealed to him.

LEFT **Alexander is seen on this amphora** (*c.* 330–320 BCE) in helmet and body armor in battle against Darius III. Darius was a formidable opponent yet the Macedonian leader crushed his army three times: at the battles of the Granicus, Issus, and Gaugamela.

Nile River to the ancient capital of Memphis, where the Persian satrap, Mazaces, surrendered both the city and the treasury to Alexander without a fight.

The reception Alexander received in Egypt, and the timing of his arrival at the end of 332 BCE, made Egypt the ideal location for the king and his army to spend the winter. The impressive religious and historical past of Pharaonic Egypt seems to have considerably affected Alexander, and this was reflected in his approaches to rulership throughout the vast empire he would eventually conquer. Alexander may have been crowned King of Egypt but the sources do not mention it. At the time Alexander arrived, it had been tradition for almost 4,000 years in Egypt for the king to be treated as a living god, and this linked closely with Alexander's growing cultivation of the image of his own kingship as being in some way divine.

The Oracle of Ammon at Siwa

Alexander also visited the Oasis of Siwa in the harsh desert to the west of the Nile. The famous Oracle of Ammon was located there, and Alexander had cultivated close links with Zeus-Ammon. Ammon was equated by the Greeks with Zeus, father of the gods. It was common throughout Egypt and the ancient Near East for local deities to be allocated Greek equivalents to facilitate intercultural worship. When Alexander arrived at Siwa he was welcomed as the son of Ammon, and this further encouraged Alexander in the promotion of the idea that he was the son of Zeus. The ancient sources tell us that Alexander consulted the Oracle in private so we do not know the exact questions he put to it. Given his strategy when cutting the Gordian Knot nearly two years before, the Oracle was perhaps wise to give Alexander the answers he wanted. Alexander returned from Siwa via the Mediterranean coast where it is said that he personally supervised the planning of the city of Alexandria, a city that would emerge later as one of the most important in the whole of the Near East. Having spent six months in Egypt, Alexander and his army departed in April 331 BCE. The final destruction of Darius III and the capture of the heartland of the Persian king's empire now lay before the Macedonian king.

The Final Battle at Gaugamela

After Alexander left Egypt, he marched quickly across Syria, probably crossing the Euphrates at ancient Thapsacus. His primary aim was to

RIGHT **The Oasis of Siwa** lies in the Western Desert, 30 miles (48 km) east of the Libyan border. The oracle's proclamation of Alexander's divinity greatly assisted his claim to rule over all Asia.

confront Darius and the remnants of his army and force their surrender, and this was to take place in northern Mesopotamia. The area of ancient Mesopotamia currently lies in Iraq, northeastern Syria, and southeastern Turkey. The last great battle between Alexander and Darius III took place at Gaugamela in the vicinity of Arbela (modern Irbil) in northern Iraq, on October 1, 331 BCE. Because of the severity of the losses suffered at the Granicus and Issus, Darius was no longer able to rely on his Greek mercenaries who had previously been the strength of his infantry forces. He was now forced to rely on the cavalry and chariots with sharp scythes on their wheels, a new weapon devised to counter the formidable *sarissa*-armed phalanx of the Macedonians. Alexander planned the battle at Gaugamela more carefully than those at the Granicus and Issus. He waited four days before attacking with an army numbering 40,000 infantry and 7,000 cavalry. The discipline of Alexander's army was superior to that of the unwieldy Persian force which Darius was not able to position correctly to meet the Macedonian charge. The Persians were defeated, but Darius escaped.

Onwards to Babylon

The victorious Macedonian army now stood on the threshold of the Persian Empire. Babylon and Susa in southern Mesopotamia fell easily, as did the royal capital of Persepolis late in 331 BCE. The vast treasury at Persepolis gave Alexander the funds he needed in order for him to put his plan to advance further east into action over the next seven years. In just three years, Alexander and the Macedonian army had captured an enormous territory, and the implications this would have for the region would be profound for centuries to come.

ABOVE **Persepolis has been settled since the sixth century BCE.** Alexander looted the treasury and, some sources claim, set fire to the palace, the ruins of which can be seen above.

Entry into Babylon

Darius III fled to Babylon after his defeat by Alexander at Issus in November 333 BCE. After another crushing defeat at Gaugamela in 331 BCE, Mesopotamia lay open to the young conqueror.

The origins of Babylon can be traced back to *c.* 3000 BCE. The ancient city lies approximately 50 miles (80 km) south of Baghdad today. Babylon was one of the most important cities in the Persian Empire, and a city of great antiquity. Babylon rose to prominence as the capital of the Neo-Babylonian Empire, with King Nebuchadnezzar II (reigned 605–562 BCE) investing considerable time and resources into its enlargement. The city is thought to have boasted a population of 200,000 during this period, and Nebuchadnezzar is credited with constructing the famed Hanging Gardens of Babylon, considered to be one of the Seven Wonders of the Ancient World.

A Hero's Welcome

As Alexander made his way toward Babylon, he was met by Mazaeus, the Persian governor of the city, who had fought at Gaugamela with Darius and fled back to the city after the Persian army's defeat. Mazaeus surrendered Babylon, himself, and his family to Alexander and was treated well by the Macedonian king.

The majority of the population of Babylon welcomed Alexander when he arrived with his army. Indeed, as Alexander and his men approached the city they were greeted by cheering crowds assembled along the walls, and the road into the city was strewn with flowers. Silver altars had been erected in the streets and were laden with offerings to the gods in thanks for Alexander's arrival, and the commander of the citadel presented gifts to Alexander and his men. The famous Chaldaean astrologers and magi chanted hymns, accompanied by musicians singing praises to Alexander.

Babylon was a well-defended city, and its complete surrender to the Macedonians was of great benefit to Alexander as a prolonged siege would have taken a toll on his army. Alexander had proceeded with some caution, having surrounded himself with his bodyguard in case this reception was a trap. Alexander ordered the townspeople to enter the city before him and he entered in a chariot which he drove to Darius's

BELOW **The Striding Lion of Babylon frieze** of decorated tiles once lined the route from the Ishtar Gate to the Marduk Sanctuary (*c.* 600 BCE). This wall has since been reconstructed in Berlin.

palace in the center of the city. The opulence that lay before Alexander and his men, and the reception they received in one of the greatest cities of the ancient world, must have prompted them to reflect on how much they had achieved since their departure on an uncertain venture from far-flung Macedonia only a few years before.

The Riches of Babylon

The extent of Babylon's wealth did not become fully apparent to Alexander until he spent some time touring its streets and walls. Babylon's walls were said to be approximately 32 ft (10 m) thick, allowing two chariots to pass by each other along their tops. The walls were around 75 ft (23 m) in height and were claimed by ancient writers to cover a distance of 40 miles (64 km), which is clearly an exaggeration. An important feature of ancient Babylon at this time was cultivated fields within the city walls. These fields allowed the provisioning of the city in time of siege. In addition, the Euphrates flowed through the city, guaranteeing the water supply. The banks of the river had been retained to reduce the effects of flooding, which was a significant problem for all the cities on the alluvial plain of southern Mesopotamia.

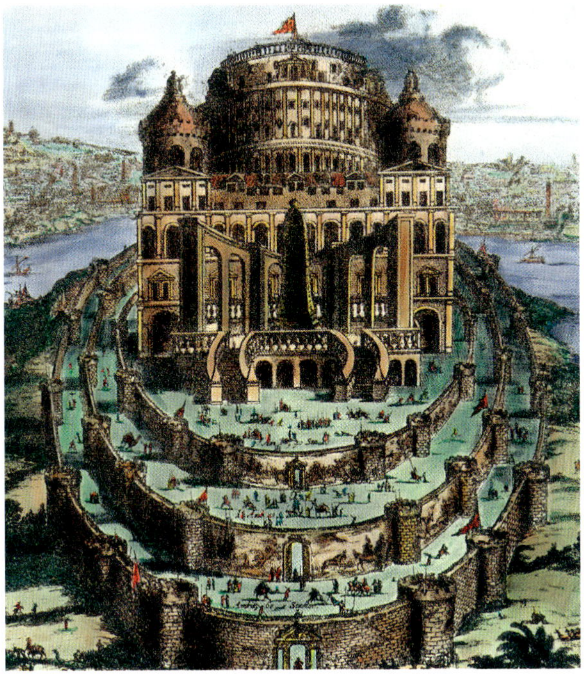

LEFT **Descriptions of the Hanging Gardens of Babylon** vary from source to source, but they were certainly impressive, prominent, and a triumph of irrigation, as this late seventeenth-century Dutch copper engraving illustrates.

The Hanging Gardens

A particularly important feature of Babylon was its citadel, which sat on an artificially constructed mound that was approximately 80 ft (24 m) in height. According to estimates by ancient writers, the citadel measured 2 miles (3 km) at its base and on one of the highest terraces were the famous hanging gardens. The citadel on which they were located was a massive architectural undertaking, and the gardens themselves contained fully grown trees claimed to be 50 ft (15 m) tall. In the flat landscape, the hanging gardens were an artificially created high place which dominated the whole of Babylon.

Alexander was so impressed by Babylon that he seems to have established it as a capital of his vast empire before his death at the city in 323 BCE. The king and his army stayed in Babylon for five weeks and, during this time, ancient writers complained that the army became lazy and indulged too much in the pleasures the city had to offer. Reinforcements from Macedonia arrived while Alexander was there and he appointed one of his Companions, Agathon, to command the citadel with 1,000 men. A special donative was distributed to the army, while Mazaeus, the Persian governor of Babylon who had surrendered the city before Alexander's arrival, was rewarded with the governorship of the satrapy of Babylonia. Alexander and his army left Babylon in December 331 BCE to campaign in Central Asia and India. They would not return to the city for almost seven years.

LEFT **Alexander enters Babylon in a chariot** pulled by a war elephant in this painting by Charles Le Brun. 1665. Alexander probably had his first encounter with these beasts at the Battle of Gaugamela.

The Eastern Conquests

Departing Babylon toward the end of 331 BCE, Alexander set out to capture Susa, another of the key centers of Achaemenid power. Like Babylon, Susa was a city of great antiquity and contained a Persian royal treasury.

In an incident similar to what had happened as he approached Babylon, the satrap of Susa met Alexander before he arrived at the city, informing him that the entire city had surrendered. Alexander and his army reached Susa 20 days after leaving Babylon. In the same manner as at Babylon, the governor of Susa met Alexander. The treasury at Susa contained 50,000 talents of silver, and a number of personal possessions of the Persian king were also found. Alexander discovered statues at Susa, which had been taken by the Persians from Athens when Xerxes invaded Greece 160 years before. He organized for their repatriation to Athens where they were placed on the Acropolis. This gesture underlined Alexander's claim of waging a just war in retribution for Persia's invasion of Greece.

Alexander Captures Persis

The territory and major cities of Persis itself (today, southwest Iran) were Alexander's next goal. The Achaemenid royal dynasty originated in the satrapy or kingdom of Persia centuries before, and Persis retained its importance in the ideology of the dynasty during this period. The two most important cities of Persis at this time were Persepolis and Pasargadae. When Alexander reached the Persian gates, a pass in the Zagros Mountains traditionally seen as the main entry point into Persis, he was confronted by the satrap of Persis, Ariobarzanes, with 40,000 infantry and 700 cavalry. With his characteristic brilliance, Alexander overcame the force of Ariobarzanes and marched towards Pasargadae and Persepolis. At Pasargadae, a city founded by the first great Achaemenid ruler, Cyrus, Alexander discovered a treasury of 6,000 talents. From there, he moved on to Persepolis where he captured another large imperial treasury. For the next month Alexander used the city as a base from which to subdue the whole of Persis.

BELOW **These desolate mountains form the western Hindu Kush.** Alexander and his army crossed them on their way into India.

The Death of Darius III

Despite the successes of the previous four years, Alexander was yet to capture Darius III. The Persian king had fled to Ecbatana in Media following his defeat at Gaugamela and, with Persis now subdued, Alexander set out to deal with Darius once and for all. In the spring of 330 BCE, Alexander began a pursuit of Darius so intense that it almost wore out his own army. He finally caught up with him at Hecatompylus on the southeast shore of the Caspian Sea just after the Persian king had been betrayed and murdered by Bessus, satrap of Bactria (modern Afghanistan). Alexander was clearly angered at Bessus's actions and sent Darius's body to Persepolis to be buried. Bessus responded by taking the traditional royal Persian title, King of Kings, and organized a revolt in Bactria and Central Asia. Alexander responded by invading Bactria. As more modern invaders of Afghanistan can confirm, this was a significant challenge as the area is mountainous and notorious for extreme weather conditions. Indeed, the invasion did not get under way until March 329 BCE due to the harsh conditions of winter. Bessus was unable to gain sufficient support from the Bactrian nobles which meant that he could

ABOVE **These gold plaques, found in Tajikistan,** are from the Oxus Treasure (*c.* 350 BCE). It is the most important collection of silver and gold to have survived from the Achaemenid period.

not raise an army large enough to challenge that of the Macedonians. Alexander took control of Bactria with barely a fight, while Bessus fled across the Oxus River into Sogdiana (modern Uzbekistan). Bessus was betrayed by his bodyguard and taken captive by Ptolemy who was then commander of Alexander's bodyguard. He would later become King of Egypt. Bessus was eventually executed in Ecbatana in Media.

Five years after leaving Macedonia, Alexander was in control of all of the territorial possessions once held by the Persian King of Kings. In the west these territories included Asia Minor, Syria, and Egypt, and in the east Mesopotamia, Persis, Media, and Bactria. Alexander was not prepared, however, to stop with the demise of Darius III and the subjugation of Bactria. This was in spite of the fact that his empire had become so huge that problems were emerging with its organization and administration. Alexander had attempted to balance the rule of the various regions he had conquered by appointing Persian satraps and Macedonian garrison commanders. The further Alexander went east, however, the more his Macedonian troops became concerned about his promotion of Persians to leading civil and military roles. They had also become concerned that his appearance was taking on more elements of Persian royalty (he had taken to wearing the diadem, white robe, and Persian sash) along with a growing reluctance to

THE ROYAL PALACE AT PERSEPOLIS TORCHED

Persepolis, as the city's Greek name indicates, was effectively the capital of Persis, and its capture by Alexander held great symbolism for him and his army. However, according to ancient writers, following an excessive drinking bout, Alexander torched the royal palace at Persepolis and forbade his soldiers to extinguish the flames. The palace was built mostly of cedar and it was completely destroyed. Alexander attempted to justify reducing the palace to ashes as revenge for the Persian destruction of Greek cities during Xerxes's invasion, but he was never able to escape criticism for his shameful and wanton destruction.

ABOVE **The western threshold to the Gate of All Nations** (a huge hall) in Persepolis is guarded by two lamassus—bulls with the heads of bearded men (*c.* 470 BCE).

campaign into the trackless wastes of Asia. They were probably unaware that they still had a further three and a half years (329-325 BCE) of fighting ahead of them which would take them as far east as India.

Alexander Campaigns in Central Asia

The campaigns into Central Asia were a consequence of the capture of Bactria in the summer of 329 BCE. Soon after Bessus was captured, a revolt against Alexander took place, not only in Bactria but also in neighboring Sogdiana where one of Bessus's main supporters, Spitamenes, had based himself. The rebellion in Bactria was dealt with swiftly, but Sogdiana took longer to subdue. Alexander's forces now arrived at cities which would later become famous for their roles in the overland silk trade from China including Maracanda (Samarkand) and Bukhara. In an attempt to capture Spitamenes, some small parties of Alexander's army ventured into areas as far north as the Aral Sea. Spitamenes was eventually murdered by his own supporters, but elements of resistance in Sogdiana held out and it took the Macedonians until late spring, 327 BCE to subdue the territory.

Alexander's Army Reaches India

Following the conquest of Sogdiana, Alexander returned to Bactria and planned his next significant military venture which was the conquest of India. The expedition to India was well organized as Alexander was aware that his army would be fighting in terrain different from that it had encountered previously. He retired a number of his Macedonian troops and added more Persian cavalry, a move which would later rankle with the Macedonian and Greek troops who

RIGHT **Alexander rode Bucephalus into all his major battles.** It was said the stallion was afraid of his own shadow but Alexander tamed him. This first-century BCE bronze statue is from Herculaneum, Italy.

accompanied him to India. The most significant battle Alexander waged in India was against the powerful Indian king, Porus, ruler of Paurava. This took place when Alexander and his army crossed the Hydaspes, a tributary of the great Indus River, in the area known today as the Punjab in northern India. Porus is represented by ancient writers in exotic and clearly exaggerated terms. He was said, for example, to be five cubits in height (approximately 7.5 feet).

The sizes of the armies of Porus and Alexander are variously estimated, and it is difficult to be conclusive on this issue. Conservative estimates of Alexander's army suggest 45,000 soldiers and cavalry; most of the sources suggest that the Indian force numbered around 30,000. Despite a clear determination, Porus was unable to stop Alexander crossing the Hydaspes. Once across the river, however, the Macedonian forces were confronted by the sight of 85 war elephants, the first time they had faced elephants used en masse to check a cavalry charge. In addition, the battle which followed was fought during a violent thunderstorm, with conditions in stark contrast to those in which the Macedonian army was used to fighting. Alexander's army eventually triumphed (albeit with significant casualties, some sources estimating 12,000 deaths), as a result of its superior cavalry and the ability of the *sarissa*-armed phalanx to stop the charge of the Indian war elephants. The Macedonian horses were terrified of the elephants, even their smell.

Perhaps the most tragic outcome of this battle for Alexander himself was the death of his horse Bucephalus, which, it is claimed, he had ridden into every battle since the crossing into Asia Minor eight years before. Alexander had broken in the horse when he was only ten years old and it had served him as a trusted companion ever since. Alexander founded the city of Bucephala on the east bank of the Hydaspes in honor of the horse. Although he had defeated the army of Porus convincingly, Alexander had great admiration for the Indian king and he allowed him to rule in a reduced satrapy.

The Army Revolts

Alexander now set his sights on crossing the Ganges River some 300 miles (400 km) further to the east, but his troops finally revolted at the Hyphasis (Beas) River in northern India. Alexander was furious, took to his tent for three days and would not speak to anyone. The soldiers were adamant in their refusal to continue, leaving the king little choice but to organize the army's return to Persia. In June 325 BCE, the army turned back to the Hydaspes River, where a fleet of approximately 2,000 river craft were arranged to transport them to the mouth of the Indus near Karachi in modern Pakistan. The return journey took them across the harsh Gedrosian Desert in a march of 60 days. Alexander underestimated the rigors of the desert, and, as a result, suffered many unnecessary casualties among the weary veterans. Some scholars believe that Alexander chose this route through the desert as a way of punishing the army for its mutiny at the Hyphasis.

In March 324 BCE, the army reached Susa and Persepolis, the cities it had captured six years before. Together with 80 of his Companions and generals, Alexander married wives from the Persian nobility. Some scholars see these marriages as indicative of how Alexander sought to govern his now enormous empire. To succeed in this he would need the Persian nobility. In spring, 324 BCE, Alexander left Susa and sailed up the Tigris to Babylon. Early in 323 BCE, he returned to Babylon and received embassies from all over the known world, congratulating him on his success. Alexander now began planning an invasion of the Arabian Peninsula, the most significant area of the Middle East unconquered by his army.

ABOVE **This detail shows the feet of one of the archers** from the glazed brick Frieze of the Archers (*c.* fifth century BCE) from Darius's Palace in Susa.

ABOVE **The figure on the left of this silver coin** (*c.* 324 BCE) is said to be Alexander driving away two war elephants.

Ai Khanoum

Plaque of Cybele

Cybele was often seen as a deification of Mother Earth. This early third-century BCE gilded silver ceremonial plaque was found at Ai Khanoum.

According to ancient sources on his life, Alexander is said to have founded 70 cities across the territory he conquered. The best-known example is Alexandria in Egypt, one of the most significant cities in the Hellenistic and Roman periods, and still an important city today. Many of the cities reputedly founded by Alexander took his name. However, there are some in the literature which took other names such as Bucephala, the city Alexander founded on the Indus River in honor of his beloved horse Bucephalus. These cities were usually centered on a Macedonian garrison and demobilized Macedonian and Greek soldiers whom Alexander retired at regular intervals during his campaigns. Not all of the cities established by Alexander grew into thriving metropolises and many are difficult to identify in modern times.

The extensive remains of a large city were discovered in the 1950sin northeastern Afghanistan at a site called Ai Khanoum. When the site was excavated in the 1960s and 1970s, a Greek city was revealed, which traced its origins either to Alexander's campaigns in Bactria or the period immediately following his death. The city is the most easterly yet discovered of all the Greek cities founded by Alexander and his successors. Ai Khanoum's location and remains meet all of the criteria which characterize an ancient Greek city, and its discovery is perhaps the most vivid indication of the remarkable phenomenon of Greek city establishment in the territories conquered by Alexander and his successors in the Middle East, Mesopotamia, and Central Asia.

Occident Meets Orient

These earrings were discovered at Ai Khanoum. There is some evidence indicating that the city's location enabled it to trade with India and China, as well as with the regions in the west.

Ai Khanoum is thought to be Alexandria on the Oxus but its ancient name has not been revealed in excavations at the site to date. It is located on the Oxus River at its confluence with the Kokcha River in the far north of Afghanistan, close to the modern border with Uzbekistan. Most of the evidence from the city dates to the third and second centuries BCE, so it was certainly an early foundation, and probably by Alexander himself.

From the Ruins of War

Many remains and artifacts from Ai Khanoum were destroyed during the Soviet invasion of Afghanistan in the late 1970s and 1980s. Work has started on restoring some of them.

Ai Khanoum had all the features of a Greek city, including a strongly defended wall circuit measuring approximately one and a half miles (3 km), a heavily fortified citadel in the middle of the city, a theater which could seat approximately 5,000 people, a large gymnasium, temples to Greek gods, and impressive private dwellings Some important architectural and artistic remains were excavated, including Corinthian-style columns, mosaics, and Greek sculpture. A number of Greek inscriptions from the third century BCE indicate the extent to which Greek culture at the city, early in its history, was strongly reflective of ongoing Classical Greek practices thousands of miles to the west in Greece itself.

Graeco-Bactrian Culture

Some evidence at Ai Khanoum indicates the influence of local culture and how this became more pronounced over time. Among the discoveries were a large palace which drew more on Persian architectural traditions, and a temple dedicated to Zeus, demonstrating strong elements of Mesopotamian religious architecture. There is evidence to show that when Bactria broke away from the Seleucid Empire in the second half of the third century BCE, Ai Khanoum became an important city to the kings of the new Graeco-Bactrian kingdom. Coins appear to have been minted at Ai Khanoum during much of its life and they signal the extent to which the city's culture became more syncretized with the local environment as its history progressed. Ai Khanoum is likely to have been the capital of one of the Graeco-Bactrian kings, Eucratides (reigned 170–145 BCE), but evidence from the site suggests that it was totally abandoned by 125 BCE. This was probably the result of significant invasions by nomads, known as the Yueh Chih, who devastated northern Bactria and eventually established the Kushan Empire in northern India during the following century.

Foreign Currency

A variety of coins from different regions have been discovered at Ai Khanoum. Some have Graeco-Bactrian provenance, and others even have depictions of Indian deities.

The Death of Alexander

As Alexander approached Babylon in the spring of 323 BCE, he is said to have received warnings from the Chaldaean astrologers that his life would be in danger if he entered the city.

Some scholars believe that the Babylonian priesthood may have discouraged Alexander from establishing himself in Babylon because of their concerns that the considerable revenues received by their temples would be diverted by Alexander for other purposes. Keenly conscious of the warnings of his death, Alexander entered the city from the east, which was used much less than the western approach. Numerous bad omens were reported as Alexander approached the city, such as ravens falling dead at his feet, and an ass kicking one of his tame lions to death.

The ancient sources represent Alexander paying more attention at this time to strange events and becoming concerned about potential plots against his life by close associates. The king began to surround himself with soothsayers and priests, and he sacrificed to the gods even more regularly than he had before. Alexander also indulged increasingly in heavy drinking bouts. He had always drunk heavily, but in Babylon it became even more noticeable. While the sources tend to highlight and perhaps exaggerate aspects of Alexander's behavior pointing to his death, there is a sense that he was becoming more and more frustrated by the fact that his eastern campaigns were effectively over. He spent some of this time in Babylon planning a military expedition into the Arabian Peninsula but it is uncertain as to how realistic these plans were.

BELOW **This gold drinking cup (*c.* 200 BCE) from Thrace,** in the shape of a woman's head, is an excellent example of Hellenistic metalworking.

Conflicting Versions of Alexander's Death

A number of differing accounts exist as to how Alexander died. On the basis of the four main surviving accounts, which all date from the Roman period, there were three versions of the cause and progression of the illness. In one version Alexander drank so much wine that he simply collapsed and died. In another, which is more accepted in modern scholarship, Alexander engaged in a particularly heavy drinking bout with the commander of his fleet, Nearchus, on an evening late in May. He drank throughout that evening and the next day, and by the evening had started to develop a fever. The fever grew worse, and on the evening of June 2, he slept in the bathroom in an effort to reduce it. In the following days, the fever increased, and he took to the bathroom where he had ready access to cool water. On June 9, Alexander was so unwell that he was unable to sacrifice without assistance, and his Companions and senior officers spent the evening outside the palace waiting for news of his condition. The day after, he was taken to the royal palace on the other side of the Euphrates, and by the evening of June 11, he was unable to speak. On receiving this news, the Macedonian commanders and regular soldiers demanded to see him and finally broke into the palace to witness their king not far from death. Each one of them filed past Alexander as he lay bedridden and virtually motionless. Two days later, towards the evening of June 13, 323 BCE, Alexander died. This account is recorded in Plutarch, who claimed that it was taken verbatim from the Royal Journals, but anachronistic

ABOVE **The marble Alexander Sarcophagus** (*c.* 320–300 BCE, from Sidon, now in Istanbul) is adorned with scenes of Macedonians and Persians in battle.

LEFT **Alexander on his deathbed** is depicted surrounded by grieving generals in this fourteenth-century copy of a fifth-century Armenian manuscript, now in Venice.

elements of the journals have caused some modern scholars to doubt their authenticity and veracity.

Was He Poisoned?

There is a third version, often popular in the modern imagination, which claimed that Alexander was poisoned. According to Plutarch, stories about Alexander's poisoning surfaced some five years after his death, and his mother, Olympias, is said to have exacted harsh vengeance against those accused of being implicated. Alexander's chief cup-bearer, Iolas, was a son of Antipater who was ruling as Alexander's representative in Macedonia. Relations between Alexander and Antipater were said to have become very strained in the last months of Alexander's life, and eventually the claim was made that Antipater had conspired with his son, Iolas, to murder Alexander by poisoning his wine. Stories of conspiracy, poisoning, and intrigue are always attractive, but there is little evidence that Alexander was the victim of such a plot. His excessive drinking, and regular exposure to water- and food-borne pathogens in southern Mesopotamia are more likely causes of his death than a conspiracy conducted over 1,500 miles (2,400 km).

The untimely nature of Alexander's death is, however, underlined by the fact that he had no practical succession plan in place at the time of his death. His Bactrian wife, Roxane, whom he had married four years earlier, was pregnant with a child who would later rule for a brief time as Alexander IV. Alexander's mentally incapacitated half brother, Philip Arrhidaeus, ruled jointly with Alexander's infant son, but neither had any hope of survival in the cut-throat world of wars, deceit, and succession which marked the years following Alexander's death.

The Diadochoi

The years following the death of Alexander the Great in 323 BCE were characterized by treachery and conflict. Competition for control of his vast empire was fierce as his newborn heir could not rule unassisted. It is said that in the days before his death Alexander was asked to whom he was leaving his empire. He replied "the strongest." This would prove to be prophetic.

BELOW **Lysimachus came to rule Thrace and western parts of Asia Minor** by aggression and politicking. This marble bust (*c.* 300 BCE) is from the Archaeological Museum in Naples, Italy.

Most of the territory Alexander conquered was eventually ruled by monarchies established by his senior military commanders. These would be known in Greek as the *diadochoi* which means "successors", and it would take approximately 50 years for the division of the empire between them to be complete. Immediately after Alexander's death, Perdiccas, one of Alexander's generals, acted as the overall regent of the empire, with others established as viceroys or satraps. Antipater had been Alexander's viceroy in Macedonia and remained so; Antigonus, a senior military commander, was satrap of Phrygia and the western parts of Asia Minor; Ptolemy, companion and bodyguard of Alexander, was made satrap in Egypt; and Lysimachus became satrap of Thrace.

It did not take long for an alliance to form against Perdiccas, and he was killed in 321 BCE. An agreement was reached at Triparadeisos in Syria in the same year that saw Antipater as regent in Macedonia for Philip III Arrhidaeus (Alexander's half-brother) and Alexander IV (Alexander's son by Roxane) who were made joint kings. Antigonus was given the command over Asia; Seleucus, who had been the commander of Alexander's *Hypaspists* (shield-bearers or elite infantry unit) was given control of Babylon and the eastern territories; Ptolemy was confirmed in Egypt; and Lysimachus in Thrace.

In Macedonia, Antipater died in 319 BCE and was succeeded by his son Cassander in 317 BCE. In the same year, Alexander's mother Olympias raised an army and attacked Cassander. She had her stepson Philip III killed in the process, but Cassander defeated her in 316 BCE and she was later executed. In the meantime, Antigonus ejected Seleucus from Babylon which drew a response from the main power brokers demanding his reinstatement. Seleucus fled to Ptolemy in Egypt who assisted him in regaining Babylonia in 312 BCE. Seleucus did not take the title of king for some years, but he would mark the beginning of the Seleucid Empire and dynasty from 312 BCE which inaugurated the most widely used dating system in the Hellenistic and Roman Near East. Following more conflict, a treaty was agreed upon in 311 BCE which confirmed Cassander's rule over Greece and Macedonia, Ptolemy's rule in Egypt, Antigonus's control over Asia Minor and Syria, Seleucus in the eastern territories, and Lysimachus in Thrace. Cassander murdered Alexander IV in 310 BCE. The new order was beginning to take shape, but there were many years of fighting ahead.

Antigonus Defeated

An important development took place in 306 BCE which demonstrated the longer-term aims of Alexander's successors. Demetrius, the son of Antigonus, defeated Ptolemy in a sea battle off the coast of Cyprus which resulted in the local population hailing both father and son as kings.

ABOVE **Demetrius Poliorcetes (337–288 BCE),** seen here on a silver tetradrachm coin, crushed Ptolemy's naval forces in the Battle of Salamis (Cyprus) in 306 BCE.

LEFT **Olympias of Molossia** fought for the rights of her grandson, Alexander IV, after the death of Alexander the Great. This gold medallion (*c.* 300 BCE) is part of the Aboukir treasure.

Not surprisingly, Cassander, Ptolemy, Lysimachus, and Seleucus took the title soon after. This development, which was probably carefully stage-managed by Antigonus, is a further indication of his ambition to re-form Alexander's empire under his own rule. At this time Antigonus controlled Asia Minor and Syria, and after 306 BCE he controlled most of the Aegean. He now aimed to capture Greece and Macedonia, and his actions ten years earlier had demonstrated his plans to take control of the eastern territories from Seleucus. In 301 BCE, however, at the battle of Ipsus in Phrygia, all of his designs came to an end. The combined forces of Cassander, Lysimachus, and Seleucus defeated the Antigonid army, and Antigonus himself was killed at the age of 81. Antigonus's territory was divided up: Lysimachus took part of Asia Minor; Seleucus took Syria; and Ptolemy gained Palestine and southeastern Asia Minor. Demetrius survived Ipsus and was able to retain some of the possessions his father had held in south coastal Anatolia.

The Antigonids Prevail in Macedonia

In 298 BCE, Cassander died, and Demetrius saw this as an opportunity to begin restoring the empire formerly held by his father. In 294 BCE, he became king of Macedonia and followed this up with an attempt to regain the territory his father had held in Syria. However, his dream of restoring his father's empire was not to be realized, for he was captured by Seleucus in 288 BCE. Lysimachus, who had remained in control of Thrace since 321 BCE now took control of Macedonia and western Asia Minor. In 281 BCE, however, he was killed in battle against Seleucus at Corupedion. Seleucus himself was assassinated in the same year, when he sought the Macedonian throne. Finally, in 277 BCE Antigonus II Gonatus, the son of Demetrius and grandson of Antigonus, took control of Macedonia, and from this time Macedonia and Greece were ruled by the Antigonids. The Antigonid dynasty would remain in power until the Romans captured Macedonia and northern Greece following the battle of Pydna in 167 BCE.

The Seleucid Empire

The Seleucid Empire was the largest of the successor kingdoms to emerge from the intense period of conflict over Alexander's empire following his death in 323 BCE. Like the other successor kings, the Seleucids established a dynasty that would last for centuries, but the empire was slow to take shape as the fighting between Alexander's successors continued.

Seleucus came from a noble background in Macedonia, and had been commander of the *Hypaspists*, an elite infantry fighting force, during Alexander's campaigns. The fortunes of the Seleucids fluctuated throughout the third century BCE, and by the last decades of that century the empire faced some major problems. The arrival of the Romans in the eastern Mediterranean, together with the rise of the Parthians in eastern Iran, eventually saw the demise of the Seleucid Empire in the middle of the first century BCE. At the time Seleucus established the empire, it embraced a wide variety of cultures, and over the course of its existence numerous elements of syncretism between Greek, Levantine, and Mesopotamian cultures are observable.

FOUNDATION OF CITIES BY SELEUCUS I

Seleucus founded many cities and fortifications in an attempt to establish a network of Greek centers linking together his vast empire. Many of these were named after himself, including Seleucia on the Tigris near Babylon, which was the most important city in the eastern portion of the Seleucid Empire. He also named cities after his father Antiochus, including Antioch on the Orontes in northern Syria (modern Turkey), which was the most important city in the western part of the empire. Apamea in the middle of the Orontes Valley was one of the cities named after his Persian wife. The ruins can be seen today near Hama in northern Syria.

ABOVE **This view of Apamea** shows the stretch of the Roman cardo maximus *c.* 150 CE. The city was built to guard the major highway from the coast at Antioch into the interior.

Foundation of the Seleucid Empire

The Seleucid Empire was officially founded when Seleucus established himself in Babylon at the head of an empire comprising most of the Iranian, Central Asian, and Indian possessions of Alexander the Great. Seleucus established a new dating system, which marked the foundation of his empire in Babylon in 312–311 BCE, although he did not take the title of king until all other successors did in 306 BCE. The Seleucid dating system was used widely in the Hellenistic world afterwards, and was still in use well into the Islamic period.

In 304 BCE, Seleucus decided to consolidate his empire. He turned his focus west, giving up his Indian possessions in a deal with the Mauryan ruler, Chandragupta. Chandragupta gave Seleucus 500 war elephants in exchange for his Indian possessions. These elephants were a considerable asset to Seleucus as he sought to expand and consolidate his empire further west. (They were used to protect against cavalry attack.) Following the defeat of Antigonus by Seleucus and Lysimachus at Ipsus in 301 BCE, Seleucus controlled territory stretching from the Aegean coastline in the west to Afghanistan in the east. His ambition to extend his empire further to the west continued throughout his reign, and in 281 BCE he was victorious in battle over Lysimachus, taking the latter's possessions in western Asia Minor and threatening to cross into Thrace and Greece. His European ambitions were cut short, however, when he was assassinated.

Seleucus's queen was Apama, the Persian wife he had taken at Susa when Alexander, his officers

LEFT **Mercenaries, such as this one on the funeral stele of Dioscorides of Balboura (c. 200 BCE),** were recruited by Seleucus and other Diadochoi to fight in their internecine wars.

and Companions all took Persian wives following the return of the Macedonian army from India in 324 BCE. Most of these marriages were repudiated after Alexander's death, but the marriage of Seleucus and Apama was an exception. Despite this Persian link, the dynasty which Seleucus established was Greek in all its essentials, as was that established by Ptolemy in Egypt. There was no intermarriage with local ruling classes, marking a sharp point of difference from their Roman successors.

The Successors of Seleucus

In an effort to ensure the ongoing survival of a Seleucid dynasty, Seleucus elevated his son Antiochus to the position of coruler in 292 BCE. As a stark indication of his desire to ensure dynastic continuity, Seleucus also gave his young wife Stratonice (Apama had died in 300 BCE) to Antiochus prior to his death in 281 BCE. Antiochus I (reigned 281–261 BCE) faced a difficult challenge in maintaining the empire established by his father. He engaged in two wars with Ptolemy II over the disputed territories of southern Syria and Palestine, and by the end of his reign the situation in Central Asia and Bactria (Afghanistan) was also becoming difficult. Toward the end of the reign of Antiochus II (reigned 261–246 BCE) the Seleucids faced an invasion by Celtic tribesmen from Central Europe, while the satrapies of Bactria and Parthia broke away, initially to govern themselves within the empire, ultimately to win their independence under native rulers. When Seleucus II succeeded his father in 246 BCE, he not only faced the

BELOW **The soldier Menas (dedicated on this tombstone from Nikaia in Turkey),** was killed at Corupedion in 281 BCE. The forces of the two elderly Diadochoi, Lysimachus and Seleucus, met head-on here and Lysimachus was killed.

ABOVE **Antiochus III inherited a fractured state.** He formed alliances, but he underestimated the power of the Romans, which was his downfall. This replica of a marble bust (*c.* 250 BCE) is in the Louvre, France.

recent loss of Bactria and Parthia, but was also confronted with breakaway kingdoms in Asia Minor, including Pergamum. There were ongoing problems with the Gauls who were eventually established in a self-governing province in central upland Anatolia later to be known as Galatia (land of Gauls). Seleucus II was defeated by Ptolemy III in the Third Syrian War (246-241 BCE) and faced a civil war against his brother Antiochus Hierax who seized Anatolia.

The problems for the Seleucids continued through the reign of Seleucus III (reigned 245–223 BCE), and following his assassination Antiochus III came to power at the age of 19. He ruled for almost 40 years, and in the first half of his reign succeeded in reversing some of the earlier losses of the Seleucid Empire in the east. However, he also suffered a sharp and unexpected defeat at the hands of Ptolemy IV at Raphia in south coastal Palestine in 217 BCE. In the decade following the battle of Raphia, however, Antiochus attempted to deal with the Bactrian and Parthian rebellions in the east and was partially successful in doing so. He even made an expedition to India in an effort to reassert some influence there. On his return west in 205 BCE, Antiochus began planning the final defeat of the Ptolemies in southern Syria.

RIGHT **Antiochus IV, seen here on a tetradrachm coin** (*c.* 175 BCE from the Israel Museum in Jerusalem), was determined to Hellenize all the eastern elements of his kingdom to strengthen it against Rome. He fell foul of Jewish particularism.

At the battle of Panion in 200 BCE he scored a decisive victory over them, and the Seleucids took control of coastal and southern Syria permanently. For these reasons he earned the epithet "Megas" which means "the Great."

Rome and the Seleucids

Antiochus antagonized Rome on two fronts and this would prove a serious problem for the Seleucid Empire over time. After the Roman forces of Scipio Africanus defeated Hannibal at Zama in 202 BCE Antiochus gave Hannibal asylum. In addition, he took the opportunity to invade Greece following the Roman defeat of Philip V of Macedonia in 197 BCE. In 191 BCE Antiochus lost a major battle against Rome at Thermopylae in Greece, and in the following year a more crushing defeat at Magnesia in western Anatolia. In 188 BCE, he was forced to sign the Treaty of Apamea. By the terms of this treaty he had to pay steep financial penalties to Rome and send one of his sons as a hostage to Rome. In order to pay these penalties he taxed his subjects heavily. Symbolic in some ways of Antiochus's financial problems was his death while attempting to seize bullion from the Marduk temple in Babylon in June 187 BCE. Seleucus IV then ruled until 175 BCE and much of his reign was spent attempting to pay the crippling indemnity.

Antiochus IV and the Jews

The reign of Antiochus IV began after the death of Seleucus IV in 164 BCE and it is significant for his confrontation with Rome, and his dealings with Jerusalem.

From 170–168 BCE, the Seleucids were challenged by the Ptolemies for control of southern Syria. After defeating Ptolemy VI at Pelusium in 169 BCE, Antiochus plundered the Temple in Jerusalem on his return to Syria. He further antagonized the Jewish populations when, subsequent to suppressing a minor revolt by the High Priest Jason, he established a Greek garrison in the holy city of Jerusalem for the first time. Later in that year, he sponsored the construction of a pagan altar in the Temple which was referred to as the Abomination of Desolation by the Jews.

Not all Jews reacted negatively to Antiochus IV's involvement in Jerusalem. Some saw it as a way of better integrating Jewish society within the Hellenistic Greek world. One group, however, opposed all compromise with Greek culture. In 167–166 BCE the Maccabean revolt flared into life against all forms of Seleucid control. The revolutionaries were led by Judas Maccabeus and they became so intent on their revolt that Antiochus reversed his attempts at religious reform in Jerusalem.

Conflict between Antiochus IV and Rome was the result of the renewed fighting over southern Syria and Palestine with the Ptolemies. Rome's power had become so strong that in 170 BCE, Antiochus IV and Ptolemy VI sent separate embassies to the Romans claiming the right to control southern Syria and Palestine. Because Rome was conducting a significant campaign against the Macedonians at this stage, it refused to become involved. In October 170 BCE, Antiochus undertook a bold invasion of Egypt and even captured Pelusium, the main fortress guarding Egypt at this time. He continued to take advantage of Rome's preoccupation in Greece, and inflicted more losses on Ptolemy in 169 BCE. When the Egyptians appealed to Rome for assistance, Antiochus invaded again in 168 BCE but Rome was now able to provide support to Egypt as it had that summer successfully defeated the Macedonians.

ABOVE **Antiochus IV receives representatives from the Hebrew people** in this eleventh-century Latin manuscript from the Book of Maccabees from Abbaye St Vaast. It is now in the Bibliothèque Municipale in Arras, France.

The Empire Declines

After the death of Antiochus IV in 164 BCE, the Seleucid Empire entered a decline from which it would never recover. The arrival of Rome and the growing power of Parthia in the east were to spell the eventual demise of the kingdom. A series of civil wars was symbolic of this decline, and in 139 BCE, Demetrius II was captured in battle against the Parthians. Iran and most of eastern Mesopotamia were now lost to the Parthians, and by 129 BCE, the Seleucids had lost Babylonia when the Parthians captured Babylon itself.

The Seleucid Empire also faced major problems in the west. In 83 BCE Tigranes, the king of Armenia, invaded Syria. The Romans defeated both Tigranes and his father-in-law, Mithridates, king of Pontus in north coastal Anatolia, in 69 BCE and restored a small Seleucid kingdom under Antiochus XIII which consisted of little more than Antioch and its immediate surrounds. Pompey arrived in the east in 66 BCE and eventually abolished the Seleucid kingdom in 63 BCE. In its place he established the Roman province of Syria. This was based on all former Seleucid lands west of the Euphrates River then under some form of Greek control.

The Ptolemaic Empire

After the wars between Alexander's successors, Ptolemy I established a dynasty that ruled over Egypt for nearly three centuries. During the Ptolemaic period a mix of Egyptian and Greek cultures emerged. However, the system of government was tightly controlled by a Graeco-Macedonian elite.

In any consideration of the history of Ptolemaic rule it is important to understand the nature of the land of Egypt and the overwhelming importance of the Nile River. The river's source lies to the south in the mountains of far-off Ethiopia, the fabled land of Punt. From there it flows north to the Mediterranean. The Nile covers a distance of approximately 4,000 miles (6,500 km), making it one of the longest rivers on earth. The river breaks up, in the vicinity of ancient Memphis, into a number of smaller branches which form the Nile Delta. This is the most fertile area in Egypt and was important for farming in antiquity. Irrigation was practiced along considerable stretches of the Nile, making the irrigated floodplain the agricultural heartland of the kingdom. In the desert west of the Nile were a number of oases, which supported significant populations and served as important links in trade with territories further to the west in North Africa.

ABOVE **Ptolemy I Soter,** seen here on a silver tetradrachm coin, was one of Alexander's most trusted generals. His aim was to hold Egypt and, where possible, establish a buffer of Asiatic territory to secure its borders.

The Legacy of Ptolemy

Ptolemy I Soter (Savior) (reigned 323–285 BCE) emerged as one of the main rulers of what remained of Alexander's empire after two decades of fierce fighting following Alexander's death. Ptolemy also held territory in southern Syria, which the Seleucids would fight to gain control over during the following century. As with all of the successors, Ptolemy cultivated his image as the legitimate successor of Alexander. He did this by inventing an ancestral link to Alexander, which was a myth, and he also took the calculated risk of seizing Alexander's coffin on its way back to Macedonia. Ptolemy had the body placed in an enormous funerary monument at Alexandria, and he used this to his advantage as an indication of Alexander's approval of his kingship in Egypt.

Ptolemy established a hereditary dynasty that lasted for almost 300 years. He was careful to have his son, Ptolemy II, acknowledged as king and co-regent two years before his death in 283 BCE. Ptolemy II was then married to Arsinoe, his sister, as an indication of the tight control of the imperial dynasty in Egypt. Ptolemy II Philadelphus ruled until 246 BCE and during his

THE CITY OF ALEXANDRIA

Particularly significant to Egypt under the Ptolemies was the city of Alexandria, which was the main center of administration. It was founded by Alexander after he took control of Egypt at the end of 332 BCE, but it was during the reigns of the early Ptolemies that the city really developed. Ptolemy I encouraged elites from mainland Greece to relocate to Alexandria, and as a result of major investment under Ptolemy II Philadelphus (reigned 285–246 BCE), the city emerged as one of the most important in Graeco-Roman antiquity. Over time, the cultural impact of Alexandria on Egypt and the whole of the Near East was undeniable.

reign he consolidated his father's steps to ensure the success of the dynasty in Egypt.

A noteworthy feature of the reigns of both Ptolemy I and Ptolemy II was the successful relationship between the Macedonians and the Egyptian temple priesthood, the effective rulers of much of the land. The temples were vital to Egypt's economy as they controlled large amounts of land. They were not only important for food production but also to the provision of taxation revenue to the Egyptian kings.

Conflict with the Seleucid Empire

In the third century BCE, one of the key issues for Ptolemaic Egypt was the conflict with the Seleucid Empire which held territories in Syria. In the upshot of the final phase of wars between the Diadochoi, Ptolemy seized much of the southern Levant, and added many of the islands in the Aegean Sea. In addition, he was active in southeast Asia Minor. When Ptolemy II endeavored to expand these interests, the Seleucids went to war with Egypt in what became known as the First Syrian War (274–271 BCE). The outcome of this war was inconclusive. However, it marked the beginning of almost a century of armed conflict between these two powers.

The Second Syrian War (261–253 BCE) was also fought over Ptolemaic possessions in Asia Minor, but it is better known for the terms of the peace agreement that followed it. The terms of this agreement, struck between Ptolemy II and the Seleucid king Antiochus II, provided that Ptolemy's daughter, Berenike, be given in marriage to Antiochus. The marriage eventually broke down, which became one of the causes of the Third Syrian War between the Ptolemies and Seleucids. Ptolemy II and Antiochus II both died in 246 BCE, generating a serious succession crisis

LEFT **Ptolemy II and his full sister Arsinoe** married but were childless. This cameo (*c.* 278 BCE) is from the Kunsthistorisches Museum, Vienna, Austria.

LEFT **The Nile River is** central to all activity—agricultural, political, and social—in Egypt, and remains its lifeblood to this day.

in the Seleucid Empire of which the Ptolemies took advantage by invading Syria. Antiochus II and Berenike had produced a son. However, they were estranged and Antiochus had a son, Seleucus II, by another marriage, and he was promoted as the heir to the Seleucid throne. The new Ptolemaic King, Ptolemy III, invaded the Seleucid Empire to save his sister, Berenike, and to have her son and his nephew proclaimed king. The Third Syrian War lasted from 246 to 241 BCE, and at one stage Ptolemy III penetrated deep into the heartlands of the Seleucid kingdom, reputedly as far as Babylon. Despite this territorial success, Ptolemy was unable to save his sister or his nephew, and they were both murdered soon after the invasion began.

Ptolemy IV (reigned 221–205 BCE) fought another round of these wars, when his newly reconstituted army somewhat unexpectedly defeated the very able Antiochus III in a major battle at Raphia in 217 BCE. Ptolemy IV was victorious, mostly as a result of the skill of native Egyptian forces. It seems, however, that their newly discovered importance caused them to revolt, and for the next 25 years much of upper Egypt was in revolutionary turmoil. During the reign of Ptolemy V (204–180 BCE) Egypt lost its possessions in Asia Minor and the Aegean Sea, while the defeat of the Egyptians at the battle of Panion in Palestine in 200 BCE heralded the end of Ptolemaic ambitions in Syria. The early decades of the second century BCE marked the beginning of Rome's rise to power in the eastern Mediterranean.

The Relationship with Rome

Rome became increasingly involved in the politics of the Hellenistic kingdoms and was focussed on curtailing the ambitions of the

BELOW **Ptolemy XV, (Caesar's son Caesarion),** stands on the right, his mother, Cleopatra, behind him, offering incense to the Goddess Hathor. Octavian had him murdered at age 14 in 31 BCE.

Seleucid and Macedonian Empires, Ptolemaic Egypt's greatest threats. During Rome's darkest hours in the Second Punic War when the Carthaginian general Hannibal threatened the city of Rome itself, the Seleucids and the Macedonians had supported the Carthaginians. Following the defeat of Hannibal in 202 BCE, Rome turned to deal with the Seleucids and Macedonians, using the pretext of protecting Egypt as a means of curtailing Seleucid power.

The Line in the Sand

The most famous confrontation between Rome and the Seleucids over Egypt came in 170 BCE when the Seleucid king, Antiochus IV, invaded Egypt and overthrew Ptolemy VI, replacing him with his younger brother, Ptolemy VIII. Rome responded by sending Gaius Popilius Laenas to deal with the situation. Laenas requested Antiochus to leave Egypt, and the Seleucid king replied that he would consider the request. Laenas responded by using his sword to draw a circle in the sand around Antiochus and informed him that he must give his answer before stepping out of the circle. Antiochus prudently withdrew.

Because Rome had assisted the Ptolemaic dynasty against the Seleucids, it now had a pretext for more direct involvement in Egypt's politics. As a result of Antiochus's withdrawal, Ptolemy VI and Ptolemy VIII reached an agreement to jointly rule over Egypt. This became problematic, and Rome used it to increase its power and influence in Egypt. Ptolemy VI died in 145 BCE and was succeeded by his son Ptolemy VII who was soon overthrown by Ptolemy VIII. The latter then ruled in Egypt as a tyrant under the watchful eye of Rome until his death in 116 BCE. The instability and wrangling had taken its toll, and over the next 60 years a succession of Ptolemaic rulers assumed the throne at young ages and did not survive long. This worked in Rome's favor, and by the time Ptolemy XIII and his sister Cleopatra VII came to power jointly in 51 BCE, Rome was a powerful force in the kingdom.

ABOVE **In the naval Battle of Actium** (September 2, 31 BCE), shown here in a frieze from the House of Vettii in Pompeii, Italy, Mark Antony lost, and forfeited all authority when he abandoned his fleet, fleeing after a prudent Cleopatra.

Cleopatra and Her Roman Liaisons

The story of Cleopatra and her relationships with two of Rome's most powerful generals is a famous one. Following Julius Caesar's arrival in Alexandria in 48 BCE, he and Cleopatra embarked on a relationship which resulted in the birth of a son, Caesarion. In 45 BCE Cleopatra and Caesarion moved to Rome to live in a palace built for them by Julius Caesar. Soon after Caesar's death, Octavian (Caesar's adopted heir, later Augustus) and Mark Antony divided the Roman realm in two, with Antony controlling the eastern half. Cleopatra began a liaison with Antony in the early 30s BCE, which came to spell doom for her and for the rule of the Ptolemies in Egypt. In the civil war which took place between Antony and Octavian, Antony and Cleopatra lost a major naval engagement at Actium and both committed suicide. The wealth of Egypt was claimed as personal possession by Octavian. No Roman (not even a senator) could enter the country without the permission of Octavian.

The riches of Egypt, such as gold and grain, were to serve Octavian well in his struggle to consolidate his hold over Rome, ushering in the age of empire.

LEFT **Victorious at Actium, Octavian** consolidated his power in Rome and later became the first Roman Emperor—Augustus. This marble bust (*c.* CE 75) is from the Roman theater in Arles, France.

Hellenic States

The city-states of Greece sought to maintain a level of independence during the period of the Hellenistic kingdoms, but were often pawns in the machinations of the larger players in the Hellenistic world. They were regularly the source of dispute between Macedonia and Ptolemaic Egypt, and sometimes attempted to play the two powers off against each other.

Macedonia remained a significant factor in the history of the city-states of Greece in the third and second centuries BCE. Antipater had ruled Macedonia in Alexander's absence. After the death of Antipater, his son Cassander took control in 317–316 BCE and ruled until his death in 298 BCE. Following a period of internecine warfare and several assassinations, Antigonus II Gonatus, grandson of the Antigonus who briefly threatened all of the first-generation Diadochoi, finally secured power in 276 BCE. His dynasty remained in power in Macedonia until unseated by the Romans in 167 BCE. One of the ways the Greek cities sought to counter the power of Macedonia was by forming regional alliances or leagues. The Achaean League would emerge as the most important unifying force in southern and central Greece by the end of the third century BCE. The iconic city of Athens maintained a separate status during this period and, because of its identification with the "Golden Age" of Greece, it was able to trade on past glories to remain aloof from the struggles of the third and second centuries BCE.

Difficulties for Athens

The predicament that Athens and many of the Greek cities found themselves in was demonstrated early when Cassander in Macedonia limited the power of the democratic governments in a number of cities, including Athens. Ptolemy attempted to strengthen his position against Macedonia in 308 BCE, by intervening on behalf of the Greek city-states against Cassander. In 307 BCE, another of the Diadochoi, Antigonus, sent his son Demetrius Poliorcetes to "liberate" Athens by removing the Macedonian garrison. Following the defeat of Ptolemy I by Demetrius in 306 BCE at Salamis, and the defeat of Cassander in 304 BCE, Demetrius also "liberated" the city-states of Chalcis, Corinth, and Sicyon. While Demetrius and Antigonus received honours from the Athenians, including gold statues of themselves erected in the Agora, the Greek city-states continued to seek true freedom from the magnates and dynasts who regularly intervened in their politics. The precarious nature of their "liberation" by power brokers such as Demetrius was demonstrated in 301 BCE when Antigonus and Demetrius were defeated at the Battle of Ipsus. Cassander now ruthlessly reinstated Macedonian authority at Athens, but, following his death in 297 BCE, Demetrius put the city under siege and removed the Macedonians again.

The city-states of Greece continued to face difficulties throughout the third century BCE. With Demetrius out of the picture after 287 BCE, Macedonia reestablished control over many key centers, although Ptolemaic Egypt began to seek influence via an ever-strengthening naval presence in Aegean waters. The emergence of Antigonus II Gonatus in control of Macedonia in 276 BCE resulted in Macedonia consolidating its power over the cities of Greece. By 272 BCE, Gonatus had

BELOW **Off Salamis** in Cyprus in 306 BCE, Demetrius, son of Antigonus, defeated Ptolemy's navy. This victory saw Antigonus and Demetrius hailed as kings, which led other Diadochoi to adopt royal titles.

garrisons in Thessaly, Euboia, Piraeus, Corinth, Argos, and Megara. An alliance of Athens and a number of Peloponnesian cities, backed by Ptolemy II, went to war with Macedonia in 267 BCE in an attempt to free the Greek cities under his rule. The war was not successful and Athens itself came under Macedonian control once again.

The Aitolian and Achaean Leagues

While leagues of Greek cities had existed for a variety of reasons for hundreds of years, two leagues emerged in the third century BCE that aimed to achieve the strength to match Macedonia militarily, and thus preserve their independence. These leagues were established not only to stand together against Macedonian dominance but also to limit each other's power, especially the designs of Sparta. The Aitolian League included the cities of classical Aitolia in south central Greece, but grew to include island communities, such as Chios in the eastern Aegean. The Achaean League comprised most of the cities in Achaea itself, but in 251 BCE it admitted Sicyon, the first city to be a member which was not in Achaea. It was under the leadership of Sicyon that the Achaean League took an anti-Macedonian stance. The Achaean League became the most important power in Greece, incorporating most of the Peloponnese and central Greece by the beginning of the second century BCE under the leadership of Corinth. Athens expelled her Macedonian garrisons in 229 BCE with help from Egypt, and although publicly claiming neutrality, was in fact a virtual Egyptian client thereafter.

Rome and the Cities of Greece

With the Roman arrival in the eastern Mediterranean following the defeat of Hannibal in 202 BCE, both Macedonia and Greece faced a new political and military reality. Philip V of Macedonia had allied with Hannibal, and after Hannibal's defeat, Rome moved to chastise his Greek ally. The Achaean League was initially supportive of the Romans against Macedonia, but it became the main opposition to Rome in Greece. Following a significant Roman military victory in 146 BCE over the Achaean League, which included a particularly savage destruction of Corinth, and looting of many Greek artworks on a massive scale, Greece came under formal Roman control. Macedonia had been captured 21 years earlier when the Roman army defeated Perseus at Pydna.

ABOVE **The Greek city-state of Corinth** became the capital of the Achaean League in the second century BCE, but it was brutally sacked by Roman invaders in 146 BCE.

LEFT **Philip V of Macedonia** was respected at home and abroad. He made various alliances with the leagues and then with Hannibal against Roman influence.

The Parthians

Little is known of Parthia until the middle of the second century BCE. In 245 BCE, Andragoras, the Satrap of Parthia, threw off Seleucid control, but was soon overthrown in turn by Arsaces, a chief of the Parni tribe, in 238 BCE. Arsaces is seen as the founder of the dynasty which ruled Parthia for the next 450 years.

ABOVE **The Parthian archer, shown here on a tomb** in Sichuan, China (*c.* 200 BCE–CE 200), executes the famous "Parthian shot." The rider pretends to retreat, then turns and shoots over his shoulder. It required superlative horse skills.

The Parthians eventually took control of Iran, Mesopotamia, Bactria, and areas further to the west and north, such as Armenia and Georgia. The growth of the Parthian kingdom came at the expense of the Seleucid Empire, and it also emerged as a serious, long-term challenge to Roman imperial ambitions in the east. While Greek culture and language remained important in the Parthian kingdom, the Iranian cultural influence became more significant over time. The Arsacid Parthian dynasty linked itself more with the Achaemenids than with Alexander, and by the first century BCE claimed descent from them. The Parthian king's official title provides a good indication of the mixture of Greek and Iranian elements in Parthian culture. He was the King of Kings, as the Achaemenids had been known. However, in addition he also took Greek epithets such as *Philhellenos* (Friend of the Greeks) and *Epiphanos* (Manifest God).

Much of what is known of the Arsacid Parthians comes from the surviving Greek and Roman sources; the Parthians themselves seem not to have developed a strong literary tradition. The Greek and Roman sources only report events in Parthia when the Hellenistic and Roman empires had contact with them, usually in a military context. This is demonstrated in the reign of the Seleucid king, Antiochus III, who launched a series of campaigns in 209–208 BCE to return Parthia to Seleucid allegiance, with some success. In 208 BCE, the Parthians were defeated in a series of engagements with the Seleucids, and Antiochus III marched against Bactria and India, where he enjoyed considerable success. He was not able to sustain the gains, and after the crushing losses at the hands of the Romans, Seleucid strength drained away, and the eastern territories once more broke free.

Parthia: A New Regional Power

It was during the reign of Mithridates I (171–138 BCE) that Parthia emerged as an important regional power. From 160–155 BCE Mithridates campaigned successfully against the Graeco-Bactrian kingdom, and in 148 BCE conquered Media. The first steps in establishing a new Iranian empire had been taken. By 141 BCE, the Parthians had taken control of Babylonia from the Seleucids, and Mithridates was crowned king at Seleucia. When the Seleucids attempted to recapture Mesopotamia in 139 BCE, Mithridates captured their king, Demetrius II. During the course of his 43-year reign he succeeded in making Parthia a formidable world power.

During the reign of Phraates II (139–128 BCE), the Seleucids made one last attempt to regain their eastern territories. In 130 BCE, Antiochus VII succeeded in regaining Babylonia and Media, freeing Demetrius II in the process. This success was not to last long when Antiochus suffered a major defeat and was killed in battle.

ABOVE **Mithridates II** (depicted here on a silver tetradrachm coin *c.* first century BCE) enjoyed a long and successful reign. His expansionist aspirations embraced both east and west: he negotiated with China and Rome.

The Parthians themselves faced difficulties on their northeastern frontiers because of migrations from southern Central Asia. The activity of the Huns in inner Asia caused these migrations in the direction of Parthia. The Yueh Chih, as the Chinese sources called them, were the strongest of these groups as they conquered the Graeco-Bactrian kingdom and established what later became known as the Kushan Empire in northern India and Bactria. Both Phraates II in 128 BCE and his successor Artabanus I (reigned 127–*c.* 124 BCE) died in battle against the Yueh Chih. At the same time, Hyspaosines, the ruler of the kingdom of Characene in the Persian Gulf, seized territory in southern Mesopotamia, penetrating as far north as Babylonia.

Mithridates II Expands the Empire

The succession of Mithridates II in 124–123 BCE represented the beginning of one of the most significant reigns in the Parthian dynasty. He ruled for nearly 40 years (until 88–87 BCE), during which time he consolidated and expanded on the successes of Mithridates I. Mithridates II defeated Hyspaosines of Characene in 122–121 BCE, and soon after the kingdoms of Adiabene, Corduene, and Osrhoene in northern Mesopotamia became vassals of the Parthian kingdom. It was during his reign that Parthia's long-term interest in Armenia began. In 97 BCE Mithridates removed the Armenian king and replaced him with Tigranes, his own son.

During the reign of Mithridates, the Parthians began to forge links with major powers to the west and the east. In 115 BCE, Mithridates was visited by an embassy from the Chinese emperor Wu-ti, and some scholars claim that this marked the beginning of long-distance trade between the two empires and the opening up of the Silk Roads. In 96 BCE, the Roman general Sulla met a Parthian envoy on the Euphrates River. The envoy offered friendship and an alliance on behalf of Mithridates.

LEFT **Mithridates I, here seen with Heracles in stone relief (*c.* 70 BCE), southern Anatolia, Turkey,** consolidated the power and reach of Parthia. He was a strategic and diplomatic leader.

Roman Expansion

Rome's military and political involvement with the Hellenistic kingdoms was the result of the Second Punic War (220–201 BCE) when Hannibal of Carthage almost succeeded in destroying Rome's power. Philip V of Macedonia formed an alliance with Hannibal during this critical period, and once Rome broke Carthage's power forever, they turned their attention towards Philip.

Rome had a pretext for war against Philip as it could claim to be intervening on behalf of Egypt, Pergamum, and Rhodes, all of which had appealed to Rome for assistance as a result of Philip's aggression towards them. The Roman Senate declared war on Macedonia in 200 BCE, and after a series of battles, the Roman general Flamininus defeated Philip at Cynoscephalae in 197 BCE. Thirty years later, following the battle of Pydna, which was fought against the last Macedonian king, Perseus, Rome took control of Macedonia and turned it into a province. Central and southern Greece came under Roman control in 146 BCE when Rome put down a revolt by the Achaean League and sacked the city of Corinth in the process.

BELOW **Antiochus IV** is best known for his attempts to Hellenize Judea and take over Egypt. This bronze bust (c. 184–175 BCE) is from the Archaeological Museum, Tehran, Iran.

Rome and the Seleucids

Hannibal and Philip V of Macedonia were also to cause problems for the Seleucids. Antiochus III entered into a secret pact with Philip in 202 BCE, in which the two powers agreed to divide the possessions of Egypt in Palestine and the Aegean. Rome intervened on behalf of Egypt, and also became concerned when Antiochus took advantage of the Roman victory over Philip and invaded Thrace in 196 BCE. Further inflaming Roman suspicions, Antiochus gave Hannibal refuge and in 193 BCE invaded Greece. The Romans responded with a declaration of war. The Seleucids were defeated in two significant battles against the Romans: the first in 190 BCE at Thermopylae; and the second in 189 BCE at Magnesia. The Treaty of Apamea, which followed in 188 BCE, was ruinous for the Seleucids and forced them to surrender most of their holdings in Asia Minor.

The Treaty of Apamea is often seen as marking the beginning of the end for the Seleucids. Asia Minor was lost forever, being divided between Rome's allies Pergamum and Rhodes. The Roman strategy of supporting these smaller kingdoms was highly effective as it justified their intervention in the eastern Mediterranean whenever the smaller powers were attacked by the Seleucids. Antiochus was also required to pay a large indemnity and give up one of his sons as a hostage in Rome to ensure his good behaviour. The first of these hostages was the future king (Antiochus IV) who received a traditional Roman education and became well-connected in the city. In 175 BCE when his brother Seleucus IV was murdered, Antiochus returned from Rome and succeeded his brother. During the reign of Antiochus IV, Rome continued to keep Seleucid power in check by intervening on behalf of Egypt. The best known example of this took place in 169–168 BCE when Antiochus attempted to take control of Egypt. The Roman authorities demanded immediate evacuation, and an enraged Antiochus had to comply. The Maccabean Revolt in Judea during the reign of Antiochus IV also provided Rome with an opportunity to intervene in the affairs of the Seleucid Empire. In the early reign of Antiochus's successor, Demetrius I (reigned 162–150 BCE), the Maccabeans appealed to Rome for assistance against the Seleucids, and the Romans once more intervened to reduce Seleucid influence.

Rome and the Near East

Despite serious political trouble at home, Roman power expanded almost inexorably throughout the eastern Mediterranean from the middle of the second to the middle of the first century BCE. Throughout this period, the Seleucid Empire began to crumble in the face of Roman and Parthian expansion. The emergence of regional powers in northern Anatolia contributed to the demise of the Seleucids. The Romans eventually conquered Pontus, but dealing with Armenia was a far more difficult proposition, as this royal house was closely related to the Parthian rulers. Rome brought the Seleucid kingdom to an end in 65 BCE, forming a Roman province of Syria out of the wreckage, based on Antioch as capital.

A similar situation arose in Egypt, which Rome had protected from Macedonian and Seleucid aggression since the early years of the second century BCE. The developments which finally led to Egypt's absorption into the growing Roman empire are well known. Egypt's last monarch, Cleopatra VII, became directly involved in Roman politics through her relationships with both Julius Caesar and Mark Antony. Cleopatra bore Caesar a son, called Caesarion, and at Caesar's invitation she and her son took up residence on the Palatine in Rome in 45 BCE. Following Caesar's assassination, Cleopatra fled back to Egypt, but soon became embroiled once more in Roman power politics. A protracted war

LEFT **Pompey the Great** reorganized the East, quelling several long-running wars—foreign and civil. However, his skillful compromises did not long outlive him.

ROME AND PERGAMUM

One of Rome's key allies in the eastern Mediterranean in the second century BCE was Pergamum. The rulers of Pergamum broke away from the Seleucids in the first half of the third century BCE and under Attalus I (reigned 241–197 BCE) became a major regional power in Asia Minor. Pergamum, along with Rhodes, turned to Rome for support against Antiochus III, and both Pergamum and Rhodes were one of the main beneficiaries of the Treaty of Apamea in 188 BCE. The last king of Pergamum, Attalus III, took the extraordinary step of bequeathing his kingdom to Rome in 133 BCE.

LEFT **Pergamum is situated** in northwestern Anatolia, Turkey. It was ruled by the Attalid dynasty after the death of Lysimachus of Thrace.

ABOVE **Palmyra was situated on a trade route** linking India, Persia, and Mesopotamia. Its location made the city valuable, and eventually attracted interest of the great powers. This view shows the theater (*c.* CE 175).

between Caesar's heir, Octavian (later Augustus), and the two lovers ensued. The war ended with Antony and Cleopatra's defeat by Octavian in 31 BCE at the Battle of Actium. Both Antony and Cleopatra committed suicide in the following months and Egypt became a Roman province.

The Romans now had formal territories in Egypt and Syria, and it was from these bases that Roman power would expand over the following three centuries. Roman power was further expressed through a number of Syrian client-kingdoms, reordered under their authority. The status of these client-kingdoms in relation to Rome vacillated during the first half of the first century CE. The kingdoms of Cappadocia, Commagene, and Emesa had all become client-kingdoms of the Romans by the beginning of the first century CE, but in the following years this approach varied. Cappadocia and Commagene both became provinces early in the reign of Tiberius (CE 14–37), but were converted back to client-kingdoms during the reign of Claudius (CE 41–54). Rome also ruled through client-kings in Judea from the time of Pompey until CE 6, when the kingdom was turned into a Roman province and ruled by a procurator. Judea, like Commagene and Cappadocia, was also turned into a client-kingdom early in the reign of the emperor Claudius.

The situation in southern Syria during this period was more complicated. Pompey's assault on Jerusalem in 63 BCE had been a diversion from the stated aim of attacking the Nabataeans who exercised considerable influence in Judea and southern Syria. Early in the reign of Tiberius however, Rome appears to have been on good terms with the Nabataeans when their king lavishly entertained Tiberius's nephew Germanicus in CE 18. Sixteen years later, when the Apostle Paul visited Damascus, the city was

LEFT **Claudius came to power unwillingly at the age of 50.** His reign is noted for successful management of Rome's client-kingdoms. This bust is from Nicomedia, now in the Archaeological Museum, Istanbul, Turkey.

under Nabataean control, and Rome's power in southern Syria was under some threat. It would take another 70 years for Rome to deal permanently with the Nabataeans. The city of Palmyra, in the middle of the Syrian desert, was on good terms with the Romans by the beginning of the first century CE, despite suffering an attack from Mark Antony in 42 BCE. Palmyra's status is ambiguous in the first century CE, as it appears not to have been a part of the province of Syria, and there is still debate about its status as a client-kingdom.

Reorganization under Vespasian

The immediate catalyst for change in Rome's organization of territory in Syria and the Near East was the war of reconquest of Judea which came in the wake of the ferocious uprising known today as the First Jewish revolt (CE 66–73). This full-scale revolt began in CE 66, and the future emperor Vespasian was sent by Nero with three legions to crush the revolt. Vespasian's son Titus took command when his father headed west to claim the throne left vacant by Nero's death and a year of civil war between rival claimants from across the empire. Following a protracted siege, Jerusalem fell to the Romans in August CE 70, but it was not until CE 73 that the last of the Jewish rebels were dealt with. The Parthians exploited the opportunity of the Judean war to destabilize the Roman arrangements in Commagene and Cappadocia. At the conclusion of the Jewish revolt, the emperor Vespasian initiated a significant territorial reorganization. The client-kingdom of Commagene became part of the province of Syria, Cappadocia became a new province, and Emesa was incorporated into the province of Syria. Four Roman legions were concentrated on the upper Euphrates: XII Fulminata at Melitene; VI Ferrata at Samosata; IV Scythica at Zeugma; and XVI Flavia Firma at Satala. This development was motivated by both defensive and offensive reasons. One of the motives was to reinforce Rome's strength on the borders of Armenia which, by common agreement with the Parthians, had been a Roman protectorate since CE 64. This reorganization under Vespasian was directed to block the major invasion routes across northern Syria from Parthia.

The Annexation of the Nabataean Kingdom

The next significant development for the Romans in the Near East was the annexation of the Nabataean kingdom. The Nabataeans had besieged Jerusalem in 66 BCE before they were forced to withdraw from Rome, and three years later Pompey set out to invade their kingdom before being diverted to Jerusalem. The relationship between Rome and the Nabataeans from this period fluctuated. The Nabataeans had clear interests in southern Syria, and it was here that they first came into direct conflict with the Romans. The city of Damascus, probably the most important in the region of southern Syria, was clearly under Nabataean control in the mid CE 30s when the Apostle Paul visited the city. This would not have been to Rome's liking. The reason for the absorption of the Nabataean kingdom into Roman provincial territory is obscure, but in CE 106, the emperor Trajan annexed the kingdom and converted it into the Roman province of Arabia. The metropolis or capital of the province was at Bostra, more centrally placed than Petra, where a legionary garrison (III Cyrenaica) was positioned.

ABOVE **Vespasian founded the new Flavian dynasty,** which ruled Rome CE 69–96. This late first-century CE bust is from Rome.

Petra

Petra is located in the northern section of the Rift Valley which was created by the collision of two vast continental plates. This explains the spectacular geographical environment in which Petra sits. It is dominated by dramatic cliffs and high places and a series of wadis (intermittent desert streams), in particular Wadi Musa.

The first historical reference to Petra dates to 312 BCE when it is mentioned in relation to the wars of the successors of Alexander the Great. At this stage, Petra was inhabited by the Nabataeans who are thought to have originated in northwestern Arabia. The Nabataeans managed to stay politically independent of the Seleucids and the Egyptians despite centuries of conflict between the two great powers over southern Syria and Palestine. The cultural influences of both the Seleucid and Ptolemaic empires were, however, significant at Petra and throughout the Nabataean kingdom.

The establishment of the province of Syria by Pompey in 65 BCE eventually had significant ramifications for Petra and the Nabataean kingdom. The Nabataeans under their kings Aretas II (reigned 110–96 BCE) and Aretas III (reigned 86–62 BCE) had been active politically in Judea and southern Syria, and Pompey embarked on a military campaign to deal with them in 63 BCE. The campaign was diverted to Jerusalem and never reached the Nabataean kingdom but it seems from this time, the Nabataeans adopted a conciliatory stance towards Rome.

El Khazneh

The Treasury (or El Khazneh) is a burial monument hewn spectacularly into the sandstone cliffs. The rock gives it the rose-red tint for which Petra is famous. The site was unknown to Europeans until the early years of the nineteenth century.

The kingdom prospered from 100 BCE to CE 100 because of trade, but politically it was effectively a client-kingdom, one that was eventually absorbed into the Roman provincial system. In CE 106, Emperor Trajan annexed the Nabataean kingdom and turned it into the province of Arabia. No evidence of conflict between the two powers exists, with the exact mechanism whereby Rome annexed the kingdom still obscure.

From the middle of the first century BCE up to the period following Trajan's annexation, Petra acquired many of the features which make it a breathtaking archaeological site. During this period the Great Temple and a large rock-cut theater were constructed. The Khazneh or Treasury façade was probably completed in the first half of the first century CE, while some of the most spectacular of the rock-cut tombs for which Petra is famous were carved after the Roman annexation.

Other important features at Petra are complex hydraulic and water collection systems. The

Nabataean Theater

The amphitheater (*c.* 50 BCE) has been cut into the sides of the rose-colored mountainside. It provides further evidence for the Hellenization of the Nabataean citizenry.

Colonnaded Street and Royal Tombs

The colonnaded street (*c.* CE 100) runs through the middle of the city, and a paved pathway continues down the Siq (the narrow principal entry into Petra), past the Khazneh and north to Amman and Syria.

Nabataeans developed advanced means of channeling and storing water which was necessary both to prevent flash-flooding of the wadis (the main entry and exit points for the city) and to compensate for the lack of rainfall.

It is sometimes suggested that the importance of trade to Petra declined after the Roman annexation, but it seems that trade continued to flourish well into the third century CE. Petra recovered much of its former status during the early Christian era, being the center of a bishopric by CE 313. Several beautiful churches have been excavated, most dating from the CE 500s. Fine stonework, polychrome mosaics, and a cache of parchment documents are only some of the recently uncovered riches. The city remained strategically significant during the Crusades, with remains of at least two small forts known from that time. Petra declined during the Ottoman period, when Bedouin groups from northern Arabia occupied the city.

Byzantine Mosaics

Petra flourished during the Byzantine period, with art, trade, and religion all playing a part in ongoing prosperity. This early sixth-century CE mosaic comes from one of the several beautiful Christian churches.

Incense

Particularly important to Petra's development as an urban center from the second century BCE was its ability to attract trade in incense and spices originating in south Arabia bound for the Hellenistic and Roman worlds. Incense, such as frankincense and myrrh, was used extensively in religious and domestic contexts throughout the Mediterranean, and spices such as cinnamon and cardamom were also in demand. South Arabia was the main source of these. The Nabataeans also established a port at Ayla (modern Aqaba) which attracted the growing sea trade from India, generated by the Greek discovery of the Indian Ocean monsoon in the mid-first century BCE.

The Romans in Palestine

Rome's first involvement in Palestine came as a result of the Maccabean rebellion during the reign of the Seleucid king, Demetrius I. The leaders of the rebellion appealed to Rome for support in 161 BCE and Rome obliged. By so doing, Rome had a pretext to intervene in the affairs of the Seleucid kingdom, but it would cause Rome problems in the centuries to follow.

When Pompey undertook an expedition against the Nabataeans in 63 BCE, he was sidetracked by problems in Palestine and forced to intervene in a civil war in Jerusalem. Pompey confirmed John Hyrcanus as *ethnarch*, effectively making Judea a Roman client-kingdom. In 40 BCE, the Parthians invaded Syria and captured Judea, replacing Hyrcanus with their own client-king. Herod, a senior official in Judea, fled to Cleopatra in Egypt and successfully secured the support of Mark Antony to return to Judea as king. Antony convinced Octavian to recognize Herod as King of Judea, and sent his best general, Ventidius Bassus, with Herod to drive the Parthians out of Syria in 38 BCE.

ABOVE **Masada, built as a fortified palace retreat by Herod**, was seized by the Zealots during the First Revolt. It was used as a base for raids against the Romans.

Judea: A Client-Kingdom

When the civil war broke out between Octavian and Mark Antony, Herod, and several client-kings in the Near East, supported Octavian, in spite of the fact that they were allies of Mark Antony. Following Mark Antony's defeat in 31 BCE, Herod was rewarded by Octavian with increased territory in Phoenicia and southern Syria. As Rome's nominee in Judea, Herod faced numerous problems. These mainly revolved around his lack of qualifications to serve as High Priest, and the resentment of some groups at the gradual Hellenization of Jewish culture.

During Herod's long reign over Judea, a number of building projects were embarked upon which were designed to transform the kingdom and align it further with the secular ruling elites fostered by Rome. Herod constructed both a theater and amphitheater at Jerusalem, and in 22 BCE undertook a major enlargement of the temple. The western wall of the massive stone terrace on which Herod placed the rebuilt temple is all that survives in Jerusalem today and is known as the Wailing Wall.

Augustus (formerly Octavian) continued to reward Herod for his loyalty, and Herod himself was, for the most part, a capable ruler. All of the major decisions made by Herod required the emperor's approval, and Herod committed a grave error in 9 BCE when he invaded the Nabataean kingdom without that approval. This weakened Herod's standing with Augustus, and when Herod died in 4 BCE his kingdom was divided three ways between his sons. Each of Herod's successors attempted to undermine the other, and the situation became so unstable that Augustus ordered the abolition of the kingdom and its conversion into a province governed by procurators. Roman control of Judea was never secure. One of its procurators, Pontius Pilate, who ruled from CE 26–36, was to discover just how challenging it would be. During the reign of Claudius (CE 41–54) Rome reestablished the client-kingdom of Judea under the rule of Herod's grandson, Agrippa I. On Agrippa's death in CE 44 the heartland of Judea was once again given over to full Roman control, with ultimately dire consequences for both the Romans and the local citizenry.

The First Jewish Revolt

The changing nature of Roman rule in Palestine contributed to growing resentment among various Jewish factions which protested against Roman control. More traditional Jews always had a problem with the religious elements of Greek and Roman culture with which they were

required to comply, such as participation in state cult. This became a significant issue, and other concerns emerged which heightened Jewish resentment of Roman rule. After a series of disturbances, a full-scale rebellion took place throughout Palestine in CE 66. It was led by anti-Roman revolutionaries called Zealots or Sicarii, who had a history of resistance to the religious aspects of Greek and Roman rule in Palestine.

Emperor Nero entrusted command of the Jewish war in CE 67 to Vespasian, one of the more effective generals. Once the civil war erupted on Nero's death, Vespasian handed over the siege of Jerusalem to his capable son, Titus, and moved on to Rome. The significance of the war was reflected in the fact that 40,000 Roman troops were committed to the siege of Jerusalem in CE 70. In August of that year Jerusalem fell. Much of the city was destroyed, including most of the temple which had only recently been refurbished. The war ended in CE 73 when the hilltop fortress of Masada was eventually captured by a Roman legion under the command of Flavius Silva after a three-year siege.

ABOVE **The Western Wall** is in the Old City of Jerusalem. It contains huge stones of the terrace on which Herod built the new temple. The site is one of the most sacred places for both Judaism and Islam.

THE BAR KOKHBA REBELLION

The rebellion of CE 66–73 was followed by an even more savage rebellion (CE 132–135) in the reign of Hadrian. Simon Bar Kokhba, a Jewish national leader, objected to Hadrian's reestablishment of Jerusalem in CE 130 as a Roman colony because it included a temple to Jupiter. Hadrian became increasingly concerned with Jewish opposition and banned circumcision in CE 132. These events precipitated a revolt, led by Bar Kokhba, which lasted for the next three years. Hadrian responded by sending an army numbering approximately 30,000 men in CE 134. It took until CE 135 to quell the rebellion, and Hadrian ruthlessly suppressed Jewish practices, including a ban on teaching the Mosaic law. The province of Judea was renamed Syria Palaestina and Jerusalem became known as Aelia Capitolina.

LEFT **The Emperor Hadrian,** depicted here in a marble bust *c.* CE 135, viewed Judaism as a threat to the Hellenization of the east and tried to reform the faith to make it more amenable to foreign influence.

The Diaspora

The beginnings of the Jewish diaspora are difficult to establish precisely but there are some pivotal developments in the history of Judaism which contributed to the emergence of Jewish communities outside Palestine. One of the most important for the history of the Jewish diaspora was the capture of Jerusalem by Nebuchadnezzar II in 586 BCE.

Following the capture of Jerusalem, Nebuchadnezzar deported thousands of Jews to Babylon. While these deportations were the most significant during this period, smaller deportations of sections of the Judean nobility had been taking place since *c.* 605 BCE. During this period of Babylonian attacks on Judea, some Jews fled to Egypt where there is evidence of a Jewish military colony on the island of Elephantine in the Nile River dating back to 594 BCE. Indeed, the exiled Jewish community at Elephantine built a temple on the island which was destroyed in 410 BCE but rebuilt with the permission of Egypt's Persian satrap (governor) in 400 BCE.

Following the defeat of the Neo-Babylonian empire by the Persian king Cyrus, he proclaimed in *c.* 538 BCE that the various exiles taken by Nebuchadnezzar could return to their homelands. It is claimed that around 40,000 Jews returned to Judea as a result of Cyrus's proclamation; however, many Jews stayed in Babylon. Some rose to positions of prominence in the Babylonian and Persian civil administration, including Daniel and Nehemiah. Over the following centuries the Babylonian Jewish community emerged as an important one and produced its own version of the Talmud. It would continue to remain active and grow through the Persian, Seleucid, Parthian, and Sasanian periods, and continued to flourish throughout the Islamic period.

BELOW **Elephantine Island hosted a Jewish colony** in the Persian period (*c.* 500–350 BCE).

Diaspora Communities in Ethiopia and the Red Sea

A number of traditions exist regarding the origins of Jewish communities in Ethiopia. One holds that a Jewish kingdom was established there following a visit by the Queen of Sheba to King Solomon in the tenth century BCE. Another claims that, during the exodus from Egypt led by Moses, some Jews broke away and headed south rather than crossing the Red Sea to the Promised Land. On the basis of these traditions, Ethiopia became a refuge for Jews fleeing the Babylonian attacks of the sixth century BCE. An appropriate context for the appearance of Jewish communities in Ethiopia remains elusive, although trade seems the most likely motivation. Some historians believe that they may have emerged there in the fifth century BCE. There is evidence for Jewish traders operating throughout the Red Sea and around the Arabian Peninsula to Yemen, and it is possible that they established specific communities in Ethiopia.

The diaspora in Egypt, Ethiopia, Babylon, and also Asia Minor gave Jews a choice of havens to move into when problems emerged in the Hellenistic and Roman periods. Jews also left Judea of their own accord in pursuit of trade and better living conditions. When the Ptolemies of Egypt were in control of Palestine and southern Syria (301–198 BCE), many Jews moved to Alexandria, as the new city offered economic opportunities, and the chance to avoid the factionalism which dominated the Jewish political scene in Jerusalem. The problems

LEFT **This wonderfully preserved synagogue** contains illustrations of Old Testament stories. It was buried beneath a siege ramp at Dura-Europos on the Euphrates River.

experienced in Jerusalem and throughout Judea during the reign of the Seleucid king Antiochus IV (175–163 BCE) also encouraged some Jews to flee to the established diaspora centers.

The Diaspora During the Roman Period

It was during the Roman period of control of Judea that a considerable number of Jews became part of the diaspora. The First Jewish Revolt (CE 66–73) leading to the Roman siege and capture of Jerusalem in CE 70, contributed significantly to the number of Jews leaving Judea and joining diaspora communities. The revolt had its origins in the Seleucid period when a section of the Jewish population protested against the increasing impact of Hellenization. This uprising became a serious problem for the Romans, and the eventual destruction of Jerusalem and reorganization of the procuratorial province of Judea were major military and political events. The Jewish diaspora communities grew as a result, including the Jewish community in the city of Rome.

The First Jewish Revolt was followed by an even more damaging Second Revolt in CE 132–135 during the reign of Hadrian, under the leadership of Simon Bar Kokhba. Based in the desert steppe lands south and west of the Dead Sea, it required considerable effort by the Roman army to quell. Rome moved to eradicate all visible symbols of the Jewish faith, rebuilding Jerusalem as the Roman colony of Aelia Capitolina, and equipping it with a prominent temple to Jupiter. Jews were forbidden to enter the new Roman city. As a result of this, many of the remaining Jews fled to the diaspora, and may even have started new diaspora communities.

At the site of Dura-Europos on the Euphrates River in eastern Syria, the spectacular remains of a Jewish synagogue were uncovered in the 1920s. (Finds from this site are so well preserved that it has been dubbed Pompeii of the Desert.) This synagogue (dating around CE 220–240) contains numerous large, colorful wall paintings of Old Testament scenes, and was relocated to the National Museum in Damascus in the 1930s. The building and the frescoes may be the work of descendants of Jews fleeing Judea during and after the First and Second Jewish Revolts.

ABOVE **This detail from the Arch of Titus in Rome** (*c.* CE 83) commemorates the fall of Jerusalem. The menorah is from the temple at Jerusalem.

The Spread of Christianity

Christianity began as an offshoot of Judaism in the broader political context of Roman imperial expansion. Jesus always styled himself a reforming rabbi, preaching a message that the temple authorities opposed. His following grew large enough to concern the Roman civil authorities when he brought reform to the capital in CE 26.

Judea in the first century CE was a hotbed of intense religious contention, and it was in this context that the message Jesus preached began to flourish. Jesus's challenge to the religious authorities was rejected by the temple priesthood, but accepted by a small community, which spread what effectively became a new faith in the two decades following the crucifixion. The Apostles seem to have been effective evangelists, bringing the message of renewal to much of the Jewish diaspora by the mid-first century CE. This religion would eventually be identified as Christianity.

The development of Christianity in its earliest days was in many ways a function of the Hellenized world in which Judaism had been operating for centuries. Although the Romans had established military and political authority over Syria and Palestine for almost a century, Hellenistic culture remained the ruling ideology, actively promoted as a socially cohesive force by the Roman authorities. The Christian message was initially directed at Jews, but Hellenizing tendencies evident in Palestine since the second century BCE, together with the presence of a Jewish diaspora in other parts of the Hellenistic world, increasingly accentuated its importance for nonJews. This gave Christianity a universal relevance beyond the narrow confines of Jewish theology, which became a key feature of Christian missionary activity.

BELOW **The Apostles, and later missionaries, Paul and Peter** are depicted on this fifth-century CE ivory relief from Campania, Italy. They spread the teachings of Jesus from Britain to Arabia.

The Importance of Missionaries

The missionary nature of Christianity was demonstrated by Christ himself in Luke 10:1 when he sent out 72 individuals to Judea and beyond to spread the message of Christianity. Following Jesus's death, Acts 2 reports that at the day of Pentecost in Jerusalem, the gift of tongues (or glossolalia) was given to the Apostles so that people who were in Jerusalem at the time who had come from many different places could understand the Christian message. The passage claims that there were visitors from across the known world, emphasizing the universal message of the Christian creed. The implication in this description is the accessibility of the Christian message for people of all nations, and not just the Jews.

Missionary activity was an important feature of the early church. In the decades after Christ's death Christianity slowly began to spread throughout Palestine, Syria, Asia Minor, Egypt, and even beyond the Euphrates to Mesopotamia. The dominant figure in missionary activity to the Gentiles was Paul, a Hellenized Jew from Tarsus in Cilicia, who had been a zealous persecutor of the early Christians until sudden conversion on the road to Damascus. Paul also emerged as the most important figure in the early development of Christian theology and community organization of the church. He undertook missions to Arabia and Damascus (CE 35–38), Antioch, Syria, and Cilicia (CE 38–39), and Greece and Asia Minor (CE 52–57) before his execution at the hands of the Romans around CE 62. Other significant missionaries were: Peter in Antioch, Greece, and Rome; and Barnabas in Cyprus.

LEFT **This fourteenth-century Coptic icon from the Church of Saint Barbara, Cairo,** Egypt, shows the Day of Pentecost when the Holy Spirit entered the Twelve Apostles.

ABOVE **Emperor Nero** is portrayed by early historians as a persecutor of Christians. Peter and Paul were both executed during his reign.

Thomas is also said to have preached in Mesopotamia and as far east as India.

Early Evidence for Expansion

Despite the spread of Christianity, the overall number of believers was still small. The religion would come to be increasingly problematic for the Roman authorities, however, because of the Christians' refusal to sacrifice to the emperors as gods, which smacked of treason or at least ill-will towards the rulers, something they could not tolerate, especially if publicly avowed. The emperors claimed that paying due honor to the gods ensured the security of the state. The refusal by the Christians to do so was interpreted as a potential threat to the safety of the state.

The first nonChristian reference in ancient texts to Christians comes from the Roman historian Tacitus who refers to events in Rome in CE 64. Christianity had come to the attention of Nero, and Tacitus claims that Nero tried to blame the Christians for starting the fire of the same year which was one of the most destructive Rome had ever experienced. The Christians as they are depicted in Tacitus are an obscure sect of which little was known.

The letters of Pliny the Younger to the emperor Trajan provide important evidence for the early spread of Christianity. Pliny was sent by Trajan as governor of the province of Bithynia in northwest Asia Minor in CE 111. Pliny wrote a number of letters to the emperor asking advice,

CHRISTIANITY IN THE PERSIAN EMPIRE

Imperial support for Christianity in the Roman Empire in the fourth century CE had an indirect impact on the growth of Christianity in the Persian Empire. Christianity within the Persian Empire in the third and fourth centuries CE grew, despite suffering persecution at the hands of the Sasanian kings in the 270s and 330s. In CE 411, the Persian church held its first synod, which 36 bishops attended.

THE EMPERORS BECOME CHRISTIAN

Perhaps the most significant event for the spread of Christianity was the decision by the emperor Constantine in CE 312 to offer imperial patronage to the Christian church. Constantine went to considerable efforts to rehabilitate the church after the damage it had suffered during the Great Persecution, and during his reign Christianity was increasingly politicized. As a result of the adoption and support of Christianity by all but one of the Roman emperors in the fourth century CE, Christian churches sprang up everywhere, and the imperial interest in the religion elevated its significance socially and politically.

ABOVE **The fourteenth-century fresco** from the Church of S. Zeno Maggiore in Verona, Italy, shows the baptism of Constantine by Pope Silvester I.

and providing details on issues associated with his administration of the province. The problems with Christians in the province was one such issue; he mentions that some refused to sacrifice and pay due honor to the cult of the emperor. Pliny had dealt with the Christians in various ways and had executed some. In the process of informing Trajan and asking his advice, he says that there were so many Christians in the province that the pagan temples were, for a time, deserted. Modern scholarship considers this an exaggeration on the part of Pliny to protect himself from the emperor's anger if he had acted inappropriately. Trajan replied that he had done the right thing, and that if Christians came to Pliny's attention for publicly refusing to sacrifice in the emperor's name, then they should be punished, but he need not seek them out, if they maintained their views privately.

Edessa and the Spread of Christianity

Over the following 150 years, Christianity continued to spread to the point where there were Christian communities in cities and towns all around the Mediterranean, and also in Mesopotamia and the Parthian kingdom. The size of this community remained relatively small. One of the important cities for the spread of Christianity throughout the modern Middle East during this period was Edessa. Edessa is known today as Urfa and is in southeastern Turkey. Christians claim that Edessa was evangelized by the Apostle Thomas in the early years of the Christian movement. The church historian of the fourth century CE, Eusebius of Caesarea, claimed that Jesus himself had corresponded with the king of Edessa, Abgar V, and that Abgar had become a Christian. Most scholars consider this to be an apocryphal story; however, Edessa does appear to have become significant as a center of Christian theological development and missionary activity in the second and third centuries CE. Some scholars believe that Abgar VIII (reigned CE 179–214), rather than Abgar V, became a Christian, or at least took a keen interest in the religion. One of the earliest references to a church building comes from the Chronicle of Edessa which refers to a church at the city being damaged by a flood in CE 201.

The House Church at Dura-Europos

Further evidence for the spread and impact of Christianity in the Middle East in the third century CE derives from archaeological excavations in the walled city of Dura-Europos on the Euphrates River in eastern Syria. The city was a Seleucid military foundation of *c.* 300 BCE built on important trade routes. It was captured by the Parthians *c.* 120 BCE, and garrisoned by the Romans after CE 165. Excavations have unearthed many pagan temples of both Greek and Semitic origins, together with a synagogue, a mithraeum (a place of worship for the followers of Mithras), and a Christian church. Dura was sacked by the Sasanians in CE 256/7 and thereafter lost much of its previous importance. Almost all the evidence from the site dates to CE 256/7 and earlier. The Christian church was a house converted into a church *c.* CE 235. It was relatively small compared with the synagogue and temples, and its decoration more rudimentary than that found in most of the other religious buildings. These observations have led scholars to conclude that the Christian community at Dura-Europos in the third century CE was relatively small and not as influential in the life of the city as other religious groups.

Expansion and Persecution

Christians were becoming more problematic in the eyes of the emperors, and as a result there were a number of persecutions in the third century CE. The most vicious was that prosecuted in CE 250 by the emperor Decius (reigned CE 249–251). Decius required all his subjects to publicly sacrifice for the well being of the emperor and the security of the state. He ordered that certificates would be issued as proof of sacrifice. Those who would not comply would be executed. The evidence for this persecution comes from Egypt and is often used as an indication of the growth of Christianity. When the Sasanian Persian king Shapur I invaded the Roman provinces of Mesopotamia, Syria, and Asia Minor in the CE 250s, thousands of captives were taken back to Persia. Among them were Greek-speaking Christians who established a new church which later developed as a branch of Nestorian Christianity. This is used as an indication of the spread of Christianity up to this point.

In *c.* CE 303, Emperor Diocletian undertook what became known as the Great Persecution, and of all the persecutions of Christianity this would be the most serious. The persecution was at its most intense in the eastern provinces and also in North Africa. We are told by the church historian Eusebius of Caesarea that the church in Nicomedia, which was effectively Diocletian's capital, was in full view of the imperial palace which is indicative perhaps of Christianity becoming more prominent in the cities of the eastern provinces.

ABOVE **Emperor Decius**, seen here on a third-century CE gold coin, believed in worshipping the ancient gods to restore Rome to its former glory.

BELOW **The Redoubt at Dura-Europos** overlooks the Euphrates River. The site provides evidence of the unofficial tolerance of many different faiths, even in a Roman garrison town.

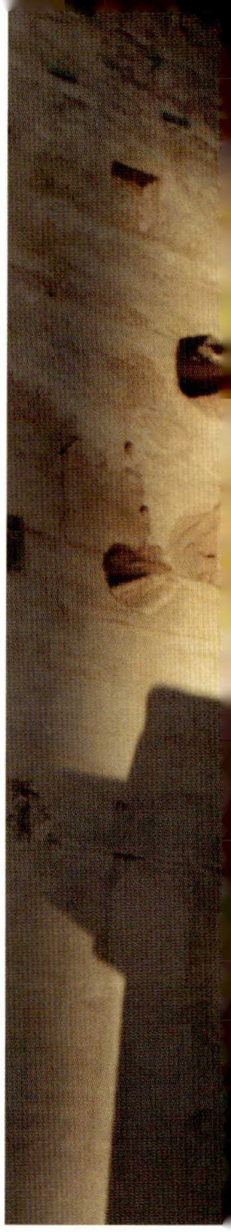

The Parthian Wars

In the middle of the first century BCE, when the Seleucid Empire was formally abolished, two relatively new powers in the Middle East—Rome and Parthia—stood in opposition to one another. Over the next 300 years, they were regularly in conflict, often at the instigation of the Romans.

The upper course of the Euphrates River as it flows through modern Turkey and northern Syria effectively formed a boundary between Roman and Parthian interests in the first century BCE. In 53 BCE, however, the Roman ex-consul and general, Marcus Licinius Crassus, crossed the Euphrates with 35,000 men in an attempt to conquer new territory from the Parthians. Although the Parthians were outnumbered, they defeated the Roman force near Carrhae in southern Turkey using effective light-armed cavalry. The defeat was one of the worst ever suffered by the Romans: 20,000 soldiers dead and 10,000 taken captive. Crassus himself and his son were both killed in the battle.

Crassus's defeat at Carrhae lived on in Roman memory, and the upshot, a decade of Parthian reprisal raids, kept large-scale military activity off the agenda for some time. It was also from this period that the kingdom of Armenia emerged as a long-term source of dispute between Rome and Parthia. Armenia was strategically located between the two empires, and for the most part managed to retain some autonomy. Numerous agreements were reached between Rome and Parthia over control of Armenia, and the Armenian kings sought to play the two empires off against each other.

ABOVE **The final military campaign of Trajan,** who is depicted on this first-century CE aureus, meant Mespotamia was conquered from the Parthians.

The Parthians Invade Syria

In 40 BCE, the Parthians successfully invaded Asia Minor and Syria before Mark Antony responded by sending Publius Ventidius Bassus to expel them, and by 38 BCE the Parthians had withdrawn back across the Euphrates.

In 20 BCE, Augustus and the Parthian king Phraates IV struck a deal which recognized the upper and middle Euphrates as the boundary between each empire's interests. Under the terms of the agreement the Parthians returned the Roman military standards captured in the defeat of Crassus and the invasion of Syria in 40 BCE. This agreement heralded a period of relative peace between Parthia and Rome which was to last until the middle of the first century CE.

Following the upsurge in conflict over Armenia during the reign of Nero, Rome and Parthia came to an understanding over the appointment of the Armenian king. The Parthians would nominate the ruler in consultation with Rome, and the Roman emperor would crown the Armenian king in Rome. In CE 66, Nero had the Parthian nominee Tiridates crowned king of Armenia in Rome, a sharing of authority that kept the peace for many years.

Trajan's Invasion

Three major conflicts erupted between Rome and Parthia in the second century CE. In CE 114, the Parthians installed their own king in Armenia without reference to Rome, and Emperor Trajan responded by sending an army. This army was much larger than that needed to settle the situation in Armenia and was clearly designed for a large-scale invasion of the Parthian Empire itself. In CE 116, two Roman forces under Trajan's command attacked the Parthians in Mesopotamia. One marched across northern Mesopotamia and down the Tigris, while the other (under Trajan's command) marched down the Euphrates. Trajan's forces captured the Parthian royal capital of Seleucia-Ctesiphon and marched as far south as the Persian Gulf. This campaign included the formation of the province of Mesopotamia in northern Iraq and Assyria in central Iraq, together with an unsuccessful siege of the independent kingdom of Hatra, an oasis town in the steppe west of the river. Trajan's gains were short-lived, and most of them were given up shortly after his death in CE 117. Despite this, Trajan's campaign was seen as a benchmark for Roman emperors for centuries to come.

LEFT **Three Parthian prisoners** are depicted on the Triumphal Arch of Septimius Severus in the Forum in Rome. The arch was built in CE 203 to celebrate Rome's victories in Parthia.

Lucius Verus and Septimius Severus

The next conflict between Rome and Parthia arose in CE 163, soon after the accession of Marcus Aurelius and Lucius Verus as co-emperors. The Parthians took the opportunity to destabilize the situation in Armenia while the new emperors consolidated their power. The emperors responded by sending an army under the command of the governor of Syria, Avidius Cassius. The Parthians were once again ejected from Armenia, and a major invasion of their territory by the Romans followed. Cassius marched down the Euphrates in CE 164–165 following a series of major field engagements in northwestern Mesopotamia along the Euphrates River where it flows closest to the city of Antioch. Seleucia-Ctesiphon was sacked once again, and Roman power was extended along the Euphrates to Dura-Europos and beyond. Roman power also became stronger across the Euphrates in the band of lowland territory between the two rivers, that lay immediately south of the Anatolian Mountains, the traditional route of invaders from time immemorial.

The third confrontation between Rome and Parthia came during the reign of Septimius Severus (CE 193–211). He invaded Parthia from CE 197–199, and captured Seleucia-Ctesiphon in December CE 197. The Romans besieged Hatra twice during this period, but in each case without result. The most important outcomes of the Severan campaigns against Parthia were the formal establishment of the Roman province of Mesopotamia in northern Iraq, southeastern Turkey and northeastern Syria. The Parthian client-kingdom of Osrhoene was split in two: a western province under Roman rule, and an eastern client-kingdom, based around the city of Edessa, but now tributary to Rome. Severus created two smaller provinces, Syria Phoenice and Syria Coele, out of the original Syrian province, in line with a tendency to reduce the military power of larger provincial centers.

LEFT **The Parthian warriors** were skilled horsemen and archers. This first-century CE bronze statue is from Shami, Iran, and is now in the Archaeological Museum in Tehran.

The Byzantines

The Byzantine period is sometimes held to begin with the reign of Emperor Constantine (CE 306–337), who founded Constantinople in CE 330. This act was a re-foundation of the existing city of Byzantium, hence the term Byzantine to describe the later history of the eastern Roman Empire.

However, the term Byzantine is a modern one, and in antiquity the Byzantines called themselves Romans up until the final capture of Constantinople by the Ottoman Turks in CE 1453. The choice of Constantine's reign as a marker for the beginning of the Byzantine Empire is arbitrary, but reflects the profound changes reverberating through the empire during his reign. Some advocate the reign of the emperor Justinian (CE 527–565) as the point at which the pagan Roman world finally gave way to a Christian empire.

Byzantium and the Early Sasanians

In the third century CE, Rome had suffered serious losses on its eastern frontier at the hands of the new Sasanian kings. At the end of the third century CE, Diocletian had recovered all lost territories and expanded the area of Roman control to include territories as far east as the Tigris and as far north as Colchis in the Caucasus. In the first half of the fourth century CE, Rome and Persia conducted a low-grade war over Mesopotamia and Armenia which escalated in CE 359–360. The Sasanian king, Shapur II, invaded Roman Mesopotamia at this time with a view to marching into Syria and capturing important cities such as Antioch. The attack failed, but not before inflicting devastation on the fortresses of Roman Mesopotamia. Three years later, following the disastrous invasion of Persia by emperor Julian, Rome would lose Mesopotamia forever. Armenia was finally partitioned and annexed by Rome and Persia in CE 387 and, for the next 150 years, conflict between the two empires was less intense than it had been.

BELOW **The Hagia Sophia in Istanbul (Constantinople)** was completed in the early CE 530s. It was intended to be the Christian equivalent of Solomon's temple—the center of worship for the entire empire.

The Persian Wars of Justinian and Heraclius

In the years from CE 530 to CE 540, during the reign of the emperor Justinian, the Persian king Croesus I campaigned throughout Syria and captured Antioch, among other important cities. Justinian's armies eventually succeeded in driving the Persians out, and Justinian followed this up with a major overhaul of the defensive system in the east. A number of important fortifications were strengthened over the next decade across the eastern marches of the empire. The walls and defenses of many towns and cities were also strengthened, including Edessa, Resafe, Apamea, Palmyra, and Antioch itself.

The Byzantine Empire faced some of its greatest challenges in the first half of the seventh century CE. The Persians again invaded under the leadership of their king, Croesus II. In CE 611 they captured Antioch, and over the following decade took Egypt, Syria, and large sections of Asia Minor. Mounting a challenge to Persia's control of this territory, the Byzantine emperor Heraclius commenced a campaign in CE 622, and over the following five years recovered all the imperial territories conquered by the Persians. Only a few years after Heraclius had restored Egypt, Arabia, and Syria to Byzantine rule, the armies of the Prophet Mohammed emerged from Arabia to take control of all of these territories. The Byzantines would never recover them.

Christianity and the Crusades

Christianity was one of the key cultural and political institutions throughout the provinces under Byzantine control. This translated into the construction of hundreds of churches throughout Syria, Arabia, and Egypt, and these churches continued to be active well into the Abbasid (ninth century CE) period. Three of the most important cities to the Christian church—Alexandria, Jerusalem, and Antioch—were now under Islamic control, but Christianity continued to influence cultural developments in the evolving Islamic community. The Byzantine Empire continued to exercise cultural and political influence in the territories it once occupied through its links to the Christian religious authorities in the regions under Islamic control. Constantinople continued to be the most important city in the east in Christian terms, and Christians outside of the Byzantine Empire still looked to it for leadership.

Following the Islamic invasions, the Byzantine Empire was confined to Asia Minor, Greece, Illyricum, and parts of Italy. It continued waxing strong in the tenth century CE, before collapsing before the onslaught of the Ottoman Turks in the twelfth century CE. Constantinople itself fell to the Turks in 1453, but the importance of the empire had long since extinguished. Perhaps the most important development in the intervening period was the arrival of the Crusading armies from Western Europe toward the end of the eleventh century CE. While the Byzantines were unable, perhaps unwilling, to reconquer territory in the Holy Lands and in western Syria that they had once controlled, the Crusaders succeeded in establishing kingdoms based around Edessa, Antioch, Tripoli, and Jerusalem. They also built many fortifications, large and small, throughout western Syria, and as far south as Petra. Despite the relative success of the First Crusade in 1099, and the establishment of Latin kingdoms and fortifications over the following 80 years, the Crusaders were eventually unable to hold their gains. With the Crusades becoming ever more difficult to fund, the Venetians, who bankrolled the Fourth Crusade, diverted that Crusade in 1204 to loot Constantinople, and partition the remaining territories of the Byzantine empire. A series of small but surprisingly long-lived Latin kingdoms grew up in Greece, Crete, and Cyprus, alongside the fragments of Byzantium that remained true to the Orthodox rulers.

LEFT **Justinian built the Hagia Sophia,** revived the eastern empire, and reconquered Africa, Italy, and parts of coastal Spain. He is depicted here on a gold denarius (*c.* CE 550).

BELOW **The Fortress of Krak des Chevaliers in Syria** is regarded as the best-preserved Crusader fortress in the Middle East. It was built by the Knights Hospitalier (*c.* 1200).

The Sasanian Empire

In the third century CE, the Sasanian dynasty in Persis rose up against the Parthians in Iran. The spur came from the Sasanian king Ardashir I, who came to power *c.* CE 209. Ardashir and the last Parthian king Artabanus V met in battle in CE 223 and Artabanus was defeated. Ardashir was crowned King of Kings (*Shahanshah*) and the new Sasanian Empire was born.

While the Parthians had occasionally caused considerable damage during lightning raids on Roman territory, the new Sasanian dynasty was a far more dangerous proposition. Within a few decades of defeating the Parthians, the Sasanians mounted devastating attacks on Rome's eastern provinces. Coupled with this, the Sasanians were keen sponsors of the Zoroastrian religion. The Sasanian kings gave considerable power to the Zoroastrian High Priest (Mobed) and established Zoroastrianism as a state religion which they promoted as part of their ruling ethos.

BELOW **Ardashir I** is seen here on horseback receiving a ribboned crown from the god Ahura-Mazda in a relief from Naqsh-i Rustam. He expanded his empire into Central Asia and the Caucasus region.

Shapur I Invades the Roman Empire

The new Sasanian regime soon began attacks on recently acquired Roman territory, particularly the province of Mesopotamia. Following the death of Ardashir in CE 241–242, his son Shapur I came to power, and a decade later mounted a series of devastating invasions of the eastern Roman provinces. Dozens of cities were captured across Mesopotamia, Syria, Asia Minor, and Cappadocia. Antioch, the metropolis of Syria and the third most populated city in the Roman Empire, was captured in CE 252–253, and, in a battle outside Edessa in CE 260, the Roman emperor Valerian was captured.

On his return to Persia, Shapur put up a large inscription at Naqsh-i Rustam in three languages which gave a detailed account of his campaigns. In the inscription Shapur claimed to have captured more than 70 cities, destroyed two Roman armies (numbering a total of 130,000 soldiers), and taken thousands of captives, including the Roman emperor himself. Naqsh-i Rustam was near Persepolis and was a center of Sasanian imperial monumental construction, designed to advertise the power of the new dynasty. Ardashir had carved rock reliefs depicting his defeat of Artabanus V, and now Shapur commissioned reliefs showing himself with the captive emperor Valerian and the emperors Gordian III and Philip the Arab whom he had defeated earlier in his reign. Many of the captives taken back to Persia by Shapur were skilled artisans, craftsmen, and builders. Evidence of their labors can still be seen today in Iran, including a bridge constructed in Roman style at Shushta, and mosaics at Shapur's palace at Bishapur.

While the Sasanians captured territory from the Romans they did not retain it, and they seem to have been interested only in taking booty and captives. Instability in the Sasanian leadership following Shapur's death in CE 272, and problems on their eastern frontier in Central Asia, meant that the Sasanians did not pose any further problems for the Roman Empire until the mid-CE 290s. During this period the strength of the Zoroastrian Mobed Kartir was growing in Sasanian Persia. At the behest of Kartir, the Sasanian king Bahram II began persecuting Christians. This persecution would recur in the fourth century CE under Shapur II.

Sasanian Challenges to Roman Power

In CE 298 the Roman emperors Diocletian and Galerius defeated the Sasanian Persians in Mesopotamia. Rome now claimed control of territory east of the upper Tigris, and in Armenia. This situation would remain the status quo for the next 60 years. The Romans had built a large number of fortifications in Mesopotamia and despite many of them being captured by Shapur II in CE 359–360, the Persian army could advance no further. However, following the Persian campaign of the emperor Julian in CE 363, during which he died, the Romans were forced to cede control of their northern Mesopotamian provinces. This represented a major victory for the Sasanians. In CE 387, Persia and Rome came to an agreement over Armenia in which the kingdom was partitioned, with the east going to Persia, and the west going to Rome.

ABOVE **Valerian, at left, is captured by Shapur I** in this fourth-century CE sardonyx cameo (now in the Bibliothèque Nationale in France).

Croesus II and the Roman Response

Over the following 200 years, conflict between the Sasanians and Romans was at a much lower level than it had been in the third and fourth centuries. This all changed when Croesus II launched an unprecedented war of conquest against the Byzantine East in CE 610. Under him, the Persians captured Roman cities and provinces, including Antioch in CE 611, Damascus in CE 613, Jerusalem in CE 614, and the whole of Egypt in CE 618. In CE 622, the Roman Emperor Heraclius set out to recapture the territory that Croesus had taken. After five years of intense fighting, Heraclius succeeded in inflicting a major defeat on the Sasanians at Nineveh, and in the following year the Romans regained all the territory previously lost to them. Within ten years, the Sasanian Empire came under unrelenting attack from Islamic forces from Arabia, and within 20 years it ceased to exist.

BELOW **King Shapur I is depicted leading nine followers**, including his son Ormuzd, in this carved relief from Naqsh-i Rustam.

Sasanian Art and Architecture

Shapur's Victory Immortalized in Stone
The rock bas-reliefs at Naqsh-i Rustam celebrate the victories of the Sasanian kings. Here Shapur I lords it over the defeated Philip the Arab, who is kneeling, and the captured Valerian. This relief is one of seven at the site.

The art and architecture of the Sasanian period is visually impressive and well known for the production of certain styles of carving and metalwork. Sasanian silverware is particularly distinguished in its style and technical execution, gracing important museum collections around the world. The Sasanians are also renowned for the execution of large rock carvings which detail the victories of various Sasanian kings over domestic and foreign opponents. In addition, the Sasanian kings invested considerable resources in constructing palaces, the remains of which can still be seen in Iran today.

Another notable feature of Sasanian art was the carving of rock reliefs by the early Sasanian *shahanshahs* illustrating their victories over a variety of enemies. The site of Naqsh-i Rustam near Persepolis in modern Iran is famous for its rock-relief carvings celebrating the victories of the first Sasanian *shahanshah*, Ardashir I (reigned CE 224–241) and his son, Shapur I (reigned CE 242–272). Naqsh-i Rustam had been an important center for the Achaemenid Persian kings centuries earlier, and the early Sasanian kings attempted to link themselves with the Achaemenids by adopting the site as an important center of their own regime. One of the rock reliefs depicts Ardashir unhorsing the last of the Parthian kings, Artabanus V. Another shows Shapur I on horseback with two Roman emperors humbled before him. One of the emperors, Philip the Arab (reigned CE 244–249), is kneeling before Shapur begging for mercy, and the other, Valerian (reigned CE 253–260), is being held by Shapur's right hand, indicating his capture by the *shahanshah* in battle near Edessa in CE 260. The rock reliefs were not only carved at Naqsh-i Rustam, but also at Bishapur, to the west, where Shapur I built a large palace. At Bishapur, a surviving rock relief depicts Shapur on horseback with Valerian held behind him, Philip kneeling before him, and another Roman emperor, Gordian III (reigned CE 238–244) trampled

Sasanian Silverware

The silver plates, bowls, and drinking cups from the Sasanian era appear to have been first produced in the fourth century CE. They often depict royal hunting scenes, or occasionally animals alone, which are thought to represent the gods of the Zoroastrian pantheon. Some silver vessels are also gilt, with rare examples that are primarily made of gold. These vessels were produced until the end of the Sasanian dynasty in the seventh century CE, and it seems that elaborate metallurgy was produced in and distributed from royal workshops. The silver and gilt dish (left, *c.* CE 200–600) depicts a king (flanked by two ibex), seated in a pavilion supported by two winged horses.

to death under the horses hooves, representing his death in battle against Shapur in CE 244.

The Sasanian kings were also famous for their palaces. Ardashir built an impressive palace at Firuzabad, Shapur I built one at Bishapur, and the remains of a number of Sasanian imperial palaces have been found throughout the Sasanian Empire. Perhaps the most famous is the palace of Croesus I (reigned CE 531–579) at Ctesiphon, the effective capital of the Sasanian Empire. Arab writers later described the palace as the most beautiful ever built. Part of the façade of the palace still stands and is dominated by an enormous barrel vault measuring 115 ft (35 m) in height with a length of nearly 165 ft (50 m). The external façade is decorated with blind architecture including columns, niches, and crenellations. This part of the structure originally stood to a height of six stories. The walls inside the palace were decorated with marble taken from one of the churches in Antioch in Syria following Croesus's capture of the city in CE 540. The walls were also decorated with glass mosaics depicting his successful capture of the city. The floors were made of thick marble and covered with silk carpets.

The Gigantic Glory of Ctesiphon
For 700 years the city of Ctesiphon was the imperial capital for different empires: the Seleucid, the Parthian, and the Sasanian.

Ruins of Bishapur
King Shapur I is reputed to have founded Bishapur on the trade route between Persis and Elam. Captured Roman soldiers and artisans are said to have labored for 20 years to build the city.

The Arab Conquest

The Arab conquest of the Byzantine and Sasanian Persian Empires in the seventh century CE was one of the most important developments in the history of the Middle East. In only 20 years the armies of Mohammed succeeded in bringing these vast territories under their control.

At the time the armies of Islam emerged from Arabia, the two great Middle Eastern powers, Byzantium and Sasanian Persia, had recently fought a ferocious 20-year war. Under Croesus II (reigned CE 591–628) the Persians had taken control of large sections of the Byzantine Empire by CE 619, and the Byzantine Emperor Heraclius (reigned CE 610–641) succeeded in recapturing most of this territory by the time of Croesus's death. The protracted and bloody wars between these two empires had left them both weak and impoverished, and it was just at this point that Islamic power was burgeoning in Arabia.

BELOW **A cave on Mount Hira in Saudi Arabia** is said to be where the Prophet Mohammed received the first revelations from Allah via the angel Gabriel (*c.* CE 615–620).

The Emergence of Islam in Arabia

The beginning of Islam is dated from the time that the Prophet Mohammed began teaching his revelation, around CE 620. The Arabian oasis trading centers in the Hejaz had been steadily growing in wealth and power during the fifth and sixth centuries CE, and Mohammed was born into one of the more powerful trading families. Mohammed first preached his revelation in Mecca, but local hostility forced him to flee north to the oasis town of Yathrib in CE 622, where he found sanctuary. Yathrib became the Prophet's base, and was known thereafter as "the city" (Medina). Mohammed died there in CE 632. By the time of his death, his message was spreading throughout Arabia, aided by the successful generalship of Mohammed's allies. While Mecca later emerged as the holiest city in Islam, Mohammed's move to Medina (known as the *Hijrah*) is considered to have been such a significant event that it marks the beginning of the Islamic calendar. Medina is now considered to be the second holiest city in Islam, after Mecca, because it is the burial place of the Prophet Mohammed.

Mohammed was succeeded by the first Caliph Abu Bakr who preached a holy war (*jihad*) to extend the power of Islam beyond Arabia. His successor, the Caliph Omar, took the first serious steps to make this a reality. His military assaults were assisted by the fact that in both Sasanian Persia and the Byzantine Near East there were many groups who were disaffected with the ruling authorities. In Byzantine Syria, Monophysite Christians and Jews had suffered persecution at the hands of the Byzantine authorities, and in Persia some sections of the military were disillusioned with the Sasanian rulers. These groups began to look to the Muslims of Arabia as liberators.

The First Attacks on Sasanian Persia

In CE 633, the first Islamic attack on Sasanian Persian territory took place. This was directed at the city of Hira (in northern Saudi Arabia today),

LEFT **The mosque at Medina** is depicted on this glazed eighteenth-century painted panel. It was found in Iznik, Turkey and is now in the Louvre, France.

LEFT **The Prophet Mohammed and Abu Bakr** are depicted in a cave in this seventeenth-century Turkish miniature. Abu Bakr guided the Islamic forces to victory after the Prophet's death.

but by the following year the Islamic army had been ejected by the Sasanian General Mirhan. This was followed by an invasion of Mesopotamia in CE 635 in which the Islamic invaders were again defeated at the Battle of the Bridges on the Euphrates River. This was the last battle in which the Sasanian Persians would emerge victorious. In CE 637, after significant Islamic victories over the Byzantines, Caliph Omar was able to send more forces to bolster the army attacking Sasanian territory. A Sasanian army was sent from the imperial capital of Ctesiphon to engage the Islamic army under the command of Saad ibn Abi Waqqas at Qadisiyyah in northern Iraq. Following a four-day battle, in which approximately 4,000 elite Sasanian troops defected to the Arabs, Waqqas defeated the Sasanian army. The battle took a heavy toll on both sides, but the Sasanians were clearly much weaker in the aftermath. According to legend a sandstorm blew up during the last day, blinding the Sasanian forces. In CE 638, Waqqas marched an army of approximately 60,000 men on Ctesiphon, the most important city in the Sasanian Empire. The forces of the Sasanian *shahanshah* Yazdegird III (reigned CE 632–651) were unable to withstand the Arab siege and the city finally fell. This victory by the Islamic forces was the first against the Sasanian Persians which resulted in the capture of large amounts of booty, including the crown jewels of Croesus II.

The next engagement took place in CE 639 at Jalula in southwestern Iraq. The fighting was ferocious, and once again the forces of Yazdegird III were crushed. It seems that in this battle, former soldiers, officers, and cavalry commanders of the Sasanian army were of considerable assistance to the Arab commander, al-Hashem. Yazdegird retreated to the vicinity of modern Tehran, and the Islamic armies advanced into Persis, the heartland of the Sasanian Persian dynasty. Persis did not surrender without a long struggle, and resistance to the invaders continued for nearly 20 years.

RIGHT **During his reign (CE 610–641), the Byzantine Emperor Heraclius** strove to quell the advances of both the Persians and the forces of Islam.

The Defeat of Yazdegird III

In CE 641, the Sasanian Empire's last major battle was fought against the Islamic armies at Nihavand in northwestern Iran. The Sasanians are claimed to have marshalled 150,000 troops in a desperate attempt to gain a victory over the Arab forces. The Arab army numbered some 100,000 troops, and included soldiers of Sasanian origin, together with troops recently freed up after victories over the Byzantines. The Islamic army had initial problems with maintaining adequate supplies, and the Sasanians held out valiantly. Eventually, the Arab forces staged a mock withdrawal in an attempt to trick the Persian forces into a pursuit which would draw them away from their supply bases. The plan worked, and the Sasanian forces were defeated for the last time. The Islamic armies now entered Iran proper but they met considerable resistance in northern Iran which was to take them several generations to subdue. The Sasanian Empire had now been destroyed, and the Sasanian royal family and many aristocratic followers fled east into Chinese Central Asia.

The First Attacks on the Byzantine Empire

In the Byzantine Near East, which mostly comprised Syria and Palestine, the effects of the wars with the Persian forces of Croesus II had been devastating, and at the time of the Prophet Mohammed's death in CE 632, Byzantine rule had only been recently reestablished. The first military encounter between the Islamic armies and the Byzantines was similar to the first encounter with the Sasanians. In CE 629 at Mu'tah, in what was little more than a skirmish, the Byzantines inflicted defeat on a small army sent by Mohammed. Despite this defeat, Mohammed created the momentum which was eventually to see Syria fall to the Muslim armies after his death. Mohammed's successor, his companion and adviser, the first Caliph, Abu Bakr, sent an army into Syria soon after the Prophet's death, and by CE 640, the whole of Byzantine Syria had fallen to the Islamic armies.

The figure to whom much of the Islamic success in Syria is often attributed is the general, Khalid ibn al-Walid, but Abu Abayda's generalship was also important. Walid marched from Iraq to Syria in CE 634 under the orders of Abu Bakr to assist in the capture of Syria. He is portrayed in the Arab sources as eventually uniting the Arab forces and devising the tactics necessary to achieve the conquest of Syria. The first major victory was at the important trading city of Bostra, which went over to Walid without a fight. The Byzantine forces under the overall command of the emperor Heraclius attempted to halt the Islamic advance, but were defeated in a battle at Ajnadayn before withdrawing to Damascus. Damascus was put under siege and eventually surrendered. The outcome for the residents of Damascus was essentially the same as it had been in Bostra: the inhabitants of the city were left to their own devices, but were required to pay tribute to the Caliphate. The first Caliph, Abu Bakr, died in Medina soon after and was replaced by Caliph Omar who was seriously opposed to Walid's command. After protracted negotiations with Omar in Medina, Walid returned to Syria to resume the attack on the Byzantines.

Heraclius had retreated to Antioch following the fall of Damascus where he planned his last major challenge to the invading Islamic armies. Marching an army of 20,000 men south, Heraclius met an Islamic army of 24,000 men under the command of Walid in the vicinity of the Yarmuk river valley separating modern Syria from Jordan. This would be the most important single battle between the Byzantine and Islamic armies. The battle was actually a series of engagements throughout the summer of CE 634, and it culminated in a major confrontation in late August. The Byzantine army was soundly defeated after Walid's employment of an innovative cavalry formation, and Syria now lay open to the victors. The city of Homs was soon

THE ISLAMIC CONQUEST OF EGYPT

The Islamic conquest of Egypt was similar to the conquest of Syria and Mesopotamia. In December CE 639, Caliph Omar sent his general Amr ibn al-As with an army of 4,000 men to attack Egypt. Heraclius had isolated Egypt after its recapture in CE 629 as its divergent Monophysite Christian administration was by no means reconciled to Byzantine rule. Al-As quickly established the authority of the Caliphate in Egypt, receiving 5,000 reinforcements in CE 640 with which he defeated the remnants of the Byzantine army at Heliopolis. Alexandria surrendered peacefully in November CE 641.

LEFT **Heliopolis (or City of the Sun),** was the site of one of the final battles between the Byzantines and the Islamic invaders. The Muslims triumphed and won much booty.

taken, and then Chalcis, which Walid would later turn into his own power base.

Heraclius Abandons Syria

Following the defeat at the Yarmuk and the advance of the Islamic forces, Heraclius appears to have resigned himself to the permanent loss of Syria. He moved from Antioch to Edessa, before heading back to Constantinople. Antioch, one of the most important cities in the Byzantine Empire, soon fell to the Islamic army without a fight, but the cities of coastal Syria and Palestine did not give in so easily. Gaza offered stiff resistance, as did Caesarea Maritima and Laodicea (modern Latakia). The surrender of Jerusalem in CE 638 was highly significant to the history of Islam. The siege lasted four months. The Caliph Omar was personally involved in the siege, and the importance of the city for Islam would grow considerably afterward.

In CE 641, Heraclius died, and a succession crisis ensued which further weakened the Byzantine Empire. The Islamic armies crossed the Euphrates and captured territory in northern Mesopotamia, including the cities of Edessa, Diyarbakir, and Raqqa. An uneasy boundary emerged which left the Byzantines in control of most of Asia Minor, but Syria and Palestine were now clearly under the control of the Caliphs. The first powerful Islamic Caliphate of the Umayyads emerged in Syria and Mesopotamia and was based in the city of Damascus where it would sponsor the construction of the Great Mosque early in the eighth century CE.

ABOVE **The Dome of the Rock, located on the Temple Mount in Jerusalem,** is sacred to Islam, as it is from this rock that the Prophet Mohammed ascended into Paradise. The Dome of the Rock was built in CE 691 and is one of the finest Umayyad monuments.

Search for Origins: The Rediscovery of the Middle East

Introduction

Historians may dispute Napoleon's objective in conquering Egypt in 1798, but the cultural impact of this event was incalculable. The Middle East now seems so central to our understanding of the ancient world, that it is easy to forget it had been ignored by the West for more than 500 years.

Much of the region had become a cultural backwater under Ottoman rule and its fabulous antiquities were neglected. Following Napoleon's invasion, Europe's attention once again turned eastward to the world's earliest civilization. But it was an economic rather than a military incursion that brought the civilizations of Mesopotamia to the attention of Europeans. Claudius Rich (1787–1820) of the East India Company explored the ancient Near East and captured the attention of his British countrymen as well as the Germans and the French. Another East India employee, Henry Creswicke Rawlinson (1810–1895) eventually made ancient Near Eastern history accessible to Westerners by deciphering cuneiform.

RIGHT **Sir Henry Creswicke Rawlinson (1882),** British soldier and orientalist, was the first person to decipher the cuneiform script.

Plundering the Ancient Near East

The work of the early "code-breakers" resulted in what can only be described as a looting spree. The French consul in Mosul, Paul-Emile Botta (1802–1870), sent the treasures of Nineveh and Khorsabad to the Louvre. Austen Henry Layard (1817–1894), appropriated Assyrian reliefs, texts, and sculpture from Nineveh for the British Museum. The Germans opened huge excavations at ancient Assur and Babylon, exporting the remains of entire buildings to Berlin.

Although the Ottoman Empire had nominal control over the region, it acquired antiquities only on an ad hoc basis from foreign explorers.

Nineteenth-century America was religiously conservative so it was not surprising that the US contribution to exploration of the Middle East was driven by a desire to demonstrate the truth of the Bible. In 1842, Edward Robinson (1794–1863), an audacious explorer of the Holy Land, was the first Westerner to publish descriptions of the region. Not long after, another neglected civilization—ancient Persia—was revealed more methodically when Marcel-Auguste Dieulafoy (1844–1920), the first in a long line of French excavators, began to work on the site of ancient Susa.

The First Modern Archaeologists Enter the Scene

The shift from a geographical focus on finding sites to an archaeological focus on recovering information was stimulated by the influential work of W. M. Flinders Petrie (1853–1942). Toward the end of the nineteenth century, Petrie had made advances in establishing relative chronologies through careful study of the different strata and types of pottery occurring together in the same deposit. Petrie's legacy was one of methodical excavation, and rapid and often insightful final publication. His countryman Leonard Woolley (1880–1960) is more famous for the wonderful discoveries at Ur. Finding the "Royal Tombs of Ur" with their incredibly rich assemblage of artifacts in gold, silver, carnelian and lapis lazuli, came in the middle of a long and distinguished career that eventually earned him, like Petrie before him, a knighthood. Later in the twentieth century, excavations in Syria, Lebanon, Iraq, Iran, and Palestine began to reveal the connections between the ancient Near East and European culture through the conduit of ancient Aegean civilizations. Woolley was among the first to pursue this line of inquiry, having worked with Sir Arthur Evans (1851–1941), excavator of the site of Knossos on Crete, very early in his career. Petrie and Woolley, both from religious backgrounds, laid the foundations for the discipline of biblical archaeology, which became centered on Palestine and Jordan.

American scholars quickly rose to prominence in the post-war period, with major excavations at Megiddo and Beth Shean dominating fieldwork. The pre-eminent scholar among these newcomers was William Foxwell Albright (1891–1971) who dominated the developing field of biblical archaeology for a generation.

The Ancient Near East Becomes Middle Eastern

With the partitioning of the Ottoman Empire after World War I, the peoples of the Middle East began to experience a marked political transformation. Interventionist Western bureaucrats intent on "modernizing" the region had replaced inattentive Eastern overlords. As a result, this was a period of instability, turmoil and emerging national identities. The local Arabic peoples of the Middle East were spurred by growing pride in their archaeological heritage towards measures that would put them in control of their own heritage. In 1933 newly independent Iraq placed restrictions on foreign excavations. Western excavators began to look elsewhere, and Syria, Lebanon, Palestine, and Iran benefited, in terms of new discoveries, from an influx of European and American scholars. It took up to 30 more years for other nations to follow the Iraqi model, but by the early sixties, foreigners who worked in the region faced far more stringent local oversight and a sharp reduction in the number of finds exported to foreign institutions. The era of indiscriminate acquisition on behalf of foreign governments and institutions had officially come to an end.

BELOW ***Pardoning the Rebels at Cairo, 23rd October 1798*** by Pierre-Narcisse Guerin is a popular depiction of Napoleon Bonaparte who brought the Middle East to the attention of Europe.

Anatomy of a Tell

Ancient peoples all over the world built up mounds, intentionally or accidentally, that testify to their presence. Mesolithic barrows in England, early earthwork temples in Mesoamerica, and tumuli built over burials, were all constructed in the landscape. Middens, accumulations of trash, and that unique feature of Middle East archaeology, the tell, are accidental creations.

The term "tell" means "artificial, or man-made mound" in both Arabic and Hebrew ("tel"). Tells are man-made structures. They are the result of both the accumulation of debris that is a feature of most archaeological sites, and the alternation of dry and wet seasons that provides both the perfect environment to create mudbrick buildings in summer, and the optimum conditions to wear them down, during rainy winters. The principle that newer strata lay on top of older ones applies to tells as it does to most archaeological sites, but archaeologists working on tells might find themselves rapidly excavating through thousands of years of successive cultures within very small depths.

The unique challenge a tell presents to the archaeologist is best illustrated by a description of work at a hypothetical tell site. This starts with the workers roping off small squares at the top of the tell. Within these areas they collect all material from the surface of the squares. Mostly potsherds, these artifacts are from various periods dating from Ottoman times back to the Iron Age. Surface pottery is not necessarily an accurate indicator of what lies beneath, but it can give a clue as to the most potentially productive areas. The workers start by removing the surface

Tel Hazor in Israel

Evidence of a thriving city that was a leading city of a number of pre-Israelite kingdoms can be found here. There are 21 levels of occupation from *c.* 2600–200 BCE.

Tell Harari (Ancient City of Mari)

On the western banks of the Euphrates River in Syria, this site was discovered by accident in the 1930s. More than 20,000 cuneiform clay tablets found here have allowed accurate dating of events in ancient Mesopotamia.

within those squares where the largest number and variety of potsherds were found. Up to 6 in (15 cm) below the surface, the pottery is nineteenth-century Ottoman. From 6 to 12 in (15 to 30 cm) below the surface, the pottery is Byzantine. Below the Byzantine level, Hellenistic stone walls are found along with abundant pottery of the period. These walls look like part of a small but elaborate building. Figurines and other ritual objects confirm that it is a temple. Below lies what appears to be an earlier structure, dating from the period of the Persian Empire. Beneath that are found the remains of what seem to be mudbrick houses built upon stone foundations dating from the Late Bronze to Late Iron Ages. From the material culture excavated from the different layers of a tell archaeologists can construct what is called a "sequence of occupations."

The archaeologists know that the formation of a tell is not a process of building up even layers one upon the other. Rather, it is quite conceivable that different parts of the tell were occupied during different periods of time. In other areas material from those time periods where gaps seem to occur might be found. The extent of occupation of most tells has a lot to do with where they are located. Dependable water sources, fertile soils, defensible positions, cultural and religious associations, trade routes, and natural barriers are all important. A large proportion of these sites have no prehistoric levels because tells are related to farming cultures and the aggregation of humans into towns and villages. Also, gaps in occupation are common when these sites are destroyed. They can remain unoccupied until the same factors that encouraged settlement there in the first place appeal to a new generation that has no memory of the events that caused the site to be abandoned.

Lamgi-Mari, King of Mari
This statue, (*c.* 2500–2400 BCE), is from the Temple of Ishtar in Mari, Syria, a city that was purpose-built to house local, previously nomadic, peoples alongside incoming city dwellers from further upstream.

Hebrew Ostracon
An ostracon (potsherd), *c.* 750 BCE, from Tel Qasileh north of Tel Aviv is inscribed with the words: "Gold from Ophir to Bethhoron–30 shekels."

Interpreting Tells

In our hypothetical tell, we would find:

1. Continuous occupation from Late Bronze (*c.*1500 BCE) to Middle Hellenistic (*c.* 200 BCE);
2. Gap of 700 years;
3. A settlement of the Byzantine Period (CE 500 to CE 700); and
4. Another gap of 1,000 years until Ottoman Times (CE 1800).

Neo-Babylonian Excavations

The Neo-Babylonians (also known as the Chaldeans) were not the first visitors to the ancient land of Mesopotamia to express an interest in its antiquities. Acquiring beautiful and exotic objects, and preserving them for future generations, had been the custom of royalty there going back to the Sumerians in the third millennium BCE.

The gathering of ancient documents into royal libraries was a practice that was already over 1,000 years old by the time the Assyrian king, Ashurbanipal, began to amass his formidable collection at Nineveh. Amassing fine libraries of epic and religious literature allowed monarchs to proclaim their civilization as well as their martial virtue, and the new Chaldean kings of the Neo-Babylonian Empire were no exception.

It had been some time since Babylon had been ruled by true Babylonians—speakers of the Semitic Babylonian language who originated in the heartland of Mesopotamia. For 1,000 years, the city had been a prize that passed from the hands of one foreign group to another. The Old Kingdom Hittite king Mursili I led a raid on Babylon around 1595 BCE. One of his key allies, the Kassite peoples, then resident in upper Mesopotamian river valleys, stayed on in Babylon after Mursili withdrew.

The Kassite dynasty ruled Babylon for the next 400 years until they were conquered by the Elamites, another people from the Iranian Plateau who, in turn, surrendered the city to Assyrian control. The Assyrians, at least, were a people with cultural and linguistic affinities to Babylon. Assyrian domination ended with the rebellion of Nabopolassar. He was the first of the great Neo-Babylonian kings, whose origin was more acceptable than that of the Assyrians. Although the Chaldeans were from the southern Euphrates River Valley—as opposed to the northern Tigris where the Assyrians originated—they were not, strictly speaking, Babylonian. Like most of the conquerors of that splendid city, they soon succumbed to the charms of its age-old civilization. There is little to distinguish Neo-Babylonian rulers from their Babylonian subjects—they clearly respected the integrity of the city's culture.

Nebuchadnezzar II: Collector and Curator

The greatest of the Neo-Babylonian kings, Nebuchadnezzar II, took his name from the most notable king of a dynasty that had ruled Babylon almost 400 years before. Nebuchadnezzar I's most lasting achievement was driving the Elamites out of Babylon and securing its borders, and, like Ashurbanipal, he was interested in scholarship and accumulated a large library of documents.

What is most significant about him was his religious devotion. The *Enuma Elish*, the account of the earth's creation and the destruction of the serpent goddess, Tiamat, by Marduk most certainly was codified during his reign. Marduk was now established as the city's primary god.

Nebuchadnezzar II was also dedicated to the worship of Marduk. As well as a major rebuilding program for all of Babylon, he rebuilt the temple of Marduk in grand style. Marduk had already returned the favor by conferring divinity upon him.

The Assyrians had all but destroyed Babylon during the last

BELOW **Glazed brick relief of a winged lion,** from the Processional Way in the palace at Babylon that was completed by Nebuchadnezzar.

LEFT ***Nebuchadnezzar in the Hanging Gardens*** is an illustration from *Myths of Babylonia and Assyria* by Ernest Wallcousins (1883–1976).

years of the kingdom, and what they did not tear down was devastated during constant rebellions. Nebuchadnezzar II, continuing in his father's footsteps, built up the city of Babylon and completed the palace, which became the focal point for his own mania for collecting. Not only were the reputed Hanging Gardens filled with plants imported from throughout the empire, but a large museum was established within the palace, housing exhibits from almost 2,000 years of Mesopotamian history.

Nabonidus

Nebuchadnezzar died in 562 BCE and was succeeded by his son Amel-Marduk, who is known as Evil-Merodach in the Old Testament. He seemed to display some rather alarming tendencies toward compassion, having, among other things, pardoned and released the Judahite king Jehoiachin, according to the Book of Kings, and, as a consequence, was soon murdered by his more ruthless brother-in-law, Neriglissar.

An able general, Neriglissar (reigned 559–556 BCE) invaded Anatolia, was victorious in Cilicia, and even crossed the Taurus Mountains. Despite this success, he was not able to guarantee the throne to his son, Labashi-Marduk, after he either died, or was deposed. Nabonidus easily took the throne away from the child.

Some accounts suggest that Neriglissar was merely a wealthy commoner, while Nabonidus was of royal blood. Nabonidus does not seem to have had an easy time on the throne, although it is more than likely that traditional accounts are heavily biased against his actions. It remains a mystery why he left Babylon for the isolated oasis of Tayma, in present-day Saudi Arabia, but speculation has suggested severe illness (perhaps periodic insanity or disfiguring disease) prevented him from carrying out the normal, and very public, ceremonies of the ruler at Babylon. These were performed by his son, Belshazzar, whose hedonistic feast, according to the Old Testament, was disrupted by the "writing on the wall" with its prophecy of doom (Daniel 5:1–31).

Nabonidus preferred to worship the god of his fathers, the moon-god, Sin. The fact that the state-sanctioned deity was Marduk did little to endear Nabonidus to the powerful priests of Babylon. The *Nabonidus Chronicle* appears to confirm this. He failed to show up for the New Year's Festival that celebrated Marduk's supremacy, staying in the desert to rebuild the moon temple.

Nabonidus had retreated to Tayma, causing much speculation as to what he was doing there other than engaging in building programs. Some suggest that this move was his attempt to reinforce the Neo-Babylonian presence on an important trade route that existed between Mesopotamia

BELOW ***The Hanging Gardens of Babylon*** is given an imagined reality in *The Seven Wonders of the World* by British archaeologists John and Elizabeth Romer.

ABOVE **Ashurbanipal and his queen enjoy a banquet** in this relief from the North Palace at Nineveh. It is unusual for women to be represented in Assyrian sculpture.

and Egypt. Rather, it seems that his interest in Tayma had to do with what he perceived as a divine command that he secure the southern borders of the empire.

However, despite his singular devotion to Sin, it is probably not true that Nabonidus spurned other gods. He seemed to have displayed a particular interest in the accomplishments and religion of his predecessors, and he restored the sanctuaries to the gods Eanna and Marduk at Sippar and Erech. It is apparent that Nabonidus considered himself as a worthy successor to the earlier Neo-Babylonian kings.

The Persians and the Greeks, as well as the Old Testament, have contributed to our negative view of Nabonidus, but none of these accounts can be considered as either authoritative or objective. The fact that the Persian king Cyrus claims to have easily wrested the Babylonian Empire away from its king may disclose more about Cyrus's braggadocio than Nabonidus's incompetence. A number of texts written by Babylonians during the final days of the empire suggest that Nabonidus had merely made some strategic mistakes out of his desire to protect his borders, rather than to purposely flout the authority of the priests or the will of the people.

The Excavations of Nabonidus

Unlike earlier Neo-Babylonian kings, it is not Nabonidus's political or religious policies that have most interested archaeologists. Rather, it is his status as possibly the world's first excavator of past cultures. He seemed to share the ancient Mesopotamian proclivity for collecting, reportedly gathering cult statues from all over the kingdom, supposedly to save them from attacks by foreign powers. We don't know if they were ever returned, but this act seems to have been one among many that have branded him in history as a crazed blasphemer.

RIGHT **The moon-god, Sin, is shown in this** limestone relief from Tell Ahmar in Syria. Nabonidus favored Sin over the god Marduk, who was, at that time, regarded by the state as the supreme power.

In any event, a Nabonidus text that tells of his repairs to the Sin sanctuary suggests that his status as a scholar, if not as a king, may very well be underrated. He relates that, during construction, he searched scrupulously for the foundation deposits, or votive offerings, from the earlier temples. In doing so, he discovered an inscription relating to the last King of Assyria, Ashurbanipal, which, at that time, would have been 75 years old. He says that he "anointed it with oil, performed a sacrifice, placed it with my own inscription, and returned it to its place."

Nabonidus then describes how, in removing the debris of an older temple, he again looked carefully for its old foundation deposit, and, instead, stumbled upon an inscribed statue of Naram-Sin who had died about 1,800 years before. Naram-Sin (reigned 2255–2219 BCE) was the grandson of Sargon of Akkad, and under his rule, the Akkadian Empire had reached its zenith. He established the tradition of Mesopotamian kings, claiming divinity and also referred to himself as "King of the Four Quarters of the Earth," an appellation that was to appeal to many succeeding generations of rulers.

While Nabonidus may have been the first archaeologist to exaggerate the antiquity of his find, he certainly was not the last. His account says:

> *"No king among my predecessors had found [it] in three thousand and two hundred years... The inscription in the name of Naram-Sin, son of Sargon, I found and did not alter. I anointed it with oil, made offerings, placed it with my own inscription and returned it to its original place. I excavated, surveyed, and inspected the old foundations...I cleared its foundations and laid its brickwork."*

It appears that, in addition to being credited with the first archaeological excavation, he may also have been the first historical preservationist. He is also, rather poignantly, aware of his responsibility to contribute to future generations of scholars. His excavation account ends with these words:

> *"Whoever you are whom Sin...will call to kingship, and in whose reign that temple will fall into disrepair and who build it anew, may you find the inscription written in my name and not alter it."*

Nabonidus and Assyria

Nabonidus was an unusual figure among the Neo-Babylonian kings and his background is not completely clear. Texts relating to his reign have been interpreted as suggesting that he was, somehow, related to the Assyrians. He referred repeatedly to Ashurbanipal, and he also had a particular interest in Haran, the city to which the Assyrians retreated after the Fall of Nineveh. As readers of the Old Testament will recognize, Haran was the first stop on the patriarch Abraham's trip to Canaan from the Mesopotamian city of Ur. Haran was also an ancient city of great importance because it was on the trade routes that ran both north–south and east–west through Mesopotamia.

Excavations have confirmed that the site was settled as early as the third millennium BCE. It was a center for the worship of the sun and the moon from the sixteenth century BCE and remained so throughout domination by the Mitannians (fifteenth to thirteenth centuries BCE) and the Assyrians, who did little to change its religious affiliations.

BELOW **Naram-Sin, king of Akkad (*c.* 2255–2219 BCE), and grandson of Sargon I, tramples on his defeated enemies in this victory stele.**

Classical Accounts

Before the middle of the nineteenth century, our knowledge about the ancient Near East came primarily from ancient Greek accounts. Names of regions, cities, pharaohs, and kings have all come down to us through Greek writers.

BELOW **Greek historian Herodotus** (c. 485–425 BCE) is regarded as "the Father of History" in the West. He traveled widely and claimed to report only what was told to him.

The land of Assyria and Babylon, for which the Greeks gave us the name of Mesopotamia or "between two rivers," had a distinct allure for Classical and Post-Classical Greek writers. The subsequent histories that have been written about these two civilizations originated with these inquisitive travelers of antiquity.

Archaeological evidence indicates that there were Greeks in southwest Asia as early as the eleventh century BCE. The stories of the Trojan War are considered to reflect Greek incursions into Asia Minor that eventually brought them further east, perhaps even to found colonies. From the second half of the tenth century BCE, Greek artifacts are found everywhere at Near Eastern sites. In the ninth century BCE, they declined in numbers, but the presence of eastern goods in Greece may reflect the rise of Phoenicia as an economic power.

One significant piece of evidence about Greece's presence in the Near East uncovered in the 1950s provided evidence that the connection was older than previously thought. This was an eighth-century BCE bilingual inscription found at the site of Karatepe. Just as the Rosetta Stone had been the key that unlocked Egyptian hieroglyphic writing, this inscription allowed scholars to decipher the Hittite language. The inscription speaks of the Kings of Adana (in southern Turkey) as being of the "house of Mopsos." According to Greek mythology, Mopsos was a legendary Greek warrior who founded cities in Asia Minor after the Trojan War.

The Classical Historians

Of the Greek classical travelers, Herodotus of Halicarnassus (a city on the coast of Asia Minor) was the first to report on "Babylon and the rest of Assyria." Herodotus came to Babylon some 180 years after the Assyrian empire had disappeared, and 90 years after the Neo-Babylonians had succumbed to the Achaemenid Persians. Of Babylon, Herodotus says:

> *"Such is its size, in magnificence there is no other city that approaches to it. It is surrounded, in the first place, by a broad and deep moat, full of water, behind which rises a wall fifty royal cubits in width, and two hundred in height..."*

Herodotus went on to describe the city's massive fortifications, which so impressed him that they undoubtedly colored his description of the Persian conquest of the city. He believes the rather suspect account of Cyrus that there was no necessity to breach the defenses of Babylon because the Persians were welcomed

HERODOTUS AND WOMEN

When confronted with Babylonian religious practices, Herodotus was more shocked than awed. "The Babylonians have one most shameful custom," he moralized. "Every woman born in the country must once in her life go and sit down in the precinct of Venus [Ishtar], and there consort with a stranger." No subsequent scholar has given any credence to this story, but it has been pointed out by many that Herodotus was at his worst when reporting on either customs or history relating to women. He was under the impression, for example, that Semiramis, a somewhat legendary figure identified with the consort of an Assyrian king of the ninth century BCE, built the city of Babylon.

is the best account we have of how ziggurats functioned as places of worship. The temple, he wrote, had

> *"a tower of solid masonry, a furlong in length and breadth, upon which was raised a second tower, and on that a third, and so on up to eight. The ascent to the top is on the outside, by a path, which winds round all the towers. When one is about half-way up, one finds a resting-place and seats, where persons are wont to sit some time on their way to the summit. On the topmost tower there is a spacious temple, and inside the temple stands a couch of unusual size, richly adorned, with a golden table by its side."*

Xenophon, the Athenian historian, visited Asia some thirty years after Herodotus, as part of an expedition of Greek mercenaries to Anatolia. They traveled down the Euphrates as far as Baghdad, and returned up the Tigris after the Battle of Cunaxa. Xenophon and his battalion found themselves stranded in Mesopotamia and they were forced to march over land, fighting their way through hostile Persians, Armenians, and Kurds, to the coast of the Black Sea from where they sailed back to Greece. Xenophon's record of the entire expedition, the *Anabasis*, was used as a guide by Alexander the Great during the early phases of his campaign against Persia.

Post-Classical Greek Sources

The last of the Greek travelers was Strabo, a first-century-BCE geographer and historian. His mother's family was from Pontus and possibly related to King Mithridates, who was so brutally defeated by the Romans. It appears he managed to ingratiate himself with his new Roman overlords, which provided him with an opportunity to travel to Asia Minor and Egypt. Strabo's geography is among the most useful of ancient sources for archaeologists and historians in locating sites even today. His history, which might have proved similarly informative, has never been found.

ABOVE ***View of the City of Babylon*** by Athanasius Kircher (1602–1680), based on the descriptions by Herodotus, was published in 1679 in Amsterdam, the Netherlands.

BELOW **Athenian historian Xenophon** is shown with Socrates, Euthyphro, Plato, and Alcibiades in this Neo-Classical drawing.

Islamic Travelers

Given the requirement of pilgrimage to the Holy Places, and the central location of many of the great centers of learning, it is only natural that travelers from the earliest Islamic times frequently covered the length and breadth of the Middle East.

ABOVE **At the center of the Great Mosque** complex in Mecca sits Kaaba, towards which all Muslims pray.

Travel was always seen in a positive light by Islamic writers. It is not surprising, therefore, that the benefits of travel are extolled in Muslim culture. Students and scholars, especially, were encouraged to travel, not just to expand their own knowledge of the world, but also to represent the best of their religious culture abroad. In the early Medieval Period, a genre of travel literature in Arabic, known as *rihla*, appeared and remained popular down the ages. This was a time when Islamic influence was at its zenith and travelers could expect to be treated well by their co-religionists from Spain to China. Another important reason to travel, at least once in a lifetime for believers, was the great hajj or pilgrimage to Mecca.

One of the prominent early Islamic travelers was Al-Ya'qubi, whose *Book of Countries*, which was completed in the ninth century CE, supplies the names of places, people, and rulers, and charts the distances between towns, the taxes levied by them, the topography, and water resources.

The tenth century CE seems to have a been a particularly busy time for Muslim travelers. During this period the legendary Ibn Fadlan visited Scandinavia and Russia on a mission from

RIGHT **The Dome of the Rock in Jerusalem** is regarded as one of the world's great architectural achievements. The Haram es Sharif (the Noble Sanctuary) is sacred to Islam, Judaism, and Christianity.

the Caliph of Baghdad. Several decades later, the famous Al-Muqaddasi, originally from Jerusalem, set off from the Holy City to visit virtually every part of the known Muslim world. He was interested in presenting a complete picture of the lands he visited for the benefit of merchants and people of culture who followed him. His writings are an incomparable source of information about the traditions, practices, and cities of the Early Islamic Middle East.

Eleventh and Twelfth Centuries

The political control of the Middle East changed dramatically during the eleventh and twelfth centuries. Although central control over Muslim lands was weakening, the religion was expanding. Under attack from European Crusaders from the West and Seljuk Turks from the East, travelers could no longer feel protected. Eventually, the Seljuk Turks settled down and adopted Islam, leaving at least the former Muslim lands in the East generally secure for their co-religionists. Inquisitive scholars like poet Nasir-i-Khusraw, an eleventh-century Persian, traveled to Palestine, Arabia, Egypt, Jerusalem, and Mecca, describing them in detail. His work, like that of others before him, provides little in the way of detail of the monuments of past civilizations.

Ibn Jubair, a Spanish Arab traveler, displayed more antiquarian interest than some of his predecessors. During the twelfth century, he began his journeys with a visit to Alexandria and describes its lighthouse, built over 1,400 years earlier and named as one of the Seven Wonders of the Ancient World. The magnificent structure was destroyed by an earthquake only 140 years later. Having been born in the West, and witnessing the decline of Islamic power there, Ibn Jubair was particularly gladdened by the sight of Damascus, but cities that had fallen into Crusader hands depressed him greatly. To Islamic eyes, medieval Christians were unhygienic and hedonistic. He describes the once-beautiful city of Acre in Palestine as having become a filthy refuse pit. We know more about his first journey than his second, but in commemoration of the latter, there is an extant poem celebrating Saladin's victory at Hittin.

Ibn Battuta

The most famous Muslim traveler of the Medieval Period was the fourteenth-century polymath Ibn Battuta. Born in Tangier, as a young adult he made a pilgrimage to Mecca. He traveled along the usual route from Morocco—through North Africa and Upper Egypt to the Red Sea where a local skirmish prevented his crossing. He diverted his route to Palestine and Syria, and from there he visited Iraq, Iran, and was finally able to go to Mecca, where he stayed for two years.

He visited more than 40 countries, including Spain, Afghanistan, India, and China, in the course of making four journeys to Mecca. His descriptions of Palestine, only recently recovering from Crusader rule, are particularly vivid. Among other sites he visited Hebron, Bethlehem, and Jerusalem, which was a fairly small city at the time. Though he found it less cosmopolitan than other places he had visited, he found the site of the Dome of Rock, built in CE 698, to be particularly transcendent. "One prayer here is equivalent to five hundred times the prayers in any other mosque except for the Haram Mosque in Mecca and the Prophet's [An-Nabawi] Mosque in Medina," he wrote. It was, he said, "...the most marvelous of buildings, of the most perfect architecture."

LEFT **Salah Al-Din Al Ayyubi,** also known as Saladin, was a twelfth-century Egyptian ruler of Kurdish descent. He is said to have taught the Crusaders much about chivalry.

Missionaries and Envoys

The Middle East appealed to missionaries and diplomats from the time of Napoleon's invasion of Europe, if not before. The attraction for these two very different professions overlapped in some areas, and came sharply into conflict in others.

In both cases, the opportunities created by the Ottoman Empire's determination to modernize agriculture and industry in the early nineteenth century CE, and its slow decline under pressure from Imperial Russia in the later years of the century, allowed for more incursions into the Middle East by foreigners. Diplomats pursued Middle Eastern alliances between the Crimean War and World War I because of its strategic importance to the West. Missionaries aimed to convert Eastern Christians, Jews, and Muslims to the new Victorian Protestant creeds—unlike the medieval Crusaders who evinced little interest in the religious beliefs of their subjects.

British and French Envoys

Claudius James Rich was appointed at the height of the East India Company's powers in 1807. His mission was to promote its economic interests against the rising power of the Napoleonic French Empire. He was able to strengthen British interests in Mesopotamia and at the same time pursue his real passion, the ancient writings of Mesopotamia. Like all wealthy connoisseurs of ancient art, Rich amassed a large collection of Mesopotamian antiquities, which eventually went to the British Museum in 1825.

Henry Creswicke Rawlinson, who was expected to surpass the accomplishments of his predecessor, Rich, went to Mesopotamia with instructions to produce results that would strengthen British interests both diplomatically and culturally. In Europe, particularly in France and England, the Assyrian discoveries were seen as acceptable returns for Europe's "contribution" to Mesopotamia. For the British there was the additional impetus to justify the presence of the East India Company in more than simple mercantile terms.

In 1841 the situation changed with the opening of a French consulate in Mosul. Paul-Emile Botta

BELOW **The British East India Company was granted** a Royal Charter from Queen Elizabeth I in 1600. This eighteenth-century depiction of its London headquarters is by Samuel Wale.

LEFT **Paul-Emile Botta (1802–1870),** the French orientalist and archaeologist, is reputed to be the first person to excavate an Assyrian palace.

was appointed to Mosul with the support of Jules Mohl, a diplomat and a founder of the French Asiatic Society—an organization dedicated to studying Near Eastern Antiquity. Botta eagerly explored the ancient ruins around Mosul. He first excavated at Nineveh in 1842, but it was his discovery and excavations at Khorsabad that made his reputation.

Rich and Botta were followed by Austen Henry Layard, destined to be the most famous of the early explorers of Assyria. Layard first came to the region as an enthusiastic scholar-explorer in 1840. It was several years before he was able to begin excavations at ancient Nimrud in 1845, but his discoveries and their publication in 1849 took Britain by storm.

The Missionaries

The increasing security and freedom of movement afforded to British and French travelers from the 1840s onwards, proved to be a magnet for a great number of Christian missionaries. Both before and after World War I, they were bent on spreading the new Protestant doctrines. Some of them, especially in the Holy Land, wanted to explore the remains of ancient civilizations, but this was a secondary concern. Throughout much of the nineteenth century, the field of biblical archaeology was dominated by men who worked with a Bible in one hand and a trowel in the other. Even though the fieldwork became more scientific, the excavation of some sites remained in the hands of those more concerned with demonstrating the veracity of the biblical narrative. This was, perhaps, the most lasting influence of the marriage of religion and archaeology in the Middle East.

Frederick Jones Bliss

Frederick Jones Bliss best exemplifies the combination of antiquarian and missionary. A student of Flinders Petrie, he worked at Meidum in Egypt and Tell el-Hesi in Palestine. He is best known for his work with the Palestine Exploration Fund. After continuing for several seasons at Tell el-Hesi after Petrie returned to Egypt, Bliss turned his attentions to Jerusalem in 1894. He worked for four years with Archibald Dickie exploring the Western Wall of the Temple Mount, the ancient walls of the city, the pool of Siloam, and several large churches. In 1898 he returned south, excavating a number of small tells in the Shephelah region of modern Israel with R. A. S. McAllister. American archaeologist and biblical scholar William Foxwell Albright believed that Bliss was the "father" of Palestinian archaeology, although Bliss was never to achieve anything like the accolades that his great countryman later received. Albright and Bliss both came from religious families. Bliss was the son of the Rev. Daniel Bliss, the founder of the Syrian Protestant College, now the American University at Beirut. The first American to excavate sites in the Holy Land, Bliss combined many of the distinctive traits that contributed to the success of both secular and religious archaeologists in the Middle East. As an American working for the British, Bliss had access to both traditions of scholarship and religious devotion. From Petrie he learnt field technique and managerial skills. From his devout, highly educated parents, he gained fluency in Arabic and a deep knowledge of the biblical past as well as the Arabic present of the Levantine world in which he worked.

BELOW **This Phoenician ivory head** was discovered in a storeroom at Nimrud. The style and subject matter echo Egyptian originals.

Explorers and Collectors

European travelers have been marveling at the sites of the Middle East, meticulously recording their observations, and collecting some of its antiquities along the way, since the anonymous Pilgrim of Bordeaux visited in the fourth century CE.

ABOVE **Marco Polo was one of the best-known** Western travelers to the Orient. This is an illustration from the *Catalan Atlas,* which was published in the fourteenth century.

A number of other unusual personalities came for either spiritual or economic reasons. In the twelfth century, Benjamin of Tudela came for both religious and scholarly purposes, preceding by a century the more famous Marco Polo whose objective was really China. Rabbi Benjamin was much more comprehensive in his accounts of the lands and people he visited than Polo, and more inquisitive about ancient civilizations. Renaissance Europeans came for similar reasons. Pietro della Valle, who vowed to go to the Holy Land during his lifetime, added Egypt, Damascus, Aleppo, Baghdad, and Persia to his itinerary and was reportedly the man who imported the famous Persian cat into Europe.

Eighteenth- and Nineteenth-Century Explorers

Widespread curiosity about the region, and the eagerness to bring some of it back home, were products of the Enlightenment. The eighteenth and nineteenth centuries were the busiest times, as European tourists were joined by Americans on Grand Tours that soon expanded from Greece and Italy to the eastern Mediterranean and beyond. Europeans, at first attracted to the Holy Land, and later to the antiquities, were zealous in their quest for new experiences. Most of the eighteenth-century explorers were concerned with finding biblical sites and displayed little interest in civilizations other than those of Egypt. There were notable exceptions—the French

Count Francois Volney came to the Levant in the late 1700s; German-born Carsten Niebuhr visited Alexandria, Mount Sinai, Jeddah, Yemen, and other places as part of a Danish expedition.

Persia was not always on the itinerary for travelers to the Holy Land, but those who made the trip found it a rewarding, if perplexing, experience. The sites of Persia were often misinterpreted by visitors, whose fanciful ideas were based on biblical references—the Tomb of Cyrus was identified as the burial place of Solomon's mother; the famous Behistun Relief of Darius I, with its inscriptions in Old Persian, Babylonian and Elamite was seen, either as a depiction of the twelve tribes of Israel or Christ and the Apostles.

This changed in the early nineteenth century, when Georg Friedrich Grotefend, a German specialist in ancient languages, began working on the inscriptions of Persepolis and was able to identify them as the records of Achaemenid kings. Rawlinson was later able to decipher the Behistun inscriptions. Both Grotefend and Rawlinson, however, are indebted to Niebuhr who made detailed and meticulous drawings of the site.

Lady Hester Stanhope, who began her travels in the Orient a short time after Napoleon invaded Egypt, was an altogether different kind of voyager. Believing that her destiny lay in the Levant and Syria, she first came to the city of Palmyra dressed as a Bedouin, going overland to Lebanon and eventually settling near Sidon in an abandoned monastery. She became such a fixture in the local society that the independent leader Ibrahim Pasha, against whom the Ottoman rulers continually struggled, sought her advice on political decisions. Lady Hester also conducted one of the first European "excavations" in the Holy Land, putting together an expedition to Ashkelon to find buried treasure. Until her death in Lebanon, she was revered by the local community as "Queen Hester."

ABOVE **Johann Ludwig Burckhardt,** disguised as Sheikh Ibrahim Ibn Abdallah, was the first Christian in modern times to reach Medina.

Johann Ludwig Burckhardt came to the Middle East in the early nineteenth century. Originally from Switzerland, he went to England to launch his scholarly assault on Syria, Palestine, and Arabia. While there, he studied Arabic, exercised rigorously and exposed himself to the elements to prepare for his ordeals. Stopping first at Aleppo, where he sought to improve his Arabic and learn something about Islamic Law, he began his travels, like Lady Hester, by disguising himself as a Muslim, in his case, a sheikh. From his base in Syria, Burckhardt went to Palmyra, Damascus, Lebanon, and Jordan. This last location proved to be the source of his primary renown as he discovered the spectacular city of Petra. His name has become associated with that site ever since.

Sir Richard Francis Burton (1821–1890), following in the steps of Stanhope and Burckhardt, wanted not just to observe and record, but to become so deeply embedded in the societies he visited that he would not be recognized as an Englishman. Fortunately, he was unusually adept at learning languages, which served him well in many of the situations in which he found himself. He was so enamored of Islamic culture that he dared a journey to Mecca in the guise of a pilgrim from Afghanistan—inviting death if he were to be discovered. The sensual literature of the East attracted him even more and he translated both the *Kama Sutra* and the *Arabian Nights*. He was

LEFT **Lady Hester Stanhope adopted** Bedouin dress. She became a Christian mystic, exploring long-forgotten gnostic traditions of primitive Christianity.

ABOVE **The eastern staircase of the Apadana** at Persepolis, one of the capitals of the Achaemenid Empire built by King Darius I, shows peoples of the empire bringing tribute to the king.

able to present the exotic Middle East to a British audience so skillfully that he became almost a cult figure. Burton exemplified the determination that was to inspire T. E. Lawrence and Gertrude Bell several decades later.

Gertrude Bell

Perhaps the most famous of the early female explorers, Gertrude Bell concentrated her efforts on the exploration of inland Turkey, Syria, Mesopotamia, and Persia. Despite her interest in archaeology, she was able to participate in few excavations during her lifetime, though she visited and recorded details of many sites. Her observations are published in the famous and widely read travelog *The Desert and the Sown* which contains particularly vivid descriptions of Damascus, Jerusalem, Beirut, Antioch, and Alexandretta. Even more so than T. E. Lawrence, Bell brought the deserts of Arabia into the parlors of English readers. During her term as Director of Antiquities (1922–1926), she founded the Baghdad Archaeological Museum, perhaps her greatest ongoing contribution to archaeological research.

Collectors on the Scene

The many visitors who included both Egypt and Mesopotamia on their tours often wondered why so little trace of the great cities of the Tigris and Euphrates Valley could be found. If they traveled as far off the beaten path as Persepolis, they would again be confronted with the spectacular sight of an ancient city rising from the dust, but where, many would ask, could one find Ur, Nineveh, or Babylon?

The fact that the major Mesopotamian cities were difficult to locate protected them for a time, but they soon fell victim to the ravages of state-sponsored collectors, as did the antiquities of Egypt and Persia. The ancient Near Eastern Collections of the British Museum and the Louvre got an early start thanks to Napoleon, whose defeat by the British resulted in a sizable portion of his own purloined antiquities being carted off to London. The British Museum also benefited from the acquisition in 1825 of many Assyrian and Babylonian specimens from the widow of Claudius James Rich.

Several centuries of travelers' accounts created a longing in Europeans for the art and artifacts that had been described so thrillingly. Back in the seventeenth century, Pietro della Valle had brought back a few items, in addition to the famous Persian cats, that drew some attention—inscribed bricks and stones from Mesopotamia and Persepolis. But the artifacts of Persia, Mesopotamia, and Palestine, with the exception of holy relics, were not of much interest to art collectors like the Medicis and their aristocratic cohorts. By the end of the eighteenth century, many formerly private royal collections had become public museums, thus fueling even more the popular clamor for acquisitions.

In 1765, the last of the Medicis ceded their holdings to the city of Florence, and the Uffizi became a public gallery. Later, the British Museum began to allow members of the "non-discriminating" public to enter and, last but not least, the new republic in France established the Louvre, once a royal palace, as a public place.

Americans did not truly join the ranks of collectors until the nineteenth century and, as they did with most of their cultural borrowings from Europe, they greatly expanded upon the idea. By this time, individuals were amassing large fortunes and seeking ways to dispose of some of them.

Endowing museums became a popular pastime for America's financial elite. Within a short period of time museums bearing, in many cases, the names of their benefactors, sprang up in large cities all over the country. The Smithsonian, the Frick, the Morgan, the Walters, and the Whitney, were joined by the less conspicuously endowed Metropolitan and Philadelphia Museums, and the National Gallery of Art.

It took some time for these museums to begin investing in artifacts from the Middle East. In fact, it was not until Americans began to excavate at archaeological sites in the Levant, Syria, Egypt, and Mesopotamia, in the early part of the twentieth century, that examples of the art of these earliest civilizations began to attain a prominent place in museums and galleries. During the nineteenth century, the Middle East held fewer attractions for America than it did for Europeans, and citizens of this younger nation were not as enthralled by travel literature, however well written.

Crumbling antiquities in dusty, destitute but exotic lands, were never regarded as romantic by sensible Americans. Mark Twain's *Innocents Abroad* is an example of what his countrymen would view as an interesting travelog. There is no doubt that those hardy souls who did venture to the cradles of civilization agreed with Twain's assessment that the landscape of the region was "rocky, bare and dreary" and the culture "rags, wretchedness, poverty and dirt."

ABOVE **The Louvre in Paris** is one of many European museums that house extensive collections of Middle Eastern antiquities.

THE PALESTINE EXPLORATION FUND

Many of the Victorians who came to the Middle East from England did so under the auspices of the Palestine Exploration Fund (PEF), founded in 1865 and still sponsoring research in the Middle East today. The PEF's aim was to "promote research into the archaeology and history, manners and customs and culture, topography, geology, and natural sciences of biblical Palestine and the Levant." The fund's projects, and the people it sponsored, read like a compendium of the history of archaeology in the region. Excavations in Ottoman Palestine, Jordan, and the Sinai, and the people associated with it, include Charles Wilson, Charles Warren, Claude Reignier Conder, and H. H. Kitchener. Flinders Petrie's early work in Palestine, Bliss's work in Jerusalem, Conder's Survey of Palestine, and Woolley and Lawrence's pre-war surveys in the Sinai were all sponsored by the fund.

LEFT **Sir Flinders Petrie,** examining Canaanite pottery excavated by him in southern Palestine.

Cracking the Cuneiform Code

As early as the seventeenth century, interested European visitors to the Middle East had begun to note ancient inscriptions in what appeared to be a totally unknown script. Some scholars doubted whether the script represented true writing at all, but a few were intrigued enough to investigate.

ABOVE **A Hittite cuneiform clay tablet,** from the National Museum of Damascus, shows details of a Royal Divorce Decree.

One of these visitors was the German classical language scholar Georg Friedrich Grotefend. In 1777, his countryman Carsten Niebuhr had published his drawings of the Behistun cuneiform inscription, which contained three versions of the same text in Old Persian, Elamite, and Babylonian. These helped Grotefend greatly in his studies.

A friend of Grotefend, Olaf Tychsen from Denmark, thought he had understood some of the characters in the Persian section of the inscription. For Grotefend, access to information about Old Persian inscriptions at Persepolis provided a key to deciphering the cuneiform. The names of the famous kings of Persia, Darius and Xerxes, could be detected.

After this, a great deal of progress was made toward deciphering this script. A number of scholars in Europe were working on it at the same time, including the clergyman Edward Hincks, who was never able to visit the land that was the source of the material he studied. Hincks believed that the civilization that produced cuneiform was earlier than the Assyrians and Babylonians. Later, this suggested to Jules Oppert that this was an entirely different culture, which he labeled Sumerian.

All of these scholars contributed to the knowledge of Mesopotamia and Persia that was being rapidly developed at the time. However, by the mid-nineteenth century, it was Henry Creswicke Rawlinson who completed the work begun by these early pioneers.

Henry Creswicke Rawlinson

Rawlinson, a cadet with the East India Company, began his career as a cuneiform scholar when he went to the Near East in 1833. He developed a considerable reputation as a scholar, but when Lord Ellenborough, the Governor General of India, tried to persuade him to take a higher level position in Nepal, he preferred to stay in Baghdad to study cuneiform. In Baghdad, he became acquainted with Austen Henry Layard, who is best known for his excavation of Nimrud. Layard went on to publish his *Illustrations of the Monuments of Nineveh*. Disappointingly for Layard, Rawlinson was not interested in archaeological materials apart from the early inscriptions. Rawlinson found Layard's spectacular reliefs and sculpture from Nineveh "not valuable as works of art" beyond their "curiosity." It is difficult to discern if Layard reaped any benefit from the relationship but Rawlinson's research benefited linguistically from the recovery of lavishly inscribed monuments from the Assyrian empire.

LEFT **William Henry Fox Talbot** not only contributed to deciphering cuneiform, he also invented the paper-based calotype process, the first negative/positive method of photography.

French historian and linguist, Jean-Francois Champollion deciphered the Rosetta Stone in 1822. It then became obvious that the Persian provided the clue to decoding the other languages on the Behistun Inscription. The topmost text was more inaccessible than the others and Rawlinson determined to secure a copy of the inscription for himself. This proved to be the main source of his fame, and this Babylonian text was the basis for the translation that enabled future generations of archaeologists to read Assyrian and Babylonian texts.

An Accurate System of Translation

Hincks and Rawlinson made good progress with the reading of Babylonian script. Two other writing detectives then joined their exclusive society, the young Jules Oppert, and the resourceful British inventor, photographer, and philologist, William Henry Fox Talbot. The four met in London and compared their progress in deciphering the Behistun text. A panel of scholars from the Royal Asiatic Society was assigned to determine which of the four had developed the most accurate system of translation. When all were presented with a text to decipher, the similarities were striking, especially the efforts of both Hincks and Rawlinson. The panel was satisfied that substantial progress had been made in deciphering the script.

Rawlinson got ahead of the others when he was able to use a Sanskrit grammar to translate the Persian text. He then devoted his attention to the other two languages, assuming correctly that one of these was Babylonian. The Elamite script proved to be the most difficult to decipher. Although Elamite was an official language of the Persian Empire, it disappeared fairly rapidly after the early days of the empire. Grotefend was the first to surmise that this script was related to the language of Susa, as it was quite different in structure from the Old Persian or Babylonian languages.

RAWLINSON'S LEGACY

The versatility of cuneiform as a method of writing had already been demonstrated. It was used as the means of written expression for Persian, Babylonian, Elamite, Akkadian, and Sumerian. Several decades after Rawlinson's work, another language was found that used cuneiform script. Germans excavating at the site of Bogazkoy, Hittite Hattusa, found thousands of tablets written in cuneiform script, but in an entirely different language. Hittite, or Luwian as it is called, opened up a new field of cuneiform studies. Not long after the discovery of these Hittite texts, yet another form of cuneiform was unearthed by the French at the site of Ugarit. It was similar to Mesopotamian cuneiform, but seemed to have some striking differences. The letter order for this alphabet had great similarities with Phoenician, which was a later development. The Phoenician alphabet spread throughout the Aegean world and is considered to have been the origin of the Greek and Latin alphabet.

BELOW **Phoenician script is clearly legible** on the lid of this sarcophagus of King Ahiram, king of Byblos (*c.* 1000 BCE). It was discovered by French archaeologist Pierre Montet in 1923.

Pioneering Excavations

During the years before the Crimean War, the failing Ottoman Empire was in disarray. This disorganization assisted European excavators, who worked far away from the centers of power, in playing off the eminently corruptible local authorities against the distant Imperial administration.

ABOVE **Moving a winged bull statue, Nimrud, 1849** is an engraving from *Discoveries in the Ruins of Nineveh and Babylon* (1853) by Sir Austen Henry Layard.

The mounds of Babylon, Nineveh, and Persepolis had been explored in the early nineteenth century by Claudius James Rich. His notes, published posthumously, and the exhibit of his artifacts at the British Museum, were among the first researches to make Mesopotamian civilizations accessible to Europeans. Two decades after Rich's death in 1820, Paul-Emile Botta worked at Nineveh and Dur-Sharrukin (Khorsabad), when he was the French consul at Mosul. His investigations, like Rich's, were not very systematic, even though Botta also had a deep scholarly interest in ancient Assyria. Another dilettante, the lawyer and would-be diplomat, Austen Henry Layard, explored Nimrud several years later.

The result of these projects was the accumulation of a vast store of antiquities for the Louvre and British Museums, and the creation of a great public excitement over the ruins of Mesopotamia. There was little true understanding of the ancient Near East to be gained, however, until Rawlinson and his colleagues had made substantial progress with deciphering ancient cuneiform in 1851.

Nevertheless, Layard's elaborately illustrated *Nineveh and its Remains* (published *c.* 1849) was immensely popular in both Britain and France. Botta's and Layard's work became the impetus for other investigators to arrive in the Middle East seeking monumental discoveries.

Mesopotamia and Persia

In the mid-nineteenth century, European scholars, following in the footsteps of pioneers like Botta and Layard, began to arrive in Mesopotamia and Persia. William Kennet Loftus and artist William Boutcher continued with Layard's work at Nimrud on behalf of the British Museum and went on to excavate at Uruk and Larsa. Frenchman Victor Place continued Botta's work at Khorsabad and then went to Nineveh. The philologist Jules Oppert worked at the site of Kish. British Consul, J. E. Taylor, excavated the ruins of Eridu and Ur, where he discovered the ziggurat of Inanna. Henry Creswicke Rawlinson, though less interested in finding cultural remains than inscriptions, was nevertheless caught up enough in the excavation fever to work briefly at Borsippa, and, reportedly, at Ur and Nimrud as well.

In Persia, since the end of the eighteenth century when relations were established with Europe, visitors from the West had been coming in increasing numbers to the sites of Persepolis and Susa. Archaeologists began to take an interest, and the first foreign excavation was undertaken by the British at Taq-e Bustan, a cliff site on the Silk Road where the kings of the Sasanian Empire (third to seventh centuries CE) carved their images. Pascal Coust, Eugene Flanden, and Edward de Sassi, on behalf of the French Academy of Fine Arts, documented the monuments of Pasargadae and Persepolis, among others. Rawlinson also worked in Iran, at Behistun, and William Kennet Loftus, of Nimrud fame, came to excavate at Susa.

The French in the Ancient Near East

The long French liaison with Iran really began in 1881 when Marcel-Auguste and Jeanne

LEFT **The Palace of Sargon, with alabaster winged bull statues,** is shown in this photograph by French archaeologist Victor Place (1852). The statues were sawn into pieces and sent to the British Museum.

Dieulafoy continued Loftus's work at Susa. The Dieulafoys were commissioned by the French Ministry of Education to study Sasanian monuments, and they stayed on to excavate the palaces of the ancient Persian kings, Darius I and Artaxerxes II. They amassed a large collection of archaeological materials that were sent to the Louvre. Realizing the value of these splendid artifacts, the French were eager to strengthen their influence over the archaeology of Persia. When the French engineer Jacques de Morgan arrived to work at Susa, which the Dieulafoys had left six years earlier, he resolved to try to obtain a French monopoly on work in Persia. He and the French ambassador conspired to do so, but it took some time. Finally, the French persuaded the Shah of Persia to agree to a convention granting France exclusive rights to uncover ancient Persia.

The French were also prominent in nineteenth-century discoveries in the Levant. Louis Felicien Joseph Caignart de Saulcy excavated at Baalbek and explored Jerusalem, but he is known primarily for some of his more fanciful interpretations. For example, he associated the Tomb of the Kings in Jerusalem, a burial site from the first century CE, with the Jewish King David who lived around 1000 BCE. He also believed that Baalbek, a city in Lebanon, had been built long before the Romans, because

BELOW **This photo shows tombs of Achaemenid kings** Artaxerxes I (left), Xerxes I (centre), and Darius I (right) at the Necropolis of Naqsh-i Rustam in Iran.

ABOVE **Auguste Mariette, shown here in Egypt** in 1878, was sent to the Middle East to acquire manuscripts for the Louvre. He set up the Egypt Antiquities Authority and later founded Cairo's Egyptian Museum.

he wanted to connect it to the Iron Age city of Baalgad which was mentioned in the Bible.

Pioneers in the Holy Land

Tell el-Hesi in southern Israel was probably the first site in the Holy Land to be scientifically excavated, rather than simply explored and mapped. Flinders Petrie, working with the Palestine Exploration Fund in 1890, and Frederick Jones Bliss, who followed Petrie at the site, utilized Petrie's newly developed systematic techniques there. Egypt and the Holy Land were the first places where these methods were applied. This allowed excavators there to advance an ambitious agenda of archaeological research earlier than elsewhere in the Middle East. Regional and period specializations in the Bronze and Iron Ages were soon developed into a sub-discipline. It was not long before archaeology in the Levant became dominated by theologically and biblically trained scholars, some of them specialists in ancient languages, whose main interest was in biblical periods.

Auguste Mariette in Egypt

Egyptologists had a fairly close relationship with archaeologists in the Holy Land and, frequently, excavators like Petrie would work in both regions. Auguste Mariette, however, whose life and career briefly overlapped with Petrie's, preferred to stay in Egypt. He must, however, be considered as a pioneer who strongly influenced the practice of archaeology throughout the region. Unlike his other European colleagues, Mariette believed that antiquities belonged in their land of origin. Perhaps because Egyptians had a longer history of suffering from the plundering of their past by Europeans, more sensitive Western scholars were finally becoming aware of the injustice of the practice. In any event, Mariette's career in Egypt, beginning in 1850 and ending in 1881, was a portent for the future. Although he was unable to persuade Ismail Pasha, the then independent ruler of Egypt, that regulations on the export of antiquities should be imposed, Mariette did manage to limit the losses to some extent.

Hormuzd Rassam

Mariette's view on the rights of Egyptians to their own antiquities was limited to the excavated materials. As to the excavations themselves, however, he kept a stranglehold on the licenses—so much so that, at one point, only the French antiquities director was permitted to work on ancient Egyptian sites. As the Europeans working in Mesopotamia had no independent regional authority to answer to, they continued earlier policies of export and display in Western museums. However, they did manage to include indigenous scholars in their projects, if only in a secondary role. One of the most accomplished of these was Hormuzd Rassam. He was born in Mosul and was a member of the substantial Christian minority there. He worked with Layard, initially in an administrative role, but he soon displayed a real ability as an archaeologist.

Layard became Rassam's mentor and provided an opportunity for the young scholar to study at Oxford. After Layard began his political career, Rassam continued the fieldwork that they had begun together at Nimrud and made a number of important discoveries. Among these were the clay tablets containing *The Epic of Gilgamesh*, that were later deciphered due to Rawlinson and company's breakthroughs. Rassam's lifelong friend, Layard, encouraged him to pursue a career as a British diplomat, and he was sent to the British Consulate at Aden. When he was unable to negotiate the release of some British missionaries taken hostage in Ethiopia, however, his profession in the foreign service came to an abrupt end, and he returned to pursue his interest in Assyrian archaeology for the British Museum. In this subsequent archaeological career he succeeded in making a number of

THE DISCOVERY OF THE HITTITES

The Hittites are mentioned frequently in the Bible but up until the mid-nineteenth century CE, their homeland and culture were completely unknown. The first inkling that they might actually have existed came in 1894 when William Wright discovered that the script on a monument at Bogazkoy (the ancient site of Hattusa) was similar to inscriptions found at Aleppo and Hamath in northern Syria. Excavations at Tell el-Amarna in Egypt in 1887 uncovered correspondence between the pharaohs and the "kingdom of Kheta" that agreed with Mesopotamian references to the "land of Hatti." The then-unknown Hittite language (Luwian) was not to be completely translated until 1960, but in the 1880s, the inscriptions suggested to Oxford linguist Rev. Archibald Henry Sayce, that the people called Hatti or Khatti in Anatolia were identical with the "kingdom of Kheta" mentioned in Egyptian texts. Both of these were the same as the biblical Hittites. By the early part of the twentieth century Sayce's interpretation had been widely accepted and it remained only to translate the Luwian texts to discover more details about these formerly mysterious peoples.

LEFT **This sculptured relief of the Hittite storm god, Teshub,** was found in a gateway of the Hittite capital of Hattusa in central Anatolia. It is dated to *c.* 1300 BCE.

landmark discoveries, including the Cyrus Cylinder that detailed the Persian conquest of the Neo-Babylonians.

Osman Hamdi Bey

Osman Hamdi was born into the Ottoman ruling class in Istanbul, his father having served as Grand Vizier to the Sultan. At first, he studied law, but then decided that his real career lay in art. After studying in Paris, he returned to his homeland to paint and learn about the arts of the East. Though he had a successful career as an artist, he wanted to make a contribution toward preserving the ancient Turkish past. He was appointed the head of the Ottoman Imperial Museum, and was the first person in that role who had plans to develop the museum, rewrite antiquities laws to protect Turkish cultural property, and begin museum sponsored archaeological excavations.

In 1884, Osman Hamdi sponsored a regulation prohibiting artifacts from being smuggled abroad—a move that greatly angered European excavators in Turkish territory. Later, he joined the ranks of archaeologists, perhaps being better qualified by reason of his art historical training than many of his fellow excavators. He worked at Nemrud Dagh, the site of the Commagene kings' tombs, the Hecate Sanctuary in Lagina, and Sidon, the great Phoenician center in Lebanon. At Sidon, he found several carved sarcophagi, including one depicting the life of Alexander the Great. To exhibit his magnificent finds, he began the building which today houses the Istanbul Archaeology Museum and the Museum of the ancient Orient.

LEFT **The Alexander Sarcophagus, late fourth century BCE,** was found in Sidon by Osman Hamdi Bey. It is named because of the superb sculptures showing Greeks and Persians in battle, and hunting.

The Discovery of Sumer

Several generations have now grown up believing that the world's first known civilization was Sumer. Although recent excavations in Syria and Iran have modified this view to some extent, it is still broadly true that history did indeed begin at Sumer.

It is, therefore, surprising that Sumerian civilization was rediscovered less than a century ago. Sumer came to light gradually in the course of excavations aimed at recovering the remains of later cultures. Even those archaeologists who, armed with Bible and spade, attempted to locate the peoples mentioned in the scriptures, did not suspect that Sumer existed and that Ur, one of its greatest urban centers, was actually Abraham's birthplace.

The Origins of Writing

Beginning in 1842, Paul-Emile Botta and Austen Henry Layard began to recover thousands of Akkadian tablets from the sites of Nineveh, Khorsabad, and Nimrud. Henry Rawlinson, who is credited with deciphering cuneiform, at first believed that this method of writing was used exclusively for Akkadian until he discovered a different, non-Semitic language appearing on some examples. It was Edward Hincks, however, who accurately surmised, in 1850, that an earlier civilization had invented cuneiform. Jules Oppert, another student of cuneiform writing, determined that the designation "Sumerian" was most appropriate for the non-Akkadian language appearing on the tablets, based upon the honorific that frequently appeared, "King of Sumer and Akkad."

Speculation on the location of the Sumerians was interrupted for several years when excavations in the Middle East were halted by the Crimean War. From 1853 to 1856, Imperial Russia, France, the United Kingdom, the Kingdom of Sardinia, and the Ottoman Empire were locked in a struggle for supremacy. After the war ended, and Ottoman rule in the region was more or less restored, archaeological work began again in earnest. Lagash and Nippur were the first Sumerian sites to be excavated, the former by the French and the latter by Americans. Less known than the European excavators, but no less important to the rediscovery of Sumer, was the work of archaeologist Hormuzd Rassam, an Assyrian Christian who was a colleague of Layard. From 1878 to 1882, Rassam worked at Nineveh, Nimrud, Borsippa, and Sippar, among other places, and succeeded in recovering critical new evidence bearing on the Sumerian presence in Mesopotamia.

BELOW **The Great Ziggurat at Ur was a temple** to the moon deity, known as Nanna (Sumerian) or Sin (Babylonian). It is located 140 miles (225 km) south of Babylon.

Post-War Sumerian Archaeology

Under Rassam's direction, the French, the Americans, and his colleagues continued their work until World War I brought it to an abrupt halt. As European control replaced Turkish rule following the

LEFT **Among the many treasures found** in the tomb of Queen Pu'Abi (c. 2500 BCE) in Ur was this Sumerian golden bull's head harp decoration.

war, more foreign archaeologists were attracted to excavations in Mesopotamia. By that time, archaeology had advanced a long way from the days of collecting and disinterring remains for museum exhibits. The methods of German archaeologists developed before the war, combined with the steadying influence of the new Director of Antiquities under the British Mandate, the famous Gertrude Bell, were producing a more methodical approach to excavation.

Woolley and the Royal Tombs

One of this new breed of excavators was the archaeologist that people most identify with ancient Sumer, Leonard Woolley. His name is associated with many famous sites, among them Carchemish, Alalakh, and Amarna, but it was his discovery of the Royal Tombs of Ur that is chiefly responsible for his fame. In the autumn of 1927, while digging through Old Babylonian and Ur III layers, Woolley came upon the cemetery. His team was excavating burial pits, when it discovered some that were larger and more elaborately constructed than the rest.

Most of the other burials had been much smaller single-chamber structures but these were elaborate tombs, some of them with several rooms. One of these tombs was virtually undisturbed and contained items of incredible opulence. Along with these spectacular objects, with which the world is now so familiar, were many bodies. According to Woolley, these were the retainers who were sacrificed to accompany their masters in death.

Woolley will always be remembered for the discovery of the Royal Tombs, but he is hailed especially for his careful conservation of the most delicate objects, and the meticulous publication of the finds, which still continues to this day.

Sumer's Glory Revealed

After Iraq's independence, both Iraqi and foreign scholars continued to work in association. They revealed Sumer's enigmatic civilization to the world, uncovering information from the important Sumerian cities of Uruk and Nippur. It was Iraqi archaeologists, however, who discovered Eridu, the oldest Sumerian city, and who excavated a temple there that was rebuilt and reused for over three thousand years. The oldest of Sumer's religious centers, Eridu has been the site that most convincingly established Sumer as the first great civilization in southern Mesopotamia.

There is an unfortunate footnote to the history of Sumerian discovery. The great upheavals of recent times have dealt harshly with Sumerian remains, both those above and below ground. Many sites are being systematically looted by large teams using mechanical digging equipment. Umma, which remains largely unexplored by archaeologists, is being rapidly destroyed. Uruk, Eridu, Nippur, and Lagash are all in danger, as are all sites in southern Iraq where valuable artifacts are being shattered or stolen.

Antiquities markets are being flooded with tablets and precious objects, whose original contexts have been lost forever. A civilization that lasted for thousands of years, so recently discovered and restored to the light of history, is rapidly disappearing from view.

BELOW **This silver Vase of Entemena, ruler of Lagash,** was found at the ancient site of Telloh. The city-state of Lagash was one of the most ancient in Sumer.

Interwar Discoveries

Before World War I, the railroad that ran through Mesopotamia was known as the Berlin-Baghdad in Germany, the Bordeaux-Baghdad or Calais-Cairo in France, and the London-Baghdad in England. After the war, it simply became known as the Baghdad Railway.

ABOVE **Work on the Baghdad Railway** began in 1888. The final completion date, in 1914, had a considerable impact on the timetable for war in the Middle East.

The Berlin to Baghdad railway was the key axis of communication linking Europe with the Middle East, and vital to the Ottoman war effort during the Mesopotamian campaigns. In some ways, the rail was an extension of the age-old caravan routes into Europe, and it was no less celebrated for bringing the riches of the East to the West.

As the importance of the Near East was brought home to both Europeans and Americans during World War I, the land itself began to exert a great appeal to travelers after the war ended. In the interwar years, people arrived from across the globe to see the fabled Orient of biblical and literary fame. The ancient Near East, not surprisingly, had a high profile with many of these tourists. The secular travelers were lured by names like Semiramis, Sardanopolus, and Zenobia. The more devout followed the paths of Abraham, David, and Jesus.

Scholars of the Interwar Years

The scholars of the ancient Near East who, by this time, considered themselves to be "scientific," viewed this popular interest as both a blessing and a curse. As they discovered fabulous new finds almost daily, the public waited to hear some fantastic story woven by journalists surrounding the discovery. For example, the Tomb of Tutankhamun, found serendipitously by Howard Carter in 1922, and containing artifacts that should have been, in themselves, legendary, became best known to the public as the origin of the infamous "Mummy's curse."

Biblical sites continued to capture the public imagination because of their alleged associations with Judeo-Christian religion, but as the scope of exploration spread to adjacent lands, revolutionary discoveries began to occur. Although British and European scholars continued to make important discoveries, the interwar years were very much the time when American scholarship came to the fore.

In the United States, strong archaeological personalities rose to the challenge of keeping the public simultaneously at bay and fascinated—and they succeeded in garnering most of the important prizes still to be had. This was the period of truly groundbreaking work.

Yankees in the East

James Henry Breasted, founder of the Oriental Institute at the University of Chicago, was among the most important, and one of the first archaeologists to take the Baghdad Railway during the interwar years. Breasted arrived in Mesopotamia in 1919 proposing to excavate there, based on information about a new site that he had received from the redoubtable Gertrude Bell. Breasted became one of the first Western scholars to see Dura-Europos in Syria, romantically describing his visit as "... the first dash undertaken by white men after the Great War across the desert region and the newly proclaimed Arab state." The next year found the peripatetic Breasted at Khorsabad,

LEFT **This fresco depicting priests** with the family of Konon is from the Temple of Palmyrean Gods, Dura-Europos in Syria. The site was first excavated after World War I.

where he duly noted that there was still much to be accomplished at this site, hopefully by "his" Oriental Institute scholars. The institute resumed excavation at Khorsabad soon thereafter. Much of this city, the capital of Assyrian conqueror Sargon II, had not been completed before Sargon's successors abandoned the city. To this day archaeologists struggle to interpret the surviving remains.

The American excavators achieved a great deal, recovering building plans, noting building techniques made clearer by their unfinished condition, and recording intricate and fragile decorations.

Another Midwestern American, Francis Willey Kelsey of the University of Michigan, appeared on the scene at the same time as Breasted and his Oriental Institute team. Kelsey came via the famous railway, like Breasted, to the Syrian city of Aleppo and proceeded to excavate Roman sites around the Mediterranean basin in Syria, Egypt, and Tunisia. He made five expeditions to the Near East to excavate, photograph, and survey sites for possible future University of Michigan excavation.

Meanwhile, in the Holy Land, William Foxwell Albright, fresh from his doctorate in Near Eastern Studies from Johns Hopkins University, arrived in the Near East by rail only one year after Breasted and Kelsey. Albright was so taken with Jerusalem, the city where he was to achieve his renown, that he wrote to his mother in 1921 that: "There is not a spot in the whole world which suits me like Jerusalem."

Albright is acknowledged as one of the first Holy Land archaeologists to combine the science of archaeology with study of both biblical and extra-biblical texts.

European Excavations in the Interwar Years

German excavators returned to the Hittite capital of Hattusa (modern Bogazkoy) in the 1920s, and soon began to make remarkable discoveries. These included the archives of the Hittite kings, one detailing the treaty between Ramesses and Hattusili III which brought the Syrian wars to an end.

At the same time, French scholars returned to Iran. Notable among them was Andre Goddard, brought there by the new Iranian government. He stayed in Iran for 30 years and played a critical role in training Iranian archaeologists at Tehran University. Goddard designed the country's first modern archaeological museum and was appointed its first director.

BELOW **These store rooms were in the temple** dedicated to the Hittite sun goddess, in Hattusa (modern Bogazkoy), the imperial capital, located in central Turkey.

Biblical Archaeology

It was a soldier, a bureaucrat, and a diplomat who brought the lands of the Bible to the attention of nineteenth-century European and American Christendom. Whatever the motives were that spurred Napoleon, Claudius Rich, and Henry Rawlinson toward exploring the Middle East, religion was not one of them.

This is not to say that their discoveries during these early days were of no interest to men of the cloth. In fact, many clergymen greeted each new glimpse into the cultures of Mesopotamia and Egypt as confirmation of the Bible. Nevertheless, most ministers were content to stay at home and work on deciphering, while more adventurous and secular scholars took to the field. A notable exception was the American theologian Edward Robinson who set out to find the biblical sites of "Palestine, Mount Sinai, and Arabia Petraea." At this time geography took precedence over archaeology in Palestine, as the aim of most explorers was simply to find the sites.

BELOW **This Amarna letter** is from Akhenaten (reigned 1352–1336 BCE) to a Palestinian vassal prince. The language is Akkadian, and the script is cuneiform.

Late Nineteenth-Century Explorers

Unlike Robinson, the British explorers of the Victorian age were inspired to map the Holy Land by the demands of both God and country. Following the Crimean War, which implicated Palestine in the conflict between Christians and Muslims, military men came to explore Palestine, some of them more conservative and religious, such as Kitchener and Gordon, and some of less faith and, perhaps, more curiosity like Richard Burton and T. E. Lawrence. The Palestine Exploration Fund, which began in 1865, continued the tradition of mapping the Holy Land by sponsoring most of these famous people.

The discovery of ancient Near Eastern documents was accompanied by an interest among religious scholars as to whether they might shed light on the scriptures. Thus, it was not long before clergymen came to see for themselves the places they had heard about for decades, abandoning their pulpits to travel to Bible sites. At the time, "higher criticism," the view that the Bible was neither factual nor contemporary with the events it reported, was growing in popularity among scholars. The Bible was, in the view of many religious people, in danger of becoming irrelevant. People like the Rev. F. A. Klein, a German missionary who discovered the Mesha Stele that documented the existence of the biblical personalities of Omri and Ahab, were taking to the field. Also among those getting actively involved were the Rev. Archibald Henry Sayce, who worked primarily on ancient texts and Egyptian sites, and Protestant missionary Conrad Schick, who, in 1880, studied the Siloam Tunnel inscription describing the building of a water tunnel by King Hezekiah in the early eighth century BCE.

Scientific Investigation of the Holy Land

The turn of the last century saw a new generation of archaeologists who were more circumspect in their dealings with Arabs and Muslims, and much more methodical—so much so that people are not always aware of their religious backgrounds. W. Flinders Petrie, for example, came from a fundamentalist evangelical family and his Christian beliefs informed his interest in the archaeology of the Middle East. Leonard Woolley, though he was from a more moderate Christian household, was the son of a clergyman.

Petrie revolutionized the entire science of archaeology from his sites in Egypt and Palestine. He established the significance of pottery typologies in delineating archaeological periods, and recovered many of the Amarna letters. In 1896 he found the Merneptah Stele, containing the earliest mention of the word "Israel." The recovery of other important documents soon followed, including the Law Code of Hammurabi in 1901, which has been compared with the Laws of Moses in Exodus.

After World War I, biblical archaeology was dominated by William Foxwell Albright. An American, Albright was ostensibly linked with past explorers by his religious background. The child of Methodist missionaries, he was deeply religious, but his beliefs did not enter into his practice of archaeology as much as some might suppose. In fact, he questioned the associations of sites with biblical texts that many of his colleagues were irresponsibly promoting. He is best remembered for his identification of the Dead Sea Scrolls, documents found by Bedouins in the Judean Desert, as authentic. One of the greatest biblical finds ever made, the earliest of them, from around the third century BCE, gave no comfort to those who were looking for evidence of the patriarchs in the Bronze Age, but they were older than any biblical manuscript previously known.

Western Biblical Archaeology Schools

The American Schools of Oriental Research, founded in 1900, and led by Albright, was the first institute to be dedicated to archaeological research in the Holy Land. The Europeans had also established their own archaeological schools. The École Biblique, founded by the Dominicans, took its present name in 1920 and is generally considered to be the French national archaeological school. Marie-Emile Boismard, Roland de Vaux, Raymond-Jacques Tournay and Pierre Benoit were members of this organization. The German Society for the Exploration of Palestine (Deutscher Palästina-Verein), founded by Lutherans in 1877, sponsored a number of projects, including excavations at Megiddo by Gottlieb Schumacher. The Palestine Exploration Fund continued to fund interdisciplinary

ABOVE **Cave IV at Qumran is the site** where Bedouins found the Dead Sea Scrolls, identified as authentic by William Foxwell Albright.

BELOW **The remains of an early Bronze Age temple** of Canaanite construction in Tel Megiddo, Israel.

research, while the British School of Archaeology was established in 1919.

Indigenous Archaeologists

The foreign excavators of Palestine benefited from the sponsorship of their respective schools and funding from abroad. It is not surprising that Americans and Europeans led most excavations. The contributions of indigenous archaeologists during these years, though not recognized as much, laid the groundwork for the development of indigenous archaeological practices in later years. The work of scholars like Tawfiq Canaan (1882–1964), who was a friend of Albright's, Dimitri C. Baramki (1909–1984), and Stephan Hanna Stephan played a considerable role in broadening our knowledge of Palestine. The best known of these was Canaan, who accompanied one of the earlier expeditions to Petra. Baramki left Palestine in 1948 and fled to Lebanon where he taught at the American University in Beirut. He began the American University's field school in archaeology in the 1950s. Stephan was a self-taught archaeologist with a strong interest, like Canaan and Baramki, in ethnography. The Jewish Palestine Exploration Society, later to become the Israel Exploration Society, sponsored projects at Hammat-Tiberias, Absalom's Tomb, Jerusalem's Jewish Quarter, Ramat Rahel, Beth-Shearim, and Beth-Yerah. The Archaeology Department of the Hebrew University of Jerusalem was established in 1934 under the directorship of E. L. Sukenik, who is credited with a number of important discoveries in Jerusalem and elsewhere. These were the true foundations of Israeli archaeology, which is often considered as an adjunct to biblical studies but, in essence, has been more nationalist than religious in its orientation.

The Rise of Israeli Archaeology

In the 1950s and 60s, it was apparent that Israeli archaeology would fundamentally change biblical archaeology much more than it would be influenced by it. Scholars trained in Israel began to usurp the prominent place that had been held for decades by the American schools. The most notable of the Israeli scholars working during this time was E. L. Sukenik's son, the soldier-scholar Yigal Yadin. Excavations by Yadin were

BELOW **The Tomb of Absalom,** who according to the Bible was the third son of David, King of Israel, is in Jerusalem.

LEFT **The site of Masada is on the eastern edge** of the Judean Desert, where Herod the Great (37–4 BCE) built a mountain fortress.

undertaken at Hazor, Beth Shean, Megiddo, and, most memorably, Masada.

This was a time of great activity, however, and Yadin was joined by many prominent Israelis working on biblical sites, including Yohanan Aharoni at Arad, Beersheba and Lachish, Benjamin Mazar at Jerusalem and En Gedi, Ruth Amiran at Arad, Avraham Biran at Dan, David Ussishkin at Beth Yerah, Moshe Kochavi at Aphek, and Nahman Avigad in the Jewish Quarter of Jerusalem.

In this age of growing national identities, Israelis, Palestinians, and Jordanians did not completely exclude foreign excavators. Although licensing requirements varied among the jurisdictions, all have welcomed scholars from abroad as long as they collaborate with indigenous archaeologists. It was during this time that Kathleen Kenyon came to work at Jericho and the City of David, James Pritchard at Gibeon, and Albright protégés William G. Dever, and G. Ernest Wright at Gezer.

Biblical Archaeology Today

Today, the archaeology of Bible lands is still much involved with the scriptures because the public and the media are still more interested in biblical finds from this region than in any others. Inscriptions, papyri, and scrolls continue to be the most celebrated archaeological discoveries in Bible lands although, in comparison to Mesopotamia and Egypt, these are few. The most newsworthy finds of recent years have been an Aramaic inscription from eighth-century BCE Tel Dan referring to the "House of David" and an eighth-century BCE amulet from Ketef Hinnom containing the only biblical text, in this case, a fragment, that predates the Dead Sea Scrolls.

Given the attention that biblical finds still attract, archaeologists working in Israel, Palestine or Jordan will find themselves continuing to work with the implications of the Bible for their research. At the same time, more religious scholars have become open to the idea that research on ancient biblical sites, in itself, is valuable. A number of archaeological Bibles, containing scriptures annotated with descriptions of sites and artifacts, have already been published. The marriage of text and trowel will continue but, eventually, we are likely to see some transformation in the roles played by each.

ARCHAEOLOGICAL RESEARCH AND THE BIBLE

A century of biblical archaeological research has not succeeded in demonstrating the biblical text, to the dismay of some scholars that adhere to the old traditions of religiously inspired research. Sites like the pool at Gibeon, Hezekiah's tunnel under Jerusalem, the siege ramp of the Assyrian Emperor Sennacherib at Lachish, and walls of the Herodian Temple still standing in Jerusalem, were all known to exist long before any archaeologist put trowel to earth in Palestine. Finds that have been uncovered at Jericho, Hazor, Megiddo, Gezer, Bethel, Beersheba, and Arad have provided a lot of information about Bronze and Iron Age Palestine but result in a confusing picture of how biblical events might be related to them. This remains the subject of much discussion and controversy.

ABOVE **The Surrender of Lachish after a siege** by Assyrian King Sennacherib, in 701 BCE, is shown in a print based on Assyrian reliefs.

Unearthing Ancient Iran

Lord George Curzon was a British scholar who published his impressions of ancient Persia until, in 1897, the French Ambassador to Persia negotiated a treaty ceding control of all archaeological activity in Persia to the French.

RIGHT **George Nathaniel Curzon,** first Marquis Curzon of Kedleston (1859–1925) was a conservative British politician who served as foreign secretary and Viceroy of India.

Curzon was the first European to connect the site of Pasargadae in Fars Province to Cyrus the Great and the Achaemenid Empire. This was not accepted by other scholars, so he was eager to see the site explored further. It was to be some time, however, before archaeologists turned their attention to Fars Province as the birthplace of the first Persian Empire. Archaeological excavations were in the hands of the French and they were preoccupied with uncovering ancient Susa.

Marcel Dieulafoy, working at Susa from 1884, was able to reveal much of the Achaemenid occupation of that site. He explored the city wall and the Apadana, the great audience hall built by Cyrus. There, he discovered the famed glazed brick frieze of Cyrus's "royal archers." Jacques de Morgan, a French scholar and Director General of the French Archaeological Mission, continued with Dieulafoy's excavations at Susa. He had ample time to make use of this site, as he remained the head of the French mission for 15 years. Realizing the possibilities inherent in establishing the interconnections between famous Near Eastern empires, de Morgan decided to pursue collaborations with Assyriologists. One of these scholars, Father Vincent Scheil, a French Dominican, assisted him with his most celebrated discovery, that of the Code of Hammurabi that they found at Susa.

Finding the Achaemenid Empire

De Morgan's work at Susa also resulted in new attention being given to the site's earlier levels. They had expected to eventually reach pre-Persian occupations at the site, but they continued to find major Achaemenid artifacts. Their ongoing discoveries of objects from the Achaemenid period suggested that Susa was one of the earliest of the empire's cities. The chronological connections between Persian Empire sites could not be made clear until other sites, such as Persepolis and Pasargadae were investigated. With the French occupied at Susa, German-born archaeologist Ernst Herzfeld came to Persia in the 1920s to excavate Cyrus the Great's capital, Persepolis. His team opened trenches at the main gate, as well as in two of the palaces, and established a new benchmark for analyzing the construction of Achaemenid monuments at Persepolis. Later, Herzfeld returned to Persepolis to direct the excavations of the Oriental Institute of Chicago, and his team found the famous reliefs on the north side of the Apadana. They also unearthed the gold and silver foundation plaques from the audience hall, and a number of Elamite cuneiform tablets that are now known as the Persepolis Fortification Texts.

One of Herzfeld's successors at Persepolis, Ernst Schmidt, excavated the Treasury and found the reliefs that had once formed part of the façade of the Old Apadana, another collection of clay tablets in Elamite, and a profusion of other

items, including bronzes, glassware, and stone tableware. Schmidt also exposed the throne hall, and the fifth-century BCE square structure called the "Tower of Zoroaster." Through the use of aerial photography, almost unknown in the region at the time, Schmidt was the first to create a complete record of all the monuments of the Persepolis region. Under Herzfeld and Schmidt's direction, Persepolis was excavated throughout the 1930s. In the 1940s, however, the excavations were taken over by the Iranian Archaeological Service and directed first by Andre Goddard, and later by Ali Sami.

The British at Pasargadae

Herzfeld had come to Pasargadae in 1905 and published his dissertation on the site three years later. In 1928, he also conducted the first excavations at Pasargadae. He believed the argument made by Lord Curzon some 30 years before that there was a strong correlation between the site and Cyrus. Following Herzfeld's work, Aurel Stein examined several of the mounds there, and Schmidt was responsible for taking the first aerial photographs of this site as well. Pasargadae was only intermittently examined by the Oriental Institute, however, and eventually Ali Sami of the Iranian Antiquities Service took over the site in the 1940s. He was able to locate and draw accurate floor plans of two of the palaces at Pasargadae.

In 1961, the British Institute of Persian Studies was founded, and, for the first time since Lord Curzon had studied the site, the British came to investigate Pasargadae under the direction of David Stronach, with the intention of continuing Herzfeld and Sami's fieldwork. Their objective was to re-examine each of the site's main monuments, including the gardens of the palace and excavate the Tall-e Takt, the stone platform on the west side of the hill that was left unfinished by Cyrus. This is thought to be either a prison of the Achaemenid era, or the mausoleum of Cyrus's mother. In the garden area, a hoard of jewelry and other precious objects was found. Stronach was able to work at the site for only two seasons, but work has resumed very recently under the direction of the Iranian Archaeological Service.

The French Return to Susa

Jean Perrot, a famous French excavator, was made head of the

ABOVE **This sculpture of a sphinx** is on a balustrade of the Trypolon (Triple Gate) at Persepolis.

BELOW **The Tower of Zoroaster** is a fifth-century BCE structure at Naqsh-i Rustam—the site of the tombs of the Achaemenid kings.

French Archeological Mission in Iran in 1968. One of his priorities was to establish a defined stratigraphic sequence at Susa where the French had been working since the nineteenth century. Under Perrot's direction, the excavation team recovered two marble foundation tablets from the palace of Darius the Great. They also excavated the Palace of Artaxerxes II and found a large statue of Cyrus the Great, cut from stone that had originally come from Egypt. The French love affair with Susa, the city where they began unearthing the treasures of ancient Iran, lasted for almost 100 years.

Locating the Elamites and Anshan

In the spring of 1901, an exhibition of the discoveries Jacques de Morgan and Vincent Scheil had made at Susa was held at the Grand Palais des Champs Elysées in Paris. The displays consisted of inscribed bricks, reliefs, stelae covered with cuneiform writing, and other works of art in an unusual style. Scheil identified Susa as the place where "the history of the country of Elam begins." A deep excavation at the Ville Royale at Susa had, early on, revealed a succession of Elamite strata going back to the second millennium BCE.

The Elamites did not truly come to light until their famed home city of Anshan (modern-day Tal-e Malyan), which is north of Shiraz in the Zagros Mountains of Fars Province, was located. The University of Pennsylvania sponsored excavations at the site throughout the seventies. Conceived as a preliminary exploration, the team was interested in establishing a chronological sequence, conducting systematic topographic, surface, and magnetometer surveys of the site, and identifying economic and social characteristics in different quarters of the city. With the evidence from Tal-e Malyan and Susa, the Elamites, though still remaining somewhat mysterious, have taken on a more defined character. What seems clear is that Elam was one of the oldest of the world's civilizations, rivaling in antiquity those of Mesopotamia. Elamite civilization probably grew up east of the Tigris and Euphrates Rivers. Very early in their history, the Elamites seem to have spread out onto the

BELOW **The Palace of Darius the Great at Susa** contains many magnificent examples of colored glazed brick friezes such as this one of a troop of archers.

FOREIGN EXCAVATORS IN IRAN TODAY

After isolation from Western scholarship for more than 25 years, the government of Iran has recently begun to permit international archaeological teams to work in the country again in collaboration with Iranian scholars. The Iranian Cultural Heritage and Tourism Organization has been a primary force in sponsoring this move and, at their urging, the government invited professors from Harvard University, the University of Chicago, and the University of Pennsylvania, as well as European universities, to tour sites in the country and set up new excavations. The requirement that an equal number of Iranians and foreigners participate in the digs is not particularly difficult to meet these days as increasing numbers of Iranian scholars have been well trained over the past few decades. There are currently several collaborative projects under way. They include one with the German Archaeological Institute to explore copper mines from the fourth millennium BCE at a site near Isfahan, a project with Japanese archaeologists to survey the city of Jalaliyeh where an important site from the Lower Paleolithic was recently found, French researchers are working again at Pasagardae, and Australians are investigating early Elamite sites near the border between Iran and Iraq.

ABOVE **Sargon of Akkad was an Akkadian minister** of the Sumerian king of Kish. This victory stele, *c.* 2350 BCE, made of diorite, tells of his conquest of Sumer.

Iranian plateau. An Elamite kingdom emerged during the third millennium BCE. It was centered around the cities of Susa and Anshan, and remained a vital and important force in the region for almost 2,000 years.

Earliest Iran–Jiroft

Recent discoveries of indigenous Iranian archaeologists are at least equal to the major discoveries of Ali Sami at Achaemenid sites—they might well change our concept of civilization having begun in the Tigris and Euphrates River valleys. Youssef Madjidzadeh is credited with finding the site of Jiroft in the southeast Iranian desert a few years back and, after two years of excavations, seems confident that this site will be the basis for defining the rise of Early Bronze Age cities in the ancient Near East. Madjidzadeh has speculated that Jiroft is, in fact, a city of the lost Aratta Kingdom. Aratta was the name of an ancient state, which appears in texts going back to 2500–2100 BCE. Sumerian legends, particularly that of Enmerkar and the Lord of Aratta, describe the kingdom as mountainous and ruled by a mythical king, Ensuh-keshdanna, who competes with Enmerkar, ruler of Uruk. The Aratta identification is disputed by other archaeologists who have connected the site to the city state of Marhashi, a Proto-Elamite site that is known from Mesopotamian sources.

Monumental architecture and a distinct style of writing seem to clearly differentiate Jiroft from other early civilizations. The famous incised chlorite vessels of Jiroft turn up at widely dispersed ancient sites that include Mari in Syria, Nippur, and Ur in Mesopotamia, Soch in Uzbekistan, and on the Saudi island of Tarut just north of Bahrain. The center of production of these vessels was a mystery for some time, but it seems reasonable to assume that, because so many examples have been recovered at Jiroft, this is where they were manufactured. This 4,500-year-old city may yet succeed in clearing up a number of mysteries about the connections between earliest Mesopotamia and Iran.

LEFT **The Code of Hammurabi,** cuneiform script on black basalt, is one of the earliest law codes from ancient Babylon that has been discovered.

The Spoils of War

With every new imperial power that arose in the Middle East, the treasures of conquered countries found their way to the new imperial capitals. The Bible says that valuable objects from the Temple of Solomon were sent to both the Assyrian capital of Nineveh, and to Chaldean Babylon.

ABOVE **Napoleon's attempts to remove** this colossal bust of Ramesses II (*c.* 1250 BCE), were unsuccessful, but in 1815 the British Consul General in Cairo organised its removal to Britain. It is now in the British Museum.

The famous stele of the Code of Hammurabi, taken by the French to be exhibited in the Louvre, was found at Susa because it had been purloined 3,000 years before by the Elamites when they conquered ancient Babylon in the twelfth century BCE. Records of the earliest cultures in Mesopotamia indicate that royalty and aristocrats were in the habit of carrying off many things that struck their fancy from conquered territories. The first systematic spoils of war system, however, arose under Roman rule.

Roman Spoilers

The Romans were as aggressive in their appropriation of art as they were in their annexation of territory. They began looting sites in the early days of the Republic with the sack of the Etruscan city of Veii in 396 BCE. Pontus, in present-day Turkey, was also plundered by the Romans. The king, Mithridates, killed himself and his entire family, after which the Romans brought back a large gold statue of the ruler along with other valuables. This institutionalized avarice may have affected the future course of the Roman Empire.

Of course, looted art, particularly when it was publicly displayed as it was in Rome, has always represented the victory of the conqueror. The prominent exhibits in the Roman Forum, which became a museum of sorts, and later the Hippodrome at Constantinople, testify to the proclivity of Romans to create material displays that demonstrated their prowess. Among the favored antiquities, the Romans singled out political representations—statues of conquered kings, victory stelae, Greek images of Nike, and the obelisks that recorded the deeds of the pharaohs. They were all used to testify to the fact that, in the end, the Romans were superior.

Venetian Looters

After the Fall of Rome, the Venetians inherited the Roman taste for spoils. The sack of the Christian city of Constantinople, a singularly outrageous act in a litany of outrageous acts perpetrated during the Crusades, was the brainchild of Venetians. The façade of the church of the city's patron saint incorporates many valuables taken from Constantinople. In addition, other churches in Venice were presented with a large collection of beautiful gemstone-decorated cameos, a jeweled golden screen created by Byzantine artists, and a golden tabernacle from the Church of the Holy Apostles. The most magnificent prize was four gilded bronze horses, replicas of which are now installed on St. Mark's Basilica.

Napoleon, Hitler, and the Spoils of War

Napoleon has entered annals of history as a great pilferer of the past. The Levant and Syria presented few opportunities for readily accessible antiquities, but this was not the case in Egypt. Because of the great scientific work that resulted from Napoleon's expedition, the *Description D'Egypte*, his role in removing monuments and artworks from the Land of the Pharaohs is not emphasized as much as that of other famous looters, but he was able to fill an entire large section of the massive Louvre Museum with Egyptian antiquities. After France's defeat at the hands of the British, many of these stolen items found their way to the British Museum.

There was a debate, at least among the British, in the early nineteenth century as to whether the international laws of war permitted such wholesale theft of what we now refer to as cultural property. Napoleon's crime, however, in the eyes of the West, had been his aggressive acquisition of art and artifacts from other European nations. Few were prepared to question

the theft of items from places such as Egypt and Mesopotamia. While the Ottomans, who controlled these regions, displayed little interest in plundering themselves, they were not very concerned about others doing it. They fought for territory, and then only when it was absolutely necessary, and were content to collect taxes and stay at home. It was not until the time of the Third Reich and the Nazi seizure of art, from their own citizens as well as from conquered European nations, that the situation was clearly seen as a violation of International Law. By 1939, the Hague Convention on the Laws of War was amended to cover the confiscation of art and antiquities.

The Looting of the Baghdad Museum

The looting of the National Museum of Iraq in Baghdad in April 2003 caused international outrage. Statues, stelae, and friezes were taken from the museum and thousands of vessels, shards, and small portable objects in boxes were removed from its storerooms.

Estimates vary, but it appears that between one quarter and one half of the stolen items have been recovered. The Baghdad Museum tragedy, though clearly a result of warfare, cannot be classified as the taking of spoils by a conquering power. Investigations have indicated that American soldiers were not among the looters, though there is still some controversy as to their role in the incident. The museum was unprotected, the country was in turmoil, and the opportunity was tempting to people who were willing to take a chance to gain a profit that was substantial, no doubt, considering their economic situation.

ABOVE **These are the original four gilded bronze horses** of St. Mark, which were removed by Napoleon. Replicas now stand on the basilica's façade in Venice.

LEFT **Parts of a beheaded sculpture** lie among rubble after looters ransacked the Baghdad Museum on April 13, 2003.

The Treasures of Nimrud

A fabulous hoard of jewelry and gold was found in 1988 at ancient Nimrud in Iraq. The journey of these exquisite artifacts from their creation almost 3,000 years ago to the present day is an unusual one.

The Medes and Scythians, who had sacked the palace at Nimrud in 612 BCE, and had missed very little in the way of valuables while doing so, did not find the treasures. British archaeologist Max Mallowan, who should have been more adept at solving mysteries than most archaeologists, being married to Agatha Christie, did not find the treasures, in spite of the fact that he excavated beneath the floor of the room in which they were hidden.

Only a handful of royals and trusted servants would, in antiquity, have had any inkling as to where these fabulous things were hidden. The secret died with them until Iraqi archaeologist Muzahim Mahmud discovered that the floor tiles in the palace room where they were found, had been relaid in the past. He looked beneath them and found a number of tombs, including that of Ashurbanipal's queen as well as two other queens from the preceding century. The obligatory curse warned the discoverer of the hoard that his spirit would "wander in thirst" if he broke the seals of the tombs but, to date, there have been no reports of physical harm to the excavators as a result of the discovery, as there were with Tutankhamun's tomb.

This spectacular find was briefly exhibited in Baghdad in 1989, but concerns about security prevented it being put on permanent display there. Proper storage cabinets were on their way to the museum when Saddam Hussein invaded Kuwait, precipitating the first Gulf War (1990–1991). At the same time, the treasure disappeared from view, and was placed in a secure vault of the Iraqi Central Bank. The bank and museum officials then reportedly flooded the area with sewage in order to deter looters.

In 2003, just before the battle for Baghdad, stories circulated that Saddam's youngest son,

Guarding the Treasures
Seventy-seven-year-old Iraqi guard Abed Atiya al-Shemari makes his rounds past the damaged remains of a statue in Baghdad's National Museum in 2004. In 2003, he was forced to flee when looters attacked the museum after the fall of Saddam Hussein's regime. The museum was established in 1926 by Gertrude Bell.

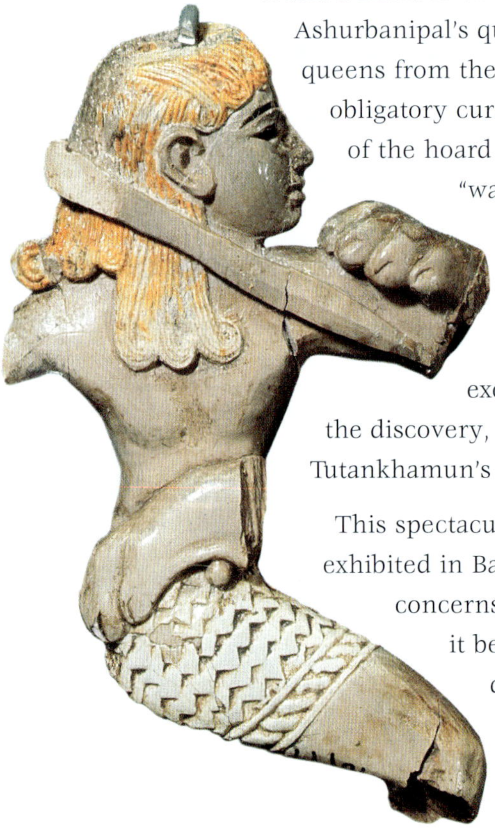

Fragment of Ivory
This Phoenician ivory figurine is one of many ivory and bone sculptures found in the Palace of Nimrud. The Phoenicians were renowned for the beauty of such carvings.

Gold Bracelets

These gold bracelets were found at Nimrud in 1988. The exquisite detail of the work can be seen in the abutting lions' heads on each bracelet.

Qusay, had made off with the Nimrud treasure when he withdrew millions from the bank, but bank officials denied this. The fate of the treasure was again in question when it was initially reported that the looters of the Baghdad Museum in April 2003 had taken it. Several months after the museum looting, some of the jewels were brought to the Iraqi Museum in Baghdad to assure a select group of journalists and dignitaries that they were indeed safe. This very brief viewing was the first time in 14 years, and only the second time in almost 3,000 years, that these artifacts had seen the light of day. This is the only known collection that exhibits the incredible craftsmanship of Assyrian artisans. All other examples of Assyrian metal- and jewelry-working have disappeared into the smelting fires of antiquity. Before 1988, the only Assyrian jewels ever seen were those carved on stone reliefs on the wrists and necks of royalty.

Who Hid the Treasures?

Very few people knew of the ploy to hide the jewels, perhaps not even Saddam Hussein himself. Though he was profligate with the other resources of his country, there is every reason to believe that Saddam had some respect for ancient art and artifacts. He had financed the reconstruction of ancient cities in Iraq—Babylon in particular—and on numerous occasions displayed his awareness of history by making comparisons between ancient and modern events in Iraq. He was more likely to compare himself to the Neo-Babylonian Nebuchadnezzar than to an Assyrian king like Sargon II. Either would have been fitting—Nebuchadnezzar had destroyed the Kingdom of Judah, and Sargon II was responsible for the conquest of the Kingdom of Israel and the scattering of the ten tribes. Both of their empires would have included the territory that is today occupied by Kuwait.

Inlaid Gold Cuffs

Further examples of the fine craftsmanship of the royal jewelers is apparent in these gold cuffs that are inlaid with precious gemstones. The cuffs were found in the tombs of the Assyrian queens.

Chronology

Historical dates before 500 BCE are approximate.

THE PALEOLITHIC PERIOD

2.5 MYA	Emergence of Genus Homo in Africa
1.8 MYA	Genus Homo in the Middle East
1.5 MYA	Ubeidiya (Israel) Lower Paleolithic–Oldowan
750,000 YA	Gesher Benot Ya'aqov (Israel) Lower Paleolithic–Acheulian
300,000 YA	Neanderthals Middle Paleolithic–Mousterian
160,000 YA	Emergence of anatomically modern man
90,000 YA	Modern man in the Middle East
50,000 YA	Last Neanderthal
30,000 YA	Levanto–Aurignacian culture
13,000 BCE	First settled communities
	Natufian culture

THE NEOLITHIC PERIOD

10,000 BCE	Pre-Pottery Neolithic A culture
9000 BCE	First animal domestication
8000 BCE	Pre-Pottery Neolithic B culture
6500 BCE	Ceramic (pottery) Neolithic villages
	Pottery-making cultures
	Çatal Hüyük wall paintings
5000 BCE	First townships
	Chalcolithic towns
	Elaborate copper metallurgy
	Ubaid Period in southern Mesopotamia
	Origin of the Sumerians

THE BRONZE AGE

4000 BCE	Early Bronze Age cities of Uruk, Ur, Kish, and Lagash
3500 BCE	Early Sumerian writing
	First temple-states in Sumer
	Rise of the temple-state of Uruk
3200 BCE	Unification of Egypt
	Earliest Egyptian hieroglyphics
3000 BCE	First city-states in Iran and Syria
	Collapse of the Uruk Empire
	Jemdet Nasr culture
	First Proto-Elamite texts at Susa
	City culture spreads to Syria and the Levant
2900 BCE	Sumerian Early Dynastic Period
2700 BCE	The Old Kingdom in Egypt and the pyramid age
2600 BCE	Semitic kingdoms in northern and central Mesopotamia
2500 BCE	Royal Tombs of Ur
	Rise of Mari and Ebla
	Eanuatum and Urukagina are rulers of Lagash
	First Sumerian law codes
2375–2350 BCE	Lugalzagesi of Umma unifies Sumer

THE AKKADIAN EMPIRE

2350 BCE	Rise of the Akkadian Empire under Sargon of Akkad
2250 BCE	Height of the Akkadian Empire under Naram-Sin
	Destruction of Mari and Ebla
2200 BCE	Fall of the Akkadian Empire

THE EMPIRE OF UR III

2110–2045 BCE	Rise of the Ur III Empire under Ur-Nammu and Shulgi
	Ziggurat of Nanna at Ur
	Law codes of Shulgi
2000 BCE	Collapse of the Ur III Empire
	Rise of Sukkulmahs of Elam
	Cities of Isin and Larsa are prominent in Sumer
1900 BCE	The Middle Kingdom in Egypt
	Old Assyrian Colony Period in Anatolia
	Hurrians in northern Mesopotamia

THE OLD ASSYRIAN KINGDOM

1814–1781 BCE	Shamshi-adad I of Assyria controls northern Mesopotamia
***c.* 1800 BCE**	Rim-Sin (1822–1763 BCE) of Larsa controls Sumer
***c.* 1750 BCE**	Hittite Anitta is ruler of Kusara in southeastern Anatolia
	Rise of Aleppo and Qatna in Syria

THE BABYLONIAN KINGDOM

1792–1750 BCE	Rise of Babylon under Hammurabi
1763 BCE	Hammurabi destroys Mari
1755 BCE	Hammurabi controls all of Mesopotamia

THE WESTERN STATES

1650 BCE	Rise of the Hittite Old Kingdom
1650–1625 BCE	Hittite leader Hattusali I refounds Hattusa as the capital and conquers Kizzuwadna and Mukish (Alalakh), Syria
1625–1595 BCE	His grandson Mursili I conquers Aleppo and raids Babylon
1650–1540 BCE	Asiatic Hyksos rule northern Egypt
	Rise of the Kassites
1550 BCE	Horses and compound bows are employed in warfare

THE EGYPTIAN NEW KINGDOM

1540 BCE	Expulsion of Hyksos from Egypt
1540–1500 BCE	Rise of the Theban New Kingdom in Egypt
1500 BCE	Collapse of the Hittite Old Kingdom
	Chariot horses are widely employed in warfare
1500–1480 BCE	Shaustatar is king of Mitanni
1400 BCE	Rise of the Hittite New Kingdom
1363–1328 BCE	Assyria becomes independent under Ashuruballit
1360–1330 BCE	Decline of Mitanni under Tushratta
***c.* 1300 BCE**	Hittite conquest of Syria under Suppiluliuma
	Assyrian conquest of Babylon
	Decline of the Kassite kingdom
1290 BCE	Adad-nirari I of Assyria conquers Mitanni
1275 BCE	Battle of Qadesh between Egypt and the Hittites
1220 BCE	First appearance of the Arameans
1208 BCE	First migrations of the Sea Peoples are defeated under pharaoh Merneptah
1210 BCE	First mention of Israel in Palestine

THE SEA PEOPLES

1190 BCE	Fall of the Imperial Hittite Kingdom
	Neo-Hittite states independent in Syria
	Mass migrations of the Sea Peoples
	Destruction of the Hittite capital Ugarit
1176 BCE	Defeat of the Sea Peoples in the Egyptian delta by pharoah Ramesses III
	Philistine settlements begin
1155 BCE	Fall of the Kassites
1130 BCE	End of the Egyptian Empire
1124–1103 BCE	Nebuchadnezzar I restores Babylon
1115–1077 BCE	Tiglath-pileser I restores Assyria
1090 BCE	Appearance of the Phrygians
1070 BCE	Collapse of the New Kingdom in Egypt
1050 BCE	Rise of the Aramean kingdoms
	Collapse of Assyria
	Decline of Babylon
1020–1000 BCE	Saul is king of Israel
1000 BCE	Phoenician kingdoms (Tyre and Sidon) prominent
	Use of alphabetic writing
	Rise of Neo-Hittite states in northern Syria (Carchemish, Aleppo, and Hama)
1000–960 BCE	David is king of Israel
950 BCE	Rise of the Aramean kingdom of Damascus
960–920 BCE	Rise of the Israelite kingdom under Solomon (Israelite United Monarchy)
934–912 BCE	Ashur-dan II restores Assyria
900-852 BCE	Omrid dynasty rules Israel

THE NEO-ASSYRIAN KINGDOM AND EMPIRE

883-859 BCE	Ashurnasirpal II reorganizes Assyrian kingdom
856 BCE	Battle of Qarqar—Assyrian King Shalmaneser III (858–824 BCE) is defeated by Hama/Damascus/Israel coalition army
852–838 BCE	Decline of the Israelite kingdom
810-785 BCE	Rise of Urartu under Menua
800-750 BCE	Eclipse of Assyria
756-730 BCE	Expansion of Urartu into northern Syria under Sarduri II
743 BCE	Tiglath-pileser III (744–727 BCE) defeats Sarduri II and expels Urartu from Syria
740–729 BCE	Tiglath-pileser III conquers Arpad (740 BCE), Hama and Unqi (738 BCE), Damascus (732 BCE), and Babylon (729 BCE) creating the Neo-Assyrian Empire
721–705 BCE	Sargon II continues the campaigns of expansion
713–706 BCE	Construction of the Neo-Assyrian capital of Dur-Sharrukin (Khorsabad)
704–700 BCE	Loss of Anatolian and Iranian provinces
704 BCE	Sennacherib (704–681 BCE) abandons Dur-Sharrukin (Khorsabad) and moves the capital to Nineveh
	Judah revolts
702–688 BCE	Nineveh is rebuilt and the Neo-Assyrian Empire is reorganized under Sennacherib
680–669 BCE	Esarhaddon resumes expansion of the empire
668–627 BCE	Ashurbanipal is the last great king of Assyria
640–609 BCE	Josiah reforms the kingdom of Judah
626–605 BCE	Rise of the Neo-Babylonian kingdom under Nabopolassar
625–585 BCE	Rise of the Median kingdom under Cyaxares
615 BCE	Coalition of Babylon and Media against Assyria
614–605 BCE	Destruction of the Neo-Assyrian Empire

THE NEO-BABYLONIAN KINGDOM

604 BCE	Babylonian King Nebuchadnezzar II (605-562 BCE) conquers Ashkelon
601 BCE	Neo-Babylonian army invades Egypt, but is repulsed
597–587 BCE	Judah revolts unsuccessfully in 597 BCE and 587 BCE
586 BCE	Jerusalem is destroyed—the Judean kingdom is abolished
553–552 BCE	Neo-Babylonian King Nabonidus (556-539 BCE) conquers northern Arabia (553 BCE) as well as Ammon, Moab, and Edom (552 BCE)
c. 550 BCE	Revolt of Persia from Media under Cyrus the Great

THE ACHAEMENID PERSIAN EMPIRE

539 BCE	Conquest of the Neo-Babylonian kingdom by Cyrus
539–530 BCE	Eastern conquests of Cyrus
525 BCE	Cambyses II (530–522 BCE) conquers Egypt
518 BCE	Darius I (the Great) (522–486 BCE) conquers the Punjab
515 BCE	Construction on the Persepolis palace begins
513 BCE	Scythian Wars
500 BCE	First coinage
	Persian Royal Road is built and provincial system is overhauled
	Old Persian script is developed
499–494 BCE	Ionian Revolt
490 BCE	Persian defeat by the Greeks at the Battle of Marathon
482 BCE	Xerxes I (486–465 BCE) launches invasion of Greece
479 BCE	Persians are defeated at the battles of Salamis, Plataea, and Mycale—the Persians withdraw from Greece
475 BCE	Formation of the Delian League
470 BCE	Rise of Athens
460–450 BCE	Athenian-led revolts in Cyprus and Egypt
449 BCE	Peace of Callias between Persia and Athens
387 BCE	King's Peace between Sparta, Athens, and Persia

THE MACEDONIAN EMPIRE

359–336 BCE	Rise of Macedonia under Philip II
356 BCE	Birth of Alexander the Great
337 BCE	Macedonian-led League of Corinth declares war on Persia
336 BCE	Assassination of Artaxerxes III
	Revolt of Egypt and Babylon
	Assassination of Philip II
334 BCE	Alexander crosses into Asia
334–323 BCE	Alexander conquers Anatolia, Syria, Egypt, Mesopotamia, Babylon, Persia, Bactria, Sogdiana, and the Punjab
330 BCE	Death of Darius III of Persia
323 BCE	Death of Alexander at Babylon
323-277 BCE	Wars of the Successors

THE HELLENISTIC KINGDOMS

277 BCE	Formation of three main successor kingdoms of Egypt (Ptolemys), Asia (Seleucids), and Macedonia (Antigonids)
274–271 BCE	First Syrian War between the Ptolemys and the Seleucids
261–253 BCE	Second Syrian War
240–220 BCE	High point of the Ptolemaic Empire
198–189 BCE	Roman intervention in Greece
188 BCE	Peace of Apamea strips the Seleucids of Anatolia
188–133 BCE	Rise of the Pergamene kingdom in Anatolia
168 BCE	Rome expels the Seleucids from Egypt
	Revolt of the Maccabees in Judea
167 BCE	Macedonian kingdom is abolished

THE PARTHIAN KINGDOM

171–138 BCE	Rise of the Parthian state under Mithridates I
160–148 BCE	Parthians conquer Bactria (155 BCE) and Media (148 BCE)
146 BCE	Roman province of Greece is established
133 BCE	Roman province of Asia is established after the Pergamene kingdom is abolished
139–130 BCE	Seleucids lose Mesopotamia to Parthia after a long struggle
129 BCE	Hasmonean Jewish kingdom is independent
128 BCE	Mithridates II (124–87 BCE) abandons Bactria to Huns
124–120 BCE	Parthian conquest of all Mesopotamia
97 BCE	Parthians in western Armenia
96 BCE	Sulla leads a Roman embassy to the Parthians
90–70 BCE	Rise of the kingdoms of Armenia and Pontus

THE ROMAN EMPIRE

66–63 BCE	Pompey's Eastern campaigns
63 BCE	Seleucid kingdom is abolished, and the Roman province of Syria is created
53 BCE	Crassus is defeated by the Parthians at Carrhae
47 BCE	Caesar reorganizes the East, and destroys the kingdom of Pontus
44 BCE	Caesar is assassinated
42–30 BCE	The Roman East is ruled by Antony
40–38 BCE	Antony's Parthian Wars
37–4 BCE	Herod the Great is king of Judea
31–30 BCE	Octavian defeats Antony at Actium (31 BCE), and conquers Egypt (30 BCE)
20 BCE	Octavian agrees to a treaty with Parthians
CE 6	Judean kingdom is abolished
CE 35–62	Apostle Paul's mission to Gentiles
CE 66–73	First Jewish Revolt against Rome
CE 106	Rome abolishes the Nabataean kingdom
CE 114	Parthians invade Armenia
CE 116–117	Trajan conquers Mesopotamia (CE 116) and Hadrian abandons it (CE 117)
CE 120–130	Hadrian reorganizes the eastern provinces, and abolishes many small client kingdoms
CE 132–135	Second Jewish Revolt against Rome
CE 164–165	Antonine Parthian Wars
CE 165–168	Roman province of Mesopotamia is founded
CE 197–199	Septimius Severus invades Parthia
	Expansion of Roman province of Mesopotamia
CE 199–204	Eastern provinces are reorganized again

THE SASANID PERSIAN KINGDOM

CE 209–241	Rise of the Sasanid Persian kingdom under Ardashir I
CE 223	Collapse of the Parthian kingdom
CE 244–260	Sasanian King Shapur I (CE 242–272) wins victories over the Roman Emperors Gordion III (CE 244) and Philip the Arab (CE 248), and captures Emperor Valerian at the Battle of Edessa (CE 260)
CE 286	Foundation of Tetrarchy by Diocletian and division of Roman Empire into eastern and western halves
CE 287–299	Ongoing conflict between the Sasanians and the Romans
CE 301–304	Diocletian reorganizes eastern Roman provinces
CE 303–305	The Great Persecution of Christians

THE BYZANTINE EMPIRE

CE 307–312	Constantine becomes the Western Roman Emperor (CE 307) and conquers Rome (CE 312)
CE 312	Edict of Toleration of Christians
CE 324	Constantine conquers the Eastern Roman Empire
CE 359–360	Sasanian King Shapur II reconquers Roman Mesopotamia
CE 476	Fall of the Western Roman Empire
CE 527–565	Justinian rebuilds much of Constantinople
CE 530–540	Justinian's Sasanian Wars
CE 540	Sasanian King Croesus I conquers Antioch
CE 545–550	Roman recovery
CE 535–565	Justinian attempts reconquest of Western Roman Empire and is largely successful
CE 575–590	Exhaustion and decline of Eastern Roman Empire
CE 611–618	Sasanian King Croesus II (CE 591–628) attacks the Eastern Roman Empire, and conquers Antioch (CE 611), Damascus (CE 613), Jerusalem (CE 614), and Egypt (CE 618)
CE 622–627	Heraclius (CE 610–641) recovers the Eastern Roman Empire
	Exhaustion of both the Byzantine and Sasanian states

THE ISLAMIC CONQUEST OF THE MIDDLE EAST

CE 624–634	Rise of Islam throughout the Arabian Peninsula
	Islamic armies launch wars of conquest against the Byzantine and Sasanian states
CE 638	Heraclius abandons all Byzantine holdings in Syria and Egypt to the Islamic armies
CE 641	Arab conquest of entire Sasanian kingdom
CE 660–700	Islam spreads across North Africa and into Central Asia under the Umayyad dynasty
CE 750	Collapse of the Umayyad dynasty

Further Reading

Introducing the Middle East

Burns, R. *Monuments of Syria: An Historical Guide*. I. B. Tauris: New York, 1992.

Butcher, K. *Roman Syria and the Near East*. British Museum Press: London, 2003.

Campbell, S. and Green, A. (eds.). *The Archaeology of Death in the Ancient Near East*. Oxbow, 2005.

Curtis, J.E. and Tallis, N. *Forgotten Empire: The World of Ancient Persia*. University of California Press: Berkeley, 2005.

Dalley, S. (ed.). *The Legacy of Mesopotamia*. Oxford University Press, 1998.

Gates, C. *Ancient Cities: the archaeology of urban life in the Ancient Near East and Egypt, Greece and Rome*. Routledge: London, 2003.

Harper, P.O. *In Search of a Cultural Identity: Monuments and Artifacts of the Sasanian Near East, 3rd to 7th century AD*. Bibliotheca Persica: New York, 2006.

Howard-Johnston, James. *East Rome, Sasanian Persia and the End of Antiquity Historiographical and Historical Studies*. Ashgate Publishing: Abingdon, 2006.

Kozlowski, S. K. and Aurenche, O. *Territories, Boundaries and Cultures in the Neolithic Near East*. Archaeopress/MOM: Oxford/Lyon, 2005.

Levy, T.E. (ed). *The Archaeology of Society in the Holy Land*. Leicester University: London, 1995.

MacDonald, B., Adams, R., and Bienkowski, P. (eds.). *The Archaeology of Jordan*. Sheffield Academic Press: Sheffield, 2001.

Moorey, P.R.S. *Ancient Mesopotamian Materials and Industries: The Archaeological Evidence*. Oxford, 1994.

Potts, T., Roaf, M., and Stein, E. (eds.). *Culture through objects: Ancient Near Eastern Studies in Honour of P. R.S. Moorey*. Griffith Institute: Oxford, 2003.

Richardson, Peter. *City and sanctuary: religion and architecture in the Roman Near East*. SCM Press: London, 2002.

Roaf, M. *Cultural Atlas of Mesopotamia and the Ancient Near East*. Facts on File, 1990.

Schwartz, Glenn M., and Nichols, John J. (eds.). *After Collapse: The Regeneration of Complex Societies*. The University of Arizona Press: Tucson, 2006.

Stager, L.E., Greene, J.A., and Coogan, M.D. (eds.). *The Archaeology Of Jordan And Beyond: Essays In Honor Of James A. Sauer*. Eisenbrauns: Winona Lake, 2000.

Stein, G. *Rethinking World-Systems: Diasporas, Colonies, and Interaction in Uruk Mesopotamia*. The University of Arizona Press: Tucson, 1999.

Van de Mieroop, M. *A History of the Ancient Near East ca. 3000–323 BC*. Blackwell: Oxford, 2004.

Wilkinson, T. J. *Archaeological Landscapes of the Near East*. University of Arizona Press: Tucson, 2003.

The Fertile Crescent: Birthplace of Agriculture

Bar-Matthews, M., Ayalon, A., Kaufman, A., and Wasserburg, G.J. "The Eastern Mediterranean paleoclimate as a reflection of regional events: Soreq cave, Israel." *Earth and Planetary Science Letters* 166, 1999, pp85–95.

Bar-Yosef, O. "From sedentary foragers to village hierarchies: The emergence of social institutions" in *The Origin of Human Social Institutions*. Runciman, G., Proceedings of the British Academy 110, 1992, pp1–38.

Bar-Yosef, O. and Goren-Inbar, N. *The Lithic Assemblages of 'Ubeidiya*. Qedem 34. The Hebrew University of Jerusalem: Jerusalem, 1993.

Bar-Yosef, O. and Valla, F.R., (eds.). *The Natufian Culture*. International Monographs in Prehistory: Ann Arbor, 1991.

Bar-Yosef, O. et al. "The excavations in Kebara Cave." *Current Anthropology* 33(5), 1992, pp497–550.

Bar-Yosef, O. "The lower Paleolithic of the Near East". *Journal of World Prehistory* 8(3), 1994, pp211–265.

Belfer-Cohen, A. "The Natufian in the Levant." *Annual Review of Anthropology* 20, 1991, pp167–186.

Belfer-Cohen, A. "Rethinking social stratification in the Natufian culture: The evidence from burials." Campbell, S. and Green, A. (eds.). *The Archaeology of Death in the Ancient Near East*. Oxbow Monographs 51: Edinburgh, 1995, pp9–16.

Bergman, C.A. *Ksar Akil, Lebanon: A Technological and Typological Analysis of the Later Palaeolithic Levels at Ksar Akil and Abu Halaka (Levels XIII–VI)*. Bar International Series 329: Oxford, 1987.

Boyd, B. "On 'sedentism' in the Later Epipalaeolithic (Natufian) Levant." *World Archaeology* 38(2), 2006, pp164–178.

Byrd, B.F. "Public and private, domestic and corporate: The emergence of the Southwest Asian village." *American Antiquity* 59(4), 1994, pp369–666.

Byrd, B.F. "Spanning the gap from Upper Paleolithic to the Natufian: The Early and Middle Epi-Paleolithic." Henry, D.O. (ed.). *The Prehistoric Archaeology of Jordan*. B.A.R. International Series 705. Archaeopress: Oxford, 1998, pp64–82.

Byrd, B.F. and Monahan, C.M. "Death, mortuary ritual and Natufian structure." *Journal of Anthropological Archaeology* 14, 1995, pp251–287.

Campana, D.V. and Crabtree, P.J. "Communal hunting in the Natufian of the Southern Levant: The social and economic implications." *Journal of Mediterranean Archaeology* 3(2), 1990, pp223–243.

Clark, J.D. "The middle Acheulian site at Latamne, northern Syria". *Quaternaria* 9:1, 1967, p68.

Copeland, L. "The Middle and Upper Paleolithic of Lebanon and Syria in the light of Recent Research." Wendorf, F. and Marks, A.E. (eds.). *Problems in Prehistory: North Africa and the Levant*. Southern Methodist University Press: Dallas, 1975, pp317–350.

Copeland, L. "The Lower Paleolithic of Jordan." Henry, D. (ed.). *The Prehistoric History of Jordan* vol. 705, B.A.R. International Series. Archaeopress: Oxford, 1998, pp5–22.

Edwards, P.C. "Problems of recognizing earliest Sedentism: The Natufian example." *Journal of Mediterranean Archaeology* 2(1), 1989, pp5–48.

Eshed, V. et al. "Has the transition to agriculture reshaped the demographic structure of Prehistoric populations? New evidence from the Levant." *American Journal of Physical Anthropology* 124, 2004, pp315–329.

Garrard, A.N. and Gebel, H.G. *The Prehistory of Jordan: the state of research in 1986*. B.A.R. International Series. Archaeopress: Oxford, 1998.

Garrod, D.A.E. and Bate, D.M.A. (eds.). *The Stone Age of Mount Carmel vol. 1: Excavations in the Wady el-Mughara*. Clarendon Press: Oxford, 1937.

Gilead, D. "Handaxe Industries in Israel and the Near East." *World Archaeology* 2(1), 1970, pp1–11.

Gilead, D. "Cleavers in Early Paleolithic Industeris in Israel." *Paleorient* 1, 1973, pp73–86.

Gopher, A. *Arrowhaeds of the Neolithic Levant*. American School of Oriental research dissertation series 10. Eisenbrauns: Indiana, 1994.

Goren-Inbar, N. and Sharon, G. (eds.). *Axe Age: Acheulian Tool-making from Quarry to Discard*. Equinox: London, 2006.

Goren-Inbar, N. and Speth, J.D. (eds.). *Human Paleoecology in the Levantine Corridor*. Oxbow Books: Oxford, 2004.

Goren-Inbar, N., Werker, E., and Feibel, C.S. *The Acheulian Site of Gesher Benot Ya'aqov, Israel: Vol. I. The Wood Assemblage*. Oxbow Books: Oxford, 2002.

Goring-Morris, A.N. and Belfer-Cohen, A. (eds.). *More than meets the eye: studies on upper Palaeolithic diversity in the Near East*. Oxbow/David Brown Book Co.: Oxford, 2003.

Goring-Morris, A.N. *At the Edge, Terminal Pleistocene Hunter-Gatherers in the Negev and Sinai*. B.A.R. International Series 361(i). Archaeopress: Oxford, 1987.

Goring-Morris, A.N. "The Harifian of the Southern Levant" in Bar-Yosef, O. and Valla, F. R. (eds.). *The Natufian culture in the Levant*. Ann Arbor, 1992, pp173–216.

Goring-Morris, A.N. *At the Edge: Terminal Pleistocene Hunter-Gatherers in the Negev and Sinai*. British Archaeological Reports: Oxford, 1987.

Goring-Morris, N.A. et al. "Patterns in the Epi-Paleolithic of the Levant: Debate after Neeley and Barton." *Antiquity* 70, 1996, pp130–147.

Grosman, L. "Preserving cultural traditions in a period of instability: The Late Natufian of the Hilly Mediterranean." *Current Anthropology* 44, 2003, pp571–580.

Grosman, L. and Belfer-Cohen, A. "Zooming onto the Younger Dryas." Cappers, R. T. J. and Bottema, S. Berlin (eds.). *The dawn of farming in the Near East*. Ex Oriente, 2002, pp49–54.

Henry, D.O. (ed.). *Neanderthals in the Levant: Behavioral Organization and the Beginnings of Human Modernity (New Approaches to Anthropological Archaeology)*. Continuum Pub Group: New York, 2003.

Horowitz, A. *The Quaternart of Israel*. Academic Press: New York, 1979.

Hovers, E. "Settlement and subsistence patterns in the Lower Jordan Valley from Epi-Paleolithic to Neolithic times." Hershkowitz, I. (ed.). *People and culture in change: The second symposium on Upper Paleolithic, Mesolithic and Neolithic populations of Europe and the Mediterranean Basin*. B.A.R. International Series 508. Archaeopress: Oxford, 1989, pp37–51.

Levy, T.E., (ed.). *The archaeology of society in the Holy Land*. Leicester University Press: London, 1995.

Marks, A.E. *Prehistory and paleoenvironments in the central Negev, Israel*. Southern Methodist University Press: Dallas, 1976.

Marks, A.E. *Prehistory and Paleoenvironments in the Central Negev, Israel*. Southern Methodist University Press: Dallas, 1983.

Moore, A.M.T. et al. *Village on the Euphrates: From foraging to farming*. Oxford University Press: Oxford, 2000.

Richerson, P.J. et al. "Was agriculture impossible during the Pleistocene but mandatory during the Holocene? A climate hypothesis." *American Antiquity* 66, 2001, pp387–411.

Rollefson, G.O. "The last Aceramic Neolithic of the Levant: a synthesis". *Paleorient* 15, 1989, pp168–173.

Sharon, G. *Acheulian Large Flake Industries: Technology, Chronology, and Significance*. B.A.R. International Series 1701. Archaeopress: Oxford, 2007.

Valla, F.R. "Natufian behaviour in the Hula Basin: The question of territoriality." Goren-Inbar, N. and Speth, J. D. (eds.). *Human Paleoecology in the Levantine Corridor*. Oxbow Books: Oxford, 2004, pp207–220.

Mesopotamia: The Cradle of Civilization

Adams, R.M. *Land Behind Baghdad: A History of Settlement on the Diyala Plains.* University of Chicago Press: Chicago, 1965.

Adams, R.M. *Heartland of Cities: Surveys of Ancient Settlement and Land Use on the Central Floodplain Of the Euphrates.* University of Chicago Press: Chicago, 1981.

Adams, R.M. and Nissen, H.J. *The Uruk Countryside: The Natural Setting of Urban Societies.* University of Chicago Press: Chicago, 1972.

Algaze, Guillermo. *The Uruk World System: The Dynamics of Expansion of Early Mesopotamian Civilization.* University of Chicago Press: Chicago, 1993.

Armajani, Yahya and Ricks, Thomas. *Middle East: Past and Present.* Prentice-Hall: Englewood Cliffs, 1986.

Averbeck, R.E., Chavalas, M.W., and Weisberg, D.B. (eds.). *Life and Culture in the Ancient Near East.* CDL Press: Baltimore, 2003.

Bahn, P.G. *The Cambridge Illustrated History of Archaeology.* Cambridge University Press: Cambridge, 1996.

Barondes, R. *The Garden of the Gods: Mesopotamia, 5000 B.C.: An Anthology of Sumerian, Akkadian and Babylonian Literature.* Christopher Publishing House: Boston, 1957.

Beaulieu, P. *The Reign of Nabonidus, King of Babylon 556–539 B.C.* Yale University Press: New Haven, 1989

Ben-Arieh, Y. *The Rediscovery of the Holy Land in the Nineteenth Century.* Israel Exploration Society: Jerusalem, 1983.

Black, J. and Green, A. *Gods, Demons and Symbols of Ancient Mesopotamia.* British Museum Press: London, 1992

Bottéro, J. *Religion in Ancient Mesopotamia.* University of Chicago Press: Chicago, 2001.

Briant, P. *From Cyrus to Alexander: A History of the Persian Empire.* Eisenbrauns: Winona Lake, 2002.

Ceram, C.W. and Marek, Kurt W. *Gods, Graves, and Scholars: The Story of Archaeology.* Vintage Books: London, 1986.

Cohen, R. and Westbrook, R. *Amarna Diplomacy: The Beginnings of International Relations.* Johns Hopkins University Press: Baltimore, 2000.

Cook, J. *The Persian Empire.* Schocken Books: New York,1983.

Dalley, S. *Myths from Mesopotamia,* Oxford University Press: Oxford, 1989.

Davis, T. *Shifting Sands: The Rise and Fall of Biblical Archaeology.* Oxford University Press: New York, 2004.

Donbaz, V. and Grayson, A. *Royal Inscriptions on Clay Cones from Ashur Now in Istanbul.* University of Toronto Press: Toronto, 1984.

Drower, M. *Flinders Petrie. A Life in Archaeology,* 2nd ed. University of Wisconsin Press: Madison, 1996.

Killebrew, A. *Biblical Peoples and Ethnicity: An Archaeological Study of Egyptians, Canaanites, Philistines, and Early Israel.* Society of Biblical Literature: Atlanta, 2005.

Knapp, A.B. *The History and Culture of Ancient Western Asia and Egypt.* Dorsey Press: Chicago, 1988.

Mackey, S. *The Reckoning: Iraq and the Legacy of Saddam Hussein.* W.W. Norton and Co.: New York, 2002.

Mellaart, J. *The Neolithic of the Near East.* Thames and Hudson: London, 1975.

Oates, D. and J. *The Rise of Civilization.* Elsevier-Phaidon: Oxford/London, 1976.

Pollock, S. and Bernbeck, R. (eds.). *Archaeologies of the Middle East.* Blackwell Studies in Global Archaeology. Blackwell: Oxford, 2005.

Postgate, J. N. *The First Empires.* Elsevier-Phaidon: Oxford, 1977.

Redford, D. *Egypt, Canaan, and Israel in Ancient Times.* Princeton University Press: Princeton, 1992.

Snell, D. *Life in the Ancient Near East.* Yale University Press: New Haven, 1997.

Stiebing, W. *Uncovering the Past: A History of Archaeology.* Prometheus Books: Buffalo, 1993.

Power Struggles: Kingdoms at War

Arnold, B. *Who Were the Babylonians?* Society of Biblical Literature: Atlanta, 2004.

Bryce, T. *The Kingdom of the Hittites.* 2nd ed. University Press: Oxford, 2005.

Chavalas, M. and Younger Jr., K.L. (eds.) *Mesopotamia and the Bible: Comparative Explorations.* Continuum: London/New York, 2002.

Collins, B.J. *The Hittites and their World.* Society of Biblical Literature: Atlanta, 2007.

Drews, R. *The End of the Bronze Age.* Princeton University Press: Princeton, 1993.

Moran, W. *The Amarna Letters.* The Johns Hopkins University Press: Baltimore, 1992.

Saggs, H. W. F. *The Might that was Assyria,* 2nd ed. Sidgwick and Jackson: New York, 1990.

Van de Mieroop, M. *King Hammurabi.* Blackwell: Oxford, 2005.

Westbrook, R. *Amarna Diplomacy: The Beginning of International Relations.* The Johns Hopkins University Press: Baltimore, 2000.

Wilhelm, G. *The Hurrians.* Aris and Phillips: Westminster, 1989.

Masters of the Known World: The Age of Empires

Aubet M.E. *The Phoenicians and the West: Politics, Colonies and Trade,* 2nd revised ed. Cambridge, 2001.

Briant, P. *From Cyrus to Alexander: A History of the Persian Empire,* translated by Daniels, P. (English translation of French original, published in 1996). Winona Lake, 2002.

Cawkwell, G. *The Greek Wars: The Failure of Persia.* Oxford, 2005.

Curtis, J.E. and Reade, J.E. (eds.). *Art and Empire: Treasures from Assyria in the British Museum.* New York, 1995.

Dalley, S. and Oleson, P. "Sennacherib, Archimedes and the Water Screw: The Context of Invention in the Ancient World." *Technology and Culture* 44.1, 2003, pp1–26.

Dalley, S. "Nineveh, Babylon and the Hanging Gardens: Cuneiform and Classical Sources Reconciled". *Iraq* 56, 1994, pp45–58.

Fuchs, A. and Parpola, S. *The Correspondence of Sargon II, Part III. Letters from Babylonia and the Eastern Provinces.* State Archives of Assyria 15: Helsinki, 2001.

Gallagher, W.R. *Sennacherib's Campaign to Judah: New Studies.* Leiden, 1999.

Grayson, A.K. *Assyrian and Babylonian Chronicles.* Locust Valley: Winona Lake, 1975 (2nd ed. 2000).

Hallo, W.W. (ed.). *The Context of Scripture 2. Monumental Inscriptions from the Biblical World.* Leiden, 2000.

Joannès, F. *The Age of Empires: Mesopotamia in the First Millennium BC.* Edinburgh, 2004.

Kuhrt, A. *The Ancient Near East c.3000–330 BC.* London, 1995.

Lipinski, E. *The Aramaeans: Their Ancient History, Culture, Religion.* Louvain, 2000.

Liverani, M. (ed.). *Neo-Assyrian Geography.* Rome, 1995.

Luckenbill, D.D. *Ancient Records of Assyria and Babylonia.* Chicago, 1989.

Markoe, G. *Phoenicians.* London, 2000.

Melchert, H.C. *The Luwians.* Leiden, 2003.

Millard, A. *The Eponyms of the Assyrian Empire 910–612 BC.* Helsinki.

Miller, M. *Athens and Persia in the fifth century BC: A study in cultural receptivity.* Cambridge, 1997.

Oates, D. and Oates, J. *Nimrud: An Assyrian Imperial City Revealed.* London, 2001.

Parpola, S. and Porter, M. *The Helsinki Atlas of the Near East in the Neo-Assyrian Empire.* Helsinki, 2001.

Root, M.C. *The King and Kingship in Achaemenid Art.* Leiden, 1979.

Russell, J.M. *The Writing on the Wall. Studies in the Architectural Context of Late Assyrian Palace Inscriptions.* Winona Lake, 1999.

Stolper, M.W. "Persepolis Fortification Archive Project Annual Report." *Oriental Institute 2006–2007 Annual Report,* 1999.

Tadmor, H. *The Inscriptions of Tiglath-pileser III King of Assyria.* Jerusalem, 1994.

Wiesehöfer, J. *Ancient Persia from 550 BC to 650 AD* (translated by Azodi, A. and Taurus, I.B.). 2001.

Zimansky, P.E. *Ecology and Empire: The Structure of the Urartian State.* Chicago, 1985.

Under Occupation: Hellenistic and Roman Conquerors

Austin, M.M. *The Hellenistic World from Alexander to the Roman Conquest,* 2nd edn. Cambridge, 2007.

Ball, W. *Rome in the East.* London and New York, 2000.

Bosworth, A.B. *Alexander and the East: The Tragedy of Triumph.* Oxford, 1996.

Bosworth, A.B. *Conquest and Empire: The Reign of Alexander the Great.* Cambridge, 1988.

Bosworth, A. B. *The Legacy of Alexander: Politics, Warfare and Propaganda under the Successors.* Oxford, 2002.

Bowersock, G. *Roman Arabia.* Harvard, 1993.

Bowman, A.K. *Egypt after the Pharaohs.* Oxford, 1990.

Butcher, K. *Roman Syria and the Near East.* London, 2003.

Downey, G. *A History of Antioch in Syria.* Princeton, 1961.

Edwell, P.M. *Between Rome and Persia: The Middle Euphrates, Mesopotamia and Palmyra under Roman Control.* London and New York, 2007.

Grainger, J.D. *Seleukos Nikator: Constructing a Hellenistic Kingdom.* London, 1990.

Green, P. *Alexander to Actium: The Hellenistic Age.* London, 1991.

Green, P. *Hellenistic History and Culture.* Berkeley, 1993.

Hammond, N.G.L. *A History of Macedonia* (vols 1–3). Oxford, 1972–1988.

Isaac, B. *The Limits of Empire: The Roman Army in the East.* Oxford, 1990.

Jones, A.H.M. *Cities of the Eastern Roman Provinces,* 2nd edn. Oxford, 1971.

Kennedy, D. and Riley, D. *Rome's Desert Frontier from the Air.* Austin, 1990.

Kennedy, H. *The Great Arab Conquests.* London, 2007.

Lieu, S.N.C. *The Roman Eastern Frontier and the Persian Wars,* Revised edn. London and New York, 1994.

Mahaffy, J.P. *A History of Egypt under the Ptolemaic Dynasty.* London, 2001.

Millar, F. *The Roman Near East: 31 BC–AD 337.* Harvard, 1993.

Parker, S.T. *Romans and Saracens: A History of the Arabian Frontier.* Winona Lake, 1986.

Pollard, N. *Soldiers, Cities and Civilians in Roman Syria,* Ann Arbor, 2000.

Ross, S.K. *Roman Edessa.* London and New York, 2000.

Sartre, M. *The Middle East under Rome.* Belknap: Harvard, 2005.

Sherwin-White, A.N. *Roman Foreign Policy in the East, 168 BC to AD 1.* London, 1984.

Shipley, G. *The Greek World after Alexander.* London and New York, 2000.

Stoneman, R. *Palmyra and its Empire.* Ann Arbor, 1994.

Yarshater, E. (ed.). *The Cambridge History of Iran* (7 vols). Cambridge, 1983.

Index

Plain page numbers indicate references in the body text. *Italicized* numbers indicate references in image captions, while **bold** numbers indicate references in colored feature boxes.

B

T

Acknowledgments

Global Book Publishing would like to thank Dannielle Viera for editing the index, as well as Scott Forbes, Marie-Louise Taylor, and Dr John Tidmarsh for their help during the conceptualization process prior to production.

Managing Director:	Chryl Campbell
Publishing Director:	Sarah Anderson
Art Director:	Kylie Mulquin
Project Manager:	Sophia Oravecz
Chief Consultant:	Dr Stephen Bourke
Contributors:	Maree Browne, Professor Mark W. Chavalas, Dr Kate da Costa, Dr Peter Edwell, Dr Yosef Garfinkel, Dr Leore Grosman, Dr Lloyd Llewellyn-Jones, Dr Kevin M. McGeough, Dr Karen Radner, Dr Seth Richardson, Dr Sandra Scham, Dr Gonen Sharon, Dr Matt Waters
Commissioning Editor:	David Kidd
Editors:	Emma Driver, Victoria Fisher, Judith Simpson, Russell Thomson
Map Editor:	Alan Edwards
Cover Design:	Alex Frampton, Kylie Mulquin
Designers:	Kerry Klinner, Lena Lowe, Avril Makula, Thomson Digital
Junior Designer:	Althea Aseoche
Design Concept:	Alex Frampton, Stan Lamond
Cartographer:	John Frith
Graphics:	Althea Aseoche
Picture Research:	Sarah Anderson, David Boehm, Emma Driver, Sophia Oravecz, Maria Stanco
Index:	Michael Ramsden
Proofreader:	Kevin Diletti
Production:	Ian Coles
Contracts:	Alan Edwards
Foreign Rights:	Kate Hill
Publishing Assistant:	Christine Leonards

Captions for Cover, Preliminary Pages, and Openers

Front cover: An archer, from the Frieze of Archers from Susa, Iran
Back cover: Vase of Entemana, ruler of Lagash from Telloh, Iraq
Page 1: Relief on Apadana staircase, Persepolis, Iran
Page 2: Temple of Hadrian along Curetes Way, Ephesus, Turkey
Pages 4–5: The site of Masada, Israel
Pages 6–7: Detail from Royal Standard of Ur mosaic from the Sumerian royal graves, Early Dynastic Period
Page 9: Detail of rock sculpture from Petra, Jordan
Pages 10–11: Sculpture of myth bird, Persepolis, Iran
Pages 22–23: Tributary of the Euphrates River near Haditha, Iraq
Pages 56–57: Detail from Royal Standard of Ur mosaic from the Sumerian royal graves, Early Dynastic Period
Pages 104–105: Fresco detail of priest leading bull to sacrifice, Mari, Syria
Pages 158–159: Reconstructed column, Persepolis, Iran
Pages 246–247: Relief of river god Cestrus, Perge, Antalya, Turkey
Pages 310–311: Fortress built by King Herod, Judean Desert, West Bank

Picture Credits

The Publisher would like to thank the copyright owners for permission to reproduce their images. Every attempt has been made to obtain permission for use of all images from the copyright owners. However, if any errors or omissions have occurred Global Book Publishing would be pleased to hear from copyright owners.

t = top; b = bottom; l = left; r = right; c = center

AA = Picture Desk/The Art Archive
AAAC = Ancient Art and Architecture Collection
BAF = Bilderberg Archive de fotographen
BM = Trustees of the British Museum
CB = Corbis Australia
GBP = Global Book Publishing
GI = Getty Images
HI = Heritage Image Partnership
NGS = National Geographic Society
PL = Photolibrary
PM = Picture Media
WF = Werner Forman Archive
VE = Visible Earth/NASA

FRONT COVER AA/Archers Musée du Louvre Paris/Gianni Dagli Orti.
BACK COVER AA/Musée du Louvre Paris/Gianni Dagli Orti.
1 GI, **2** GI, **3**, GI, **4** GI, **5** GI, **6** GI, **7** GI, **8** GI, **9** GI, **10-11** GI, **12** PL, **13t** GI, **13b** PL, **14** AA, **15t** AA, **15b** GI, **16** GI, **17t** PL, **17b** C, **18** GI, **19t** GI, **19b** CB, **20** CB, **21t** GI, **21b** GI, **22-23** GI, **23** AA, **25t** PL, **25b** CB, **26** GI, **27t** Kenneth Garrett, **27b** Kenneth Garrett, **28** AL, **29t** Kenneth Garrett, **29b** GI, **30** PL, **31t** Kenneth Garrett/NGS, **31t** PL, **32t** courtesy of Dr. Leore Grosman, **33** courtesy of Dr. Leore Grosman, **34** Courtesy of Dr. Leore Grosman **35t** Courtesy of Dr. Leore Grosman, **35b** Courtesy of Dr. Leore Grosman, **36** The Evatt Collection/Flinders University Library, **37t** AA, **37b** Yosef Garfinkel **38** AAAC, **39t** AA, **39b** Berthold Steinhilber/Bilderberg Archive de fotographen, **40** PL, **41t** akg-images/Erich Lessing, **41b** NG/GI, **42t** AA, **42b** Yosef Garfinkel, **43** AA, **44** P. Dorsellands/courtesy of Dr Gary O. Rollefson, **45t** Curt Blair/courtesy of Dr Gary O. Rollefson, **45b** John Tsantes/courtesy of Dr Gary O. Rollefson, **46** AA, **47t** Catalhoyuk Research Project, **47b** AA, **48** CB **49t** AA, **49b** Sake Elzinga/Hollandse Hoogte Agency, **50t** CB, **50b** Sake Elzinga/Hollandse Hoogte Agency, **51** AAAC, **52t** Yosef Garfinkel, **52b** AA, **52b** PL, **53** BM, **54** GI, **55t** akg-images/Erich Lessing **55b** Yosef Garfinkel, **56-57** WF, **57t** AA, **59r** AA, **59b** CB, **60t** HI, **60b** CB, **61** AA, **62t** CB, **62b** AA, **63b** Aladin Abdel Naby/Reuters/PM, **64** akg-images/Erich Lessing, **65t** AA, **65b** PL, **66** AA, **67t** AA, **67b** AA, **68b** CB, **68-69** CB, **69r** AA, **70t** AA, **70b** GI, **71** akg-images/Werner Forman, **72t** AA, **72b** akg-images/Erich Lessing, **73t** akg-images/Erich Lessing, **73b** AA, **74** CB, **75t** AA, **75b** AA, **76** akg-images/Erich Lessing , **77t** AA, **77b** CB, **78** AA, **79t** GI **79b** AA, **80t** CB, **80b** GI, **81** akg-images/Erich Lessing, **82** AAAC, **83t** WF **83b** AA, **84** AA, **85t** AA, **85b** PL, **86** akg-images/Erich Lessing, **87t** AA, **87b** AA, **88** akg-images/Erich Lessing, **89t** HI, **89b** AA, **90** GI, **91t** akg-images/Erich Lessing, **91b** PL, **92b** CB, **92-93** WF, **93r** akg-images/Erich Lessing, **94** akg-images/Erich Lessing, **95t** HI, **95b** AAAC, **96t** GI, **96b** PL, **97t** CB, **97b** GI, **98t** GI, **98-99** akg-images, **99t** AA, **100** AA, **101t** GI, **101b** akg-images/Erich Lessing, **102t** AA, **102b** HI, **103t** akg-images, **103b** akg-images, **104-105** AA, **105t** GI, **107t** AA, **107b** AA, **108** GI, **109t** AA, **109b** AA, **110** akg-images/Erich Lessing, **111t** AA, **111b** akg-images/Erich Lessing, **112t** GI, **112b** AA, **113t** AA, **113b** AA, **114** AA, **115t** AA, **115b** GI **116t** AA, **116b** GI, **117** GI, **118** AA, **119t** GI, **119b** AA, **120** GI, **121t** akg-images/Gerard De George, **121b** PL, **122** PL, **123t** akg-images/Erich Lessing, **123b** akg-images/Erich Lessing, **124** AA, **125t** AA, **125b** AA, **126** PL, **127t** AA, **127b** AA, **128t** AA, **128b** German Archaeological Institute/Hattusa Project/Bekir Kösker, **129t** CB, **129b** CB, **130** PL, **131t** AA, **131b** GI, **132** AA, **133t** AA, **133b** CB, **134** CB, **135t** GI, **135b** BM, **136** AA, **137t** akg-images, **137b** AA, **138** PL, **139t** CB, **139b** GI, **140** PL, **141t** CB, **141b** PL, **142** AA, **143t** AA, **143b** BM, **144** WF, **145t** CB, **145b** GI, **146** GI, **147t** AA **147b** AA, **148** CB, **149t** GI, **149b** GI, **150** AA, **151t** AA, **151b** AA, **152** GI, **153t** akg-images/Erich Lessing, **153b** WF, **154** BM, **155t** AA, **155b** CB, **156** GI, **157t** akg-images/Erich Lessing, **157b** CB, **158-159** GI, **159t** GI, **161t** AA, **161b** AA, **162** GI, **163t** AA, **163b** AA, **164** AA, **165t** akg-images/Erich Lessing, **165b** akg-images/Erich Lessing **166t** AA, **166b** akg-images, **167** AA, **168t** akg-images/Werner Forman, **168b** AAAC, **169** akg-images/Erich Lessing, **170t** AA, **170b** GI, **171** AA, **172t** CB, **172b** CB, **173** GI, **174t** AA, **174b** AA, **175t** AA, **175b** AA, **176b** AA, **176t** BM, **177** Thorne Anderson/CB, **178** AAAC, **178-179** akg-image/Erich Lessing, **179t** AAAC, **180** GI, **181t** WF, **181b** WF, **182t** HI, **182b** GI, **183** AA, **184** PL, **185t** PL **185b** PL, **186t** AA, **186b** akg-images/Erich Lessing, **187** GI, **188** AA, **189t** AA, **189b** AA, **190** AA, **191t** AA,**191b** AA **192** AA, **193t** akg-images, **193b** AA, **194** akg-images/Erich Lessing, **195t** akg-images, **195b** WF, **196t** akg-images/Erich Lessing, **196b** AA, **197** PL, **198t** AAAC, **198b** PL, **199** AA, **200** AA **201t** CB, **201b** PL, **202** WF, **203t** akg-images, **203b** CB, **204t** AA, **204b** akg-images/Erich Lessing, **205** AA, **206** PL, **207t** BM, **207b** PL, **208** AA, **209t** PL, **209b** GI, **210t** CB, **210b** CB, **211** akg-images/British Library, **212** GI, **213t** AA, **213b** GI, **214** GI, **215t** CB, **215b** PL, **216t** AA, **216b** AA, **217** AA, **218t** akg-images/Bildarchive/Steffens, **218b** akg-images/Erich Lessing, **219** GI, **220t** CB, **220b** CB, **221** AA, **222** akg-images/Erich Lessing **223t** AA, **223b** AA, **224** GI, **225t** CB, **225b** CB, **226t** AA, **226b** AA, **227** CB, **228** akg-images/Suzanne Held, **229t** GI, **229b** PL, **230t** AA, **230b** AA, **231t** CB, **231b** WF, **232** PL, **233t** AA, **233b** PL, **234** GI, **235t** akg-images/Erich Lessing, **235b** GI, **236t** AA, **236b** akg-images/Erich Lessing, **237** CB, **238b** GI, **238t** GI, **239b** AA, **240** CB, **241t** akg-images/Erich Lessing **241b** CB, **242t** AA, **242b** WF, **243** AA, **244** AAAC, **245t** AA, **245b** CB, **246-247** GI, **247t** GI, **249t** AA, **249b** AA, **250t** AA, **250b** akg-images, **251** AA, **252** PL, **253t** akg-images/Peter Connolly, **253b** AA, **254t** AA, **254b** Jacques Descloitres/MODIS Land Rapid Response Team/ VE, **255** CB, **256** AA, **257t** AA, **257b** Frank and Helen Schreider/National Geographic Stock, **258t** CB, **258b** AA, **259** GI, **260t** AA, **260-261** AA, **261** akg-images, **262** CB, **263t** HI, **263b** PL, **264** AA, **265t** AA, **265b** AA, **266t** CB, **266b** GI, **267t** CB, **267b** CB, **268b** AA, **268-269** AA, **269t** AA, **270t** AA, **270-271** AA, **271t** AA, **272** GI, **273t** AA, **273b** akg-images/Erich Lessing, **274t** GI, **274b** akg-images/Erich Lessing, **275** AA, **276t** AA, **276-277** GI, **277t** akg-images/Nimatallah, **278** akg-images/Erich Lessing, **279t** AA, **279b** AA, **280** AAAC, **281t** CB, **281b** GI, **282** WF, **283t** AA, **283b** akg-images/Gerard Degeorge, **284** AA, **285t** AA, **285b** PL, **286** AA, **287t** AA, **287b** AA, **288t** GI, **288b** GI, **289t** WF, **289b** CB, **290** GI, **291t** CB, **291b** GI, **292** CB, **293t** akg-images/Erich Lessing, **293cr** AA, **294** akg-images/Electa, **295tl** AA, **295tr** GI, **296t** akg-images/Electa, **297t** AA, **297b** AA, **298** GI, **299t** AA, **299b** AA, **300** GI, **301t** AA, **301b** AA, **302** AA, **303t** akg-images/Erich Lessing, **303b** AA, **304t** AA, **304b** GI, **305t** PL, **305b** PL, **306** CB, **307tl** akg-images, **307tr** Marie-Lan Nguyen/Wikimedia Commons **308** AA **309t** PL, **309b** AA, **310-311** GI, **311t** GI, **312b** HI **313** GI, **314t** CB, **314b** AA, **315t** AA, **315b** akg-images/Erich Lessing, **316** AA, **317t** PL, **317b** PL, **318** AA, **319t** AA, **319b** AA, **320** AA, **321t** AA, **321b** PL, **322t** GI, **322b** GI, **323** AA, **324** AA, **325t** GI, **325b** WF, **326** GI, **327t** GI, **327b** GI, **328** GI, **329t** GI, **329b** GI, **330** CB, **331t** GI, **331b** akg-images/Erich Lessing, **332** AA, **333t** AA, **333b** AA, **334** akg-images/Coll. B. Garrett, **335t** AA, **335b** AA, **336** GI, **337t** AA, **337b** GI, **338** GI, **339t** AA, **339b** AA, **340** AA, **341t** GI, **341b** CB, **342** CB, **343t** GI, **343b** AA, **344** AA, **345t** CB, **345b** CB, **346b** GI, **347t** AA, **347b** AA, **348** CB, **349t** CB, **349b** GI, **350t** Faleh Kheiber/Reuters/ PM, **350b** CB, **351t** GI, **351b** GI.
Feature Page Background Graphic GBP.